To Michael
with gratitude
and appreciation.

Gail

PALEO-
ANTHROPOLOGY

PALEO-ANTHROPOLOGY

G. E. Kennedy

Assistant Professor of Anthropology
University of California,
Los Angeles

McGRAW-HILL BOOK COMPANY

New York St. Louis San Francisco Auckland Bogotá Hamburg Johannesburg London Madrid
Mexico Montreal New Delhi Panama Paris São Paulo Singapore Sydney Tokyo Toronto

This book was set in Palatino by Black Dot, Inc. (ECU).
The editors were Richard R. Wright and Susan Gamer;
the designer was Joan E. O'Connor;
the production supervisor was Dennis J. Conroy.
The drawings were done by Fine Line Illustrations, Inc.
R. R. Donnelley & Sons Company was printer and binder.

PALEOANTHROPOLOGY

1234567890 DODO 7832109

Library of Congress Cataloging in Publication Data

Kennedy, G. E., date
Paleoanthropology

Bibliography: p.
Includes index.
1. Fossil man. 2. Human evolution. I. Title.
GN282.K46   569'.9   79-15398
ISBN 0-07-034046-3

To
Joseph Birdsell
and
Michael Day

CONTENTS

Preface   xi

**1 EVOLUTIONARY BIOLOGY, TAXONOMY,
    AND PALEOANTHROPOLOGY**   1
    Introduction   1
    Feedback Model   2
    Evolutionary Biology   6
    Taxonomy   15
    Summary   20
    Suggestions for Further Reading   21

2 THE ORDER PRIMATES   23
    The Mammals   23
    The Primates   28
    Summary   61
    Suggestions for Further Reading   62

3 EARLY PRIMATES: CRETACEOUS TO OLIGOCENE   63
Introduction   63
Ecologic Background   63
Cretaceous Primates   70
Paleocene   72
Eocene   82
Oligocene   99
Summary   110
Suggestions for Further Reading   112

4 MIOCENE HOMINOID RADIATION   114
Introduction   114
Ecologic Background   116
Miocene Hominoids: Morphology and Classification   128
Radiation in the Middle Miocene   144
Summary   166
Suggestions for Further Reading   167

5 THE FAMILY HOMINIDAE   169
Introduction   169
Geographic Origins   170
Characteristics   171
Theories of Hominid Origins   190
Summary   202
Suggestions for Further Reading   204

6 HOMINIDS OF THE PLIO-PLEISTOCENE   205
Introduction   205
Earlier Classifications   207
Current Taxonomy   212
Summary   247
Suggestions for Further Readings   248

7 PLIO-PLEISTOCENE HOMINID LOCALITIES   250
Introduction   250
Tools of the Plio-Pleistocene   252
Sites   256
Summary   303
Suggestions for Further Reading   304

8 HOMINIDS OF THE MIDDLE PLEISTOCENE
(0.7 TO 0.2 M.Y. B.C.)   306
Introduction   306
Pleistocene Ecology: The Ice Ages   308

Homo Erectus (1.5±c.0.25m.y.B.P.) 311
Characteristics 312
Behavior 335
Summary 348
Suggestions for Further Reading 349

9 HOMINIDS OF THE EARLY UPPER PLEISTOCENE 351
Introduction 351
Ecologic Background 353
Cultural Traditions 354
Human Evolution in the Early Upper Pleistocene 364
Hominids of the Third Interglacial 388
Hominids of the Early Würm 393
Summary 406
Suggestions for Further Reading 407

10 SUMMARY 409

Appendix: Dating Techniques 417
Glossary 426
Bibliography 431
Index 469

PREFACE

During the second half of this century many scientific disciplines have undergone rapid and even revolutionary development: new data and information and new analytical methods have led to the formulation of new ideas, new theories, and inevitably new conclusions. Paleoanthropology, the study of primate and human evolution, has been no exception.

Until very recently the study of fossil hominids focused almost entirely on the organic remains of earlier populations. The structural, functional, and comparative anatomy of jaws, teeth, and bones was the subject of most such studies. Beginning in the early 1960s, however, studies of early humans began to focus on broader objectives and more comprehensive areas of inquiry; and paleoanthropology, as an interdisciplinary science, was born.

While jaws, teeth, and bones still form much of the empirical base of the study of human evolution, the questions asked of these materials, and of organic and inorganic materials found associated with them, are both more comprehensive and more detailed than before. For example, paleo-environmental reconstructions to determine climate, geography, and contemporaneous plants and animals form an important new area of inquiry. And more subtle questions are now asked of the bones, jaws, and teeth themselves than were asked in earlier studies. Thus, locomotor patterns, posture, bone structure, and dietary habits are all vital new areas of anatomical investigation. Additionally, the models and concepts of population genetics have permitted these data to be cast in new analytical frameworks. Finally, there is a new meeting ground for the fossil evidence and archeological evidence of human evolution and the theories which attempt to explain evolutionary processes in the application of feedback models. Feedback models are theoretical constructions which allow us to interrelate evolution at various levels and in various systems. Having determined these evolutionary relationships, we may then ask how changes at different levels may affect and effect one another.

This book is an inquiry into the process of primate evolution in general and human evolution in particular, using data from comparative, structural, and functional anatomy in combination with various kinds of paleoenvironmental information. When, in later phases of human emergence, cultural materials and archeological remains become available, then these too are incorporated. Ideally, the elucidation of such fossil and archeological data in their environmental context will permit the development of feedback models so that interactions between evolutionary stimuli and biological and behavioral adaptations will become, if not visible, at least comprehensible.

This book is intended for students who have completed an introductory course in physical anthropology or biology. Much basic information about biological structure and evolutionary theory has not been included here. Although the ultimate focus of this book is human evolution, humans do not appear as a separate, recognizable entity until relatively recently in the long span of mammalian and primate history. Therefore, Chapters 1, 2, and 3 deal with the earlier phases of primate evolution within the ecological perspective of the early and middle Cenozoic. Thereafter, the evolutionary line leading to the higher primates is explored in greater detail. The extensive geographic diversification of the great apes in the Miocene forms the subject of Chapter 4. From this radiation emerged the ancestors of the modern apes and humans. In Chapters 5 through 9 the focus is on the humans themselves: their morphological structure, subsistence patterns, living sites, and cultural materials are examined in some depth. Chapter 9 examines the emergence of anatomically modern *Homo sapiens* in the Upper Pliestocene. Chapter 10 is a summary. An appendix discusses dating techniques; and a glossary is also included.

The emphasis here is on the fossil record itself. This emphasis means that other, possibly important, aspects of evolutionary studies have not been included. Thus, subjects like statistical analysis and biochemical or molecular research are not treated in detail here. *Paleoanthropology* is, then, a search of the fossil record in all its material manifestations; its goal is the reconstruction of the environmental milieu in which the close and distant ancestors of *Homo sapiens* existed.

ACKNOWLEDGMENTS

The help, cooperation and advice of a number of people and institutions made this book possible. My greatest thanks go to Professor Joseph Birdsell and Professor Michael Day, to whom this book is dedicated. Their advice, conscientiously given if not always sensibly taken, has been of great importance. My thanks must go to others who have read all or parts of the manuscript and made helpful suggestions: Ralph Holloway, Philip Stein, James Sackett, and Reiner Berger. Hans Kummer made many vital and enlightening suggestions which have been incorporated into Chapter 5.

My thanks must also go to individuals who allowed me to examine fossil materials in their care: Richard Leakey of the Kenya National Museum; Peter Andrews and Theya Molleson at the British Museum (Natural History); D. A. Hooijer at the Rijksmuseum van Natuurlijke Historie; Elizabeth Vrba and Bob Brain at the Transvaal Museum; Philip Tobias at the University of Witwatersrand; and Dave Golz at the Los Angeles County Museum.

Assistance, varied and generous, was also given by my graduate students Jan Austen and Tommy Thomas; and by my children, Mark and Karen.

G. E. Kennedy

PALEO-ANTHROPOLOGY

EVOLUTIONARY BIOLOGY, TAXONOMY, AND PALEOANTHROPOLOGY

INTRODUCTION

Paleoanthropology has the paradoxical distinction of being both a very new scientific discipline and a rather old one. Its roots extend into the mid-nineteenth century when anatomists, medical doctors, and "natural historians," stimulated by the discovery of "Neandertal Man" in 1856, were first confronting the implications of extinct human types. Charles Darwin's *Origin of Species*, published in 1859, at once reinforced speculations on human development while providing a theoretical framework within which the process could be explained.

The analytical approaches of the early workers consisted mainly of anatomical descriptions and metrical comparisons, reflecting the scope of the science of paleoanthropology at that time. Within the last two or three decades, however, burgeoning and even exponential progress in many scientific areas has stimulated the development of a number of new investigative tools and techniques, so that our current understanding of the events and processes of human evolution now has a depth and range not previously possible. Moreover, important recent fieldwork in Europe, India, and east Africa has increased the material evidence of human evolution; this evidence has added new areas of thought and investigation.

Paleoanthropology today represents a **synthetic**[1] science in the same sense that Huxley has termed the current theory of evolution a "synthetic" theory (1942). In both usages, the meaning of "synthetic" is the same: it is applied to a body of philosophy or data which has been elucidated and amplified by scientific advances in other fields. Developments in evolutionary biology, population genetics, biochemistry, geochronology, paleontology, ecology, biomechanics, multivariate statistics, and cybernetics have made perhaps the most important contributions to the development of the field of paleoanthropology. To this synthesis of methodologies, techniques, and concepts have been added the more traditional approaches of biometrics and descriptive, functional, and comparative anatomy. Thus our understanding of the evolutionary process in humans is now much more complete than ever before.

The implications of the synthetic viewpoint for the study of the events and processes of human evolution are several. Previously, emphasis has been focused mainly on the fossil evidence—that is, on the bones themselves. While it is true that the bones are still the vital part of the study, our new tools, methods, and concepts have provided many new ways to increase the data available from the fossil sample itself.

Three of these areas of scientific thought are relevant to understanding the evolutionary process itself which is the subject of this chapter. **Evolutionary biology** describes the processes by which evolutionary change occurs. **Taxonomy** relates to the practice of identifying and naming these evolutionary changes. Third, these and other areas of evolutionary knowledge are bound inextricably within the fabric of the **feedback model.**

FEEDBACK MODEL

Beyond analysis of the fossil sample, the synthetic approach demands that the history of human development be viewed in a broad and highly eclectic way. For example, data and information from social and cultural anthropology and archeology have been added to the models and theories of cybernetics and communications theory to provide a new approach to understanding the forces, directions, and relationships among differing types of evolutionary stimuli. The resultant constructions, called "feedback models," have been highly instructive in delineating the interrelationships that may exist between several levels of organization (Maruyama, 1963; Holloway, 1966, 1967).

By definition, feedback results when an action on one level influences an action or actions on other levels. Feedback systems may be of two types.

[1]Terms of particular importance in this text are set **boldface** when they are introduced. They are defined either in context or in the Glossary, pages 426–430.

In one type, deviations or alterations are eliminated, thus maintaining the status quo; these systems are referred to as "negative feedback systems." For example, a drop in temperature may trigger a thermostat which in turn ignites a furnace, thus causing the temperature to rise again to the desired level. Obviously, change is not permitted under such negative feedback systems, since they eliminate deviations.

The second type of feedback system is more relevant to the analysis of progressive changes; it is termed "positive feedback." In this model, any deviation from the norm is amplified and increased. In economics, compound interest is an example of such deviation amplification. Evolutionary studies provide excellent applications of this sort of feedback.

When a viable new situation arises, whether it is a genetic mutation, an environmental change, or a behavioral modification, adjustments must be made, since the original status quo is altered. The former pattern of relationships and interactions between environment and organism is changed, and new patterns must be established if the organism is to continue successfully. The adjustments may occur on several levels in living organisms.

In the human case, these levels represent biological development, behavioral patterns, and cultural manifestations (Figure 1-1). Within such a feedback model lies the suggestion that human beings have evolved not only physically and intellectually but also in terms of their social and cultural patterns. It is an obvious but sometimes overlooked fact that social and cultural traditions and structures did not arise suddenly, *de novo*, but were themselves subject to slow development and emergence. It is therefore important to view the development of humans on several levels: the behavioral, the cultural, and the physical, all of which are interactive within the external environment. Yet, it is also important and valuable to consider that these levels are all part of a single, yet multifaceted, process. For example, cultural development in terms of consistent, learned patterns of tool manufacture could not proceed without certain necessary biological prerequisites, such as coordinated eye-hand movement, depth perception, and manual flexibility and dexterity. Finally, brain development must have proceeded to a level capable of advanced associations, memory, planning, and communication.

In the same way, increases in the complexity of social organization reinforced, and were in turn reinforced by, the biological necessities of long-term dependency of the young, the need to communicate information about tool manufacture and use, and the exigencies of the later hominid pattern of big-game exploitation.

It can, in fact, be argued that the biological foundations for complex and stable social organization can be found in the greater maturation time characteristic of the order Primates. Such an increased development period extends the contact time between generations and expands the opportuni-

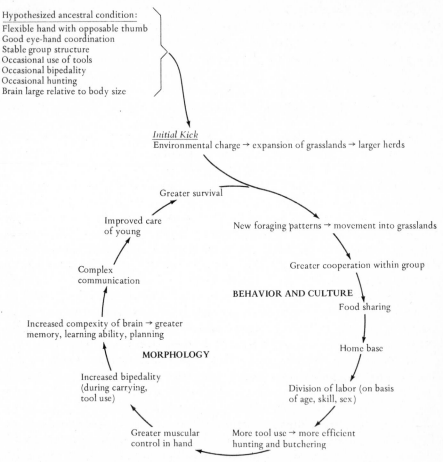

FIGURE 1-1 Feedback model. This hypothetical structure uses environmental change as an initiating event favoring greater use of hunted meat. The fossil record indicates that such an event could have occurred 9 to 10 million years ago; this event may have led to progressive evolutionary change in the hominids.

ty for the exchange of learned behavior patterns. The term "exchange" is a proper one in this context because information surely must flow both ways between generations. Primarily, of course, it is the older generation which passes on learned behavior. Also, however, the younger generation, with the curiosity and playfulness so characteristic of developing primates, must have made innovative additions to the behavioral repertoire of the whole group. Such play-based behavior has been termed "effectance motivation" (see Campbell, 1966). Finally, although the innovations may arise in a variety of ways, it must be the increased time of contact between generations that allows behavioral modification to be incorporated into the group behavioral structure.

One of the most interesting aspects of the theory of feedback structures is that such interactive patterns require an initiating event. Such an event, termed an **"initial kick,"** involves a deviation from a previously established set of interactions (see Maruyama, 1963; Holloway, 1966). The "initial kick" may involve environmental change, new genetic patterns, or a behavioral modification, such as a different location of nest site, a different time of feeding activity, or an alteration of food preparation.

There are, in fact, numerous examples of behavioral modifications in primates. Frisch (1968) reports that the practice of eating wheat spread through one troop of Japanese macaques within a period of 4 hours. Another troop of Japanese macaques, those on Koshima Island, acquired the ability to swim, so that within a period of 2 years, 37 of the 50 adult members of the troop were swimming in the sea. Even more interesting is the practice these same macaques developed of washing their sweet potatoes in the sea. The pattern was apparently initiated by a 16-month-old female who began washing her potatoes in a small brook; other young members of the troop started washing theirs in the sea, and eventually about 90 percent of the troop members sea-washed their food. As this pattern became more firmly established, bipedal locomotion grew more common. Frisch observed some members of the troop walking bipedally for distances of up to 50 meters carrying their sweet potatoes.

Another type of dietary and behavioral modification has been observed in a troop of baboons in Kenya. These baboons have recently begun to demonstrate predatory patterns that were not common in the group previously. Farmers in the area of Kekopey, northern Kenya, have eliminated most of the carnivores that kept the local antelope herds in check. In the absence of carnivore predation, the antelope began to expand in number, and with this expansion the baboons apparently assumed the role of predator (Harding and Strum, 1976). Most primates will kill and consume small game on an occasional and opportunistic basis, but the Kekopey baboons doubled their number of kills in a 2-year period. Moreover, although the adult males appeared to have initiated the behavior, eventually both adult females and juveniles also demonstrated predatory behavior. Harding and Strum observed that the predation has gradually taken on a more organized and cooperative aspect; now, several baboons may act together to capture the game. A further important aspect of this cooperation is that captured meat is now shared within the group; previously, hunted meat was consumed by the killer alone.

Obviously, we do not have the time perspective necessary to know whether these behavioral modifications will provide the basis for new evolutionary patterns. However, such modifications could provide the background for an entirely new set of selective pressures favoring the adaptation of new genetic patterns if they occur. Progressive evolutionary change depends on the incorporation of such genetic variation into the gene pool. But the selective advantage for new variations may arise from behavioral modifications of the type just described.

Equally often, selective advantage may arise from changes within the external environment. Such changes may involve temperature (warmer or colder), rainfall (drier or wetter), or the arrival (or departure) of organisms, and thus may alter the balances in the local ecosystem. Other environmental changes may involve drought, flood, famine, or disease. Whatever the source of the pressure, once the balance has been disturbed, however slightly, new adaptive patterns will emerge.

EVOLUTIONARY BIOLOGY

As outlined here, feedback models provide a comprehensive and interrelated way of viewing the evolutionary process. The comprehensive, synthetic approach is made up of many component parts. Of the various scientific disciplines that have contributed to the synthetic theory of evolution, biology has been, perhaps, the most productive.

Evolutionary biology is the study of dynamics of change in organic systems, and one of its conceptual keystones is the theory of natural selection.

NATURAL SELECTION

The theory of evolution in its most widely accepted form rests with Charles Darwin's concept of natural selection.

The process of natural selection begins with genetic variation, which may arise through either recombination of existing genetic material or entirely new genetic patterns called "mutations." Individuals carrying these new variations are subjected, like the rest of the population, to competition for food, water, space, and mates. If the new variation makes the individual more successful (more "fit," in Darwin s terms) in such competition, the individual will have a greater chance of surviving and passing on genetic material to the next generation. If this occurs, increasingly large numbers of individuals in future generations will carry the new genetic pattern. Gradually the population will be characterized by an increased frequency of the particular genetic pattern.

Speciation

Darwin, in naming his major work *The Origin of Species by Means of Natural Selection*, defined the importance of the process of speciation in the evolutionary process. Many definitions of the species exist in the literature, but most of them rest on the concept that a species is reproductively isolated from other species; that is, members of one species cannot interbreed with members of other species and produce fertile offspring. While it is true that interspecific crosses do occur (between tigers and lions, for example, and between horses and asses), this fact does not diminish the validity of the concept of species as reproductive isolates. Rather, it reinforces the fact that speciation is a continuing dynamic process, and that the genetic barriers between diverging populations may exist in varying degrees of effectiveness.

Many models exist in which the processes leading to the formation of new species have been theoretically defined. Although there are different "theories" of speciation, all revolve around one of two modes. Speciation may occur through a gradual morphological transformation from one level into another **(phyletic gradualism)** or it may occur when populations split and occupy different geographic areas **(multiplication of species)**.

Phyletic Gradualism   In Darwin's view, speciation involves the slow and gradual transformation of an ancestral population into a new descendant species. He called this process "descent with modification"; more recent workers have used the term "phyletic gradualism" (Eldredge and Gould, 1972). The transformation involves most or all populations within the species range. Because of continuous and frequent interbreeding among the local populations, favorable genetic patterns and mutations would eventually spread throughout the entire species. In this way, evolution would proceed at a slow and even pace, gradually adapting the species through time to any changes occurring in the environment. Thus the ancestral species A would ultimately become the descendant species B. Multiplication of species, or splitting, would not occur; one species would simply evolve into another.

The key concepts here are the slow, gradual emergence of one species from another without the intervention of geographic isolation and without an increase in the number of species. As a result of the gradual changes, time-successive populations will show few differences; it is only when a long series of populations is viewed in the continuum of geologic time that the changes become pronounced and visible. It is obvious that lines between time-successive species will be arbitrary and will be very difficult to define empirically. Under this sort of slow evolution, environmental changes are assumed to be minimal at any particular time. Consequently, selective pressures for quick, radical changes will also be assumed to be minimal.

Obviously, to validate this sort of theory from the fossil record, one must have long sequences of time-successive populations showing gradual alteration from one form to another. Such evidence is very difficult to obtain, and the explanation for this was originally proposed by Darwin himself. He recognized that such evidence would have to be forthcoming if his theory of the gradual "unfolding" of new species was to be accepted. However, in pointing out that the fossil record is very incomplete and is broken by long spells of nondeposition, erosion, volcanic activity, etc., he at one stroke countered any possible criticisms based on this lack and explained why such proof could never be given. Darwin concluded that all the intermediate forms had been present in the geologic past but were now irrecoverably lost.

It is, in fact, very difficult to document gradual phyletic changes in the fossil record; more often, the record shows abrupt morphological changes even between time-successive populations. Although Darwin and others have attempted to explain these discontinuities, still others have used this negative evidence in a new and positive way by suggesting that evolution may sometimes occur so rapidly that the few intervening forms have only a small chance of surviving in the fossil record (see Eldredge and Gould, 1972, and below).

Multiplication of Species   The second mode of speciation involves the multiplication, or splitting, of populations so that the number of species increases. This is the type of evolution more often identified in the fossil record, and hence it is of greater interest here.

SYMPATRIC SPECIATION   Some workers have proposed that multiplication of species can occur within geographically contiguous populations. Thus, sympatric speciation occurs when certain populations within the species develop progressive adaptations for certain local niches within the species range. These adaptations lead to greater inbreeding and behavioral isolation, which in turn, through time, lead to genetic isolation and the formation of new species.

The possibility that speciation will occur within geographically contiguous populations has been very strongly challenged by Mayr (1963, 1970). He has, in fact, argued that every case of proposed sympatric speciation can equally well, and perhaps more validly, be explained by geographic or allopatric speciation. He summarized his position as follows: "In not a single case is the sympatric model clearly superior to an explanation of the same natural phenomenon through geographic speciation" (1970, p. 273).

The dispute over the possibility of speciation in sympatric populations is of some interest in the evolution of the australopithecines of the Plio-Pleistocene. Members of that genus can be divided into gracile and robust groups which many workers have recognized as distinct species: *Australopithecus africanus*, *A. robustus*, and *A. boisei*. However, in most cases where a relatively large number of these hominids are present, the robust form occurs in association with the gracile form. Although we surmise that the robust group diverged from the gracile group, our knowledge is not complete enough to tell us where or when it did so. If Mayr's position against the likelihood of sympatric speciation is valid, we must assume that, at some point in time, a population of gracile australopithecines became geographically isolated and, under such conditions, developed the more specialized adaptations present in the robust group. Later, probably between 2 and 3 million years ago, this population reentered into the local coexistence that is particularly well documented in east Africa. We have not, however, identified the conditions and circumstances that may have led to such isolation. The problem remains open.

ALLOPATRIC OR GEOGRAPHIC SPECIATION   This mode of speciation depends on the evolution of new species in populations which have split off or become isolated from the central parent group. Such splitting may occur when populations invade new ranges or habitats; the conditions encountered in the new area will provide a set of selective pressures different from those to which the group had originally adapted. Isolation, here, would be a natural consequence of populations existing in peripheral or outlying areas. By virtue of their distance from the greater part of the population, it would be more likely, in a statistical sense, that a new, favorable genotype would be passed on to future local generations. In this model, the accumulation of favorable genotypes in the new environment would eventually lead to biochemical, morphological, and behavioral modifications of such magnitude that interbreeding with the parent population would ultimately no longer be successful. At the point where such interbreeding ceases to produce viable and fertile offspring, then, by definition, speciation has occurred.

This model of evolutionary change, instead of focusing on slow speciation throughout the range of an entire species, focuses on changes in local, isolated populations of the species. Therefore the emphasis is on peripheral, rather than central, populations. This is an important distinction and reflects underlying evolutionary processes rather different from those seen in the phyletic gradualism model.

Evolutionary change in peripheral populations may lead to the multiplication of species; this is a basic process through which **adaptive radiation** may occur. Adaptive radiation takes place when populations encounter ecosystems different from those in which they originally developed. The ecosystems may be old ones that are newly vacant. An example of this sort of adaptive radiation occurred in the Late Mesozoic when the ruling reptiles, previous occupants of many diversified niches, became extinct. With reptilian competition absent from marine, freshwater, arboreal, and ground habitats, the way was open for the mammals, still small and generalized, to expand. In the Early Cenozoic, the mammals underwent an explosive radiation and filled most of the habitats previously occupied by the reptiles. When the marsupials invaded Australia, they too underwent a similar phenomenon. Here, it was not a question of taking over previously occupied habitats but, rather, of moving into an area without competition or predation from placental carnivores. In Australia, the marsupials have radiated to occupy virtually all the habitats that placental mammals occupy elsewhere. There are "flying," grazing, burrowing, climbing, carnivorous, and insectivorous marsupials; nowhere else have they attained such diversity.

Adaptive radiation may also occur when existing ecosystems expand; such processes may have involved the angiosperm forests in the Early Cenozoic, the European tundra of the Pleistocene, and the grasslands of the Late Miocene and Pliocene. In all cases, forests, tundra, and grasslands had existed previously, but changes in the environment (mainly temperature and rainfall) resulted in their widespread expansion. As they widened, new habitats and new areas opened up for animals to exploit. The early hominids were among the animal groups that progressively occupied the newly expanding grasslands in the Late Miocene and Pliocene. It seems probable that the human lineage underwent an adaptive radiation at this time; such a radiation would explain the wide degree of diversity apparent in the hominids by Early Pleistocene times.

A second distinction between allopatric speciation and the phyletic gradualism model involves the rate or pace of the changes. In peripheral populations, evolution can, and occasionally must, proceed relatively rapidly. In recognition of such uneven evolutionary speed, Eldredge and Gould (1972) proposed the term **"punctuated equilibrium."** By this term they indicate that evolution under such conditions may proceed rapidly during the initial exploitation of the new habitat, then will slow as the population settles into the local ecosystem. The selective pressures in a new environment may be strong at first, and if a population, recently arrived, is to survive and succeed, it must change; the alternatives are to leave or become extinct. Second, such peripheral populations are, by definition, smaller than the total parent species. Such small population size would provide an advantageous situation for random gene changes, in the form of random genetic drift, to be incorporated into the gene pool (see Mayr, 1970). Such changes would tend to separate and further reinforce the differences between the parent and peripheral populations.

This model demands relatively rapid evolutionary change in peripheral populations. Under such conditions, it is unlikely that the intermediate forms would be preserved; thus, the absence of such forms from the fossil record is incorporated into the theory, rather than dismissed as in the phyletic gradualism model.

The evolution of *Homo sapiens* from *Homo erectus* may be an example of such variable rates of evolution. The earliest clear evidence of *Homo erectus* dates to about 1.5 million years (m.y.) ago; a well-preserved skull from

Lake Turkana[2] is not significantly different from that of "Peking Man" more than a million years later in time. In fact, throughout most of the species' range of over 1.25 million years, little progressive change is evident. Then, around the beginning of the Third Interglacial, a period of active evolution seems to have occurred. From this spurt of activity emerged the highly variable groups of early *Homo sapiens*, containing both Neandertals and groups of more modern appearance.

Although the evidence is much more fragmentary, this pattern of stasis, counterpointed by rapid changes, may also have occurred in the earliest hominids. The genus *Ramapithecus* was widespread throughout many areas of the Old World, yet little regional differentiation is apparent among the far-flung groups. Moreover, the earliest known members of the genus, about 15 million years ago, differ little from individuals living about 9 million years ago. More interesting, however, is the evidence that hominids with a ramapithecine dental pattern (particularly a third premolar with an enlarged outer cusp) occur as recently as 3 to 4 million years ago at Hadar and Laetolil. Thus a very consistent hominid dental pattern can be identified over an 11-million-year period.[3] After this long period of stasis, a rapid evolutionary diversification occurred between 2 and 3 million years ago; this resulted in diversification of the early hominid line and the appearance of the genus *Homo*.

Thus, in these two cases in hominid evolution, a punctuated equilibrium model seems applicable. Moreover, the demonstration that it does work in an explanatory framework rests, in these cases, not on negative or absent evidence but on empirical evidence of long-term morphological stasis punctuated with rapid bursts of evolutionary activity and diversification.

Evolutionary Change above the Species Level

Until recently, most evolutionary biologists have concluded that once the genetic isolation of the species had occurred, the foundations for higher levels of taxonomic differentiation—such as new genera, families, and orders—had also been laid. This approach takes the point of view that all evolution, whether below or above the species level, proceeds by a similar set of natural selective processes. However, some evolutionary biologists have proposed that evolution above the species level may involve a somewhat different set of competitive interactions. These newer models stress that in achieving higher levels of taxonomic differentiation, competition among related species may be more important than interactions

[2]Lake Turkana, formerly called Lake Rudolf, was renamed in 1976 by a decree of President Kenyatta of Kenya.

[3]Since our knowledge of the genus *Ramapithecus* is limited to jaws and teeth, we do not know what evolution (if any) was occurring in the rest of the body.

among populations and the physical environmental factors which are influential in the process of speciation (Bock, 1965, 1970, 1972; Stanley, 1973). This emphasis rests on the concept that the pressures and stresses of the physical environment are relatively finite and limited, and while the environment may show gradual and long-term change, these alterations are too slow and too slight to demand continuing and progressive evolutionary differentiation in local populations. Once an adaptation to an environment is made, natural selection will act to keep the population in equilibrium. Thus, the dynamic evolutionary pressures needed in the production of new genera, families, orders, etc., may come from other species in the same geographic area that may be in competition for the same basic resources. These competitive interactions may lead to ever more precise adaptations to niches within the habitat. The first change, under such conditions, could be a very small one involving only behavioral alteration: a change in nesting site, emphasis on one food over another, or a change in the daily rhythm of activities, for example. Such a change, however small, could set up an entirely new pattern of selective pressures which would, at the same time, reinforce and support the original behavioral alteration and provide a new selective background for morphological or functional change. Such a process, since it involves closely related groups, may be at least one of the evolutionary modes underlying adaptive radiation. Clearly, a feedback system is in operation in such cases, with the "initial kick" toward a new higher level of differentiation having been derived from a behavioral modification. Alternatively, however, the "initial kick" could have been derived from a new and advantageous genetic pattern.

Possible direct evidence that such a model may be in operation in the production of higher levels of taxonomic differentiation may be seen in **character displacement** (W. L. Brown and Wilson, 1956; W. L. Brown, 1958; Schaffer, 1968; Bock, 1970). This concept, which Darwin called "character divergence," suggests that closely related species living in the same area (in sympatry) will show more morphological difference than the same two species living apart (in allopatry). One explanation of character displacement is that, under the effect of competition for the same basic resources, each species may be forced into more intense and efficient exploitation of local niches (Lack, 1947). In this way, the two species may remain in geographic contiguity, but they may not, in fact, be dependent on identical resources within that area. In such a way, sympatry can be maintained because the effects of competition have been diminished.

An example of character displacement was proposed by Lack (1947). He noted that the Galapagos ground finches *Geospiza fortis Gould* and *Geospiza fulginosa Gould* differ from each other mainly in body size and beak proportions. In areas where the two species co-occur, they can easily be distinguished; the single parameter of beak depth gives a clear bimodal curve. Where only one species occurs, as on a number of small islands, this same measurement shows a single, unimodal curve intermediate between the distribution on the other islands. Lack concluded that the islands which contain only a single species may be too small to support populations of both species. However, since food resources appropriate to both species are locally present, an intermediate beak form would allow exploitation of multiple food sources.

The implications are that, under sympatry, competition may force a certain degree of specialization, so that the range of resources utilized by each species becomes narrowed. Under more relaxed allopatric conditions, all appropriate resources may be used, thus resulting in a less specialized morphology. Continued sympatric competition would favor and reinforce more specialized adaptations, thus driving the populations further apart.

For such a model of competitive interactions to be applied to the fossil record, it would be necessary to demonstrate that two or more closely related species were living in the same area at the same time. There are a number of situations in primate evolution where this may have occurred. In Middle Miocene times, for example, several different species of apes were living contemporaneously in the same area in east Africa (see Table 4-2). Primate paleontologists think that among these apes can be found the ancestral forms of living gibbons, chimps, gorillas, and humans.

It is possible that the model outlined here, which stresses the effect of competitive interactions among related species, forced these apes into more efficient exploitation of local niches. The ancestors of the chimps, for example, may have become (or remained) fruit- and leaf-eating forest dwellers; the gibbon ancestors may have occupied the high tree canopy; and the ancestral gorillas may have become less arboreal (because of their size) and more herbivorous. The ancestors of humans may have been forced, through continued competition, to the forest margins and eventually onto the grasslands where they adapted to a way of life almost unique for primates.

Thus, the effects of competition among several species of Miocene ape may have forced each species to occupy progressively more defined portions of the habitat. It is therefore significant that in Middle Miocene times in east Africa, a variety or mosaic of such niches was available. At Fort Ternan in Kenya, for example, lakeside environments, dense forests, and more open grasslands were all available to the local fauna (see Andrews and Walker, 1976, and Chapter 4). It is perhaps not an accident, then, that *Ramapithecus*, the earliest probable hominid, was part of such a mosaic environment both in east Africa and elsewhere.

GENERALIZATION AND SPECIALIZATION

The terms **"generalization"** and **"specialization"** are important in any discussion of evolution and are of special interest in primate history. These terms can be defined in a variety of ways. The most common definition involves the amount of evolutionary differentiation from an ancestral form. For example, a five-fingered hand is considered to be generalized, since five digits were present in the early terrestrial vertebrates. In the same way, the opossum is regarded as a generalized animal, since it has altered very little from the early marsupials in the Mesozoic. In this same form of usage, the term "specialization" would refer to an organ, a body part, or an animal that has changed greatly from the ancestral form. The foot of a horse is a good example of a specialized body part. The number of toes has been reduced from five to one and the remaining toe has itself become very much altered.

In these examples, the terms "generalization" and "specialization" have been used to describe visible levels of morphological organization. However, there may be subtler levels of biological organization that are less apparent and that do not correspond to the external pattern. The human hand is a good example of such paradoxical organization. It is little altered in its gross morphological structure from that of the early vertebrates; the flexible five rays, or the five-fingered form, is a constant feature. However, in terms of its underlying muscular and neurological organization, it is vastly different from the hand of the early vertebrate ancestors and, in this sense, must be regarded as a highly specialized body part (see Chapter 2).

The terms may also be used to describe functional capability. For example, a type of locomotion that is very limited in its range of expression is regarded as specialized. Within the mammalia, an extreme example would be the cetaceans, the aquatic mammals; evolutionary changes have altered them from quadrupedal terrestrial mammals in the Eocene to the fish-like animals of today (Romer, 1945). In this case, evolutionary changes have restricted their locomotion to a single mode, that of swimming. A less extreme example would be the hoofed mammals, such as horses and cows. Their five-fingered ancestors in the Early Cenozoic could move in a variety of strata, including trees. Living hoofed mammals have lost this capacity and now move efficiently only over more-or-less flat surfaces. Many primates, on the other hand, have relatively generalized locomotor patterns. A "modified brachiator," such as the orangutan, can move with speed and agility, using its forelimbs to propel it through the trees; it may also use its hindlimbs to support or suspend the body while in the trees. On the ground surface, orangutans may move quadrupedally or they may move bipedally, using only the hindlimbs for support and propulsion. The human form of bipedality must be regarded as a specialization in terms of both structure and capability. A number of modifications have occurred in the human skeleton at the hip, knee, and foot, involving the centering of body mass in a plane perpendicular to the ground surface. Moreover, the shortening of the forelimb relative to the hindlimb and changes in the pelvis mean that, while a quadrupedal stance is still possible, as in babies, it is uncomfortable and inefficient for adults. It is interesting that we have not entirely lost the brachiating ability of our ancestors; our shoulder joints are still highly mobile and flexible.

TAXONOMY

One of the traditional goals of biological studies, whether of living or fossil populations, has been the naming or classification of groups. In this context the terms of "systematics," "taxonomy," and "classification" are often, and incorrectly, used interchangeably. Systematics is the scientific study of the diversity of organisms and of the relationships among them.[4] Systematists thus study the structure and diversity of organisms and from these data try to determine the relationships among groups of animals. This study forms the raw material of classification, which is the practice of naming animals and, in so doing, formalizing their relationships with other animals. Taxonomy is the theoretical study of the theory and principles of naming animals.

Much of this text will be concerned with classification; the reason for this is twofold. First, classification provides a semantic device—a name—that gives a convenient and widely understood reference. Second, classification provides a categorizing tool that allows the indication of what something is by placing it within a nominal framework that relates it to other specimens. Thus, classification, or the naming of animals, is a vital component in any evolutionary study in that a name at once provides a point of reference and an indication of relationships.

LINNAEAN SYSTEM

Although various naming systems have been suggested since the time of Aristotle, the one proposed by Linnaeus in 1735 has gained the most widespread acceptance. Building on Linnaeus's work, taxonomists have developed a seven-level system of formalized relationships called the "Linnaean hierarchy" (Table 1-1).

Biospecies

From a biological standpoint, the last of the Linnaean categories, the species, is the most important. The Linnaean concept of the species centered on the demonstration of reproductive isolation; that is, members of one species may not interbreed with members of other species to produce fertile offspring. This definition recognizes that genetic differences between two species are so great that reproduction cannot be successful. Such a definition of the **biospecies** is almost universally applied by

---

[4]These terms have been discussed and defined by Simpson (1961).

TABLE 1-1   The Linnaean Hierarchy of *Homo Sapiens*

Kingdom	Animalia
Phylum	Vertebrata
Class	Mammalia
Order	Primates
Family	Hominidae
Genus	*Homo*
Species	*sapiens*

Note: The Linnaean hierarchy is a conventional way of indicating levels of relationships in a descending order; thus all animals are included in the animal kingdom, but only those with backbones are placed with the vertebrates.

biologists in studies on living populations. Included within the scope of the biospecies definition are two other important concepts: the **type** and the ecological niche, the **econiche**.

Type   The concept of type is a basic one in Linnaean taxonomy. The idea derives, initially, from the philosophy of Plato, who envisioned the "real world" as a pale and muted reflection of reality and taught that to seek truth means to search for underlying and hidden meanings. Thus, ultimate truth or ultimate essence, in Plato's thinking, existed in the realm of the gods, but only a mongrelized version of these truths was available to humans.

This concept of an ultimate, but unreachable, reality has become embedded in both the philosophical and the practical aspects of Linnaean taxonomy and classification. The concept of typology states that every natural group shares a basic complex of features which does not vary; when variations on this pattern do occur, they are to be regarded as accidental and without meaning. Thus, every group has an underlying, idealized basic pattern or plan.

Translated into the practical terms of classification, this concept means that when a new species is proposed, it is based on a "type" against which all future and potential members of the species are to be compared. Technically, the type is the first example found of the new species. Thus, the characteristics of the first-found specimen becomes the model or ideal against which all future and potential members of the species will be compared. If they meet all the criteria (a rare occurrence), the new specimen can be included within the existing species; more often, however, a new group must be proposed. Such a situation has led to a proliferation of unneeded names because of a very narrow application of the type-species concept; that is, no account has been taken of the very wide range of variation that may exist within species.

Ecological Niche   Also relevant to the Linnaean biospecies concept is the concept of the ecological niche. The ecological niche has been called an organism's "profession"; it is "the position or status of an organism within its community and ecosystem resulting from the organism's structural adaptations, physiological responses and specific behavior (inherited and/or learned)" (Odum, 1959). Thus, a niche is what an organism does within an ecosystem; it refers, in a precise way, to how organisms obtain their sustenance and how they interact with other organisms in the same system.

An obvious extension of such a definition is that no two species can occupy the same econiche. This is the concept of **competitive exclusion,** which was developed by Gause in 1934 and sometimes called "Gause's principle." If two species are in competition for a particular complex of resources within the same local area, Gause thought it impossible that interactions could continue indefinitely. More likely, one species would be excluded from exploiting at least some of the resources and would thus alter its niche requirements. The excluded species could either alter its niche, leave the area, or become extinct.

Fossil Species

In keeping with scientific doctrine and the perspective of his day, Linnaeus viewed species as fixed and immutable or unchanging. Moreover, he also regarded them as having been specially created. This view was indeed appropriate at a time when neither the theory of evolution nor the vast scope of geologic time was known. The Linnaean system thus deals only with living, contemporaneous species and is based on a horizontal time perspective. It does not deal with populations or species in the vertical dimension of time. Because Linnaeus saw species as unchanging, he understandably provided no method of indicating the evolution of one species to another.

It is one of the great paradoxes in paleontological theory that a naming system that ignores the existence of change came to be the basic tool in the identification of rock strata that contain the proof of just such evolutionary change.

The practice of recognizing and defining rock strata by the fossils contained within them was first devised by William ("Strata") Smith in 1799. In 1816 he even more firmly and clearly laid the foundations for the use of **index fossils** in the identification of rock strata.

In the use of index fossils, the age of rock strata is determined by the kinds of fossils contained in them. Thus, one of the index fossils used to identify Early Eocene beds in the north-central United States is the fossil prosimian *Pelycodus* (see Chapter 3). In the same way, the presence of the three-toed horse *Hipparion* defines strata of the Vallesian or late Middle Miocene age in Europe.

Since index fossils were designated by Linnaean names, classification became a basic tool of paleontologists and geologists in the study of earth history. Indeed, this practice seemed perfectly valid in the early days of both geology and paleontology, when most stratigraphic successions were incompletely or imperfectly known and the gaps in the fossil record appeared to reflect major morphological discontinuities between species. But as the stratigraphic record became more completely known, it appeared that the morphological discontinuities in evolving lineages were not real but, rather, reflected breaks in the depositional process. Thus, as the fossil record became more completely known, it grew progressively clearer that any separation of an evolving lineage into different species was largely arbitrary.

The paradox thus becomes this: While biospecies, by definition, cannot interbreed with one another, the process of evolution demands the occurrence of just such events. For example, most hominid paleontologists accept the theory that *Homo erectus* evolved into *Homo sapiens*, and yet, by placing them in different species, we deny, by definition, the possibility of such an event. This paradoxical situation is complicated by the impossibility of proving (or disproving) genetic exchange between fossil populations. The fragmentary fossil record simply cannot give such information.

In order to resolve these problems at least partially, new species definitions were proposed to deal with observable differences rather than with unobservable breeding success.

The term **"morphospecies"** (see Cain, 1954) is based on the concept that morphological distinctiveness may be used as a species criterion. Morphological differences are therefore equated with specific distinctiveness.

This point of view can be criticized on the ground that morphological distinctions are secondary to genetic distinctions; morphological differences are, therefore, an effect of genetic isolation rather than its cause (Mayr, 1970). Moreover, in the absence of clear-cut, empirical evidence of the genetic isolation that is possible in living populations, definitions of morphospecies become subjective and even arbitrary. There is no agreement among paleontologists regarding just what features and what allowable ranges of variation may be included in any particular species.

In an effort to circumvent the difficulties of applying the concept of a morphospecies, some paleontologists have proposed the use of another concept: the **chronospecies** or **paleospecies**. Both terms are applied to successive, transitory, vertical populations, each of which at any single time level is a valid biospecies; they are "integrated phyletic successions of biospecies" (George, 1956). Theoretically, this is an attractive concept, and the use of a defined time level would provide an empiricism absent in the other concepts of fossil species. In the reality of practical application, however, the concept of a chronospecies is as difficult to use as the other approaches.

How, for example, can a decision be made on when one evolving species ends and its successor begins? This is a very real problem in paleontology, particularly in species that were widespread geographically. In such species, some populations may become either partially or completely isolated; with separation of the gene pools, evolutionary changes and the rates of such changes may proceed rather differently in each population. Such a case, for example, may have occurred in hominids during the Middle Pleistocene. We know that populations of *Homo erectus* occupied the island of Java more than 1 m.y. ago (see Chapter 8). Presumably they entered the island over a land bridge during a period of low sea level. Later, when the sea level rose, the island and the human population became isolated. In the early Upper Pleistocene, the Solo population on Java retained many features characteristic of *Homo erectus* at a time when fully modern *Homo sapiens* populations had appeared elsewhere.

Recently, attempts have been made by a number of paleontologists to place the classification of fossil groups on a more objective and empirical base. Some of these attempts have involved the use of **cladistics**.

CLADISTIC TAXONOMY

In the approaches described above, the emphasis most often is placed on defining ancestor-descendant relationships. In order to do this, a variety of information is often included in the decision-making process. Information, such as facts on chronology, behavior, and environment, is often added to morphological or structural data. Thus, quite logically, most students of evolution have attempted to place specimens under study within a phylogenetic or evolutionary framework. While admirable in intent, such hypotheses of phylogeny are essentially untestable (see Delson, Eldredge, and Tattersall, 1977). Paleontologists can never know, with any degree of real certainty, that one form was actually ancestral to another. Moreover, chronology, while accurate within broad ranges, is never precise in limited ranges (see the Appendix, page 417). Behavior and environment, while important and interesting areas of paleontological inquiry, should not be included within taxonomic decisions, since these features can only be inferred from the fossil record.

The recognition of these problems has led to the development of the cladistic approach to taxonomy (a "clade" is defined as a group of closely related organisms). Cladistic taxonomy was first defined by Hennig in 1950 and expanded in a later book (1966). Others, such as Remane (1961), Le Gros Clark (1962), and R. D. Martin (1968), have applied Hennig's methodology to the order Primates. More recently, a number of papers have attempted to apply a cladistic approach to problems in hominid taxonomy (Eldredge and Tattersall, 1975; Delson, 1978, Delson et al. 1977).

The cladistic methodology does not seek to define ancestor-descendant relationships as most other techniques do, but, rather, tries to identify closely related or "sister" taxa on the basis of shared morphological traits. Cladistic taxonomies do not include time or other information in the relationships drawn.

In the terminology of cladistics, characters or character sets can be of two types. Conservative, unspecialized, primitive, or **symplesiomorphic** characters have been inherited unchanged from an ancestral form. Such symplesiomorphic characters help to define large groups of related forms. For example, the Hominoidea (including the great apes and humans, both fossil and living) are grouped together because they all share certain dental, cranial, and postcranial features (reduction of honing ability of the lower third premolar, enlargement of incisors relative to molars, increase of brain size relative to body size, among others) (see Delson and Andrews, 1975). Similarly, the Eocene adapids are included within the Lemuriformes because they share a number of distinctive features: among them, inclusion of a free tympanic bone within the auditory bulla and small promontory artery (see Chapter 3).

The second type of character set in cladistic taxonomy is termed **"synapomorphic."** These characters represent more advanced, more specialized features which were derived after an evolutionary or genetic split. The presence of such advanced or derived features signifies that evolution has occurred and that a new group has emerged. For example, the Hominidae (including *Ramapithecus*, *Australopithecus*, and *Homo*) are placed together because they all share a distinctive morphological pattern found in no other group. These features, in part, include reduced canines, two cusps on the the lower third premolar, cheek teeth with thick enamel, greater wear gradient, and a short, nonprognathous face (see Delson et al., 1977).

Cladistic taxonomy, based on the identification of shared character sets, thus has an empirical, nonsubjective base. It is the approach which will be used, either explicitly or implicitly, throughout this text.

SUMMARY

In this chapter we have looked at some of the theoretical and practical problems associated with paleoanthropology.

The feedback model will provide both the implicit and the explicit framework for the following survey of primate and human evolution. It is a basic concept of the view of evolution brought forward here that the organism is just one component in a dynamic environment composed of food resources, climate, and other organisms. Moreover, the organism itself is composed of different levels of organization, each interacting with other levels of organization in mutual cause-and-effect patterns. All these factors and their interrelationships must be evaluated in any study of the evolutionary process.

The theory of evolution has itself been shown to be dynamic and subject to change. While the basic tenets of Darwinian natural selection are basically unchanged, several new ideas have slightly altered our perception of the ways in which evolution proceeds. For example, the process of speciation, a basic event in the evolutionary progression, was viewed by Darwin as a slow and steady, step-by-step transformation of one species into another. More recent ideas, however, have suggested that speciation may not be such a stately progression, but may, in fact, proceed at highly variable speeds. Thus, the punctuated equilibrium model is now posing a challenge to Darwin's phyletic gradualism model.

This chapter has also described some of the basic semantics, ideas, procedures, and problems involved in the naming of organisms. Taxonomy is an integral part of any study on evolution because it at once provides a name for a specimen and places that specimen in relationship to other specimens.

In the classification of living organisms, species boundaries are usually clear-cut and definable; when they are not, experiments can be conducted to test whether or not barriers to breeding are present. No such luxury exists in paleontology, however, and often classification proceeds on the slimmest of evidence. Moreover, that evidence is frequently equivocal in that it is incompletely known and imperfectly understood.

However, the chapter has emphasized that in the practice of classification, independently acquired, or synapomorphic, characters are the ones that should be used when possible in drawing boundaries between organisms. Such unique or distinctive characters indicate that genetic isolation has occurred, and such genetic isolation is a basic requirement in the formation of new taxa.

SUGGESTIONS FOR FURTHER READING

Gould, S. J. 1977. *Phylogeny and Ontogeny*. Cambridge, Mass.: Harvard University Press. (An important book that is forcing a new look at certain evolutionary processes, particularly neoteny.)

Huxley, J. 1942. *Evolution, the Modern Synthesis*. London: Allen & Unwin. (A major work that laid the groundwork for the integration of the biological sciences, particularly population genetics, with the theory of evolution.)

Le Gros Clark, W. E. 1962. *The Antecedents of Man* (2d ed.). Edinburgh: Edinburgh University Press. (Although somewhat out of date, still a sound theoretical approach to primate evolution.)

Martin, R. D. 1968. "Towards a New Definition of Primates," *Man*, **3,** 376–406. (An important paper, building on earlier work of Le Gros Clark and emphasizing the necessity of understanding the origin of characters before they are used in classification.)

Mayr, E. 1963. *Animal Species and Evolution*, Cambridge, Mass.: The Belknap Press, Harvard University Press. (An important statement of the application of evolutionary theory.)

Mayr, E. 1976. *Evolution and the Diversity of Life*, Cambridge, Mass.: The Belknap Press, Harvard University Press. (A series of essays discussing various aspects of evolution.)

Rensch, B. 1960. *Evolution above the Species Level*. New York: Columbia University Press. (A major statement of the concept that evolution both below and above the species level proceeds in the same way.)

Schopf, T. (ed.). 1972. *Models in Paleobiology*. San Francisco: Freeman, Cooper and Co. (An important collection of papers dealing with the application of the principles of evolutionary biology to paleontology.)

Simpson, G. G. 1945. "The Principles of Classification and a Classification of Mammals," *Bulletin, American Museum of Natural History*, **85,** 1–350. (The basic work on the classification of the mammals.)

Simpson, G. G. 1961. *Principles of Animal Taxonomy*. New York: Columbia University Press. (A more up-to-date and more theoretical work than Simpson's 1945 paper.)

Sylvester-Bradley, P. C. (ed.). 1956. *The Species Concept in Palaeontology*. London: Systematics Association Pub., no. 20. (A collection of papers on this important problem.)

2

THE ORDER PRIMATES

THE MAMMALS

ORIGINS OF THE MAMMALS

The history of the order Primates should ultimately be viewed not only in terms of the history of the class Mammalia but also within the full perspective of vertebrate evolution (Table 2-1). For, although the primates represent just one of the many diversified lines within the Mammalia, the class, as a group, shares many evolutionary features.

Although some aspects of mammalian origins are still subject to controversy, there is little doubt that the class originated from the mammal-like or therapsid reptiles in the Triassic. The therapsids sit on the boundary between the reptiles and the mammals and share characteristics with both classes. Reptiles, for example, are characterized by having just one type of tooth, which is conical in shape. The mammals and the therapsids have a differentiated dentition consisting of incisors, canines, and molars with multiple cusps. Reptilian limbs sprawl out to the side of the body; the mammals and the therapsids have limbs which are brought under the body. Reptiles are cold-blooded, but both therapsids and mammals are warm-blooded. On the other hand, the therapsids still have the multiple openings in the skull, including one for the pineal gland, typical of the early reptiles.

One question of particular interest is just how many lines of therapsid

TABLE 2-1   Geologic time scale

PERIOD			DESCRIPTION
	Quaternary	Recent	Diversification of *Homo*
		Pleistocene	First *Homo sapiens*
Cenozoic m.y. B.P.	Tertiary	Pliocene	Expansion and diversification of hominids
			First hominids
		Miocene	Expansion and diversification of apes and monkeys
		Oligocene	
			First anthropoids
		Eocene	Expansion and diversification of prosimians
		Paleocene	
Mesozoic 70 m.y. B.P.	Cretaceous		First primates
			First flowering plants
	Jurassic		First mammals
			First birds
	Triassic		First dinosaurs
Paleozoic 230 m.y. B.P.*	Permian		Extinction of many forms
	Pennsylvanian		First insects — Large coal-forming swamps
	Mississippian		First reptiles
	Devonian		First land plants and animals — Expansion of bony fishes
			First amphibians — Scorpions, millipedes
	Silurian		
	Orodvician		First vertebrates — Corals, cephalopods
	Cambrian		Trilobites, sponges, Brachiopods
Proterozoic 600			First invertebrates
			First life
Archeozoic			

*B.P. = before the present.

reptiles were involved in the development of the mammals. Some workers (Olson, 1944) have documented the development of mammal-like characters in several separate lineages of therapsids, giving rise to the hypothesis that separate groups of later mammals had separate ancestors within the reptiles. This **polyphyletic** theory of mammalian origins would therefore see the living placentals, marsupials, and monotremes as probably having been derived from separate lineages of therapsids; they have thus had a long and independent history. Alternatively, Hopson and Crompton (1969) have proposed a **monophyletic** theory suggesting that all mammals came from a single group of therapsids; still others, such as Kielan-Jaworowska (1975), have suggested that all living mammals have come from two reptilian groups.

In terms of evolutionary history, the reptiles represent the primary phase in the acquisition, by the vertebrates, of a totally terrestrial way of life. Less advanced land vertebrates, such as the amphibians, must return to the water for reproduction, but the reptiles, having a hard-shelled egg (the **amniote egg**) which is laid on dry land, are totally divorced from aquatic environments. The amphibians, therefore, live in two worlds, the aquatic and the terrestrial, and their morphology represents something of a compromise between these two habitats. They can become fully specialized to neither. But the reptiles, fully independent of water, can pursue, in an evolutionary sense, adaptations to and specializations in a terrestrial way of life to a degree not previously possible. This freedom permitted them, in the increasingly dry and desiccated conditions of the Late Paleozoic and Mesozoic, to move great distances away from permanent water sources. This liberation from aquatic environments allowed them the geographic range necessary to develop the extreme diversification the group was to undergo during the course of the Mesozoic.

During the Mesozoic the reptiles radiated to occupy virtually every kind of habitat. Members of the class Reptilia made adaptations to grasslands, to forests, to deserts, to the air; others, coming full circle, resumed life in the water. The dinosaurs became carnivores, herbivores, omnivores, and insectivores. We don't know why so many of these forms, after such a long period of evolutionary success, became extinct; but none of the dinosaurs survived the end of the Mesozoic.[1]

RADIATION OF THE MAMMALS

During the florescence of the ruling reptiles, the mammals remained small and inconspicuous animals. The strong competition of the reptiles proba-

---

[1]Some authors have recently made the fascinating suggestion that the dinosaurs are not extinct but still exist as the birds. This is part of a larger theory which appears to demonstrate successfully that the dinosaurs were not cold-blooded, as are living reptiles such as lizards and snakes, but were warm-blooded, like birds and mammals. (See Bakker, 1975; Seymour, 1976; Desmond, 1975.)

bly prevented them from radiating into too many niches. But with the extinction of the ruling reptiles, the mammals reacted with almost explosive evolutionary vigor and soon filled most of the vacant niches.

The class Mammalia (Table 2-2) represents a second phase in vertebrate adaptations to terrestrial life. Unlike the reptiles, the mammals nurture their young, thus improving their chance for survival. The process of nurturing necessitates a longer period of contact between generations, thereby increasing the opportunities for the exchange of information. Thus, the biological process of providing sustenance for the young also provides an environment in which learning can occur. It is from this biological background that the complex behavior patterns characteristic of the mammalia have emerged.

Other external factors were also at work in the survival and success of the mammals. One of the vitally important factors in the Cenozoic radiation of the mammals in general and the primates in particular was the expansion of the angiosperms. The angiosperms, one of the major divisions of the plant world, are distinguished by having their seeds enclosed in capsules; the group contains almost all deciduous and flowering plants, including the fruit and vegetable groups. By Early Cretaceous times, such trees as the cinnamon, magnolia, fig, and poplar

TABLE 2-2 Class Mammalia

Class: Mammalia
  Subclass: Prototheria
     Order: Monotremata: egg-laying mammals: duck-billed platypus
  Subclass: Theria
   Infraclass: Metatheria
     Order: Marsupialia: pouched mammals: opossums, kangaroos, koala "bears"
   Infraclass: Eutheria: placental mammals
     Order: Insectivora: moles, shrews, hedgehogs
     Order: Dermoptera: "flying lemurs"
     Order: Chiroptera: bats
     Order: Primates: prosimians, monkeys, apes, humans
     Order: Edentata: sloths, anteaters, armadillos
     Order: Pholidota: pangolins (scaly anteaters)
     Order: Lagomorpha: pikas, hares, rabbits
     Order: Rodentia: squirrels, gophers, rats, mice, porcupines, beavers
     Order: Cetacea: whales, dolphins, porpoises
     Order: Carnivora: dogs, cats, bears, raccoons, pandas, mink, skunks, civets, hyenas, weasels, badgers, seals, sea lions, walruses
     Order: Tubulidentata: aardvarks
     Order: Proboscidea: elephants
     Order: Hyracoidea: coneys, hyraxes
     Order: Sirenia: manatees or "sea cows"
     Order: Perissodactyla: horses, asses, zebras, tapirs, rhinos
     Order: Artiodactyla: pigs, hippos, camels, deer, giraffes, bovids (sheep, goats, bison, cows)

existed; and by Middle Cretaceous times, forests consisted largely of trees belonging to modern genera (Dunbar, 1956).

The development of arboreal ecosystems, made up largely of fruiting and flowering angiosperms, was a vital step in the development of animals dependent not only on the safety and refuge of the trees but also on their food products. Several arboreally dependent groups exist within the mammalia: insectivores, squirrels, bats, and primates are among them. Without the Mesozoic expansion of the angiosperms, it is doubtful that the evolution of a number of mammalian groups, including the primates, would have followed the course that it did.

By the Late Mesozoic, the adaptive radiation of the mammals was well under way.

Paleontologists today agree that the order Primates developed from a more generalized mammalian form within the order Insectivora. The insectivores, which now include such forms as tree shrews, hedgehogs, and moles, are a very generalized group whose Mesozoic members probably provided the ancestors of a number of mammalian orders. In fact, the insect-eating mammals of the later Mesozoic supplied the ancestral populations for the major radiation of plant-eating mammals that occurred in the Late Mesozoic and Early Cenozoic. This early radiation of herbivorous mammals filled many of the niches previously occupied by the plant-eating dinosaurs (Colbert, 1973).

The primates were among the first to emerge from the insectivore stem, but they were soon followed, in the Early Cenozoic, by bats, lagomorphs (rabbits), and horses (Romer, 1945). A number of bizarre forms were part of this early herbivore radiation. The South American pyrotheres developed an elephant-like trunk; the rhinoceros-like arsinotheres were about 3.35 m (11 ft) in length and had two huge horns on the tops of their heads; the widespread uintatheres were enormous and their heads were topped by three horns (Colbert, 1973; Romer, 1945).

The radiation of the early mammals was formidable; in the Late Cretaceous there were 13 families of mammals, but by the end of the Paleocene, the first epoch of the Cenozoic, there were 41 families (Kurten, 1971).

Within the insectivores, the family Tupaiidae, which contains the tree shrews, shares a number of characteristics with the primates. Some of these characteristics are so similar, in fact, that there has been a continuing controversy over whether the tree shrews should be placed within the order Insectivora or the order Primates. Napier and Napier (1967), Le Gros Clark (1965), Hill (1953–1962), and Goodman (1962a, b, and 1963) have favored including the tree shrews within the prosimians as the most primitive form of living primate. Others, however, have argued that the tree shrews should be included within the insectivores (R. D. Martin, 1975; Buettner-Janusch, 1973).

The final placement of the tree shrews will depend, however, on the selection of traits used to define the order Primates and, in the trait complex used here, the tupaiids will be excluded from the primates. However, the major question is not ultimately to determine to which group the tree shrews belong, since this is arbitrarily determined in the selection (or exclusion) of traits assumed to be ordinal significance. What is important is the recognition that the tree shrews, by virtue of their morphological complex of primate and insectivore traits, may resemble, in a general way, the ancestor from which the order Primates was derived. They appear to be a form of somewhat transitional morphology, and the significance of that morphology should not be minimized by demanding that they be placed within one group and excluded from the other. The usefulness of taxonomy as a categorizing tool should not be allowed to obscure or minimize the importance of transitional or compound forms when they occur. The tree shrews may well sit on the morphological boundary between the order Insectivora and the order Primates.

THE PRIMATES

ORIGINS OF THE ORDER

A number of students of evolution have tried to identify the selective pressures underlying the initial divergence of the primates. One of these was Grafton Elliott-Smith, a neuroanatomist who was chiefly concerned with the emergence of the primate brain. He hypothesized (1912) that the ancestors of the primates were terrestrial forms which eventually came to occupy arboreal habitats. He argued that the selective pressures in such a habitat would differ from those encountered in a terrestrial way of life. One of the major changes involved the usefulness of the olfactory sense. Terrestrial animals depend largely on their sense of smell to detect both food and enemies. However, an acute sense of smell, while still useful in the trees, is not sufficient in a habitat that demands a variety of rapid and precise motor and sensory responses. Thus, with the acquisition of arboreal life, Elliott-Smith argued, vision and touch became the predominant senses. Moreover, the hand, grasping and flexible, came to perform the functions formerly served by the lips and mouth in obtaining food. Elliott-Smith, then, viewed the primates as mammals adapted to arboreal life through the elaboration of the visual, tactile, and motor areas of the brain. This proposal has come to be called the **"arboreal theory"** of primate origins.

Frederick Wood-Jones, a student of Elliott-Smith's, shared his teacher's functional-arboreal explanation of primate origins. Wood-Jones, however, placed his emphasis on the development of the primate hand and foot (1916). He reasoned that the arboreal habitat would place selective pressure on the development of a hand specialized for precise grasping abilities; this ability is called **"prehension"**. Thus the primate hand functioned not only as an organ of locomotion but also as a food gatherer. Wood-Jones conceived of the primate adaptation as being constructed, at the base, of a flexible hand but also including some of the changes necessary for arboreal life, such as stereoscopic vision with overlapping visual fields and upright posture. He argued that the diminution of the olfactory sense resulted in a decrease in the length of the snout. The loss of the large snout permitted the eyes to be drawn together toward the center of the face so that the visual fields could become superimposed.

The major concepts of the arboreal theory were later crystallized by Le Gros Clark (1965). However, he did not view the primates as representing a new stage of arboreal adaptation but, rather, as a continuation of arboreal life within a generalized mammalian group. Indeed, much of Le Gros Clark's application of the arboreal theory stressed the generalized nature of primate morphology and the lack of locomotor and dietary specializations typical of many members of the class Mammalia.

The question of the arboreal origins and adaptations of the primates can be approached from a slightly different perspective. Matthew (1904; see also Gregory, 1920), in reviewing the morphology of the early placental mammals, concluded that originally they were arboreal. Therefore, occupation of arboreal habitats would be very ancient in the placental mammals. Matthew argued that arboreal life allowed the early mammals to retain a primitive and unspecialized morphology. Terrestrial adaptations, on the other hand, almost invariably involve a number of specializations, especially in the locomotor systems. There is, for example, a tendency in terrestrial forms to compress and elongate the limbs; grasping and flexible hands and feet which are advantageous in the trees may face negative selection on the ground. Terrestrial movement is more rapid and efficient if the limbs move only in a fore-and-aft plane; a shoulder or hip which freely rotates would be a hopeless impediment in running on solid ground. But, in the multiple strata of the trees, flexibility of movement is demanded. The presence of a clavicle, of five free digits, of unfused radius and ulna, and unfused tibia and fibula would all be advantageous in the trees; they are all basic characteristics of the primates. Under this model, it is not remarkable, then, that humans, the most terrestrial of the primates, are also among the most specialized in terms of locomotion. Many morphological characters of humans are associated with bringing the body into a plane perpendicular to the ground surface. The shortened and backwardly curved ilium on the pelvis, the laterally compressed foot without the divergent big toe of the other primates, and the downward-directed foramen magnum (in the base of the skull) are all manifestations of this adaptation (Figure 2-1).

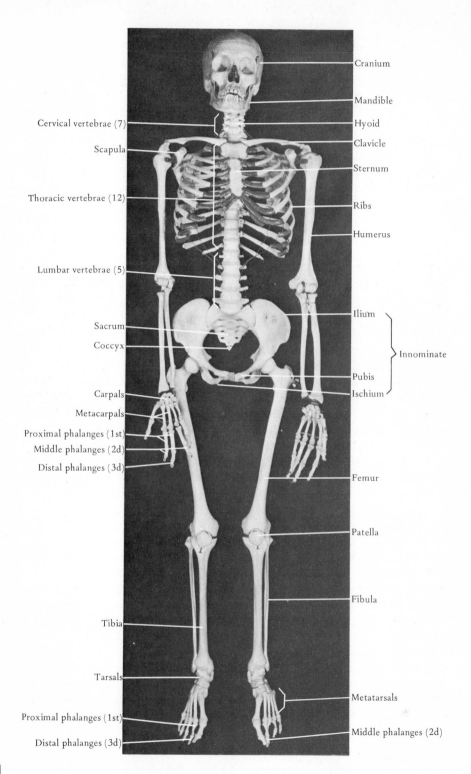

Cranium

Mandible

Cervical vertebrae (7)

Hyoid

Scapula

Clavicle

Sternum

Thoracic vertebrae (12)

Ribs

Humerus

Lumbar vertebrae (5)

Ilium

Innominate

Sacrum

Coccyx

Pubis

Ischium

Carpals

Metacarpals

Proximal phalanges (1st)

Middle phalanges (2d)

Distal phalanges (3d)

Femur

Patella

Fibula

Tibia

Tarsals

Metatarsals

Proximal phalanges (1st)

Middle phalanges (2d)

Distal phalanges (3d)

Recently, however, the arboreal theory of primate origins has been questioned. Cartmill (1972, 1974) has pointed out that many mammals are arboreally adapted and yet do not have the major ordinal characters of primates. Tree squirrels (Sciurinae), for example, have laterally facing eyes, no stereoscopic vision, no significant reduction of the olfactory sense, claws on all digits except the thumb, and no opposability of either thumb or big toe. Yet, the tree squirrels are well-adapted and successful arboreal mammals. Cartmill has therefore suggested that the characteristic primate traits may be more validly explained in terms of visually directed predation on insects rather than as strictly arboreal adaptations. He has stated that "visual conveyance and correlated neurological specializations are predatory adaptations comparable to the similar specializations seen in cats and owls and allowing the predator to gauge its victim's distance accurately without having to move its head" (1974, p. 440).

Cartmill has thus argued that the primate morphological pattern represents not a complex of arboreal adaptations but, rather, an adaptation to feeding patterns visually directed primarily on insects. He pointed out (1972) that the Cretaceous expansion of the angiosperms provided new habitats for both insects and their predators and that several separate lineages of insectivorous vertebrates came to exploit new habitats in the undergrowth and lower forest canopy.

Cartmill's visual-predation theory of primate origins has several important implications. Primarily, he demands that since the feeding pattern represents the source of the basic primate adaptation, evidence of such feeding patterns must be present in all members of the order. He would therefore use as ordinal characters:

Internal ear structures enclosed within the petrosal bone in the skull (petrosal auditory bulla) (see Figures 2-2a and 2-9).

Encirclement of the eyeball by a continuous bony ring (complete postorbital bar) (see Figure 2-2b, c, and 2-3).

Divergent thumb and first toe with flattened nails.

The grasping hands and feet and the complete postorbital bar (which Cartmill loosely, but never explicitly, relates to eye convergence and stereoscopic vision) are said to be closely related to the demands of visually

---

FIGURE 2-1   Skeleton of *Homo sapiens*. Note the presence of the clavicle and the free and mobile bones of the lower arm and lower leg. These features are characteristic of the primates. The low, rounded shape of the ilium and the short arm, relative to the leg, are characteristic of the bipeds. The laterally compacted foot, with a nonopposable big toe, is also part of this locomotor pattern. (Photograph courtesy of William A. Richardson; labeling by Jan Austin.)

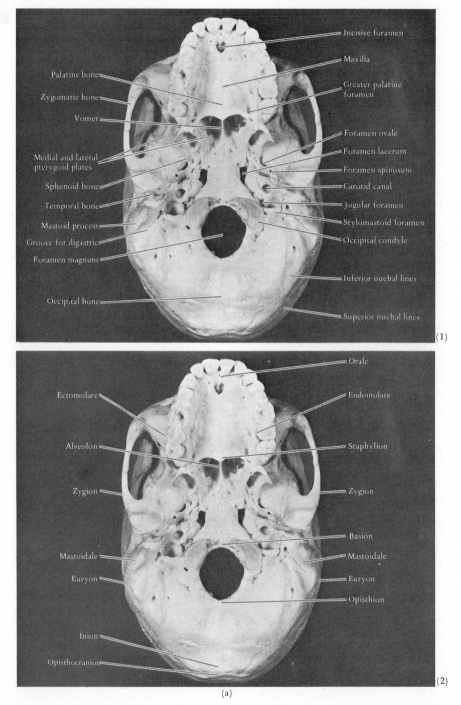

FIGURE 2-2   (a) Skull of *Homo sapiens*, basal view: (1) bones, (2) anthropometric landmarks.

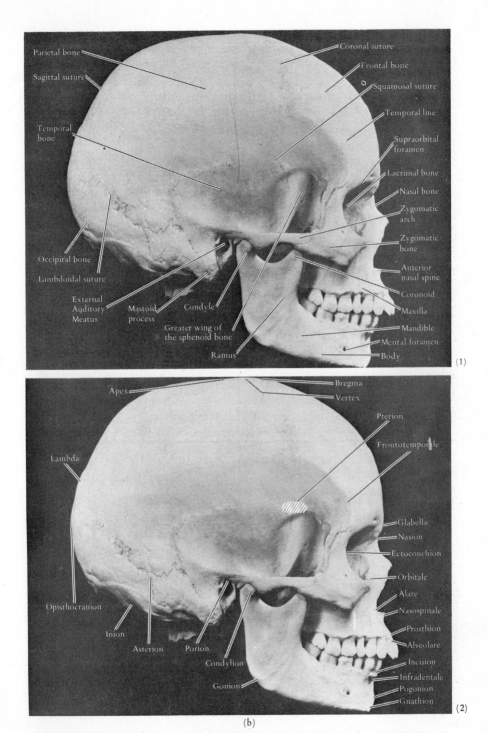

FIGURE 2-2 **(b)** Skull of *Homo sapiens*, lateral view: (1) bones, (2) anthropometric landmarks.

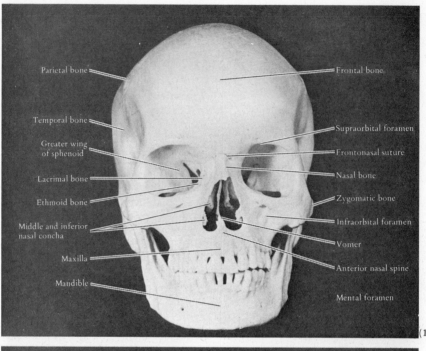

Parietal bone

Temporal bone

Greater wing
of sphenoid

Lacrimal bone

Ethmoid bone

Middle and inferior
nasal concha

Maxilla

Mandible

Frontal bone

Supraorbital foramen

Frontonasal suture

Nasal bone

Zygomatic bone

Infraorbital foramen

Vomer

Anterior nasal spine

Mental foramen

(1)

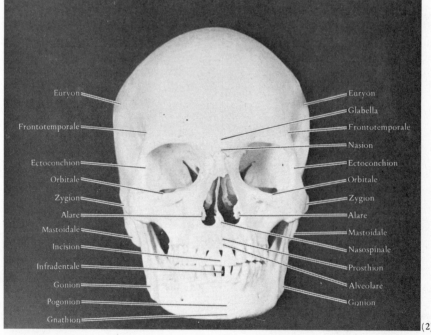

Euryon

Frontotemporale

Ectoconchion

Orbitale

Zygion

Alare

Mastoidale

Incision

Infradentale

Gonion

Pogonion

Gnathion

Euryon

Glabella

Frontotemporale

Nasion

Ectoconchion

Orbitale

Zygion

Alare

Mastoidale

Nasospinale

Prosthion

Alveolare

Gonion

(2)

(c)

FIGURE 2-2 **(c)** Skull of *Homo sapiens*, frontal view: (1) bones, (2) anthropometric landmarks. (Photographs for Figure 2-2*a,b,c* courtesy of William A. Richardson; labeling by Jan Austin.)

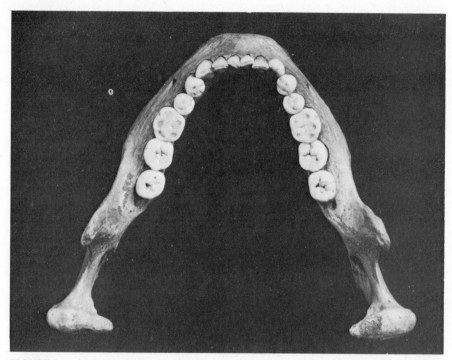

FIGURE 2-3 Mandible of *Homo sapiens*, occlusal view. All Old World monkeys, apes and humans have a dental formula of 2123; but the small canines and identical premolars (homodonty) are characteristic of humans alone. Note that the molars are worn to different degrees; such "differential wear" is characteristic of the hominids and reflects their long maturation period. (Photograph courtesy of William A. Richardson.)

directed predation. How, or if, the petrosal auditory bulla is related to this adaptive pattern is not made clear.[2]

The demand for this complex of traits would have the effect of removing from the order many early forms long considered to be primates in terms of their total pattern of traits shared with other undoubted primates. Cartmill has argued that certain forms, particularly within the extinct primate family Plesiadapidae (see Chapter 3), do not show evidence of a postorbital bar and grasping hands and feet; and, thus, since they lack this "adaptive" pattern, they should not be included within the primates. He would therefore conclude that the primate fossil record began in the Eocene, not the Cretaceous, as other evidence, based largely on dentition, appears to indicate.

[2]Cartmill should not, however, be criticized too severely for this omission. Although the petrosal bulla is a well-recognized and consistent synapomorphic primate character, its adaptive significance or importance is not known.

Cartmill's position that these three characters indicate a shift to visual predation and insectivory may be criticized on several grounds.

First, while recognizing that the character complex, rather than the individual traits, must form the unit of analysis, can we also associate any of these separate traits with other dietary modes? If the answer is yes, the strength of this pattern as an adaptive complex can be questioned. The encirclement of the eye with a bony ring is, according to Cartmill, associated with convergence of the eyes toward the center of the face and stereoscopic vision. In fact, many nonprimate forms without stereoscopic vision have a complete postorbital bar. Many hoofed animals, such as camels, deer, bovids, and hippos, as well as sirenians (aquatic mammals), have complete postorbital bars and are demonstrably both noninsectivorous and nonpredatory. The fact that none of these animals has grasping hands and feet is a further indication that grasping ability and the postorbital bar are not functionally interrelated (see Szalay, 1975a).

Second, as pointed out in Chapter 1, taxonomic relationships at all levels within the Linnaean hierarchy must be based on shared, ancestral characters. Yet the plesiadapids, a group Cartmill would exclude from the primates, demonstrate characters shared in common with all early primates and shown by no other group. The plesiadapids have a petrosal auditory bulla as well as a number of distinctive and definitive primate characters in the dentition. Such a pattern of shared symplesiomorphic characters would appear to confirm their affinity with the primates.

DEFINITION OF THE ORDER PRIMATES

As an order, the Primates (see Table 2-3) are difficult to define, since no single feature characterizes all members. In noting this, Le Gros Clark (1962, 1965) suggested, in fact, that probably the most distinctive feature of the primates is their lack of specialization. But neither does generalization characterize the entire order, for some members show a high degree of specialization in at least some features. In the human, for example, the complex and large brain clearly represents a specialization of a very important type. In the aye-aye (genus *Daubentonia*), the extremely elongated, insect-grubbing middle finger of the hand is another specialization.

Linnaeus chose the term "primate," perhaps egocentrically, from a Latin word meaning "first" or "chief." In his original definition of the order, he included both the Chiroptera (bats) and the Dermoptera ("flying lemurs"). In Mivart's later description of the order (1873), he excluded both these groups and characterized the primates as:

> Unguiculate claviculate placental mammals, with orbits encircled by bone; three kinds of teeth, at least at one time of life, brain always with a posterior lobe and calcarine fissure; the innermost digits of at least one pair of

extremities opposable; hallux with a flat nail or none; a well-developed caecum; penis pendulous; testes scrotal; always two pectoral mammae.

With little modification, this definition still stands today. It is valid because most of these characters are found in most members of the group. However, the possession or exclusion of a single feature does not alone determine membership in the order. What determines membership is the possession of a complex or compound of certain features. This group of features, taken together, tells us something about the total adaptive, behavioral, and morphological pattern of the order. This is the concept of the **total morphological pattern** developed by Le Gros Clark. The concept basically relies on the fact that one feature, characteristic, or anatomical trait exists as part of a functional complex. In the analysis of organisms, either fossil or living, it is the functional complex that must provide the element of study, not the individual components.

It seems paradoxical, however, that in studying fossils, which are almost always incomplete and fragmentary, we are often reduced to the analysis of just these individual components. But in paleontology, the paradox is more apparent than real. In studying fossil components and comparing them with similar components in the functioning complexes of living organisms, our understanding of the total, but now incomplete, fossil complex can be improved. This mating of comparative anatomical analyses of living forms and paleontological analysis of fossil forms is one of the foundations of modern evolutionary biology. Their degree of complementation is so great that one should not exist without the other.

CHARACTERISTICS OF THE ORDER

Limb Anatomy

Nails   Mivart (1873) began his description of the order Primates with the term "**unguiculate**"; it describes animals possessing nails or claws on the hands and feet, as opposed to highly specialized structures such as hooves. An unguiculate condition is indeed a basic and long-term characteristic of the order. Most members possess flattened nails, however, rather than claws. Many prosimians retain either one or two claws for feeding and grooming activities, and all the marmosets (order Callithricidae) also possess claws.

Opposability of the Digits   The primate hand (Figure 2-4 shows the human hand) is characterized by a high degree of flexibility. In fact, a number of animals—such as raccoons, squirrels, rabbits, and tree shrews—also have flexible hands with the ability to converge the digits,

TABLE 2-3 Classification of the primates

ORDER	SUBORDER	INFRAORDER	SUPERFAMILY	FAMILY	SUBFAMILY	GENUS
	Prosimii	Tarsiiformes				*Tarsius*
		Lorisiformes	Lorisoidea	Lorisidae	Lorisinae	*Loris* *Arctocebus* *Nycticebus* *Perodicticus*
					Galaginae	*Galago*
		Lemuriformes	Lemuroidea	Lemuridae	Lemurinae	*Lemur* *Hapalemur* *Lepilemur*
					Cheirogaleinae	*Cheirogaleus* *Microcebus* *Phaner*
				Indriidae		*Indri* *Avahi* *Propithecus*
			Daubentonioidea			*Daubentonia*
					Cebinae	*Cebus* *Saimiri*
					Alouattinae	*Alouatta*
					Aotinae	*Aotus* *Callicebus*

Order	Suborder	Superfamily	Family	Subfamily	Genera
Primates	Anthropoidea	Ceboidea	Cebidae	Atelinae	*Ateles* *Brachyteles* *Lagothrix*
				Pitheciinae	*Pithecia* *Cacajao* *Chiropotes*
			Callithricidae		*Callithrix* *Callimico* *Cebuella* *Leontopithecus* *Saguinus* *Tamarinus*
		Cercopithecoidea	Cercopithecidae	Cercopithecinae	*Cercopithecus* *Cercocebus* *Macaca* *Papio*
				Colobinae	*Colobus* *Nasalis?* *Presbytis* *Pygathrix* *Rhinopithecus?* *Simias?*
		Hominoidea	Pongidae		*Pongo* *Pan* *Gorilla*
			Hylobatidae		*Hylobates* *Symphalangus*
			Hominidae		*Homo*

Source: Adapted from Buettner-Janusch, 1973.

39

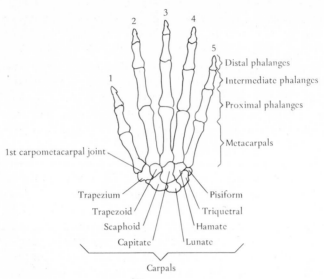

FIGURE 2-4   Hand of *Homo sapiens*.

thus allowing the manipulation of food and other objects. In these animals the thumb acts in conjunction with the other digits; thus, while they can hold objects, they cannot stabilize them by the opposition of the thumb. Therefore, they require both hands in any manipulative or holding action.

All primates, however, have a thumb which acts independently of the other digits, thus allowing the stabilization of objects held in the hand.[3] In some primates, such as the marmosets and the prosimian genus *Tarsius*, the divergence of the thumb is very limited but is sufficient for one-handed feeding and the stabilization of objects. The thumb of the marmosets and tree shrews is termed "nonopposable," indicating the very limited rotational function of the thumb.

All other primates have thumbs with a greater degree of opposability and the capability of being rotated around to face the other digits. This facility permits a high degree of manipulative ability.[4]

Two types of opposability have been defined (Napier and Napier, 1967): pseudo-opposability and true opposability.

PSEUDO-OPPOSABILITY   Pseudo-opposability is found in all New World monkeys (except marmosets) and the prosimians (except *Tarsius*). This

---

[3]The spider monkeys of the New World (genus *Ateles*) do not have an external thumb and therefore cannot grasp objects as other primates do.

[4]Opposability of the digits, however, is not a prerequisite for tool use. Sea otters, for example, frequently and efficiently use stones to break open the carapaces of shellfish, yet they do not have opposable digits and, in fact, do not even have a very flexible hand.

term refers to movements of the thumb that are not related to rotation at the first carpometacarpal joint. In the prosimians and the New World monkeys, opposition is achieved through a hinge joint at the first carpometacarpal articulation. Since the saddle-shaped facet, typical of the Old World primates, is missing, true rotation is not possible. However, this type of opposability can be very effective. In the organ-grinder monkey (genus: *Cebus*), small objects, such as coins or nuts, can be easily and quickly picked up and manipulated even without full rotation of the thumb.

TRUE OPPOSABILITY   True opposability is found in all Old World monkeys, apes, and humans. It occurs when the pulp surface of the thumb can be placed in contact with the pulp surface of at least one of the fingers. This results in a **precision grip**. Another functional manifestation of opposability is the **power grip**, which occurs when all the fingers are tightly curved over an object and the thumb is folded over the fingers. This grip permits power but less precision than the precision grip.

Functionally, true opposability is made possible by the presence of a saddle-shaped or concave facet on the proximal surface of the first metacarpal; this facet articulates with a convex articular facet on the trapezium (see Figure 2-5a, which shows the human thumb).

True opposability in the thumb of the Old World anthropoids is based, in part, on a new feature of one of the hand muscles. In the Old World anthropoids, the flexor pollicis brevis muscle, which acts to flex and rotate the carpometacarpal joint, has developed a second, deep head. This new deep head originates on the trapezoid and capitate bones in the wrist and inserts into the base of the first proximal phalanx. This deep head adds to the ability to rotate and flex the thumb. The deep head is found only in the Old World anthropoids that have the ability to oppose the thumb; it is absent in the prosimians and the New World monkeys (Day and Napier, 1961, 1963).

The saddle-shaped carpometacarpal joint is a unique feature in the hand of the Old World monkeys and apes (except for the hylobatids) and represents an important and unique specialization in the structure and function of the thumb (see Figure 2-5b, which shows the thumb of *Papio*).

The hylobatids, including the two genera *Hylobates* and *Symphalangus*, have developed true opposability in a different way. In these genera, the carpometacarpal joint has a ball-and-socket conformation rather than the typical convex-concave articulation typical of other Old World primates (Jouffroy and Lessertisseur, 1960).

Anatomically, the hylobatid thumb (Figure 2-5c) has a very high degree of opposability; and although it is very short relative to the fingers, it is used with great precision.

It is therefore interesting that while true thumb opposability occurs in no other animal group, it has arisen within the Hominoidea at least twice

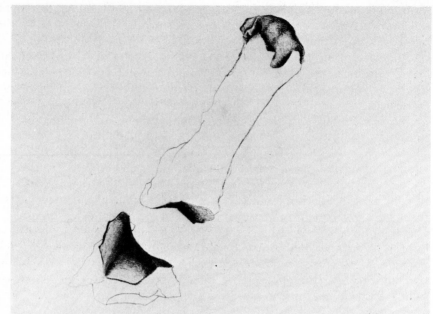

(a)

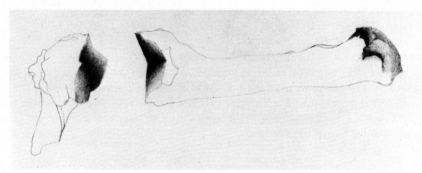

(b)

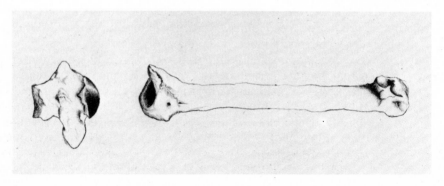

(c)

in different ways. Both the saddle-shaped thumb joint of the Old World monkeys, pongids, and hominids and the ball-and-socket joint of the hylobatids represent different pathways to full rotation of the thumb. It is clear that this action, which results in a fully flexible and highly manipulative hand, has had important selective advantage within the higher primates. Yet, it is equally clear that the fully opposable thumb, while associated with tool making in the later hominids, arose long before the emergence of any tool-using practices in primates. Neither can the opposable thumb be directly related to arboreal habitats, since other animals, such as squirrels, successfully occupy trees without such capability.

However, when taken as part of the full morphology of the primate hand, thumb opposability seems more understandable.

Hands   Primate hands are characterized by having ridges (reflected in fingerprints) which are highly sensitive to touch. The palms are also well supplied with sweat glands to moisten the skin and to provide additional friction for handling objects. Hill has pointed out the significance of such ridge-bearing skin:

> Being moist and abundantly supplied with sensory (tactile) nerve endings, it endows the extremities, especially the digits, with a high degree of sensibility, supplying the brain with information concerning the texture, size and other features of external objects, including food items. It also encourages the manual exploration of the environment and of the possessor's own body and those of its mates. Primates in possession of these faculties enter an entirely new and richer world of experiences. Coupled with the acquisition of stereoscopic vision, a much implemented three-dimensional view of the environment is attained. This intimate association between visual and tactile exploration has profound significance in the evolution of the higher primates (including man). (1972, p. 44)

When viewed from the perspective of structural flexibility, perceptual acuity, and physiological capabilities, the primate hand seems a perfect

---

FIGURE 2-5   (a) Trapezium and first metacarpal of *Homo sapiens*. The convex surface of the first metacarpal fits neatly into the saddle-shaped facet of the trapezium (one of the carpals or wrist bones). The congruence at this joint allows the full rotation of the thumb around toward the palm of the hand. (b) Trapezium and first metacarpal of *Papio*, a cercopithecoid monkey. Although the saddle-shaped facet is shallower and less defined than in *Homo sapiens*, the overall morphology is very similar. (c) Trapezium and first metacarpal of *Hylobates*, the gibbon. This line of great apes had a long period of separation from the other great apes. Here, full rotation and true opposability of the thumb occur in a parallel, yet fascinatingly different, way. The first carpometacarcal joint in *Hylobates* is a unique ball-and-socket joint which permits complete rotation of the thumb. (Drawings by Christopher Pircher.)

machine for exploration, perception, and manipulation. Thumb opposability is just part of this endowment, and tool use is merely a late by-product.

Clavicle Mivart's second descriptive term (1873) for the primates was "claviculate," and all primates retain a clavicle or collarbone. The clavicle is an important component of the shoulder girdle and has been found in some terrestrial vertebrates since the Paleozoic amphibians. It exists in forms that have the ability to rotate the upper limb, and the presence of a clavicle indicates a wide range of movement in the upper limb. The clavicle has been lost in forms that habitually move their limbs forward and backward rapidly over hard ground; carnivores (such as dogs and cats) and the hoofed mammals (such as horses, cows, and antelopes), for example, do not have clavicles.

The radius and fibula are present and separate in primates, although partial fusion of the tibia and fibula has occurred in the hindlimb of *Tarsius*.

Locomotion

The locomotor categories of the primates (Table 2-4) have been described by Napier and Napier (1967). As indicated below, the living members of the order practice several different types of locomotion, encompassing both terrestrial and arboreal quadrupedality and terrestrial bipedality. Although the locomotor categories given here are clearly defined, the primates seldom confine themselves entirely to any single form of movement. They often adopt different forms of locomotion in different habitats. For example, a chimp may use the hindlimb as a suspensory organ while in the trees, but once on the ground, it may use the hindlimbs to support its body in a quadrupedal or, occasionally, in a bipedal mode. Similarly, the gibbons, whose locomotion while in the trees depends upon forelimb suspension, often switch to the use of the hindlimbs while on the ground and move bipedally.

The following are the major categories in Napier and Napier's (1967) classification of primate locomotion.

Vertical Clinging and Leaping "A type of arboreal locomotor behaviour in which the body is held vertically at rest and pressed to the trunk or main branch of a tree; movement from place to place is effected by a leap or jump from one vertical support to another. The forelimbs take no part in propelling the body during leaping. Vertical clinging and leaping primates usually hop bipedally when moving rapidly on the ground, but assume a quadrupedal gait when moving slowly" (p. 387) (Figure 2-6a).

Quadrupedalism "A type of locomotion which can take place on the ground or in the trees; its principal component is four-legged walking or

TABLE 2-4   Locomotor categories of primates

CATEGORY/SUBTYPE	ACTIVITY	PRIMATE GENERA
1. Vertical clinging and leaping	Leaping in trees and hopping on the ground	Avahi, bushbabies, hapalemur, lepilemur, sifaka, indri, tarsier
2. Quadrupedalism		
(i) Slow-climbing type	Cautious climbing—no leaping or running	Golden potto, potto, slow and slender lorises
(ii) Branch-running and walking type	Climbing, springing, branch running	Mouse lemur, dwarf lemur, forked lemur, lemur, all marmosets and tamarins, night monkey, titis, sakis, uakaris, cebus, squirrel, guenons
(iii) Ground-running and walking type	Climbing and ground running	Macaques, baboons, mandrill, gelada, patas
(iv) New World "semi-brachiation" type	Arm swinging with use of prehensile tail, little leaping	Howler, spider, woolly spider, woolly
(v) Old World "semi-brachiation" type	Arm swinging and leaping	Colobus, all langurs, proboscis, snubnose
3. Ape locomotion*		
(i) True brachiation		Gibbon, siamang
(ii) Modified brachiation	Arm swinging and quadrumanous climbing	Orangutan
(iii) Knuckle walking	Occasional brachiation, climbing, knuckle walking	Chimpanzee, gorilla
4. Bipedalism	Standing, striding, running	Human

*Ape locomotion is defined as what each genus does. It is disputed whether to lump chimpanzee and gorilla with orangutans, or to separate them as terrestrially adapted knuckle walkers.

Source: Napier and Napier, 1967.

running. In an arboreal situation the hands and feet may be used, in a prehensile fashion, to provide stability. The movements of springing, jumping and leaping are associated with this mode of locomotion. Quadrupedalism also involves the vertical movement of climbing using all four extremities. Movement may be rapid as in galloping on the ground or it may be cautious and slow. Quadrupedal primates in certain situations show a variable amount of arm-swinging with or without the additional use of a prehensile tail" (pp. 387–388).

During quadrupedal locomotion the monkey hand can be positioned in one of two ways. The more terrestrially adapted monkeys, such as the mandrills (Mandrillus) and patas (Erythrocebus), often walk on the fingers;

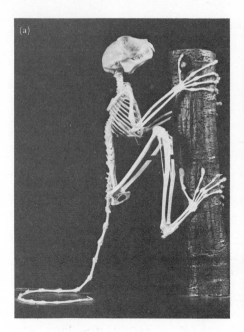

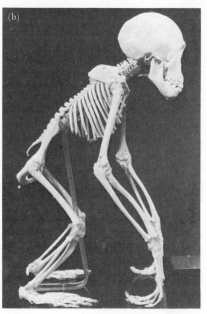

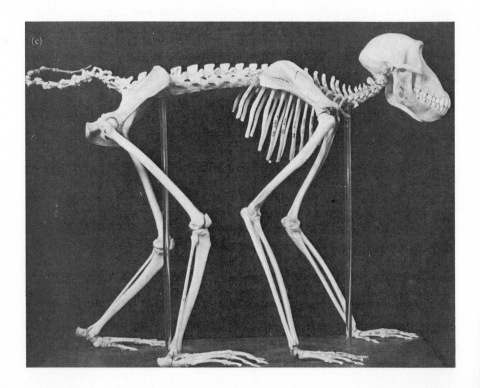

this is **digitigrade** locomotion. Other monkeys, such as baboons (*Papio*), usually move with the fingers extended and the palms more or less flat on the ground in **palmigrade** locomotion (Figure 2-6*b*).

Brachiation   In this form of locomotion, the typical component is arm swinging, by which means the body, suspended from above, is propelled through space. The hindlimbs are used to support the body in the trees or on the ground either in the erect or in the quadrupedal position. In some brachiating primates the hindlimbs may be used to suspend the body.

Napier and Napier (1967) recognize two subtypes of brachiation. In the "true brachiators," the gibbons and siamangs, locomotion depends almost entirely on suspension and propulsion by the forelimb. The "modified brachiators," the chimps, gorillas, and orangs, involve the lower limb more in support and suspension of the body (Figure 2-6*c*).

During ground locomotion, the true brachiators often move in a bipedal mode with their long arms held to the sides or above their bodies for balance. The modified brachiators, however, often assume a special type of quadrupedal locomotion when on the ground. The chimps and gorillas hold the hands tightly flexed and only the backs of the first two finger joints come into contact with the ground surface (Tuttle, 1969). Such a hand posture is termed **"knuckle walking."** Orangs, when on the ground, also flex the hand tightly but roll it over so that weight is borne more on the back of the hand; this is termed **"fist walking."**

In all types of terrestrial locomotion, the joints are subjected to constant shocks of a compressional nature. This compression will cause dislocations if the joints are not adequately stabilized. In knuckle walkers, the wrist is stabilized by close packing of the wrist bones **(carpals)**, and the distal radius and ulna are tightly bound together with a thick fibrous

---

FIGURE 2-6   **(a)** Skeleton of *Tarsius*. Note the partially fused tibia and fibula; this is the only primate in which such fusion of limb bones occurs. All other primates retain a very generalized skeleton. The upright posture of the trunk is typical of a vertical clinger and leaper. **(b)** Skeleton of *Pan troglodytes*, a "modified brachiator." While progression through the trees in this form may be done by arm-swinging, the hind limbs too play an active part in locomotion. Note that in *Pan* the arms are longer than the legs and that the postures of the hands and feet are different. While the feet remain palmigrade, the fingers are curled in a specialized form of ground movement called "knuckle walking." Note the short coccyx, characteristic of the tailless hominoids. **(c)** Skeleton of *Papio*, a quadruped. Note the long, rectangular ilium and long ischium. The large muscles on the back of the thigh, the hamstrings, originate on the ischium, and the greater length of this bone provides greater efficiency for these muscles. The ischium is broadened and thickened to form support for the characteristic "ischial callosities," or sitting pads, of some Old World monkeys. The more or less equal length of the fore and hind limbs is also characteristic of quadrupeds. The hands and feet of this specimen are in a palmigrade posture, in which the palms and soles rest flat on the ground surface. (Photographs courtesy of William A. Richardson; skeleton in *a* from Carolina Biological Supply.)

wrist capsule. The finger joints are additionally stabilized by very strong flexor tendons which leave high ridges imprinted on the palm surfaces of the finger bones. The elbow joint also needs additional stabilization in quadrupedal primates. This joint, in primates, is hook-like, with the tightly curved top of the ulna fitting into a depression (**olecranon fossa**) in the lower end of the humerus. Stabilization at the elbow joint involves making the depression in the humerus deeper and enlarging the bony crests which surround the depression. In this way, the chance of dislocation to the outside (laterally) is minimized; dislocation to the inside (medially) is unlikely because the radius, on the inside of the forearm, prevents it.

Bipedalism "A form of locomotion in which the body is habitually supported on the hindlimbs which move alternately to propel it through space; the gait is characterized by the act of striding which involves a heel-toe propulsive movement" (Napier and Napier, 1967, p. 389).

Indicators of Locomotion Relative limb length is a good indicator of locomotor category and can be used in the reconstruction of possible locomotor patterns in fossil material. For example, limbs which are long relative to trunk length are advantageous in terrestrial locomotion in that they effectively lengthen the stride. Long arms, relative to trunk length, serve the same function in arboreal brachiation. Arboreal quadrupeds, on the other hand, have relatively short limbs so that the center of gravity is lowered, thus providing additional stability in the trees (see Napier and Napier, 1967).

Various indices, such as the humero-femoral index (Table 2-5) and the

TABLE 2-5   Humero-femoral index*

TAXA	MEAN
Old World monkeys	
Rhesus	84.7
Pongidae	
Gorilla	116.2
Pan	102.0
Pongo	135.7
Hylobatidae	
Hylobates	113.7
Hominidae	
Homo sapiens	74.2
Fossil forms	
Oreopithecus	117.0
Australopithecus	83.9
(gracile form, AL 288)	

$$*\frac{\text{Humerus length} \times 100}{\text{Femoral length}} = \text{humero-femoral index}$$

Sources: Homo sapiens (figure represents the mean for males), Schultz, 1937; *Oreopithecus*, Straus, 1963; *Australopithecus* (AL 288), Johanson and Taieb, 1976.

TABLE 2-6   Intermembral index*

TAXA	INDEX
Vertical clingers and leapers (legs longer than arms)	50–80
Quadrupeds (arms and legs nearly equal)	80–100
Brachiators (arms longer than legs)	100–150
Fossil forms	
Plesiadapis	≈ 100.0
Pliopithecus	94.1
Oreopithecus	118.6

$$*\frac{\text{Humerus} + \text{radius length} \times 100}{\text{Femur} + \text{tibia length}} = \text{intermembral index}$$

Sources: Vertical clingers and leapers, quadrupeds, and brachiators, Napier and Napier, 1967; *Plesiadapis*, Russell, 1967; *Pliopithecus*, Zapfe, 1958; *Oreopithecus*, Straus, 1963.

intermembral index (Table 2-6), have been developed to describe the relative length of the limbs. These indices have been especially useful in attempts to reconstruct the locomotor patterns of fossil forms.

Tails

Tails are present in most primate groups although they have been lost in all living hominoids. Some New World monkeys have developed a tail that has the ability to grasp objects and that can thus act almost as a fifth limb. This **prehensility,** found in some New World forms, is absent in all Old World forms. This finding may indicate that the anatomical characters allowing the grasping actions of the ceboid tail are very old, indeed, in the New World forms. The hominoids, as a group, apparently lost their tails in Late Oligocene or Early Miocene times. *Aegyptopithecus,* the earliest known hominoid (from the Middle Oligocene) retained a long tail, but the Middle Miocene form, *Dryopithecus,* apparently had none, to judge from the available fossil evidence.

Skull

During the course of primate evolution, there has been an increased centering of the eyes on the face, associated with the development of overlapping visual fields and stereoscopic vision. Additional protection for the eyes has been developed through the production of a complete bony socket or **orbit** for the eye (Figures 2-7*a* and 2-8*a*).

In many mammals the bony socket that contains the eye is open at the side; but throughout primate history, there has been a tendency to surround the eye completely with a bony ring. This has been accomplished in two separate processes. First, a bony bar has enclosed the eye at its outer margin, forming a complete bony circle. This postorbital bar has been

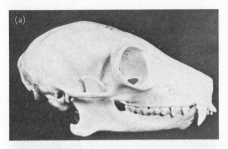

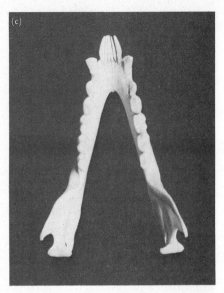

FIGURE 2-7 **(a)** Skull of *Lemur*, lateral view. In the primates a bony bar completely encircles the orbits, but in the Prosimians there is no bony plate to complete the postorbital closure behind the eye. **(b)** Skull of *Lemur*, basal view. Note the enlarged bulla, or bony cavity, which encloses the ear structures. Note also, however, that there is no bony tube leading from the bulla as there is in the higher primates of the Old World. The absence of the postorbital plate can also be seen in this view. **(c)** Mandible of *Lemur*, occlusal view. In this genus the enlongated incisors and canines form a dental comb. The dental formula is 2133. (Photographs courtesy of William A. Richardson.)

formed by a downward extension of the supraorbital portion of the frontal bone and an upward extension of the cheekbone or jugal. The complete encircling of the eye is first seen in the Eocene prosimians *Adapis* and *Notharctus*. (See Chapter 3.)

The development of a postorbital plate, which encloses the eye on the side of the skull behind the bar, completes the bony eye socket in the anthropoids. This plate is composed of the jugal, the alisphenoid, and the frontal. Evidence of complete lateral closure of the orbit does not occur until the Miocene, although *Aegyptopithecus*, in the Oligocene, shows nearly complete closure.

Such protective structures for the eye have been developed, in varying degrees of completeness, in many different mammalian orders. The function of these structures seems to be to protect the posterior portion of the eye from the stresses of highly developed chewing muscles. The major chewing muscle, the temporalis, originates near the top of the skull, and as it travels to its insertion area at the back of the mandible, it passes just behind the eye.

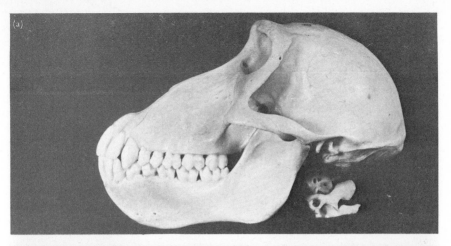

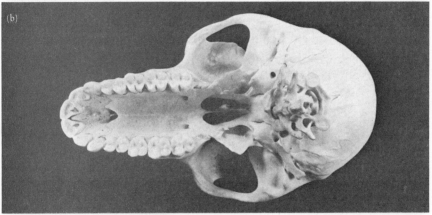

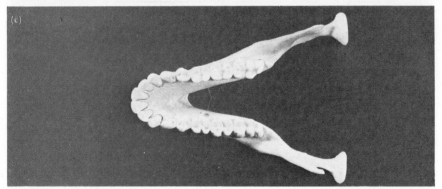

FIGURE 2-8 **(a)** Skull of *Papio*, an Old World monkey, lateral view. In the higher primates, the postorbital region has become entirely enclosed by bone. **(b)** Skull of *Papio*, basal view. Note that in the ear region a long bony tube extends to the side of the skull from the bulla; this long, external meatus is characteristic of all Old World higher primates, including humans. **(c)** Mandible of *Papio*, occlusal view. The front and rear pairs of crests on the molars are joined by a transverse crest; this condition, called "bilophodonty," is characteristic of most Old World monkeys. (Photographs courtesy of William A. Richardson.)

Ear

Originally, the mammals lacked a bony protection for the delicate structures of the middle ear region. During the course of the Cenozoic, however, different orders have evolved a variety of ways to protect these structures. In some insectivores, such as the tree shrew *(Tupaia)*, this area is protected by an entotympanic bone, a new bone developed in the base of the skull expressly for this purpose. All known primates, living and fossil, have developed this protection in a cavity **(bulla)** within the petrous portion of the temporal bone. Thus all primates are characterized by having the middle ear region contained within a **petrosal bulla** (Figure 2-9).

The tympanic bone, which supports the eardrum, has acquired two different forms within the primates. In the lemurs, this bone has a ring-like form and is contained entirely within the bulla; the petrosal bone itself forms the lateral wall of the ear cavity. Such a structure is seen in the fossil prosimians *Adapis* and *Notharctus* of the Eocene age (see Figure 3-11); it is also seen in the anthropoids *Aegyptopithecus* and *Apidium* of the Oligocene age (Gingerich, 1973). This similarity in ear structure among living and

FIGURE 2-9 Comparative ear structures: variation in the structure of the middle ear in primates. Arrows indicate possible developmental series, according to Szalay. **(a)** Hypothetical eutherian morphotype; **(b)** hypothetical intermediate between primate and primitive eutherian morphotype; **(c)** ancestral primate pattern represented by Lemuriformes; **(d)** *Megaladapis*: **(e)** *Galago*; **(f)** *Loris*; **(g)** Paramomyidae; **(h)** Tarsiiformes; **(i)** *Tarsius*, a specialized Tarsiiformes; **(j)** Platyrrhine; **(k)** Catarrhini. (By permission of Fred Szalay.)

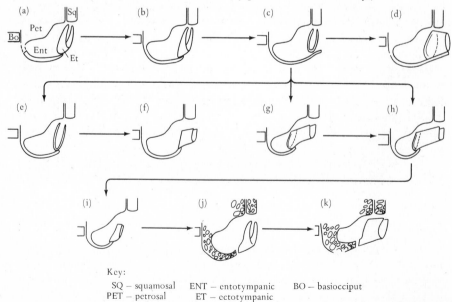

Key:
SQ – squamosal   ENT – entotympanic   BO – basiocciput
PET – petrosal   ET – ectotympanic

fossil lemurs and the early anthropoids has important implications for theories of the origins of the anthropoids, as we will see in Chapter 3. In both living and fossil tarsiers, in the lorises, and in all living higher primates including humans, the tympanic ring forms the lateral margin of the ear cavity. In the New World monkeys and the lorises, the tympanic ring extends to the side as a very short tube, but in all living Old World primates, including humans, this tube is considerably longer (see Figures 2-7b and 2-8b). This laterally extended tympanic ring is called the **"ectotympanic bone,"** and it forms the auditory canal, or **external auditory meatus.**

Brain

Some of the most remarkable and important trends in primate evolution have affected the structure and organization of the brain. This is the one area of primate anatomy that has shown persistent specialization through-out the history of the group.

Problems of brain evolution are complicated by the fact that the brains themselves are not preserved in the fossil record. Our knowledge of brain evolution comes from two sources, and both are, in effect, indirect. The first is the study of brain **endocasts**, which are models of the interior surface of the skull. Such endocasts reflect the size and shape of the interior of the skull, but this space is only a general reflection of the brain itself. In life, the brain is covered with several layers of tissue and is surrounded by fluids.

The second way to approach brain evolution is through what might be called **"comparative neurology."** This approach is based on analysis of brains of living animals, and extrapolations are made back to interpret the fossil data. Thus, the brain of a living prosimian might be used as a comparative model for the brain of an Eocene tarsioid. This is not, however, an entirely valid method, since prosimians have experienced at least 50 million years of evolution since the Eocene. Since this is the only available method of reconstructing neurological function, however, it is perhaps better than no method at all. But the limitations of the approach must be understood.

All brains, which are ultimately an expansion of the upper end of the spinal cord, have basically the same components.

Cerebellum
Controls balance, motor activities, and, in combination with the brain stem, innate reflexes.

Cerebrum
Occipital lobe: The visual cortex, which is separated from the rest of the cerebrum by the **lunate sulcus**. Visual signals are analyzed here.

Temporal lobe: The auditory cortex, where both visual and auditory memory are recorded; this is a means of recording experience.

Frontal lobe: Having little or no motor or sensory function, much of this lobe appears to be dispensable. But the frontal area does seem to control drive, initiative, and the ability to plan. It seems also to govern the ability to sustain and direct attention toward a planned goal.

Parietal lobe: Important association areas where input from other areas of the brain are correlated.

Although these same components (and many others not discussed here) occur in all animals, they show remarkable differences among groups. For example, in a fish the cerebrum is quite small in relation to the optic lobe, but in the chimps, the relationship is reversed and the optic lobe is relatively smaller. In a general way, such differences in relative proportions reflect the relative degree of development of these brain areas.

During the course of the Cenozoic, brains in many mammalian orders have demonstrated both relative and absolute increases in size. The ungulates (hoofed mammals), proboscideans (elephants), cetaceans (whales and dolphins), some carnivores, and the primates have all shown enlargement in brain size. Part of this increase is allometric; that is, it is associated with a general increase in body size. Throughout the mammalia, in fact, brain size is highly correlated with body size: big animals tend to have big brains. But, more important, part of this increase goes beyond a simple adjustment to body size. A good way to express this increase is to compare brain weight and body weight. Bauchot and Stephan (1966, 1969; summarized by Radinsky, 1975) have developed a **progression index**, which is a logarithmic expression of the increase using a "basal insectivore" as a comparative reference point. Such a generalized insectivore is assumed to be similar to the primate ancestral group. Table 2-7 shows the results of such a comparison. Thus, the living anthropoids demonstrate increases in total brain size and in the size of the neocortex, visual cortex, and cerebellum which are not tied simply to an increase in body size. A human being, for example, has a neocortex which is 156 times larger than would be expected for an insectivore of similar body size. The size of the olfactory lobe has decreased in most prosimians and in all anthropoids relative to body size. This decrease undoubtedly reflects the diminished importance of the olfactory sense in primates. The relative size of the visual cortex is about the same throughout the primates, possibly reflecting the fact that all primates have a similar high degree of dependency on the visual sense.

Beyond these alterations in size, changes in brain structure and complexity have also occurred during primate evolution. Brains in many of the lower vertebrates have essentially a linear, cylindrical arrangement of their components. But in the higher vertebrates, such as the mammalia,

TABLE 2-7   Relative brain size in the primates

		RELATIVE SIZE			
	PROGRESSION INDEX*	NEOCORTEX	OLFACTORY LOBE	VISUAL CORTEX	CEREBELLUM
Living prosimians	2.4– 7.0	8.3–26.5	1.3–0.13	1.0–4.6	2.9– 8.1
Living anthropoids	5.3–11.7	21.0–61.0	0.2–0.02	3.0–7.5	4.3–11.5
Humans	28.76	156.0	.02	5.0	20.9

*The progression index is computed by the equation: log brain weight (grams) = −1.37 + 0.63 log body weight (grams). The comparative point is the ratio of brain weight to body weight in the smallest-brained living insectivores (Bauchot and Stephan, 1969).

Sources: Neocortex, olfactory lobe, and cerebellum, Bauchot and Stephan, 1969; visual cortex, Stephan, 1969.

there has been a tendency to form the brain into a more spheroidal shape. This spheroidal shape is very pronounced in the primates, where the brain is broad and nearly round. Such a shape may reflect the need to pack more brain tissue into a skull without significantly lengthening it.

Primate brains have also changed in terms of their complexity. For example, it would be logical to assume that when an area of the brain enlarges, the functional components within it would similarly increase in number. (The functional cells of the brain are called "**neurons**.")

Since the brain of *Homo sapiens* is roughly 4 times the size of a chimp brain, such an assumption would lead us to believe that the human brain has 4 times as many neurons. The human, however, has only about 1¼ times as many neurons as a chimp (Shariff, 1953). In the human, the distance between the neurons has expanded and the neurons themselves have increased in size. The human neurons also show an increase in the number of **dendrites** issuing from them. It may be this larger number of dendrites that has permitted the complex behavior patterns characteristic of humans (Holloway, 1966).

The actual number of functional neurons seems, in fact, to have little importance in brain function. For example, a human has about 1.4 billion more neurons than a chimp, but more than this number can be removed during surgery without the person's subsequently demonstrating nonhuman behavioral traits. Moreover, there is good evidence that the processes of aging involve the loss of neurons; as many as one-third the entire neuron number (or about 2 billion) can be lost because of age changes without the loss of human behavior patterns (Brady, 1955).

Another highly important reflection of the increase in brain complexity in primates is seen in the neocortex. Reference to Table 2-7 will show that the neocortex has increased more than any other part of the brain, relative to the basal insectivore datum. Much of this greater volume is contained within the folds and wrinkled surface **(convolutions)** of the brain. In most lower animals, including most nonhuman primates, the surface of the brain is unwrinkled or, as in the case of the pongids, contains only a few convolutions and fissures. In monkeys, for example, just 7 percent of the brain surface is found within the fissures; in the human, 64 percent of the surface is contained within the fissures, demonstrating the highly convoluted surface of the human brain (Campbell, 1966). This higher degree of fissuration has allowed the neocortex to expand without causing the brain surface to become impossibly large.

Dentition

Many of the early mammals had a greater number of teeth than are found in living members of the class. Most mammals have four types of permanent teeth: incisors, canines, premolars, and molars. The numbers of these teeth are written in a literary convention called the "**dental formula**." Many of the unspecialized early mammals had 3 incisors, 1 canine, 4 premolars, and 3 molars in each half of the jaw; the dental formula would thus be written 3143. Such a formula would indicate that the numbers of teeth in the upper and lower jaws were equal. If there was some modification in the number in either the upper or lower jaw, it would be written, for example,

3143

2143

thus signifying the loss of one pair of incisors in the lower jaw. The primates have reduced the total number of teeth: most living members of the order have a dental formula of either 2133 (most New World monkeys and many prosimians) or 2123 (all Old World monkeys, great apes, and humans). (See Figures 2-7c and 2-8c.)

Along with the loss of certain teeth, a relatively unspecialized cusp pattern has been retained. The reptilian ancestors of the mammals had teeth consisting of a simple, single cusp, the **protocone** (see Figure 2-10a). One dental characteristic of the early mammals was the addition of two extra cusps to this structure. Thus, from the single reptilian conical tooth, the early mammals came to have a three-cusped tooth, a **trigon** (Figure 2-10b). In the upper jaw of the early mammals, the protocone was located at the inner **lingual** side of the tooth and the two new cusps, the **paracone** and **metacone**, were on the outer, or **buccal**, side of the tooth. Similar terms are used for the equivalent cusps in the lower jaw, except that the suffix "id" is added, thus giving **paraconid, metaconid**, and **protoconid**. In the lower jaw the cusp arrangement is reversed, so that the protoconid is on the buccal side and the metaconid and paraconid are on the lingual side.

As the mammals diversified in the Cretaceous and Cenozoic, many

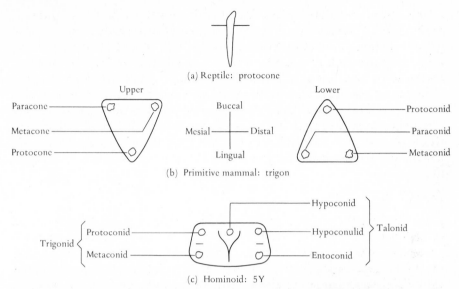

(a) Reptile: protocone

Upper   Lower

Paracone ——— [diagram]   Buccal   [diagram] ——— Protoconid

Metacone ———   Mesial —+— Distal   ——— Paraconid

Protocone ———   Lingual   ——— Metaconid

(b) Primitive mammal: trigon

                                                      ——— Hypoconid

Trigonid { Protoconid ——— [diagram] ——— Hypoconulid } Talonid

            Metaconid ———   ——— Entoconid

(c) Hominoid: 5Y

FIGURE 2-10 Cusp morphology of the molars. One trend in mammalian dental evolution is an increasingly complex cusp morphology on the molar teeth. The earliest primates, in the Cretaceous, demonstrated this trend by the addition of a heel or talonid of enamel at the rear of the lower molars. This was accompanied by the addition of new cusps. Cusps on the upper and lower molars can be distinguished by the addition of the suffix *-id* for the lower teeth.

groups, including the primates, added extra cusps to the primitive three-cusped molar. The primates added on a heel, or **talonid**, of enamel at the rear of the lower molars. On the talonid were positioned at least three additional cusps, called the **hypoconid, hypoconulid**, and **entoconid**. The higher primates have tended to lose the paraconid on the trigonid while adding additional cusps to the talonid. Most modern Old World and New World monkeys now have four cusps on their lower molars.

In the hominoids (great apes and humans), the hypoconulid on the talonid has become enlarged to form a fifth cusp on the lower molars. These five cusps are usually arranged with three cusps on the outer (buccal) surface and two cusps on the inner (lingual) surface of the tooth. The fissures between the cusps form a Y configuration with the open end of the Y pointing in the buccal direction; this type of molar cusp formation is termed the "5Y" and is an important characteristic of all fossil and living apes and humans (Figure 2-10c). It must be pointed out, however, that while most hominoids do have five cusps on the lower molars, this is not an invariable rule. Some individuals, both apes and humans, have as many as six or more cusps or as few as four.

Although the cusp morphology of the early primates and their probable insectivore ancestors was quite similar, several important differences distinguish the two groups. Insectivore teeth have high, sharp cusps, some of which are connected by strong, well-marked crests, and a steep drop between the trigonid and the talonid. Such a pattern would be well suited to piercing, shearing, and cutting with the teeth. The primates, on the other hand, have lower, more rounded (**bunodont**) cusps and less pronounced crests between the cusps, and the shelf between the trigonid and talonid is less steep. This dental pattern would be more advantageous in crushing and grinding actions (Szalay, 1972a, b). These distinctions would appear to support the idea that the emergence of the primates was related to a dietary or habitat shift which placed greater emphasis on plants than on insects as a source of food. This possibility will be discussed in more detail in Chapter 3.

Development

As a group, the mammals are defined by the dependence of the young on the mother for sustenance. As a result, the length of contact time between generations is longer in the mammals than it is in nonmammalian groups. The length of contact time reaches a maximum in the primates, where infant survival goes beyond the demands of nutrition. In the primates, survival depends also on the acquisition of learned, rather than innate, behavior patterns. Obviously, then, the length of time that the generations are in contact has a significant effect on the amount of information which can be transmitted, and can therefore have an important effect on survival. Learned behavior patterns are most vital to survival in the hominoids, and it is undoubtedly no accident that growth and development take longest in that group.

Therefore a direct and inverse correlation appears to exist between the rate of growth and the importance of learned behavior patterns in survival. As the demands for sophisticated behavioral responses increase, the rate of growth slows; maximal complexity of behavioral development and the slowest growth rates co-occur in the human. Table 2-8 summarizes these data.

Placentation The term "placentation" refers to the way in which a mammalian embryo is attached to the uterine wall of its mother. It is through the placenta that the embryo receives its nourishment and oxygen and expels its waste. In the primates, there are two types of placentation. In the **epitheliochorial** placenta of the lemurs and lorises, the placental membrane is diffuse over the inner surface of the uterus; the outer membrane surrounding the embryo invades the uterine wall to only a limited extent. Thus the maternal and fetal bloodstreams remain separate, and very little exchange of proteins or other blood-carried chemicals occurs

TABLE 2-8 Duration of primate life periods

| | PHASES | | | | |
	FETAL, DAYS	INFANTILE, YEARS	JUVENILE, YEARS	ADULT, YEARS	LIFE SPAN, YEARS
Lemur	126	?	2?	11+	14
Macaque	168	1½	6	20	27–28
Gibbon	210	2?	6½	20+	30+
Orangutan	233	3½	7	20+	30+
Chimpanzee	238	3	7	30	40
Gorilla	265	3+	7+	25	35?
Modern human	266	6	14	50+	70–75

Source: Napier and Napier, 1967.

between the embryo and the mother. This type of placenta is also termed "nondeciduate" because no maternal tissue is lost at birth.

The second type of primate placenta, termed "haemochorial," is found in tarsiers and all higher primates including the human being. This type of placenta is attached to a restricted area of the uterine wall but invades the wall more deeply. There is thus a great opportunity for the exchange of blood-carried materials between the embryo and the mother. This type of placenta is also termed "deciduate" because, when it pulls away from the uterine wall at birth, maternal tissues are lost.

The work of Morris Goodman (1963) has indicated that important evolutionary ramifications have resulted from the different types of primate placentation. Among these ramifications is the efficiency of oxygen delivery through the placental connection to the embryo.

In the brain, the neocortex is easily injured by oxygen deprivation, while the phylogenetically older areas, such as the paleoencephalon, are less easily damaged. The neocortex, which is relatively larger in the anthropoids than in the prosimians (see Table 2-6), thus requires a constant and reliable flow of oxygen. This flow cannot be supplied by the epitheliochorial placenta, since the maternal and fetal bloodstreams are not in intimate contact. A rich and constant oxygen flow can, however, be assured with a haemochorial type of placenta. Goodman (1963) has argued that the large, complex brain of the higher primates could not have evolved without this improved type of placentation.

Another factor related to placental structure is isoimmunization (Goodman, 1963). Isoimmunization refers to a process whereby some of the proteins produced by the developing embryo and passed through the placental membranes may be incompatible with those of the mother. The mother's immune system produced antibodies against the "foreign" proteins produced by her own embryo. These maternal antibodies, designed specifically to attack a certain fetal protein, pass back through the placental membrane and cause death or injury to the embryo. Isoimmunization is a relatively common occurrence in a variety of incompatible protein situations; ABO and RH reactions are among the most frequent.

Isoimmunization may also appear when a new genetic pattern occurs in the embryo through genetic mutation. This mutation results in an alteration of the structure of a protein, thereby increasing the chance that the maternal immune system will regard it as foreign. In the epitheliochorial type of placentation in lemurs and lorises, there is little opportunity for problems to occur. The maternal and embryonic bloodstreams are not in contact; there is no real exchange of protein material between them, and isoimmunization does not occur.

In the case of a haemochorial placenta, however, the situation is quite different. With the relatively greater exchange of blood proteins, isoimmunization is much more likely to occur. If the embryo carries a protein that is foreign to the mother, her antibodies will attack it and may damage or kill the embryo. This means that genetic variation, which is the raw material of all evolution, has less chance of survival in primates that have a haemochorial type of placenta. Consequently, there could be little variation in the proteins, such as albumin, that appear before birth. Proteins that appear after birth, such as gamma globulin, would not be affected by the process of isoimmunization. Goodman states:

> Therefore, the mutant genes which act only in the postnatal organism have the selective advantage of not provoking the maternal immunological system. On the other hand a delay in the appearance of adult proteins would increase the helplessness of the offspring. Genetic codes which retarded the maturation of the new born could only be selected if there were corresponding increases in the protective care of the young by the mother or other adults. The primates with their expanding cerebral cortex and their increasing ability for adaptive psychological responses were uniquely suited for this development. (1963, p. 214)

A feedback relationship is taking place here. Mutations affecting proteins that occur in the postnatal state have a much greater chance of survival than do those which affect embryonic proteins. Thus, factors that retard the biochemical development of the embryo will be selected for, and the embryo will be born at an immature developmental stage. However, although such a pattern has positive selection working for it, environmental factors would work against the survival of such immature individuals. They could survive only if given careful, long-term care. Thus there is a feedback system occurring between the biochemical demand for immaturity and the primate behavioral pattern of long-term infant care. Goodman points out that "it is not by chance" that of all the primates, humans have the most retarded development (1963, p. 215). This phenomenon of retarded development is called **"neoteny."** It is an important one in primate and human evolution, and we will return to it in Chapter 5. Here, however, Goodman has pointed to the important and necessary biochemical base for such slowed development.

SUMMARY

The major characters of the order Primates may be summarized as follows:

1. Retention of the ancestral mammalian limb condition characterized by five digits on the hands and feet, presence of a clavicle and an unfused radius in the arm, and unfused fibula in the leg
2. Ability to hold the trunk upright
3. Presence of flattened nails, rather than claws
4. Enclosure of the internal ear structures in a bulla formed within the petrosal bone
5. Simple cusp pattern on the molars
6. Presence of 32 or 36 teeth in most members of the order
7. Reduced olfactory ability, reflected in a reduction of the snout
8. Stereoscopic vision (overlapping visual fields)
9. Enclosure of the eye in a bony orbit, with the bony plate (behind the eye) not complete, but the bony bar (to the side) complete, in all living groups
10. Enlarged and complex brain, especially those areas involved with vision, muscle coordination, tactile sensations, memory, and learning
11. Lengthened period of gestation (relative to most other mammals)
12. Lengthened period of infant dependency
13. Lengthened period of maturation

In the overview, the primates, as a group, are notable for their lack of limiting morphological specializations. They have maintained a flexibility of behavior, morphology, and physiology that has allowed them a large amount of environmental and, as we shall see, evolutionary mobility. In no other single order is it possible to find such a large range of behaviors and locomotor patterns. In the following chapters, we shall see that this overall morphological generalization and the ability to adapt to changing environmental conditions may have played a crucial role in the primates' evolutionary success.

Again and again in the primate fossil record, we will see evidence of adaptation without the loss of flexibility; of diversification without true specialization. Such features characterize the initial prosimian radiation, the Miocene anthropoid radiation, and the hominid radiation of the Late

Miocene and Pliocene. Surely such diversification without specialization is one of the major features of primate evolution. It may, in fact, be unique in mammalian evolution.

SUGGESTIONS FOR FURTHER READING

Desmond, Adrian. 1976. *The Hot-Blooded Dinosaurs: A Revolution in Palaeontology.* New York: Dial. (Although the subject of this book is not dinosaurs, Desmond's book contains fascinating insights into the history of paleontology as a science.)

Hill, W. C. Osman. 1953–1962. *Primates, Comparative Anatomy and Taxonomy.* New York: Interscience. 5 vols. (A series that is basic to any study of the primates; the most complete publication available.)

Jerison, H. J. 1973. *Evolution of the Brain and Intelligence.* New York: Academic. (An individualistic but scholarly approach to the study of brain evolution.)

Jolly, Allison. 1972. *The Evolution of Primate Behavior.* New York: Macmillan. (Well-presented and well-documented study on primate behavior patterns.)

Napier, J., and P. Napier. 1967. *Handbook of the Living Primates.* London: Academic. (More concise than Osman Hill; basic reference material.)

3

EARLY PRIMATES: CRETACEOUS TO OLIGOCENE

INTRODUCTION

Paleontological evidence now indicates that the order Primates first diverged from its insectivore ancestor in the Late Cretaceous. Although this earliest evidence is limited to a single molar tooth, the amount and diversification of primate fossil material available in the following Paleocene epoch strongly support a Cretaceous origin of the order. During the Late Mesozoic and Early Cenozoic (see Table 3-1), a number of environmental and ecological factors influenced the development and distribution of the early primates.

ECOLOGIC BACKGROUND

During the geologic history of the earth, the continents and seas have gradually changed their relative positions. The current theory of plate tectonics indicates that in the Paleozoic, all the earth's land was joined together in a single supercontinent called "Pangaea." In the Late Paleozoic, this single continent broke into two land masses: Laurasia in the north

63

Table 3-1 Cenozoic chronostratigraphy

M.Y. B.P.	EPOCH	MAMMAL STAGES — NORTH AMERICAN	MAMMAL STAGES — EUROPEAN	
	Pleistocene	Irvingtonian	Villefranchian	
	—— 1.8 ——			
5	Pliocene	Blancan	Ruscinian	
	—— 5.5 ——	Hemphillian	Turolian (Pontian)	
10			Vallesian	"Hipparion Datum"
15	Miocene	Clarendonian	Vindobonian	
		Barstovian	Burdigalian	
20		Hemmingfordian	Aquitanian	
	—— 22.5 ——	Arikareen		
25			Chattian	
	Oligocene	Orellan	Rupelian	
30		Chadronian	Sannoisian	

64

Ludian	Duchesnean	—36.—
Bartonian	Uintan	Eocene
Lutetian	Bridgerian	
Ypresian	Wasatchian	—53.5—
Sparnacian	Clarkforkian	
Thanetian	Tiffanian	Paleocene
Montian	Torrejonian	
Danian	Puercan	—65—
		Cretaceous

35 — 40 — 45 — 50 — 55 — 60 — 65 —

Source: From Van Couvering, 1972.

65

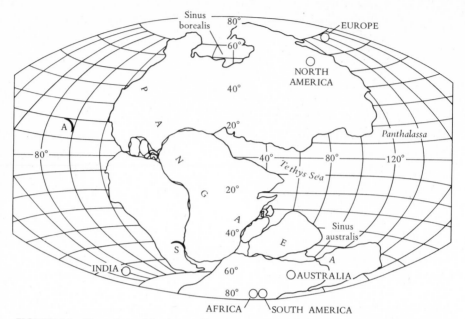

FIGURE 3-1 The universal land mass Pangaea may have looked like this 200 million years ago. Panthalassa was the ancestral Pacific Ocean. The Tethys Sea (the ancestral Mediterranean) formed a large bay separating Africa and Eurasia. The relative positions of the continents, except for India, are based on best fits made by computer, using the 1,000-fathom isobath to define continental boundaries. When the continents are arranged as shown, the relative locations of the magnetic poles in Permian times are displaced to the positions marked by circles. Ideally these positions should cluster near the geographic poles. The hatched crescents (A and S) serve as modern geographic reference points; they represent the Antilles arc in the West Indies and Scotia arc in the extreme South Atlantic. (Reproduced by permission of Scientific American.)

and Gondwanaland in the south (Figure 3-1). Gondwanaland itself began to fragment at this time into the continents of South America, Africa, Australia, India, and Antarctica. Laurasia began to break up somewhat later, probably by Triassic times, into North America, Greenland, and Eurasia. This fragmentation was a slow process, however, and a land connection remained between North America and Eurasia at Greenland until Middle Eocene times (Figure 3-2) (see Kurten, 1969).

In the Cretaceous, much of Europe was covered by a vast and ancient sea, the Tethys. Remnants of the Tethys exist today as the Mediterranean, the Black Sea, and the Caspian Sea. In Paleocene times, mountain building, associated with plate movements, resulted in the regression of the Tethys from its former extent. For example, in the Early Paleocene, about 63 m.y. ago, the Iberian plate collided with the European plate, and mountain building in the area of the Pyrenees began. Probably Africa and the Iberian plate were also united for a time (Figure 3-3) as a result of this

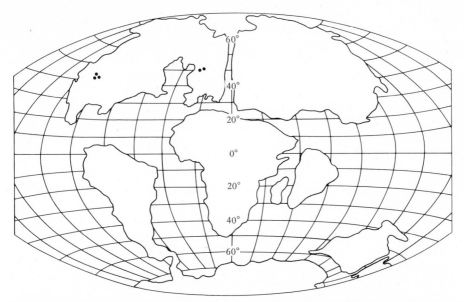

FIGURE 3-2 Primate distributions from the Paleocene through the Middle Eocene. Note that Europe and North America are joined but that Europe and Asia are separated by the Turgai Strait, which ran north and south from the Tethys Sea to the Arctic Ocean. (Redrawn from Frakes and Kemp, 1972.)

FIGURE 3-3 Primate distributions in the later Eocene. Note that the Turgai Strait in Europe has closed, opening a land connection with Asia, and that Africa has joined briefly with southern Europe. (Modified from Frakes and Kemp, 1972, with permission.)

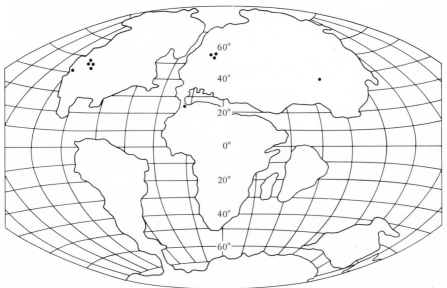

pattern of movement (Dewey, Pittman, Ryan, and Bonnin, 1973). Although much of Europe and Africa were emergent in the early Paleocene, long seaways still extended to the north and east, isolating Europe. To the north, the Turgai Strait opened into the waters of the Arctic Ocean separating Europe from Asia; to the east, a vast seaway connected the Tethys with the Indian Ocean.

By Middle Paleocene times, several primate genera were common to both North America and Europe. This distribution confirms the evidence, seen in the continental drift, that these two areas were joined in the Early Cenozoic. The faunal similarities between these two areas are so strong, in fact, that Simpson (1947) has regarded North America and Europe as a single zoogeographic region during this time. These faunal similarities do not, however, extend into Asia, and it is probable that Europe and Asia were geographically separated until Middle Eocene times (Kurten, 1966), when a land bridge developed across the Turgai Strait. It is interesting, however, that, although many faunal similarities existed between North America and northern Asia in the Late Mesozoic and Early Cenozoic, no primates are known to have been in Asia before the Late Eocene. Many types of large vertebrates, such as dinosaurs and early placental mammals, were common to both areas. This fact may indicate that the Bering Strait land bridge, intermittently in existence during the Mesozoic and Cenozoic, was a "filter" bridge (Simpson, 1953). The term "filter" is used in an environmental sense, meaning that some species could cross, but that others, including the primates, probably could not. It is probable that some geographic factor, such as lack of continuous forest cover or cool temperatures, may have made the Asian–North American land connection unsuitable for the primates.

Various lines of evidence have combined to indicate that worldwide temperatures in the Early Cenozoic (Table 3-2) were considerably warmer

TABLE 3-2   Cenozoic mean annual temperatures

REGION	CHRONOLOGY	TEMPERATURE, °C
Northwestern Europe	Present	9–10
	Pliocene	14–10
	Miocene	19–16
	Oligocene	20–18
	Eocene	22–20
Western United States	Pliocene	8–5
	Miocene	14
	Oligocene	18–14
	Eocene	25–18
	Paleocene	14
	Cretaceous	20

Sources: Northwestern Europe, Schwartzback, 1963; western United States, Nairn, 1961.

than they are today. The warmer, more equable climates of the Early Cenozoic were due to a combination of factors. With the continents grouped largely in circumequatorial areas, there was a free exchange of cooler polar waters with warmer waters of the temperate oceans. Consequently, the steep temperature gradients that exist today between polar and equatorial regions were absent. Moreover, the very fact that much of the continental land areas were in equatorial regions meant warmer climatic conditions. However, with the northward drift of the Laurasian land masses and the resultant diminution of free exchange between polar and equatorial oceans, there was a steady trend toward cooler climates throughout the Cenozoic.

Still another very important factor in early primate evolution was the development and radiation of the angiosperms. By Early Cretaceous times, they had largely replaced the formerly dominant cycads, ferns, conifers, and ginkgos (Dorf, 1955). This major radiation of the angiosperms in the Late Mesozoic allowed the development of an entirely new ecosystem. Insects, birds, and several mammalian groups, among them the primates, made major adaptive radiations into the expanding and diversifying angiosperm forests. This movement was not merely the occupation of now vacant "dinosaur niches" but also the development of totally new sets of environmental interactions. These new interactions, with interdependencies among angiosperms, insects, birds, and mammals, laid the foundation for the forest ecosystems that have become one of the major characteristics of the Cenozoic.

Present evidence indicates that the first primates appeared near the end of the Cretaceous in North America. Evidence from studies on various plant and animal groups indicates that the latter Cretaceous was a time of far-reaching geologic, ecologic, and climatologic changes affecting many life forms. An examination of this evidence may suggest something about the environments from which the earliest primates emerged.

The final stage of the Cretaceous began in western North America with widespread seas and warm or temperate climatic conditions. Ferns and cycads were the dominant plant types, but the angiosperms were becoming more numerous. During the final part of the Cretaceous, the Laramide Revolution began. This "revolution" represents a major phase of volcanic activity and mountain building, culminating in an early form of the Rocky Mountains. Laramide mountain building extended from Alaska to New Mexico and from Colorado to eastern Nevada. An important effect of this uplift in the western part of the continent was that the vast inland sea, a major feature throughout the Mesozoic, now regressed to the south, leaving swamps and forests behind it. As the end of the Cretaceous approached, other changes followed and the climate seems to have become somewhat cooler and drier. In eastern Montana, where the earliest known primates have been found, the number of species of ferns decreased by one-half between the Late Cretaceous and the Early Paleocene; other

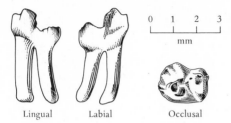

FIGURE 3-4 *Purgatorius ceratops;* RM₂ of the oldest known primate, from Cretaceous beds in Montana. (Redrawn by permission of Leigh Van Valen.)

plants, dependent on warm and moist conditions, also declined in number. On the other hand, the conifers increased from 12 percent of the total plant species in the Cretaceous to 30 percent in the Paleocene in the same area (Hall and Norton, 1967). Other studies in the area have confirmed large extinctions of plant forms at this time; one study in Wyoming showed that of 74 Cretaceous plant species, only 7 existed in both the Cretaceous and the Paleocene (Dorf, 1940).

Many extinctions also occurred in the animal world at the end of the Cretaceous. On a worldwide scale, many marine invertebrates, such as the ammonites and reef-building clams, became extinct; others, such as the tiny foraminifera, were drastically reduced in species numbers. The extinction of the ruling reptiles was perhaps the most remarkable event in the Late Cretaceous. These reptiles continued to show active evolution and diversification right up to the end of the Cretaceous, when they simply disappeared from the fossil record. Not one species of the ruling reptiles, flying, aquatic, or terrestrial, crossed the terminus of the Mesozoic.

Out of that changing world emerged the first primates. In 1964, a single molar of *Purgatorius ceratops*, the earliest known primate, was found in the Late Cretaceous–age Hell Creek Formation in McCone County, eastern Montana (Van Valen and Sloan, 1965) (Figure 3-4). This earliest primate was found in a stream channel that flowed southeast from the early Rocky Mountains. The specific name of *ceratops* was bestowed because a *Triceratops* skeleton had been found in the same stream gravels. In fact, six species of dinosaur lived contemporaneously with *Purgatorius* in eastern Montana, including a *Tyrannosaurus rex* 609.6 cm tall.

CRETACEOUS PRIMATES

Suborder: Prosimii
  Infraorder: Plesiadapiformes
    Superfamily: Plesiadapoidea
      Family: Paromomyidae

These earliest known primates differed little from their insectivore ancestors. The insectivores are predators and their dentition reflects the ability to pierce and slice their prey with speed and effectiveness. The earliest primates retained tritubercular molars, like the insectivores, but enlarged the chewing surface of the tooth with the addition of a heel of enamel (the talonid) at the rear of the tooth. The new cusp on the talonid, the hypoconulid, is small and the wall between the trigonid and talonid is steep and sharply defined. The trigonid is therefore high relative to the deeper talonid basin.

The Cretaceous species *Purgatorius ceratops*, its Paleocene descendant *P. unio* (Figure 3-5), and several other genera have been placed in the family Paromomyidae. This family represents the initial shift from order Insectivora to order Primates. Although the fossil evidence is limited, there are some indications of the adaptive nature of the shift. The Insectivora and the earliest paromomyids have sharply defined trigonids and talonids; the cusps are high and acute. The chewing area of the early primate molar has been somewhat increased, but its functions appear to have changed little. However, later paromomyids have lower trigonids with lower, more rounded cusps. As a result, such a tooth has less surface relief and less shearing and piercing capabilities. These later paromomyids often show specialized development at the anterior portion of the jaw, with both enlarged incisors and the loss, in some genera, of the lateral incisors and one pair of premolars. Such a pattern might suggest that dental preparation of food was concentrated on the molars rather than on the anterior teeth. In fact, the later paromomyid molars appear to be effective grinding

FIGURE 3-5 Right P_2-M_3 of *Purgatorius unio*: (a) occlusal view; (b) labial view. In this Paleocene paromomyid there is still a steep shelf between the high trigonid and low talonid. Note, however, that the slightly raised cusps on the talonid have somewhat decreased the discrepancy in height between the front and rear of the teeth. This is an early indication of the primate evolutionary trend which changed the molars from shearing to grinding teeth. (Scanning electron micrograph taken by M. T. Maglio; photograph courtesy of W. Clemens.)

(a)

(b)

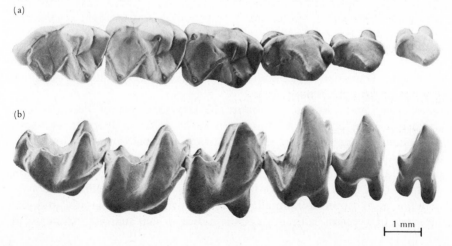

1 mm

and crushing teeth, well suited to chewing harsh, fibrous foods or crushing tough outer coverings.

These changes indicate that a dietary shift had occurred from Insectivora to Primates. *Purgatorius ceratops*, its molars slightly enlarged by a talonid, shows the initial stages of this transition (see Szalay, 1968a, for an excellent discussion of this material).

SUMMARY: CRETACEOUS

Within the Cretaceous we see the first evidence of an adaptive shift which led one group of insect-eating mammals toward a subsistence pattern more dependent on plant foods. This adaptive shift resulted in the emergence of the first primates near the end of the Cretaceous. It seems logical to correlate this shift in one group of mammals with the expansion of the angiosperm plants that occurred at about the same time.

PALEOCENE

ECOLOGIC BACKGROUND

By the Early Paleocene the primates had undergone considerable expansion and diversification—so much so, in fact, that this time has been referred to as the "first radiation" of the primates (Simons, 1972a). During this first radiation, members of the order became specialized for a variety of subsistence patterns and came to be important constituents of the fauna on two continents, Europe and North America. No primates are known from Africa or Asia in the Paleocene. Despite their effective radiations, most of the early primates were small and some were indeed very tiny; a few, however, may have reached the size of a domestic cat.

Europe

Although primates have been found in a number of European areas, one particularly important site is at Cernay in France; this site, of Middle Paleocene (Thanetian) age, provides considerable paleoecological evidence of early primate habitats.

Cernay, near Reims, is about 128 km northeast of Paris; several Paleocene collecting sites are known in the area. These deposits represent the deltaic sediments of a river moving from the east through a low-lying landscape. Near the river there were gallery forest stands of willows, poplars, alders, elms, and palms, but away from the river the vegetation seems to have been more brush-like. The total aspect of the climate appears to have been tropical. Rainfall, however, was only moderate, and the presence of gypsum in these deposits indicates that seasonal dryness did

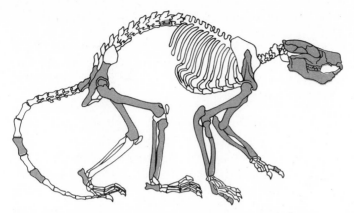

FIGURE 3-6 Skeletal reconstruction of *Plesiadapis*. Shaded parts are preserved. Scale: 0.25. (Reproduced from Tattersall, 1970, by permission.)

occur (Kurten, 1971). At least two primate genera, *Plesiadapis* and *Chiromyoids*, were present. *Plesiadapis* (Figure 3-6) is, in fact, the most common mammal in the Cernay deposits; this is a possible indication that these primates were living in troops of relatively large numbers. These early prosimians were joined, however, by a peculiar group of animals, many of which are now extinct. A reptile, not a dinosaur but still perhaps 457 cm (15 ft) long, was present in the form of *Champosaurus*; reptiles of more modern aspect, such as turtles, lizards, and crocodiles, were also present. Only one clearly carnivorous mammal is present at Cernay; this is the condylarth *Dissacus*. Among the most interesting animals in these Middle Paleocene deposits are members of the genus *Diatryma*, also called the "terror crane," a flightless bird as much as 243 cm (8 ft) tall; Kurten has suggested that these animals filled the carnivorous niche left vacant by the extinction of the dinosaurs.

This site, then, represents, in microcosm, the world of the Middle Paleocene European primates. One other site should be mentioned, however, since it reveals further information about early habitats of this time. A member of the genus *Pleisiadapis* was recovered from coal deposits at Puy-de-Dôme in southern France (Russell, 1967). The presence of this primate in coal clearly indicates its existence in an arboreal habitat surrounded by heavy vegetation and swamps.

North America

Few paleoecological studies are available for North American Paleocene deposits in the Rocky Mountain areas where the earliest primates existed (Figure 3-7). Dorf (1940), in analyzing the botanical differences between the Late Cretaceous (Lance Formation) and Paleocene (Fort Union Formation),

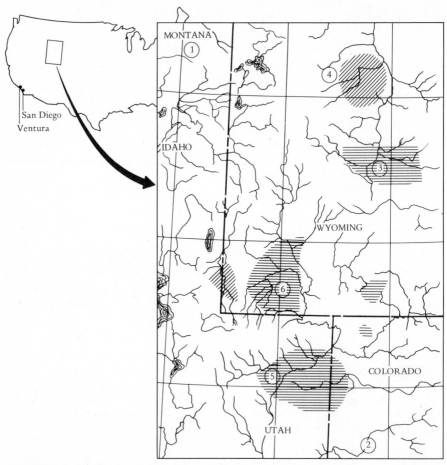

FIGURE 3-7 Distribution of Paleocene and Eocene primates in North America; major early Cenozoic depositional basins. (1) Gidley Quarry, Montana; Middle Paleocene age: *Elphidotarsius, Palaechthon*. (2) Mason Pocket, Colorado; Later Paleocene: *Plesiadapis, Carpoadaptes, Phenacolemur*. (3) Wind River Basin, Wyoming, Early Eocene: *Loveina, Shoshonius*. (4) Big Horn Basin, Wyoming; Early Eocene: *Tetonius, Absarokius, Elphidotarsius, Pelycodus*. (5) Uintah Basin, Utah; Early-Late Eocene: *Uintalacus, Ourayia*. (6) Bridger Basin, Wyoming; Middle Eocene: *Notharctus, Smilodectes, Anaptomorphus, Hemiacodon, Omomys, Washikius*.

pointed out that fewer than 10 percent of plant species are common to both time periods within the same local areas. This finding means that about 90 percent of the Cretaceous plant species had disappeared by the Paleocene. The extinction rate for local vertebrate species was also high. But the earliest primates, members of the genus *Purgatorius*, crossed the Mesozoic-Cenozoic boundary with very few apparent morphologic changes.

Faunal lists from the Purgatory Hill local fauna, of Early Paleocene age, show a wide variety of both aquatic and terrestrial forms in association with *Purgatorius unio*. A number of chondrichthyes and osteichthyes indicate the permanent presence of water. Reptiles, amphibians, marsupials, insectivores, condylarths, and multituberculates[1] suggest the wide range of terrestrial forms present (Van Valen and Sloan, 1965).

PALEOCENE PRIMATES

Suborder: Prosimii
  Infraorder: Plesiadapiformes
    Superfamily: Plesiadapoidea
      Family: Paromomyidae
      Family: Picrodontidae
      Family: Carpolestidae
      Family: Plesiadapidae

Four primate families, all within the suborder Prosimii, are known from the Paleocene; three of these families appear in the fossil record for the first time in the Paleocene, and the fourth, the Paromomyidae, had continued from the Cretaceous. Szalay (1972a, 1973) has made the suggestion that these four families should all be placed within a separate suborder, the Paromomyiformes.

Paromomyidae

Two genera within the family Paromomyidae (Table 3-3) are particularly well known in the Paleocene. *Purgatorius unio*, the presumed descendant of the Cretaceous species *P. ceratops*, has now been identified from two sites in eastern Montana. The confirmation of this genus as a primate is now based on more than 100 teeth and several jaw fragments (Clemens, 1974). Although the incisors are not yet known, it is apparent that *P. unio* had four premolars; thus the dental formula is ?143. Also, in this species the trigonid cusps are lower (bunodont) and are thus more like later primates. In assessing the morphology of this form, Clemens (1974) pointed out that it shared many similarities with the Middle Paleocene (Torrejonian-age) *Palaechthon* and *Palenochtha*, and he concludes that *P. unio* is probably ancestral to these forms.

The genus *Phenacolemur*, also within this family, is of considerable importance. This genus is well-known from both hemispheres, and at least one species continued on into the Late Eocene (P. Robinson, 1968). The cranium is low and broad (Simpson, 1955), reflecting the typical primate brain shape. However, no Paleocene primate skulls are complete enough for actual analysis of probable brain structure. Both saggital and nuchal

---

[1]The condylarths and multituberculates were primitive mammalian groups; they are now extinct.

TABLE 3-3   Paleocene primates: Paromomyidae

EPOCHS	STRATIGRAPHY			PRIMATE GENERA		
	NORTH AMERICA	EUROPE	AFRICA	NORTH AMERICA	EUROPE	AFRICA
Eocene	Duchesnean Uintan Bridgerian Wasatchian	Ludian Bartonian Lutetian Ypresian Sparnacian				Azibius ↓ ?
Paleocene	Clarkforkian Tiffanian Torrejonian Puercan	Cernay Walbeck Montian Danian		Phenacolemur Paromomys Palaechthon Palenochtha ↑	Phenacolemur	
Cretaceous	Lance			Purgatorius		

crests are present, indicating strongly developed chewing and neck musculature. The nature of the paromomyid ear region is demonstrated in *Phenacolemur* (see Figure 2-9g). As in all primates, the bony case for the ear, the auditory bulla, is formed by the petrosal bone, but in *Phenacolemur* the lateral portion of the middle ear region is outside the bulla. Thus, while the inner two-thirds of the middle ear was contained within the petrosal bulla, the lateral one-third was covered by an ectotympanic plate. The condition of having the ectotympanic plate outside the bulla is seen in all prosimians except the lemuroids, and in all higher primates including humans. Szalay (1971) has suggested that this, rather than the lemuriform intrabullar ectotympanic, is the primitive condition for the order. This presents an interesting problem to which we will return shortly. Since the first anthropoids, in the Oligocene, do not have an ectotympanic plate, it is possible that forms such as *Phenacolemur, Necrolemur,* and *Rooneyia* may have developed this structure earlier and independently of the higher primates.

Picrodontidae

The second of the Paleocene families, the Picrodontidae (Figure 3-8; Table 3-4) was possibly derived from the paromomyids (Szalay, 1971). They are rather bizarre primates; so unusual, in fact, that one genus *(Zanycteris)* of

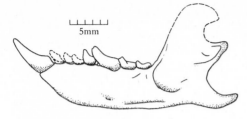

FIGURE 3-8 Mandible of *Picrotus*, a picrodontid primate from the Paleocene. This tiny prosimian may have been adapted to feeding on pulp, nectar, or other soft foods. (Redrawn by permission of Elwyn Simons.)

TABLE 3-4 Paleocene primates: Picrodontidae

AGES	GENERA
Clarkforkian	
	Zanycteris
Tiffanian	
Torrejonian	Picrodus
Puercan	

the family was originally placed in the bats. The picrodontids have a highly specialized dentition which suggests that they fed on nonabrasive foods, such as fruit pulp and nectar (Szalay, 1968a). The anterior teeth of *Picrodus*, for example, are very long and procumbent, with enlarged and flat premolars and molars (Figure 3-8). These primates appear to have a very limited distribution and were restricted to the New World.

Carpolestidae

The family Carpolestidae (Table 3-5), also known only from North America, probably diverged from the Plesiadapidae in about the Middle Paleocene (Simons, 1972a; Rose, 1975). Only three genera are known, *Elphidotarsius, Carpodaptes,* and *Carpolestes;* they seem to form a linear ancestor-descendant sequence. Members of the family were extremely small. The smallest mandible is just 1.5 cm long, and the largest only 2.5 cm (Simons, 1972b). Total body size could not have exceeded that of a mouse. (Figures 3-9 and 3-10.)

The family is defined on the basis of its extremely specialized dentition, particularly the P_4.[2] The anterior dentition is reduced with the

[2]A note on the terminology of the premolars: The original mammals had four premolars, but in the course of primate evolution, the first and often the second premolars have been lost. Thus, the living Old World anthropoids have retained P3 and P4, but have lost P1 and P2.

TABLE 3-5   Paleocene primates:
Carpolestidae

NORTH AMERICA	
AGES	GENERA
Clarkforkian	
Tiffanian	Carpoadaptes
	Carpolestes (to early Eocene)
Torrejonian	Elphidotarsius
Puercan	

exception of a large and procumbent medial incisor. The P_4 is large, blade-like, and multicusped; some individuals have as many as nine cusps on this tooth. The upper premolars have rough, saw-like occlusal surfaces. Such a dental pattern is termed **"plagiaulacoid"** after the multituberculate

FIGURE 3-9   Reconstruction of the skull of *Carpolestes,* a Paleocene primate, showing highly specialized cheek teeth. (Rose, 1975, fig. 33. Used by permission of Kenneth Rose.)

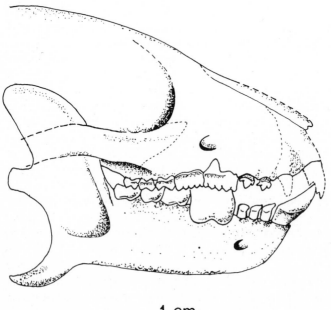

1 cm

FIGURE 3-10 Dentition of *Carpoadaptes hazelae*, lateral view. (Rose, 1975, fig. 12. Used by permission of Kenneth Rose.)

suborder Plagiaucoloidea, which has a similar morphology. Similar dental patterns are also found in some marsupials and the plesiadapoids *Plesiadapis* and *Saxonella* (Rose, 1975). Rose, in his fine monograph on this group, has concluded that the premolars acted in a saw-like fashion to cut or shear food. Such a dentition may have been useful in a diet containing a large proportion of coarse, fibrous vegetable foods or seeds (Szalay, 1972a; Rose, 1975).

Plesiadapidae

The Plesiadapidae (Table 3-6) was a widespread and very successful family in the Paleocene. This family is interesting particularly because some workers (McKenna, 1961; A. Wood, 1962) have suggested that the rodents may have originated from within this group. Szalay (1972a), however, has contended that the similarities between the early rodents and plesiadapid primates are due to evolutionary convergence rather than to similar ancestry. Members of the Plesiadapidae are characterized by having large, multicusped incisors, often with the loss or reduction in the canines and anterior premolars. This results, in *Plesiadapis*, in a large diastema, or gap, in the tooth row between the anterior and posterior teeth.

Within this family, the genus *Plesiadapis* is well known from both the eastern and western hemispheres. Moreover, the discovery of associated cranial and postcranial material has allowed a fuller reconstruction of this primate than of any others at this early date (Figure 3-6).

The intermembral index of *Plesiadapis* was slightly below 100, giving it approximately the body proportions of the New World monkey *Ateles* (Russell, 1967). The feet were fissured like a dog's paws, and they had large, arched claws; these features are not known in any living primate.

TABLE 3-6   Paleocene primates: Plesiadapidae

			EUROPE	NORTH AMERICA
EOCENE	Duchesnean	Ludian		
	Uintan	Bartonian		
	Bridgerian	Lutetian		
		Ypresian		
	Wasatchian	Sparnacian	Platychaerops	
PALEOCENE	Clark–Forkian	Cernay (Thanetian)	Saxonella Plesiadapis Chiromyoides	Plesiadapis
	Tiffanian	Walbeck (Thanetian)		
	Torrejonian			
		Montian		Pronothodectes
	Puercan	Danian		

Simons (1972a) has concluded that *Plesiadapis* must have moved much like a squirrel or rat; that is, it had the ability to move well both on the ground and in the trees. The very wide distribution of this genus would indicate that its method of locomotion was somewhat flexible.

The cranium of this form had no postorbital plate or bar; thus the orbits were entirely open to the side. In the ear region, an ectotympanic plate is present, taking the form of a long, tubular external auditory tube. Although this feature is similar to that of the living higher primates, as pointed out in the discussion of *Phenacolemur* earlier in this section, it may be an independently acquired parallelism. The arteries within the bulla show a primitive feature in that they are not enclosed in bony tubes, as in living primates. In *Plesiadapis*, both the stapedial and the promontory branches of the internal carotid artery lie in shallow grooves on the petrosal (Szalay, 1972a).

With reference to the dental structures of this genus, Simons (1972b) has pointed out that it shares a number of functional dental similarities with the kangaroos. In both groups, the lower incisors form a shearing arch within the arcade of the upper incisors; the premolars are nonproject-ing in both groups. The living kangaroos use this dental mechanism for grazing and browsing and it seems a good analogy, according to Simons, that *Plesiadapis* was a similarly practicing herbivore. The Plesiadapidae seem to have been a quite specialized branch which, in fact, continued to show progressive dental specializations throughout their known history. The last known members of this group in the Eocene had lost a total of eight teeth in the anterior portion of each jaw; the canine, two premolars, and one incisor were all eventually lost. This evidence of continued specialization would suggest that the Plesiadapidae were off the main stream of primate evolution.

SUMMARY: PALEOCENE

Several things are very remarkable about primate evolution in the Paleocene. The first is the amount of morphologic diversification and adaptation present at this early time. Each of the four families present shows a particular and distinctive pattern of characters indicating that by Paleocene times, the order Primates already had a long evolutionary history behind them. The very presence of such diversification at approxi-mately 50 to 60 m.y. ago is a strong indication of their earlier origins. Clearly, the order could not have emerged just 60 m.y. ago, as Sarich concluded on the basis of his immunological data (Sarich, 1968; Sarich and Wilson, 1967).

The second important aspect of the primate fossil record in the Paleocene is their widespread distribution. These primates, most of them no larger than a mouse, are found in deposits in both western North America and northern Europe. After their Late Cretaceous beginning, they must have spread more or less continuously from North America to northern Europe, presumably by way of the land connection in the Greenland area. Such distribution indicates the presence of favorable habitats, such as warm or temperate forests, throughout this area.

The morphologic developments in the order at this time are also interesting. Although the picrodonts may have developed a specialized feeding behavior and morphology, it is clear that the remainder of the order in the Paleocene were exploiting a dietary base consisting largely of coarse vegetable foods and possibly seeds. The evidence for such a diet is present in the mandibular, dental, and cusp morphology. First, there is a trend in the Paleocene prosimians to reduce the relative trigonid-talonid height, so that the molar teeth have a more level occlusal surface. The cusps and crests became lower and more rounded. There is often loss of the lateral incisors and one pair of premolars, resulting in the presence of plagiaucoloid dental patterns in both plesiadapids and carpolestids. There appears to be a diminution in the vertical bite and piercing action (orthal shear component) in mastication from early Paleocene times on (see Szalay, 1973). Orthal shear is an important masticatory component in the insectivores and *Purgatorius*; its deemphasis in later primates may indicate that insect predation was less important in diet than herbivory. Lack of predation may also be indicated by the decrease in canine size; a smaller canine is less effective for the holding or piercing actions necessary in predation.

Correlated with these dental changes are alterations in the mandibular form. The mandible became more robust and heavily built during the Paleocene. This trend, later reinforced by fusion of the two halves of the mandible, suggests that the jaw was being subjected to greater chewing stresses. Fusion of the mandible at the midline is presumably related to the presence of greater horizontal or grinding masticatory actions. The unfused jaw halves of the insectivores appear to be present when the vertical bite or shear component is the predominant masticatory action; when horizontal actions become stronger and more important in chewing, additional stability seems to be necessary at the anterior portion of the jaw. This total morphological pattern of dental structures does not support Cartmill's (1974) hypothesis that the early primate adaptations reflect predation rather than herbivory.

EOCENE

ECOLOGIC BACKGROUND

The Eocene represents a germinal time in mammalian evolution when the radiation of the class reached its peak. In the Late Paleocene, 41 mammalian families were in existence, but by the Late Eocene, this number had risen to 91 (Kurten, 1971). Moreover, for the first time, mammalian faunas take on a modern appearance and familiar, recognizable forms appear in the fossil record. Seven new orders emerged in the Eocene and all of them are still in existence. The first appearance of the true carnivores, bats, elephants, cetaceans, rodents, and both major orders of ungulates (Perissodactyla and Artiodactyla) probably occurred at this time (Kurten, 1971). Also, the primates, sharing in this almost explosive Eocene mammalian diversification, experienced their second major radiation; possibly 45 genera of primates are known from the Eocene (Simons, 1963).

In the Early Eocene, North America and Europe still formed essentially a single faunal community. The faunas contained within the North American and European deposits were very similar indeed, indicating that the North Atlantic land connection in the Greenland area was still open. But by Middle Eocene times, plate movements had broken the connection and no further major faunal exchanges took place between Europe and

North America subsequently. For a brief span of time in the Middle Eocene, however, Asia and Europe were united by a land bridge over the Turgai Strait (see Figure 3-3). It is probable that primates were involved in the faunal exchanges that occurred between Europe and Asia at this time; thus the primates probably entered Asia from Europe in the Middle Eocene. Fossil evidence for primates in eastern Asia is limited to a very few fragments, all probably dating to the Late Eocene: *Lushius, Hoanghonius,* and "Kansupithecus"[3] are known from China, and *Amphipithecus* and *Pondaungia* are from Burma (pages 96, 97).

In addition to the faunal exchange between Europe and Asia in the Eocene, it is apparent that a limited contact also occurred between Europe and North Africa, probably in Late Eocene or Early Oligocene times. No mammalian groups are known to have left Africa at this contact, but it seems probable that members of two, and possibly three, groups entered Africa (Coryndon and Savage, 1973). During the Paleocene and Eocene, African land mammal faunas are very poorly known and the only available information comes solely from the northern part of that continent. This information, however, indicates that African land mammals were highly endemic, or locally developed, in the Early Tertiary. The possibility of a Paleocene contact between Africa and Europe has already been mentioned. In the Late Eocene or Early Oligocene, several new elements appeared in the north African faunas; in fact, 20 percent of the known mammals at this time were apparently immigrants (Coryndon and Savage, 1973). Creodonts (primitive carnivores) and anthracotheres (artiodactyls often associated with water) both apparently entered Africa in this period. It also seems possible and geographically plausible that higher primates or their direct ancestors also may have moved into Africa. These two contacts—one between Europe and Asia and the second between Europe and Africa (Figure 3-3)—are extremely important in primate evolutionary history. They will be explored in more detail in the following discussion.

Europe

In the Early Eocene, the high temperatures of the Paleocene continued, but by the middle of the epoch a number of geographic and climatic changes were occurring. By Middle Eocene times, the arm of the Tethys Sea, which had previously extended to the warmer waters of the Indian Ocean, had become restricted by the initial stages of mountain formation in southern Europe and western Asia. By the Late Eocene, the Alps, the Pyrenees, and the Vosges mountains had risen to the extent that they formed major barriers to the rain-laden winds coming in from the Atlantic. Such barriers

[3]The nomen "Kansupithecus" is not italicized and is placed in quotation marks because it is technically an invalid genus. Bohlin, who proposed the name in 1946, did not provide a type species for the genus.

form "rain-shadow" areas where amounts of rainfall and precipitation are low. Now, although warm, tropical, and subtropical conditions still prevailed in parts of Europe, the presence of various types of evaporite deposits, such as gypsum and phosphorites, indicate that greater season-ality was occurring, with occasional drought in some areas. Evaporite deposits are particularly important in the area of the Paris Basin and in south-central France; primate fossils have been found in both areas. In the Parisian district of Montmartre, Late Eocene gypsum deposits form the famous "plaster of Paris". These deposits contain a vast storehouse of Early Tertiary fossils for students of evolution. Indeed, Cuvier's studies of fossils in the Montmartre gypsums laid the foundation for the science of paleontology over 150 years ago.

Gypsum ($CA\ SO_4\ 2H_2O$) is formed when water evaporates at tempera-tures of less than 34°C (Green, 1961); thus, gypsum deposits are important paleoclimatologic indicators. Studies of the Montmartre deposits indicate that waters within the Paris Basin were subject to frequent evaporation, and the gypsum is the chemical residue left behind. It is likely that animals were then living in a period of seasonal drought, and the presence of evaporite deposits in many parts of Europe at this time confirms wide-spread climatic change during the Late Eocene.

In contrast with the seasonal dryness in France, the southeastern portion of the British Isles was experiencing warm, tropical, and humid conditions; the mean temperature was approximately 21°C, whereas the same area has a mean of 10°C today. Late Eocene levels in this area are called the "London clay deposits." Floral studies (Reid and Chandler, 1933, Edwards, 1936) indicate a tropical rain forest with the presence of mangrove swamps and the remains of many seeds and fruits. The closest comparison with a floral assemblage today is that of the Indo-Malayan area (Muller, 1968).

North America

The great mountain-building activity of the Late Cretaceous resulted in a highly variable geography in the interior of western North America. And, as in the Paleocene, this area contains considerable evidence of Early Tertiary primates. Much of the fossil evidence is concentrated in a series of depositional basins, collectively called "Fossil Lake," located in Wyoming, Montana, Utah, and Colorado (see Figure 3-7). Less abundant material from this time has been collected from a number of sites in southern California.

Of the depositional basins in the Fossil Lake area, the Green River Basin is perhaps the best known. By the Late Eocene, the lake in the Green River Basin covered an area of more than 12,950 sq km (5,000 sq mi) (Kurten, 1971). More than 135 plant species are known from these deposits; they include ferns, cycads, palms, and many other plants that grow under tropical conditions today. Trees, such as willow, walnut, birch, and oak, were also present, indicating more temperate local conditions also.

Eocene primate sites in southern California are located in a variety of environments. Southern California is bisected by a plate boundary marked by the San Andreas Fault. Much of California lies to the east of the fault, on the North American plate. But coastal California, south of San Francisco, lies west of the fault on the Pacific plate. The two plates are slowly moving past each other, with the Pacific plate moving toward the north. In Eocene times, this Pacific plate was far to the south at approximately the latitude of Sonora, Mexico, today. Most of the southern California primate sites represent tropical or subtropical environments (Golz, 1976). Several primate sites in San Diego County (Friars Formation) were located very near lagoons, and fringing reefs may have been offshore, thus protecting the shoreline (Golz, 1976). Other sites to the north in Ventura County (Sespe Formation) represent habitats located along rivers or streams (Golz, 1976).

The Eocene primates from the interior of the continent and those from coastal southern California are very similar in morphology, and, in at least one case, the same genus occurs in both areas. This finding would indicate that an equable environment for these tiny prosimians must have existed between the interior and coastal areas, which were not separated by any major mountain ranges (Golz, 1976).

While the discovery of earlier Paleocene primates has been almost entirely confined to western North America and western Europe, the Eocene fossil evidence suggests that these primates were a much more cosmopolitan group than the earlier ones. They had spread not only to the western coast of North America, but also to eastern and southern Asia and into north Africa.

EOCENE PRIMATES

Within the order Primates during the Eocene, the infraorders Lemuriformes and Tarsiiformes made their first appearance. The infraorder Plesiadapiformes continued on from earlier times. It is difficult to ascertain the direct Paleocene ancestors of the new Eocene infraorders; it is possible, in view of the incompleteness of the fossil record, that we do not have the remains of the immediate ancestors. It is clear, however, that both the Picrodontidae and the Carpolestidae, from the Paleocene, are too specialized to have provided the ancestral populations for the new Eocene groups. Of the remaining groups, the Paromomyidae and Plesiadapidae, it is also probable that the Plesiadapidae were so specialized in their dental morphology that they could not have provided the necessarily generalized ancestral populations. The remaining group, the Paromomyidae, are thus the most likely of the known groups to have supplied the ancestry of the new Eocene forms.

Suborder: Prosimii
   Infraorder: Lemuriformes
      Superfamily: Adapoidea
         Family: Adapidae
            Subfamily: Adapinae
            Subfamily: Notharctinae
   Infraorder: Tarsiiformes
      Superfamily: Tarsioidea
         Family: Tarsiidae
            Subfamily: Microchoerinae
         Family: Anaptomorphidae
            Subfamily: Anaptomorphinae
            Subfamily: Omomyinae
   Infraorder: Plesiadapiformes
      Superfamily: Plesiadapoidea
         Family: Paromomyidae

Infraorder Lemuriformes (Table 3-7)

Family Adapidae   Most primate paleontologists would agree that the ancestors of the living lemuroids can be found within the family Adapidae. Gingerich (1973) has recently suggested that the ancestors of the higher primates may also be found within this group.

Both living lemuroids and the adapids have a free ring-like tympanic bone and a long muzzle, and they share a number of dental features. Most of the adapids had a dental formula of 2143, with incisors that were vertically implanted rather than slanting outward. Resemblances between the adapids and living lemuroids extend also to the circulatory patterns within the ear. The auditory bulla is served by the internal carotid artery; as the artery enters the bulla, it divides into two branches: the promontory and stapedial arteries. In *Notharctus*, *Adapis*, and *Lemur*, the inferior branch of the stapedial is lost and the remaining portion of this artery is much reduced. The remaining branch of the internal carotid, the promontory artery, is also very small. The implication of this pattern is that the structures of the cranium, above the bulla, were supplied with blood drawn mainly through the vertebral arteries and not the carotid (Gregory, 1920). This supposition is important because in *Tarsius* and all anthropoids, the stapedial artery is very much reduced or even absent, but the promontory artery is very large. As Szalay (1972a) has stated, the

TABLE 3-7 Eocene Lemuriformes: Family Adapidae

	STRATIGRAPHY			PRIMATES			
				SUBFAMILY ADAPINAE		SUBFAMILY NOTHARCTINAE	
m.y. B.P.	PERIOD	NORTH AMERICA	EUROPE	NORTH AMERICA	EUROPE	NORTH AMERICA	EUROPE
37	Upper Eocene	Duchesnean	Ludian		*Adapis* *Pronycticebus* *Caenopithecus*		*Pelycodus*
		Uintan	Bartonian				
45	Middle Eocene	Bridgerian	Lutetian		*Anchomomys*	*Notharctus* *Smilodectes*	
49	Lower Eocene	Lost Cabin	Ypesian				
		Wind River Graybull	Sparnacian		*Protoadapis*	*Pelycodus*	

87

tarsier-anthropoid system may represent an improved method of supplying blood to the brain. He has pointed out that one large vessel will carry more blood than three smaller ones. Such an increased flow of blood would be necessary to deliver nutrients and oxygen to the brain. It is possible, then, that the circulatory patterns of the internal ear region may indirectly reflect one of the physiological requirements of the larger anthropoid brain.

The family Adapidae is divided into two subfamilies according to their different geographic distributions. The subfamily Adapinae is known only from Europe, and the subfamily Notharctinae only from North America. A possible exception to this geographic distinction is that the notharctine *Cantius* is known from France (Simons, 1972a.)

Subfamily Adapinae   The best-known of the Eocene adapinaes is the genus *Adapis*. The original specimen came from the "plaster of Paris" gypsum deposits at Montmartre; others have been recovered from the Quercy phosphorites, the London Clay, and other sites in western Europe.

Gregory (1920), in describing the dental morphology of *Adapis*, suggested that the molar teeth would have been very effective in cutting and shearing but not in grinding. The structure of the jaw, which is short and robust, suggests a powerful chewing action which probably moved almost entirely in an up-and-down, or orthal, plane; rotatory or grinding activities seem to have been less important (Gingerich, 1972). The major chewing muscles in *Adapis* appear to have been well developed. The nearly vertical relationship between the origins of temporalis on the sagittal crest and its insertion on the posterior angle of the jaw shows that this muscle could have developed a powerful bite. The broad flare to the cheekbones (the malar bones) and the large area of origin of the masseter confirm the presence of a strong chewing mechanism, especially in the front of the mouth. Gregory concluded that such a dental morphology indicated that *Adapis* had a diet of tough, fibrous vegetable foods.

Functionally, this pattern and that of later hominids share at least one similarity in that both groups have a short, robust jaw capable of exerting a powerful bite. They differ in that the hominids, instead of emphasizing the vertical component of the bite as the adapids did, have developed a strong rotatory chewing mechanism.

An endocranial cast of a member of this genus has been studied by Le Gros Clark (1945). He noted a combination of primitive and more advanced features. The primitive features include enlarged and projecting olfactory bulbs, a cerebrum small in relation to the cerebellum, very small frontal lobes, and small lateral cerebellar lobes. Le Gros Clark pointed out that such a morphology is intermediate between tree shrews *(Tupaia)* and the mouse lemurs *(Microcebus).* On the other hand, the *Adapis* brain shows at least one advanced feature: the temporal lobe is relatively larger than it is in nonprimates.

Subfamily Notharctinae This subfamily is known from only three genera, all of which appear to be closely related. The earliest, *Pelycodus*, is clearly ancestral to *Notharctus*, and the transitional processes from one form to the other have been well documented (Osborn, 1902; Simons, 1972a). Gregory (1920), especially has discussed aspects of this transition, which may reflect dietary changes within the lineage. He regarded *Pelycodus* as a largely insectivorous form with relatively great piercing power in the anterior portion of the mouth and with relatively less grinding and cutting power in the region of the cheek teeth. This interpretation is reinforced by the fact that of all the Adapidae, only *Pelycodus* does not show fusion of the suture at the front of the mandible **(mandibular symphysis).** Such a condition at the anterior portion of the lower jaw would indicate that rotary or grinding actions during chewing were relatively minimal and that the emphasis was on a more vertical type of mastication. The dental apparatus of *Notharctus*, on the other hand, shows a progressive molarization of the premolars. This development, along with fusion of the mandibular symphysis, would suggest greater efficiency of grinding or rotary chewing actions during mastication. This morphology, Gregory argued, reflected a diet of leaves or soft-rind fruit. *Notharctus*, in turn, shares many features with the slightly later *Smilodectes* and presumably provided the ancestral population for this genus.

The transition in the North American Notharctinae is well documented largely because *Smilodectes*, *Pelycodus*, and *Notharctus* are very common forms in their respective and successive assemblages. *Pelycodus* is so common, in fact, that it is regarded as an index fossil to the Early Eocene beds of western North America. Both *Notharctus* and *Smilodectes* are found in the Bridger Basin deposits in Wyoming, where exceptional conditions have led to the preservation of virtually whole animals. These two genera are undoubtedly the most completely known pre-Pleistocene primates.

As a subfamily, the Notharctinae are characterized by a dental formula of 2143. The presence of the P1 is interesting. This tooth, which erupted with the deciduous teeth, was small and had only a single root. It apparently was never replaced by a permanent tooth (Gregory, 1920). A further characteristic of this group is that the hypocone on the upper molars arose from the protocone; in the Adapinae and most other mammals, the hypocone develops from the lingual **cingulum,** a ridge of enamel around the inner side of the tooth.

The type genus of this subfamily, *Notharctus*, is very well known. Numerous cranial and postcranial remains of this genus were the subject of a very fine monograph by Gregory (1920).

The cranium of *Notharctus* shows completion of the bony orbit around the eye. Closure was achieved by downward expansion of the orbital process of the frontal bone to meet the orbital process of the malar bone. This is the first time that the completed bony ring of the primate orbit appears in the fossil record.

The total functional pattern of the postcranium of *Notharctus* (Figure 3-11) suggests that the locomotor pattern was of the vertical clinging and leaping variety; indeed, the intermembral index of 60-61 demonstrates that the limb proportions were similar to living practitioners of this method of locomotion, such as *Tarsius*. Other anatomical characters support such a locomotor interpretation. There is, for example, a protuberance on the front border of the ilium for the origin of rectus femoris. This muscle is a strong flexor of the hip joint and, in concert with other muscles of the thigh, acts also to straighten or extend the knee. Such a development of rectus femoris would provide a strong thrust of the leg in leaping. Moreover, the humerus is short and robust, with a large crest for the major shoulder muscle, the deltoid; the deltoid lifts and rotates the forelimb, and having this function, it would be a strong climbing muscle. The nearly circular head of the radius indicates that considerable rotation of the forelimb was possible. This rotation adds another element of flexibility in the locomotion of *Notharctus*. This locomotor pattern is completed by a big toe (**hallux**) that is strongly divergent and a thumb (**pollex**) that is less so. The distal phalanges of both the hands and feet are broad and flat, indicating the presence of flattened nails, rather than claws.

Infraorder Tarsiiformes (Table 3-8)

Family Tarsiidae   In Eocene times, prosimians similar to living tarsioids were widespread in both North America and western Europe. Morphological features of living tarsioids are particularly apparent in members of the subfamily Microchoerinae. These similarities include a similar dental formula (2133), very large, forward-directed orbits with complete postorbital closure, and a number of similarities in the ear region, including a long external auditory tube and a similar pattern of circulation within the bulla. Four genera are known from the subfamily Microchoerinae: *Necrolemur*, *Pseudoloris*, *Microchoerus*, and *Nannopithex*. Of these, the best known is *Necrolemur*. Although this genus bears many similarities to living tarsiers, it has several specializations, especially in the dentition, which remove it as a potential ancestor of that group. The very distinctive molars of this genus have inflated cusps and appear swollen. The trigonids are high, while the talonid basins are small and unexpanded. However, similarities between *Necrolemur* and *Tarsius* occur in the ear region. There is a long external auditory tube; and in the circulatory system in the ear, the stapedial branch of the internal carotid artery is smaller than the promontory.

Necrolemur and *Tarsius* also have important similarities in the eye region in that both genera show complete postorbital closure. This closure has been caused largely by an outward and downward expansion of the frontal bone; the orbital plate of the maxilla has also contributed, but to a very small degree. Although the size of the orbits relative to the rest of the skull is somewhat smaller in *Necrolemur* than in *Tarsius*, the pattern of

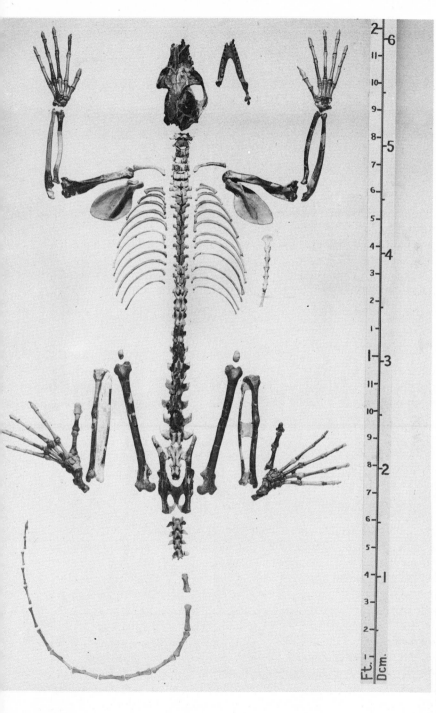

FIGURE 3-11 Skull and postcranium of *Notharctus osborni*, recovered from the Bridger Basin, Middle Eocene deposits in Wyoming. This beautifully preserved specimen is one of the best known of all Tertiary primates. Note the fully generalized limb structure. (Photograph, American Museum of Natural History.)

TABLE 3-8 Eocene Tarsiiformes

M.Y. B.P.	CHRONOLOGY			FAMILY: ANAPTOMORPHIDAE					FAMILY: TARSIIDAE	
				ANAPTOMORPHINAE		OMOMYINAE			MICROCHOERINAE	
	NORTH AMERICA, AGES	EUROPE, AGES	ASIA, FAUNAS	EUROPE	NORTH AMERICA	EUROPE	NORTH AMERICA	ASIA	EUROPE	NORTH AMERICA
37 / 40 (UPPER)	Duchesnean	Ludian	Irdin Manha, Pondaung				Ourayia	Amphipithecus (?), Podaungia (?), Kansupithecus (?), Lushius (?), Hoanghonius (?)	Microchoerus	
45 (MIDDLE)	Uintan	Bartonian					Chumashius			
49 (MIDDLE)	Bridgerian	Lutetian					Utahia, Stockia, Washakius, Omomys, Hemiacodon, Anemorhysis		Necrolemur, Nannopithex, Pseudoloris	
55 (LOWER) WASATCHIAN	Lost Cabin, Wind River, Graybull	Ypresian, Sparnacian	Ulan Bulak	Berruvius	Uintanius, Uintalacus, Absarokius, Tetonius, Tetonides	Teilhardina	Shoshonius, Loveina			

92

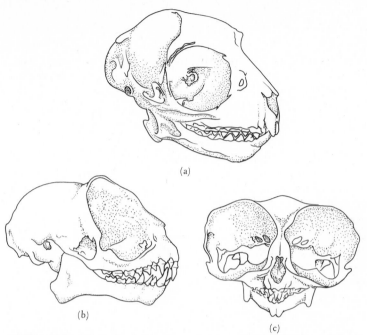

(a)

(b)

(c)

FIGURE 3-12 **(a)** Skull of *Necrolemur* in comparison with that of **(b, c)** *Tarsius*. (*a*, by permission of Elwyn Simons; *b* and *c*, by permission of John Buettner-Janusch.)

closure nevertheless is clear (Figure 3-12). In the higher primates, postorbital closure has occurred with important contributions from several skull and facial bones, such as the frontal, malar, and alisphenoid. Thus, although closure has occurred in both groups, it has been developed in rather different ways (Buettner-Janusch, 1966, Simons and Russell, 1960).

The postcranial morphology of this subfamily is known from the genus *Nannopithex*, from Middle Eocene–age coal deposits in east Germany. In this specimen, several anatomical features point to a hopping, or a vertical clinging and leaping, mode of locomotion. The heel bone **(calcaneum)** is long and the foramen magnum is located well under the skull, a position that would indicate an erect posture of the trunk. Living tarsiers, which practice a hopping mode of locomotion on the ground, have an erect body posture; they have also developed fusion of the tibia and fibula, a specialization that had not yet occurred in the Eocene (Simons, 1961a).

Family Anaptomorphidae This Eocene family, too, shows many similarities with living tarsiers. As a family, the Anaptomorphidae are characterized by a dental formula of 2123 or 2133; thus, there has been some loss in the premolar series relative to the Adapidae. Associated with this reduction in the premolars is the occasional loss or reduction of the lateral incisors. Geographically, this family has a wide distribution in North America, western Europe, and possibly China.

SUBFAMILY ANAPTOMORPHINAE   This subfamily of the Anaptomorphidae is known only from sites in Colorado, Wyoming, and Utah. With the exception of an excellently preserved skull of the genus *Tetonius,* the subfamily is known entirely from dental remains. The dental characters of this group include enlarged central incisors and fourth premolars with loss or reduction of the lateral incisors and second premolars.

The skull of *Tetonius* (Figure 3-13), found in the Big Horn Basin, Wyoming, shows a number of similarities with living tarsiers. The orbits are large, the postorbital bar is complete, and the overall dental pattern resembles that of the tarsiers. Radinsky (1967) has studied an endocranial cast obtained from this skull. He has pointed out that the brain of *Tetonius* was, in fact, very modern in form and showed expansion of the brain areas that deal with optic and auditory functions; Radinsky has suggested that such sensory specializations and improvements "may have been one of the critical adaptations responsible for the early Eocene radiation of the Primates" (1967). However, as pointed out earlier, this sensory-perceptual pattern may be of even greater antiquity in the order.

SUBFAMILY OMOMYINAE   Members of this subfamily are known from many sites in the northern hemisphere; it is the most widely distributed of the

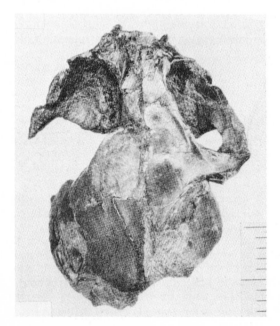

FIGURE 3-13 Skull of *Tetonius homunculus,* an early Eocene tarsioid (or anaptomorphid) primate, recovered from the Greybull Formation, Bighorn Basin, Wyoming. Note the completed postorbital plate and bar and the evidence of very large chewing muscles. (Photograph used with permission of Leonard Radinsky.)

Eocene groups. Two of its possible members are known from China, others from western Europe including Switzerland, and both the western and Pacific Coast areas of North America.

Very few cranial fragments are known for this subfamily, and portions of the postcranium are known from only a single individual. Therefore, the major characteristics of this subfamily are defined almost entirely on the dentition. Within the Omomyinae, the molars often have wrinkled or crenulated enamel, and the dental formula is, in all known cases, 2133. There appears to have been an adaptation to enlarge the chewing surface of the cheek teeth; the molars have enlarged talonid basins, the premolars often have molariform heels of enamel, and additional cuspules are often present on the molars. A particular feature of the Omomyinae is the addition of an extra cusp on the anterior inner cingula of the upper molars; this extra cusp is called a **"pericone."**

Within the subfamily, three genera form a close and interesting group: *Washakius*, known from both Wyoming and southern California; *Shoshonius*, from Wyoming; and *Dyseolemur*, from southern California. *Shoshonius* is the earliest of this group, known from Early Eocene beds in the Wind River Basin; it is very likely ancestral to the Middle and Late Eocene *Washakius*. By the Late Eocene, members of this genus occur in beach or shore deposits in San Diego County in southern California. The Late Eocene *Dyseolemur*, known from inland deposits in Ventura County, southern California, was probably locally derived from *Washakius* (Stock, 1934). These three genera would appear to document a westward-moving radiation of primates beginning in the Middle Eocene. The cheek teeth of all three are omomyid in the sense that they have wrinkled enamel and show extra cusps; as a group, they all demonstrate a crowded appearance to the cheek teeth and the presence of an extra cusp on the back of the metaconid. This extra cusp is called a **"metastylid."** With such a dental morphology, it is possible that the three genera were exploiting a particularly harsh and fibrous vegetable diet. Gazin (1958) has thought that one member of this little trilogy, *Washakius*, could have been near the ancestry of the ceboids. Although this is an interesting idea, particularly in view of the minor radiation experienced by members of this genus, additional morphological evidence is needed. This is particularly true since an Oligocene genus of this subfamily, *Rooneyia* from west Texas, shows a long, external auditory tube and other features not known in living New World monkeys (J. Wilson, 1966; Hofer and Wilson, 1967).

Perhaps a second radiation within the omomyids can also be documented. The Early Eocene genus *Teilhardina* is known from a number of sites in western Europe, particularly in France and Belgium. The dentition of this form is typical of omomyids except that, in some individuals at least, a first premolar is present. The dental formula would thus be 2143. Primates very similar to *Teilhardina*, of Early and Middle Eocene age, are known from the Bridger Basin deposits in Wyoming. The genera *Omomys* and *Hemiacodon* are part of this evidence, but poorly known forms, such as *Utahia* and *Stockia*, may also belong to this group. These genera have lost the first premolar, but other dental and jaw features are very like *Teilhardina*. *Chumashius*, from Late Eocene deposits in southern California, would appear to document the westward movement of this group. Most interesting, however, is the resemblance of the European-American genera to two genera known from Late Eocene deposits in Honan Province, China. *Hoanghonius* (Woo and Chow, 1957) and *Lushius* (Chow, 1961) would appear to indicate the spread of this type of omomyid prosimian throughout the northern hemisphere (see Simons, 1963, 1972a).

It is interesting to speculate on the significance of the resemblances between the California *Chumashius* and the Asian *Hoanghonius* and *Lushius*. The mammal faunas of Asia in the Late Eocene show a number of similarities with contemporaneous North American faunas. These resemblances are particularly marked in the large herbivores, especially the browsers. Studies on these Late Eocene Asian faunas (Simpson, 1947) have indicated that, while a few European forms are present, the major similarities are with North American forms. The question then centers on the geographic origin of these Late Eocene Asian primates. Are they part of the European faunas that entered Asia over the Turgai land bridge, or did they use a land bridge in the Bering Strait area, as did many forest-dwelling animals of larger size? Only a total review of the Late Eocene mammalian assemblages from coastal North America and north Asia, with particular reference to the smaller mammals, will resolve this interesting question.

The question is made even more challenging by the presence of three other primate genera in Early Tertiary deposits in Asia. Both *Pondaungia*, described by Pilgrim in 1927, and *Amphipithecus* (Figure 3-14), described by

FIGURE 3-14 Mandible of *Amphipithecus*, occlusal view. This specimen, from the Eocene of Burma, may represent the earliest known anthropoid. The compression of the tooth row and the cusp morphology of the molars support this attribution. (Photograph courtesy of Fred Szalay.)

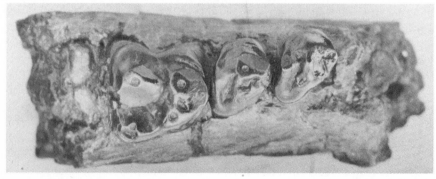

Colbert in 1938, are from the Pakokku district in Burma. They appear to be Late Eocene in age. The third reported primate is "Kansupithecus" from Oligocene deposits[4] in Taban-buluk, China.

A number of workers have claimed that *Amphipithecus* is an anthropoid primate (Colbert, 1938; Simons, 1963, 1972a; Hill, 1968). If it is, then it is the earliest known member of the suborder that contains the higher primates. Van Valen (1969), in fact, thought the genus might be assigned to the Pongidae, and Simons (1972a) has placed it tentatively within the Hominoidea. In suggesting such affiliation, Simons has emphasized, in particular, the depth of the mandible and the compression of the tooth row in *Amphipithecus;* these features would indicate a shortening of the face typical of the hominoids. Moreover, the cross section of the mandible and cusp morphology on both the molars and premolars would seem to support such an affinity. Simons has pointed out that the jaw fragment of *Amphipithecus* bears a number of similarities to later undoubted hominoids from the Egyptian Oligocene, such as *Oligopithecus* and *Aegyptopithecus*. Szalay (1970) has disagreed with this attribution. While not questioning that similarities do exist, he has stressed the possibility that they reflect convergent or parallel evolutionary changes rather than a close phylogenetic relationship. The issue will remain unsolved until more fossil material is recovered from southeast Asia.

The Burma form differs from later Old World anthropoids, however, in the possession of a third premolar. This, by itself, would not deprive it of anthropoid status since early cercopithecoids from the Egyptian Oligocene also possess a third premolar, as do the living New World monkeys.

With regard to *Pondaungia*, Simons (1972a) has pointed out that it bears resemblances both to prosimians, such as *Notharctus* and *Pelycodus,* and to some hominoids. It cannot, however, be definitely placed within either group. Simons (1963) concluded that although "Kansupithecus" is very poorly known, it may be "a primitive pongid somewhat similar to Amphipithecus" (p. 97).

Therefore, although the evidence is very limited and fragmentary, it is possible that higher primates, members of the suborder Anthropoidea, were present in Asia as early as the Late Eocene. If the evidence is correctly interpreted and these primates truly were anthropoids, it is probable that they did not evolve in Asia. As pointed out earlier, European mammals did not enter Asia until the Turgai Strait closed briefly in later Eocene times. Therefore, evolution from prosimian to anthropoid must have occurred there very rapidly, or else the anthropoids evolved elsewhere. The question of the ancestors of the anthropoids was long thought settled, but, as we will see shortly, it is now open again. At the present time, not only

---

[4]Thenius (1958) has suggested that these deposits may be of mid-Miocene age.

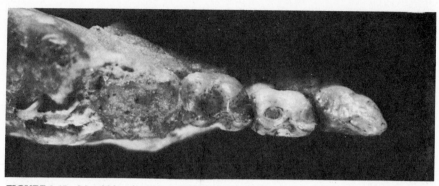

FIGURE 3-15   Mandible of *Azibius trerki*, occlusal view. This paromomyiform primate is the earliest evidence of the order Primates on the African continent . (Photograph courtesy of J. Sudre.)

do we not know who the ancestors were; we are not even sure when or where the grade change from prosimian to anthropoid occurred.

Superfamily Plesiadapoidea

Family Paromomyidae   The family Paromomyidae has only recently been documented to extend into the Eocene. *Azibius trerki* (Sudré, 1975) has been found in beds of Early or Middle Eocene age at Hammada du Dra, Algeria (Figure 3-15). This is the earliest evidence of the existence of the primates in Africa and may represent ancestors of forms that entered that continent during a brief land connection between northern Africa and southern Europe during the Paleocene or Early Eocene.

PROBLEMATIC EOCENE PRIMATES

Among the Eocene primates, the Microsyopidae are problematic members. This group has variously been placed within the order Insectivora (Szalay, 1968b; McKenna, 1960, 1966) and with the primates (Simons, 1972a; Szalay, 1971, 1972a; Bown and Gingerich, 1973). Simons has placed this group within the tarsier-like Anaptomorphidae.

Difficulties have arisen because the group demonstrates a complex of insectivore-primate features. Dentally, for example, it shares with the primates its bulbous molar cusps, expanded talonids, and enlarged, procumbent incisors. The auditory bulla, on the other hand, is formed from the entotympanic, not the petrosal, as in primates (McKenna, 1966). In justification of their placement of this group within the primates, Bown and Gingerich (1973) have argued that the characteristic primate dental pattern emerged before the petrosal bulla developed. It must be pointed out, however, that the genus *Notharctus*, Middle Eocene contemporaries of this group, already had a petrosal bulla similar to that found in some modern prosimians, such as the lemurs (Gregory, 1920).

Most members of this group are from North America, with a single genus known from Europe. One North American genus, *Uintasorex*, is known from both Wyoming and southern California. Thus, *U. montezumicas* documents the westward expansion, if not of the primates, at least of other small mammal groups in the Middle Eocene (see Lillegraven, 1976).

SUMMARY: EOCENE

Several observations can be made about the course and progress of primate evolution in the Eocene. The evolutionary vigor of the order, which was apparent in the Paleocene radiation, became even more remarkable during the Eocene when the geographic range of the order extended to the limits of the northern hemisphere. The route of entry into Asia is a tantalizing problem. The primates may have entered from Europe, during the later Eocene, over the Turgai land bridge or via the Bering land bridge from North America. This interesting question needs further investigation.

The higher primates, the anthropoids, may have emerged during the Eocene; they were clearly in Egypt in the Early Oligocene (see the following section) and were possibly present earlier in Asia. Their place of origin is not clear. The anthropoids could have emerged in Africa from local prosimian groups that entered during the Paleocene or Eocene period of connection with Europe. It should be pointed out, however, that the only African primates known prior to the Oligocene are members of the Paromomyidae. On the basis of evidence outlined in this chapter, this group seems unlikely to have contained the ancestors of the higher primates. Alternatively, the higher primates may have emerged from Eocene lemuroid stock in Europe.

OLIGOCENE

ECOLOGIC BACKGROUND

In the Oligocene our attention is inevitably drawn toward the Old World—to north Africa, in particular. Few primates are known from Oligocene deposits in the New World: the excellently preserved *Rooneyia* skull from Texas, with a potassium-argon date of 35 m.y., and *Branisella*, a possible early ceboid from Bolivia, are two known genera (see Simons, 1972a). Both these forms are, however, off the mainstream of primate evolution leading to humans. For that reason, they will not be discussed here.

In general, mammalian evolution during the Oligocene demonstrated not only a leveling off but an actual reduction in the number of known families. By the Early Oligocene, the number of mammalian families had risen to 95, but by the end of the epoch, this number had dropped to 77 (Kurten, 1971). It seems that a critical point in temperature and climatic conditions had been reached in the Oligocene; this was an epoch of selective environmental filtration through which a number of mammalian families, some of them quite old, could not pass. The primates, especially, were affected by this filtering process. By the end of the Oligocene, the order had a very modern configuration; many of the early prosimian groups died off, but both monkeys and the great apes emerged during this epoch.

THE FAYUM

In the Old World, virtually all fossil evidence for primate evolution during the Oligocene comes from a single unique site located in Egypt about 100 km south of Cairo, called the "Fayum" (Table 3-9). Apart from the newly described *Azibius* from the Eocene, the only land mammals known from Africa prior to the Early Oligocene are members of the order Proboscidea (elephants) (Coryndon and Savage, 1973). Of the 31 genera of land mammals known from Africa during the Middle and Late Oligocene, 25 are found only in Africa. These facts would indicate that Africa experienced a long period of isolation prior to the Oligocene.

Although today the Mediterranean coast is about 250 km north of the Fayum area, in Oligocene times the sea was very near. The Fayum deposits apparently represent a riverine-deltaic area where a large, permanent river entered the sea. Many large fossil tree trunks are in the deposits; all indications are that in Oligocene times the Fayum was a well-watered, tropical gallery forest (Cachel, 1975; Simons, 1967). Both aquatic and terrestrial animals are present. In the former category, there are crocodiles, fish, and dugongs; and in the second, primates, elephants, rhinos, and rodents.

The primary Fayum deposits are located in the Jebel Qatrani escarpment, which contains about 488 m (1600 ft) of exposed sediments. The lower 213 m (700 ft) are referable to largely marine Eocene deposits, and the remaining 274 m (900 ft) to the river-delta deposits of Oligocene age. The Jebel Qatrani formation contains a remarkably varied record of animal life: 73 species of mammal are recorded, comprising 16 families and 9 orders (Cooke, 1972). Two mammalian orders show particular florescence: the proboscideans contain 9 separate species, and the fantastically varied hyraxes, 24 species. The Fayum primates are similarly varied, and although both early cercopithecoids and anthropoids are present, no prosimians are known from these deposits.

TABLE 3-9   Oligocene (Fayum) primates

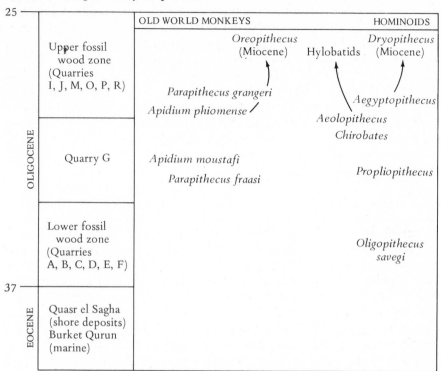

From the perspective of primate evolution, the Fayum deposits of the Egyptian Oligocene are extraordinarily important. These deposits are not only the single adequate record of primate evolution during that entire epoch in the Old World, but they contain the earliest clear evidence of the prosimian-anthropoid split. With the possible and very tentative exception of *Amphipithecus* and *Pondaungia*, all primates until the Oligocene were of the prosimian grade of evolution. At Fayum, however, we suddenly see no more prosimians but, instead, a diversified array of higher primates at the anthropoid grade of evolution. Prosimians certainly did not die out, since they exist today, yet they are oddly absent from the Fayum assemblage.

In the earliest anthropoids, the distinctions between members of the two major suborders within the primates are very small indeed. There is a general tendency among the anthropoids, for example, to shorten or lower the height of the incisors; the cheek teeth tend to be enlarged but have low cusps; and there is little or no differentiation in height between the trigonid and the talonid. Such changes may be related to increasing the grinding efficiency of the cheek teeth and the deemphasis of such feeding activities as juicing or shredding (Simons, 1972a). The anterior cusp (the paraconid) on the lower molars tends to be reduced or absent; the talonid usually has three cusps. The P_3 (or the P_2 in ceboids) is enlarged and tends to have two cusps, one of which is enlarged and acts as a hone to sharpen the upper canine. Such a pointed tooth is termed **"sectorial."** The postorbital plate is complete and is made up of the frontal, alisphenoid, jugal, and maxillary components. The face is usually shortened, with reduction of the snout. The brain is relatively larger and more convoluted than in prosimians, and it has a central (rather than coronal) sulcus (Radinsky, 1975). The two halves of the mandible are fused, as are the two halves of the frontal bone in adults.

ORIGIN OF THE ANTHROPOIDS

When considering the emergence of any new taxonomic group, whether it be a new species, new genus, or new suborder, it is important to try to define the evolutionary significance of the characters underlying the new level of organization. Darwinian theory tells us that a new level of organization should render the population more adaptively secure within its particular environment. Thus, these Oligocene anthropoids in the Fayum should be more "fit" for their particular way of life than were the prosimians. Since the Eocene prosimians were a successful and highly diversified group of long duration, we can assume that some external change occurred that necessitated a new complex of adaptations. We can further assume that the response to this change included those features that characterize the anthropoids. What happened to require such a new level of organization?

The ecologic and anatomic evidence covered so far suggests that the prosimian primates of the Early Tertiary were predominantly arboreal in habitat and most were herbivorous in diet. A few forms, such as *Plesiadapis*, may have adopted a more terrestrial way of life, but on the whole, most seem to have been dependent on the trees. Moreover, subsistence appears to have relied largely on those foods available in a tropical or subtropical forest, with the emphasis on leaves but also including insects and fruits. A tropical forest habitat is characterized by a constant and reliable supply of food. Fruiting is not confined to a single season, as it is in temperate regions, but occurs year round with different trees fruiting at different times. Moreover, tropical plants are, for the most part, evergreen, and therefore do not drop all their leaves in the fall.

By the Late Eocene, as we have seen in the European deposits, seasonal climatic differences were becoming greater and periods of dryness and aridity were occurring. These changes must have had an effect on the faunal groups long dependent on the warm, humid, and well-stocked Early Tertiary forests. These animals, including the primates, had either to make adaptations that would allow them to use the seasonally changing forest environments and foods—or to die. Many did die out. But some followed the tropical forests southward, where seasonality was less pronounced, and today they remain prosimians. Some adapted to the changed seasonal conditions, and it is possible that the anthropoids represent that group of primates that made such an adaptation. Napier (1970) has made a similar suggestion concerning anthropoid origins from a slightly different perspective.

Although it is true that the earliest definite anthropoids are African, this fact does not necessarily indicate that the suborder emerged there. Indeed, on the basis of known ecological factors, Africa seems an unlikely place for anthropoids to have originated. Environmental conditions in north Africa were stable, warm, and tropical or subtropical. No strong environmental pressures can be identified there at the appropriate time, as they can be in Europe. As pointed out previously, there is abundant information that Europe, in those areas where primates are known to have existed, experienced strong seasonality and even drought conditions in Late Eocene times. Moreover, appropriate ancestral groups seem to have been present; on the basis of ear region morphology and dentition, the lemuroid *Pelycodus,* or a closely related form, is one such possibility (Gingerich, 1973).

Such a place of origin for the anthropoids seems plausible from the biogeographic point of view also. If anthropoids were present in Asia in the Late Eocene and in Africa in the Early Oligocene, then Europe, more-or-less centrally located between the two areas, seems a logical point of dispersion.

Most prosimians today live in tropical forests where seasonality has little effect on the food supply. It therefore seems safe to conjecture that living prosimians represent the groups that did not change their subsistence patterns but, rather, continued to occupy territories climatically much like those of the Early Tertiary. Ancestors of the early anthropoids, however, may have remained generalized enough so that they could exploit a variety of food sources available at different seasons. Living Old World Monkeys and pongids have two basically different subsistence patterns: the monkeys exist predominantly on leaves, and apes predominantly on fruits (Napier, 1970). The word "predominantly" is significant, for, although monkeys subsist largely on leaves, they can and do exploit a variety of foods. Most monkeys will eat virtually anything from fruit and grass to insects and meat. Therefore, although they have food preferences, they have no forceful dietary specializations. Similarly, pongids are preferentially frugivorous, but will consume whatever mood and chance provide.

It seems reasonable to propose that such dietary generalizations were highly adaptive characteristics in a time when traditional food sources were less dependable and when the competition was intense for what food was available. The argument here is that the morphologic pattern underlying the anthropoid grade of evolution is toward greater generalization and greater laterality in diet, behavior, and perhaps in locomotion. The changes in brain structure support this hypothesis. With the relative diminution of the olfactory areas and the increase in the visual sense, it may be that the distance senses, such as vision and hearing, were undergoing additional emphasis at the expense of the proximal senses, such as smell and tactile sensitivity (see Jerison, 1973). The expansion of the neocortex may also indicate that more complex responses and patterns of behavior are essential in meeting the need to survive.

This hypothesis suggests, then, that at least part of the prosimian-anthropoid dichotomy was based on the ability of the ancestors of the anthropoids to retain generalized, flexible patterns of adaptations in the face of the increased seasonality and variable environments characteristic of the Middle Tertiary. This pattern of generalized morphological patterns, rather than specialized ones, is unique in mammalian evolution. The usual pattern of mammalian response in the face of harsh environmental selection is to specialize and to narrow and restrict the range of adaptation, focusing on what is available and appropriate in the environment. Indeed, this is the basic concept underlying the theory of natural selection, and most mammals have demonstrated this sort of progressive adaptation during the Cenozoic. Horses, for example, changed from generalized five-toed forest browsers to specialized one-toed plains grazers; the marine mammals (the cetaceans) gave up land life (and limbs) to return to the seas. One effect of such ever narrowing specializations is the minimization of competition. The anthropoids did not follow this course but, rather, "chose" to do everything. In this way, adaptive pressure was placed not on morphological specialization, but on behavioral adaptability. This latitude of behavioral response may explain the selective pressures responsible for the highly complex—and specialized—anthropoid brain.

OLIGOCENE PRIMATES

Suborder: Anthropoidea
  Infraorder: Anthropoidea
    Superfamily: Ceboidea
  Infraorder: Catarrhini
    Superfamily: Cercopithecoidea
      Family: Cercopithecidae
        Subfamily: Parapithecinae
    Superfamily: Hominoidea
      Family: Hylobatidae
        Subfamily: Pliopithecinae
      Family: Pongidae
        Subfamily: Dryopithecinae

Superfamily Cercopithecoidea

Oligocene members of the Cercopithecoidea are contained within two genera, each with two species. Simons has placed these genera within a separate Oligocene subfamily, the Parapithecinae, and, although these genera are not placed within the same subfamily as modern monkeys, they share many features with them. Both the Oligocene subfamily and modern monkeys show fusion of the mandibular and frontal sutures and the presence of complete postorbital closure. The latter condition is demonstrated in the single skull known for these early monkeys, *Apidium phiomense*. The fossil monkeys differ from living ones in their dental formula; the Oligocene forms have a third pair of premolars, resulting in a dental formula of 2133. All living Old World monkeys have a dental formula of 2123.

An important characteristic of cercopithecoids, whether Oligocene or Recent, is seen in the cusp structures of the molar teeth. In both the upper and lower molars, the teeth tend to have four cusps, arranged with two cusps across the front and two across the back of the teeth. The protocone-paracone at the front and the metacone-hypocone at the rear are usually joined together by ridges arranged transverse to the tooth row; such a condition is called **"bilophodonty"** (this condition is described in Chapter 2).

The oldest of the Oligocene monkeys is *Apidium moustafi*, which occurs in Quarry G, about midway through the Oligocene deposits at the Fayum. The later species, *A. phiomense*, has been recovered from Quarries I and M in the Upper Fossil Wood Zone. This later species, which is known from both cranial and postcranial material, had limb morphology suggestive of arboreal, rather than terrestrial, locomotion, and its hind foot seems to have been capable of springing. It appears to have been about the size of a modern squirrel monkey (Simons, 1972a). The presence of a small, centrally located cusp **(centroconule)** on the lower molars of *Apidium* may indicate this form as ancestral to *Oreopithecus*, which had a similar cusp morphology. Skull fragments of *A. phiomense* have been described by Gingerich (1973). It now appears that *Apidium* had a free tympanic ring within the petrosal bulla and that there was no external auditory tube. This pattern is similar to that in the Fayum hominoid *Aegyptopithecus* (Simons, 1972a; Gingerich, 1973) and in living and fossil lemurs. This similarity strongly suggests that the ancestors of the higher primates will be found in the lemuroids rather than in the tarsioids.

One of the most common primates in the Fayum deposits is *Parapithecus*. Despite the fact that the earlier species of this genus, *P. fraasi*, is known from a nearly complete mandible, considerable controversy has surrounded the taxonomic identity of this form. This jaw was placed in a number of different groups, including marsupials, prosimians, and hominids, before it was recognized that the jaw, apparently complete at the front, had in fact been broken at the midline and the pair of central incisors had been lost. A single pair of incisors, as was originally postulated for this species, would be very unusual (unique) for a higher primate. Later finds indicate that the genus had two pair of incisors and is apparently closely related to *Apidium* (Simons, 1972a). A later species, *P. grangeri*, of somewhat larger size than the earlier species, has been recovered from Quarry I.

The lower molars of *Parapithecus* show loss of the paraconid. This loss, along with the expansion of the entoconid and hypoconid on the talonid, resulted in a four-cusped lower molar like that seen in living Old World monkeys. The cusps, however, remained separate and distinct in *Parapithecus* and were not joined by the crests or **lophs** that characterize the living Old World monkeys (Hill, 1972).

Superfamily Hominoidea

The oldest of the Fayum primates, and indeed the earliest unquestioned ape, is *Oligopithecus savagei*. It has been recovered from Quarry E in the upper portion of the Lower Fossil Wood Zone and is therefore older than the cercopithecoids from the Fayum. Only a single specimen, consisting of half a mandible, is known. Many features of its dental anatomy clearly bear the stamp of its prosimian ancestor, and yet, features belonging to the higher primates are also present. Perhaps the most important of them are the dental formula 2123 and the presence of an elongated and blade-like P_3, which shows a wear facet on its anterior face for the upper canine. Such a wear facet also occurs in living apes, and it is a basic character of the anthropoids. However, in cusp morphology, *Oligopithecus* is not clearly an ape. The two known mandibular molars still retain the four-cusp pattern of the cercopithecoids.

Also known from a very small amount of material—two mandibular fragments—is the hominoid *Propliopithecus haeckeli*. Schlosser (1911), who recovered the type and the only described member of this genus, did not record the exact location of his find. However, the recovery by Simons of isolated teeth similar to those of *P. haeckeli*, from Quarry G in about the middle of the Jebel el Qatrani formation, suggests that its stratigraphic location is near that point (Simons, 1965, 1972a).

Propliopithecus is interesting in that it shares a number of dental characters with the hominids. It has small, vertically implanted incisors and canines, similar **(homomorphic)** premolars and low-crowned **(buno-dont)** molars. In view of these similarities, some authors have placed this genus within the human lineage. Kurten (1972), Simons (1963), and Pilbeam (1967), taking a more conservative view, have all suggested that it might be near the ancestry of the Hominidae. Others have proposed that it may be near the ancestry of *Limnopithecus*, a gibbon-like form from the

Miocene (Schlosser, 1911; Gregory, 1916). The molars are an interesting combination of both cercopithecoid and hominoid characters. The M_1 and M_2 are more or less bilophodont, although the posterior loph or ridge is separated by an extra cuspule. The M_3 appears to have a fully developed fifth cusp, a hominoid character.

It is possible that the apparent complex of hominid characters present in *Propliopithecus* may be due to adaptive parallelisms rather than to direct ancestry. Such a pattern may reflect a dietary specialization which included coarse or fibrous vegetable foods requiring considerable grinding and chewing. In fact, adaptation to such a diet may be responsible for the early hominid dental pattern as well.

Another hominoid from the Fayum is *Aeolopithecus chirobates*, known from a single mandible recovered from Quarry I, in the Upper Fossil Wood Zone. This form has many ape-like characters and may be an ancestor of the gibbons (Simons 1972a). Ape-like features of *Aeolopithecus* include a large canine and heteromorphic premolars. The P_3 in this form, as in the pongids, is sharp and acts as a hone for the upper canine. The incisors are somewhat procumbent and the M_3 is slightly reduced, as in living gibbons. The bilophodont crests are incomplete, but the full pongid cusp pattern on the molars is not yet apparent. *Aeolopithecus* has a number of close similarities with the *Limnopithecus-Pliopithecus* group of primates from the Miocene; these forms, better known than the Oligocene genus, have several gibbon features in the dentition and postcranium and are widely regarded as having been on the gibbon line (Simons, 1972a). The presence of such features in this Oligocene form may indicate an earlier origin for the gibbon line than for the rest of the great apes.

The best-known and most intriguing of the Fayum hominoids is *Aegyptopithecus* (Figure 3-16). *A. zeuxis* is known from Quarry 1 and from localities I and M in the Upper Fossil Wood Zone. The first specimen was recovered in 1906 but was not described until 1963; in 1966 a virtually complete skull was found, and a number of postcranial remains, possibly attributable to this genus, are also known. More recently, a member of this genus has been reported from Early Miocene deposits on Rusinga Island in Kenya (Andrews, 1970).

Members of this genus contain a remarkable amalgamation of primitive and advanced primate characters. In view of their advanced features, they are probably near the point of ancestry of the later great apes. In recognition of this ancestral position, Simons (1972a) has regarded *Aegyptopithecus* as the earliest member of the subfamily Dryopithecinae. This group, which experienced extraordinary diversification in the Miocene, almost undoubtedly contains the ancestors of the living chimps, gorillas, and humans. *Aegyptopithecus* was the largest of the Fayum primates and was approximately the size of a gibbon.

Its dentition is much like that of the later great apes: long, sectorial P_3,

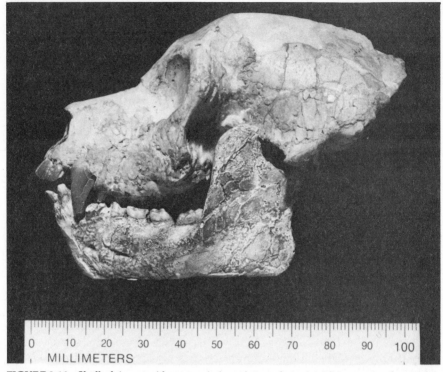

FIGURE 3-16 Skull of *Aegyptopithecus zeuxis*, lateral view, from the Oligocene age deposits at Fayum, Egypt. This genus may be near the ancestry of the anthropoids. Although its brain was organized along anthropoid lines, it retained primitive features such as the long snout and lack of a long auditory tube. (Photograph, Peabody Museum of Natural History, Yale University.)

large canines, and an increase in molar size from M1 through M3. The cusp pattern on the mandibular molars is distinct from that of the cercopithecoids but is not yet clearly that of the later hominoids. In the hominoids, both fossil and living apes and humans, a fifth cusp is present on the talonid of the lower molars. This fifth cusp has resulted from the development of the hypoconulid in the posterior lateral portion of the tooth. Lower molars of this type are termed "5Y" and are characteristic of the hominoids. In *Aegyptopithecus* the transverse bilophodont crests of the monkey's molars are not present, and yet the new fifth cusp of the hominoids is only slightly in evidence.

Only parts of the postcranium have been found. The few bones of the foot that are known are said to be similar to those of the Miocene dryopithecines (Simons, 1972a). A nearly complete ulna has recently been reported (Fleagle, Simons, and Conroy, 1975). This arm bone is very robust and shows lengthening of the top portion of the olecranon. Such lengthening provides additional leverage for the extensor muscles when the elbow is partially flexed. This additional leverage would be important in climbing. Other features, particularly in the trochlea, suggest that the elbow joint had considerable structural stability during climbing and suspensory postures. The evidence of a clear separation at the lower end of the radius and ulna suggests that the muscles that rotate the arm were well developed. This total pattern of the ulna would be consistent with a robust, yet agile, arboreal quadruped. The elbow joint had stability for climbing and swinging and yet was mobile enough so that the lower arm, in particular, could be freely rotated (see also Conroy, 1976).

It also seems probable that *Aegyptopithecus* had a long tail, a feature lost by all living apes (Simons, 1972a).

There was apparent reduction of the olfactory lobes and expansion of the visual areas of the *Aegyptopithecus* brain. Radinsky (1975) has pointed out that the brain of the genus was organized on a distinctly different level from that of the prosimians; such evidence is a very strong argument that *Aegyptopithecus* had reached an anthropoid level of organization. In the prosimian brain, a **coronal sulcus** divides the brain lengthwise. Although the full functional implications of this division are not known, it appears to separate the representation of the head and forelimb in the motor and sensory cortex. In the anthropoids and the prosimian pottos, there is no major lengthwise sulcus but, instead, there is a crosswise **central sulcus.** *Aegyptopithecus* had a crosswise central sulcus, adding to the probability that this genus was anthropoid.

Some features of *Aegyptopithecus*, on the other hand, are distinctly primitive, not only in relation to living apes, but also to the slightly later Miocene dryopithecines. For example, there was a long snout; the postorbital plate, while nearly complete, did not show total closure, and there was no external auditory tube. This last feature, in which this genus resembles *Apidium*, is of considerable importance in identifying possible ancestors for the Anthropoidea. Most paleontologists have agreed in the past that the anthropoid ancestors are to be found within the Eocene tarsioids, particularly the omomyids. Many workers, in supporting such hypotheses, have tabulated the number of similarities between tarsiers and anthropoids (see especially Simons, 1963). Living members of both groups have complete closure of the orbit, a long, tubular auditory canal, large promontory, and small stapedial branches of the internal carotid artery. Moreover, both share the same haemochorial type of placenta, which differs from the epitheliochorial type of the lemurs and lorises. Such a model of tarsioid-anthropoid relationships was strengthened with the discovery that a number of Eocene tarsioids had the long external auditory tube characteristic of the anthropoids. However, the absence of such an auditory tube in undoubted anthropoids, such as *Apidium* and *Aegypto-*

pithecus in the Oligocene and in *Pliopithecus* in the Miocene, would seem to make a tarsioid derivation of the anthropoids unlikely (Gingerich, 1973). As pointed out previously, *Apidium* has a free tympanic ring inside the bulla and no external auditory tube. In *Aegyptopithecus*, the tympanic is fused to the bulla and, in fact, forms its lateral margin; as in *Apidium*, there was no external auditory tube (Simons, 1972a). It is possible, then, that the tarsioids developed the external auditory tube earlier than, and independent from, the anthropoids. This documents the existence of a strong parallel evolutionary trend (see Chapter 1) in several primate groups. The fact that Oligocene anthropoids, such as *Aegyptopithecus* and *Apidium*, and a Miocene anthropoid, *Pliopithecus* (see Chapter 4), have short auditory tubes appears to confirm this trend. Both *Aegyptopithecus* and *Pliopithecus* may be on the ancestral lines to later groups, both of which independently developed a long auditory tube.

It therefore seems probable that the ancestry of the higher primates is to be found outside the tarsioids; that ancestor may possibly be found in some member of the lemuroid group. *Pelycodus* in particular, which is found in both eastern and western hemispheres in the Eocene, could be close to such ancestry.

SUMMARY

Paleontological evidence indicates that the first primates emerged from an insectivore ancestor late in the Cretaceous. It seems plausible that the morphological characters of the earliest primates, and indeed also of later members of the order, represent a series of adaptations away from an insectivorous subsistence pattern toward a more herbivorous pattern. Thus, the major primate dental features appear to be directed toward the production of larger, flatter chewing teeth and an increased efficiency and power of the whole dental apparatus.

By Paleocene times, four families of primates existed, all within the suborder Prosimii (Table 3-10). By this time, some of the primates had spread to Europe, probably across a land bridge which connected Europe and North America in the Greenland area. Three of these Paleocene families, the Picrodontidae, the Carpolestidae, and the Plesiadapidae, had developed progressively specialized dietary patterns and probably became extinct. But the Paromomyidae seem to have retained a more generalized herbivorous pattern and may have provided the ancestral stock for most of the Eocene primates.

The Eocene was also a very active period in primate evolution. Not only did a number of new primate families emerge, but the primates spread to both Africa and Asia during this time. By the Eocene, primates of more modern appearance had emerged; the first lemur-like and tarsier-like prosimians both date to this period.

TABLE 3-10   Primate families of the Late Mesozoic and Early Tertiary

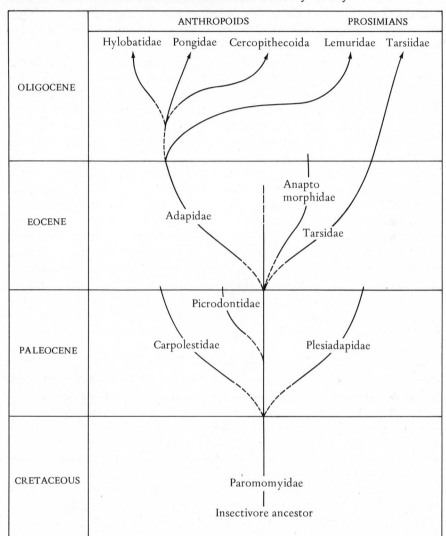

Thus, one of the remarkable features of the early primates' evolution was their geographic expansion. It is even more notable that this expansion was successfully accomplished without significant morphological specializations. While it is true that some early primate groups, such as the picrodontids, carpolestids, and plesiadapids, did develop some degree of dietary specialization, it is also true that these same groups soon became extinct. Although the primates radiated into a wide variety of geographic areas, the surviving lineages never developed patterns of morphological

features that strongly diverged from the ancestral condition. Such specializations limit the number of behavioral options available to a group of
organisms. On the one hand, specialization may fit the group more
precisely into a particular ecological space, but, at the same time, it may
prevent them from occupying other spaces. Consistent and progressive
morphological specialization and divergence have, in fact, been a pattern
in the evolution of many mammalian groups. Winged bats, hoofed horses,
and finned whales are just a few of the more familiar specialized mammals.
Yet, although the primates spanned a very wide geographic area, they
have maintained a generalized morphology. The reason for their success,
in view of this rather paradoxical evolutionary pattern, may well lie in their
behavioral flexibility and adaptability. What other mammals have accomplished through their morphological adaptations, the primates have
achieved through their broad and flexible range of behavioral responses
and learning capabilities.

It was long thought that the Anthropoidea, or higher primates,
emerged from a tarsier-like ancestor. This assumption was based, in part,
on a similar ear morphology in both tarsiers and anthropoids. However, it
now appears that the early anthropoids from the Oligocene-age Fayum
deposits did not have the long auditory tube characteristic of the tarsiers
and later anthropoids. Therefore, a tarsier derivation now seems less
likely, and, in fact, it now seems probable that a lemur-like prosimian gave
rise to the first anthropoids.

The earliest undoubted anthropoids are known from the Egyptian
Oligocene. However, tentative and very fragmentary evidence from
southeast Asia suggests that the higher primates may have appeared there
in the Eocene. More fossil evidence is needed before the time and place of
the origin of the anthropoids can be determined.

By the end of the Oligocene, both monkeys and apes had emerged
from their prosimian ancestor. The stage was now set for the extraordinary
radiation of the apes in the Miocene.

SUGGESTIONS FOR FURTHER READING

Gregory, W. K. 1920. "On the Structure and Relations of *Notharctus*, an American
Eocene Primate," *Memoirs of the American Museum of Natural History*, New
Series 3, 49–243. (A classic example of a comparative anatomical study.
Beautifully illustrated and clearly written, it amounts to a textbook on the
anatomy and reconstructed physiology of a fossil primate.)
Kurten, Bjorn. 1971. *The Age of Mammals*. New York: Columbia University Press.
(Written in an interesting way, this book provides a good background on the
environments of the Cenozoic. It is weak on references, however.)
Romer, Alfred S. 1945. *Vertebrate Paleontology*. (2d ed.). Chicago: University of

Chicago Press. (A comprehensive text on the evolution of the vertebrates; good bibliography.)

Simons, Elwyn. 1961. "Notes on Eocene Tarsioids and a Revision of Some Necrolemurinae," *Bulletin, British Museum (Natural History)*, Geology, **5**(3), 45–75. (Very detailed, but contains good discussions of the dynamics of the systematics of fossil primates.)

Simons, Elwyn. 1967. "The Earliest Apes," *Scientific American*, **217**(6), 28–35. (Review of the Oligocene Fayum primates.)

Simons, Elwyn. 1972. *Primate Evolution*. New York: Macmillan. (Contains the only comprehensive discussion, in English, of the evolution of the order Primates. Almost entirely description with no underlying ecological or theoretical base.)

Wilson, J. Tuzo (ed.). 1972. *Continents Adrift*. San Francisco: Freeman. (Contains reprints of certain *Scientific American* articles concerned with plate tectonics and the geological evolution of the earth's surface. Well-illustrated and informative.)

4

MIOCENE HOMINOID RADIATION

INTRODUCTION

The Miocene, spanning the time from 22.5 m.y. to 6 m.y. ago, was an extremely important phase in hominoid[1] evolution. Although the first apes had appeared earlier, it was in the Miocene that they achieved a period of real florescence (Table 4-1). By the Early Miocene a number of different apes had appeared in east Africa; among them were the ancestors of the living gorillas, chimps, gibbons, and humans. By the Middle Miocene, a land bridge leading the way out of Africa had developed, and some of these early apes left that continent to colonize many parts of the Old World. This proliferation of hominoid forms is perhaps a major feature of the Miocene.

It must be pointed out that this classification of the Miocene hominoids, particularly within the family Pongidae, is very tentative. This area of research is currently very active and the following classification is provisional; it may well be changed as research progresses.

[1]The term "hominoid" refers to a member of the superfamily Hominoidea, which includes all the great apes and the humans, living and fossil. The term "hominid" refers to a member of the family Hominidae, which includes humans and their close phylogenetic ancestors. The term "hominine," to be introduced in a later chapter, refers to a member of the genus *Homo.*

TABLE 4-1   Relationships of Miocene hominoids

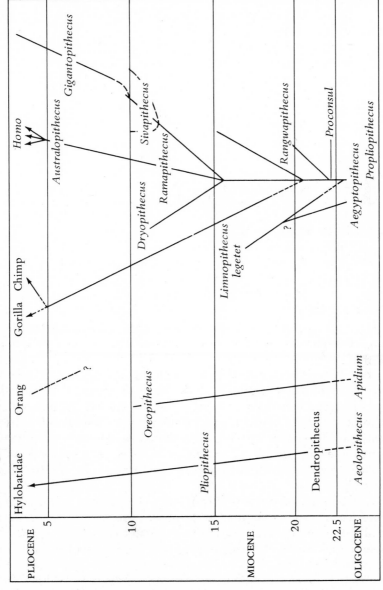

115

Suborder: Anthropoidea
  Infraorder: Catarrhini
    Superfamily: Hominoidea
      Family: Hylobatidae
          Genera: *Pliopithecus, Dendropithecus*
      Family: Pongidae
        Subfamily: *Dryopithecinae*
          Genera: *Proconsul, Limnopithecus, Dryopithecus*
        Subfamily: Sivapithecinae
          Genus: *Sivapithecus*
        Subfamily: Gigantopithecinae
          Genus: *Gigantopithecus*
      Family: Hominidae
          Genus: *Ramapithecus*
      Family: Oreopithecidae
          Genus: *Oreopithecus*

ECOLOGIC BACKGROUND

During the Miocene, some hominoids invaded new territories not previously occupied by them, while others continued to occupy dense forest habitats. *Sivapithecus, Gigantopithecus,* and *Ramapithecus* made an important habitat shift away from forests and into more open woodland areas. Such open, lightly forested regions showed extensive expansion during the second half of the Miocene and provided new habitat space for this radiation.

The Miocene was an extremely important epoch not only in the evolutionary history of the primates but also, in more general terms, in many aspects of earth history. The Miocene was a time of considerable plate tectonic and volcanic activity; one result of this activity was the development of several major mountain ranges. As was pointed out in Chapter 3, mountain building often results when tectonic plates collide. The Alps, Himalayas, and Pyrenees, and the Atlas and Zagros mountains have all been formed in this way. Such plate collisions are significant in evolutionary studies because they open up immigration routes that allow land animals to move into new areas. Dating these collision events is therefore critical in tracing the times and routes of dispersions. This is especially true in the Miocene. Although Africa was geographically isolated in the Early Miocene, the Afro-Arabian plate collided with the Asian plate in Middle Miocene times some 16 to 17 m.y. ago (Van Couvering and Van Couvering, 1976). As we will see, the ramifications of this collision for primate evolution are extremely important.

A further effect of the plate tectonic and mountain-building activity was that the vast Tethys Sea was broken up, turning much of Europe into island archipelagos. By Middle Miocene times, however, the configuration of the old Tethys had become much like the Mediterranean of today.

The end of the Miocene is marked by an extraordinary geologic event.

Thick layers of salt under the present Mediterranean clearly indicate that the sea dried up; this event has been dated to about 6 m.y. ago. The period of desiccation was short, perhaps only about 0.5 m.y. (Hsu, Ryan, and Cita, 1973), and ended when the Atlantic refilled the Mediterranean Basin.

The downward temperature trend, begun in the Early Cenozoic, continued, and temperatures may have dropped even more sharply than they had before. The first appearance of local glaciations is seen in the Miocene, with ice sheets present in Antarctica and Iceland. By the end of the Miocene, the combination of vulcanism, mountain building, and cooler temperatures on a worldwide scale meant that the widespread temperate, tropical, and subtropical forests of the earlier Tertiary were further diminishing. Forest tracts, which had once been continuous over large expanses of the earth's surface, were now broken up into smaller areas with intervening woodlands, grasslands, and savannas. Although grasslands did not become widespread until the Late Miocene, their beginnings in the earlier Miocene provided new environments and new selective backgrounds that resulted in the expansion and diversification of many groups of animals. Among them were the hominoids.

Perhaps one of the most remarkable events in Miocene mammalian evolution is the expansion and radiation of the hominoids. At the beginning of the Miocene, the subfamily Dryopithecinae, first known from the Egyptian Fayum deposits in the preceding Oligocene, had undergone extensive differentiation. Also by Early Miocene times, the family Hylobatidae, which contains the living gibbons and siamangs, had probably also emerged from its Oligocene ancestors. In character with primate evolutionary patterns in general, none of the known Miocene hominoids became truly specialized. But clearly, an adaptive radiation was under way: by Middle Miocene times, in east Africa alone, there were possibly five species of dryopithecines, one species of hominid.

With the establishment of a land bridge between Africa and Eurasia about 16 m.y. to 17 m.y. ago, the dryopithecines left Africa, their apparent homeland, and rapidly colonized many areas of the Old World. Hominoids are not known outside Africa before the Middle Miocene; by Late Miocene times, however, a variety of hominoids existed in many non-African areas. Hylobatids, pongids, and hominids, as well as two unusual and unique genera, *Oreopithecus* and *Gigantopithecus*, are known from this time. The existence of hominoids in far-flung geographic areas, separated by a diversity of habitats and ecosystems, has important implications. Primarily, it indicates that the early hominoids must have been able to subsist, move, and survive in a variety of environments. Continuous, stable forest tracts did not exist at this time over large areas of the earth's surface. A "forest bridge" of more or less continuous subtropical vegetation (Van Couvering and Van Couvering, 1976) may have eased the way out of Africa, but primate adaptability and flexibility must have been the major, if not the vital, factor in this extensive Miocene radiation.

TABLE 4-2   Distribution of Miocene hominoids in Africa

SITE	(AGE) m.y. B.P.	PONGIDAE: DRYOPITHECINAE							HYLOBATIDAE	OREOPITHECIDAE	HOMINIDAE
		Aegyptopithecus	*Limnopithecus legetet*	*P. africanus*	*P. nyanzae*	*P. major*	*P. (R.) gordoni*	*P. (R.) vancouveringi*	*Dendropithecus macinnesi*	*Oreopithecus*	*Ramapithecus*
Lukeino	6.5										X?
Ngorora	8.5–12										X?
Fort Ternan	14.0		X	X	X						X
Moroto II	14.3					X					
Losidok	14–15			X		X					
Maboko	15–16				X					X	
Napak	18–19		X			X					
Ombo	18.0		X								
Rusinga	18.0	X	X	X?			X	X	X		
Loperot	18.0			X							
Moruarot	18.0			X		X					
Koru	19.5		X	X		X			X		
Songhor	19.5		X	X		X	X	X	X		
Bukwa	22.0										
Karungu	22–23			X					X		

Sources: For references, see Andrews and Van Couvering, 1975; Van Couvering and Van Couvering, 1976.

AFRICA

The fossil evidence for Miocene hominoids in Africa (Table 4-2) is confined to the eastern part of the continent. The east African environments of Early Miocene times seem to have consisted mainly of tropical gallery forest interspersed with more open areas of woodlands and grasslands. The Early Miocene African faunas appear to have been very stable and were probably indigenous (Cooke, 1968; Coryndon and Savage, 1973). Such animals include the Proboscideans (elephants), hyraxes, and dryopithecines. However, at the end of the Early Miocene some 16 m.y. to 17 m.y. ago, two extremely important geologic events occurred which have had far-reaching effects on mammalian evolution.

The first of these events was the development of the rift zones in east Africa; they are usually termed the "eastern" and the "western" rift zones. This rifting was accompanied by much volcanic and mountain-building activity. The high mountain areas resulting from this activity had the effect of producing large rain-shadow areas (areas of low rainfall), which caused not only the expansion of the existing grasslands but also the development of semiarid desert environments. One consequence was the production of a strong mosaic of local environments in east Africa, environments which would, of course, contain their own sets of selective pressures and evolutionary potentials. This expansion of grassland areas in relation to forest areas seems to have had an initial and strong impact on the large herbivorous animals, particularly the hoofed mammals, or ungulates. In the Early Miocene, most of the herbivores were leaf-eating browsers. Since leaves do not contain large amounts of highly abrasive silica, the cheek teeth of such browsers are usually low-crowned. After the Middle Miocene, however, most of the herbivores were grazers who subsisted largely on highly abrasive grasses (Van Couvering and Van Couvering, 1976). The teeth of such animals are high-crowned, so that the "chewing life" of the teeth, and therefore of the animal, is longer.

The second major geologic event was the collision of the Afro-Arabian plate with the Eurasian plate in the area of the Zagros Mountains. This resulted in the upward thrust of the Zagros Mountains and the development of a land bridge between these major geographic areas. As a result, indigenous African forms, such as elephants, hyraxes, and the dryopithecines, left Africa. Other forms, such as pigs, insectivores, hyenas, hippos, rhinos, some rodents, and some of the cats, entered Africa for the first time (Cooke, 1968; Coryndon and Savage, 1973).

East African Sites

Of the numerous east African sites (Figure 4-1) where Miocene hominoids have been collected, several have been studied from an ecological point of view. The earliest site where hominoids have been found is at Bukwa, located on Mount Elgon in eastern Uganda. Here, a dryopithecine,

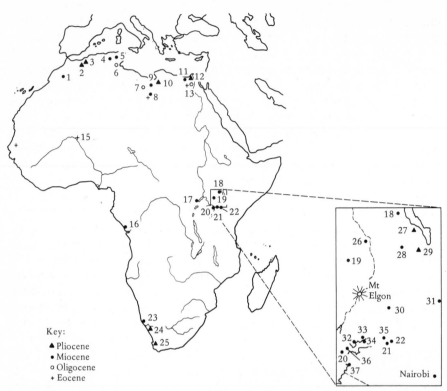

FIGURE 4-1   East African hominoid sites (the inset shows the east African localities on an enlarged scale). (1) Beni Mellal, (2) Wadi el Hammam, (3) Mascara, (4) Kouif, (5) Thala, (6) Gebel Bon Gobrinc, (7) Zella, (8) Gebel Coquin and Dor el Talha, (9) Gebel Zelten, (10) Gasr-es-Sahabi, (11) Moghara, (12) Wadi Natrun, (13) Fayum, (14) M'Bodione Dadere, (15) In Tafidet, (16) Malembe, (17) Karugamania, (18) Losodok, (19) Napak, (20) Mfwanganu, (21) Koru, (22) Fort Ternan, (23) Namib, (24) Klein Zee, (25) Langebaanweg, (26) Moroto, (27) Lothagam, (28) Loperot, (29) Kanapoi and Ekora, (30) Tambach, (31) Kirimon, (32) Chianda Uyoma, (33) Ombo, (34) Maboko, (35) Songhor, (36) Rusinga, (37) Karungu. (Redrawn by permission of H. R. S. Cooke.)

Limnopithecus legetet, was found in deposits dated to about 22 m.y. old (Walker, 1969). A variety of climatological indicators, including flora and fauna, have suggested that in Early Miocene times the area was a tropical evergreen rain forest and that a small lake probably existed nearby.

A number of important Miocene hominoid sites are located on the eastern shore of Lake Victoria; Rusinga Island contains several. In 1971 excavations were initiated in the area in an effort to define the nature of the local environments available to the dryopithecines present there. These important Early Miocene sites date to between 18 m.y. and 20 m.y. ago (Van Couvering and Miller, 1971b). Andrews and Van Couvering (1975) identified three types of local environment: a waterside community with crocodiles and turtles; a forest community with prosimians, elephant shrews, and rodents; and a third community that could have occupied a variety of habitats but probably came from a bushland or an open woodland. At Rusinga, therefore, the hominoids could have occupied either the forest habitat or the more open country. Two other sites nearby, at Songhor and Koru, seem to represent predominantly forest habitats. These date to about 19.5 m.y. (Bishop, Fitch, and Miller, 1969).

The dryopithecine site at Loperot, in northern Kenya, contains some faunal elements unexpected at a primate site. The first of these is a ziphiid or beaked whale (Van Couvering and Van Couvering, 1976). The presence of this whale at a site now in the eastern rift zone indicates the former inland extent of the Indian Ocean. In Early Miocene times, the primates at Loperot must have been living near the ocean shore.

The important Middle Miocene site at Fort Ternan, Kenya, is a good example of the changes between the early and middle phases of the epoch. This site has been dated by potassium-argon to between 12.5 m.y. and 14 m.y. old (Bishop et al., 1969; Andrews and Walker, 1976). Most field workers would place the faunal remains from the site at near the older of these dates. The mammalian fauna there is largely immigrant and shows close associations with both Asian and Spanish groups; the association with the Bugti beds in Pakistan is especially close (Hooijer, 1968). The rhinos, hippos, sciurid and cricetid rodents, and antelope are new African forms (Coryndon and Savage, 1973). The apes, too, show some evidence of Asian, rather than African, affinities. *Limnopithecus legetet* appears to show closer affinities with European *Pliopithecus* than with earlier African forms (L. S. B. Leakey, 1962; Simons and Pilbeam, 1972).

Paleoecological evidence at Fort Ternan indicates that a variety of environments probably existed in the region (Andrews and Walker, 1976). There is clear evidence of heavily forested areas: land snails, insectivores, rodents, and elephant shrews would all have been part of this habitat. More open woodland also existed thereabouts; the numerous antelope, bovids, giraffids, and ostriches are all assumed to have occupied this sort of area. Remains of crabs and crocodiles indicate the nearby presence of fresh water. A variety of primates present at Fort Ternan, *Limnopithecus*, probably two species of *Proconsul*, a loris, and the hominid *Ramapithecus* have all been recognized.[2] It is impossible to determine exactly which of the

[2]*Oreopithecus* has also been reported from Fort Ternan by Louis Leakey (1968); Andrews and Walker (1976) state, however, that these isolated teeth belong to the Suidae (pigs). Pigs and primates have a long history of getting mixed up, at least as far as their teeth are concerned. Although the occlusal (chewing) surfaces of the teeth are quite different in the two groups, in worn teeth the low crown and square shape found in both can be confused. A noted (or notorious) example was "Hesperopithecus." This tooth was found in Nebraska in 1922 and was analyzed by no less expert a team than Gregory and Hellman (1923). On the basis of anatomical and metrical comparisons, they decided that it belonged to an extinct ape, the only fossil ape known from the New World. Later reexamination showed it belonged to a fossil peccary. More recently, "Olduvai Hominid 41," a molar, also turned out to be that of a pig.

local habitats each of these primates occupied. The lorises are today forest animals, as are some descendants of the dryopithecines, such as the chimps and gorillas; it is logical to assume that they were part of this habitat.

It is interesting that one of the earliest hominids should be part of such an assemblage. As we will see, the early hominids, members of the genus *Ramapithecus*, are often found in such a mosaic environment outside the dense, unbroken forest.

One of the most significant aspects of the Fort Ternan fauna is that so much of it represents intrusive Eurasian elements. Of the 23 vertebrate families present, only 5 are exclusively African (Coryndon and Savage, 1973). In view of such a large, intrusive element, an inevitable question must be asked: Is *Ramapithecus* a native African form, or has it come from elsewhere? Did this form develop from native African hominoids such as *Proconsul*, or did the family Hominidae emerge from Indian or European groups and then enter Africa with other incoming mammals?

Hominids of later Miocene age are known from two other sites in Kenya. Both appear to represent deposits laid down near a lake; thus, aquatic communities are represented along with both forest and grassland animals. A single fragmented tooth has been recovered in the Ngorora district, about 20 miles northwest of Lake Baringo. The Ngorora tooth probably dates to about 12 m.y. ago (Bishop and Chapman, 1970; Bishop and Pickford, 1975). A hominid molar has also been recovered from the Lukeino formation in northern Kenya; the date of this deposit is approximately 6.5 m.y. ago (Pickford, 1975).

Although both the Ngorora and Lukeino teeth appear to be hominid, it is difficult to attribute them to a particular genus or species. Louis Leakey did, however, suggest that the Ngorora tooth is very similar to the slightly earlier ramapithecine teeth from Fort Ternan, and it may well belong with this group (Bishop and Chapman, 1970).

Europe

Hominoids of Miocene age have been found at a number of European sites, ranging from Greece, Turkey, Germany, Austria, and Hungary in the east to France and Spain in the west (Table 4-3).

Two recently reported sites in Turkey may be among the earliest hominoid sites known in Europe. Pasalar, southwest of Istanbul, may, in fact, be the earliest one known. Analysis of the fauna there suggests an age of between 15 m.y. and 16 m.y. (Andrews and Tobien, 1977). Candir, northeast of Ankara, may have a date equivalent to that of Fort Ternan. The remains of *Ramapithecus* have been identified at both sites; 31 isolated teeth have been found at Pasalar, and a well-preserved mandible has been recovered from Candir (Andrews and Tobien, 1977; Tekkaya, 1974). Pasalar has additionally yielded teeth of a large hominoid which has been called *Sivapithecus darwini* (Andrews and Tobien, 1977).

TABLE 4-3 Major Eurasian hominoid sites

Stage	m.y. B.P.	RAMAPITHECUS	SIVAPITHECUS	DRYOPITHECUS	PLIOPITHECUS	GIGANTOPITHECUS	OREOPITHECUS
Pikermian	6						
	7						
	8						
	9	Pyrgos, Greece	Macedonia, Greece / Potwar Plateau, Pakistan	Lérida, Spain ↕ Klein-Hadersdorf, Austria		Potwar Plateau, Pakistan	Monte Bamboli, Italy
Vallesian	10	Yunnan, China		Can Llobateres, Spain / Valles-Penendes, Spain	Haritalyangar, India		
	11						
Sarmatian	12	Rudabanya, Hungary	Rudabanya, Hungary	Eppelsheim, Germany / Saint Gaudens, France / Saint Stephen, Austria	Rudabanya, Hungary		
Vindobonian	13	Potwar Plateau, Pakistan	Potwar Plateau, Pakistan	La Grive, France / Vienna Basin, Czechoslovakia	Vienna Basin		
	14	Candir, Turkey			Touraine, France / Sansan, France		
	15	Pasalar, Turkey	Pasalar, Turkey		Neudorf, Czechoslovakia		

The fauna at both Turkish sites is composed of forest and open-country forms; this ecological situation is similar to that seen at Fort Ternan.

Sites containing Middle Miocene hominoids have also been identified in the Vienna Basin. These, however, have a rather different ecological context. Middle Miocene levels in the Vienna Basin were formed in a damp evergreen forest; these conditions lead to the production of coal. The hylobatid *Pliopithecus antiquus* and a dryopithecine have been recovered from these coal deposits (Berger, 1952; Kräusel, 1961; Zapfe, 1958).

Rudabanya in Hungary, dating to some 12 m.y. ago, has also yielded hominoids from coal deposits (Kretzoi, 1975). A hominid, originally called "Rudapithecus" but now placed within *Ramapithecus,* has been found there, as have a hylobatid and a sivapithecine (Pilbeam et al., 1977).

The very important site at Saint Gaudens, France, where the first dryopithecine was discovered in 1856, reflects a rather drier type of environment. Here, temperate forests of pine, chestnut, and oak were the major type of vegetation. The Saint Gaudens site is probably Middle Miocene and dates to between 12.5 m.y. and 14 m.y. ago (Von Koenigswald, 1962).

Miocene apes have also been found in the Valles-Penendes basin in northeastern Spain. These sites may date to between 10 m.y. and 12 m.y. ago, and the fauna in these deposits reflects the somewhat drier conditions of the Late Miocene and Early Pliocene (Crusafont-Pairo and Golpe-Posse, 1973).

The site at Pyrgos, near Athens, contains a mandible now attributed to *Ramapithecus.* Although the Pyrgos site itself has not been dated, it contains a fauna similar to that found on the island of Samos, where it has been dated to about 9 m.y. ago (Van Couvering and Miller, 1971a). This mandible was recovered in 1944 and was originally attributed to a monkey, *Mesopithecus pentelicus* (Freyberg, 1950). Von Koenigswald, in reviewing the fossil material from the Pyrgos site, recognized the mandible as hominoid and proposed the nomen "*Graecopithecus freybergi*" (1972). More recently, Simons (1974) has concluded that "there is almost no possible basis to doubt" that this specimen represents *Ramapithecus.*

The Pyrgos site is of ecological significance, since here a later Miocene hominid is very clearly in association with a grassland type of *Hipparion* fauna. The association of *Ramapithecus* with this fauna is extremely important in that it demonstrates that by approximately 9 m.y. ago, at least some hominids had moved into a grassland-savanna habitat.

The explosive radiation and expansion of *Hipparion,* a three-toed horse, was an important event in Miocene mammalian evolution. Soon after its initial appearance in North America, the genus *Hipparion* spread to Asia, India, the Near East, and Europe. So swift was this spread that the first appearance of Hipparion in a faunal assemblage can be used to date the deposits; the *"Hipparion datum"* is usually placed at 12.5 m.y. This rapid and successful expansion of a grassland-adapted animal and the forms associated with it is an excellent indicator of the importance and scope of grassland habitats in Middle and later Miocene times. It seems clear that the hominids were part of this pattern. This association of later Miocene hominids with *Hipparion* may be important from the standpoint of understanding the selective pressures affecting the Hominidae. Both horses and hominids, in fact, may have been responding to similar environmental pressures.

The horses, like the primates, had a long Cenozoic history in the forests, but in about Middle Miocene times, they too began a series of dental and locomotor adaptations through which they became highly adapted and highly efficient grassland animals. Throughout the Early Cenozoic, the horses were small animals, adapted to browsing (leaf-eating) in the forests. With the gradual diminution of the forests they, along with some other animals, began a series of adaptations to a grassland, grazing way of life. This change necessitated a number of morphological changes. Low-crowned teeth, well adapted for less harsh forest foods, would have been rapidly worn down by exposure to the fibrous savanna grasses with their silicate content. Therefore, higher-crowned teeth would have been selectively advantageous.

Other morphological changes were necessary in the grassland environment. The forest itself offers protection in the form of dense underbrush and light and shadow for camouflage. None of these advantages is available on the grassland. There, protection was available to the horses by only one means: speed. Early horses had five toes, the primitive mammalian and primate number of digits. By Miocene times, this number had diminished to three, and by Pliocene times, one-toed *Equus*, the modern genus, had appeared. The loss in the number of toes also represents part of the grassland adaptation. Five, or even three, functional toes are useful in a forest where speed is not essential and the surface may be soft. But speed would be increased if only one firm, hard toe reached the ground.

Further evidence of hominoids from eastern Europe has been reported from a site called "Ravine of the Rain" in the Macedonian area of northern Greece (Figure 4-2); this site may date to about 9 m.y. (P. Andrews, personal communication, 1977). Several mandibles have been recovered here, in association with an *Hipparion* fauna. It was first suggested that they may belong to a new species of dryopithecine, *D. macedoniensis* (de Bonis, Bouvrain, Geraads, and Melentis, 1974; de Bonis, Bouvrain, and Melentis, 1975). More recently this material, from an ape of very large size, has been placed in a new taxon, *Ouranopithecus macedoniensis* (de Bonis and Melentis, 1977). Rather than warranting a new genus, however, "Ouranopithecus" may belong with the large sivapithecines (Pilbeam et al., 1977) (Figure 4-2).

FIGURE 4-2 Mandible of a large hominoid from Ravine of the Rain, Macedonia, Greece. This specimen has been attributed to "Ouranopithecus" but may be a member of the sivapithecine group. (Photograph courtesy of L. de Bonis.)

ASIA

India

Hominoids, including *Sivapithecus*, *Ramapithecus*, *Gigantopithecus*, and possibly hylobatids, have been recovered from a number of sites in Kashmir in northeastern India and on the Potwar Plateau in Pakistan. The geologic and climatologic sequence in the Siwalik Hills, in which these fossils are found, is well known (Kyrnine, 1937). Recent work by Pilbeam on the Potwar Plateau has added to this information (Pilbeam et al., 1977). The relevant part of the sequence in the Siwaliks, which are the foothills of the Himalayas, begins with the Chinji levels (Table 4-4). During Chinji times, the Himalayan foothills had heavy but seasonal rainfall with occasional flooding; there were large rivers and heavy forestation. The faunal assemblage reflects just this sort of environment: it includes crocodiles, turtles, aquatic birds, and a number of forest-living mammals (Tattersall, 1969a, b). The succeeding Nagri levels show a decrease in rainfall, with the expected and concomitant reduction in forest habitats and forest-living forms. There are more open grassland areas, and periodic droughts seem to have occurred. The lowest levels in the Nagri deposits contain the first Indian evidence of *Hipparion*. Although no absolute dates are available for the Siwalik levels, the absence of *Hipparion* in the Chinji and its abundant presence in the following Nagri levels may be a good indicator of age. Since *Hipparion* is found in widely distributed Asian and European sites beginning about 12.5 m.y. ago, the Chinji beds probably predate this time; on faunal grounds, the total Chinji series probably covers the time from 12 m.y. to about 13 m.y. ago (Pilbeam et al., 1977). The Dhok Pathan

TABLE 4-4 Siwalik biostratigraphy

m.y. B.P.	STRATA	TAXA		
		SIVAPITHECUS	*RAMAPITHECUS*	*GIGANTOPITHECUS*
0				
1	Pinjor			
2	Tatrot			
3				
4				
5				
6	Dhok Pathan			
7				Haritalyangar, India
8				Hasnot, India
9		Potwar Plateau, Pakistan	Potwar Plateau, Pakistan	
10		Haritalyangar, India		
11	Nagri			
12		Chinji Village, Pakistan Ramnagar, India	Chinji Village, Pakistan Ramnagar, India	
13	Chinji	↓	↓	
14	Kamalial			
15				

Source: Data from Pilbeam et al., 1977.

levels, extending into the Early Pliocene, contain windblown silts, clearly indicating arid conditions. During this time, the forests continued to diminish, and savannas, steppes, and even open desert areas became the major environments of the Siwalik regions.

China

Evidence of *Ramapithecus* in China has been recovered from lignite coal deposits at Hsiaolungtan, Yunan Province; these deposits date approximately to between 8 m.y. and 10 m.y. ago (Chia, 1975). This very limited material consists of only five molar teeth and one jaw, none of which has been completely described. Nevertheless, their morphology seems to indicate that hominids were present in eastern Asia at this time (Simons and Pilbeam, 1965). Lignite coal forms when dense vegetation and moist conditions are present. Such an environment is unlike that occupied by most other ramapithecines toward the end of the Miocene. This may indicate that while other members of the family Hominidae were occupying more open, grassland habitats by the later Miocene, the family retained the morphologic and behavioral flexibility to utilize widely varying environments. Since such flexibility characterizes later hominids, there is no reason why it should not have been present at this time also.

MIOCENE HOMINOIDS: MORPHOLOGY AND CLASSIFICATION

FAMILY HYLOBATIDAE, OLIGOCENE TO RECENT

Dendropithecus macinnesi[3] (Figure 4-3)
Pliopithecus vindobonensis
Pliopithecus hernajaki
Pliopithecus antiquus

There is good evidence that the family Hylobatidae had its origins in the Late Oligocene, probably in Africa. *Aeolopithecus,* from the Fayum, is regarded by Simons as the earliest known hylobatid (1972a). Andrews, however, has regarded both *Oligopithecus* and *Propliopithecus* as possible ancestors (1976).

The earliest Miocene hylobatids belong to the taxon *Dendropithecus macinnesi,* known from east African sites at Rusinga, Koru, Songhor, and Moruarot, dated to between 19 m.y. and 23 m.y. ago. The presence of Miocene hylobatids in Asia is tentatively suggested by a single tooth recovered at Haritalyangar in the Siwaliks, India; these deposits have a probable date of 10 m.y. to 12 m.y. ago (Simons, 1972a).

The hylobatids were one part of the extensive hominoid radiation in the Miocene. They first appeared outside Africa in European deposits dating to about 12 m.y. to 14 m.y. ago. Their occurrence with an African

---

[3]*Dendropithecus macinnesi* was originally one of two species within the Miocene hylobatid genus *Limnopithecus*. *Limnopithecus legetet* was first described by Hopwood in 1933; a further species, *L. macinnesi,* was added by Le Gros Clark and L. S. B. Leakey in 1951. However, Andrews (1974) has suggested that the type species, *L. legetet,* was a pongid referable to the subfamily Dryopithecinae and was not a hylobatid. Therefore, according to the rules of zoological nomenclature, the earliest designated species name would be retained but a new generic name would have to be proposed for *L. macinnesi*. Andrews has proposed the generic name *Dendropithecus* for this hylobatid form (1978).

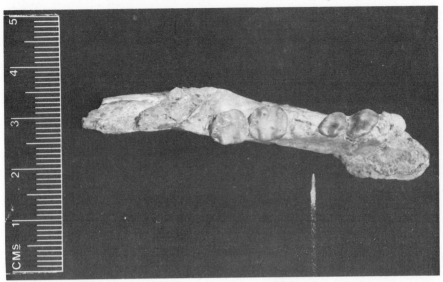

FIGURE 4-3 Mandible of *Dendropithecus macinnesi* (M16652), an early hylobatid from east Africa. The hylobatids emerged as a separate line in Oligocene times and by the Miocene were well differentiated from other anthropoids. (Photograph courtesy of P. Andrews, British Museum—Natural History.)

elephant at Sansan in France (Ginsberg, 1961) suggests that both were among the faunas which left Africa soon after the establishment of the land connection.

Two genera have been proposed for the Miocene hylobatids. The genus *Dendropithecus* contains a single species, *D. macinnesi*, and is known only from east Africa. The European genus *Pliopithecus* has the distinction of being the first fossil anthropoid to be described. Lartet in 1837 described a well-preserved mandible as *P. antiquus* from the French site of Sansan. Three species are presently recognized in the *Pliopithecus*: *P. vindobonensis*, *P. antiquus*, and *P. hernajaki*.

Characteristics

The following are important characteristics of the Miocene Hylobatidae:

Equivalent to living gibbons in size

Robust, well-buttressed jaw

Large, slender canines

Shortened snout

Low cusps on the molars (bunodont)

Short, orthognathous face

Temporal bone with short auditory tube

Elongated and slender limb bones

The best material of this group has been described by Zapfe (1958), who has discussed dental, cranial, and postcranial remains from several individuals of *Pliopithecus vindobonensis*. This material was recovered from a fissure deposit near Neudorf in Czechoslovakia and dated, on the basis of extensive faunal comparisons, to the early part of the Middle Miocene, about 15 m.y. ago (Steininger, Rogl, and Martini, 1976).

A number of interesting features have been revealed by studies of this material.

Skull and Jaw   The well-preserved skull shows the short, vertical **(orthognathous)** face; large, forward-projecting orbits; deep depression at the base of the nose; and long, slender canines characteristic of living hylobatids. The jaw is shallow and the molars have low, rounded cusps, as in modern groups (Simons, 1972a).

The ear region is of particular interest in that it is unlike that found in any living ape or Old World monkey. The external auditory tube is extremely short in comparison with the long tube found in living Old World primates and is formed by the petrosal. Zapfe pointed out that if the ear region had been found separately, it would not have been regarded as anthropoid (1958). This ear morphology is especially remarkable in view of the fact that the Oligocene ape *Aegyptopithecus* also has a short auditory tube. This finding in a Miocene hylobatid is a strong indication that the long auditory tube formed from the ectotympanic characteristic of all living Old World monkeys and apes may have been developed separately and in a parallel fashion in these groups (Kennedy, in press).

Postcranium   In the bones of the postcranium, there is a complex of modern hylobatid features in combination with other more generalized anthropoid characteristics. The humerus, for example, was straight and lightly built in the Miocene hylobatids, as in living members of the group. This is in contrast to the flexed or slightly bent humerus of *Dryopithecus;* this straightness could be an indication of some suspensory or hanging postures. The arm of *Pliopithecus* was shorter relative to the leg than that of living hylobatids. The intermembral index of African and European members of the genus was 96 (Simons, 1972a); the index in the living genus *Hylobates* is 129 (see Chapter 2). Limb proportions like these would be similar to those of both *Alouatta*, a South American semibrachiator, and to *Papio*, the baboon, which is a terrestrial quadruped. This pattern would indicate that while some hanging or suspensory postures were part of the locomotor repertoire of *Pliopithecus*, these locomotor activities were not so well developed as in living hylobatids. Zapfe (1958) concluded that *Pliopithecus vindobonensis* must have been basically a ground-living animal. He pointed out that most of the animals found with the fossil primate were also ground-living forms.

A final characteristic of the European hylobatids was the presence of a tail. Ankel's study (1965) of the sacrum, at the lower end of the spine, has indicated that *Pliopithecus* probably had a long tail, consisting of 10 to 15 caudal vertebrae. If her study is correct, then both the hylobatids and the other great apes have lost their tails independently. Zapfe (1958), however, reached the opposite conclusion and stated that *Pliopithecus* was already tailless. This belief seems to have been based on the presence of only three caudal vertebrae in the fossil remains; it can be misleading, however, to rely heavily on missing or negative paleontological data.

FAMILY PONGIDAE, OLIGOCENE TO RECENT

Subfamily: Dryopithecinae, Oligocene to Late Miocene

Classification The first description of a member of this group was made by Lartet in 1856 when he proposed the name *Dryopithecus fontani* for several mandibular fragments discovered in the same year by Fontan at Saint Gaudens, France. Lartet proposed the generic name *Dryopithecus* because impressions of oak leaves were found in the same deposits.[4]

Subsequently, other dental and postcranial material was eventually recovered from Saint Gaudens and from other sites in Europe. Discoveries of Miocene hominoids in India were made as early as 1879, when Lydekker proposed the name *"Palaeopithecus sivalensis"* for a partial palate. Pilgrim's work in 1910 and 1915 added a number of other taxa, and by the latter date he had named *Sivapithecus indicus* and three species of *Dryopithecus: D. punjabicus, D. giganteus,* and *D. chinjiensis.* The two mandibular fragments, called *D. punjabicus* by Pilgrim, were later referred to the genus *Bramapithecus* by G. E. Lewis (1937b).

East Africa has long been an important source of Late Cenozoic fossils in general (Figure 4-4), and it certainly ranks as a major collecting area for Miocene primates (Figure 4-1). In 1926, the maxilla of a large ape was recovered on a farm at Koru, in Kenya. The recognition, by Hopwood of the British Museum of Natural History, that this bone represented the maxilla of a fossil ape stimulated further fieldwork in Kenya, Uganda, and Tanganyika (now Tanzania). Hopwood, continuing the excavations at Koru, in 1931 recovered the remains of nine more primates; in 1931 and 1932 Louis Leakey and Donald MacInnes discovered Miocene fossil sites

---

[4]In Greek mythology, a "dryad" is a wood nymph, often said to inhabit oak trees.

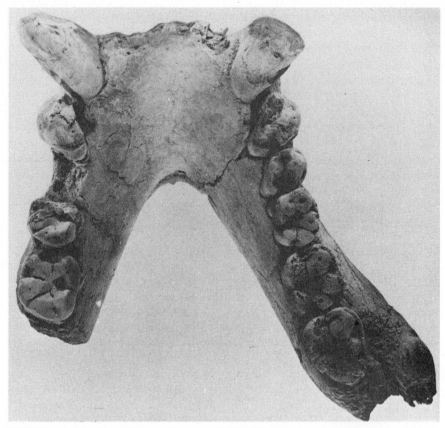

FIGURE 4-4 Mandible of *Proconsul nyanzae* (KNM RU 1087). Note that all three molars are worn to approximately the same degree. Such a lack of differential wear indicates that the period of growth was rapid. Note also the large buttress of bone at the anterior portion of the jaw; this is the superior buttress or torus characteristic of this group. (Photograph courtesy of P. Andrews.)

on Rusinga Island, in Lake Victoria, and at Songhor, not far from Koru. In 1948, during the second field season on Rusinga, Mary Leakey found the first and still most complete skull known of this Miocene ape; this skull is attributed to *Proconsul africanus* (Figure 4-5). Continuing fieldwork in east Africa has now revealed a total of 15 localities of Miocene age where at least one higher primate has been found.

By the mid-1960s, literally hundreds of fragments of Miocene apes had been recovered, resulting almost inevitably in a dazzling array of Linnaean names. By 1965, in fact, at least 39 different binomials had been given to pongids of this time period. Because of the resultant confusion surrounding the Miocene hominoids, Simons and Pilbeam sought to examine as

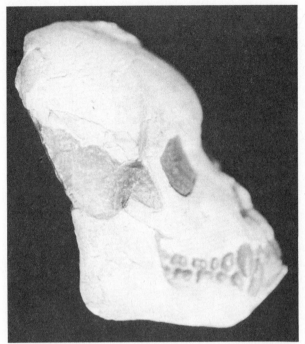

FIGURE 4-5 Face of *Proconsul africanus* (R 1948, 50). The skull of this species was very lightly built, with no pronounced muscle markings; note the absence of brow ridges.

much of the original material as possible. From this firsthand perspective, they organized much of this group into one genus, with three subgenera and seven species (Simons and Pilbeam, 1965):

Family: Pongidae
  Subfamily: Dryopithecinae
    Genus: *Dryopithecus*
      Subgenus: *Dryopithecus*
        D. fontani
        D. laietanus
      Subgenus: *Sivapithecus*
        D. indicus
        D. sivalensis
      Subgenus: *Proconsul*
        D. africanus
        D. nyanzae
        D. major

The implication of the 1965 diagnosis of the subfamily Dryopithecinae was that it contained a number of closely related groups which all showed a basically similar morphologic and adaptive pattern. Since that time, however, research has indicated that this inference was not correct. Two or more morphologic and adaptive patterns are present in the group which Simons and Pilbeam placed in a single subfamily. This diversification, which appears to indicate a very rapid adaptive radiation, is reflected in the classification used here. This classification follows that used by Andrews (1978) for the African groups.

Genus: *Proconsul*
   Subgenus: *Proconsul*
      P. *(Proconsul) africanus* (Figure 4-5)
      P. *(Proconsul) nyanzae*
      P. *(Proconsul) major*
   Subgenus: *Rangwapithecus*
      P. *(Rangwapithecus) gordoni* (Figure 4-6)
      P. *(Rangwapithecus) vancouveringi*
Genus: *Limnopithecus*
      L. *legetet*
Genus: *Dryopithecus*
      D. *(Dryopithecus) laietanus*
      D. *(Dryopithecus) fontani*

FIGURE 4-6 Mandible of *Proconsul (Rangwapithecus) gordoni* (KNM SO 1112). This is one of two newly proposed species within the subgenus *Rangwapithecus*. (Photograph courtesy of P. Andrews, British Museum—Natural History.)

The subfamily Dryopithecinae (Table 4-5) represents those apes that continued to live in a fully forested habitat; their morphology remained conservative and little changed from that of the Oligocene ancestral forms. The earliest and most primitive members of this group are found in the genus *Proconsul* and it was probably from this genus that the later, non-African hominoids diverged. Thus *Proconsul,* or a closely allied form, may have left Africa soon after the establishment of land contact at 16 m.y. to 17 m.y. ago and provided the stem groups for *Sivapithecus, Giganto-pithecus,* and *Ramapithecus.* (See Figure 4-7.)

Characteristics

The following are important characteristics of the subfamily Dryo-pithecinae (Delson and Andrews, 1975; Andrews, 1976, 1978):

Thin enamel on the teeth

V-shaped mandible with divergent tooth rows

Lightly built dental apparatus with gracile cheek region

High-crowned, vertically implanted incisors

Nonrobust canines

Cingula on the molars

Deep mandibular symphysis

Superior torus on mandible

Mandibular body thin compared with height

Large, wide-set orbits

Brain-body weight ratio apparently like modern apes (known from only one individual)

Reduction of the snout

Dentition Dentally, the subfamily is characterized by having canines that are vertically oriented, rather than slanted outward as in living pongids. The P_3 is sectorial (pointed) with a large outer cusp and a much smaller inner one; the P_4 has two cusps which are relatively equal in size. Such a condition, wherein each of the premolars has a different morphology, is termed **"heteromorphy."** The molars are usually elongated and increase in size from the first through the third. The 5Y cusp pattern is present on the lower molars. The incisors are relatively small and vertically oriented.

There was rapid eruption of the molars with little differential wear (Figure 4-4). Such differential wear is an important discriminator between pongids and hominids, living and fossil. The pongids have a short growing

TABLE 4-5 Subfamily Dryopithecinae

Genus: *Proconsul*
Early to Middle Miocene, Kenya and Uganda
Size range from gibbon to gorilla
Incisors broad, often spatulate
Molar crowns often having complex folding (crenulations)
Upper molars with lingual cingula; lower molars with buccal cingula
Enlarged buccal cusp on P^3
M$_3$, elongated, with large hypoconulid
Large superior torus on mandible; no inferior torus

Subgenus: *Proconsul*
  Proconsul (Proconsul) africanus:
    Smallest member of the genus, most gracile in build
    M^3 often reduced in size
    Postcrania with some features like chimps
  Proconsul (Proconsul) nyanzae
    Larger than *P. africanus*, approximately the size of a chimp
    Strong sexual dimorphism
    Cingula on upper molars often "beaded" or discontinuous
  Proconsul (Proconsul) major
    Largest member of the subgenus, approximately the size of a female gorilla
    Massive dental size

Subgenus: *Rangwapithecus*
  Early to Middle Miocene, Kenya and Uganda
  Approximately the size of a gibbon
  Incisors high-crowned and narrow
  Molars elongated
  Molar crowns often crenulated
  Upper molars and premolars with lingual cingula
  Marked wear gradient on molars
  Horizontal ramus of mandible deep and robust

136

Proconsul (Rangwapithecus) gordoni
  Largest member of the subgenus
  Early Miocene only
Proconsul (Rangwapithecus) vancouveringi
  Smaller in size than *P. (Rangwapithecus) gordoni*
  (According to Andrews, 1974, 1978, the major difference between these two taxa is size)

Genus: *Limnopithecus*
Early to Middle Miocene, Kenya and Uganda
Approximately the size of a gibbon
Central incisors large and broad
P_3 with single cusp; P^3 with cusps of equal size
Molars low and rounded
Upper molars with lingual cingula, buccal cingula on lower molars
M^3 slightly reduced in size
  Limnopithecus legetet
    (characters as for genus)

Genus: *Dryopithecus*
Middle to Late Miocene, Europe, western Asia
Small size, approximating that of a pygmy chimp or gibbon
Incisors small (relative to *Proconsul*)
Canine often smaller than in living apes
Molars elongated, often crenulated
Cingula present but usually less developed than in *Proconsul*
Horizontal ramus of mandible deep and robust
Inferior torus on mandible
  Dryopithecus laietanus
    Spain, north India
    Smallest member of the genus
    Cingula sometimes absent
  Dryopithecus fontani
    Widely found in Europe; also in U.S.S.R.
    Lingual cingula sometimes absent

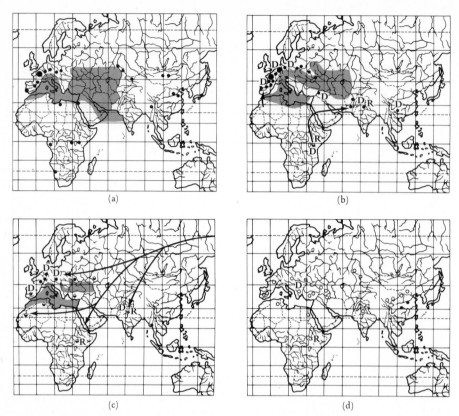

FIGURE 4-7 **(a)** Hominoid localities in the early Miocene (early Burdigalian) 21 to 18 m.y. ago. ● Predominately forested-habitat vertebrate localities; D, localities containing dryopithecine remains; the hatched area is the Tethys Sea. **(b)** Hominoid localities in the early Middle Miocene (Middle Burdigalian-Vindobonian) 18 to 12 m.y. ago. ● Predominately forested-habitat vertebrate localities; ◑ Mixed forest–open habitat vertebrate localities; D, localities containing dryopithecine remains; R, localities containing ramapithecine remains; the hatched area represents the Tethys Sea, and the arrow represents African faunal emigration routes. **(c)** Hominoid localities in the late Middle Miocene (Vallesian) 12 to 10.5 m.y. ago. ● Predominately forested-habitat vertebrate localities; ◑ Mixed forest–open habitat vertebrate localities; D, localities containing dryopithecine remains; R, localities containing ramapithecine remains; the hatched area represents the Tethys Sea, and the arrows represent the spread of *Hipparion primigenium*. **(d)** Hominoid localities in the late Miocene (Turolian) 10.5 to 6 m.y. ago. ● Predominately forested-habitat vertebrate localities; ○ predominately open-habitat vertebrate localities; R, localities containing ramapithecine remains; G, localities containing gigantopithecine remains. (Courtesy of R. Bernor and B. Campbell.)

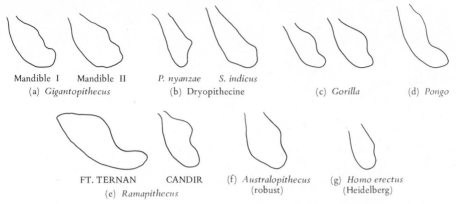

| Mandible I | Mandible II | | P. nyanzae | S. indicus | | | |
| (a) *Gigantopithecus* | | | (b) Dryopithecine | | | (c) *Gorilla* | (d) *Pongo* |

| FT. TERNAN | CANDIR | (f) *Australopithecus* | (g) *Homo erectus* |
| (e) *Ramapithecus* | | (robust) | (Heidelberg) |

FIGURE 4-8 Symphyseal cross sections of hominoid mandibles. The pongids— **(a)** *Gigantopithecus*, **(b)** a dryopithecine, **(c)** *Gorilla*, and **(d)** *Pongo*—show buttressing just below the level of the teeth; this is called a "superior torus." The hominids— **(e)** *Ramapithecus*, **(f)** *Australopithecus*, and **(g)** *Homo erectus*—show the development of a lower buttress, the "inferior torus." The inferior torus may represent additional stability for the jaw during the rotary grinding characteristic of the hominids. [a, c, Simons and Chopra, 1969; b, g, f, Simons and Pilbeam, 1965; d, e, Andrews, 1971 *(Pongo*, Fort Ternan), and Tekkaya, 1974 (Candir).]

period relative to that of the hominids. Therefore, little time elapses between the eruption of the first and third molars, so that all the molar teeth are worn to approximately the same degree. In contrast, the hominids have a longer growth period, and with the greater elapsed time between the eruption of the first and third molars, these teeth show a greater degree of differential wear.

Mandible The shape of the cross section of the mandible at the front midline is an important character. The point where the two halves of the lower jaw meet is called the **"symphysis."** The symphyseal cross section reveals the way in which the front of the jaw is buttressed (Figure 4-8). The Oligocene anthropoids had a thickening or buttress at the lower margin of the jaw; this is called an **"inferior torus."**[5] The Miocene members of the subfamily Dryopithecinae show a derived character. They have lost the inferior torus and show, instead, a **superior torus** at the top of the mandible, just under the teeth. It is interesting that the genus *Ramapithecus* and later hominids show a reacquisition of the inferior torus (see below).

The tooth rows diverge at the rear so that the distance between the canines is usually only 50 to 60 percent of the distance between the second molars (Figure 4-9). This divergence has decreased through time so that in

[5]The word "torus" (plural, "tori") means a bony bar that usually serves as a structural support to add strength to the bone in a heavily stressed area.

FIGURE 4-9 **(a)** Maxilla of *Proconsul major* (UMP 62-11), occlusal view. This species was one of the largest of the Miocene apes and may have been ancestral to living gorillas. Note the lingual cingula, particularly on $M^{2,3}$, a characteristic of the genus *Proconsul*. **(b)** Maxilla of *Proconsul major* (UMP 62-11), lateral view. The broad, spatulate incisors are apparent in this view, as is the large, projecting buccal cusp on P^3. This specimen is from Middle Miocene–age deposits at Moroto, Uganda. (Photograph courtesy of D. Pilbeam.)

modern great apes, the intercanine distance is 80 to 90 percent of the intermolar distance. This increase has resulted in the parallel-sided tooth rows of modern ape genera (Simons, 1972a).

Skull and Brain Only a single skull is known for the subfamily Dryopithecinae; it was discovered on Rusinga Island, Kenya, and is attributed to *Proconsul africanus*. The face, which is relatively complete, shows some prognathism in that the lower part projects to the front. The skull is very gracile in appearance, with very slight muscle markings. On the sides of the skull, the line of origin of one of the major jaw muscles (the temporalis muscle) is very slightly marked, and these muscles do not meet to form a sagittal crest in the middle of the skull, as often occurs in living gorillas, for example. There are no brow ridges in the frontal region and the skull bones are very thin. In terms of overall size, the skull would approximate that of a small chimp.

The ear region of the group is known from only a single specimen recovered at Rusinga Island; it has also been attributed to *P. africanus*. The specimen shows that a short external auditory tube was present. This tube is considerably shorter than in living hominoids.

A limited amount of information regarding the superficial anatomy of the brain can be derived from a study of the internal markings on the skull bones and from an endocast made from the bones. What seems to be apparent from such a study of this skull is that the dryopithecine brain shared a number of similarities with that of living apes. Radinsky (1974) has pointed out that the frontal lobe resembles that of the gibbons in several ways, lacking only one groove or sulcus found in the living genus. Radinsky has estimated that brain size in the fossil individual was about 150 cc; based on the apparent body size of *P. africanus*, this measurement would result in approximately the same ratio of brain to body size as that found in living anthropoids, except humans. Such conclusions would seem to indicate that much general anthropoid brain evolution, in terms of structural organization and size increases, had occurred by Miocene times.

Postcranial Skeleton and Locomotion A number of bones of the postcranial skeleton are known from Miocene hominoids, and much of this sample has been attributed to members of this group. Thus, we have fairly good material with which to reconstruct the probable locomotor pattern of these early apes.

In their monograph on the forelimb of the Early Miocene east African dryopithecines, Napier and Davis (1959) concluded that while the morphological heritage from a generalized arboreal quadruped was still apparent in this form, other features, possibly associated with the beginnings of more specialized forms of arboreal locomotion such as brachiation, were also present. Some workers have emphasized the characters associated with active arborealism and have pointed out that the Miocene forms showed considerable morphological similarity in the forelimb to the modern South American semibrachiators, such as *Ateles* and *Alouatta* (Schön and Ziemer, 1973). This resemblance does not imply that a close genetic relationship exists between the South American and African forms, but rather, that the New World forms have a very generalized type of arboreal locomotion without the specializations of the true brachiators.

Information about locomotion in the east African members of the genus has been derived from two specimens: the *P. africanus* forelimb from Rusinga, described by Napier and Davis (1959), and a humerus from Fort Ternan (Andrews and Walker, 1976). In both cases, the humeri are flattened or compressed from front to back and the shaft is curved with the convexity toward the outside. At the lower end of the humerus, there is a strong keel between the capitulum and trochlea, and the olecranon fossa is relatively deep. Moreover, the insertion of the deltoid muscle, which raises and rotates the upper arm, is placed relatively far down the shaft. This position is lower than it is in quadrupeds and would also seem to be a brachiating characteristic. Evidence from the newly described Fort Ternan humerus may indicate that the elbow joint was capable of being stabilized or fixed when the arm was straight. Such features are seen in the deep olecranon fossa and the strong ridge of bone on the outside margin of this fossa. These characteristics would tend to hold firmly the hook-like ulnar head and prevent lateral displacement during terrestrial movement. Walker has also suggested that some terrestrial features were present in the radius and foot of this group (see Pilbeam, 1969, p. 82).

O. J. Lewis, whose investigations have centered mainly on the wrist joint, has emphasized the ape-like characters of the dryopithecine forelimb. He has pointed out (1972) that the wrist of the living great apes and humans differs from that of the monkeys in the existence of a **meniscus** in the hominoid joint. A meniscus is a thin disc of fibrous or cartilagenous tissue found in many joints in the body. The meniscus in the hominoid wrist joint effectively prevents the lower end of the ulna from participating in wrist movements; this has the effect of allowing free, twisting movements at this joint. These twisting movements, called **"pronation"** (turning the palms down) and **"supination"** (turning the palms up), are very important in the increased range of wrist movement (through about 180°) necessary for specialized arboreal locomotion, such as brachiation. The evidence of a meniscus in the dryopithecine wrist joint, if correctly interpreted, suggests that the Miocene apes were capable of active arboreal life and had free movements of their wrist joints. The monkey's wrist joint does not have a meniscus between the radius and ulna; consequently, its more fixed and stable joint is capable of rotation through only about 90°. This limitation would seem to be an obvious advantage during the repeated biomechanical stresses of terrestrial quadrupedalism.

A number of hand bones have also been found on Rusinga Island; like other material discussed from this site, they may be attributable to *P. africanus*. Of the small bones that make up the wrist, the trapezium, capitate, scaphoid, lunate, hamate, and pisiform have been identified in the fossil material. Of the available hand bones, the trapezium is of particular interest, since it is the bone that articulates with the bones of the first digit or thumb. Analysis of this carpal can reveal much about the degree of opposability or rotation possible in the thumb. In order for the thumb to have full opposability, as in the hand of the human and the Old World monkeys, two morphological features must occur together. First, the trapezium must be concave or saddle-shaped on its distal surface; only in this way can the first bone of the thumb (the first metacarpal) fully rotate around toward the palm to oppose the other fingers. The second necessity is an obvious one: the thumb must be long enough so that the opposability action is effective. Neither of these criteria is apparently fully met in the dryopithecine wrist and hand. The distal surface of the trapezium is cylindrical, and while this allows some degree of rotation, it is not enough to bring the thumb fully around toward the palm. The cylindrical trapezium is commonly found in most living New World monkeys, the exceptions being *Ateles* and the marmosets.

As far as the second criterion is concerned, a direct measurement of the length of the dryopithecine thumb is not possible, since the bones are incomplete. The best estimate, however, suggests that it was somewhat longer in relation to the other fingers than it was in the chimps. Napier and Davis concluded that the dryopithecine hand was capable of some rotatory movement, and they use the term "passive" opposability or "pseudo-opposability" to describe this action. The human, by comparison, is capable of the full range of "active" opposability.

The lower limb of the dryopithecines is known from several foot bones and femora recovered in both east Africa and Europe. Thigh bones **(femora)** probably attributable to the subfamily are known from Eppelsheim, Germany,[6] and Napak, Maboko, and Rusinga Island in Kenya. All these specimens are remarkably similar in size and morphology. The femora are slender and straight when viewed from the front, and the side view shows a slight forward convexity of the shaft. They are clearly hominoid anatomically, although they differ from both chimps and gorillas in their very light, gracile build. One anatomical feature of the fossil femora is particularly noteworthy. About halfway along the upper back surface of the femoral neck, there is a small tubercle; such a tubercle is also present on the femur of *Pliopithecus vindobonensis* (Zapfe, 1958). This tubercle is

---

[6]This femur has been placed in at least two other taxa: in 1895 Pohlig placed it in "Paidopithex rhenanus," and in the same year Dubois proposed "Pliopithecus eppelsheimensis" to contain it. In each case, the taxon contained only this isolated limb bone. Pearson and Bell (1919) considered it to be gibbon.

commonly found in living Old World monkeys and rarely in living gibbons and humans (Le Gros Clark and Leakey, 1951); it is not found in the living African apes. The anatomical significance of this tubercle is not entirely clear, since no muscle or ligament attaches there. It may be, however, as Le Gros Clark and Leakey suggested, that it is associated with the extension of the articular surface of the hip and strong development of the ischiofemoral ligament. A function of this ligament is to stabilize or steady the hip joint in a flexed or bent position, as in a posture at the beginning of a springing leap. Many carnivores, in fact, have such a tubercle.

What conclusions can be drawn regarding the locomotor pattern of the dryopithecines? One immediately apparent fact is that the Miocene pattern probably has no direct modern parallel. Napier and Davis (1959) concluded that while the group members were probably basically arboreal quadrupeds, they may have also shown some early specializations for the brachiator patterns characteristic of some living apes. It is undoubtedly true that the Miocene hominoids were not so highly specialized as living true brachiators, such as gibbons. Rather, the Miocene form of locomotion probably involved a more generalized pattern of arboreal locomotion, with a variety of feeding and nesting capabilities. It is possible that one form of African Miocene hominoid, *P. major*, was quite large, and if this is true, this species probably spent much of its adult life on the ground, like living gorillas. After a certain body size is reached, arboreal locomotion, no matter what the structural indications, becomes unsafe.

The flexible and mobile forelimb indicated by the fossil hominoid material of the Early Miocene would have provided an excellent morphological and locomotor base from which to derive the anatomical patterns seen in later hominoids, including humans.

RADIATION IN THE MIDDLE MIOCENE

Soon after the establishment of the land contact between Africa and Eurasia (16 m.y. to 17 m.y. ago), populations of the earlier Miocene African hominoids emigrated, eventually to colonize much of the Old World. Ancestral hylobatids became widely established in Europe, and probably in Asia, as the genus *Pliopithecus*. Descendants of the genus *Proconsul* also left Africa and formed the base of a widespread radiation in Europe and Asia during this time. Interestingly, the record of hominoid evolution in Africa in the Middle and later Miocene is much less well known than in Eurasia. From the available evidence, the focus of hominoid evolution during the period from about 15 m.y. to about 8 m.y. ago was Eurasia and not Africa.

Thus, beginning some 16 m.y. or 17 m.y. ago, *Proconsul*, or a closely allied type, formed the basis of a very active period of radiation. This radiation and the appearance of new forms were so rapid that this may well be an example of punctuated equilibria. Three closely related genera are of particular interest in this radiation: *Sivapithecus*, *Gigantopithecus*, and *Ramapithecus*. *Sivapithecus* and *Ramapithecus* both appear at Pasalar, Turkey, yet these deposits are currently dated, on the basis of faunal comparisons, to 15 m.y. to 16 m.y. ago (Andrews and Tobien, 1977). If this date is accurate and if the date of the opening of the Eurasian-African land bridge is also accurate, then these new genera had appeared there in a span of 1 m.y. to 2 m.y. That would represent a period of very rapid evolution.

These three genera all share a complex of characters, yet each also has its own individually derived features, thus validating its inclusion in a separate taxon. These genera are most often found in deposits reflecting drier, more open woodland habitats than those apparently occupied by the forest-dwelling ancestral *Proconsul*. Their shared characters, which may well reflect adaptations to such drier, nonforested habitats, include:

Thick enamel on the teeth

Rotation of P_3 so that its long axis is turned about 45° to the long axis of the tooth row

Differential wear on the molars

Loss of cingula

Teeth large relative to assumed body size (**megadonty**)

Broad, robust cheek region

This dental pattern, with its thick enamel, large teeth, and robust cheek region, may represent adaptations to the stresses of chewing hard, coarse, or fibrous foods. This would be a logical and necessary pattern developed in response to drier, open-country foods, which are typically encased in hard or protective coverings.

SUBFAMILY SIVAPITHECINAE, MIDDLE TO LATE MIOCENE

Sivapithecus darwini
Sivapithecus meteai
Sivapithecus indicus
Sivapithecus sivalensis

Members of the genus *Sivapithecus* are known from sites in Europe, India, and Pakistan. *S. darwini* is the earliest and most primitive of these species (Andrews, 1976). The presence of slight cingula on the molars of this form appears to indicate a close, and recent, relationship with *Proconsul*. *S. meteai* is a very large form currently known only from Greece and Turkey (Andrews, 1976). The two remaining species, *S. indicus* and *S. sivalensis*, are both known from India and Pakistan. *S. indicus*, another very large form, may be on the ancestral line to *Gigantopithecus*.

Characteristics

In addition to the characters shared by the three genera involved in this radiation, the sivapithecines also demonstrate the following features:

Nearly parallel tooth rows

Large, sexually dimorphic canines

Broad incisors

Low-cusped molars

Crowded cheek teeth

Deep mandible with a large inferior torus and small superior torus

No skull or postcranial material has definitely been assigned to this group. Eight postcranial specimens from the Potwar Plateau, Pakistan, have tentatively been assigned to *S. indicus*, but they have not yet been analyzed (Pilbeam et al., 1977).

It is interesting, however, that several Middle Miocene hominoid arm bones from Europe may show some patterns of terrestrial adaptations (Simons and Pilbeam, 1971). At the present time, the group to which this material belongs is not clear; nevertheless, this material would seem to indicate that an adaptive pattern to some form of ground locomotion had emerged in at least one group of Middle Miocene hominoids. The European material consists of a humerus shaft from the Saint Gaudens type site of *Dryopithecus*, and a partial humerus and ulna from Klein-Hadersdorf in north Austria (Zapfe, 1960). Simons and Pilbeam (1971) concluded that this group of material shows a number of similarities with *Pan paniscus*, the pygmy chimp, which is a knuckle walker. If this is true, then it would seem possible that some degree of more specialized terrestrial locomotor patterns had developed in some Miocene European hominoids. The likelihood of some ground adaptations is supported by the drier environmental conditions under which the French and Austrian deposits were laid down. The temperate forest or open woodland indicated by these deposits clearly suggests the absence of a continuous tree canopy, and some ground locomotion would seem to have been necessary. Moreover, such a forest or woodland contains trees and plants with marked seasonality of fruiting and leafing. This fact would also seem to indicate the necessity for wider foraging for food, presumably on the ground.

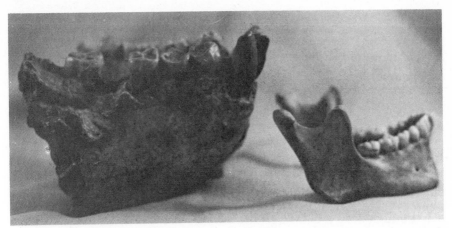

FIGURE 4-10 Mandible of (left) *Gigantopithecus blacki* in comparison with (right) *Homo sapiens*. Note that although *Gigantopithecus* was massive in size, the canines did not project above the level of the other teeth. The canine was, in fact, very large in cross section and appears to be small only because it has been ground down during chewing.

SUBFAMILY GIGANTOPITHECINAE, LATE MIOCENE TO MIDDLE PLEISTOCENE

Gigantopithecus bilaspurensis
Gigantopithecus blacki

A second member of this Miocene hominoid radiation is the genus *Gigantopithecus;* the most likely ancestral form for this genus is the Indian species *Sivapithecus indicus* (Andrews, 1976). The earlier species, *G. bilaspurensis,* is known from teeth recovered in the Hasnot area of northern India, dating to 9 m.y. to 10 m.y. ago, and from a fine mandible recovered at Haritalyangar, north India, dating to 8.5 m.y. ago (Pilbeam et al., 1977). *G. blacki* (Figure 4-10) is an Early to Middle Pleistocene form and is known from a number of sites in south China. As the name indicates, the genus is characterized by very large size; members are, in fact, larger in most dental dimensions than living gorillas.

Characteristics of the subfamily are as follows:

Large size

Canines smaller than in Dryopithecinae and Sivapithecinae

Deep mandible with well-developed superior torus, smaller inferior torus

Small incisors, vertically implanted
Large molars with deep indentation between trigonid and talonid
Crowding of the cheek teeth
Molarization of P_4

The known material of this genus consists of jaws and teeth; a humerus, recovered from the Potwar Plateau, may be attributable to it. This possibility will be discussed shortly.

The dental and mandibular pattern here is typical of the adaptive pattern seen in other members of this radiation. In this pattern, the canines are of particular interest. They appear to be somewhat smaller than in other large apes, but they are unique in the pongids in that they are worn flat through heavy chewing. The canines are still fairly large in cross section and have a deep root, but they apparently functioned as grinding teeth and are worn off to the level of the other teeth.

No diastema or gap is present between the incisors and canines; this is a reflection of the crowding at the anterior portion of the mouth. The P_3 is not a highly sectorial tooth, and although the premolars are heteromorphic, the difference between them is not marked. The molars are absolutely larger in most dimensions than those of gorillas, and the 5Y pattern is present. The molars are distinguished by an important and unique occlusal shape. They are characterized by having an indentation between the trigonid and talonid, which gives the occlusal surface a "waisted" appearance. As in all other pongids, the molars increase in size from front to back (Woo, 1962; Simons and Chopra, 1969). All the teeth are tightly packed into the jaw, with the result that where the teeth surfaces meet one another, interstitial wear facets often occur. **Interstitial wear** occurs between the teeth when they are crowded together and are subjected to heavy chewing. This pattern of mastication also characterizes the early hominids and the gelada baboon *(Theropithecus)* (C. Jolly, 1970).

The earlier species, *G. bilaspurensis,* was so named in recognition of its having been found in the former princely state of Bilaspur, northern India. The species was based on a jaw found in deposits of Dhok Pathan age. The climate in Dhok Pathan times was very dry, and these deposits seem to reflect a dry savanna or grassland habitat; *Gigantopithecus* is associated in these levels with *Hipparion* (Simons and Ettel, 1970).

This Miocene species appears to have been somewhat smaller than the later Chinese species; but it is also possible that the very limited Miocene material is all female. Alternatively, the genus may have increased in size by the Early Pleistocene. *G. blacki* was, in fact, very large; Simons and Ettel (1970) have postulated that members of this species may have reached a height of about 275 cm (9 ft) and a weight of almost 272 kg (600 lb). This reconstruction of size is extremely tentative, however, and is based on very limited materials.

A humerus recently recovered from the Potwar Plateau (mentioned earlier) may be assigned to this genus. The distal end of this humerus closely resembles that of a female gorilla and shows features that may indicate a stabilized elbow. If so, *Gigantopithecus* had a rather specialized form of ground locomotion, similar to that of living knuckle or fist walkers (Pilbeam et al., 1977).

The Middle Pleistocene Chinese species, *G. blacki*, is as remarkable for its size and morphology as for the unusual conditions of its discovery. For centuries the Chinese have used various types of fossilized materials in the preparation of traditional medicines. This fact has not escaped the notice of paleontologists working either in China or in other areas of the world that have large Chinese populations. Numerous collections of "dragon bones" or "dragon teeth," as the source materials are called, had reached European museums as early as the mid-nineteenth century. Ralph von Koenigswald became acquainted with one of these Chinese assemblages in the Haberer Collection in Munich in the 1930s. Later, while working in southeast Asia, he attempted to make his own collection of "dragon bones" from Chinese pharmacies but was unsuccessful until he obtained a prescription for dragon teeth: "Liung Tse." After that, he was able to obtain "dragon teeth" in Java, the East Indies, the Philippines, Hong Kong, Malaysia, Siam, and San Francisco, and even on Mott Street in New York City. Among material he had collected in Hong Kong pharmacies, Von Koenigswald recognized, in 1935, the tooth of a very large hominoid. He named it *Gigantopithecus blacki* (Von Koenigswald, 1952) in honor of Davidson Black, an anatomist who had worked in Peking on the "Sinanthropus" material.

The site from which these teeth had initially come remained unknown until 1956, when 50 *Gigantopithecus* teeth and 2 mandibles were recovered from caves in Kwangsi Province in southern China; in 1958, a third mandible was recovered from the same area. By 1960, more than 1000 teeth had been found in caves in Kwangsi alone, and recently more teeth have been recovered from other sites in southern China (Woo, 1962).

The south China caves that have yielded the *Gigantopithecus* remains are part of the very distinctive topography of this area. Much of south China rests on limestone; this rock type, in combination with warm and humid climatic conditions, has produced a particular type of topography called "tower-karst" (see White, 1975). Typically, the tower-karst topography consists of high, narrow pinnacles rising from a valley floor; these towers, depicted in much Chinese art, often contain caves. The so-called "Gigantopithecus cave" in the Liucheng district of Kwangsi is typical. The cave in this tower is about 90 m above the present ground surface, and its filling, rich in fossils, has been exploited for its phosphates, used in making fertilizers. The cave began as a sinkhole or cavern below ground level. As it gradually filled with surface débris and the bony remains of its occupants' meals, the surrounding land surface was slowly eroded away, leaving the former sinkhole exposed as a tower. Both predators and scavengers apparently occupied such towers. The presence of predators is indicated by the fact that much of the faunal material found in these towers is of either young or old individuals, precisely those age groups most vulnerable to predation. The porcupine (genus *Hystrix*) was evidently also active in these bone accumulations. Porcupines are not predators but accumulate bones to chew on; the very distinctive marks of their teeth are found on much of the tower-karst faunal material. Tooth roots, in particular, are often missing or damaged because of having been chewed away by porcupines.

In these Chinese cavesites, *Gigantopithecus* is almost always associated with a *Stegodon-Ailuropoda* fauna, so named because of the dominant mammalian elements present: *Stegodon* is an extinct elephant and *Ailuropoda* is the giant panda. This large faunal assemblage was widely distributed over southeast Asia, and its members seem to have been drawn from both forest and grassland environments. Forest-living elements include badgers, cats, tapirs, a langur, a gibbon, and the orangutan (*Pongo*), which is represented by more than 1500 teeth; the pandas and bears may also have been part of this forest-living group. A grassland component is also well represented: elephants, horses, rhinos, and hyenas may all have been here too.

Especially interesting is the presence of a hominid in direct association with *Gigantopithecus*; it has been named "*Sinanthropus officinalis*" by Von Koenigswald (1952), who bought a tooth in a Hong Kong drugstore. The geologic association has been confirmed by the characteristic staining of the cave material and the porcupines' root gnawing. In his monograph on *Gigantopithecus blacki*, Von Koenigswald made the following enigmatic statement:

> A few additional teeth that are not definitely classifiable with either orang or *Gigantopithecus* probably indicate the presence of forms related to the Australopithecinae in our fauna. They are of large size, too large for *Sinanthropus*, with a very simple cusp pattern and too small for *Gigantopithecus*. These teeth have not yet been studied in detail. (1952, p. 309)

Indeed, these teeth have still not been studied. Recently, more teeth of a small hominid have been recovered in association with *Gigantopithecus blacki*. Gao-Jian (1975) reported four and possibly five teeth from Hupei and Kwangsi provinces that may date to late Early Pleistocene times.

The *Stegodon-Ailuropoda* fauna is a complex one obviously drawn from a variety of habitats. It is therefore not possible to decide, on the basis of faunal associations, the ecological zone from which *Gigantopithecus* was drawn. It is very interesting, however, to note the number of dental similarities between this pongid and the giant panda. The panda has a very specialized and selected diet composed almost entirely of bamboo. In fact, bamboo, a member of the grass family (Gramineae), is a very tough material containing much siliceous material and requiring considerable mastication. The panda shows the same anterior dental reduction and posterior dental expansion (Davis, 1964) as *Gigantopithecus* and, indeed, the robust australopithecines. It may be that the morphology in all these forms arose in response to the same factor: the need to crush and grind their food. We will return to this point.

Because no appropriate minerals for absolute dating are available in the Chinese caves, the dates for *G. blacki* are somewhat uncertain. Most workers, on the basis of faunal correlations, would agree, however, that *G. blacki* dates to the Early or Middle Pleistocene. In terms of years, this designation has some flexibility and the Chinese deposits may date from about 1 m.y. to about 0.5 m.y. All the Chinese gigantopithecines may not be contemporary, however. The Bama material from Kwangsi and that from Wuming are somewhat later than the Liucheng and Hupei specimens (Chang, Wang, and Dong, 1975).

The affinities of the subfamily Gigantopithecinae have been the subject of some debate. Von Koenigswald (1952) placed this primate within the hominid lineage but regarded it as belonging to a highly specialized and aberrant side branch. In so doing, he noted a number of dental features in which this genus seems to parallel the hominid lineage; he specifically cited the low, flat molars and the relatively small canines. Woo (1962) also followed this interpretation. Dart (1960) has also accepted the hominid affinities of *Gigantopithecus* on the basis of some similarities between the molars of the robust australopithecines and those of *Gigantopithecus*. Weidenreich (1946) went a step further and placed *Gigantopithecus* in a central position of ancestry to all subsequent hominids. He argued that the family Hominidae had gone through a gigantic phase, as seen in *Gigantopithecus blacki*, followed by a somewhat smaller, but still large, stage represented by the Javan form "Meganthropus." This stage was followed by the later hominids from Java and China, now included within *Homo erectus*. Weidenreich was, in fact, wrong in his initial assumption: "Meganthropus" was earlier than *G. blacki* and is probably a very robust form of *Homo* (see Chapter 6).

The question of the hominid affinities of *Gigantopithecus* has been revived recently because of two events. First, the discovery of the earlier Indian species has placed the genus at a point in time when it conceivably could have served as a hominid ancestor. Second, the recovery of some very large dental material from east Africa, particularly from Omo and Lake Turkana, has shown that some undoubted hominids did reach rather large size, at least in the jaws and teeth. Therefore, the whole question of a gigantic, or at least very large, phase in human evolution has been reopened.

TABLE 4-6   Mandibular tooth areas

TOOTH	ROBUST AUSTRALOPITHECINES		G. BILASPURENSIS	G. BLACKI			
	OMO L-125	KNM ER 729		I	II	III	IV
C	74.9	85.9	148.8	177.1	—	196.5	148.8
P₃	182.0	150.5	172.3	226.5	262.4	278.8	172.2
P₄	221.1	205.9	190.0	228.6	290.1	306.0	189.9
M₁	314.2	244.9	241.4	295.5	345.7	349.6	241.4
M₂	291.6	342.0	305.6	323.6	402.5	445.2	313.6
M₃	269.4	383.4	315.5	—	—	402.3	317.5

Sources: Data for robust australopithecines and G. bilaspurensis from Frayer, 1973; data for G. blacki from Simons and Chopra, 1969.

The more recent studies which have supported this point of view have done so on the basis of metric resemblances between *Gigantopithecus* and certain hominids. Certain metric similarities can indeed be demonstrated, particularly in the cheek teeth (see Frayer, 1973). However, if one looks at the measurements of the canine area, the figure for a robust hominid (Omo L-125) is about one-half that for *Gigantopithecus* (see Table 4-6).

More critical, however, is the fact that studies based on such metric measurements wholly miss the morphological differences between these two groups. The size and shape of the canines are very different; the "waisted" appearance of the *Gigantopithecus* molars is absent in the hominids; and the shape, proportions, and buttressing of the mandible vary significantly between the two groups.

The alternative and probably more acceptable interpretation from a paleontological point of view is that *Gigantopithecus* represents a specialized and divergent member of the Pongidae. Remane (1950, 1960), Simons and Chopra (1969), Pilbeam (1970), and Simons (1972a) have all supported this view. This interpretation would accept the hypothesis that the similarities present in these large apes and the hominids are due to adaptations to a similar pattern of subsistence. Such subsistence would involve dependence on coarse, fibrous foods requiring considerable mastication. The adaptive pattern seen here would fit very well with C. Jolly's "seed eaters" hypothesis (1970), discussed in Chapter 5.

FAMILY HOMINIDAE, MIDDLE MIOCENE TO RECENT

Ramapithecus punjabicus

The Hominidae, which contain both living and fossil forms, first appeared in the Middle Miocene. The genus became very widespread during the Miocene, but probably only a single taxon, *R. punjabicus*, is needed to contain the group in the Miocene (Simons and Pilbeam, 1965).

Classification

The first material, now included within the genus *Ramapithecus* (Table 4-7), was recovered in the early years of this century and was attributed by Pilgrim (1910) to two new species of fossil ape, *Dryopithecus punjabicus* and *Sivapithecus indicus*, both from the Chinji levels in the Siwaliks. It is ironic now, in hindsight, that Pilgrim (1915) suggested that *Sivapithecus indicus* might be close to the ancestry of humans while, in reality, it seems that *Dryopithecus* (now *Ramapithecus*) *punjabicus* probably deserves that position.

Further collection of fossil hominoids in the Siwaliks continued during the 1931–1933 Yale–North India Expedition. At that time G. E. Lewis collected a number of fossils, some of which he later (1934) attributed to a new genus, *Ramapithecus*,[7] containing two species: *R. brevirostris* and *R. hariensis*. Both these are of Nagri age, or slightly later than the Chinji-age material. A mandible, also from the Nagri levels, was attributed to a further genus, *Bramapithecus*. Lewis believed that both new genera were very close to the Hominidae, and in his doctoral dissertation at Yale (1937a), he actually attributed *Ramapithecus* to the Hominidae. In that same year (1937b), he suggested that Pilgrim's *D. punjabicus* mandible, along with one recovered by the Yale expedition, should be attributed to *Bramapithecus*. Both "Bramapithecus" mandibles are now included within *Ramapithecus*.

Although G. E. Lewis, and to a certain extent Pilgrim, recognized the hominid characters present in this Indian material, it was not until Elwyn Simons reopened the question (1961b) that the hominid affinities of these fossils came to be more widely accepted. Simons, inspired by the recovery of Early Pleistocene hominids from Olduvai Gorge in east Africa, began to examine fossil material in the Peabody Museum for other possible early members of the family Hominidae. He pointed out that the maxilla recovered by Lewis in 1932, and attributed to *Ramapithecus brevirostris*, contained a number of morphologic similarities to later hominids. These features included reduced protrusion of the face, small incisors and canines, and no diastema in the tooth row. Shortly after Simons's paper appeared, Louis Leakey published a report (1962) on a maxillary fragment from Fort Ternan which he attributed to a further Miocene hominid taxon, *Kenyapithecus wickeri*.

Leakey's attribution of his material to a second genus within the early Hominidae posed the question of morphologic and taxonomic diversity within this group at this time. Simons and Pilbeam (1965), in their review

---

[7]The name "Ramapithecus" is derived from the name of a prince deified in the Sanskrit legend of Ramayana.

TABLE 4-7 Material now attributed to *Ramapithecus*

COUNTRY	LOCATION	FRAGMENTS PRESENT	CATALOG NUMBER*	INITIAL AUTHOR	INITIAL TAXON
India	Haritalyangar	Right maxilla, P^3–$M^{1\dagger}$	GSI D-185	Pilgrim, 1915	*Dryopithecus punjabicus*
		Left mandible, P_4–M_3	GSI D-199	Pilgrim, 1927	*Palaeopithecus sylvaticus*
		Right maxilla, M^{1-2}	YPM 13807	G. E. Lewis, 1934	*Ramapithecus hariensis*
		Right mandible, M_{2-3}	YPM 13806	G. E. Lewis, 1934	*Dryopithecus sivalensis*
		Right maxilla, P^3–M^2, alveolus of C^{-},I^1 root of I^2	YPM 13799	G. E. Lewis, 1934	*Ramapithecus brevirostris*
		Isolated M_3	GSI 18068	Prasad, 1964	*Dryopithecus punjabicus*
	Hasnot	Right mandible, M_1–M_3	YPM 13814	G. E. Lewis, 1934	*Bramapithecus thorpei*
Pakistan	Chinji Village	Mandible: RM_3, LM_2	GSI 118–119	Pilgrim, 1910	*Dryopithecus punjabicus*
	Attock	Right mandible, M_3	BMNH M–13264	Simons, 1964	*Ramapithecus punjabicus*
	Kanatti	Left mandible, M_3	YPM 13833	Gregory, Hellman, and Lewis, 1938	*Bramapithecus punjabicus*

COUNTRY	LOCATION	FRAGMENTS PRESENT	CATALOG NUMBER*	INITIAL AUTHOR	INITIAL TAXON
Pakistan (Potwar Plateau)	(1) Khaur, Locality 182	Adult mandible, LM_1–M_3; RM_3	GSP 4622/4857	Pilbeam et al. (1977)	*Ramapithecus punjabicus*
		LM^3	GSP 8702		
		RM^1	GSP 5019		
	(2) Sethi Nagri, Locality 311	LM_1	GSP 7144		
	(3) Khaur, Locality 260	RI^1	GSP 9903		
		LP^4	GSP 9906		
		Infant mandible, RC^- dP_3	GSP 12709		
		Adult mandible, LP_3, M_1; RM_{2-3}	GSP 9563/9902		
	(4) Khaur, Locality 317	Left mandibular fragment, P_3	GSP 7619		
	(5) Khaur, Locality 224	Left mandibular fragment, P_4–M_3	GSP 6153		
	(6) Khaur, Locality 227	RM^2	GSP 6206		

*, † See notes on page 157.

(Continued)

TABLE 4-7 (Continued)

COUNTRY	LOCATION	FRAGMENTS PRESENT	CATALOG NUMBER*	INITIAL AUTHOR	INITIAL TAXON
Kenya	(1) Fort Ternan	Left mandible with P_3–P_4	*KNM FT 45	L. S. B. Leakey (1962)	*Dryopithecus*
	(2) Fort Ternan	Left maxilla, P^4–M^2; roots of P^3–M^3	KNM FT 46	L. S. B. Leakey (1962)	*Kenyapithecus wickeri*
	(3) Fort Ternan	Right maxilla, M^1–M^2	KNM FT 47	L. S. B. Leakey (1962)	*Kenyapithecus wickeri*
	(4) Fort Ternan	RM_2	KNM FT 48	L. S. B. Leakey (1962)	*Kenyapithecus wickeri*
	(5) Fort Ternan	$RC_{\bar{x}}$	KNM FT 3318	Walker and Andrews (1973)	*Ramapithecus wickeri*
	(6) Fort Ternan	Right mandible with parts of P_4–M_1	KNM FT 7	Walker and Andrews (1973)	*Ramapithecus wickeri*
	(7) Fort Ternan	Left maxilla with germ of canine	KNM FT 8	Andrews and Walker (1976)	*Ramapithecus wickeri*
	(8) Ngorora	LM^-		Leakey, in Bishop and Chapman (1970)	Hominidae‡
China	Keiyuan	Right mandible with M_2–M_3	IVPP AN 612	Chow (1958)	*Dryopithecus keiyuanensis*

COUNTRY	LOCATION	FRAGMENTS PRESENT	CATALOG NUMBER*	INITIAL AUTHOR	INITIAL TAXON
Germany	Swabian Jura, Württemberg	RM^1		Branco (1897)	*Dryopithecus fontani*
Greece	Athens	Mandible without tooth crowns		Freyberg (1950)	*Mesopithecus pentelicus*
Turkey	(1) Candir	Mandible, LP_3–M_3		Tekkaya (1974)	*Sivapithecus alpani*
	(2) Pasalar	RP_4–M_3 35 isolated teeth		Andrews (1976)	*Ramapithecus*
Hungary	Rudabanya	2 maxillas 3 mandibles 4 isolated teeth	Rud-12,15 Rud-1,2,17 Rud-5,13,16,19	Kretzoi (1975)	*Rudapithecus hungaricus*

Key: BMNH = British Museum (Natural History); GSI = Geological Survey of India; KNM FT = Kenya National Museum, from Fort Ternan; YPM = Yale Peabody Museum. GSP = Geological Survey of Pakistan; Rud = Rudabanya; IVPP = Institute of Vertebrate Paleontology Peking.

†This is a conventional way of representing the teeth which are present; this entry means that all the teeth between P^3 and M^1 are present in the maxilla (just two, in this case). If the entry read "P^3–M^3," it would mean that all the cheek teeth from P^3 through M^3 were present in the maxilla.

‡Leakey noted resemblances in this tooth to *Kenyapithecus*, *Australopithecus*, and *Homo*; it is placed here with *Ramapithecus* because of its date, c. 12 m.y. B.P.

of Miocene hominoids, found evidence for only a single genus and a single species. By the taxonomic rules of priority, this taxon was called *Ramapithecus punjabicus*. While many workers have rejected the genus *Kenyapithecus* in favor of *Ramapithecus*, some have recognized the presence of different species. Some, for example, would attribute the Pasalar and Fort Ternan material to a separate species, *Ramapithecus wickeri* (Andrews and Walker, 1976; Andrews, 1976; Andrews and Tobien, 1977). The Pasalar material is, in fact, slightly more primitive in the retention of a cingulum on the inner (buccal) surfaces of the molars. This more primitive morphology may be justification for a separate species, but the ultimate decision should rest on the recovery of more early material. A mandible from Pyrgos, Greece, has been tentatively attributed to a third and slightly later species, *R. freybergi* (Simons, 1974).

The earliest hominids now known are from Pasalar, Turkey, and date to 15 m.y. to 16 m.y. ago; another Turkish site, at Candir, and Fort Ternan, in Kenya, may both date to about 14 m.y. ago (Andrews and Tobien, 1977). The earliest appearance of hominids in India and Pakistan was about 13 m.y. ago. Therefore, within about a 2-m.y. period, the hominids had spread over a wide geographic area.

Most of these early hominid sites were in areas of lightly wooded, open country. They were neither forest nor grassland. Most of the deposits, however, indicate the nearby presence of other types of habitats as well. Perhaps the best term for the environments of the earliest hominids is "mosaic," implying that a variety of local habitat space was available. We will return to this point and its significance in human evolution in Chapter 5.

The original point of dispersion of the hominids has not yet been identified, although increasing evidence is pointing to a Eurasian, rather than an African, locale. Moreover, in the whole of Africa, Fort Ternan is the single hominid site of Middle Miocene Age, and the hominids there are associated with a largely immigrant Eurasian fauna. Therefore, the evidence for an African origin of the Hominidae is neither strong nor compelling at the present time.

Just as the point of origin of the hominids has not yet been identified, neither has the ancestral form been clearly ascertained. When Africa was favored as a point of origin, *Proconsul nyanzae* was regarded as a likely candidate (Simons and Pilbeam, 1965). However, now that a non-African origin for the family Hominidae is being seriously considered, there are other possible candidates. *Sivapithecus*, particularly the early species *S. darwini*, now seems a possible ancestor (Andrews, 1976). However, it is not known for certain that this species occurs earlier in time than *Ramapithecus*. At present, the earliest occurrence of both forms is at Pasalar. In support of *S. darwini* as an ancestral form, it is interesting to note that both this form and the ramapithecines from Pasalar demonstrate molar cingula. Moreover, this primitive trait is also shared with members of the African genus *Proconsul*. Therefore, a possible lineage could read: *Proconsul→ Sivapithecus→ Ramapithecus* (Andrews, 1976). One possible alternative lineage would replace *Proconsul* with *Rangwapithecus* (Andrews, 1976). This form, however, has elongated molars and rather high-crowned teeth, a pattern that makes *Rangwapithecus* a less likely ancestor.

Characters of the Miocene Hominidae

Important characteristics are as follows (see also Figure 4-11):

Small incisors

Small canines, which may project only slightly above the other teeth

Reduction of M3 relative to M1 and M2

Shallow, robust mandible

Large inferior torus on mandible

Slightly divergent tooth rows

P_3 with two cusps; a large outer (buccal) and much smaller inner (lingual) cusp

Nonprojecting face (orthognathous)

Greater differential wear on molars (relative to other Miocene hominoids)

P_3 placed with its long axis turned 45° to the long axis of the tooth row

Thick enamel

The currently available evidence of *Ramapithecus* is limited to a few fragments of jaws and teeth and a small portion of the lower face. Yet the hominid features in this material are unmistakable; they are particularly evident on the mandible. As pointed out previously, ape mandibles tend to be high and thin in cross section. Such a structure is probably related to the fact that while many apes chew harsh, coarse foods, they masticate almost entirely in an up-and-down, or vertical, mode. Their large interlocking canines prevent any significant sideways movement of the mandible. In hominids, however, the chewing mode, and therefore the mandibular structure, is quite different. Hominid mandibles are shallow in height, yet broad in cross section (Figure 4-8). The canines are small, so that mastication is not limited to the vertical mode. Thus, hominids grind their food with a rotatory movement; the side-to-side movement of the ramapithecine jaw is confirmed by horizontal striations on the surface of the molar teeth (Andrews and Walker, 1976).

The tooth rows, or "dental arcade," in this genus are straight and

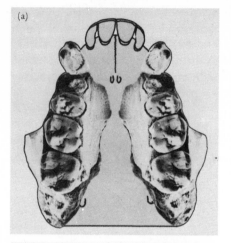
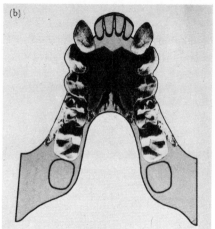
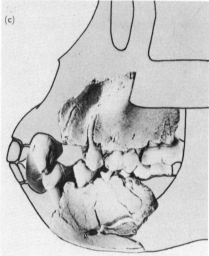

FIGURE 4-11 **(a)** Maxilla of *Ramapithecus*, based on KNM FT 46 and 47, occlusal view. Only two molars have erupted in this subadult individual. Note the front-to-back compression of the tooth rows and the fact that the long axis of the premolars is approximately perpendicular to the long axis of the tooth row. The lingual cingula, a consistent characteristic of *Proconsul*, has disappeared. **(b)** Mandible of *Ramapithecus*, based on KNM FT 45, occlusal view. Even though the M_3 has not yet erupted, note the different degrees of wear present on M_1 and M_2. By the time M_3 would have come into occlusion, the first two molars would have been very worn. This differential wear indicates a prolongation of the growth period in the rama-pithecines in contrast to other hominoids. Note also the P_3, with its large outer cusp and very slightly developed inner cusp; such a "semisectorial" premolar represents a primitive condition in these earliest hominids. **(c)** Face of *Ramapithecus* (reconstructed). Note the minimal prognathism of the lower face and the small size of the canines. Note also that the mandible was low, in contrast with the high mandibles of other hominoids. (Photographs courtesy of P. Andrews and A. Walker.)

slightly divergent toward the rear; in *Homo,* the tooth rows usually curve in toward the rear and are said to be "parabolic." The literature has revealed considerable misunderstanding of the shape of the ramapithecine jaws. Although G. E. Lewis, in his early papers on *Ramapithecus,* clearly stated that the "dental arch [was] divergent" (1937b, p. 142), he had previously said it was "parabolic" (1934, p. 162). Later workers have ignored his full description of the jaw arch of this genus and have almost unanimously used the word "parabolic" as descriptive of the jaw form. However, a reconstruction of the Fort Ternan jaw material (Walker and Andrews, 1973) and recovery of more complete material have confirmed that the sides of the jaw were divergent in *Ramapithecus* (see Figure 4-11b). In fact, divergent dental arcades seem to be the rule in most fossil hominoids, including *Dryopithecus, Gigantopithecus,* and the Oligocene anthropoids. Such posterior divergence may in fact be a primitive condition for all hominoids, and both the parabolic arcades in *Homo* and the rectangular, parallel-sided jaw in living pongids are relatively recent acquisitions (Simons, 1972a, 1974). The biomechanical implications of this jaw structure will be discussed in Chapter 5.

The incisors were small teeth and may have protruded slightly forward. The canines were small, conical, and vertically implanted; in some individuals, they extended slightly above the level of the other teeth.

The premolars are of particular interest because, while showing a definite hominid character, they retain traces of the ape ancestral form. Moreover, the premolars are different in the upper and lower jaws. In the upper jaw, they are identical to one another in size and shape. Such a condition of homomorphy is just like that found in modern humans. In the lower jaw, however, the premolars are not identical to one another; this condition is an example of heteromorphy. The P_3 has one large cusp on the outer (buccal) surface and a smaller one on the inner (lingual) surface. Such a tooth has some structural similarities to the **sectorial** P_3 in apes, which has just one large cusp. The sectorial premolars in the great apes act as a hone or sharpener for the upper canines, against which they occlude. The modified P_3 in *Ramapithecus* is termed **semisectorial,** and the tooth from Fort Ternan actually has a small wear facet on its front border where it occluded with the upper canine. In *Ramapithecus,* the P_3 is set obliquely to the long axis of the tooth row at an angle of about 45° (Andrews and Walker, 1976). Such structure of the P_3 appears to represent an intermediate position between the full heteromorphy of the dryopithecine premolars and the full homomorphy of the later hominids. In later hominids, the second, inner cusp on P_3 is enlarged and the inner, posterior portion of the tooth is expanded by development of a "heel" of enamel (talonid) and an extra rim of enamel (cingulum). Andrews (1971) has termed the P_3 morphology in *Ramapithecus* "incipient molarization"; this means that the premolars in the Miocene genus were beginning to function more as grinding teeth and less as piercing or cutting teeth. Therefore, some selective advantage must have been conferred by the added grinding capability of these teeth. The evolutionary significance of this will be discussed in Chapter 5.

The molar teeth also show clear evidence of their hominid nature. In apes, the usual arrangement is for the molars to increase in size from front to back, so that M1 is the smallest and M3 is the largest of the molar series. In hominids, the condition is reversed, so that M1 is usually the largest and M3 the smallest. This may very well reflect the fact that the lower portion of the hominid face, including the jaws, is reduced in size relative to the faces of the great apes. The ramapithecine molars are broadened from side to side, so that they are nearly square in shape. This broadening has not necessarily increased their chewing surface, but it has permitted the molars to retain a large chewing surface even though the jaws themselves have become shorter. Moreover, these broad, low-cusped molars are tightly packed into the tooth row and rub against one another during mastication. This rubbing (interstitial wear) leaves small wear facets on the adjacent teeth. The molars of *Ramapithecus* have thicker enamel than those of the dryopithecines, a condition that, again, may represent an adaptation to a harsh diet.

Recent studies with the scanning electron microscope have further emphasized the hominid character of the ramapithecine teeth. These studies, which have examined the shape of enamel prisms on the occlusal surface of the molars, have shown that there is a distinct difference between hominid and pongid teeth. The hominids, including *Ramapithecus* and *Homo sapiens*, have a tightly packed, "keyhole" prism pattern. The pongids, including chimps, gorillas, and orangs, show a loosely packed circular or hexagonal pattern (Gantt, Pilbeam, and Steward, 1977).

A final feature of the ramapithecine molars is a very good example of their hominid nature. In the apes, the period of growth and development is relatively rapid (see Chapter 2). One result is that the permanent molar teeth erupt rather rapidly. This fact can be confirmed by examining the chewing surfaces of these teeth: All three molars in the apes will show a similar amount of wear. A basic characteristic of the Hominidae, however, is a lengthening of the growth period, and this longer period is unquestionably apparent on the molars of *Ramapithecus*. In living humans, M1 erupts at about 6 years of age and M3 appears between 18 and 20 years of age. Such a long growth period, lasting 12 to 14 years, means that M1 may be very worn before M3 appears; this is termed **differential wear**. The growth period in *Ramapithecus* may not have been as long as in *Homo*, but it was clearly longer than in the dryopithecines.

Although the fossil evidence of *Ramapithecus* is extremely limited, a distinctive morphologic and functional pattern seems to be present. The teeth are crowded together so that no gaps are present in the tooth row.

The cheekbones (zygomatic arches) flare widely from the maxilla, indicating that the temporalis muscle, just behind, was large. The front of the mandible was buttressed strongly by a bar of bone along its lower surface. Such a pattern both directly and indirectly indicates that the basic subsistence foods required considerable grinding and mastication. The horizontal scratches on the tooth surfaces show that much of this grinding used a rotary movement. Such a functional morphology is unknown in the primates before the Miocene and seems to be a response to a new set of selective pressures. Such pressures may have resulted from the exploitation of a coarse, fibrous vegetarian diet. Such food items, including grasses and seeds, can be found both on the forest floor and in more open grassland country. It is possible that such a morphologic complex first appeared in the forest or forest-margin areas and then acted as a preadaptation for later expansion out of the forest and into areas where these foods were more common and plentiful. It is interesting, and perhaps highly significant, that the dental changes seen in these Middle Miocene hominids closely parallel those found in the contemporaneous herbivorous ungulates, discussed earlier. Hominid teeth have not become high-crowned, as in some ungulates; but they have adopted other ways of increasing their chewing and grinding capabilities. Hominid molars have become broad, almost square, in comparison with the narrower ape molars. The canines are no longer piercing teeth but now function as grinding teeth too.

The view outlined here is that *Ramapithecus* represents a hominid and was, indeed, the earliest known hominid. This point of view is based on the resemblances between trait patterns present in the fossil sample and trait patterns found in later and undoubted hominids. The existence of this same total trait pattern in *Ramapithecus* justifies its inclusion within the Hominidae. There is, moreover, a logical morphologic and evolutionary progression from the Middle and Late Miocene ramapithecines to the Plio-Pleistocene hominids. In some cases, the similarities between *Ramapithecus* and later hominids are so great that, on the basis of jaw and dental morphology alone, it is difficult to see any significant distinctions. Simons, in fact, has said, "Dental and facial characters are so close to *Australopithecus africanus* as to make difficult the drawing of generic distinctions between the two species on the basis of present material" (1964, p. 535). When faced with these kinds of similarities, the exclusion of *Ramapithecus* from the Hominidae is hard to justify.

However, alternative interpretations of this material do exist. Hrdlicka (1935) was the first to voice objections to the hominid status of *Ramapithecus*. He dealt with three taxa of hominoids which had been recovered in north India in 1932: "*Ramapithecus brevirostris,*" "*Ramapithecus hariensis,*" and "*Sugrivapithecus salmontanus.*" G. E. Lewis, in 1934, had suggested that these three taxa were at, or near, the ancestry of the later hominids.

Hrdlicka was correct in noting the basic pongid nature of the last two taxa; Simons and Pilbeam (1965), in fact, placed these within *Dryopithecus sivalensis*. However, his criticism of the hominid nature of the maxilla of *"Ramapithecus brevirostris"* is contradictory and difficult to understand. For example, Hrdlicka (1935) stated that the maxilla had "a greater general resemblance to the human than that of any other known fossil or living anthropoid ape," and that "the maxilla itself, in the main, was pithecoid" (p. 36). Moreover, he reached this conclusion while acknowledging that the maxilla was "nearer to man than are any of the Dryopitheci or the *Australopithecus*" (p. 36).

More recently, Sarich's research on protein evolution has provided a new source of objections. These objections rest with his interpretation of the significance of the protein differences between living hominids and pongids. He has summarized his conclusions in this way:

> To put it as bluntly as possible, I now feel that the body of protein evidence on the *Homo-Pan* relationship is sufficiently extensive so that one no longer has the option of considering a fossil specimen older than about 8 million years as a hominid *no matter what it looks like.* (1970, p. 109)

Such a statement would seem to indicate that the sciences of paleontology and comparative anatomy are no longer of any use in the interpretation of fossil material. However, the fossil evidence now implies that advanced hominids, such as members of the genus *Homo*, were present at a very early date. Material from east Africa indicates the presence of *Homo* there before 2 m.y. ago. Obviously, the slow and sedate rate of protein evolution would need more than 6 m.y. to convert a pongid into *Homo*. Therefore, these arguments, and those of Hrdlicka 40 years ago, are not valid. It is, of course, possible that *Ramapithecus* was not a hominid, but on the basis of presently available anatomical evidence, this supposition seems unlikely.

FAMILY OREOPITHECIDAE; LATE MIOCENE

It seems somehwat paradoxical that the most completely known of the Miocene apes is also the most enigmatic. The name *Oreopithecus bambolii* was first proposed by Gervais in 1872 to contain a nearly complete mandible found in a lignite coal mine at Monte Bamboli in Tuscany, Italy. These deposits, and similar ones in southern Russia that also contain *Oreopithecus*, date to Pontian times, probably about 10 to 12 m.y. ago (Straus, 1963). A possibly ancestral form has been found at Maboko, Kenya, in deposits of Middle Miocene age (Von Koenigswald, 1969); this form has been called *"Mabokopithecus clarki."* This form may have originated from the Oligocene genus *Apidium* (Simons, 1960, 1972a). All three genera (*Apidium, Mabokopithecus,* and *Oreopithecus*) share a distinctive cusp morphology on the lower molars. The most important of these shared similarities is the presence of an additional cusp near the center of the lower molar, termed the **"centroconid."**

Gervais (1872), and later, Schlosser (1887), suggested that the original mandible was that of a cercopithecoid monkey, most nearly like living macaques and baboons. Others have suggested that it was from an anthropoid ape (Schwalbe, 1915) or a hominoid (Hürzeler, 1949). Still others have placed this genus either in a position of hominid ancestry or as a full member of the Hominidae. Since most controversy over taxonomic allocation usually revolves around the problems posed by incomplete specimens, the classification of *Oreopithecus* should have been resolved in 1958 when a virtually complete individual was recovered in lignite deposits at Baccinello, Grosseto, Italy. This specimen was removed, crushed but nearly intact, by Hürzeler. Agreement over the classification and affinities was not to occur, however, because *Oreopithecus* comprises a unique assemblage of characters found today in monkeys, pongids, and hominids.

The face of *Oreopithecus* was short and vertical (orthognathous) with little projection of the lower part. The face is so short and straight, in fact, that the nasal bones project forward, roofing the nasal cavity; this is a condition seen elsewhere only in hominids. The skull was fairly large, with an estimated cranial capacity of 565 cc (Straus and Schon, 1960). With a body about 122 cm (4 ft) tall and weighing about 40 kg (88 lb), the body dimensions would be approximately those of a chimp. The ratio of brain size to body size would have been about equal to this form. There was no simian shelf in the jaws and the incisors and canines were small and vertically implanted; there was no diastema. The premolars were bicuspid and homomorphic, also a condition seen elsewhere only in hominids. The dental formula was 2123, like that of living higher primates. M3, however, was larger than M1, a pongid condition. The trunk was broad and shallow, the number of lumbar vertebrae was five, and the number of sacral segments was six—all hominoid characters. However, the lumbar and thoracic vertebrae have a central ridge or keel, which is a monkey character. The vertebral canal becomes very small near the end, suggesting that perhaps *Oreopithecus* did not have a tail. The upper limb is basically hominoid in form; the phalanges are curved with strong flexor ridges on the palm surface—a hominoid character (Straus, 1963).

The pelvis and lower limbs are of particular interest in that they have several features that are hominid in nature. The ilium was relatively low and broad, as in hominids, not long and blade-like, as in quadrupeds. Most important is the presence of an anterior inferior iliac spine on the front margin of the ilium. The ilio-femoral ligament originates here and acts to prevent backward tilting of the trunk. The ligament and its attachment area are small in quadrupeds but well developed in hominids that hold the trunk erect. The very presence of this spine on the front of the ilium is a strong indication that the trunk was habitually held upright. The overall relationship between the limbs seems to indicate pongid affinities; the intermembral index was 119, indicating arms longer than legs, and it is closest to the gorilla. The humero-femoral index, 117, was also within the pongid range (Straus, 1963).

Not only was the morphology of *Oreopithecus* unique, but its probable habitat was also an unusual one for a primate. Lignite coal, like all other forms of coal, forms under swamp-like conditions where dense vegetation is associated with shallow water. All the known European forms have been discovered in such deposits. At these sites, *Oreopithecus* was found in association with a number of swamp-living animals: fish, crocodiles, snakes, and turtles. Terrestrial mammals are rare in these deposits, but some rabbits, bear, rodents, and antelopes do occur; however, living forms related to these Miocene animals do enter swamps in the southern United States (Simons, 1972a).

The complexity and unusualness of the morphological and ecological pattern associated with *Oreopithecus* presents numerous difficulties in interpretation. Some of these features undoubtedly reflect a specialized form of locomotion required by the wet or swampy conditions. Such a form of locomotion would involve some arm swinging, as indicated by the long arms, mobile shoulder joints, and curved fingers. These characters closely parallel those found in hylobatids and some New World monkeys, such as *Ateles*. The morphology of the pelvis and lower leg, on the other hand, indicates that the trunk was habitually stabilized in an upright position. These features, and others in the lower limb, strongly suggest that this animal was capable of moving bipedally. It is difficult to explain this morphological complex in any other way. Is it possible that the wet, spongy conditions of the subsurface made bipedality, rather than quadrupedality, more selectively advantageous in a primate? Such a possibility brings up an interesting point. Bipedality is a very odd way for an animal to move, and it has evolved only a very few times. It has distinct disadvantages in that it exposes the abdominal organs to attack and makes balance precarious. Despite its rarity, it may have appeared at least twice in separate hominoid lines. In any case, *Oreopithecus* appears to have been a short-lived form and is known only from the later Miocene.

SUMMARY

During the Miocene there was a remarkable radiation of higher primates. This radiation involved both an expansion of their geographic range and an increase in the number of forms present. For example, at the Early Miocene site of Rusinga in east Africa, as many as seven species, contained in four genera, are known. With the establishment of land contact between Africa and Eurasia about 16 to 17 m.y. ago, some hominoid groups left Africa.

Among these were the ancestors of living hylobatids and humans. Although the species diversity is not known to be so great outside Africa, nevertheless two or three species are present at a number of Middle Miocene sites in India, Pakistan, Turkey, Hungary, and Spain.

Members of the genus *Proconsul*, a primitive African ape, may have provided the ancestral populations that led to the highly diversified and widespread Eurasian radiation. At least four genera resulted from this radiation. Members of the genus *Dryopithecus*, found at many sites in Europe, were little changed from the African *Proconsul*. The remaining genera of this radiation were, however, more altered.

The most interesting part of this radiation involved three closely related genera: *Sivapithecus*, *Gigantopithecus*, and *Ramapithecus*. Paleoecological evidence from sites where some specimens were found indicates that they had moved out of the forest home of the earlier primates and were living in more open woodland environments. In response to the adaptive pressures encountered in such environments, they developed a dental pattern unlike their ancestors. Distinctive characters in their dental complex include thick enamel on the teeth, large teeth, and robust chewing apparatus, presumably an adaptation for the harder or coarser foods of the more open country.

Toward the end of the Miocene, two rather bizarre primate forms appeared. *Oreopithecus*, known from coal deposits dating to about 10 m.y. ago, had an unusual combination of features. It had the long arms of a brachiator, yet some of the pelvic characters of a biped. It appeared only briefly and seems to have died without issue. *Gigantopithecus* appeared just before the end of the Miocene in India and Pakistan, and continued on at least until the Middle Pleistocene in China. As the name indicates, it was a very large ape; it too probably died without issue.

Thus in the Early and Middle Miocene, the hominoids exhibited a geographic and taxonomic diversity not subsequently seen in that group. With the increase of the more open woodlands and grasslands in the Middle Miocene, the traditional forested habitats of the hominoids decreased. Some, unable to adapt, became extinct. Others adapted and changed to live in the grasslands. Among these were *Gigantopithecus* and *Sivapithecus*, extinct without issue, and *Ramapithecus*, the probable ancestor of *Homo sapiens*.

SUGGESTIONS FOR FURTHER READING

Andrews, P., and J. Van Couvering. 1975. "Palaeoenvironments in the East African Miocene," in F. Szalay (ed.), *Approaches to Primate Paleobiology, Contrib. Primat.*, Basel, Switzerland: Karger, Vol. 5, pp. 62–103. (An excellent discussion of the environmental context of some of the African early hominoids.)

Isaac, G., and E. McCown (eds.). 1976. *Human Origins*. Menlo Park, Calif.: W. A. Benjamin. (contains a variety of papers on topics related to early humans. The most relevant to the Miocene are: Andrews, P., and A. Walker. "The Primate and Other Fauna from Fort Ternan, Kenya," pp. 279–306. Van Couvering, J., and J. Van Couvering. "Early Miocene Mammal Fossils from East Africa: Aspects of Geology, Faunistics and Paleo-ecology," pp. 155–208.)

Simons, E., 1977, "Ramapithecus," *Scientific American*, **236**(5), pp. 28–35. (Up-to-date discussion of recent ramapithecine finds.)

Simons, E., and P. Ettel. 1970. "Gigantopithecus," *Scientific American*, **222**(1), pp. 76–85. (Comprehensive discussion of this form.)

Simons, E., and D. Pilbeam. 1965. "Preliminary Revision of the Dryopithecinae (Pongidae, Anthropoidea), *"Folia Primatologica*," **3**(2–3), pp. 81–152. (Although technical, this is the most comprehensive discussion of the Miocene hominoids available.)

THE FAMILY
HOMINIDAE

INTRODUCTION

Modern humans and their close ancestors are members of the family Hominidae. At present, at least three genera are recognized as belonging within this family: *Ramapithecus, Australopithecus,* and *Homo.*

The concept of the family as a taxonomic category did not originate with Linnaeus in the 1730s but was proposed by Gray in 1825, when a growing number of biologists realized that a category was needed between the genus and the order. The category of the family, placed in this gap, is defined as a group of genera that share a number of important characteristics. Each family is based on a type genus which gives its characteristics and name to the family; thus, the type genus of the family Hominidae is *Homo.* The most important criteria for the family Hominidae center on its distinctive locomotor, dental, and brain characteristics. When dealing with fossil members of any family, however, it is obvious that the earlier forms will not be identical to later members of the group. Therefore, in examining the earlier hominids, we will see some variations from later members of the group. Clearly, there is no reason why hominids 14 or 15 million years old should be identical or even nearly identical to living members of the family, since evolution is a continuing process.

GEOGRAPHIC ORIGINS

The geographic area where the family Hominidae originated has been the subject of some debate through the years. Darwin, in *The Descent of Man* (1871), noted the morphological similarities between the living African apes and humans and postulated that humans first emerged on the African continent. Although interest in the Far East as the home of humans began in 1868 with Haeckel, it gained widespread credence only with the discovery of "Pithecanthropus" in Java in the 1890s, followed by the discovery of "Sinanthropus" in China in the 1920s. After these important discoveries, the focus of studies of early hominids was firmly switched to the Far East. With the initial discoveries of australopithecines in South Africa at almost the same time that "Sinanthropus" was being found in China, the mainstream of evolutionary thinking should again have been directed to Africa. But acceptance of the South African fossils as hominids did not occur until almost 20 years later when Le Gros Clark, in 1947, voiced his strong acceptance of their placement within the human family.

Two further events placed the spotlight of human origins even more strongly on Africa. In 1959, Louis and Mary Leakey, after more than 30 years of effort, began to uncover early Pleistocene hominids in Olduvai Gorge. Soon afterward, Elwyn Simons published his view that *Ramapithecus* was a hominid (1961b). Although Simons's material had come from India, Louis Leakey (1962) soon described a Middle Miocene Fort Ternan fossil, "Kenyapithecus wickeri," as a hominid. Clearly, with this report, a chronological sequence of human evolution could be documented in Africa as it could nowhere else in the world. Since that time, Africa has been viewed as the home of the Hominidae by most paleoanthropologists.

Although the expanding understanding of biochemistry and genetics has clearly shown that the relationship between African apes and humans is closer than between humans and any other living primate group, the controversy has not yet subsided. Weidenreich was perhaps the foremost proponent of his day in championing the point of view that hominids emerged in Asia. His conviction was based in large part on his view that hominids had come from a line of gigantic apes, fossil evidence for which had been found in Asia. This evidence centered mainly on *Gigantopithecus*, known then only from south China, and "Meganthropus," from Java. More recently, Von Koenigswald (1973) has placed hominid origins in India. The point of view rests on the fact that he rejects the African evidence of *Ramapithecus* and accepts only the Indian material as hominid. Campbell and Bernor (1976) have reviewed the geological and ecological evidence and have concluded that Africa and the Far East each contained appropriate habitats and could therefore have served as the place of hominid origins. They concluded, "It is slightly more probable that the first hominid adaptations took place in Asia" (p. 452).

The present evidence appears to indicate that the family Hominidae possibly did not emerge in Africa. That evidence is not refined enough, however, to indicate whether hominids originated in Europe or Asia. But, with the earliest known hominids now identified in Turkey, a Eurasian origin must be considered.

CHARACTERISTICS

Certain characteristics of the Hominidae are also characteristics of the great apes, but to a lesser or different degree. Among these quantitative differences is bipedality. All pongids will move bipedally on occasion, but in none of the apes is bipedality the primary mode of locomotion. Tool use and tool manufacture, long regarded as uniquely human characteristics, are also known to occur in nonhuman primates and are especially well documented in the chimps. Humans alone, however, depend on tool use for survival. Cooperative group hunting and stable male-female pairings may also occur under certain conditions not only in pongids but also in some monkeys. A large brain and a long period of maturation and development are characteristics of the primates as a whole. The human differs in these features only in degree.

There are, however, certain quantum or synapomorphic differences between the Hominidae and the Pongidae. Structured, flexible speech is one of them. Another is the loss of estrus in the human female, as is the loss of the penis bone in the male. There are also important behavioral differences between apes and humans. One of these is the fact that only humans establish and maintain a home base to which the group returns over a period of time. Finally, although other primates will make and use tools, none manufactures them according to a consistent plan, as the human does.

It is important to realize that it is the total pattern and association of this set of morphological and behavioral characters that define members of the family Hominidae, or, indeed, of any taxonomic category. It is also important to recognize that some members within populations may lack certain of these individual characters and yet not jeopardize their membership in that taxon. Thus a member of *Homo erectus* from Java, such as "Pithecanthropus 4," may have a rather large canine and a small gap or diastema in the tooth row, and still be included within the family because of the overall pattern of hominid characters present.

MORPHOLOGY

Important morphological characteristics are as follows:

Thick enamel on the teeth

Marked differential wear on molars

Loss of cingula in all but the earliest hominids

Teeth large in relation to body size in early forms; relative and absolute dental reduction in later forms

Reduced canine

Reduction of M3 relative to M1 and M2

Nonsectorial P_3 (semisectorial P_3 in some early hominids)

Shallow, robust mandible

Inferior torus on mandible

Tooth rows divergent in early forms, parabolic in later forms

Erect posture and bipedal locomotion

Brain large in relation to body size

Speech structures capable of producing flexible, structured sounds

The last three characteristics are documented only in later groups.

Dentition

Compared with pongids, the hominids show reduction in the size of the anterior dentition in relation to the posterior dentition. The incisors are small and vertically placed. Hominid canines, unlike those of the pongids, are small and do not project much, if at all, above the level of the other teeth; no diastema is present. Moreover, hominid premolars are identical or nearly so in size and morphology, and they have two equal-sized cusps; this condition is termed "homomorphy." The molars are low-crowned (bunodont) and steep-sided. The M3 is generally reduced in size, so that the M1 is usually the largest of the cheek teeth. Hominid molar teeth show a sharp wear differential, so that the M1 may be considerably worn before the M3 is fully in occlusion (Figure 4-11b).

The hominid mandible is shallow and low but thick and robust, with the body turning inward (toward the chin area) at the level of M1. The sides of the mandible diverge in earlier members of the family Hominidae but converge toward the rear in *Homo*. Finally, the dental enamel on the surface of the teeth is thicker in hominids than in pongids.

Dental Function

The morphology of the hominid dental apparatus and the implications of this morphology can be discussed from several aspects. One such method of analysis is that of its function or biomechanics.

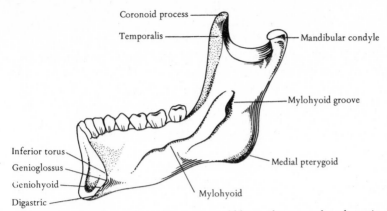

Coronoid process
Temporalis
Mandibular condyle
Mylohyoid groove
Inferior torus
Genioglossus
Geniohyoid
Digastric
Medial pterygoid
Mylohyoid

FIGURE 5-1 Interior surface of human mandible, to show muscles of mastication.

The biomechanical forces acting on any mammalian jaw have basically three components: a vertical force, a lateral force, and compressive forces resulting from occlusion of the teeth (Figure 5-1). The vertical forces are developed largely by the temporalis and masseter muscles, while the lateral forces result mainly from the medial and lateral pterygoids. The very complex action of chewing results from an orchestration of these muscles: the jaw drops and is pulled up and forward by the temporalis and masseter. The forward movement is continued by the medial and lateral pterygoids which, acting on just one side or the other, pull the jaw over; the pterygoids on the opposite side then contract to pull the chin to the other side.

Since muscle efficiency increases with the effective length of the muscle, a deep mandible is advantageous when there is a strong vertical component in chewing. The deep mandibles of the dryopithecines, living chimps, and gorillas are good examples of this; the large canines in these pongids help to lock the jaws into the vertical mode and thus diminish the lateral component. In many living gorillas and in some early hominids, such as the robust australopithecines, the effective length of the temporalis muscle was increased by the development of a sagittal crest on the skull along the area of the muscles' origin.

The hominids, including *Ramapithecus*, do not have a deep jaw but have, instead, a shallow yet robustly built mandible. This morphology, along with small canines which do not interlock, demonstrates that there was a strong lateral component in hominid jaw mechanics (see Andrews, 1971; Andrews and Walker, 1976). In other words, in contrast with the pongid mode of vertical "chomping," the hominids grind their food with side-to-side, rotary movements of the lower jaw against the upper. The implications of this procedure are clear: the hominids, including the earliest, *Ramapithecus*, subsisted on a diet different in composition and texture from that of the pongids, either living or fossil.

Although the large, rear-projecting shelf of bone on the inside of the jaw (the simian shelf) is not found in hominids, buttressing bars of bone are present. These most often take the form of an inferior torus (Figure 4-8) placed at the lower margin of the jaw at the front. This torus may be placed on the inside of the mandible, as in the robust australopithecines; or, as in later members of the genus *Homo*, it may be placed on the outer surface and thus take the form of a chin. In either position, the function of this bar of bone is the same: it acts as a buttress for the mandible against the forces of chewing, especially those that involve lateral or rotational movement.

It seems apparent from this morphological pattern that the hominid mandible is structured for strong grinding capabilities. This pattern, involving heavy dental use, is reinforced by the presence of thicker enamel on the hominid teeth. The pattern is also demonstrated by the low cusps and broad chewing surface of the molars, by the molarization of the premolars, and by the decreased size of the canines. These features mean that the cheek teeth of the hominids, from the canine through the third molar, effectively act as grinding teeth. The shearing and piercing function of the pongid canine, and of P3 to a lesser extent, has been lost in favor of greater grinding capability.

Locomotion

The erect bipedality of the Hominidae is, as has been noted, a very rare form of locomotion in the animal world. Some dinosaurs were bipedal, as are the birds; but with the possible exception of the penguins, none held the spinal column perpendicular to the ground surface. Therefore, the term "erect" does not apply to these nonhominid bipeds.

The hominid form of locomotion has many interacting components involving virtually every part of the bony skeleton. The skull, for example, has come to be more "centered" or balanced on the upright spinal column, and the spinal column itself has taken on an S-shaped curve. These adjustments mean that a human being who is standing still is more-or-less in balanced equilibrium and requires little active muscle effort to maintain an upright posture. During movements such as walking or running, muscle actions are required to maintain balance and equilibrium, but the magnitude of these actions is much less in the hominid than in a chimp walking bipedally, for example. This balanced, erect posture of humans has been acquired by a number of modifications in the bony skeleton, but the most important of them have occurred in the bones of the pelvis.

The structure and mechanics of hominid bipedality can be approached through a comparison of the hip and lower limb of a modern human with

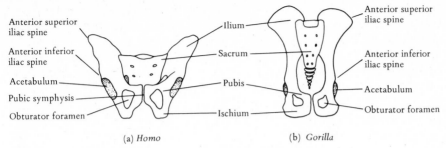

FIGURE 5-2   Os coxa, anterior view: **(a)** *Homo;* **(b)** *Gorilla.*

that of a gorilla (Figure 5-2). Although it is probable that the structures found in these two living forms will not be exactly the same as in earlier members of their respective groups, nevertheless these models can serve to outline the basic locomotor differences found within the Hominoidea.

Figures 5-3 and 5-4 show the differences in hip and leg structure between the quadrupedal hindlimb of a gorilla and the bipedal limb of a human.

Pelvis   Major alterations have occurred in the pelvis, which is made up of three bones: ilium, ischium, and pubis. These bones are separate during the growth period but fuse into a single structure called the **"os innominatum"** in the adult.

Ilium   In the quadruped, the ilium is a more-or-less rectangular bone which lies with its long axis approximately parallel with the long axis of the spinal column. The muscles on the back or outside of the ilium act to straighten or extend the hip and help to erect the trunk as they contract. At the hip joint in the gorilla, the main extensors are the three gluteal muscles: gluteus maximus, gluteus medius, and gluteus minimus. In the gorilla, gluteus maximus is quite small, but the other gluteal muscles, medius and minimus, are relatively larger; the center of gravity is forward and above the hip joint and, with the large mass in the chest and trunk, the upper body has a strong tendency to fall forward. In quadrupeds, the forward momentum is, of course, offset by the forelimb. However, when the great apes move bipedally, they use all three gluteal muscles to help counteract this momentum and hold the trunk up. In this effort, they also use the large extensor muscles, called the "hamstrings" (biceps femoris, semitendinosis, and semimembranosis) on the back of the thigh. Because of this muscular effort, a quadruped cannot move efficiently in terms of energy expenditure in a bipedal mode. The stride will be short because the lower limbs are short, and the forward momentum of the trunk must be counteracted by strong and constant muscular effort.

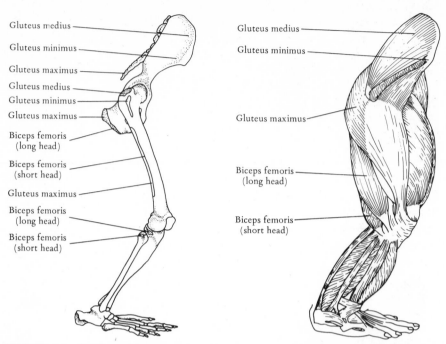

Gluteus medius

Gluteus minimus

Gluteus maximus

Gluteus medius

Gluteus minimus

Gluteus maximus

Biceps femoris
(long head)

Biceps femoris
(short head)

Gluteus maximus

Biceps femoris
(long head)

Biceps femoris
(short head)

Gluteus medius

Gluteus minimus

Gluteus maximus

Biceps femoris
(long head)

Biceps femoris
(short head)

FIGURE 5-3 Quadrupedal posture needs two sets of muscles to act as the principal extensors of the hip. These are the gluteal group (the gluteus medius and minimus in particular), which connects the pelvis to the upper part of the femur, and the hamstring group, which connects the femur and the lower leg bones. Of these only the biceps femoris is shown in the gorilla musculature at right. The skeletal regions to which these muscles attach are shown at left. In most primates the gluteus maximus is quite small. (Napier, 1967. By permission of Scientific American.)

In the human, however, the ilium is no longer blade-like but is lower and tightly curved backward and outward. This curvature, in two planes, has altered the actions of the gluteal muscles. A major effect of this curvature is to project the origin of gluteus maximus further behind the hip joint, and from this position it can now improve its action as the main extensor of the hip. Although gluteus maximus is a very visible part of human anatomy, it is not very important in normal walking, which is little impaired or altered even if this muscle is completely paralyzed (Basmajian, 1967). Gluteus maximus is mainly active in locomotion to stop the forward momentum of the body at the end of a stride and to add stability as the next stride begins (J. Robinson, 1972). More important, it gives extra power when the hip is bent or flexed. It is therefore useful in running or climbing but not vital to normal walking.

In bipedal walking, however, the changes that have affected the two smaller gluteal muscles, gluteus medius and gluteus minimus, are more

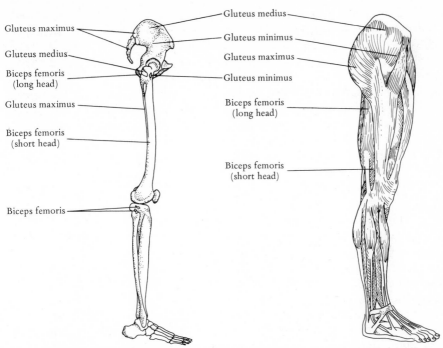

Gluteus maximus

Gluteus medius

Biceps femoris
(long head)

Gluteus maximus

Biceps femoris
(short head)

Biceps femoris

Gluteus medius

Gluteus minimus

Gluteus maximus

Gluteus minimus

Biceps femoris
(long head)

Biceps femoris
(short head)

FIGURE 5-4 Bipedal posture brings a reversal in the roles played by the pelvic and femoral muscles. Gluteus medius and gluteus minimus have changed from extensors to abductors and the function of extending the trunk, required when a biped runs or climbs, has been assumed by the gluteus maximus. The hamstring muscles, in turn, now act mainly as stabilizers and extensors of the hip. At right are the muscles as they appear in the human being; the skeletal regions to which their upper and lower ends attach are shown at left. (Napier, 1967. By permission of Scientific American.)

important. The outward and backward curvature of the ilium has completely altered the function of these two muscles in humans. The effect of the curvature means that their point of origin is now behind the hip joint rather than over it, as in the gorilla. Thus, they no longer straighten the hip but pull the top of the ilium (and the trunk) sideways; this sideways movement is called "abduction."[1] It is a vital component of bipedal walking. During bipedal locomotion, when one leg is lifted off the ground, the hip on the unsupported side tends to drop or sag and balance is lost. In a pongid moving bipedally, the pelvic drop is compounded by the high and forward position of the center of gravity. To counteract this, the hip and leg extensors contract, along with some of the abdominal muscles. The arms and shoulders are also brought into play by being swung strongly to the supported side. Thus the reestablishment of lost balance and equilibri-

[1]Technically, "abduction" is a movement away from the midline of the body.

um in pongids requires considerable expenditure of energy. In the human, however, the new abductors, gluteus medius and minimus, contract from the top of the ilium to the top of the femur on the supported side, thus pulling this side back down. Although other muscles are also active in stabilizing the trunk during human bipedality, this action of the trunk abductors minimizes the sway of the upper body, and thus equilibrium is never lost. With no pelvic drop on the unsupported side, balance is never upset and the two abductors thus function at every step to keep the pelvis level and to maintain equilibrium. The efficiency of the abduction action of the two smaller gluteal muscles has been improved by the lengthening of the neck of the femur in hominids. By lengthening the femoral neck, the leverage (or **lever arm**)[2] of the muscles' action has been increased, thus adding to their ability to abduct the trunk.

Balance is also aided, without muscular effort, by the backward curve of the ilium; this brings the human center of gravity slightly behind the hip joint and at about the same level as that joint. Thus, relative to the pongid center of gravity, the human position is lower and more posterior, and this position minimizes the tendency of gravity to pull the trunk forward. The human trunk, in fact, has a slight tendency to fall backward, but this inclination is offset by muscles and tendons on the front of the ilium. One of these tendons, that of rectus femoris, originates on the front of the ilium; its point of origin is marked by the anterior inferior iliac spine. The presence of this feature is an important indication of habitual erect posture. It is not, however, unique to the Hominidae; *Oreopithecus* also had such a feature.

Ischium   The ischium in pongids and hominids is also of different size and orientation. In gorillas, for example, the ischium is long and extends well behind and below the hip joint. In the human, it is relatively short and does not extend so far behind. The size and position of this bone relates to the efficiency and strength of the extensors, since gluteus maximus and the hamstrings attach here. The long posterior extension of the ischium in pongids acts to increase the leverage of the hamstrings and thus gives them additional power. As we will see shortly, the short ischium in the human is probably an adaptation to speed in extension, rather than in power.

The lever arm of the hip extensors extends from the center of the hip joint (the acetabulum) to the ischium. In the gorilla, the length of the lever arm is long relative to the length of the lower limb; such a limb would be structured for power rather than speed. This capability would be advantageous, for example, in climbing (J. Robinson, 1972). The situation is

---

[2]In biomechanical terms, the lever arm is defined as the distance from the point of rotation (in the joint) to the attachment area of the muscle.

reversed in the Hominidae, where the lever arm is relatively short but the lower limb is relatively long. Such a limb, in this case, would be structured for speed and rapid movement, rather than power in extension (J. Robinson, 1972).

Veterbral Column and Lower Limb In addition to the changes in the pelvis just outlined, the development of erect bipedality in the hominids has resulted in other changes in the bony skeleton. The vertebral column has, for example, developed an S-shaped curve. This curve helps to bring more of the body mass in the chest area behind the plane of the hip joint, thus adding to the postural equilibrium. The backward curve in the upper part of the spine is compensated for by the forward curve in the lower part of the spine just above the level of the hip joints.

Changes at the knee joint have involved bringing the knees inward toward the midline of the body. This feature appears to be part of the overall pattern of centering body mass, thus reinforcing skeletal, rather than muscular, equilibrium. This change is very apparent when examining the differences in load line in the lower limb between hominid and gorilla. The load line of the lower limb begins with the head of the femur in the acetabulum. In the gorilla, the femur when viewed from the front is oriented more-or-less parallel with the long axis of the spinal column, and the load line in the lower limb passes through the inner side of the knee. In the hominids, on the other hand, the femur is oriented obliquely to the spinal column and the knees come close together. The load line therefore passes to the outside of the knee. This alteration in the load line has been carried on to the foot. In pongids, the load line during standing passes between the first and second toes, and very little travels toward the outside of the foot. Moreover, the toes are long and the first toe diverges widely from the others. Such a foot is mobile, flexible, and capable of a great many activities, but it is not very efficient for rapid movement. In hominids, the foot is quite specialized and has a more limited range of capabilities. Here, the load line also passes to the inner side of the foot but passes through the first toe rather than between the first and second toes. But, the load is also transmitted through the outside of the foot, thus bringing the entire foot into use as a stabilizing element. The human foot acts essentially as a tripod, with weight being equally distributed between the first and fifth toes and the center of the heel (Figure 5-5).

A good way to examine the differences in load transmission is through the robusticity index of the metatarsals (Day and Napier, 1964). Table 5-1 shows these data. The robusticity index of 15432 in the human indicates that weight is distributed to both the inner and outer sides of the foot, while in the gorilla the index of 12345 shows that the main weight-bearing emphasis is on the inner side of the foot. In the human, the front part of the foot, the phalanges and metatarsals, has been shortened relative to the

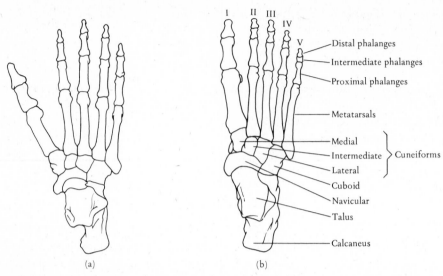

FIGURE 5-5   Foot of **(a)** *Gorilla* and **(b)** *Homo,* dorsal view. The bases of metatarsals I and II do not meet in *Gorilla* as they do in *Homo;* this indicates the divergence of the first toe in *Gorilla.*

TABLE 5-1   Metatarsal robusticity index

TAXA	INDEX
Homo sapiens	15432
Gorilla	12345
Olduvai Hominid 8	15342

Note: Robusticity index = $\dfrac{\text{metatarsal mean diameter} \times 100}{\text{metatarsal mean length}}$

The robusticity index shows the size relationship between the metatarsal bones in the foot. The numbers in the index refer to the number of the metatarsal, starting on the inside of the foot. The sequence of the numbers shows the bones' sequence in size, starting with the largest and ending with the smallest. Thus, if the first number in the index is 1, the first metatarsal is the largest; if the second number is 5, the fifth (or outer) metatarsal is the second largest, and so on.

Source: Day and Napier, 1964.

posterior portion. It is in the posterior portion of the foot that the main thrust in walking is developed. By emphasizing this portion rather than the front portion, the power capabilities of the hominid's foot are accentuated.

Brain

The basic features of primate brain evolution have been outlined in Chapter 2. As indicated there, most changes in brain structure cannot be observed directly but can be examined only through their end products, behavior. Thus, we can directly measure changes in total brain size and in the relative sizes of its component parts, but the neurological results of these changes can be examined only indirectly.

Speech One of the most important of the end products of brain evolution in the Hominidae is the acquisition of language. Obviously, we cannot document the date when hominids began to communicate verbally, but such communication represents a quantum behavioral jump from pongid to hominid. Only humans practice structured verbal communication in which the signals are variable in number and composition. The variable nature of speech patterns and the availability of an almost infinite number of verbal symbols distinguish hominid speech from all other forms of primate and animal communication.

While it is true that some chimps have learned to use verbal symbols or sign language, they have done so only through long-term and highly intensive training. This acquisition demonstrates a capability, although limited, but it is not part of a chimp's normal developmental process, as it is in hominids.

The origin and structure of human speech have been discussed by Geschwind (1964), who has argued that the hominid system of language has been made possible by the development of a new area within the brain: the posterior part of the parietal area. This new area he has termed the "association cortex of the association cortex." Not all students of brain evolution agree with Geschwind's model, which rests on a bipartite division of brain function. Still, the model provides a useful way of examining some aspects of brain function.

Geschwind (1964) has pointed out that, functionally, the mammalian brain can be divided into two systems: the **limbic** and the **nonlimbic.** The limbic system, located on the inner surfaces of the temporal lobes, deals basically with responses to nonpalpable (intangible), subjective kinds of stimuli; it is divided into two subsystems. The limbic motor response area deals with inborn reflexes to sensations, such as rage, fear, and sex; the limbic sensory response area deals with such sensations as smell, taste, hunger, thirst, and the corresponding satisfaction of these sensations. In terms of evolution, the limbic areas are the older areas of the brain. The nonlimbic system, located on the exposed surfaces of the brain, deals with responses to objective, palpable stimuli, such as vision, hearing, and touch.

These two major areas, the limbic and nonlimbic, do not directly connect with each other but, instead, connect with an association area where responses to the various stimuli are determined. It is in the association area that responses, both learned and unlearned, occur; the size and complexity of this area determine the extent and complexity of the behavioral response. The limbic and nonlimbic areas, along with the motor cortex, constitute what Geschwind calls the "primordial zones." In a mammal, such as a rabbit or a cat, the primordial zones account for much of the entire brain mass and the association area is very small. Thus, the potential for complex reactions is similarly small. In more advanced mammals, such as the primates, the primordial zones are separated by a larger association cortex, thus increasing the capability of the brain to code complex responses.

The limbic-nonlimbic associative responses may be simple, with little or no learning involved: the nonlimbic visual cue of a predator may elicit the limbic motor response of fear and flight; the visual cue of food or water may stimulate limbic responses of hunger or thirst. However, responses learned through limbic reinforcement may also occur. For example, in training a dog, obedience to the nonlimbic command to "sit" may be rewarded with food. This reward constitutes a positive reinforcement through the limbic system of gratification of the hunger sensation. Training can also occur with negative reinforcement through punishment that elicits the limbic response of fear. The same educational process may occur in a primate, such as a chimp. The chimp can be taught to choose between differently shaped objects, such as a cross and a circle; the "correct" choice will be rewarded with food. Thus the choice of the correct nonlimbic visual cue (the cross, say) will be positively reinforced with a limbic satisfaction of the sensation of hunger.

At this point in the chimp's learning process, Geschwind (1964) argued, we can demonstrate the basic and fundamental difference between the learning capability of a hominid and that of a pongid. An experiment can be constructed where the same circle and cross are put into a box; the chimp is required to reach into the box and select, by touch only, the "correct" one. This the chimp cannot do. It cannot take information learned in one nonlimbic mode, the visual, and transfer it to another nonlimbic mode, the tactile. Thus, the chimp cannot make associations between two nonlimbic modes, only between limbic and nonlimbic ones. However, a hominid can make such nonlimbic associations. A person, asked to make the same choice, can determine the cross by feel even when the only previous contact with the cross has been visual. Geschwind (1964) argued that humans can do this because they have invented a symbol, the word "cross" for the object. This symbol has reality in the various nonlimbic modes: the spoken word, the written word, and the touched object. Much human learning, in fact, takes place through such nonlimbic associations. Children learn to write, for example, by transforming an auditory cue (a spoken word) into a visual form (a written word). Reading aloud constitutes the transformation of a visual cue into an auditory one.

Geschwind (1964) has used the term **"verbal mediation"** for this process, and this ability to form a symbol that can be understood in a variety of modes may underlie the human ability to communicate. He has suggested that this naming ability, or verbal mediation, takes place in what he terms the "association cortex of the association cortex."

Holloway (1967) has suggested that once language and culture, even in incipient forms, became part of the hominid behavioral repertoire, they could have formed the basis of a new feedback system. Thus, advancement in communication ability may have allowed (or stimulated) advances in learned behavior patterns, such as tool manufacture or technology, hunting techniques, or other subsistence activities. Changes in these behavioral areas might have stimulated (or possibly demanded) further changes in language. In proposing this idea, Holloway has used data on rats which have indicated that an enriched environment can lead to greater brain development. An enriched environment for a rat includes mazes, toys, mirrors, other rats, etc. This brain development involves changes of several types: increase in total brain mass, increase in dendritic branching, and increase in the number of neurons. Thus, in a sense, "exercise" of the brain may lead to improvement of its function and an increase of its ability. We do not know whether these improvements can be passed on to future generations, but it is easy to see that such flexibility and adaptability in behavior would have a high selective advantage. In this case, then, it may have been the flexibility of behavior that was selected for rather than the advanced behavior pattern itself.

Aspects of Geschwind's model have found interesting support in the work of Bryan Robinson. Robinson's research has indicated that the vocalizations produced by nonhuman primates and by humans originate in different areas of the brain (1967, 1972). The vocalizations of the nonhuman primates originate, according to Robinson, in the deep, limbic areas of the brain, and they are thus closely tied to emotional or innate kinds of responses. As a result, they have a low informational content; such vocalizations may express fear, hunger, rage, etc., but complex responses are not possible. Robinson found that the full repertoire of vocalizations of monkeys could be elicited with direct electrical stimulation of the brain; thus, whether the sounds were elicited artificially through small electrical currents or were produced naturally by the animal, they were the same. By contrast, in humans, electrical stimulation of the brain will not produce the complex sounds and syllables of human speech. This finding indicated to Robinson that the vocalizations of the nonhuman primates are produced with little intervention of the higher (and more recently developed) areas of the brain. As we will see below, there are anatomical, as well as neurological, reasons for this difference.

In humans, vocalizations seem to be produced both by the deep limbic areas of the brain and by the nonlimbic areas; and several areas of the neocortex seem to be involved in different aspects of the production of speech (see Penfield and Roberts, 1959). The informational content of human speech is greater than that of pongid vocalization; and speech is more independent of the basic emotional responses, since it is produced largely by the higher and more evolved areas of the brain. Thus, there are basic differences in the neurological production of speech by humans and by their nonhuman relatives.

There are also anatomical differences between humans and the other primates in the production of vocalizations. Although the anatomical structures (Figure 5-6) concerned with this production are basically the same in all primates, certain important differences in the relative size and position of these structures exist. Vocalizations are produced when the flow of air coming up from the larynx, through the pharynx, and into the cavity of the mouth is constricted or impeded at any of several points. These constrictions cause variations in pitch and tone, resulting in different sounds. The constrictions may occur by movement of the two membranes called the "vocal chords" or by varying the position of the tongue in relation to other structures in the mouth. The tongue may impede the flow of air at the upper end of the pharynx or at the roof or front of the mouth (see Robins, 1964). Movements of the lips further alter the stream of air. Depending on the degree of closure and the position of the tongue in relation to the palate, lips, and teeth, different sounds are produced. When the back of the tongue impedes the air flow at the top of the pharynx, for example, the initial sounds of "come" and "go" are produced; when it rests against the top of the mouth, the initial sound of "yet" and "yeast" is made. The large size and great flexibility of the human tongue make it a vital part of the production of the wide variety of human speech sounds. The large tongue is a human feature; the tongue is much smaller in the other primates (see Lieberman, 1968, 1972)—too small to produce the many diverse sounds characteristic of humans. Moreover, in nonhuman primates, the larynx is situated high, almost at the level of the palate (Lieberman, 1968, 1972); in humans, it is situated much lower in the neck. As a result, the variety of sounds produced by the back of the tongue altering the upper end of the pharynx is not possible in nonhuman primates. Thus, the smaller tongue and shorter pharynx in the nonhuman primates result in considerable restriction of the variety of sounds they can produce. It would seem, then, that the nonhuman primates have neither the neurological nor the anatomical ability to produce the range of human speech sounds.

BEHAVIORAL CHARACTERISTICS

Hominids and other primates share a number of behavioral activities; meat eating and tool use, for example, occur not only in some apes but also in some monkeys (see Chapter 1). However, if one looks at the total behavioral set or pattern, it is possible to see that these features, and other associated behaviors, occur in markedly different proportions in human and nonhuman primates.

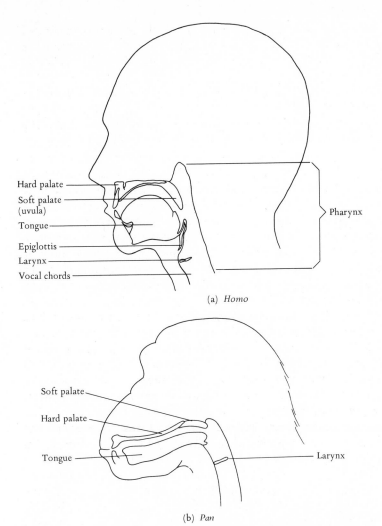

Hard palate

Soft palate
(uvula)

Tongue

Epiglottis

Larynx

Vocal chords

Pharynx

(a) *Homo*

Soft palate

Hard palate

Tongue

Larynx

(b) *Pan*

FIGURE 5-6 The almost infinite variety of human vocalizations rests in part on the anatomical structures of speech. **(a)** In humans, the upper, anterior wall of the pharynx is formed by the rear portion of the tongue. The thick human tongue can vary the shape of the upper pharynx, thereby allowing a great variety in sound production. **(b)** By comparison, in *Pan* the tongue is thinner and the upper pharyngeal space is much less variable. Sound production is, therefore, very limited.

One particular set of hominid behaviors may be interrelated in that the function of each of the behavioral components impinges upon, and may influence, the success of other components. In fact, this particular set, involving the use of a home base, food sharing, meat eating, tool use, and carrying may reflect a positive feedback system.

It is important to recognize, however, that we know nothing about the behavioral characteristics of the earliest hominids; no information has survived. Moreover, although behavioral information is preserved at some Plio-Pleistocene sites, we cannot be sure which of the two or more hominid lines existing at that time was responsible for the artifacts and living débris. Paleoanthropologists can never be entirely certain who or what occupied a particular living site. This introduces a major ambiguity into such studies, since human bones found within a site may represent prey or predator.

Home Base

Some primates, such as the gelada baboons (genus *Theropithecus*) and the hamadryas baboons (genus *Papio*), will frequently return to a particular site for certain kinds of activities. These baboons, for example, frequently reoccupy the same sleeping place on the side of a cliff. Only hominids, however, focus a variety of activities, such as eating and toolmaking, as well as sleeping, at a single site. Indeed, such sites are recognized by the scatterings of butchered and fragmented animal bones and stone tools. Thus, the establishment of a home base is an important hominid behavioral trait; such sites can be clearly identified in levels dated to as early as 2.5 m.y. ago, and may well have existed even earlier (Isaac, 1976b).

It is apparent from the archeological record that the earliest home-base sites were occupied for only short periods, perhaps only for the length of time needed to consume the fruits of a single crop or a single killed or scavenged animal. In later times, however, the débris of human activity becomes thicker, indicating longer stays during each occupation. Such sites also become stratified or layered, indicating that human groups returned again and again to the same locality.

Division of Labor

The focusing of living activities on a certain home-base site, for whatever length of time, may have other behavioral implications. For example, by focusing sleeping, feeding, and toolmaking activities on a certain site, individuals may be permitted to carry out specific activities separately during the day. This division of labor on the basis of sex, age, or skill would allow the exploitation of a much wider range of environmental products than if the entire group foraged together. Thus, with the home base clearly defined and recognized by the hominid band, smaller groups (females with infants, juveniles, and older males, for example) could move out to collect, hunt, or scavenge the variety of items necessary for the survival of the entire group. In this way, the responsibility for group survival would depend on individual activities performed within a framework of cooperative action. This pattern would reinforce the structure of the group by reinforcing a system of interdependencies and mutual obligations.

A model of the division of labor, particularly along sexual lines, has been developed by Campbell (1966, 1976). There is, however, an important negative aspect to fragmentation of the social group, especially when it occurs on a sexual basis. One of the functions of the large social grouping typical of some savanna-living primates is that it provides protection against predation. Few predators will attack a group of savanna-living baboons, although outliers or stragglers may be killed. If the group fragments, the protective element of group size is lost. Further, if the fragmented units consist largely of females and young, poorly equipped to deal with predators, loss of individuals from such groups would probably be high. Therefore, while the division of labor may be advantageous in allowing a variety of activities, it also has important disadvantages in exposing reproductively essential group members to predation.

Meat Eating and Food Sharing

The habitual and frequent sharing of food is a further important hominid characteristic. Other animals, such as birds and the social carnivores, also share food. In these animals, food sharing is most often practiced between parent and offspring or between adult male and adult female during mating or courting behavior. Food sharing is, however, a rare activity among the primates. It is an interesting and perhaps relevant observation that on those rare occasions when nonhuman primates do share food, it is almost always meat that is shared; the usual primate dietary items of fruits, leaves, and grasses are very seldom shared. Perhaps the hominid pattern of food sharing grew out of the occasional, and gradually more frequent, consumption of hunted or scavenged meat.

Hominids are the only primates to consume meat regularly and frequently, and the archeological record indicates that this pattern has a long history. As pointed out above, the earliest home-base sites; dated to about 2.5 m.y. ago, contain fragments of butchered animals; one of the oldest of these sites contains a hippo. By about 2 m.y. ago, the hominids were consuming a wide variety of animal foods. The site called "DK"[3] at Olduvai Gorge, dating to about this time, contains an amazing array of animal remains. There are animals associated with water, such as frogs, snails, crocodiles, and fish; birds, such as ostriches and flamingos; and large mammals, such as rhinos, hippos, elephants, giraffes, horses, five types of pigs, and ten types of bovids (M. D. Leakey, 1971a).

We cannot be sure whether these animals were actively hunted or were simply scavenged after dying from other causes. Both hunting and scavenging have their implicit dangers, either from the prey during the hunt or from other scavengers after the kill. It does seem more probable, however, that the very large animals, such as hippos and elephants, were scavenged, while the array of smaller animals, birds, and aquatic forms may well have been actively sought.

[3]Sites in Olduvai Gorge are named for various people; "D" in "DK" stands for Douglas, Louis Leakey's brother. "K" stands for Korongo, the Masai word for "gulley" or "ravine."

This concentration of a diversity of animal foods at Olduvai and at other early hominid sites is significant: There appears to be a logical and close relationship between meat eating and the use of a home base. The usual pattern of the nonhuman primates' feeding behaviors may take them long distances from the sleeping site, and feeding activities may be spread out over most of the daylight hours. Yet, this concentration of food remains at certain sites indicates that the hominids were not eating all the fruits of their foraging as they collected them but were returning with at least some of the food to their camp. As pointed out, food sharing may be a logical consequence of meat eating. The hunters (or scavengers), unable to consume all the meat, may have transported some to the home base for those who had been involved in other activities.

There is thus an obvious difference between hominids and other primates in their feeding behaviors, and the indications are that by 2 m.y. ago feeding had become a communal activity. It then follows that the consumption of animal foods allows feeding activities to be both concentrated in time and focused in space.

The frequent and consistent consumption of animal foods might have other ramifications. Such foods are compact and easily transportable; they are also nutritionally efficient for a hominid. The protein-calorie value of meat per unit of weight, for example, is greater than that of other foods normally consumed by primates. Moreover, meat supplies the full range of amino acids that are essential for normal hominid growth and development; no single fruit or vegetable food supplies this range of nutrients. If such a compact and efficient source of nutrition were secured by only certain members of the group, then a pattern of social and even physiological interdependencies might arise between the meat suppliers and the rest of the consuming group.

Tool Manufacture and Use

A number of animals use tools; for example, both Galapagos finches and chimps use wooden sticks as probes, and sea otters use stones as hammers to open shells. However, only hominids alter objects according to a consistent plan and design. The consistent production of manufactured, planned objects, such as tools, implies that a pattern of design and use was being transmitted not only horizontally within a contemporaneous group but also vertically between generations.

Even in the earliest stone tool tradition, the Oldowan, it is clear that detailed information about tool manufacture was being transmitted. For example, the spheroidal stone balls typical of such assemblages occur in the same form throughout Beds I and II at Olduvai Gorge, covering a period of about 1 m.y. Moreover, information regarding tool manufacture was being transmitted not only vertically through time, but also horizontally between groups. Such stone balls occur at a number of sites in both east and north Africa and at Ubeidiya in Israel. By the time the Acheulian tradition appeared about 1.5 m.y. ago, it is clear that complex, detailed information regarding flaking techniques, tool shape, and raw materials was being transmitted very widely. By Middle Pleistocene times, standardized Acheulian hand axes had become a universal stone tool throughout Africa, Europe, and parts of western Asia.

Information about tool manufacture may have been transmitted verbally; indeed, some anthropologists have seen in this possibility the origin of the human pattern of speech. Alternatively, however, the communication of such information could have been nonverbal, as by gestures. Visually demonstrating the correct way to knock flakes from a rock seems much easier than describing the process in words. Therefore, verbal communication and patterned tool manufacture and use are not necessarily interrelated activities.

Carrying

The occurrence of both food remains and tools at a certain locality implies that the ability to carry, as an anatomical capability and a behavioral activity, may be a basic and long-standing hominid characteristic. Isaac. for example, has stressed the importance of container objects, such as bags or trays, in the development and reinforcement of such transport (1971, 1976b). Thus, carrying, container objects, and a home base are necessarily interrelated features. The use of container objects meant that more materials (gathered, scavenged, or hunted foods and raw materials for tools) could be obtained at one time. Such practices would indicate planning for future needs and contingencies; it would, moreover, imply an awareness of needs beyond immediate requirements.

Loss of Estrus

"Estrus" (or "heat") is the term for the periodic sexual receptivity characteristic of all mammals except the hominids. The period of estrus is very apparent in nonhuman primates, usually resulting in olfactory or visual cues to the male, such as swelling of the skin surrounding the female genitalia. During estrus, sexual activity becomes the prime focus of activity, and other forms of behavior and interrelationships may be interrupted. In hominids, however, there is no such clearly defined period of sexual receptivity, and the human female is more or less continuously receptive to the male.

Some anthropologists have suggested that loss of estrus in the hominids may have important effects on social interactions. Campbell (1966, p. 254) has summarized the possible social effects of loss of estrus:

1. Child rearing lasts longer without loss of reproductive capability.
2. Relatively permanent male-female relationships (pair bonding) in a less competitive sexual atmosphere are possible.

3. Sexual drives become more readily subject to social control.

Thus, Campbell has tied the loss of estrus in hominids to broader categories of social structures and behaviors; he sees this loss as a vital factor in the patterning of human interactions. In his view, once the periodically disruptive effects of estrus activities are diminished or lost, more stable relationships, both between adults and between mothers and offspring, become possible.

However, this particular set of behaviors does not necessarily form an interactive or interdependent system. For example, some primate groups, such as the hamadryas baboons, form strong pair bonds without a decrease in estrus activity. Therefore, stable male-female bonds are not necessarily tied to continuous sexual receptivity (Kummer, 1971). Moreover, the presence of an estrus female does not necessarily result in the disruption of normal social interactions. In the hamadryas, for example, the presence of an estrus female does not attract males other than her own consort, and no fighting between males occurs (Kummer, 1971). Therefore, the presence or absence of estrus is not closely related to pair bonding and social stability.

The hominids are thus characterized by certain morphological and behavioral characters. Separately, few of these characters are unique and most may be found in other mammals. It is therefore the occurrence of a set or complex of characters that distinguishes the family Hominidae, or indeed, any group.

Since it is the set of characters that is distinctive, it is the set that should be used in understanding the adaptive pattern of the hominids. A number of anthropologists have tried to use this set in order to understand the ultimate origins of the family.

THEORIES OF HOMINID ORIGINS

The evidence of a close relationship between hominids and the living African great apes cannot be doubted. Comparative anatomical evidence clearly shows the presence of many shared functional and structural similarities. Comparative embryological studies have also documented the strong resemblances present during the developmental phases. Further, biochemical studies[4] have revealed that in the minute structures of body

---

[4]These studies are based on comparative analyses of various proteins, such as hemoglobin and albumin and DNA. Such studies appear to have the ability to quantify the differences (or similarities) among groups of living animals. Some workers have extrapolated from these data in an attempt to define the point in time at which certain animal groups diverged (Sarich and Wilson, 1967; Sarich, 1968; A. C. Wilson and Sarich, 1969; Sarich, 1970). This extrapolation is based in part on the hypothesis that the changes in protein structures (amino acid substitutions) occur at a regular, constant rate. This hypothesis is untestable; therefore, the usefulness of these biochemical studies to evolutionary studies is uncertain.

proteins, the African great apes and hominids show remarkable and close similarities that could not have arisen merely by chance. However, the ape line and the human line do have important distinctions, the evolutionary significance and origin of which have been the subject of continuing controversy.

CANINE REDUCTION, TOOL USE, BIPEDALITY, AND CARRYING

The hominid pattern of morphological characters forms an integrated and interactive complex. Beginning with Darwin and continuing through Washburn (1960), Bartholomew and Birdsell (1953), and others, it has been pointed out that a forelimb freed from locomotor activities may allow the manufacture, use, and transport of tools; that reduced canines and incisors may be related to such tool use; and that the continuing use of tools may both reinforce and provide new selective backgrounds for more complex brain development. The feedback model present in such interactive circularity is apparent.

Darwin formulated the earliest discussion of such a pattern. He suggested that tool use was both a cause and an effect of bipedality. The initial acquisition of even partial bipedal locomotion would have left the hands free and available for manipulating tools. This incipient tool use presumably proved so helpful and "adaptive" that it reinforced the development of bipedality, thereby allowing the more frequent and complex use of tools. As tool use became more habitual, it took over more and more of the functions of the large primate canine as a defensive and offensive weapon and in the preparation of food. Such removal of the active functions of the canine resulted in a reduction in its size.

Washburn (1960) further developed Darwin's concept and placed these changes in an anatomical and functional framework. He described, for example, how a reduction in canine size would be reflected in many parts of the skull. A large canine implies powerful jaws, which in turn require well-developed musculature. The size of this musculature is reflected in the formation of sagittal cresting, in widely flared zygomatic arches, and in deep mandibles. A large canine further implies powerful neck musculature, resulting in bony crests on the occipital bone. All these features are characteristic of the pongids.

Washburn concluded that the skull structure of the early hominids is simply

> that of an ape that has lost the structure for effective fighting with its teeth. Moreover, the man-ape has transferred to its hands the function of seizing and pulling, and this has been attended by reduction of its incisors. Small canines and incisors are biological symbols of a changed way of life; their primitive functions are replaced by hand and tool. (1960, p. 69)

Bartholomew and Birdsell (1953) have argued from much the same point of view, but they have focused on the effects of the hominid adaptation to a terrestrial habitat, rather than on the arboreal habitat characteristic of most other primates. They have pointed out that the hominid form of bipedality is so unusual in the animal world that its acquisition

> implies that a significant non-locomotor advantage must have resulted from even the partial freeing of the forelimbs. This advantage was the use of the hands for efficient manipulation of adventitious tools such as rocks, sticks or bones. Of course, the terrestrial or semi-terrestrial living primates have their hands free when they are not moving, but only man has his locomotion essentially unimpeded while carrying or using a tool. (1953, p. 482)

Such arguments are internally very cohesive, and their very circularity is compelling. However, these models, resting on an interrelationship between canine reduction, tool use, bipedality, and carrying, can be criticized from several standpoints.

First, paleontological and archeological evidence indicates that bipedality preceded tool use by a period of considerable time. A humerus from Kanapoi in Kenya (see Chapter 6), dated to between 4 and 4.5 m.y. ago, constitutes indirect evidence of early bipedality. This fragment suggests a morphologically unstabilized elbow, unlike that required in a quadruped; in fact, the humerus is very like that of *Homo sapiens*. More direct evidence of early bipedality is found in pelves from Sterkfontein, South Africa, and Hadar, Ethiopia, dated to between 2 and 3 m.y. ago (see Chapters 6 and 7). These pelves are extraordinarily well adapted to erect bipedality; by virtue of their degree of morphological adjustment, they must represent a long-term evolutionary and locomotor pattern. Tools, however, cannot be documented before about 2.5 m.y. ago. This limitation, of course, does not disprove earlier tool use, but no evidence of earlier tool assemblages is now known.

Second, although the models cited above focus on the cause-effect relationships between bipedality and carrying, bipedality in nonhuman primates and other mammals can serve functions other than carrying. For example, bipedality is often used to increase visualization during searching. Many animals, such as rats, mice, squirrels, and marmots, as well as primates, stand erect while scanning their surroundings but continue to move quadrupedally. The Koshima macaques, referred to in Chapter 1, do carry food bipedally, it is true, but such carrying actions are very rare in other primate groups. The common form of carrying in primates and other mammals is to carry the object in the mouth, clenched between the teeth. Alternatively, primates may carry an object in one hand while moving tripedally. In fact, tripedal locomotion can be rapid and is apparently efficient, at least for short distances. Field observations have indicated that bipedal carrying in primates may be limited to occasions when a number of items are being transported; single items are carried either in the mouth or in one hand (Kummer, personal communication, 1977).

The assumption of the models regarding the origins of hominid bipedality, mentioned above, is that bipedality is directly and clearly related in some way to the hominid adaptive pattern. Thus, tool use, bipedality, canine reduction, and carrying are regarded as parts of a single and integrated adaptive response. This is not necessarily true, and the Koshima macaques again provide an example. These macaques have acquired the behavioral pattern of washing sweet potatoes and wheat in the sea. This practice brought them into contact with the previously unexploited marine environment. Once they developed an intimate acquaintance with the sea, some began swimming; as familiarity increased, one macaque even swam to a nearby island (Kawai, 1965). In this case, the new locomotor pattern of swimming was not itself a direct adaptation but represented a by-product of a new feeding behavior. We cannot know, then, if hominid bipedality is a direct response to an adaptive need, such as carrying, or represents the by-product of another, but unrecognized, evolutionary response.

Third, the reduction of the canine is regarded in the models of Darwin and Washburn as being indicative of tool use. Canine reduction, according to these models, implies that the function of the canine has been replaced by a tool. Yet, marked canine reduction occurred in the hominids and some hominoids many millions of years before any documented tool use. The earliest known hominids of 15 m.y. ago, *Ramapithecus*, had such a reduced canine. In the absence of any empirical evidence, it seems very unlikely that canine reduction in this genus could have been associated with regular or habitual tool use. Moreover, in Plio-Pleistocene times, the smallest canine found in any hominid is that of the robust australopithecines (see Chapters 6 and 7). The canine in this group is very small both in absolute size and in relation to the other teeth. This group appears to represent a specialized, herbivorous side branch of the hominids, and tool use has not been indicated as part of its behavioral repertoire. Moreover, a degree of canine reduction also occurred in some dryopithecines, in the Oligocene form *Propliopithecus*, and in the Miocene forms *Oreopithecus* and *Gigantopithecus*. Yet, tool use has never been postulated for these groups either. There is, then, no a priori reason why tool use and canine reduction are necessarily related features. The reduction of the primate canine can occur, and has occurred, without tool use.

It is therefore possible to demonstrate that the components of the so-called "Washburnian syndrome"—canine reduction, tool use, bipedality, and carrying—are not necessarily interrelated in an evolutionary sense. Moreover, the seductive circularity of such a pattern clouds the fact that the demonstration of an interrelationship within a functional complex (spurious or not) does not reflect on the *origin* of any of these features. In other words, the demonstration that features may be adaptively related does not shed any light on how that morphological complex originated. The search for hominid origins may thus become the search for an "initial kick."

ENVIRONMENTAL FACTORS

Several authors have sought the source of the "initial kick" in the environmental changes that were occurring in the Late Tertiary; among them are Hockett and Asher (1964). They have correctly pointed out that the time of the protohominids was one of climatological change; drying and cooling trends continued to affect both global and local weather patterns, with the result that the nature and extent of local habitats were in the process of change. They have further emphasized that most evolution is conservative; that is, evolutionary changes often are adaptations that permit a population to maintain its existence in a changing environment. This concept has been termed "Romer's rule" after the paleontologist who first discussed it with reference to Late Paleozoic lobe-finned fishes. Romer observed that the Late Paleozoic was a time of vast climatic changes when many habitats were diminishing or disappearing entirely. The lobe-finned fishes occupied bodies of water that were subject to drying; those fishes having fins sufficiently strong (the "lobe fins") to move over the intervening dry land to the next pond were the survivors. These survivors, Romer suggested, were the ancestors of the first terrestrial vertebrates, the amphibians. These lobe-finned fishes thus used an already-existing structure to help maintain their existence in their traditional aquatic habitat. Actually, then, the lobe fins were a **preadaptation** useful in the gradual acquisition of land habitats.

In applying this theoretical construction to the origin of the hominids, Hockett and Asher (1964) pointed out that the climatic changes of the Late Tertiary effectively caused a diminution of the continuous forest environments, the traditional habitats of the primates. The acquisition of bipedality, they argued, was an adaptation to efficient movement over the intervening grassland to the next stand of forest. However, that next stand of forest was already occupied by the ancestors of the present-day pongids. Therefore, the protohominids, unable to fight aggressively for their original environment against the entrenched occupants, were forced to adapt to the savanna. The alternative was extinction. It is at this point that Hockett and Asher reverted to the usual feedback model of bipedality and carrying.

There are useful ideas in this presentation, particularly in the attempt to relate hominid origins to general paleontological theory. Too often, hominid evolution is assumed to have proceeded by a "special" category of processes. Nevertheless, the application of Romer's rule in this particular case does not seem to work. Why should bipedality be especially adaptive in the grassland? "Carrying" is not an adequate explanation, since other primates, such as baboons and patas monkeys, demonstrate effective and long-term grassland occupations that involve neither bipedality nor habitual carrying. The chief difficulty here, it seems, is in placing the major emphasis on the grassland as being, in itself, the main source of selective pressure in the emergence of the Hominidae. It would be better to investigate, in a particulate way, those factors within the grassland environment that may have provided selective pressures of sufficient force to have acted as the "initial kick."

THE DIETARY HYPOTHESIS

Clifford Jolly (1970) has attempted to identify such a selective pressure. Jolly approached the explanation of hominid origins by suggesting that two major and separate steps were involved; he calls them "phase 1" and "phase 2." Both represent complex adaptive patterns arising out of the utilization of available food resources.

In the formulation of his hypothesis, Jolly first examined the theoretical foundations of earlier models of hominid origins, which have focused mainly on the behavioral, dietary, and locomotor implications of anterior tooth reduction. If one postulates that the reduction in size of the incisors and canines reflects tool use, then one must explain why modern savanna-living chimps, which are regular tool users (Goodall, 1964; Kortlandt, 1967), have the largest relative anterior dentition of any living pongid, including the gorilla. One must also explain why the fossil apes, such as *Propliopithecus* and *Oreopithecus*, had considerable anterior dental reduction, although tool use has never been suggested for these genera. These observations, Jolly contends, suggest that there is not a direct causal relationship between relatively small incisors and canines and tool use.

Jolly has also criticized the savanna–hunting-ape model of hominid origins. He has pointed out that of those primates which have made adaptations to the savanna-grassland (baboons, patas, some chimps), none has taken up carnivory as its major subsistence base, as later hominids did. Baboons and chimps do catch and eat meat, but it never forms a consistent or major portion of their diet. He concluded from this that mere occupation of the grassland environment does not turn a primate into a hominid.

On the basis of this evidence, Clifford Jolly (1970) has concluded that the model based on tool use, anterior dental reduction, and meat eating cannot explain the origin of the morphological pattern that differentiates the Hominidae from the Pongidae. He has suggested that this morphological pattern is best explained as an adaptation to a diet consisting largely of seeds and grains, the most easily available and accessible foods in a savanna-grassland environment. This pattern of feeding on hard, small objects Jolly has termed **"granivorous";** it characterizes phase 1 hominids. Such a diet might have been supplemented by a wide range of small vertebrates and invertebrates and fruits, leaves, and vegetation that would be locally and seasonally available. Probably the most important and useful aspect of Jolly's seed-eating hypothesis (1970) is his demonstration that such a diet could, in fact, be related to just that morphological pattern present in the jaws and teeth of the earliest hominids. In the formulation of the seed-eating hypothesis, Jolly has noted the existence of a number of morphological and functional parallels between the early hominids and *Theropithecus*, the living gelada baboon. These parallels include the following:

Both occupied grassland–open-country habitats.

Both have incisors and canines which are reduced relative to the premolars and molars.

Both show crowding of the cheek teeth, with the presence of interstitial wear between the teeth.

Both have the anterior fibers of the temporalis muscle set well forward on the frontal bone, thus maximizing the efficiency and power of this muscle.

Both have a mandible which is robust and thick under the cheek teeth.

Both have a flexible hand.

Clifford Jolly concluded:

> There seems no good reason against attributing the *Theropithecus*-like incisal proportions and jaw characters of the early hominids to a similar adaptation to a diet of small, tough objects. There is no need to postulate a compensatory use of cutting tools for food preparation, until it can be shown archaeologically that such tools were being made. (1970, p. 14)

As we will see, however, the full story may be more complex than this model indicates. Jolly's hypothesis demands an initial occupation of the grassland; that is, he views the hominid morphological complex as an adaptation to grassland foods. Paleontological and paleoecological evidence indicates, however, that the earliest known hominids did not occupy a full grassland habitat but were living with other apes in woodland areas where grasslands as well as other habitats were available nearby. We will return to this important point shortly.

The phase 2 hominids, according to Jolly, arose out of populations with the adaptations and preadaptations present in phase 1, and they reflect continuing small, but nevertheless important, changes in the environment. Such changes may have meant only that the seasonal differences were more pronounced, thereby decreasing the amount of available grains during one season.[5]

Such a dietary deficit, Jolly argued, may have forced greater reliance on alternative sources of food. Of the various foods available to a primate in a grassland, meat is the most efficient in terms of protein and calories. A greater dependence on meat would have had a significant effect on the social and cultural aspects of the hominid emergence. Males, according to Jolly, would have taken over the acquisition of meat while females would have been responsible for gathering plant foods. Tool use would have occurred in response to the need for skinning and disarticulating meat without the aid of a large canine.

An interesting sidelight to this model has recently been provided by Elaine Morgan in *Descent of Woman* (1972). She has pointed out that this model, focusing as it does on the male contribution, is highly chauvinistic. Hunting and its technologic demands and ramifications are often regarded as the basic evolutionary pressure underlying hominid emergence. She emphasizes that humans are social creatures and that stable male-female relationships contribute not only to group stability, but also to support of the long-maturing young. Moreover, the male-contributed meat was probably highly supplemented with plant·foods at times.

These are valid criticisms; however, we need not dismiss hunting as an important evolutionary factor in order to build a female-oriented model. The behavioral patterns and biological roles of both sexes undoubtedly played important parts in the emergence of the human.

COMPETITION HYPOTHESES

Jolly's seed-eating hypothesis is an attractive model which fits many of the known facts of hominid development very well. It does not, however, fit the evidence of the earliest known hominids. As paleoecological and paleontological investigations of the earliest hominid sites in Africa, Europe, and India have proceeded, it has become clear that the earliest known members of the family Hominidae were associated with woodland or mixed environments and not solely with savanna habitats. While most workers have undoubtedly been aware of the fact that *Ramapithecus* was sympatric with other hominoids in east Africa, Europe, and India, they have unaccountably ignored the fact of that sympatry. Some have continued to postulate a grassland environment for the earliest hominids while accepting a forest environment for *Dryopithecus* and *Sivapithecus*,

[5]This is in concurrence with Liebig's "law of the minimum"; this ecological theorem states that populations must adapt to the availability of a major resource in its minimum quantity (see Odum, 1959).

although both were, in many cases, found in the same levels of the same site. It is undoubtedly true that after about 9 m.y. ago the hominids did occupy grasslands and that these habitats may have been very important in the course and direction of later hominid development. However, grassland adaptation cannot be responsible for the initial appearance of the Hominidae.

At Fort Ternan in Kenya, for example, *Ramapithecus* was associated with three species of dryopithecines and a loris-like prosimian. As Andrews and Walker point out, "all the living counterparts of these primates are exclusively forest living" (1976, p. 301). Animals from more open types of habitats, such as bovids and ostriches, are also present, indicating the local availability of different habitats. Similarly, in both India and Europe, *Ramapithecus* is associated with other hominoids and faunas composed largely, but not entirely, of woodland elements (Tattersall, 1969a, b). Yet, *Ramapithecus* already differed detectably and morphologically from even closely related primates. Thus, morphological change in the first hominids preceded their move to the savanna.

We may look to this demonstrated sympatry between hominoids and ramapithecines for evidence of the "initial kick" in the first appearance of the Hominidae.

Chapter 1 contained a discussion of the evolutionary and selective pressures which may occur under conditions of sympatry. When members of different species compete for the same limited environmental resources, such as food, space, and water, there may be several consequences. For example, one of the competitor species may become extinct or may simply leave the area. Either way, the competitive pressures will diminish. Alternatively, the competing species may remain in sympatry, but, through the exploitation of narrower, more restricted areas of the local habitat, competition may also decrease. This latter situation may have occurred in the divergence of the hominids from the pongids. We know that in east Africa, for example, five or more species of ape were in local sympatry for a period of at least 2 million years. Such a long-term sympatry indicates that competition among the various species must have remained at acceptable levels. Thus some primates, such as the early hylobatids, may have progressively exploited their ability to use the higher portions of the trees and the topmost canopy. Other primates, such as the dryopithecines, may have used the lower portions of the same trees as food sources, nesting places, and refuges.

With the variety of dryopithecine species contemporaneously present in east Africa during the earlier part of the Miocene, competition for food and space in the lower portions of the trees must have been intense. Therefore, some species may have begun to use more resources of the forest floor, thus diminishing competition in the trees; hominids may be descendants of one such group.

By Middle Miocene times competition would inevitably have become very stringent because the area of the forest was diminishing; especially in the marginal forest areas of east Africa and Asia, competition for the already limited forest resources would have become very strong. The behavioral and morphological features developed by the early hominids in the exploitation of food resources on the forest floor then became even more advantageous. These adaptations for forest-floor foods became usable, if not vital, preadaptations for savanna foods. The more efficient grinding teeth, initially developed for the harsher forest foods, became the imperative and essential morphological "tool" to accompany the early hominids in the exploitation of the new habitat.

It is then possible that the initial step toward hominidization occurred when a population of hominoids began to exploit foods and other environmental resources that were not traditionally a major part of their pattern; relatively soft tree foods, such as fruits and leaves, would have been gradually replaced by harsher, "chewier" forest-floor foods, such as grasses, roots, and seeds. The "initial kick" would then have been a behavioral one involving a progressive change in the selection of diet items, and this "kick" would itself have resulted from the intense competition of the sympatric and closely related primates.

Once the beginning of such a pattern had emerged, other factors may have both reinforced the dietary practices and laid the ground for still other behavioral and morphological changes. The exploitation of forest-floor foods and the occupation of the forest-grassland margin would then have provided new selective foundations for the incorporation of genetic variations into the gene pool.

The forest-grassland margin may itself have been especially influential in the selection and reinforcement of certain selective patterns. In such a mosaic of microenvironments, the behavioral flexibility characteristic of all anthropoids would have been at a selective premium. The earliest hominids occupying the forest-grassland margin may well have responded by drawing not only on their morphological preadaptations for grassland foods but also on their behavioral adaptability and flexibility.

Thus, precise morphological specializations may not have been selectively advantageous in the complex, variable, and varying microenvironments of the Middle Miocene forest fringe. What may, instead, have been advantageous was a laterality and flexibility of response in terms of diet, morphology, and locomotion.

NEOTENY

One factor which increases the behavioral flexibility of an animal is its ability to learn and to incorporate learned behavior patterns from other members of its social group. In primates, as in all other animals, the period of most intense learning occurs during growth and development. Therefore, if the growth period can be extended, it seems logical that the period of learning may similarly be extended.

In the late nineteenth and early twentieth centuries, some observers noted a close resemblance between the juveniles of certain pongids and humans. The adults of these same ape species, however, were quite unlike humans in appearance. These observations led to a number of theories postulating that the human phenotype was due to the retention of juvenile or fetal characters in the adult. The term "neoteny" was proposed by Kollmann in 1905 to describe such retention, and in 1926 Louis Bolk published an important paper which fully developed these concepts and their application to humans.

Bolk's theory rests on the retention of fetal or juvenile characters in the adult through a slowed rate of maturation. These "retarded" features of the hominids include a globular skull without brow ridges, an orthognathous face without protrusion of the jaws, the forward position of the foramen magnum, a nonopposable big toe, and a number of other features. Bolk concluded that the delayed rate of maturation was due to a hormonal alteration which slowed the rate of growth.

This theory does not explain all hominid characters. Bipedality and its associated muscular and skeletal correlates cannot, for example, be included within the hypothesis. Also, Bolk never recognized or stated a selective advantage in such retarded development.

However, the theory has been revived in a form more concordant with the theory of natural selection (see Montagu, 1962). Gould (1975, 1977) accepts slowed, neotenous growth rates in the hominids. He points out that gorillas attain 70 percent of their total brain size in their first year of life, while the human brain does not reach this percentage of final size until the third year. Other features, such as closure of the skull sutures and skeletal and sexual maturation, also occur later than in other primates. Gould differs from Bolk, however, in contending that such slowed growth rates may have an important natural selective advantage.

Gould suggests that for humans, survival depends on the ability to learn rather than on morphological specializations. By slowing the growth rate, the period of learning can be extended. This lengthens the time of contact between generations, thus increasing the opportunity for passing on learned behavior patterns and information. The delay in maturation through a slowed rate of growth would allow more information to be acquired during the active, curious period of childhood and adolescence without the physiological distractions of mating. Thus, Gould recognizes a strong selective advantage in the slowed growth rate of the hominids related to an increase in the period of learning and experimentation.

There may also be advantages of a biochemical nature in a slowed rate of development. As we have seen in Chapter 2, Goodman (1963) has suggested that the haemochorial type of placentation, typical of the higher primates, results in a greater exchange of fetal and maternal proteins than does the epitheliochorial placentation typical of the prosimians (except *Tarsius*). This means that proteins active at the fetal stage in the higher primates must be very conservative in an evolutionary sense, since mutant fetal proteins are likely to be destroyed by the maternal antibodies. The mutations with the greatest chance of survival in the higher primates would be those that were manifested after birth. However, although it would be advantageous to delay the appearance of adult proteins, this delay would also result in a very immature offspring. Therefore, any factor, such as maternal care, which aided the survival of the immature offspring, Goodman argues, would be selectively advantageous.

Both the haemochorial placenta and an increase in maturation time are characteristic of all higher primates and are not specific characters of the hominids. Maturation time, however, is longest in the hominids, and it is possible that the behavioral components in offspring survival are greater in that group.

The fossil record offers some support for the theories that base certain hominid morphological patterns on growth retardation. For example, the subadult phase of some Miocene hominoids shows a manifest hominid dental pattern. These features include a shallow, robust mandible; a short, vertically implanted canine; lack of a diastema in the tooth row; closely packed cheek teeth; and a nearly vertical ascending ramus.

The similarity of the subadult hominoid dental morphology with that of adult hominids was clearly indicated in the case of a sivapithecine mandible from northern Greece. Although this mandible has been attributed to a new hominoid genus, *Ouranopithecus* (de Bonis and Melentis, 1977), its small canine, shallow mandible, and other features caused some anthropologists to consider it a member of the Hominidae. When eight more jaws, some from adults, were recovered from the same site, it was recognized that the "hominid" features of the first mandible were due to its youth and not to any hominid affinities.

This evidence may well indicate that growth rates were slowing in at least one lineage of Miocene apes. It is logical to argue that the retention of these subadult features in the adult would result in a full hominid dental pattern. Whether or not this would result in a hominid must await further fossil evidence.

In some ways these theories centering on the significance of delayed growth are among the most satisfying of all the theories of hominid origins. They are satisfying in the sense that they rest ultimately on the most apparent of all hominid traits, the human intellect. They are also highly complementary to the theories of hominid origins based on competition and dietary adaptation. Many animals have evolved unique behavior patterns on which their survival depends. The ritualized mating behavior of some birds, the social stratification of bees and ants, the gregarious herding instincts of zebras and antelopes are all survival-oriented behaviors. Yet, in none are those behaviors as intelligently and effectively interposed between the environment and the organism as in the human. Morphologically, the hominids have no strong offensive or defensive tools. The tools of survival are intelligence and the ability to store, to correlate, to cross-reference, to communicate, and to use information. Is it not likely, then, that natural selection should have acted very strongly on those physiological, behavioral, and morphological features upon which hominid learning ability rests? Should not the intellect of the hominids have been a major focus of selection during their evolution?

The models outlined here present a functional and processual view of the emergence and development of the Hominidae. But there is something else here that is not easily touched on within the framework of empirical observation. Throughout this discussion of primate evolution, we have seen a unique evolutionary process within the order. The primates have diversified and exploited new environments, and yet they have remained among the most generalized of mammals. Adaptations have occurred, yet a flexible phenotype remains. The primates *may* usually do one thing, and yet they *can* also do another if opportunity and necessity occur. This is the unique aspect of primate evolution: adaptation without specialization.

This process has continued in the Hominidae in an even more pronounced fashion. Humans, of course, have specializations, including the vital ones of bipedality and an extraordinarily complex brain. But these same specializations combine with the supremely flexible human hand. Its intricate pattern of morphological and functional generalization and muscular and neurological specializations allow more plasticity of movement and manipulation and more variety of action than are possible in any other animal. These anatomical features, instead of limiting and restricting activities and responses, have vitally extended the human behavioral repertoire.

The final point may be, therefore, that the most important adaptive feature of the Hominidae is the lack of morphological specialization. Humans may be human because they can do so many things; and perhaps this freedom of choice to pursue different avenues toward survival is, finally, the most basic human characteristic.

SUMMARY

Important characteristics of the family Hominidae are:

Reduction of the anterior dentition, particularly the canine, relative to that of the pongids

Nonsectorial P3, with homomorphic (identical) premolars in later groups
Differential wear on molars, indicating prolongation of growth period
Shallow, robust mandible, with development of a chin in later groups
Erect posture and bipedal locomotion
Brain large relative to body weight
Structured, flexible speech

Because of limited fossil evidence, we cannot be sure that all these features (particularly the last three) were present in the earliest hominids. Nevertheless, the pattern and features which are preserved in the Miocene and Pliocene hominids do closely resemble those apparent in the Pleistocene and Recent hominids.

The early theories of hominid origins sought a relationship between these morphological and behavioral characters and the environment. The ideas of Darwin and, later, Washburn and others focused particularly on tool use, bipedality, carrying, and canine reduction as a response to the newly occupied grassland habitat. Yet, the distinctive hominid morphology had appeared before the move to the grasslands; we must therefore look elsewhere for the factors that led to the initial divergence of the hominids and the pongids.

There are several alternatives to the grassland adaptation hypotheses, and they may be regarded as highly complementary. While these, too, are hypothetical, they rest firmly on the presently available fossil evidence.

1. Competition between a variety of anthropoids for the diminishing space of the Middle Miocene forests led to increasing discrimination of habitat areas. The ancestors of the hominids were among those anthropoids that came to use and depend upon the resources of the forest floor at this time.

2. The Middle and later Miocene hominid descendants of this group are found in conditions indicating that they occupied the marginal, mosaic area between the diminishing forest and the expanding grasslands. In such areas, fixed, limiting morphological specializations would be disadvantageous. Flexibility of action and response would be demanded. It was under such conditions that strong selective pressures for increased learning and cognitive abilities emerged. Thus, prolongation of the period of growth, development, and learning may have been strongly selected for under such environmental conditions.

3. Toward the end of the Miocene, with the increased availability of savanna living space, many animals moved onto the grasslands. The hominids were among those who made full grassland adaptations at this time, bringing with them the dental adaptations for the coarse

foods of the forest floor. These served as preadaptations for the utilization of the harsh seeds, grains, and grasses of the savannas.

SUGGESTIONS FOR FURTHER READING

Geschwind, N. 1972. "The Organization of Language and the Brain," in S. L. Washburn and P. Dolhinow (eds.), *Perspectives on Human Evolution, Vol. 2.* New York: Holt. Pp. 382–384.
Lieberman, P. 1972. "Primate Vocalizations and Human Linguistic Ability," in S. L. Washburn and P. Dolhinow (eds.), *Perspectives on Human Evolution, Vol. 2.* New York: Holt. Pp. 444–468.
Napier, J. 1967. "The Antiquity of Human Walking," *Scientific American,* **216**(4), pp. 56–66.
Negus, V. E. 1949. *Comparative Anatomy and Physiology of the Larynx.* London: Heinemann.

6

HOMINIDS OF THE PLIO-PLEISTOCENE
(5.5 m.y. to 0.7 m.y. ago)

INTRODUCTION

In contrast with the hominids of the Miocene, the hominids of the Plio-Pleistocene[1] show several important differences. First, the hominids of the Plio-Pleistocene demonstrate a wide degree of morphological variability. While the Miocene hominids comfortably fit into a single genus and perhaps even into a single species, the Plio-Pleistocene hominids probably comprise at least two genera. Second, the Miocene hominids show a very broad geographic distribution, extending into tropical and temperate areas from Africa through Asia. Paradoxically,the highly diversified Plio-Pleistocene hominids are known only from east Africa and South Africa. Not until about 1.5 m.y. ago do we again see evidence of the broad geographic distribution which characterized the ramapithecines. Third, the remains of Plio-Pleistocene hominids are often found in association with stone tools; this proximity indicates that cultural activities were becoming part of the hominid behavioral repertoire. Moreover, the association of these stone tools with butchered animals, obtained by either hunting or

[1]The term "Plio-Pleistocene" refers to the Pliocene epoch and the early or lower part of the Pleistocene.

205

scavenging, signals an important dietary shift at this time. It is probable that these last two characteristics (tool use and meat eating) were then more common in one hominid line than the other.

The Plio-Pleistocene has often been viewed as a time of extreme climatic crisis involving widespread desiccation and drought. Robert Ardrey, in *African Genesis* (1961), has been particularly effective, if somewhat overdramatic, in the development of a picture of severe drought conditions during this time and their effect on the emerging hominids. It is true, however, that worldwide temperatures were lower than the previous Cenozoic highs. Moreover, both temperate and tropical forests continued to diminish, yet no dramatic drop in temperature or rainfall occurred in Plio-Pleistocene times. With the decrease of the forests, however, grasslands and savannas did expand in area and deserts developed in some areas, particularly in north and south Africa. Some animals closely associated with the savanna-grassland environments, such as the pigs and antelopes, experienced an "almost explosive divergence" during the Plio-Pleistocene, a situation no doubt directly due to the expansion of their habitat area (Cooke, 1972). Some primates, such as the macaques and savanna-living baboons, also expanded at this time (Napier, 1970). The hominids, now also adapting to a savanna-grassland habitat, similarly expanded and diversified during this time.

However, despite the expansion of drier habitats and the animals associated with them, the African Plio-Pleistocene was not a time of devastating drought. Rivers and lakes existed in many areas of east Africa throughout the period; both the Omo River in Ethiopia and Lake Turkana (formerly Lake Rudolf) in Kenya existed in much the same form they do today (Bishop, 1976). Many lakes, in fact, dotted the east African landscape in the Plio-Pleistocene; the sediment of one of these lakes has preserved some of the remarkable evidence which has been excavated at Olduvai Gorge.

Undoubtedly, one of the most significant factors in hominid history during the Plio-Pleistocene was the adoption of a new habitat. Probably a number of factors were involved in this shift from the forest and woodland or forest-fringe ecosystems to the savanna ecosystem. Initially, the prime factor may have been the pressures of interspecific competition in the diminishing forest and forest-margin areas. Clearly, a variety of higher primates was in local coexistence in such areas, and competition among these groups for food and space must have been intense. But, at the same time that they were competing for the limited forest and woodland space and resources, the space and resources of the savanna were increasing and expanding.

Thus, pressures of competition and the opportunity for movement and geographic expansion may have combined to initiate the hominid occupation of the savanna. The first attempts at the occupation of a new habitat, such as the savanna, usually do not involve genetic change; behavioral or ethologic changes often occur first, followed by the incorporation of available genetic patterns that reinforce, expand, and intensify the adaptations to the new location (see Mayr, 1970, 1976, for a discussion of these processes).

As we have seen, the Miocene hominids rapidly moved out from their homeland to occupy many areas of Europe, Asia, and Africa. But, despite their wide geographic distribution, there was little morphological diversity apparent among the known Miocene hominids. Although some authors have favored the recognition of two or more species within the genus *Ramapithecus* (Simons, 1974; Andrews, 1971), these categories are more a reflection of a broad presence in time and space than of any definite morphological variation.

However, by the Pliocene, hominid diversity was so broad that a single taxon probably cannot contain all this material. This diversity is the source of one of the great and continuing controversies in paleoanthropology: the classification of the Plio-Pleistocene hominids.

EARLIER CLASSIFICATIONS

As discussed in Chapter 1, a number of problems face anyone seeking to impose order on the fossil record: This record is incomplete; the material is fragmented; our knowledge of chronology is not entirely adequate; and the Linnaean taxonomic model was not designed for application to vertical, time-successive populations. Moreover, any classification reflects the known fossil record at a particular point in time. It also is marked by the scientific background as well as the academic viewpoint of the classifier. These factors combine to explain the diversity of opinion regarding the classification of the Plio-Pleistocene hominids.

With few exceptions, most workers have proposed taxonomic divisions of these hominids at either the generic or the specific level. The anatomist Le Gros Clark (1964, 1967), for example, has suggested that the observed differences may be dealt with by allocating all the material to a single genus *Australopithecus* containing two species, *A. africanus and A. robustus*. Within the genus *Australopithecus*, the species *A. africanus* was said to be small and lightly built, while the species *A. robustus* was larger and heavier with a "coarser skeletal structure." He concluded that *A. robustus* was off the line leading to the modern human and represented a somewhat specialized side branch diverging from the more generalized human ancestor *A. africanus*.

Tobias, also an anatomist, has divided the Plio-Pleistocene material into two different genera: *Homo* and *Australopithecus*. The genus *Australopithecus* in this case would contain three species: *A. africanus, A. robustus,* and *A. boisei*. His definition of this genus is basically that of Le Gros Clark, although he has slightly modified it. He has pointed out, for example, that australopithecines tend to have a "thin-walled skull and the contour of the internal mandibular arch is in a (V) or blunt (U) shape" (1967). His definition of species within the genus *Australopithecus* is based, not on individual or distinctive characters, but on the relative development of the basic trait complex. Thus, *A. africanus* shows

> more gracile, lighter construction of the cranium . . . ectocranial superstructures and pneumatisation not as marked as in other species; . . . premolars and molars of moderate size [but] mandibular canine larger than other species, and hence more in harmony with the postcanine teeth. (1967, p. 234)

A. robustus is characterized by

> more robust, heavier construction of the cranium . . . well developed ectocranial superstructures and degree of pneumatisation (more marked than in *A. africanus* though not as pronounced as in *A. boisei*); . . . premolars and molars of very large size [but] mandibular canine absolutely and relatively small and hence not in harmony with the postcanine teeth; degree of molarization of lower first deciduous molars more complete. (1967, p. 235)

A. boisei is defined as being

> most robust, with heaviest construction of the cranium . . . very pronounced ectocranial superstructures and degree of pneumatisation (more marked than in *A. robustus*); extremely well developed supra-orbital torus with a "twist" between the medial and lateral components; well developed sagittal crest . . . premolars and molars extremely large . . . [but] maxillary canine absolutely and relatively small and hence not in harmony with the postcanine teeth. (1967, p. 235)

Both Le Gros Clark and Tobias can be criticized on the basis that species definition cannot rest on such flexible criteria as "smaller" or "larger" or "more gracile" or "more robust". As pointed out in Chapter 1, separation between taxa must rest on distinctive or derived characteristics. Thus, if reproductive isolation cannot be proven (as it must be to define living species), then morphological space between groups must be demonstrated in the bones themselves.

The second genus in Tobias's classification, *Homo*, in the Plio-Pleistocene would contain the single species "*H. habilis*". The taxon "*H. habilis*" was first proposed after Louis Leakey recovered the remains of what he considered to be an advanced type of hominid from Bed I, Olduvai Gorge; the type specimen OH 7 was dated to about 1.75 m.y. B.P.[2]

---

[2]OH stands for "Olduvai hominid"; the number 7 indicates that this was the seventh individual found at Olduvai.

The basic characters of this species include:

> Mean cranial capacity greater than that of members of the genus *Australopithecus* but smaller than that of *Homo erectus*; . . . maxillae and mandibles smaller than those of *Australopithecus* and within the range for *Homo erectus* and *Homo sapiens*; dentition characterized by incisors which are relatively large in comparison with those of both *Australopithecus* and *Homo erectus*; canines which are proportionately large relative to premolars; . . . molars in which the absolute dimensions range between the lower part of the range in *Australopithecus* and the upper part of the range in *Homo erectus*; . . . the hand bones[3] differ from those of *Homo sapiens sapiens* in robustness, in the dorsal curvature of the shafts of the phalanges, in the distal attachment of flexor digitorum superficialis, in the strength of the fibrotendinous markings, in the orientation of the trapezium in the carpus. (L. S. B. Leakey, Tobias, and Napier, 1964, p. 7)

The generality of this definition was criticized by J. Robinson (1965), who pointed out that no evidence was presented which clearly separated "*H. habilis*" from existing taxa. More damaging to the validity of the new taxon, Robinson noted, was that the authors had suggested a close morphologic affinity between "*H. habilis*" and several existing specimens (Olduvai hominids, 4,6,8,13,14, and hominids from Kanam, Chad, and Ubeidiya), thereby confirming that "*H. habilis*" was not distinctive and did not deserve a new Linnaean nomen. Despite these criticisms, Tobias (1965b, 1972), Howell (1969), and others have continued to attribute material to this taxon. In particular, it has been asserted that "*H. habilis*" may also include a further Olduvai hominid, OH 24 (Tobias, 1972), material from the Sterkfontein Extension site in South Africa, *Sinanthropus officinalis, S. lantianensis, Hemanthropus peii, Homo modjokertensis, Pithecanthropus dubius* from Asia (Tobias, 1965b), and material from the Omo region in Ethiopia (Howell, 1969). The Kanam jaw was removed from this taxon by Tobias himself, who noted that its modern "chin" was undoubtedly due to a pathological condition (osteogenic sarcoma) (Tobias, 1960). The inclusion of OH 24 has been questioned on the basis of its very close morphologic and metric similarity with MLD 6,[4] a gracile australopithecine from South Africa (Anon., 1972). Moreover, the Chad fragment is so damaged through erosion that its affinities are very difficult to determine (Coppens, 1961a, b, 1962, 1965).

[3]Fifteen hominid hand bones recovered from FLK NN I were described by Napier (1962) and were included within the type material of "*Homo habilis*" as OH 7. Day has pointed out (1976) that at least two hominids are present, since seven of the bones are clearly juvenile and two are adult; the others are of uncertain age. Moreover, the two adult proximal phalanges are unlike the other phalanges: they show strong dorsal curvature, very small heads, and prominent ridges for the attachment of fibrous flexor sheaths. Day concluded that they most closely resemble the phalanges of the black-and-white colobus monkey *Colobus polykomos*, although they are considerably larger.

[4]MLD is the museum designation for material from the Makapangat Limeworks dump in South Africa.

At the present time, the usefulness and validity of the taxon *"Homo habilis"* is under reexamination. Part of the problem is that a more advanced hominid, *Homo erectus*, is now known to have existed at the same time and perhaps earlier than *"Homo habilis"*. With a more advanced form present contemporaneously, *"H. habilis"* can hardly have been ancestral to modern *H. sapiens*. Some workers would now place other "habilines," such as OH 24, in the gracile australopithecine group while placing others, such as OH 13, within *Homo*. This question cannot be resolved without further fossil material.

Campbell (1972) has suggested a further solution to the classification of the early Pleistocene hominids. He too recognizes a dichotomy within the fossil record and divides the material into a gracile lineage leading to the modern human and a more robust and specialized side branch, which became extinct about 1 m.y. ago, represented by *Australopithecus boisei*. The interesting factor in his approach lies in his dividing the gracile lineage not by empirical, morphological criteria but by time lines, thus: *A. africanus* became *"H. habilis"* at 2 m.y., and *"H. habilis"* became *H. erectus* at 1.3 m.y. ago. This chronospecies approach suggests a debt to the "morphological dating" technique practiced by some workers earlier in this century. In morphological dating, a specimen of unknown age is assigned to a time period because of its morphology; therefore, a "primitive" specimen is placed earlier in the time scale and a "modern" one is placed later. Campbell's approach also suggests a relationship between time and morphology in that a particular taxon is, by definition, confined to a particular time zone. Underlying such an approach would be the phyletic gradualism model discussed earlier. As we will see, phyletic gradualism may not work too well in all phases of hominid evolution. With the better control over dating now possible, we see that populations in different geographic areas may change at different rates. This may be especially true in southeast Asia (see Chapters 8 and 9). A final blow to such a time-line approach is the demonstration that *Homo erectus* overlapped or even preceded *"Homo habilis."*

Still other paleoanthropologists have advocated placing all the hominid material into a single taxon. Such classifications would attribute the visible variations to sexual dimorphism, temporal variations, or subspecific or racial categories. The idea was first proposed by Ernst Mayr (1950) and later developed by Wolpoff (1968b, 1970b, 1971a, 1973); Buettner-Janusch (1966, 1973) has also advocated the acceptance of a similar scheme.

J. Robinson, whose research has centered mainly on the South African material, has structured the Early Pleistocene fossil evidence into a bigeneric system. In analyzing the cranial, dental, and postcranial material, he has proposed the existence of two different masticatory and locomotor adaptations; these adaptations overlie somewhat different levels in brain development. He argues that because these morphologies demonstrate different adaptational patterns, the material should be divided into two taxa, *Homo africanus*[5] and the robust form, *Paranthropus robustus*. Robinson has contended that the dentition and associated chewing musculature in the two genera are adapted to quite different diets, *Homo* being a generalized omnivore and *Paranthropus* a more specialized herbivore. Although the posterior dentition in both groups may be quite large (see also Wolpoff, 1973), there are important distinctions in size relationships between the front and back teeth. *Paranthropus* is characterized by having very reduced front teeth (incisors and canines) in relation to the posterior teeth (premolars and molars). *Homo*, on the other hand, has front teeth that are considerably larger in comparison with the posterior dentition. Moreover, the chewing muscles in *Paranthropus*, particularly the temporalis and masseter muscles, are large, and the attachment areas on the skull and mandible often show cresting and torus development. Robinson also suggested that the locomotor system, while bipedal in both forms, may not have been exactly equivalent. He noted that while *H. africanus* was essentially like modern humans in terms of locomotor capabilities, *Paranthropus*—having a shorter lower limb and a more flexible foot—still possessed some climbing ability. Although endocranial volume seems not to have been significantly different, he suggested that brain development may have reached rather different levels in both groups. J. Robinson has proposed that the vault height—that is, the extent to which the vertex rises above the upper margin of the orbits—in *Paranthropus* is close to the value for living great apes, while that in *H. africanus* is nearer the values for living hominines. This low vault would seem to suggest that the frontal and parietal regions of the brain were smaller in *Paranthropus* than in early *Homo*; this point has been disputed by Holloway (1973), who sees no significant difference in these areas.

    J. Robinson (1953b, 1954, 1955) has been the main proponent of including the Pleistocene Javan mandibular and dental material referred to as "Meganthropus" with *Paranthropus* and the robust australopithecines. Such a suggestion is important because it would indicate the existence of this group outside of Africa; others (Weidenreich, 1945a; Le Gros Clark, 1964, 1967), however, have suggested that this material should be included

[5]The procedures for nomenclatural revision are contained within the International Code of Zoological Nomenclature; it states that when a genus is "sunk" or eliminated, the original specific name must be retained. Thus, when J. Robinson "sank" the genus *Australopithecus* in favor of *Homo* (1965), he properly should have kept the trivial or specific name *africanus*, first used by Dart in 1925. However, under the assumption that the nomen *Homo africanus* was "occupied," having been used by Sergi in 1908, he took the next available specific name, *transvaalensis*, proposed by Broom in 1936. In a comprehensive review of the literature, J. Robinson later (1972) discovered that Sergi's usage was not Linnaean in that he used three levels of binomials concurrently for the same group: *Homo afer, Homo eurafricus, Homo africanus*. Therefore, the nomen *Homo africanus* was available, and J. Robinson returned to this usage in 1972.

within *Homo erectus*. On the basis of dental anatomy, particularly the relatively small premolars and the lack of molarization of these teeth, this latter suggestion at present seems most likely.

In summary, none of these classifications appears to fit exactly the fossil evidence and material presently available. Very probably two genera were present, but their apparent configuration does not correspond exactly with any of the previous classifications.

The following discussion will attempt to delineate the morphologic and adaptive features of the genera *Australopithecus* and *Homo* in the Plio-Pleistocene.

CURRENT TAXONOMY

Australopithecus and *Homo* share a number of features and character complexes that must have been derived from their common, and as yet poorly understood, ancestor. It is therefore useful to look at the characters which they share.

In the dentition, for example, low-crowned, usually square molars are present, as is the 5Y cusp pattern. The canines, although projecting slightly in some individuals, are always significantly smaller than in the great apes. The maxillary premolars are usually homodont. There is no significant diastema in the dental arcade. There is a pronounced wear differential between M1 and M3, which suggests the elapse of considerable time between the eruption of the first and last molars. This, in turn, suggests that the growth period of the Plio-Pleistocene hominids was considerably extended over that of nonhuman primates. M3 is usually the smallest molar, as in modern humans, although the very robust individuals may have molars of nearly equal size. This is in clear contrast to the great apes in which M3 is the largest.

Our knowledge of the locomotor patterns of both genera of Plio-Pleistocene hominids is not complete, but in terms of broad functional complexes, some facts are clear. The limited evidence available from the upper limb gives no indication of weight transmission through the arm. The elbow joint, which in knuckle-walking great apes shows some morphological features to prevent displacement during weight bearing, is generalized and without such stabilization features. In terms of the lower limb, there are important variations between *Homo* and *Australopithecus* in the hip and foot, but the evidence of bipedality is clear in both genera. It is also clear that in both, the knees were near the midline of the body during standing and that complete straightening of the hip and knee joints was possible, and probably habitual. At the ankle joint, weight seems to have been transmitted evenly over the surface of the talus, as in modern humans, and not predominantly through the inner side, as in the living great apes.

Although it is true that in terms of absolute brain size, many Plio-Pleistocene hominids were still within the range of modern pongids, it is also clear that very significant changes in brain structure and organization had taken place by this time. Within both genera of Plio-Pleistocene hominids, many of the features of the modern human brain were present. There was expansion of the parietal and temporal lobes and increased complexity of the frontal lobe; the area of the visual cortex was reduced; and the cerebellar lobes showed basically human configuration (Holloway, 1974).

A number of studies have shown that while the absolute size of the Plio-Pleistocene hominid brain was within the limits of pongid brain size, at this time the size of the hominid brain relative to body weight seems to have been within the modern human range (see Chapter 2). Thus, the very important point emerges that significant evolutionary changes in the hominid brain had occurred prior to the beginning of the Pleistocene and that subsequent human evolution was, in fact, based on these earlier changes. Therefore, whatever the selective pressures for brain development—tool manufacture and use, improved conceptualization and communication, complex social behavior and organization—such development seemingly existed prior to the generic divergence of the Plio-Pleistocene and is a basic component of the hominid pattern.

It is therefore apparent that many of the features characteristic of modern humans were also present in the Plio-Pleistocene Hominidae. It seems probable, then, that such features as bipedality, a large and complex brain, and the distinctive human dental pattern have considerable antiquity extending back into the Pliocene and possibly the Miocene. Whatever the pressures for the development of these features, they existed, in a more-or-less developed fashion, in the ancestral group that gave rise to the Plio-Pleistocene hominids.

We know almost nothing about the history of these two genera between the latest definite ramapithecine, about 8 m.y. ago, and the earliest definite australopithecine, between 3 m.y. and 4 m.y. ago. The little evidence available comes from several east African sites, and all this material is closer to the gracile form of australopithecine than to any other group.

HOMINIDS OF THE EARLY PLIOCENE

One of the very few pieces of information from this time is a small mandibular fragment from Lothagam in Kenya, dated to about 5.5 m.y. ago. This fragment has only a single tooth crown, making taxonomic attribution below the family level impossible. The tooth, however, is small, low-crowned, and little differentiated from earlier ramapithecines (Patterson, Behrensmeyer, and Sill, 1970).

A temporal bone from Chemeron, near Lake Baringo in Kenya, also shows a pattern without any distinctive morphological features and is, in fact, much like the later "gracile" australopithecines (Martyn and Tobias, 1967). The Chemeron deposits may date to about 4.5 m.y. ago (Bishop and Chapman, 1970; Tobias, 1976a).

These two specimens, along with the Lukeino and Ngorora molars discussed previously, seem to indicate that the progenitors of the later Pliocene hominids were gracile and lightly built; beyond that, the ancestral morphology can only be inferred.

The distal humerus found at Kanapoi, Kenya, is an extremely interesting piece of evidence. This fragment is dated to between 4 and 4.5 m.y. B.P. (Patterson et al., 1970). Various studies have shown that the specimen, in the preserved parts, is virtually indistinguishable from a comparative sample of modern *Homo sapiens* (Patterson and Howells, 1967; McHenry, 1972).

While we cannot be sure of the precise taxonomic attribution of the Kanapoi humerus, its close similarity to the humerus of modern humans has some noteworthy implications. The Kanapoi humerus shows no evidence of specialized features at the elbow joint, such as stabilization for either quadrupedal movement or brachiation. This would appear to indicate that full bipedal locomotion, without aid from the forelimb, had emerged by 4 m.y. ago. Firm and unequivocal confirmation of early, well-adapted bipedality is seen in the hominid footprints from Laetolil, dated to about 3.7 m.y. ago (M. D. Leakey and Hay, 1979). These footprints, indicating an arch and fully adducted first toe, clearly show that bipedality is a long-term feature of the hominid line.

HOMINIDS OF THE LATER PLIOCENE AND EARLY PLEISTOCENE

By Middle Pliocene times the morphological diversity within the Hominidae was very broad, and by at least 2 m.y. ago, two distinct hominid genera, *Homo* and *Australopithecus*, had appeared.

The presence of two hominid genera by Late Pliocene times indicates that the family had experienced a period of vigorous, active evolution which coincided with the occupation of the savannas. This evolution may have been due to pressures of competitive interactions, described previously, or to adaptations to changing environmental conditions. It may, additionally, reflect underlying behavioral changes: change in food preference and the exploitation of somewhat different environmental resources. If different populations within a single ancestral species acquired even slightly different dietary habits, new selective pressures would have been developed, resulting eventually in rather different morphologies. The reason for the emergence of two separate genera—the "initial kick"—may have been any, or a combination, of such factors.

Genus Australopithecus

The genus was proposed by Raymond Dart in 1925 to contain a juvenile individual discovered at Taung in South Africa.

Genus: *Australopithecus*; 3.7 m.y. to 1 m.y.
  Australopithecus afarensis
  Australopithecus africanus
  Australopithecus robustus
  Australopithecus boisei

Morphology Morphological characteristics are as follows:

Thin bones in skull and post cranium

Cranial capacity 440 to 700 cc

Bell-shaped, globular cranium with maximum breadth at lowest point of skull

V-shaped nasofrontal suture, opening downward

Nasal bones flattened

Face concave or "dished"

Face large in relation to cranial length

No chin

Arms longer relative to legs than in *Homo*

Femur with flattened neck, no flare on greater trochanter; femoral head smaller and femoral neck longer than in *Homo*

Pelvis with laterally flaring ilium and small acetabulum

Fully erect posture and bipedal locomotion

The genus displays a remarkable amount of diversity, and the full biologic and taxonomic significance of this diversity is unclear. It is probable that, as indicated, more than one species can be included within the genus. Current classifications of this group often list four species, the format followed here. However, it is by no means clear that the two robust forms, *A. robustus* and *A. boisei*, are distinctive from each other at the species level. They could well be geographic variants or subspecies of one taxon. Moreover, the gracile forms, *A. africanus* and *A afarensis* may not warrant separate species since they share many features.

The gracile forms were lightly built and retained a primitive, generalized morphology. *A. afarensis*, the earlier and more primitive of the two groups (Johanson, White and Coppens, 1978; Johanson and White, 1979) retained a highly heteromorphic P_3, widely divergent dental rows, and other dental characters little changed from the ramapithecines. *A. africanus* may have showed a slightly more advanced morphology in these characters, especially a tendency toward a more homomorphic P₃. Both gracile forms were clearly bipedal; and some individuals may have been of very small size, measuring less than 122 cm (4 ft) in height. *A. afarensis* is known first from Laetolil, Tanzania, at about 3.7 m.y. and from slightly later deposits at Hadar, Ethiopia. *A. africanus* first appears at about 3.0 m.y. at Sterkfontein and Makapan, South Africa, and later at Olduvai and the Omo River Valley of Ethiopia. (See Table 7-1, page 251, for the distribution of the Plio-Pleistocene hominids.)

Other groups within the genus *Australopithecus* were more robustly built. These groups, *A. robustus* and *A. boisei*, demonstrate dental specializations for a coarse, herbivorous diet; their dietary specializations are apparent in their larger cheek teeth, very much reduced front teeth, and large areas of muscle attachment on the skull and jaw.

In east Africa, a "superrobust" form, *A. boisei*, had appeared by about 2 m.y. ago. This group shows extreme enlargements and specializations in the jaws and teeth. The latest known members of this east African group were from Lake Natron, Tanzania, and Chesowanja, Kenya, dating to about 1.4 or 1.5 m.y. ago (Isaac, 1967; Bishop and Pickford, 1975).

The sites at Swartkrans and Kromdraai in South Africa contain *A. robustus*, a slightly less massive form than its east African counterpart. These sites may date to about 1.8 m.y. ago.

No evidence of any australopithecine is known after about 1 m.y. ago, when it apparently became extinct.

CRANIUM The skull of the australopithecines is globular or rounded in shape in contrast with that of *Homo*, which has expanded laterally. Overall, the bones of the skull are thin. However, they may show localized thickening due to one of two processes: crest development or **pneumatization.**

The skull bones may demonstrate large crests or bony ridges raised as a result of muscle development. In the case of such bony crests, only the outer table of the skull bones is enlarged; the middle layer (the diplöe) and the inner table remain thin (Figure 6-1*a*, *b*, *c*). In early members of the genus *Homo*, the skull bones, and even some bones of the postcranium,

FIGURE 6-1 Comparative skull thickness. **(a)** In this individual, a *Homo erectus* from Choukoutien, the skull bones are very thickened. This is a characteristic of the early hominines and has affected both the inner and the outer tables of bone. **(b)** OH 5. Although this robust australopithecine had a well-developed sagittal crest, only the outer table of bone has enlarged. The remaining areas of the skull bones have remained very thin. **(c)** OH 7 ("*Homo habilis*"). The skull bones in this individual are very thin and quite unlike those found in early *Homo*. (Drawings by Christopher Pircher.)

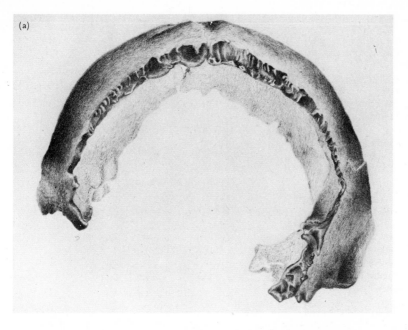

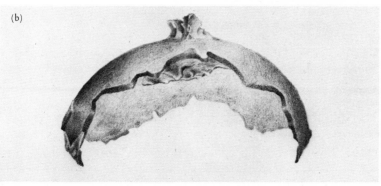

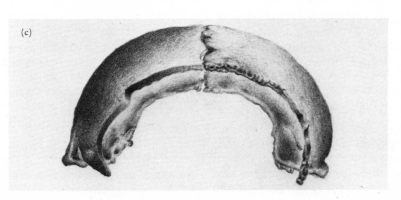

TABLE 6-1   Thickness of the cranial vault bones

SPECIMEN	THICKNESS, MM	
	AT BREGMA*	AT ASTERION*
Modern Europeans	5.5 (mean)	4.01 (mean)
Neandertals:		
Spy 1	7.1	7.0†
Fontechevade 2	8.0	6.0
La Ferrassie	4.0	5.0
La Chapelle	5.0	5.0
Solo 4	—	15.9†
Solo 7	—	13.0
Solo 8	—	17.8
Bodo	13.0	—
Homo erectus		
Choukoutien	8.8 (mean)	13.5–17.4 (range)
Bilzingsleben	8.0	16.0
Swanscombe	7.0	8.0
Lantian	16.0	—
Australopithecus		
OH 7	4.0	4.0
OH 24	4.0	6.5
OH 5	5.5	6.5†
South African graciles	3.0–7.7 (range)	
KNM ER 1470	6.0	7.0

* See Figure 2-2.

† Taken at mastoid angle.

Sources: Modern Europeans, Neandertals, and Swanscombe: Weiner and Campbell, 1964. Solo: Weidenreich, 1951. Bodo: Conroy et al., 1978. Choukoutien: Weidenreich, 1943a. Bilzingsleben: Vlcek, 1978. OH 5 and South African data, Tobias, 1967. Lantian: Woo, 1965. Other data by author on originals.

such as the femur, show remarkable thickness which is unrelated to muscular development. (See Table 6-1.)

In the robust, but not the gracile, australopithecines, bony crests or tori are built up on the outer table of the skull bones. These crests mark areas of muscle attachment and their large size is an indication of the superdevelopment of certain muscles. Temporalis, a major chewing muscle which closes the jaw, is particularly important in this regard.

In *Homo*, temporalis extends from the sides of the skull to the front margin of the jaw ramus, just in front of and below the jaw joint. In the robust australopithecines, temporalis was enlarged greatly and, in fact, originated along the top of the skull. Its area of origin in both *A. robustus* and *A. boisei* is marked by a sagittal crest which runs along the midline of the skull (Figure 6-2a). In these forms the sagittal crest began very far

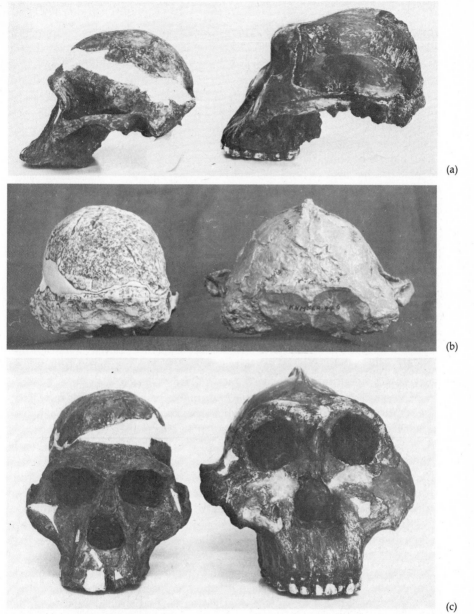

(a)

(b)

(c)

FIGURE 6-2 (a) Skull of *Australopithecus*, lateral view (STS 5 and OH 5). This view shows the development of the sagittal crest in the robust group. Note also the concave or dished face in both the robust and the gracile individuals. (b) Skull of *Australopithecus*, posterior view (STS 5 and KNM ER 406). The small, globular cranium characteristic of the genus is apparent here, as is the typical bell shape of the skull. (c) Skull of *Australopithecus*, anterior view (STS 5 and OH 5). The sagittal crest of the robust individual is again apparent, as are the broad, flaring cheekbones which are characteristic of the group. These features of the robust australopithecines may be associated with hyperdevelopment of the muscles of chewing (Photographs *a* & *c* by Gary Feinstein, *b* by Thomas.)

forward, just behind the brow ridges. Gorillas and other large pongids also have sagittal crests similarly developed by large temporalis muscles, but in these forms the crests begin further back on the skull (Tobias, 1967). The forward placement of the front part of the muscle in the robust australopithecines would mean that the anterior fibers of the muscle were acting in nearly a vertical orientation. Thus, in these forms the muscle was capable of delivering more power than in the more obliquely oriented pongid temporalis.

The bar of bone over the eyes, called the "brow ridge" or "supraorbital torus," is very large in both the South and east African robust australopithecines. In these forms where anterior fibers of the temporalis muscle begin just behind the brow ridge, the crest of that muscle defines the posterior margin of the brow ridge (Tobias, 1967). This is very different from brow ridge structure in early members of the genus *Homo*. In this group the frontal bone is larger and more vertically oriented than in the australopithecines, so that a considerable amount of forehead always intervenes between the brow ridge and temporalis.

Pneumatization, a further characteristic of the australopithecine skull, is a type of bone growth where air sacs or air cells are incorporated within the center of the bone tissue. Thus, pneumatized bones contain hollow, air-filled spaces of various sizes surrounded by a more dense layer of bone. The air cells may be very large, in which case they are called "sinusus," or very small, resulting in bone of "spongy" appearance.

The skull of *Australopithecus* is pneumatized in the frontal, maxillary, zygomatic, and temporal bones. This pneumatization is developed to a remarkable degree in *A. boisei* (Tobias, 1967) and is seen to a lesser degree in *A. africanus* (Broom, Robinson, and Schepers, 1950). Some early hominine skulls also show pneumatization, but it is never developed to the extent seen in the australopithecines. The Javan *Homo erectus* and hominids from Petralona, Greece, and Rhodesia show, for example, well-developed frontal sinuses but lack heavy pneumatization of the other skull bones.

The function of pneumatization is not entirely clear. Tobias (1967) has suggested that in *A. boisei* the remarkable amount of pneumatization may be related to the large size of the jaws and teeth. Thus, it may have lightened the bones so that sufficient bone mass would be available to support the dental structures without the increased weight of solid bone.

Pneumatization has caused the distinctive shape of the australopithecine skull when viewed from the rear (Figure 6-2b). In this view, the skull has a bell-shaped outline which flares at the bottom. The point of maximum skull breadth is thus at or near the lowest point of the cranium and corresponds with the maximum area of pneumatized bone. This differs from the condition in *Homo* where the lack of pneumatization in the mastoid and temporal bones, combined with the lateral expansion of the skull as a whole, has resulted in the point of maximum skull breadth occurring somewhat higher.

The capacity of the cranium is usually between 440 and 530 cc, although some larger individuals had capacities of over 700 cc. The mean for the gracile form is about 496 cc, while the mean for the robust forms (*A. robustus* and *A. boisei*) combined is 517 cc. (See Table 6-2). The larger mean for the robust forms is probably correlated with their larger body size. Thus, in terms of absolute size, the skull capacity of both the robust and gracile forms was smaller than that of modern humans. It may be, however, that relative to body weight, the australopithecine skull capacity was equivalent to that of *Homo sapiens*. Although the reconstructed body weights given in Table 6-2 are speculative, available evidence indicates that they are probably generally correct.

The available evidence does not indicate any significant structural differences between the australopithecine brain and the modern human brain. By the time of the earliest known australopithecine skull (from Sterkfontein, c. 3 m.y. old), the brain was organized essentially along modern lines (Holloway, 1966, 1972, 1973). For example, the lunate sulcus which separates the posterior parietal association cortex and the occipital lobe was placed low, as in modern humans. This placement indicates that the important posterior parietal association cortex had already enlarged by this time (see Chapters 2 and 5). Moreover, the area that has motor control over speech is enlarged, as in modern humans (Holloway, 1972). This area, called "Broca's area" for the French anatomist who first described its

TABLE 6-2   Relative brain size in the hominids

HOMINID	BRAIN SIZE, CC	ESTIMATED BODY SIZE, LB	PROGRESSION INDEX*
Homo sapiens	1361	150	28.8 (mean); 19–53 (range)
Homo erectus			
OH 9	1067	108	22.1
OH 12	727	74	27.6
Australopithecus			
Taung	440	45	19.8
STS 60	428	43.5	19.6
STS 71	428	43.5	19.6
STS 5	485	49	20.6
OH 7	687	69.9	21.2
SK 1585	530	54	20.8
OH 5	530	54	21.2
KNM ER 406	510	52	23.9
KNM ER 732	500	50.9	20.9

*See Table 2-7

Source: Progression index, Bauchot and Stephan, 1969; data for *Homo sapiens*, Bauchot and Stephan, 1969; data for *Homo erectus*, Holloway, 1973; data for Taung, Holloway, 1970.

action, is contained in the third inferior frontal convolution. Whether or not these conditions indicate that the australopithecines possessed speech, we cannot be sure. However, this area is clearly different from that of pongids and at least indicates that the motor capability of speech was present.

From this evidence we can therefore conclude that the main events in the evolution of the hominid brain had occurred sometime prior to 3 m.y. ago. It would seem that the evolutionary pressures for complex behaviors, such as learning, memory, planning, and communication, occurred early in human history. Thus the hominid repertoire of complex behavioral responses and actions is an ancient one.

In the facial region, an important distinction of this genus is the fact that the facial portion of the skull is large relative to the cranial length (Figure 6-2c). The relationship between facial size and cranial length can be seen in Table 6-3. This relationship is reversed in *Homo*, where facial size has decreased absolutely and relative to skull length and the cranium itself has enlarged. This disproportion between the face and cranium in *Australopithecus* has resulted in extreme constriction of the frontal bone

TABLE 6-3 Facial height–cranial length index

SPECIMEN	INDEX
Homo sapiens	30.0–45.0 (range)
Predmost	38.3
Skhul 5	38.0
Neandertals	
La Chapelle	41.3
Gibraltar	40.6
Tabun	43.1
Rhodesian	45.3
Homo erectus	
Choukoutien	39.7 (mean)
Australopithecus	
STS 5	51.0
OH 5	64.5
KNM ER 1470	59.0

Note: Facial height index = nasion-alveolare height/glabella-opisthion length (see Walker, 1976).

Sources: Homo and *Australopithecus:* Walker, 1976. Skhul 5, Neandertals, and Choukoutien: Weidenreich, 1943a. Predmost and Rhodesian: by author, from casts.

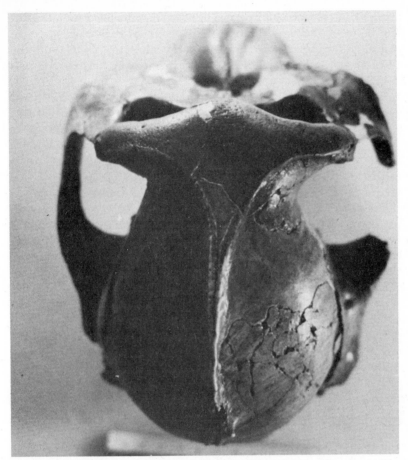

FIGURE 6-3 Skull of *Australopithecus*, superior view (OH 5). This view again shows the sagittal crest of the robust group; note also the tight postorbital construction, another feature indicative of the large chewing musculature. (Photograph of a cast, Kenya National Museum.)

behind the eyes (Figure 6-3). This post orbital constriction is a further distinctive characteristic of the australopithecine cranium. In *Homo* the lateral expansion of the frontal bone and the decrease in the size of the face has diminished this constriction.

The central portion of the australopithecine face is concave or "dished"; this is due to two separate features. First, the nasal bones do not protrude as in *Homo* but lie flat or even concave at the root of the nose. Second, the protrusion of the jaws (prognathism) brings the lower part of the face forward. In *Homo* the smaller size of the jaws and changes in the nasal bones have resulted in greater relief of the central part of the face.

A further characteristic of the nasal bones is that the nasofrontal suture (the suture between the frontal and nasal bones) has an inverted V shape. In the australopithecines, then, the nasofrontal suture forms a V (with the point upward). By contrast, in *Homo* this suture usually lies more or less horizontal (Walker, 1976).

The occipital condyles lie behind the midpoint of the skull while those of modern humans are approximately at the middle of the skull. From this position in the australopithecines, Tobias (1967) has concluded that the head of *A. boisei* was not so well balanced on the spinal column as in *Homo sapiens*. Therefore the large weight of the face and teeth meant, according to Tobias, that the head sagged slightly forward.

There is some evidence that the australopithecines possessed a premaxillary bone. This facial bone carries the incisors but in modern humans it becomes fused with the maxilla before birth. However, STS 5[6] shows evidence of having a premaxilla as an adult. Broom and Schepers (1946) claimed that a portion of the suture between the maxilla and premaxilla was present on the face of this individual; on the other hand, Le Gros Clark (1947) was unsure. However, a clear line of the suture exists on the palate of STS 5. This suture line is only very rarely present in modern humans after birth.

A premaxilla is clearly present in the face of *Proconsul africanus* (Le Gros Clark and L. S. B. Leakey, 1951). Its presence in *Proconsul* and in the australopithecines (at least in the gracile form) would indicate that *Ramapithecus*, too, had such a feature. This prediction remains to be confirmed in the fossil record.

The tympanic plate was vertically oriented, as in *Homo sapiens*. This vertical orientation of the plate can be seen both in robust forms (OH 5, and several individuals from Swartkrans), in MLD 37/38 (Tobias, 1967), and in gracile forms (STS 5). In contrast with sapiens, however, the plate was concave; in both modern humans and the apes, the tympanic plate is convex (Tobias, 1967).

JAWS AND DENTITION   Throughout the Hominidae the basic dental morphology is very similar, although differences in relative and absolute tooth size may distinguish certain groups. For example, the maxilla of *Ramapithecus*, the gracile australopithecines, and *Homo* shows a very similar overall pattern and size. In fact, on the basis of the maxilla alone, it may be almost impossible to distinguish between the gracile australopithecines and *Homo*. Indeed, the maxilla of *Ramapithecus* differs little from that found in this group. Although the more specialized robust australopithecines do show enlargement of the cheek teeth, their overall dental pattern is also typically hominid. (See Table 6-4).

---

[6]"STS" stands for the Sterkfontein Type site in South Africa; "SES" signifies the Sterkfontein Extension site, at the same locality but of more recent age.

TABLE 6-4 Crown areas* of the maxillary teeth

| GROUP SPECIMEN | CROWN AREAS, mm² | | | | | | | | | RATIO C/P³ |
	I^1	I^2	C	P^3	P^4	M^1	M^2	M^3	
American white	63.0	38.4	60.8	65.5	59.8	126.3	105.8	91.2	92.8
South African gracile australopithecine (mean)	78.0	44.2	90.5	110.7	117.2	173.4	212.6	205.8	81.7
OH 5	80.0	51.7	84.4	185.3	212.4	269.0	361.0	336.0	45.5
South African robust australopithecine (mean)	71.4	49.0	81.7	139.7	163.0	200.1	230.9	252.0	58.5
Gorilla, male (mean)	131.5	95.3	339.5	180.1	173.6	238.6	273.8	249.5	188.5
Gorilla, female (mean)	101.2	68.2	163.9	153.0	145.2	203.0	231.0	195.8	107.0
Homo erectus (Peking; mean)	79.3	66.4	96.9	98.8	90.1	136.3	138.4	110.4	98.0

*Crown area = Mesiodistal length × buccolingual width

Source: Data from Tobias, 1967.

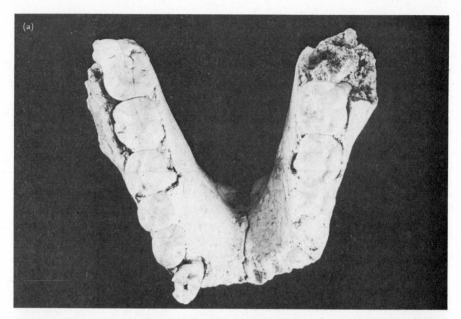

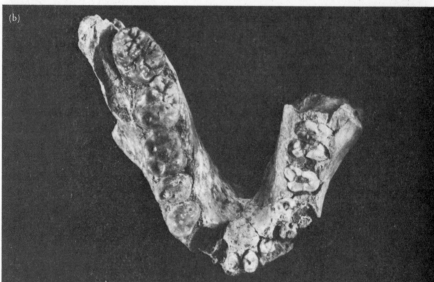

FIGURE 6-4   **(a)** Mandible of *Australopithecus* (LH 4), an early gracile form from Laetolil, Tanzania. A characteristic of this form is the oblique rotation of the P_3, the enlargement of its outer cusp, and the divergent tooth rows. These features are also found in the ramapithecines. (Photograph courtesy of M. D. Leakey and T. White.) **(b)** Mandible of *Australopithecus* (AL 288). Although this gracile individual ("Lucy") from Hadar, Ethiopia, is later than LH 4, it shares a remarkably similar morphological pattern, particularly the rotated P_3 and the divergent tooth rows. Both specimens are now placed in the species *A. afarensis* (Photograph courtesy of D. Johanson.)

In the mandible of the australopithecines, however, the P_3 shows an interesting variation between the robust and gracile groups. In the gracile group, particularly in such early members as AL 288 ("Lucy")[7] and in the Laetolil hominids, attributed to *A. afarensis* the P_3 is semisectorial (Figure 6-4a, b) (Johanson and Taieb, 1976; White, 1977). The P_3 of these individuals has a large outer (buccal) cusp and a much smaller inner (lingual) cusp. This may well represent an extreme evolutionary conservatism in the gracile lineage, since the same feature occurs in the ramapithecines. The robust australopithecines show a deviation from this premolar form, which undoubtedly reflects part of their dental specialization for chewing very harsh or coarse foods. The P_3 in both *A. robustus* and *A. boisei* is enlarged by side-to-side (buccolingual) expansion. This buccolingual expansion has resulted in molarization of P_3 and P_4 so that they function as grinding teeth like the molars (Figure 6-5a, b).

The dentition of the robust and the gracile groups is also distinguished by differences in both absolute and relative tooth size. In *A. robustus* and *A. boisei*, both the mandibular and maxillary cheek teeth (premolars and molars) are enlarged relative to the anterior teeth (incisors and canines). The relative size of the front and back teeth is shown in the C^-/P^3 ratio (Table 6-4). In modern humans this ratio is 92.8, indicating that the canine and P^3 are of nearly equal size. The slightly lower ratio for the gracile australopithecines show that the P^3 is somewhat larger in this group than in modern humans but is not greatly enlarged. In the superrobust group, however, that ratio is 45.5, clearly demonstrating the enormous enlargement of P^3 relative to the canine.

The australopithecine mandible shows features that seem to be associated with improved efficiency of the chewing muscles; these features are particularly pronounced in the robust groups. The significance of the anterior position of the temporalis muscle has already been described. The structure of the mandible, particularly of the vertical or ascending ramus, enhances the biomechanical advantage provided by the vertical orientation of this muscle. The vertical ramus is tall in both the gracile and the robust group, providing a longer power arm for temporalis and for other chewing muscles which attach to the mandible below this muscle.

The mandible is well supported internally with both inferior and superior buttresses. The mandible of *Homo* is also well buttressed, but in this genus the buttress is inferior, placed either on the inner or outer surface of the mandible. In *Homo sapiens*, the outer buttress takes the form of a chin.

Some australopithecine mandibles show the presence of multiple foramina at the lower, anterior margin of the jaw approximately under the premolars. These small holes, or **mental foramina,** are points where nerves and blood vessels go through the bone to supply the outer tissues of the

---

[7]"AL" stands for the Afar locality in the Hadar region of Ethiopia.

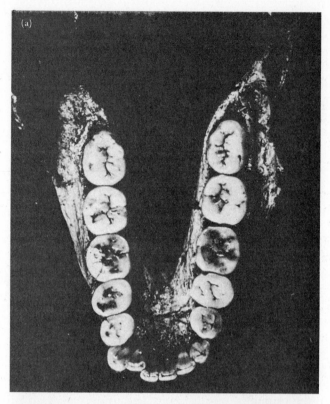

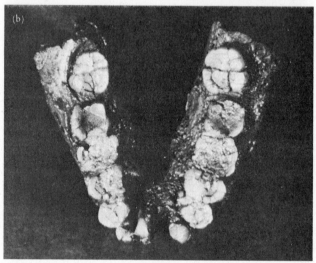

FIGURE 6-5 **(a)** Mandible of *Australopithecus* (SK 23). This jaw shows the anterior dental reduction and posterior dental expansion characteristic of the robust group. This is particularly evident in the molarization of the premolars, which indicates that these functioned as grinding teeth. The molarization of P_3 in the robust group is in strong contrast with the semisectorial pattern seen in LH 4 and AL 288. (Photograph courtesy of M. Wolpoff.) **(b)** Mandible of *Australopithecus* (KNM ER 818). In this east African "superrobust" form the reduction of the anterior dentition has apparently progressed further than in the South African form (SK 23). (Plate, Kenya National Museum.)

lower face. Modern sapiens usually have a single foramen on each side of the lower jaw. These multiple mental foramina reach a frequency as high as 12 percent in some modern populations, but they usually occur in only about 2 to 3 percent of individuals (Riesenfeld, 1956). They were, however, much more common in fossil hominids (see Chapter 8). It has been suggested that they were in some way related to the absence of a chin (Warick, 1950). In the South African australopithecines, multiple mental foramina are found in gracile forms from Sterkfontein (Broom and Schepers, 1946; Broom, Robinson, and Schepers, 1950), and in robust forms from Kromdraai (Broom and Schepers, 1946).

Finally, in the australopithecine jaw, the horizontal ramus is deepest toward the front. In *Homo*, the mandible is usually about the same depth, front and back.

UPPER LIMB At present, the most complete australopithecine individual is AL 288 ("Lucy") from Hadar; more fragmentary individuals are also known from Lake Turkana (KNM ER 1500)[8] and Sterkfontein, South Africa (STS 14). Remains from one individual are of great interest because they give some indication of body proportions and relative length of limbs.

Evidence from AL 288 indicates that the upper limb was slightly longer, relative to the lower limb, than in modern humans (Johanson and Taieb, 1976). Thus, the humero-femoral index (see Table 2-5) of AL 288 is 83.9, while that of modern humans averages about 74.2; in contrast, all the living great apes have indices in excess of 100.

The australopithecine elbow joint, comprising the lower end of the humerus and the upper end of the ulna, shows no evidence of stabilization during weight bearing. However, muscle markings on the shaft of the humerus, particularly for the flexor muscles, are well marked and indicate considerable power in the hand, forearm, and shoulder (Day, 1976).

Some of the australopithecine humeri are very robust and massively built. KNM ER 739 is a good example of this sort of morphology (R. E. F. Leakey, 1971). This bone is both very long and very large in cross section.

[8]KNM ER is a museum acquisition code; it indicates a Kenya National Museum specimen from Lake Turkana.

TABLE 6-5   Mean robusticity index of hominoid humeri

| HOMO | PAN TROGLODYTES | GORILLA | | PONGO | | KNM ER 739 | STS 7 |
		MALE	FEMALE	MALE	FEMALE		
n=63	n=42	n=25	n=41	n=13	n=21		
19.71	23.56	23.78	22.69	20.79	18.70	25.60	23.2

Note: Robusticity index = $\dfrac{\text{circumference at midshaft} \times 100}{\text{maximum shaft length}}$

Sources: All data from McHenry, 1973, except for STS 7, from J. Robinson, 1972.

The relationship of these two parameters is indicated in the robusticity index, in which circumference (at midshaft) is divided by total length (Table 6-5). This index exceeds the range of variation for gorillas (McHenry, 1973). Despite its robust size, however, the lower end of this humerus shows none of the specialized features that stabilize the elbow joint during quadrupedal locomotion. The limb, therefore, appears not to have been used in locomotion. Other specimens from Lake Turkana, such as KNM ER 1504, are smaller than KNM ER 739 but show a similar morphological pattern (R. E. F. Leakey, 1973a; Day, 1976).

While most of the bones of the australopithecine postcranium indicate erect posture and bipedality, the evidence of the ulna is somewhat contradictory.

The best-preserved australopithecine ulna is SH 40-19 from the Omo River Valley in Ethiopia. It presumably is from a robust form. This bone shows several features that ally it with knuckle walkers, rather than with bipeds. For example, the bone does not have a strong interosseous ridge. This ridge, which runs down the shaft of ulna, is the attachment area for the interosseous ligament, which strongly binds the radius and ulna together. Chimps and gorillas also do not have a strong interosseous ridge, but humans do. Moreover, the bone is very elongated and is strongly curved, also as in knuckle walkers. Other features, such as the lack of elongation at the top of the olecranon, are more like the hominids (Howell and Wood, 1974).

This ulna is important in demonstrating a combination of characters which is not found in any living hominoid group. This evidence may well reinforce the hypothesis (discussed below) that australopithecine bipedality was of a unique variety with no exact modern parallel.

Thirteen hand bones, probably from a single individual, are known from Bed I, Olduvai Gorge. This hand was originally attributed to "Homo habilis," but in the absence of more comparative material, it cannot definitely be assigned to any particular hominid group. Day (1976) has pointed out that the hand was capable of strong flexion and grip. A saddle-shaped trapezium indicates a fully opposable thumb. Indications of strong finger flexion are also present in the hand of AL 288; this undoubted australopithecine hand has not yet been described, however.

LOWER LIMB AND LOCOMOTION   Clear evidence of bipedal locomotion is present in the lower limb of *Australopithecus;* in fact, very few features of locomotor significance separate the known lower limb elements of *Australopithecus* from those of *Homo.* The major evolutionary changes in the hominid pelvis, such as reorientation of the ilium and the shortening of the ischium, are clearly present in *Australopithecus* (Figure 6-6*a*). A more subtle, yet no less important, change distinguishes the australopithecine and hominine pelvis from that of the other primates. In nonhuman primates, the muscle rectus femoris has a single point or "head" of origin on the pelvis just anterior to the acetabulum. In hominids, the rectus femoris has two heads of origin; to the "reflected" head, common to all quadrupeds, the bipedal hominids have added a "straight" head. The rectus femoris, along with several other muscles which extend from hip to knee, acts to flex the hip joint and extend or straighten the knee. A roughened tuberosity on the anterior inferior iliac spine of the pelvis clearly shows that the australopithecines had acquired the human "straight" head; this is further confirmation of their bipedality.

The australopithecine ilium, however, shows several distinct differences from that of the hominines. The ilia in *Homo* are tightly curved in toward the midline, while in the australopithecines they show a strong lateral, outward flare. Another distinct australopithecine feature, a strong forward extension (or beak) of the anterior superior iliac spine, may be related to this lateral flare. The anterior superior iliac spine gives origin to the inguinal ligament and to the sartorius muscle. (The inguinal ligament helps to stabilize the front of the pelvis, and the sartorius rotates the thigh and flexes the hip and knee.) The beak may bring this point of origin back toward the body midline so that the structures are in correct biomechanical alignment (Lovejoy, 1973, 1978). The lateral flare and "beak" are found in both robust and gracile australopithecines and are particularly well demonstrated in the SK 50 ilium (Figure 6-6*b*).

The ilium of *Australopithecus* also differs from that of *Homo* in its buttressing. In *Homo sapiens,* the ilium has two buttresses or areas of reinforcement. The acetabulo-cristal buttress (or "iliac pillar") is more or less vertical and extends from the acetabulum to the top of the iliac spine. The acetabulo-spinous buttress is directed more anteriorly toward the anterior superior iliac spine. In *Australopithecus,* only a single, anteriorly directed buttress appears, and it extends into the beaked area. This strongly developed buttress may act to compensate for the greater lateral flare and forward extension of the ilium. (See J. Robinson, 1972; Day, 1978; and Lovejoy, Heiple, and Burnstein, 1973, for a discussion of the lower limb and gait of the australopithecines.)

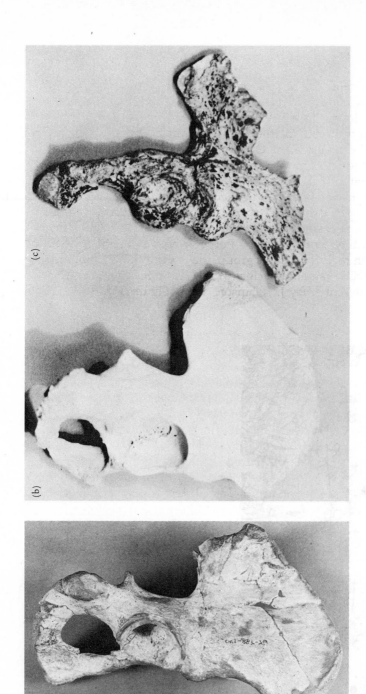

FIGURE 6-6 **(a)** Pelvis of *Australopithecus* (AL 288). This pelvis shows a number of features which are strictly characteristic of bipeds: the short, broad ilium and the well-developed superior and inferior spines on the front of the ilium are among them. (Photograph courtesy of D. Johanson.) **(b)** Pelvis of *Homo sapiens* in comparison with that of **(c)** *Australopithecus* (SK 50). Although the pelvis of this South African robust form shows a basic bipedal pattern, it differs from that of the gracile form (as in AL 288) in the greater forward extension of the ilium. The forward extension of the ilium was buttressed by a strong pillar of bone. The crest of the ilium was lost after death. Note also the backward and downward extension of the ilium, resulting in the V-shaped sciatic notch characteristic of the hominid pelvis.

The ischium, too, may have been slightly different in the australopithecines, although the considerable controversy which surrounds this bone is due to its poor representation in the hominid fossil record. J. Robinson (1972), on the basis of the pelvis from Swartkrans (SK 50), has argued that the ischium was longer in the robust australopithecines than in *Homo*. If this is true, then the australopithecine ischium might have functioned to add power to the hamstrings. Others, such as McHenry (1975), have suggested that the ischium was indeed absolutely longer than in other hominids, but that in relative and biochemical aspects, it did not function differently. More fossil material is needed to resolve this problem.

The lower portion of the vertebral column is of particular interest in the australopithecines, since this is an area where specialized adaptations to upright bipedality would appear. Portions of only a single vertebral column have been reported for this group; the lower or lumbar portion of a spine from a gracile australopithecine (STS 14) from Sterkfontein in South Africa has been described by J. Robinson (1972) (Figure 6-7).

FIGURE 6-7 Lumbar spine of *Australopithecus* (STS 14). The lumbar portion of this australopithecine spine contained six vertebrae; that of the modern human spine usually contains only five. Note the forward curve to the spinal column; this resulted in the distinctive lordotic or S-shaped curve found in all bipedal hominids (Photograph courtesy of M. Wolpoff.)

There are six lumbar vertebrae in the spine of this individual; five is the usual number for modern humans, although six do appear in a small number (fewer than 5 percent) of *Homo sapiens* (Schultz, 1930). Obviously, the fossil sample is too small to show whether the australopithecines usually had more lumbar vertebrae than modern humans.

Of greater interest is the fact that this australopithecine spine demonstrates the same S-shaped, or lordotic, curve as the spine of modern humans. The lordotic curve is an essential component of upright bipedality since it acts to redistribute body weight in the pelvic area. The presence of this curve in an australopithecine is virtually irrefutable evidence of erect bipedality, as well as clear indication that bipedality was efficient.

The morphology of the australopithecine femur (Figure 6-8) is now

FIGURE 6-8 Femur of *Australopithecus* (SK 82 and SK 97). The proximal portion of the australopithecine femora was characterized by a long neck and small head; the greater trochanter does not flare from the shaft as it does in modern *Homo sapiens*.

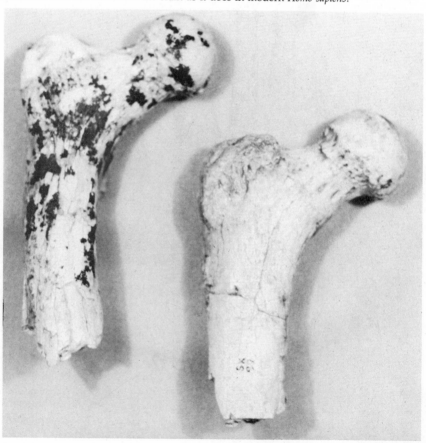

well documented in many specimens from East Africa and South Africa. Although there is a considerable size range, a clear trait pattern is present. The head of the femur is small (this is reflected in a small acetabulum in the pelvis); the femoral neck is long and flattened. The greater trochanter does not flare out from the shaft, as it does in *Homo*, but is flattened; and the ridge between the greater and lesser trochanters, the inter trochanteric line, is only slightly developed or is absent. The femoral neck appears to meet the shaft at a more acute angle than in modern humans. The femoral shafts were angled in toward the knees; this fact indicates that weight transmission down the lower limb must have been approximately the same as in *Homo* (Day, 1969a; Walker, 1973; Kennedy, 1973).

The structure of the foot is now known from a number of specimens. A nearly complete foot (Figure 6-9) was recovered from Bed I, Olduvai

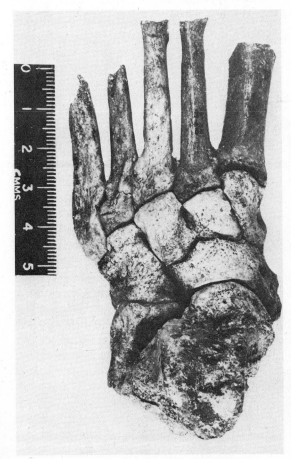

FIGURE 6-9 Foot of *Australopithecus* (OH 8). This foot, beautifully preserved except for the toes, was found in Bed I, Olduvai Gorge. The big toe lies close to the other toes (is adducted), unlike the condition found in the apes, where the big toe is widely divergent (is abducted). In OH 8, the toes lie so close together that the first and second metacarpals form a contact facet at their bases; no such facet occurs in nonhuman primates. A transverse arch is also present. This foot, along with the lumbar spine from South Africa (Figure 6-7) form virtually irrefutable evidence of erect bipedality by at least 1.75 m.y. ago (Photograph courtesy of M. H. Day).

Gorge, and originally attributed to *"Homo habilis,"* but more recently placed in *Australopithecus* (Day, 1976; Wood, 1974). A number of tali have been found which may also be attributed to *Australopithecus*.

The talus (Figure 6-10) is a particularly interesting and informative bone. It is an important bone of the foot since it acts as a hinge joint between the lower leg and the foot. In such a position, it can reveal much about the weight-bearing and weight-distribution systems of the leg and foot. Basically,the talus consists of a grooved top (the trochlea), which receives the bottom of the tibia, and a short neck with a semispherical head. The head articulates with the navicular, a bone on the inner side of the foot.

The grooved trochlea in *Australopithecus*, as in *Homo*, is symmetrical, since weight in a biped must be received and transmitted evenly. In the

FIGURE 6-10   Tali. The talus at the bottom *(Homo)* shows how the horizontal neck angle is determined. A high value for this angle (see Table 6-6) indicates that the first toe was abducted or divergent from the other toes, as in the great apes. A low value indicates that the first toe was adducted, or carried close to the other toes, as in *Homo*. The low value for *Homo* and KNM ER 813 (right) indicates their high degree of adaptation for bipedal walking. The higher value for the Kromdraai talus (on the left) may mean that the first toe was divergent in this robust australopithecine. (Photograph courtesy of T. Thomas.)

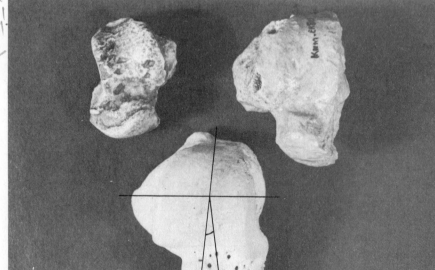

TABLE 6-6 Horizontal neck
angle of the talus

Homo sapiens (mean)	19.6
Neandertal (Spy)	11.0
Shanidar 2	29.0
OH 8	19.0
Kromdraai	32.0
Gorilla	30.1
Pan	31.2

Source: All data from Day and
Wood, 1968, except Shanidar 2,
from Stewart, 1977.

gorilla, on the other hand, weight is carried predominantly on the inner
side of the leg and foot, and therefore the outer lip of the trochlea is
enlarged. The symmetrical trochlea in australopithecine tali, such as KNM
ER 1476, OH 8, and one from Kromdraai (TM 1517)[9] in South Africa, are
added anatomical support of their bipedality.

Other features of the australopithecine talus are not like those of the
modern human, however. The degree of deviation of the neck of the talus
from a plane through the midline of the trochlea (Table 6-6) indicates
whether or not the first toe was divergent. Gorillas, for example, have a
wide angle between the trochlear midline and the talar neck, indicating a
divergent (or abducted) first toe. Their "horizontal neck angle" measures
about 30° (Day and Wood, 1968). Modern humans, with their fully
adducted first toe, have an angle of about 19°. The Kromdraai talus shows
an angle of 32°; OH 8 shows 28°. This comparatively wide angle is a strong
indication that the first toe in these individuals was divergent.

This is not the full story, however, since the OH 8 talus is part of a
nearly complete foot and the other evidence from that foot shows,
unequivocally, that the first toe was not divergent. In this foot, the bases
of the first and second metatarsals meet and have formed a small facet at
the point of their joining. This does not occur in the foot of a gorilla.

The OH 8 foot might be described as the foot of a biped superimposed
on the foot of a quadruped. The first toe is not abducted because the head
of the talus (but not the neck) has rotated around toward the outside of the
foot, thus bringing the first toe in close conjunction with the other toes.

The Kromdraai and OH 8 tali indicate that the australopithecines had a
foot well suited to the biomechanical necessities of bipedal locomotion
while retaining some of the prehensility and flexibility of their ancestors.

[9]TM stands for the Transvaal Museum in Pretoria, South Africa. Most of the South African
australopithecines are stored there.

In summary of all these features, the australopithecines present a picture of extreme diversity. Yet, under that diversity there appears to be a single morphological template. Available evidence suggests that we might reconstruct their history in the following way.

The early members of the gracile group, which first appear in the fossil record around 3.7 m.y. ago in east Africa, were little changed from their ramapithecine ancestors. The very small size of *A. afarensis* and some aspects of their dentition suggest great evolutionary conservatism. But at some point during the Plio-Pleistocene, this conservative gracile group entered a phase of rapid adaptive radiation. Perhaps this period of swift evolution coincided with entry into full savanna-grassland habitats. In any case, by about 2 m.y. ago, and perhaps earlier, the conservative gracile lineage had diversified. One group, *A. africanus*, remained similar to the earlier gracile form but showed increases in cranial capacity and body size and lost the primitive features in the dentition. Although this later gracile group is found in deposits indicative of grassland habitats, they show no clear pattern of dietary adaptation to the savanna foods. The robust forms, another part of this radiation, do, however, show remarkable dental specializations for the coarse or hard foods of the savannas. The final partner in this Plio-Pleistocene radiation of the Hominidae is the genus *Homo*.

Genus *Homo*; 2 m.y. B.P. (+?) to present

Homo (species indeterminate)
Homo erectus

Some preliminary reports have suggested the existence of *Homo* before 3 m.y. ago. Aaronson et al. (1977) and Johanson and Taieb (1976), for example, reported *Homo* in the early levels at Hadar, Ethiopia. However, later and more complete study of this material resulted in its being placed in *Australopithecus afarensis*, the primitive australopithecine species. *Homo* has also been suggested to be present at an early data at Lake Turkana, but the dates of the early levels in that area are presently disputed (see Chapter 7).

However, there is strong evidence of *Homo* by about 2 m.y. ago from both the Omo River area and Lake Turkana. In the Omo River area, the first evidence of *Homo* overlies a tuff dated to 1.93 m.y. ago (Howell and Coppens, 1976). At Lake Turkana, a well-preserved hominine skull was discovered in levels dated to earlier than 1.5 m.y. ago (R. E. F. Leakey and

Walker, 1976). This skull is /particularly important because it closely resembles the skulls of later individuals from Asia and Europe, as well as Africa, which have been attributed to *Homo erectus*.

Since *H. erectus* is a relatively advanced hominine and is the immediate precursor of modern humans, this would imply a considerable time depth for the genus *Homo*. Following this line of reasoning, the emergence of the genus could well have occurred more than 3 m.y. ago.

In contrast with the restricted geographic distribution of the australopithecines, members of the genus *Homo* moved out of Africa to occupy other areas of the world. This emigration may have first occurred sometime before 1.5 m.y. ago. At the present time, the earliest clear evidence of *Homo* outside Africa appears on the island of Java and may date to about 1.3 m.y. to 1.5 m.y. ago. Although *Homo* logically should have been in Europe and on mainland Asia before arriving in Java, the first evidence for *Homo* in these areas is slightly later in time. In fact, the earliest occupation sites in both areas date to about 1 m.y. ago (see Chapter 7).

This second group of hominids within the Plio-Pleistocene may have followed a different evolutionary course in adapting to the savanna. The genus *Homo*, rather than adhering to the earlier and basically herbivorous diet, became much more omnivorous, exploiting a broader range of foods, including meat.

This group may have depended less on the ramapithecine and australopithecine diet of seeds, grains, and grasses and may have begun to rely more on other savanna food resources. Once the behavioral trend toward omnivory, including meat eating, had been initiated, a whole new selective background formed. Certain characters and features, subjected previously to negative or neutral selection, now were positively selected for and incorporated into the gene pool, and entirely new genetic mutations may have added further reinforcement to the new adaptive pattern.

By Middle Pleistocene times, the diet of *Homo* clearly contained substantial amounts of meat, and this pattern undoubtedly had emerged in the Plio-Pleistocene. The use of animal foods, either hunted or scavenged, requires different strategies, different exploitative techniques, and different intellectual and learning abilities from those relating to the use of vegetable foods. As was discussed in Chapters 1 and 5, a positive feedback system may exist between tool use, meat eating, food sharing, carrying, and the home base. Bipedality and verbal communication may also be fed into this system of mutually and positively interacting factors. For example, the increased ability to learn may be enhanced by a flexible hand, freed from the constraints of locomotion. Such a hand would have an increased opportunity to manipulate and alter natural objects, thus opening up new behavioral and exploitative realms.

Morphology   Important morphological features are as follows:

Bones varying from thick (in early groups) to thin (in modern groups), but nearly always thicker than in *Australopithecus*

Cranial capacity: 750–2300 cc

Laterally expanded cranium, with point of maximum low in the temporal region (in early groups) and high (on the parietals in modern groups)

Nasofrontal suture nearly horizontal

Face smaller (relative to cranial length) than in *Australopithecus*

Face convex (not dished) in midportion

Chin formation in later groups; chin absent in earlier groups

Arms shorter relative to leg length than in *Australopithecus*

Femoral head larger and femoral neck longer than in *Australopithecus*

Large acetabulum on pelvis

Fully erect posture and bipedal locomotion

CRANIUM   In *Homo* the bones of the cranium vary from thin to very thick; even the thinnest bones, however, are thicker than those in *Australopithecus*. Maximum thickness is reached in *Homo erectus* (see Figure 6-1).

The skull in *Homo* is often marked with large brow ridges (see Figure 6-11*a*), supraorbital tori, and large nuchal crests on the occipital bones. Although the impressions along the area of origin for the temporalis muscle may be pronounced, these impressions never meet to form a sagittal crest, as they do in some apes and australopithecines.

In the posterior view (Figure 6-11*b*), the skull is somewhat more laterally expanded than in the australopithecines; the point of maximum skull width may be located low, at the level of the mastoids in early members of the genus, or high on the parietals as in *H. sapiens*. The size of the skull is extremely variable, with a total generic range from about 750 to

---

FIGURE 6-11   (a) Skull of *Homo*, lateral view (KNM ER 3733). A number of features present here show the close relationship of this individual to later members of *Homo erectus*. Note the visor-like brow ridges, the platycephalic skull, and the sharply angulated occiput. Note also the forward protrusion of the nasal bones and the relief of the central face; these features are unlike those found in *Australopithecus*. (b) Skull of *Homo*, posterior view (KNM ER 3733). In early forms of the genus, the point of maximum skull breadth is low and the skull walls slope gently inward. Contrast this with Figure 6-2b. (c) Skull of *Homo*, anterior view (KNM ER 3733). Note that the nasofrontal suture is gently curved and does not "V" sharply as in *Australopithecus*. (Photographs courtesy of R. E. F. Leakey and Kenya National Museums.)

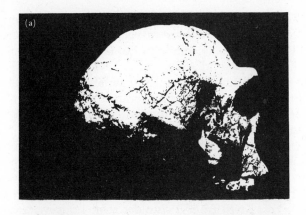

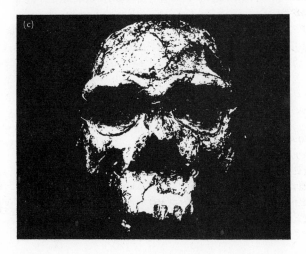

2300 cc; the range in *H. sapiens* is about 900 to 2300 cc. Since cranial capacity is highly correlated with body size (especially stature), it is not a useful taxonomic discriminator. In modern humans there is no correlation between cranial capacity and intelligence.

The nasofrontal suture is usually horizontal and does not "V" upward as in the australopithecines. A further contrast with the australopithecines is the fact that the facial portion of the skull in *Homo* (Figure 6-11*c*) is small relative to the cranial length (see Table 6-3).

It is interesting that skull form in Plio-Pleistocene hominines often closely resembles that of later Middle Pleistocene members of the genus. For example, the cranium of KNM ER 3733 is very similar to the skulls from Peking, which have been attributed to *Homo erectus* (R. E. F. Leakey and Walker, 1976). Yet, KNM ER 3733 is older than 1.5 m.y., and the Peking skulls may date to about 0.35 m.y. Such evolutionary conservatism in the early hominines is supported by other skeletal evidence, particularly the pelvis.

JAWS AND DENTITION   The form and proportion of the masticatory system in early *Homo* closely resemble those of modern humans (Figure 6-12). The most apparent difference between the dentition of early *Homo* and *Australopithecus* is the absence of disproportion between the anterior and posterior teeth. In *Homo*, the premolars have two cusps and lack the broad,

FIGURE 6-12 Mandible of *Homo*, lateral view (KNM ER 730). This partial mandible, recovered below a tuff dated at 1.5 m.y. ago, shows the presence of a chin. This is the earliest known evidence of chin formation and supports the attribution of this individual to *Homo*. The molar teeth are very heavily worn, and a considerable degree of periodontal disease is present.

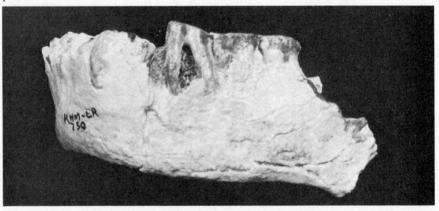

flat molariform structure seen in the robust australopithecines. The canines are usually slightly larger than in the robust australopithecines; in a few individuals, such as Sangiran 4, the canine may extend beyond the occlusal level of the other teeth and be associated with a gap or diastema in the tooth row.

Evidence of very large chewing musculature is not present and the attachments of the temporalis and masseter muscles are not enlarged. The ramus of the mandible is usually short, and relative to the australopithecines, it is more obliquely oriented. The upper and lower margins of the mandible are usually parallel so that the depth of the mandible is more-or-less constant from front to back. Buttressing occurs, in later members of the genus, at the front of the mandible but on the outer rather than the inner surface, thus resulting in the human "chin" (Walker, 1976).

The human chin also reflects a reduction in dental size. As the teeth have become smaller during human evolution, the top tooth-bearing portion of the mandible (the **alveolus**) has regressed, resulting in an apparent protrusion of the lower portion of the jaw. This complex of dental and mandibular traits indicates that the chewing mechanism in *Homo* did not function with the same strength as in *Australopithecus*. This entire pattern suggests a lesser degree of dental specialization in this group.

LOWER LIMB AND LOCOMOTION   The basic hominid locomotor pattern has been described in Chapter 5. That pattern is the same for the genus *Homo;* however, a few features distinguish it from that of the australopithecines.

A considerable number of early hominid femora are now known from both Africa and Asia, and the African material quite clearly falls into two morphological categories. The australopithecine pattern has already been discussed. In *Homo*, the femoral head is larger, the femoral neck shorter and rounder; the greater trochanter flares out slightly from the shaft. The neck leaves the shaft at a more open, less acute angle than in the australopithecines. There is considerable variation in size among early hominines, as in living man. One femur from Lake Turkana (KNM ER 999) may have belonged to a man 175.26 cm to 177.8 cm (5 ft 9 in or 5 ft 10 in) tall, while others appear to have come from considerably shorter individuals.

Femora of Early and Middle Pleistocene hominines, in many instances, have very thick shaft walls. In many cases the thickness of the shaft walls (the cortex) exceeds the range of variation for modern humans (Kennedy, 1973). Although few studies are available on bone thickness, the known evidence indicates that thick bone cortex was a consistent feature of the early hominines (see Chapter 8). The tibiae of early members of the genus *Homo* also appear to be thickened (Chia, 1975).

The evidence of the pelvis agrees with that of the femur in indicating that the postcranium of the early hominines was much like that of modern humans. Two east African pelves are particularly interesting in this regard. KNM ER 3228 (R. E. F. Leakey, 1976) from Lake Turkana and OH 28 (Day, 1971a) from Bed IV, Olduvai Gorge, both show a similar pattern. In both, the acetabulum is large, indicating a large femoral head. Both have a large, thick buttress which extends from the top of the acetabulum to the top of the ilium. This pattern would indicate a hip joint very like that of modern humans but perhaps more heavily muscled.

The close similarity between OH 28 and KNM ER 3228 is important because these two individuals may be separated in time by as much as 1.5 m.y. OH 28 is dated to about 0.5 m.y. ago, and KNM ER 3228 may be less than 2 m.y. old. This would suggest that once the genus *Homo* had appeared, prior to 2 m.y. ago, the line was characterized by considerable evolutionary stability. As discussed earlier, this stability is also suggested in the form and shape of the skull.

At least two tali have been attributed to early populations of *Homo*; both are from Lake Turkana. KNM ER 803 and KNM ER 1464 show a morphological pattern that differs in no significant way from that of modern humans (Wood, 1974; Day, 1976).

The origin of the genus *Homo* is, egocentrically, one of the more interesting events in paleontological history. Yet, the evolutionary stimuli that brought this emergence about are not clear. One possible explanation, the "hunting hypothesis," has often been sensationalized by picturing humans as aggressive killer apes. While this portrayal may be an overestimate of our killer instincts, there are important ramifications of the frequent and consistent consumption of meat. Meat consumption is an important component of a feedback mechanism that may have had far-reaching effects during human evolution in the Plio-Pleistocene. Those hominids who favored meat and desired it in their diet responded to evolutionary pressures in ways unlike those of their more herbivorous relatives.

Hunting by a primate without strong morphological weapons, such as canines, claws, and speed, requires less aggression than it does cooperation, communication, and reliable, mutual interdependencies. Strong aggression in an animal lacking aggressive equipment would be nonadaptive, to say the least, unless it was supported by reliable and consistent patterns of group action.

Consequently, the emergence of the genus *Homo* may be based, in part at least, on the social ramifications of meat consumption. These ramifications include cooperation and the recognition of interdependencies within a stable group. Such a pattern would allow and enhance long-term care of the young and the exchange and perpetuation of learned behavior. Such patterns would be reinforced by the acquisition of verbal communication. The cultural by-products of meat consumption include the establishment of a home base and tools for butchery.

Thus, while habitual and consistent consumption of meat may not be the only explanation of the origins of *Homo,* it does explain the majority of the characteristics of this genus, including its major morphological, social, and cultural attributes.

TAXONOMIC PROBLEMS

The question inevitably arises as to the number of species present within these Plio-Pleistocene genera. As discussed in Chapter 1, there is often little empirical justification for the recognition of many fossil species. Within the genus *Australopithecus,* specific names, such as *A. afarensis, A. africanus, A. robustus,* and *A. boisei,* have been proposed and are used here. It is true that some individuals and populations do closely correspond to the type definitions for these taxa. For example, KNM ER 406 is very like OH5 and both very probably belong to the same group, in this case *A. boisei;* KNM ER 732 is sufficiently like both to be considered a female of the same group. Such specific usages do not involve the demonstration of genetic isolation, merely of phenotypic similarity. There are, however, many other cases where association is not clear and attribution to one taxon (and exclusion from others) may obscure important and informative morphological features. KNM ER 1813, for example, has a small cranial capacity—no more than about 500 cc—yet the dental pattern shares a number of similarities with *Homo* (R. E. F. Leakey, 1974).

The cranium of KNM ER 1805 is particularly interesting. This skull has a cranial capacity of 582 cc (Holloway, personal communication, 1976). It has small teeth showing none of the specializations of the robust australopithecines. Moreover, the bones of the skull are thick, as in early *Homo.* These characters would seem to ally it with the genus *Homo* although the skull capacity is smaller than is usual in the genus. However, the skull shows markedly developed temporal lines which very nearly form a sagittal crest. No member of the genus *Homo* is known to have had such a crest. Moreover, with such small teeth, what is the need for a sagittal crest? Crests are associated with large and heavy chewing apparatus. KNM ER 1805 probably dates to between 1.5 and 1.6 m.y. ago, and at such a time can be neither an ancestor nor a hybrid. This specimen will undoubtedly remain controversial for some time, as will KNM ER 1470.

When the skull of KNM ER 1470 was first described (R. E. F. Leakey,

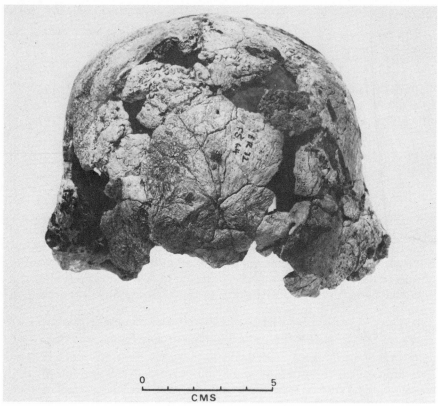

0   5

CMS

FIGURE 6-13 Skull of KNM ER 1470, posterior view. Note the bell-shaped flare of this cranium. Such flaring at the lower margin of the skull is typical of *Australopithecus* and is a strong indicator that this individual belongs with that genus rather than with *Homo,* as was originally thought. In the broken areas, the thinness of the skull bones can be detected; this also is a characteristic of *Australopithecus.* (Photograph courtesy of R. E. F. Leakey and Kenya National Museums.)

1973b), it was widely regarded as the earliest known member of the genus *Homo.* It was attributed to this genus because of its large cranial capacity (over 700 cc) and its straight, almost orthognathous face.

However, reevaluations of the skull since have indicated that, in fact, it shares many similarities with the australopithecines rather than with the hominines. Such features in the skull include thin cranial bones, large face-to-cranium ratio (see Table 6-3), V shape of the nasofrontal suture, and the bell-shaped outline of the skull (Figure 6-13). (See Walker, 1976; Corruccini, 1975; Wells, 1973.)

With the suggestion that KNM ER 1470 may be a large-skulled australopithecine, the taxonomic position of OH 7, "Homo habilis," should also be reconsidered. The skull of this individual was placed within the genus Homo also on the basis of its large cranial capacity of 687 cc (Tobias, 1971). This skull is much less complete than that of KNM ER 1470 and the individual was not fully mature. The parietal bones of OH 7 are well-rounded and the skull bones are thin. The possibility must be considered, then, that both KNM ER 1470 and OH 7 represent large-skulled australopithecines, rather than hominines, and that the full range of the cranial capacity of the genus Australopithecus was greater than originally recognized.

Other fossils, while of surer generic attribution, have proven difficult to identify at the specific level. Some early members of the genus Homo, for example, such as KNM ER 3733 and 3228 and OH 9 (see Chapter 8), are unequivocably members of Homo erectus on the basis of their similarities with other individuals so defined and so attributed. Others have a Homo-like trait pattern without demonstrating the full suite of characters present in Homo erectus. KNM ER 1805, for example, has hominine teeth but a smaller cranial capacity than is usual for Homo erectus.

On the basis of the known fossil record, it is pointless to argue the precise and specific attribution of such individuals. It is more useful to recognize the basic, underlying adaptive and morphological complexes.

SUMMARY

The model outlined here is based on an adaptive radiation of hominids into the Pliocene savannas. As a result of this radiation, two separate and distinct morphological complexes emerged. One was a progressively specializing herbivore built on a preadaptive morphological complex present in the ramapithecines: this was Australopithecus. These preadaptations permitted a habitat change from forest to savanna, while a similar dietary pattern of grasses, seeds, and vegetable foods was still maintained. Once in the savanna, greater dependence on the harsher and more fibrous elements in this diet led to a higher degree of dental specialization in some groups.

The second complex, based on the same preadaptations, followed a less specialized dietary course and relied on a very broad subsistence base: this was Homo. As indicated by the lack of dental specializations, this group became more omnivorous. This generalized, omnivorous subsistence base in turn provided the preadaptations for the human's later development of meat-eating and hunting practices.

Such a model is supported by the fossil evidence of the Early Pliocene. Although this earlier material is very limited, none of the morphological specializations present in the robust australopithecines of the later Pliocene and Pleistocene is apparent in it.

The evidence of the Kanapoi humerus and the australopithecine pelvis, femur, and lumbar spine is a strong indicator that bipedality appeared very early in human history. The degree of efficient adaptations for erect bipedality in the australopithecine fossil material suggests a great time depth for this locomotor mode. Bipedality and its functional precursors may well be ancient features of the family Hominidae. The presence of so rare a locomotor pattern in two slightly different forms of early hominids would be plausible only if it had been derived from a common ancestor.

It is a fascinating feature of the fossil record that greater evolutionary vigor, in terms of morphological diversity, was present, not in the line which leads to modern humans, but in a collateral side branch. Most known members of this group, the australopithecines, are probably too late in time to represent the ancestors of modern humans. It seems likely that the gracile members of this group maintained a morphology not too different from their earlier ancestors; yet they gave rise to rapidly evolving and specializing side branches of hominids, the robust australopithecines.

The hominine line, on the other hand, never demonstrated such morphological diversity and was much more conservative overall. It seems likely that the direct ancestors of modern humans developed behavioral complexities, rather than morphological ones, in order to cope with the demands of the environment. It may have been this range of behavioral adaptability that led the way out of Africa.

SUGGESTIONS FOR FURTHER READING

Day, M. H. 1977. *Guide to Fossil Man* (3d ed.). Chicago: University of Chicago Press. (A useful, up-to-date listing of the major fossil hominids; it includes information on classification, history, and anatomy of each specimen. It is also a good bibliographic source.)

Jolly, C. (ed.). 1978. *Early Hominids of Africa*. London: Duckworth. (A series of up-to-date papers on the African hominids.)

Le Gros Clark, W. E. 1947. "Observations on the Anatomy of the Fossil Australopithecinae," *Journal of Anatomy* (London), **81**, 300–333. (Both a classic and a prototype for the analysis of fossil hominids.)

Le Gros Clark, W. E. 1967. *Man Apes or Ape Men?* New York: Holt. (A concise introduction to the anatomy of the australopithecines.)

Robinson, J. 1972. *Early Hominid Posture and Locomotion*. Chicago: University of Chicago Press. (Concerned mostly with the South African material, this is a good discussion of the australopithecine postcranial material.)

Tobias, P. V. 1967. *Olduvai Gorge*, Vol. 2. Cambridge, England: Cambridge University Press. (Contains the comparative and anatomical description of "Zinjanthropus.")

7

PLIO-PLEISTOCENE HOMINID LOCALITIES

INTRODUCTION

A number of important localities, or sites, in east Africa and South Africa have yielded remains of Plio-Pleistocene hominids (Table 7-1). During the early part of this period human occupation seems, in fact, to have been focused entirely on Africa. However, by about 1.5 million years ago we see the first skeletal evidence that humans had moved beyond the African continent to other areas of the Old World.

Human cultural evolution began in the Plio-Pleistocene; and we must now add a new element to our study of human evolution: tools.[1]

---

[1]"When flaked stone is under discussion, the term 'artifact' includes all objects believed to have been formed by humanly induced fracture, whether as purposive target forms or as by-products. However, the term tool is reserved for objects with a series of trimming scars believed to indicate designed modification for use. Most flakes and other items of debitage have sharp edges and corners which give them high potential for use in cutting, piercing, or whittling" (Isaac, 1976a, p. 554).

TABLE 7-1 Hominid localities of the Plio-Pleistocene

	OMO	LAKE TURKANA	OLDUVAI	HADAR	OTHER SITES	MAKAPANSGAT	STERKFONTEIN	SWARTKRANS	KROMDRAAL	TAUNG	EUROPE	ASIA
PLEISTOCENE 1.1			H		Chad' H?							Java: Djetis Beds (H)
1.4	H	(H) Acheulian tools	?		Chesowanja R			← R →	← R →			
1.8			(H) G R		Natron R (Peninj)		← H Extension Site					
PLIOCENE 2	H · R	Oldowan tools H? G R →	G · G	G								
2.5	G · G · First artifacts			G ? · H?		← GR? →	← G Type Site →			← G? →		
3	G				Laetolil G							
4					Kanapoi G Chemeron G							
5					Lothagam G							
5.5												

Key: G = gracile Australopithecines   R = robust Australopithecines   H = *Homo*   (H) = *Homo erectus*

251

TOOLS OF THE PLIO-PLEISTOCENE

There are three categories of stones which may be classified as tools: (1) A **core** is a piece of rock which has had one or more chips removed to form a cutting, shearing, or chopping surface. (2) A **flake** is a chip or sliver of rock, removed from a larger piece, which has been trimmed or retouched on the cutting edge. (3) **Debitage** describes the material wasted when chipping rocks: these chips can be used as tools without further preparation.

The stone tool industries of the Plio-Pleistocene are highly variable, and this variability may be due to a number of causes. A primary cause may be differences in the physical properties of the raw materials used. Indeed, there seems to have been little selection for appropriate raw materials in the earliest assemblages. Some lavas and the quartzes, for example, break with a distinctive conchoidal or concave fracture and will almost automatically give a sharp edge. Isaac (1976a) has made the point that the "discovery" of conchoidal fracture in some types of stone was an important step in human cultural development, since such a cutting edge is sharp and very predictable. Other lavas and granites, however, may break with a straight (or nonconcave) edge and will result in a tool of very different appearance. Still other types of rocks will fall into many small pieces when struck.

Tools may also vary according to the way in which they are used. Isaac has pointed out (1976b) that only a sharp, pointed chip is needed to cut effectively through most animal material. Therefore, large, sophisticated tools are not a necessary part of human hunting or scavenging activities. Other activities, however, may require larger or differently shaped tools. The battering of nuts and seeds or bones (to remove the marrow) may require larger and heavier stones. Weapons, both offensive and defensive, are more effective when they are larger and heavier. The scraping and preparation of animal skins, if indeed such processing was done at this period, would require yet another type of stone tool.

Finally, differences in stone tool assemblages may reflect the cultural traditions and heritage of the hominids. While this relationship is clearly a factor in explaining later variations (as in the Upper Paleolithic), it may not be an important aspect of the variation at this early date.

The earliest stone tools occur at about 2.5 m.y. B.P. in Member C of the Shungura Formation in the Omo River Valley in Ethiopia. These are very small tools, apparently consisting of randomly broken rocks, that were used for some purpose, perhaps butchering. Other early tools occur at the CPH site at Lake Turkana (Isaac, Harris, and Crader, 1976). This site is approximately 8 to 10 m below the KBS tuff, which has been provisionally dated to 1.8 m.y. B.P. (see below). Stone tools from later than about 2 m.y. ago occur at a large number of sites in east Africa and South Africa.

At least three distinctive tool complexes existed in Plio-Pleistocene times; of these, the Oldowan and Acheulian are the most important. The third, termed the "Karari," has a very limited distribution and its significance is unclear at present. The Oldowan, discussed below, is known to occur in east and South Africa and, later, in north Africa (Ain Hanech) and at Ubeidiya in Israel. The Acheulian, discussed in Chapter 8, first appears about the middle of Bed II at Olduvai Gorge and later throughout Europe and the Near East. The Karari, at present, is known only from sites near Lake Turkana.

OLDOWAN

Typical Oldowan

The term "Oldowan" was first applied to industries from Bed I and lower Bed II at Olduvai Gorge. This early stone tool industry has several characteristics. First, there is a limited number of tool types; about six have been identified (M. D. Leakey, 1971a). These types are choppers, polyhedrons, scrapers (both heavy-duty and light-duty), spheroids, and discoids (Figure 7-1a). Second, when the Oldowan tools occur, there are usually few of them. In the earliest sites they generally are thinly scattered over a small area. This distribution may indicate that toolmaking was not frequently or easily accomplished at this period. It is in contrast to distributions in later sites where numerous tools may occur in relatively dense concentrations over a site. Third, the tools vary widely in appearance and lack the standardization that appears later in Acheulian assemblages, for example. This diversity may further reinforce the second observation that tool manufacture was neither frequent nor very important at this time.

Ecologically, these early artifact assemblages are often associated with water sources. At Olduvai and Lake Turkana, many of the archeological sites are near the lakeshore; in the Omo area, they are near watercourses, such as stream channels. Concerning this association, Issac has observed:

> It is almost a metaphysical point, but there is some interest in the fact that hominids, while colonizing the savanna, may have preferred to keep their home bases in strips of woodland that extended out into more open country, rather like tourists transporting themselves into Hilton hotels in alien lands! (1976b, p. 501)

In many of these sites the tool assemblages are associated with the remains of animals. It is an almost inescapable conclusion that the tools were used to dismember or butcher the animals. Between 2.5 and 2 m.y. ago, such tool-animal sites increased in number, a fact that very likely represents a rise in the importance of meat in the hominid diet during this period. We cannot determine, however, whether the butchered animals were deliberately killed or were scavenged after death from some other cause. But by this time, hominids were apparently adding meat to their diet on a more regular and frequent course.

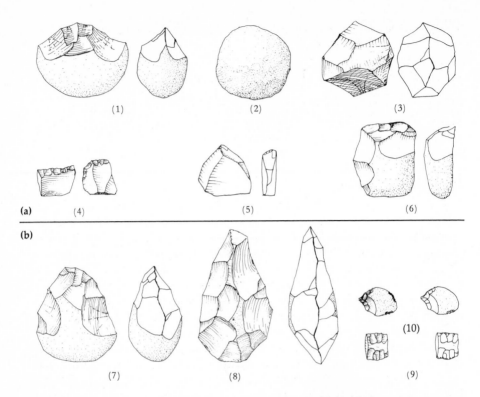

FIGURE 7-1 Oldowan tools. Oldowan tools were first identified in Bed I, Olduvai Gorge; they are now known from many sites in east and South Africa. Two subcategories of tools exist within the Oldowan: "Typical" and "Developed." **(a)** Typical Oldowan. "Typical" assemblages are characterized by a small number of tool forms; the most common of these is the chopper. (1) Chopper: In this tool a few large flakes were removed from a core of chert, basalt, or quartzite to form a cutting or chopping edge. The butt end was usually left unworked to form a comfortable handle. (2) Spheroid: A stone ball battered into a more or less rounded shape. Spheroids were usually made on lava and may have served as missiles or "bolas" stones. (3) Discoid: This tool is characterized by radial flaking of the entire circumference of the cobble. (4) Light-duty scraper: One end of this small stone tool usually shows additional small-calibre flaking (retouch) to form the working edge. These scrapers were usually made of quartzite or lava cores. (5) Burin: This has a small, pointed working surface at one end. (6) Heavy-duty scraper: Larger scrapers were made in the same way as light-duty scrapers, often with an unworked butt. **(b)** Developed Oldowan. In the "Developed" assemblages, a few new tool types appeared, the most important of these being the bifacial hand axe. (7) Developed Oldowan A: These "protobifaces" are typical of the earliest Developed assemblages in Upper Bed I. These are highly variable but usually have a relatively small number of flakes and an unworked butt. (8) Developed Oldowan B: These "true bifaces" first appeared in Middle Bed II. They are more finely made, are more consistent in pattern, and usually show working over the entire surface. (9) These small laterally trimmed flakes also represent a new tool type in Developed Oldowan B assemblages. (10) Small, pointed burins or awls are also new items. (Scale: 0.5; drawn by Ross Sackett.)

A final important point must be made. During this time period, at least two forms of hominid were in local coexistence. Indeed, many of the tool-animal sites contain skeletal evidence of one or more hominids, and we do not know which hominid form was responsible for the stone tools or the animal remains. On the basis of the dietary assumptions outlined in Chapter 6, it seems that the tool-animal assemblages are more likely to have been due to *Homo*. This assumption does not mean, however, that the australopithecines were incapable of tool use and manufacture.

Developed Oldowan

The typical Oldowan assemblages of Bed I and lower Bed II at Olduvai Gorge were followed, in the middle and upper parts of Bed II, by industries that have been termed the "Developed Oldowan" (Figure 7-1*b*). This group consists of two separate assemblages, termed "Developed Oldowan A and B." The Developed Oldowan assemblages seem to represent a gradual and local development from the typical Oldowan assemblages of the earlier series. There are two basic differences between the earlier Oldowan assemblages and the later Developed Oldowan series: greater diversity of tool types and greater quantities of tools at the sites.

In Developed Oldowan industries, three new tool forms appear: awls, cleavers, and a rudimentary, crudely chipped hand ax. Other components of the Developed Oldowan also occur in the earlier series but are numerically much less important. Thus, burins, cleavers, and spheroids all occur earlier but show important increases in the Developed Oldowan series; on the other hand, fewer choppers are found. The numerical increase of the spheroids or "symmetrical stone balls" is considered by Mary Leakey to be highly significant. She regards them as "missiles" that were either thrown singly or tied together with thongs and then thrown in bundles of two or three. As "bolas," they would, if the modern analogy holds, be thrown about the legs of an animal to immobilize it, thus allowing an easier kill (M. D. Leakey, 1971a.)

Nonlithic Tools[2]

A number of animal bones in the Olduvai deposits show evidence of modification and use. Of the 113 modified bones known from both Typical and Developed Oldowan sites, only 15 have come from Beds I and lower II. Among the earlier series are a polished horse rib and a few long bones which show evidence of chipping or smoothing. The remainder of these modified bones occurs at the Developed Oldowan sites. Of particular interest are a number of hippo canines and incisors that show chipping and

[2]The term "lithic" refers to stone; nonlithic tools are made from wood or bone.

flaking, especially at the pointed end of the tooth. Several giraffe scapulae show flaking around the edges; Mary Leakey speculates that with such modification, the scapulae would have made efficient shoveling or digging tools (M. D. Leakey, 1971a.)

SITES

SOUTH AFRICA

Hominids of Plio-Pleistocene age were first discovered in South Africa; therefore, the five South African sites have historical preeminence.

Much of the southern interior of the African continent rests on a plateau of dolomite (limestone), which has been mined commercially for many years. Dolomite characteristically forms solution cavities or caverns where water seeps down from the surface and dissolves the minerals. The plane of water seepage may gradually widen to form a shaft connecting with the surface. When it does so, the cavities will gradually fill with surface materials and then contain a valuable record for paleontologists. This "fill" material, consisting of surface debris and minerals dissolved from dolomite, then solidifies into a hard, dense mass (much like concrete) called **"breccia"**.

The caves may fill in several ways. They may act as catchment basins where surface material is washed or blown in or simply falls in. They may act as refuges for animals, such as leopards, hyenas, porcupines, owls, and humans, which leave behind records of their activities. Leopards, owls, and humans may leave the bony débris of their meals; hyenas and porcupines, their scavenged bone collections. Humans may, in addition, occupy such caves and leave evidence of their cultural activities, such as stone tools and utilized bone fragments. Clearly, most of the material in the five South African caves was either collected through the actions of scavengers and predators or brought from the surface by natural agencies. Plio-Pleistocene hominids did not occupy caves in the same way that later hominids did; probably only part of one of these caves, the Sterkfontein Extension area, acted as a living site. (See Sampson, 1974, for a detailed discussion of these sites.)

Several problems surround the interpretation and dating of the South African caves. First, all these sites represent former lime mines, and most of the fossil material has been derived from mining dumps outside the caves. Therefore, almost nothing has been found *in situ*, and we know very little about the stratigraphic and temporal relationships of this material. In the last few years, however, some new material has been recovered from Sterkfontein (by Philip Tobias) and Swartkrans (by C. K. Brain), and the stratigraphic position of this material is known. But the vast amount of the material recovered earlier cannot be placed in any precise stratigraphic framework.

The second major problem surrounding the South African cavesites is that the caves have not been precisely dated. Appropriate minerals for potassium-argon dating are not present and the deposits are too old for radiocarbon or racemization dating. In order to solve this problem, Partridge (1973) proposed an imaginative dating technique based on geomorphological evidence. He attempted to calibrate the geologic process of valley formation and in this way tried to date the time at which the caves became open and thus available to receive surface materials. Although this approach has been strongly criticized (Helgren and Butzer, 1974), Partridge's results correspond in a general way with dates derived from faunal correlations with other African sites. Thus the faunal assemblage at Sterkfontein Type site and Makapan (particularly the pigs and elephants) corresponds in many ways with faunas from sites absolutely dated to between 2.5 to 3 m.y. ago (Cooke, 1967; Maglio, 1973). Swartkrans Member I, on the same basis, may date to about 1.8 m.y. ago (Cooke, 1967). Vrba's analysis (1974, 1975) of the bovids corresponds broadly to this same framework.

Thus, although different investigators may vary in the exact placement of these sites, an oldest-to-youngest sequence of Makapan-Sterkfontein-Swartkrans-Kromdraai is usually agreed upon. The placement of Taung, however, continues to arouse controversy. This site was the first to be discovered and has now been totally destroyed by mining activities. Most early investigators believed that Taung was the oldest of the known sites, but Wells (1969) and, more recently Partridge (1973) have disputed this assertion.

Taung

The lime workings at Taung[3] in Cape Province provided the first evidence of hominids in the Plio-Pleistocene. Mining activities in these deposits had revealed the presence of a fossil species of baboon; some of the findings were shown to Raymond Dart, in the Anatomy Department of the University of Witwatersrand, Johannesburg, South Africa. Dart, who was interested in paleontology, asked to be informed of any further discoveries. In late 1924, blasting at Taung uncovered part of the face and brain case of a then unknown type of primate. Dart's preparation of these remains revealed a face and jaws in nearly perfect condition (Figure 7-2). The presence of a full deciduous dentition with the first molars just coming into wear indicated that the individual was about 6 years old. Dart published a preliminary report of this find in *Nature*, February 7, 1925. In this report, he

---

[3]"Taung" is Bantu for "place of the lion."

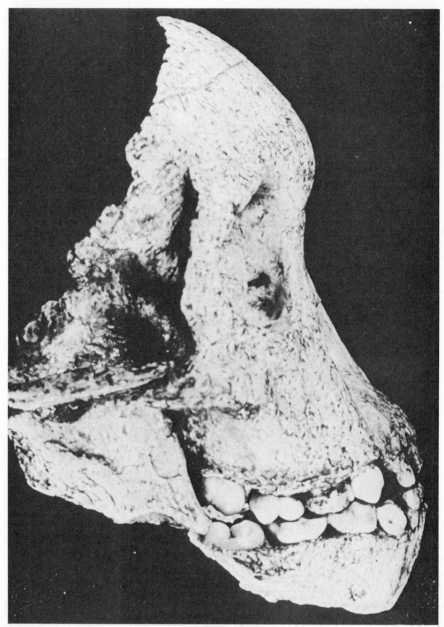

FIGURE 7-2 The Taung child, the first australopithecine to be discovered. When Raymond Dart suggested, in 1925, that the child was a hominid, he pointed out the forward position of the foramen magnum, the relatively high and rounded forehead, the large braincase, and the human characteristics of the teeth, including a small canine. (Photograph courtesy of M. Wolpoff.)

stated that the remains were those of a human-like ape with features intermediate between living anthropoids and humans. He pointed out that the brain was large (525 cc) and that its general structure was more like that of humans than of apes.[4] In particular, the lunate sulcus, a groove on the rear portion of the brain which demarcates the visual portion of the brain, occupied a posterior position, as in humans. He noted that the foramen magnum was located forward of its position in the apes; this placement suggested a whole syndrome of characters associated with bipedality and freedom of the hands. Moreover, the dentition had a distinctly human appearance. He supported his locomotor interpretation by noting that at the time the child had lived, the Taung area was a "near desert," so that the arboreal life typical of most primates would have been impossible. Dart concluded by proposing the taxon *Australopithecus africanus*, meaning "southern African ape." He also proposed a new primate family, the "Homo-simiadae," to indicate its transitional morphology.

Dart was severely criticized for his conclusions and interpretations regarding this individual. Only Sollas in England and Robert Broom, a fellow South African, offered support. Broom, in his book *Finding the Missing Link* (1959), argued:

> In England, many took little interest in the discovery of what might be a being closely related to man's ancestors, but they were greatly interested in the pedantic question of whether the name Australopithecus was good Latin! Prof. Dart might or might not be a great anatomist, but they were sure he was not a great classical scholar. As if it mattered in the least! Even one of the leading scientists in the British Museum wrote as follows in *Nature*, June 20, 1925: 'If you want to join in a game, you must learn the rules.' But even worse was his statement: 'Prof. Dart does not yet realize the many-sideness of his offences.' Here was a man who had made one of the greatest discoveries in the world's history—a discovery that may yet rank in importance with Darwin's *Origin of Species*; and English culture treats him as if he had been a naughty schoolboy. (pp. 26–27)

Among Dart's "crimes" was the mixing of Greek and Latin in the term "Australopithecus" and his proposing a transitional taxonomic family to contain the specimen. Among his harsher critics was Arthur Smith-Woodward, who concluded that the skull belonged to a fossil chimp and that it had "little bearing" on human evolution. Smith-Woodward is to be remembered also for writing the definitive work in support of the human status of "Piltdown Man."

As time passed, a few more scientists came to support Dart's conclusions; one of the most important of them was William Gregory at the American Museum of Natural History. After studying the dentition of the

---

[4]Holloway (1970) has recently revised his figure for brain size to 405 cc.

Taung jaw, Gregory and Hellman (1939a) concluded that it shared 2 characters with gorillas, 1 with chimps, and 20 with primitive humans.

General acceptance of *Australopithecus* as a hominid did not come, however, for over 20 years. Prior to the First Pan African Congress on Prehistory in 1947, Le Gros Clark went to South Africa to examine the original material. Later, at the Congress meetings in Nairobi, he stated his conclusion that this first specimen, and others discovered subsequently, were in fact hominids and therefore relatives of humans. The prestige of Le Gros Clark, professor of anatomy at Oxford, was such that his viewpoint gained wide credence. Such restraint in the acceptance of a valid hominid fossil is ironic, when a fraudulent fossil such as Piltdown was accepted enthusiastically and almost without question.

The Taung child is the only hominid to be recovered from that site, and although its hominid status is no longer in question, its date and precise taxonomic position remain in dispute.

As pointed out previously, the traditional chronologic position of Taung as the oldest of the South African hominid sites has recently been questioned. These doubts have been raised by the geomorphological evidence that points to a possible opening of the Taung cave at less than 0.9 m.y. ago (Partridge, 1973) and by faunal comparisons that indicate that the Taung material is much younger than Sterkfontein. Butzer, using both geomorphological and paleoecological evidence, has also provided evidence that the Taung site is "no older than Swartkrans and Kromdraai" (1974). Butzer's studies suggest that the Taung hominid-bearing breccias were deposited during a wet period, rather than a dry one as previously thought.

Thus, the site cannot be dated precisely at present. If it is in fact the youngest, rather than the oldest, of the South African sites, the Taung child would be the youngest of all known australopithecines, postdating by perhaps 200,000 years the most recent individuals known from east Africa.

The second problem associated with the Taung site is the taxonomic allocation of its one hominid. After Dart's description, the Taung child became the type of the taxon *Australopithecus africanus*, the gracile group of the australopithecines. Since then, it has been suggested that the type of the gracile australopithecines may, in fact, be a juvenile of the robust form, usually called *A. robustus* (Tobias, 1973; Sperber, 1974). Indeed, the only adult tooth present, the first molar, does show the distinctive side-to-side expansion characteristic of the robust group. If this identification is correct, the robust australopithecines would now have to be called *A. africanus* according to the rules of zoological nomenclature, a nomen associated for more than 50 years with the gracile variety. Further, the gracile group would have to be renamed, presumably as *A. transvaalensis*. The resulting confusion would be considerable, to say the least. The question of whether the "gracile" features of the Taung child are due to actual affinity with that group or to its youth has yet to be resolved.

Sterkfontein Valley

Three major Plio-Pleistocene hominid sites are located within sight of one another in the Sterkfontein Valley, about midway between Johannesburg and Pretoria, in South Africa. Initial investigations at Sterkfontein, Kromdraai, and Swartkrans were made by Robert Broom, a medical doctor and amateur paleontologist, in the 1930s and 1940s.

Sterkfontein Cave   By 1934 Broom had relinquished his medical practice to become a full-time paleontologist at the Transvaal Museum in Pretoria. During his work there, especially on the Permian-aged reptiles of the Karoo, he learned of a lime-mining cave at Sterkfontein, about 65 km from Pretoria. Broom later (1959) made the poignant observation that although this cave had been known since the 1890s as a paleontological site, no investigations had taken place there for nearly 40 years, during which time uncounted and invaluable fossils had undoubtedly been burned in the lime kilns.

In his first 9 days of work at Sterkfontein, Broom recovered most of an australopithecine face and skull, and in less than a year had recovered cranial remains of eight more individuals. For the first of these, he proposed the nomen *Australopithecus transvaalensis* (1936). However, after more thorough study of the teeth, he decided that the differences between Taung and Sterkfontein were at the generic level and proposed the taxon *Plesianthropus transvaalensis*.

Extensive excavations have revealed the existence of two hominid sites within the Sterkfontein locality that appear to represent distinct depositional phases. The earliest of these is called the "Type" site and the somewhat younger deposits are called the "Extension" site. Both sites are contiguous and the Extension site overlies the Type site in one area (Table 7-2).

Analyses of faunal remains from the Sterkfontein Valley hominid sites have been carried out by Vrba (1974, 1975). Her analyses, which are focused particularly on the bovids, involved the size of the taxa preserved and the condition and completeness of the remains. From these data she has tried to reconstruct both the ecological requirements of the fauna and the conditions surrounding its inclusion in the site deposits.

In her analysis of the Sterkfontein Type site, Vrba has pointed out that the remains of the bovids there are from large genera, and that fewer than half of them are of juveniles. The large size and maturity of the remains found in these breccias probably reflect the feeding activities of a large carnivore, such as a sabertoothed cat. Furthermore, the bovids there were

TABLE 7-2 The Sterkfontein Formation

MEMBER	AGE (m.y.)	HOMINIDS	CULTURAL ASSOCIATIONS
5 Extension site	1.5–2.0	*Homo:* skull (STW 53), isolated teeth, fragmented metacarpal	Developed Oldowan or earliest Acheulian
4 Type site	2.5–3.0	*A. africanus* (parts of more than 60 individuals)	None
3		None	None
2		None	None
1		None	None

Source: Data from Hughes and Tobias, 1977.

dependent on a reliable water supply and are usually found in areas of dense bush cover. Although a number of hominids have been recovered from the Type site, neither stone tools nor occupational débris have been found. The interpretation of the Type site is, then, that it reflects the lair of a large cat, possibly a saber-toothed cat, and the hominids, like the bovids, represent the remains of their feeding activities.

Depositional conditions at the Sterkfontein Extension site appear rather different, however (Vrba, 1975). The bovid remains from this area of the site are very fragmented and show a wide distribution in both age and size. Vrba concluded that this material would be best interpreted as representing bones scavenged from carnivore kills. The large number of stone tools at the Extension site would indicate that the scavenging had been done by a hominid.

The stone tool assemblage from the Sterkfontein Extension site resembles the Developed Oldowan series from middle and upper Bed II, Olduvai. The basic Oldowan components are present, as well as a few bifacial hand axes (M. D. Leakey, 1970). These tools, and the ones from the Swartkrans "Brown" breccia (Member II), are somewhat larger than the Olduvai materials, however. Virtually no flakes are present, suggesting that the tools were made elsewhere, perhaps at the site where the raw materials were collected. A single bone tool has been identified from the Sterkfontein Extension site; this bone flake has been shaped and worked to a point at one end.

Over the past few years, a number of small isolated hominid teeth have been recovered from the Sterkfontein Extension site; and in August 1976, precisely 40 years to the day after Broom's first visit to the site, a skull

(STW 53) was found *in situ* in Member 5 (see Table 7-2). Tobias (1976b) and Hughes and Tobias (1977) have attributed this skull to "Homo habilis." The skull is small, although too incomplete at present for any measurement, and its walls are thin. These features are found more often in the australopithecines than in early *Homo*.

In summary, the hominids from both Sterkfontein sites are small and lightly built; whether they belong to two genera is not clear. The dental material, particularly within the Type site, shows a considerable range of variation from very small to large. Such variation probably reflects sexual dimorphism, since the morphological complex seems to be constant.

Postcranial material is relatively well represented at the Type site; all this material seems to be from very small and lightly built individuals. In particular, the pelvis of STS 14 is very gracile and has a number of similarities with the pelvis of AL 288 from Hadar, Ethiopia (see Figure 6-6a). The femoral (see Figure 6-8) and vertebral remains from Sterkfontein also reflect this type of morphology. Of particular interest in the Sterkfontein vertebral material (see Figure 6-7) is the indication that the lower part of the spine had the same S-shaped curve found in living humans. This is a further substantiation of upright bipedality.

Swartkrans The most productive of the South African cavesites is Swartkrans, just across the valley from the Sterkfontein cave. Paleontological excavations were begun here after lime mining had ceased in the late 1940s.

The geology of the Swartkrans cave has long been a source of some confusion. Most studies have concluded that all the cave fillings were roughly contemporaneous and that therefore the faunal remains, hominids, and stone tools represent a single depositional phase. The presence of a clearly advanced hominine, originally called "Telanthropus," in association with robust australopithecines added further confusion to the picture.

However, recent studies have shown the existence of two separate depositional sequences at Swartkrans (Vrba, 1975; Brain, personal communication, 1975) (Figure 7-3). The earlier of these sequences is represented by Member I of the Swartkrans Formation; this sequence was formerly called the "Primary" (or "Pink") breccia. Member II, initially known as the "Brown" or "Secondary" breccia, probably dates to the Middle Pleistocene. Member I may be broadly contemporaneous with Bed I at Olduvai Gorge (see Table 7-1).

Vrba's faunal analyses have revealed that the bovids here are predominantly juveniles of medium-sized genera; all available evidence suggests that the faunas in Member I, including more than 60 hominids, were accumulated by a large species of carnivore. On the basis of weight and age distribution of the bovids (Vrba, 1975) and other lines of evidence

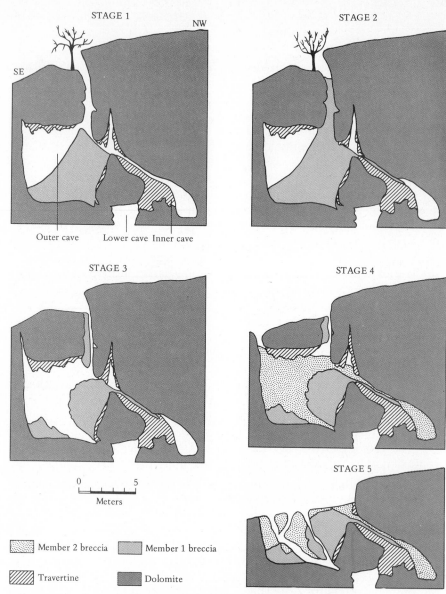

STAGE 1

NW

SE

Outer cave Lower cave Inner cave

STAGE 2

STAGE 3

STAGE 4

0 — 5
Meters

STAGE 5

Member 2 breccia   Member 1 breccia

Travertine   Dolomite

FIGURE 7-3 The evolution of the Swartkrans cave; such development is typical of cave formation in dolomitic limestone areas. *Stage 1:* Outer cave opens through a vertical shaft to the surface. Debris from the surface enters this shaft and will eventually become the older breccia. *Stage 2:* Vertical Shaft becomes clogged with surface debris. *Stage 3:* Percolation of rainwater reopens part of the vertical shaft and erodes the older breccia. *Stage 4:* A new vertical shaft forms to the surface, allowing the entry of new materials which will become the younger breccia. *Stage 5:* Erosion of the hillside above the cave exposes the breccias on the surface. Fragments of about eighty-eight robust australopithecines, a single *Homo* (SK 847), and a few rough stone tools were recovered from the Member I breccias. Only members of the genus *Homo* and a few bifacial hand axes have been recovered from Member II. (Courtesy of C. K. Brain.)

(Brain, 1970), this carnivore was probably a leopard. The fact that leopards preyed upon the Sterkfontein Valley hominids is dramatically demonstrated in the hominid cranium SK 54. The skull of this juvenile robust australopithecine shows two round perforations in the rear of the cranium. The distance between these two holes exactly corresponds to the distance between the mandibular canines of fossil leopards from the same site. Brain has suggested that the canines of the leopard's upper jaw would have been placed in the child's orbits.

Most of the 60 hominids from Member I are clearly robust australopithecines. Although some of these individuals were very heavily built, none reached the degree of robusticity seen in the very large east African individuals. However, two specimens are tentative evidence of the presence of *Homo* during Member I times. The first of these, SK 45, is a small fragment of mandible with M_1 and M_2 present. These teeth do not show the expansion characteristic of the robust australopithecines, and there is no thickening or buttressing of the mandible. The second piece of evidence is a cranium, SK 847, composed of three separate fragments. Two of them were originally attributed to a robust australopithecine *(Paranthropus)*; the maxillary fragment was attributed first to "Telanthropus" and later to *Homo erectus*. On fitting these individual fragments together, it was decided that they all belonged to a more advanced hominid, probably *Homo* (Clarke, Howell, and Brain, 1970). Wallace (1978) has suggested that SK 45 and SK 847 are, in fact, part of the same individual.

The evidence for stone tools from Member I is tentative. Brain reports that possibly six tools have been identified from these deposits. Most of them are "pebble choppers" (personal communication, 1975).[5]

A rather different ecological and cultural situation appears to be present in Member II. These deposits may be much younger than Member I, perhaps about 0.4 m.y. old (Vrba, 1975). Within these deposits the bovids are mostly the juveniles of small species. The predator here, then, was probably small also. Such selection of prey may indicate that these juveniles are not scavenged remains of carnivore kills; the juveniles of small species would be logical prey for a human hunter. An interpretation of the Member II deposits as indicative of hunting is also supported by the relatively many tools from this site. About 50 stone tools have been identified. Overall, these tools resemble the Developed Oldowan from Olduvai Bed II; the basic Oldowan components are present, with the addition of a few hand axes, cleavers, and heavy-duty picks.

Stone tools and a very few hominid remains are known from Member II, and all appear to belong to *Homo*. The mandible SK 15 (Figure 7-4),

---

[5]In her discussion of the Swartkrans stone tools, Mary Leakey (1970) reported that the only tools from this site were "unquestionably" from the "Pink" breccia (now Member I). More recent work has shown that most, if not all, of the stone tools are from the later Member II deposits (Brain, personal communication, 1975).

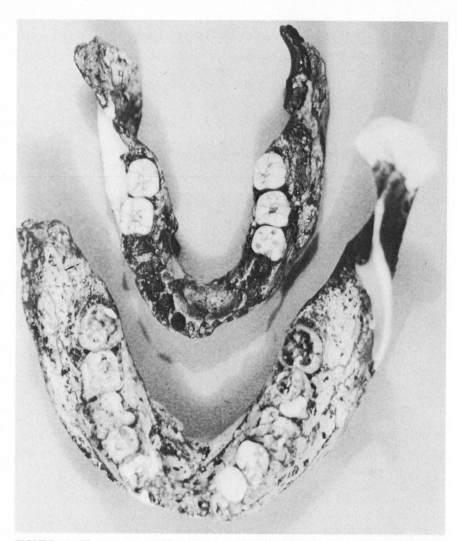

FIGURE 7-4 These two mandibles show the range of variation between the older Member I hominids and those from Member II. SK 12 (at the bottom) is a robust australopithecine from Member I; SK 15 (first called "Telanthropus"), from Member II, probably belongs to *Homo erectus*. Note the divergence of the mandibular rami and the thick buttressing at the front of the robust australopithecine jaw; these features are absent in SK 15.

originally called "Telanthropus," is the best evidence for this allocation; this specimen has the low, parallel jaw borders and the low ramus characteristic of early *Homo*, particularly *Homo erectus*. The teeth are small and no buttressing is present. SK 15 presents a very different morphological pattern from the robust australopithecine mandibular material in Member I.

Kromdraai The third hominid site in the Sterkfontein Valley, Kromdraai, was discovered in 1938 by a schoolboy who picked up a fossilized maxilla from the surface about a mile from the Sterkfontein site. The news of the discovery reached Broom, who bought the maxilla (and four fossilized teeth the boy had in his pocket). Upon examining the site, now on a private farm and no longer being excavated, Broom recovered much of the left side of a face and part of a lower jaw. This material belonged to a large, robust form of hominid which Broom named *"Paranthropus robustus"* (1939). The total hominid assemblage from Kromdraai is extremely limited and was probably derived from a very few individuals. All this material shows the typical robust australopithecine pattern: sagittal cresting is present on the cranial fragments and the jaws show the posterior enlargement of the cheek teeth characteristic of this group.

Two separate sites are in fact recognized at Kromdraai. Kromdraai A has no hominid remains and may have been a carnivore lair (Vrba, 1975); Kromdraai B is the hominid site. A number of faunal remains have been recovered from Kromdraai B, and, as at Member II at Swartkrans, this faunal assemblage is dominated by the juveniles of small species. This may indicate, as it did at Swartkrans, that a small-sized predator was active here too. At Kromdraai, however, the only hominid known is australopithecine not *Homo*. Could this indicate that the australopithecines were part of the prey of a carnivore or of a hominid not represented in the deposits? Or, alternatively, does this finding indicate that the robust australopithecines, for all their dental specializations, were also carnivorous on occasion? There is insufficient evidence to decide.

Makapan This site, also known as the "Makapan Limeworks," is located approximately 200 miles north of Pretoria. Table 7-3 shows the stratigraphic sequence at Makapan. Although the deposits have proven as difficult to date as those at other South African sites, various data indicate that the maximum age for the australopithecine-bearing levels may be about 3 m.y. Paleomagnetic results also support this date and bracket these deposits to be between 1.8 m.y. and 3 m.y. (Brock, McFadden, and Partridge, 1977).

Early investigations at this lime quarry were initiated by Raymond Dart, who was first made aware of the paleontological potential of the site by a collector who sent him blackened and possibly burned ungulate bones in 1925. On the basis of these bones, Dart postulated the existence of a fire-using hominid which he named "Australopithecus prometheus" (1943a, b).

The existence of a fossil hominid in the early levels at Makapan was not demonstrated, however, until James Kitching's recovery of an australo-

TABLE 7-3 The Makapan Formation

DATES, m.y. B.P.	MEMBER	DESCRIPTION	SPECIMENS
2–1.8	Member V	Red breccia	Australopithecine maxilla, stone tools
	Member IV	Pink breccia	Australopithecine occiput (MLD 1), stone tools
2.5	Member III	Gray breccia	Most of the australopithecines, Osteodontokeratic materials, no stone tools
3	Member II	Brownish-red breccia	No hominids, abundant animal bones
	Member I	Travertine	No hominids, very few animal bones

Sources: Sampson, 1974; Brain, 1958; Brock and McFadden, and Partridge, 1977.

pithecine occiput in 1947 (Dart, 1948b). This discovery stimulated further explorations both within the lime mine itself and in the miners' dumps nearby. This work revealed the presence of several more hominids and a large quantity of stone and bone material, possibly containing evidence of human modification.

Two major controversies have long surrounded Dart's interpretation of the material found at Makapan. When he was shown the blackened faunal material in 1925, he concluded that these bones had been burned by hominids. Dart (1948a) later reported on chemical analyses which showed the presence of free carbon in the bones, thus seeming to confirm that they had been burned. The full results of these examinations were never published, and in 1956, Kenneth Oakley, of the British Museum, attempted to resolve the question. He concluded, after analyzing several samples from Makapan, that no free carbon was found and that the blackening was probably due to manganese dioxide staining. Oakley (1956) attributed the earlier results to contamination, perhaps from the miners' blasting or from modern hearths. There is, finally, no evidence of any deliberate use of fire by Plio-Pleistocene hominids at Makapan or anywhere else; such evidence first occurs in association with *Homo erectus* in the Middle Pleistocene.

Certainly the most controversial aspect of the Makapan deposits is Dart's claim that they contain large amounts of occupational debris of early hominids. He contended that the broken animal bones in these deposits included not only the remains of australopithecine meals but also their tools. These tools, Dart asserted, were made of such raw materials as bone, teeth, and horn; being an inveterate coiner of words, he proposed the term **"Osteodontokeratic"** to describe this assemblage (Figure 7-5). To support this contention, Dart pointed out that the nonhuman bones in the deposits do not represent a random sample of parts of the skeleton; furthermore, he argued, they demonstrate a consistent pattern of breakage and modification. There are, for example, bovid and ungulate jaws whose sharply

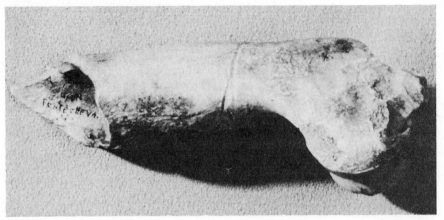

FIGURE 7-5 An Osteodontokeratic tool from Makapan. This antelope leg bone shows possible signs of having been altered by humans. The pointed end shows some microscopic signs of wear and chipping, and the deep incision encircling the shaft probably could not have been made by nonhuman agencies.

serrated teeth show chipping or smoothing; there are limb bones which have been broken, so that they appear to be "scoops." Many of the bone flakes show signs of abrasion. There are some "compound tools," which are composed of two separate fragments. In some cases, for example, a smaller bone has been rammed into the marrow cavity of a larger one. In others, a piece of stone or stalagmite has been wedged between the condyles of a limb bone. The most striking of these tools is the skull of a hyena with a bone (an antelope calcaneus) thrust up between the zygomatic arch and the skull. Many of the long bones have been broken in a manner which strongly suggests torsional or twisting kinds of actions.

Dart's interpretation[6] of the Makapan assemblage was supported by Tobias (1965a, 1967), who has clearly shown the presence of localized wear on the edges and tips of some of the bone fragments; such localized wear, Tobias argued, could have occurred only with deliberate use. He also emphasized that there are 5 times as many antelope humeri as femora and 10 times more distal humeri than proximal humeri. Therefore the distal end of the humerus, with its heavy double condyles, seems to have been selected for some purpose, Tobias concluded. He pointed out that more than 80 percent of the baboon skulls from Makapan, Taung, and Sterkfontein show skull fractures made on fresh bone with depressions which fit these double condyles. Some of the distal humeri, moreover, show signs of battering. It should be pointed out that if these humeri were "clubs," they must have been wielded from very close quarters indeed. Most are not

[6]Wolberg (1970) has provided a comprehensive discussion of various interpretations of the Osteodontokeratic assemblage.

more than 10 to 12 cm long, and a small australopithecine that clubbed a large Pleistocene baboon would have required considerable courage, at the very least.

While some workers have supported Dart's claims, others have rejected them. Some have contended, for example, that both hyenas and porcupines may have accumulated these bone collections. Washburn (1957), for example, has observed that similar bone accumulations occur at carnivore kill sites and has postulated that the Makapan cave may have served as a carnivore lair.

Other work has been conducted in order to examine those factors that may affect the types of bones preserved within a site. Brain (1967, 1976a, b) has studied the remains of goat kills at a Hottentot village in southwest Africa (Table 7-4). He concluded that the more resistant (to weathering, chewing, and scavenging) a bone is, the more likely it is to be included in an archeological deposit. He has related this survival to the age at which the growth of the bone ceases and fusion occurs.[7] In the Hottentot goat kills, the distal humerus and proximal radius (the parts of the bone nearest the elbow) fuse before their opposite ends do. Therefore, they should be more resistant to destruction. Hence, they should occur in greater proportions than the opposite ends. This is exactly the observed situation with regard to the antelope forelimbs at Makapan and at the Hottentot village. However, Brain acknowledges that the modern analogy does not fully explain the Makapan accumulations. For example, he points out that fewer distal tibiae occur at Makapan than would be expected, and distal metacarpals and metatarsals are more common than the expected proximal portions.

In the end, the explanation of the Makapan bone accumulations and the validity of the Osteodontokeratic as a cultural assemblage is undoubtedly a complex one. It is probable that no single answer is adequate to explain all the qualitative and quantitative features of these deposits. It is likely, for example, that carnivores and porcupines have contributed some elements. But they have not contributed all. In a study of a modern porcupine lair, Hughes (1954) noted that about 70 percent of all bones had gnaw marks left by porcupine incisors; less than 1 percent of the Makapan bones have been gnawed.

The analogy with goat remains from modern Hottentot settlements suggests that scavenging (by hyenas or hominids?) may have played an important role in the accumulations; but the modern analogy does not explain the much smaller proportion of distal tibiae in the Makapan deposits. It does not explain the "compound tools" or the "scoops."

In the end, it seems valid to suggest that the early hominids at Makapan contributed something to the Osteodontokeratic assemblage in

---

[7]Growth of bone occurs between the end of the shaft and the articular area. Thus, during growth, the shaft and its ends remain separate so that the growth can occur. Once growth is complete, the separate portions fuse into a single bone.

TABLE 7-4   Bone survival: Hottentot goats versus Makapan antelopes

	HOTTENTOT GOATS	MAKAPAN ANTELOPES
Half mandibles		
Humerus: distal		
Tibia: distal		
Radius and ulna: proximal		
Metatarsal: proximal		
Scapula		
Pelvis		
Metacarpal: proximal		
Axis		
Atlas		
Metacarpal: distal		
Radius and ulna: distal		
Metatarsal: distal		
Femur: proximal		
Astragalus		
Calcaneus		
Ribs		
Tibia: proximal		
Lumbar vertebrae		
Femur: distal		
Cervical 3–7 vertebrae		
Thoracic vertebrae		
Phalanges		
Sacrum		
Humerus: proximal		
Caudal vertebrae		
Other parts		

Hottentot goats axis: 0   20   40   60   80   100
Makapan antelopes axis: 0   20   40   60   80

Percentage survival of parts

Source: Courtesy of C. K. Brian.

the way of deliberate selection and modification of some of the animal bones.

   The conclusion that at least some of this material has been deliberately and artificially worked seems inescapable, once the original material has been examined. It is, in fact, difficult to understand the reluctance of some anthropologists to accept at least some small part of the assemblage as tools when one realizes that just such a group of tools is demanded by most earlier models of human evolution. It is implicit, for example, in Washburn's writings, from about 1950 on, regarding the role of tool use in hominid evolution.

   Most anthropologists have agreed that stone tool manufacture represents a later stage in human cultural development for two reasons. First, stone is relatively difficult to work, requiring some skill to remove properly shaped flakes. Second, a stone tool (a hand ax, a chopper, etc.) is not apparent within the raw material of the stone; the tool must be visualized and a plan of manufacture formulated before tool production can be undertaken. The situation is quite different, however, with such materials as bones, teeth, and horn. During feeding, the long bones would be broken, perhaps by twisting, to obtain the marrow. This action in itself would result in sharply pointed bone fragments with obvious and immediately visible uses. Manipulation of an animal skull to obtain the brain and tongue, for example, would expose the teeth. The uses of sharply serrated occlusal surfaces of some ungulate teeth again may be readily visualized.

It is only logical, then, that the evolutionary precursor of stone tools, or the replacement of stone tools in areas where raw materials are poor, would be the remains of food animals. The Osteodontokeratic assemblage, while justifiably criticized on some grounds, does fulfill such a model.

The hominids from Makapan are generally placed with the gracile australopithecine group, but this allocation is not entirely satisfactory. The human remains from these deposits show a great range of variability. On one occipital bone (MLD 1), for example, the attachment lines for the temporalis muscle are just 5 mm apart; although the top part of this skull is missing, it is possible that, further forward, the temporal muscles may have met to form a sagittal crest. Such cresting is not known for the gracile australopithecines but is found in the robust group. The juvenile mandible (MLD 2) also shows some robust characteristics; and both Tobias (1967) and Aguirre (1970) have suggested that this individual may belong within that group rather than with the gracile australopithecines. The most marked robust feature of this mandible is the side-to-side (buccolingual) expansion of the M_2.

East Africa

A number of important Plio-Pleistocene hominid sites are known in east Africa. These sites center in two geographic areas: northern Tanzania and southern Ethiopia–northern Kenya.

Olduvai Gorge, Tanzania In historical perspective, undoubtedly the most important of all east African sites is Olduvai Gorge[8] (Table 7-5). The Gorge was apparently first seen by a non-African in 1911 when a German entomologist named Kattwinkel reportedly nearly fell into it while pursuing butterflies with a net (Cole, 1975, p. 80). Kattwinkel collected some paleontological specimens, along with his insects, which were taken back to Germany. Later, Hans Reck, a geologist with the Geological Survey of

[8]In the Masai language, *ol duvai* means "place of the wild sisal."

TABLE 7-5   Biostratigraphy of Olduvai Gorge

DATE, m.y. B.P.		BED	HOMINIDS	CULTURAL ASSOCIATIONS
0.15	Recent			
0.32	Naisiusiu		OH 1	
0.4	Ndutu			
0.6	Masek			
0.8	Bed IV	Tuff IV B .7 m.y.	OH 2, 11, 12, 22, 23, 28	Acheulian
1.15	Bed III			
	Upper Member		OH 3, 9, 19	Developed Oldowan B
1.5	Bed II	Faunal	OH 13, 14, 15, 18, 32	Acheulian
		Break		Developed Oldowan A
	Lower Member		OH 16, 20, 30	Oldowan
1.7		Tuff II A 1.71 m.y.		
	Bed I	Tuff I B 1.75 m.y.	OH 10, 26, 27, 31	Oldowan
			OH 5, 6, 7, 8, 35 OH 4	
2.1			OH 24	
	Precambrian	basement		

German East Africa, visited Olduvai during explorations in 1913. While working at Olduvai, he discovered the nearly complete skeleton of "Oldoway Man" (Olduvai Hominid 1), which later was also taken to Germany.[9] Louis Leakey, while studying bows and arrows in Munich in 1925, saw "Oldoway Man," and after discussing with Reck the Pleistocene fauna apparently in association with the skeleton, he determined to do his own exploring there.

Louis Leakey, born in east Africa of missionary parents, began studying his surroundings at an early age. After taking a distinguished double-first degree at Cambridge, with majors in anthropology and modern languages (French and Kikuyu), he returned to east Africa in 1926.

[9]This modern *Homo sapiens* skeleton probably dates from the Upper Pleistocene.

By 1931 he had organized the First East African Expedition which went to Olduvai.

Leakey is a germinal figure in the history of studies of early hominids. Although some of his interpretations in areas of taxonomy and evolutionary theory resulted in active controversy, he envisioned east Africa as a home of early hominids, and in this he was indisputably right. His early archeological work and the recovery of the Gamble's Cave, Kanam, and Kanjera material reinforced his idea that east Africa was the place to look for evidence of early hominids. From 1931 to 1959 he worked sporadically at Olduvai. He was joined there in 1935 by Mary Nicol (later to be his wife), who had previously illustrated stone tools for one of his books. During this period, they recovered a large collection of stone tools and Pleistocene faunas but only two fragments of human skull and two human teeth. His foresight and persistence in searching for early hominids at Olduvai was rewarded in 1959 with Mary Leakey's recovery of the skull of "Zinjanthropus" (Olduvai Hominid 5), a superrobust australopithecine. Since that time, more than 50 Early and Middle Pleistocene hominids have been recovered from the Gorge. Although it has long been fashionable in academic circles to criticize Louis Leakey for some of his not-well-considered pronouncements, it is worth estimating what the extent of our knowledge of Early Pleistocene hominids would be without him, Mary Leakey, and their son Richard.

Beyond the historical perspective, the deposits at Olduvai are important for other reasons. First, they contain recurring series of volcanic deposits, making possible the use of absolute dating techniques, such as potassium-argon. Second, almost all the hominid material has been recovered while still *in situ*, so that its exact geologic and stratigraphic provenance is known. In both these factors, Olduvai Gorge and, indeed, the rest of the east African sites contrast strongly with the South African sites. Finally, excavation techniques used at the Gorge are very precise and some are very extensive, leading to a much richer and more varied picture of early human activity than we have from anywhere else at this time level.

Olduvai Gorge represents a stream-cut valley about 65 km long and between 50 and 80 m deep. Stratigraphically, it is divided into seven levels. Bed I, along with the lower portion of Bed II, forms a single ecological and depositional sequence and, as such, they will be discussed together. In middle Bed II times, geological and ecological changes occurred which are reflected in different archeological and environmental contexts in middle and upper Bed II.

BED I AND LOWER BED II (1.9 TO 1.5 M.Y. B.P.)   During the deposition of Bed I and lower Bed II (Table 7-6), a large alkaline and fresh-water lake existed on the vast plain of the Serengeti. Available evidence suggests that the climate was somewhat wetter at that time than at present. In the lakebed

TABLE 7-6 Hominids from Bed I 3–1 lower Bed II, Olduvai Gorge

POSITION	HOMINID NUMBER (OH)	DATE OF DISCOVERY	PARTS PRESERVED	ORIGINAL TAXONOMIC STATUS	ASSOCIATED INDUSTRY
Lower Bed II					
FLK	16	1963	Skull parts, upper and lower dentition	*Australopithecus?*	Inferred Oldowan
HWK	20	1959	Femur, proximal portion	*A. boisei*	—
Maiko Gully	30	1969	Skull parts, deciduous and permanent teeth	*"H. habilis"*	Inferred Oldowan
Upper Bed I					
FLK North	10	1961	Terminal phalanx, first toe	?	Oldowan
FLK West	26	1969	RM_3	*A. boisei*	—
HWK	27	1969	RM_3	*"H. habilis"*	—
HWK East	31	1969	Broken molar	?	—
Middle Bed I					
FLK	5*	1959	Skull	*A. boisei*	Oldowan
	6	1959–1960	2 teeth, skull fragments	*"H. habilis"*	Inferred Oldowan
FLK NN	7*	1960	Mandible, parietal, hand bones	*"H. habilis"*	Oldowan
	8*	1960	Foot	*"H. habilis"*	Oldowan
FLK	35	1960	Tibia and fibula	*"H. habilis"*	Oldowan
Lower Bed I					
MK	4	1959	1 molar, 2 tooth fragments	*"H. habilis"*	Inferred Oldowan
DK East	24	1968	Skull, several teeth	*"H. habilis"*	Inferred Oldowan

*See Figures 6-1, 6-2, 6-3, and 6-9.
Source: M. D. Leakey, 1971a.

deposits are abundant remains of crocodiles, fish, turtles, aquatic birds, and floral remains suggesting reeds and papyrus (L. S. B. Leakey, 1967a; M. D. Leakey, 1971a). At present, 10 occupation sites and 2 kill or butchering sites are known in Beds I and lower Bed II, thus giving abundant information regarding the behavioral attributes of Early Pleistocene hominids. Most of these sites were located on the margins of the lake or the banks of stream channels, in contrast to the location of later sites, which seem to have existed in drier areas.

The site at DK (Douglas Korongo) in lower Bed I (Figure 7-6) is the earliest known hominid site in the Gorge; it rests directly on a basalt dated to 1.9 m.y. ago (Hay, 1976, M. D. Leakey, 1971a). A well-preserved, though crushed, skull of a gracile australopithecine (OH 24) was recovered from this site; its extremely flattened condition when recovered led to its being named "Twiggy" after a toothpick-slim British model of the 1960s.

Besides this hominid skull, perhaps the most interesting aspect of excavations at DK was the exposure, in 1962, of possible evidence of an enclosure or structure. During excavations a roughly circular group of stones, about 30 cm high, was uncovered. This circle measured 4 to 5 meters in diameter; Mary Leakey reports that structures with similar stone foundations are still constructed by some African groups today. She thus interpreted the stone circle at DK as representing the remains of a temporary shelter, with the stones serving as the foundation for branches or twigs that formed a windbreak; these, in turn, may have been covered with skins or grasses for added protection. If this interpretation is correct, and it is difficult to see any reasonable alternative, this stone circle is the earliest evidence of any structure made by humans.

Numerous artifacts and faunal remains were found both within the stone circle and in concentrations outside it. The tools, mostly of lava, are of Oldowan type and consist mainly of choppers, scrapers, and utilized flakes. No bifacially flaked tools are present (M. D. Leakey, 1971a). The faunal remains at DK are exceedingly fragmented but consist mostly of crocodile (65 percent); tortoises, bovids, giraffes, rhinos, and other large animals are found in lesser numbers.

Further evidence of a shelter-like structure has been found at FLK (Frida Leakey Korongo) in the same level in which "Zinjanthropus" and a hominid tibia and fibula were found. "Zinjanthropus" was recovered at the close of the 1959 season, and in the following year extensive excavations were undertaken at the site. As at DK, the Oldowan tool kit is present, but here the tools are made mainly from quartz and quartzite. At FLK there is a dense concentration of faunal and artifactual material (including much débris or debitage from tool manufacture), which is surrounded by a nearly barren semicircular area. Mary Leakey interprets this area as having been occupied by a windbreak, possibly of thorn bushes, which would have partially enclosed the central part of the campsite.

At least two butchering or kill sites involving large animals are known in Bed I and lower Bed II. It is impossible to determine whether these animals were scavenged by hominids or were deliberately killed for food. Two lines of evidence, however, point to the latter explanation. A butchered *Deinotherium* (an extinct relative of the elephant) was found in association with numerous Oldowan tools; the head was uppermost in the lakeshore clay deposits and the legs and feet were lowest, indicating that the animal had sunk, in an upright position, into soft, swampy ground. A second butchered elephant was also found, lying on its side in the lake clays. Since large animals do not usually venture into swampy areas that will not support their weight, it is possible that they were driven into these areas where they could be either killed more easily or allowed to drown. Finally, three skulls of the extinct antelope *Parmularius* were found with depressed skull fractures. Mary Leakey reports that these skull fractures each occurred similarly and accurately over the right eye, in the most vulnerable part of the skull. Consequently, she concluded, they indicate deliberate hunting activity at close quarters by hominids.

Approximately 14 hominids have now been described from Bed I and lower Bed II; most of them are represented only by isolated teeth and therefore reveal little morphological information. In this sequence of deposits, it is clear, however, that at least two forms of australopithecine were locally coexisting. The skull of "Zinjanthropus" (OH 5), here called "*Australopithecus*," represents the east African superrobust form; the presence of this robust form in lower Bed II times also may be documented by the upper portion of a femur, OH 20.

Also evidence of the gracile form *Australopithecus* in OH 24 is seen in the crushed skull from lower Bed I.

The evidence for *Homo* from Bed I and lower Bed II is both controversial and equivocal. The type specimen of "*Homo habilis*," OH 7, was obtained from a level about 56 cm below that of OH 5. The skull of OH 7, although incomplete and juvenile, has a cranial capacity of 687 cc (Tobias, 1972). This rather large skull size was a major reason for the attribution to *Homo*. However, as pointed out previously, large skull size is not necessarily unique to *Homo*. The very thin skull bones of OH 7 (see Figure 6-1c) are much more like those of other australopithecines than those of contemporaneous members of the genus *Homo* from Lake Turkana. On the basis of available evidence, then, there seems to be no clear reason to place OH 7 within the genus *Homo* as it is defined here.

FIGURE 7-6 *Following pages:* Plan of the living floor at DK, Olduvai Gorge, Bed I. This is the oldest site in the gorge, dating to about 1.9 m.y. ago. The symmetrical concentration of stone in the lower portion of the diagram may represent the base or foundation of a brush-covered shelter. (Stones, including artifacts, are shown in black; fossil bones are shown in outline.) (Courtesy of M. D. Leakey and Cambridge University Press.)

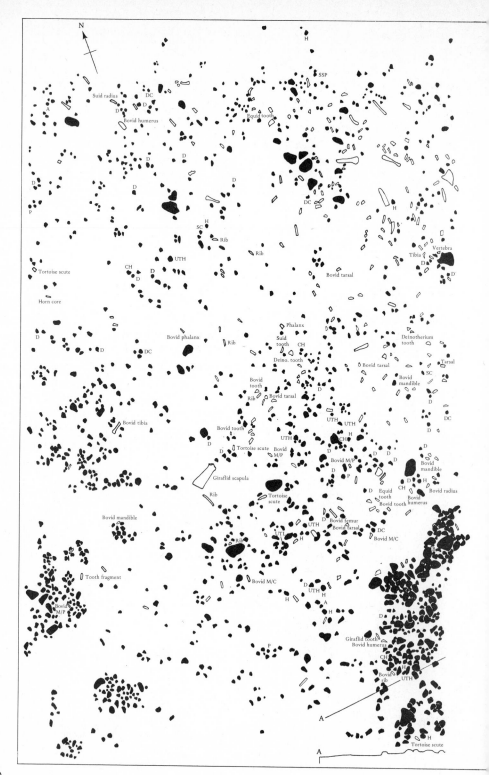

278

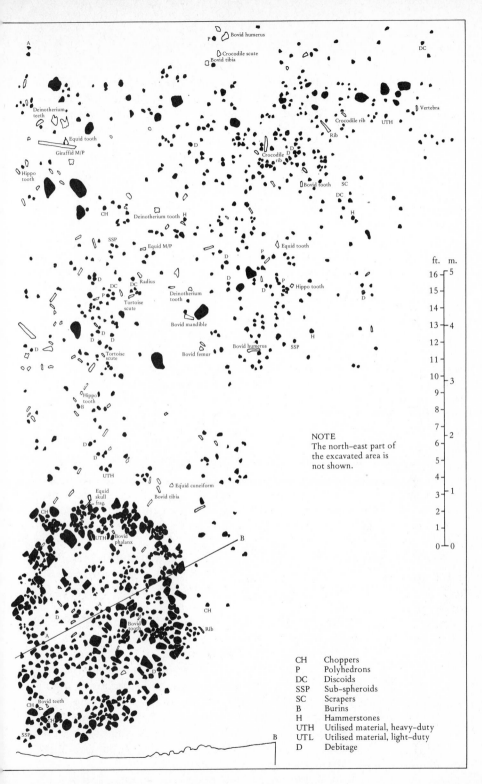

NOTE
The north–east part of
the excavated area is
not shown.

CH	Choppers
P	Polyhedrons
DC	Discoids
SSP	Sub-spheroids
SC	Scrapers
B	Burins
H	Hammerstones
UTH	Utilised material, heavy-duty
UTL	Utilised material, light-duty
D	Debitage

Some interesting resemblances appear when the hominids from Bed I and lower Bed II are compared with others from sites outside east Africa. For example, OH 24 very closely resembles STS 5 from Sterkfontein, and both of them, in turn, show close resemblances to the small facial and dental fragment MLD 6 from Makapan.

MIDDLE AND UPPER BED II (1.5 M.Y. TO 1.1 M.Y. B.P.) A number of important changes occurred in Bed II between the lower and middle series of depositions. Geologic activity, either volcanic or seismic, seems to have altered drainage patterns on the Serengeti Plain, thereby causing the lake to become increasingly saline and alkaline. The increase of flamingos, which feed on alkaline-dependent microorganisms, is one reflection of this change. Moreover, the fresh-water elements of the lake decrease after the beginning of middle Bed II times, and in the land deposits there is an increase of grassland forms, such as horses and antelopes. By the end of Bed II times, about 1.1 m.y. ago, the lake seems to have been drastically reduced, and extensive grasslands existed (M. D. Leakey, 1971a).

Several significant changes occurred in the characteristics of the hominid occupation between the earlier and later sequences. First, the faunal remains in the middle and late Bed II occupation sites (Table 7-7) are fewer in number but consist of larger species, such as hippos, horses, rhinos, and giraffes. This shift in population may reflect not only changed environmental conditions but also alterations in hunting patterns and dietary preferences.

A very interesting kill site occurs at SHK in upper Bed II. Here a small herd of antelope has been fossilized in a clay deposit. Although the site has not been completely excavated, it is possible that such a situation could indicate that the hominids had deliberately driven the animals into the swampy lake margin. The SHK site contains tools of Developed Oldowan B (M. D. Leakey, 1971a).

At another upper Bed II site, BK, there are the remains of *Pelorovis*, a very large bovid; one individual apparently died standing upright in a deep, swampy area. Nearby are several choppers and a single biface (M. D. Leakey, 1971a).

Such animal remains, if they indeed represent a change in hominid hunting patterns, could indicate an increase in the size and a change in the composition of the hominid group. They could also result from more cooperative hunting patterns. A small band, with perhaps one or two adult males, may feed itself by killing a few small animals and supplementing its kill with gathered foods. A larger group, with perhaps four or five adult males, may feed itself more efficiently by killing fewer but larger animals. Such hunting practices, however, require cooperation among the hunters. To drive a herd of antelopes or *Pelorovis*, or even a single elephant, requires both planning and communication of such planning.

At present, only nine hominids from middle and upper Bed II have

TABLE 7-7   Hominids from middle and upper Bed II, Olduvai Gorge

POSITION	HOMINID NUMBER (OH)	DATE OF DISCOVERY	PARTS PRESERVED	TAXONOMIC STATUS	ASSOCIATED INDUSTRY
Upper Bed II					
BK	3	1955	Deciduous canine, deciduous molar	*A. boisei*	Developed Oldowan B
LLK	9	1960	Skull	*H. erectus*	None
SC	36	1970–1971	Ulna	*H. erectus* (?)	None
Middle Bed II					
MNK	13	1963	Skull and jaw fragments	"*H. habilis*"	Oldowan
MNK	14	1963	Cranial fragments	?	Inferred Oldowan
MNK	15	1963	Canine, 2 molars	*Homo* (species unknown)	Indeterminate
FLK	18	1969	Hand phalanx	?	Indeterminate
FC West	19	1963	Molar fragment	?	Developed Oldowan B
MNK	32	1969	Molar fragment	?	Indeterminate

Source: Data from M. D. Leakey, 1971a.

been reported; of these, only two are complete enough for any analysis. Evidence for the robust australopithecines in this series is limited to just a few teeth (OH 3) from upper Bed II.

Of the remaining material, the skull and jaws of OH 13 are the most enigmatic. The skull is small and thin-walled and bears a number of similarities with the gracile australopithecines. The mandible, however, bears some resemblance to material from Java which has been attributed to *Homo erectus* (Tobias and Von Koenigswald, 1964).

The skull of OH 9, recovered from the very top of Bed II, seems to represent important evidence of a new human population, *Homo erectus,* in the Olduvai area. The skull has a cranial capacity of 1067 cc (Holloway, 1973); it has enormous visor-like brow ridges and a long, low skull shape typical of *H. erectus* elsewhere. Perhaps its single most interesting feature is the thickness of the skull walls; in most areas of the skull, the bones are 2 to 3 times the thickness found in the same areas of australopithecine skulls. Such bone thickness is a common and consistent feature of Middle Pleistocene *Homo erectus.* OH 9 has the distinction of being the only hominid to be discovered by Louis Leakey himself.

Further evidence of *Homo erectus* in the Olduvai area at this time is seen in the ulna, OH 36. This ulna is very robust, but not very long, and is curved anteroposteriorly; it has strong muscle markings indicating a powerful forearm (Day, 1977). Although its attribution to *Homo erectus* must remain provisional until more is known about the postcranium of this form, its robusticity and relative shortness differ significantly from that seen in the hominid ulna from the Omo River Valley, SH 40-19 (discussed in Chapter 6).

While OH 9 and OH 36 may indicate that new hominid populations entered Olduvai Gorge at this time, archeological evidence also indicates the presence of a new type of stone tool technology at this same time. The change is reflected in the appearance of the first bifacially flaked hand axes of Acheulian type (see Chapter 8). Although rough "proto-bifaces" occur in the Developed Oldowan series, large and well-prepared bifaces first appear in significant numbers at EF-HR (Evelyn Fuch-Hans Reck) site near the middle of Bed II.

Laetolil   The site at Laetolil, Tanzania, about 65 km from Olduvai Gorge, has long been of interest to paleontologists. Louis Leakey visited the area in 1936, and in 1939 Kohl-Larsen, a German paleontologist, recovered a partial hominid maxilla with both premolars there. This specimen is sometimes called the "Garusi" maxilla, for a small river in the area. Kohl-Larsen, showing admirable caution, named the specimen "Australopithecus?" (1943). Weinert later renamed it "Meganthropus africanus" (1950). J. Robinson, in reviewing the specimen in 1955, pointed out its affinities with the South African gracile australopithecines, particularly those from Sterkfontein.

More recently, Mary Leakey returned to the site and recovered the dental remains of 13 more hominids (Figure 7-7; see also Figure 6-4a). Potassium-argon ratios indicate an age of the hominid-bearing levels at between 3.59 m.y. and 3.77 m.y. B.P. (M. D. Leakey et al., 1976). The original Garusi maxilla is apparently contemporaneous with these newly recovered Laetolil hominids (White, 1977).

The first reports on this newer material suggested that it had affinities with *Homo* (M. D. Leakey et al., 1976). However, such an attribution may have been somewhat premature, and a study of its morphology would seem to support an affiliation with the gracile australopithecines. Perhaps the best indication of this association is in the gently divergent tooth rows and the thickening at the anterior and interior borders of the mandibles. More important, however, is the presence of an enlarged outer cusp and smaller inner cusp on the P_3. This condition is very like that seen in AL 288 ("Lucy") (see Figure 6-4b) from Hadar. It has, in fact, been suggested that the Laetolil hominids, along with those from Hadar, Ethiopia, belong to a new and very primitive species of australopithecine, *A. afarensis* (Johanson, White, and Coppens, 1978; Johanson and White, 1979). Although there are some differences between later *A. africanus* specimens and *A. afarensis*, it is not yet clear that these differences are significant at the species level. The only apparent distinctions between the two species are in the dentition.

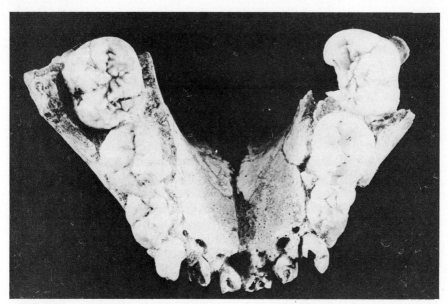

FIGURE 7-7 A number of hominid jaws have been recovered from Laetolil, not far from Olduvai Gorge. These date to between 3.5 and 3.7 m.y. old. This photograph shows Laetolil Hominid 2: only the permanent M_1 has erupted in this child's jaw; the permanent incisors, canine, and P_3 are still enclosed within the jaw. In modern humans, the M_1 erupts at about 6 years of age. (Photograph courtesy of M. D. Leakey and T. White.)

Postcranially, *A. africanus* and *A. afarensis* appear to be extremely similar (see Anon., 1979.) The Laetolil hominids are very important, however, since they are the earliest group of australopithecines known. Further study of the site should yield vital information concerning hominids of 3 m.y. to 4 m.y. ago. No tools or artifacts have been recovered from the Laetolil site.

Omo River Basin Paleontological investigations in the Omo River Basin in southern Ethiopia were begun in 1933 by the French paleontologist Camille Arambourg. Since 1959, Clark Howell and his co-workers have carried on extensive fieldwork in this area.

The Plio-Pleistocene deposits in the Omo River Basin reach a total thickness of over 1100 m and contain a very rich and varied record of events and organisms during this period (Table 7-8). Hominids have been recovered from two separate formations in this area, spanning a period from about 3.3 m.y. ago to at least 0.8 m.y. ago. The Usno Formation contains earlier deposits covering the period from about 3.3 m.y. to 2.9 m.y. ago. Most of the Usno fossils, however, are near the earlier age. The Usno Formation overlaps in time with the lower levels or members of the

TABLE 7-8 Biostratigraphy of the Omo River Valley

FORMATION	TUFF	MEMBER	DATE, M.Y. B.P.	HOMINID REMAINS				ATTRIBUTION		
				ISOLATED TEETH	JAWS	CRANIA	POSTCRANIA	AUSTRALOPITHECUS		HOMO
								GRACILE	ROBUST	
	L	L	1.27–1.41	2				?		
		K		1				?		X
	I₂		1.81–1.87					?		
		H		1				X		
Shungura	G	G	1.93	58	5	2	Femur proximal ulna	X		X
	F	F	1.99–2.06	44	1				X	
	E₁	E	2.12	16	2	1	Ulna	X	X	

		Age (m.y.)					
	D	2.16–2.60	12			Proximal humerus	X
	C		39	1	1	Middle phalange	X
	B	2.93–2.96	13		1	1	X
	A		1				
Usno	U₁₀	2.64–2.97	21				X
	U₁	3.11–3.51					
Mursi		4.05				No hominids	

Sources: F. Brown and Nash, 1976; Howell and Coppens, 1976.

Shungura Formation, which contains the main fossil-bearing deposits in the Omo River Basin. The Shungura Formation also has a maximum age of about 3.3 m.y. and continues on until about 0.8 m.y. ago (Howell, 1976; Howell and Coppens, 1976).

Ecologically, the Usno and lower members of the Shungura (Members A, B, and C) reflect a similar sort of environment. During that time, Lake Turkana, just to the south, extended further north and covered parts of what is now southern Ethiopia. Many of the fossil-bearing horizons at this time represent marsh or swamp conditions. Between the lower and middle sections of the Shungura Formation between 2 m.y. and 2.5 m.y. ago, a number of faunal and ecological changes occurred in the area. The lake and swamp deposits become much less frequent and most of the sediments of this period represent river deposits. During this time, in fact, the lower Omo River must have become much as it is today (Howell, 1976). Studies of the pollen (palynology) and plant remains (Bonnefille, 1975) show that at about 2.5 m.y. B.P., there was a decrease in the forest and woodland species and an increase in drought-resistant plants and grasses. Thus, at this time the forest environments gradually gave way to more open grasslands and bush areas. However, forests continued along the banks of the more permanent watercourses. It is very interesting, but perhaps only coincidental, that the first robust australopithecines and the first members of the genus *Homo* appeared in the Shungura deposits during this ecological change.

Hominids are represented in the Usno Formation by 21 teeth; in fact, a large portion of the Omo hominids are known from isolated teeth. These teeth have a number of resemblances with the teeth of gracile australopithecines from Sterkfontein, although they are smaller than most of the Sterkfontein teeth. Therefore, the Usno hominids probably belong to the gracile australopithecine group (Howell, Coppens, and de Heinzelin, 1974; Howell and Coppens, 1976; Howell, 1976).

The lower members of the Shungura Formation also contain hominids probably belonging to the gracile australopithecine group. The range of variation present in this group is more clearly demonstrated in these individuals than in the Usno specimens. Some of the Shungura individuals are, in fact, quite large but morphologically within the range of the gracile lineage; a similar wide range of variation is seen at Sterkfontein. The first clear evidence of a member of the robust group occurs in Member E, in the middle of the Shungura series, and throughout the middle portion of this series this group is well represented. Several very robust mandibles are known, as well as an ulna, possibly referable to *Australopithecus boisei*.

Around 2 m.y. ago, hominids, probably referable to *Homo*, appear in the Shungura deposits. Therefore, at about that time both gracile and robust australopithecines, as well as *Homo*, appear to have been in the Omo River Basin.

The earliest archeological material from the Omo River Basin occurs in Member C of the Shungura Formation and dates to approximately 2.5 m.y. ago (Chavaillon, 1976). A number of archeological sites have also been excavated in Member F, dating to about 2 m.y. ago. These assemblages consist of low-density scatters of very small artifacts; the mean maximum length of the fragments is less than 20 mm (Merrick and Merrick, 1976). The tools seem to represent pieces of quartz which were shattered and then used without further chipping or preparation. None of these artifacts has a standardized appearance or even recognizable tool form. This diversity is probably due to the poor quality of the quartz from which they were made; better raw materials were evidently not present nearby. Several pieces of flaked and chipped bones were recovered from Member E, and Chavaillon (1976) thinks they may represent bone tools. There is no clear evidence of butchering at any of these early Omo sites.

It is very interesting that the first tools occur in the Omo River Basin deposits long after the first hominids appeared in the area. There could be several explanations of this sudden appearance (Howell, 1976). Various geological factors and conditions of sedimentation could mean that tools were washed away or "lost" so that they do not now occur in any recognizable concentrations. Also, tool use may have been infrequent and sporadic; this possibility would also result in a lack of identifiable concentrations. Finally, the sudden appearance of tools may reflect the presence of a new hominid in the area, one with a way of life more dependent on frequent and constant tool use.

Hadar Plio-Pleistocene deposits at Hadar in the Afar region of eastern Ethiopia (Table 7-9) have been investigated only since 1973, but in the few field seasons to date, the area has revealed enormous paleontologic potential. Part of this potential is based on the fact that the conditions for preservation of animal remains in these deposits are excellent. A large lake occupied much of this area during Plio-Pleistocene times and much of the sediments therefore reflect either lake or lakeshore environments. Many of the organisms included in these deposits are nearly complete; in some cases even crocodile and turtle eggs are preserved. Paleontologic material from other east African Plio-Pleistocene sites is almost always much broken and fragmented—in great contrast to some of the Hadar material.

All hominid material recovered from the Hadar area appears to be older than 2.6 m.y., and a basalt about midway through the Hadar series has been dated to about 3 m.y. (Aaronson et al., 1977). Therefore, all hominid material from Hadar is now dated to between 2.7 m.y. and 3.2 m.y. B.P. The faunal correlations between the Hadar series and the Usno and lower members (A-C) of the Shungura are close and support such dates, based on potassium-argon and fission-track dating techniques.

TABLE 7-9
Hadar
biostratigraphy

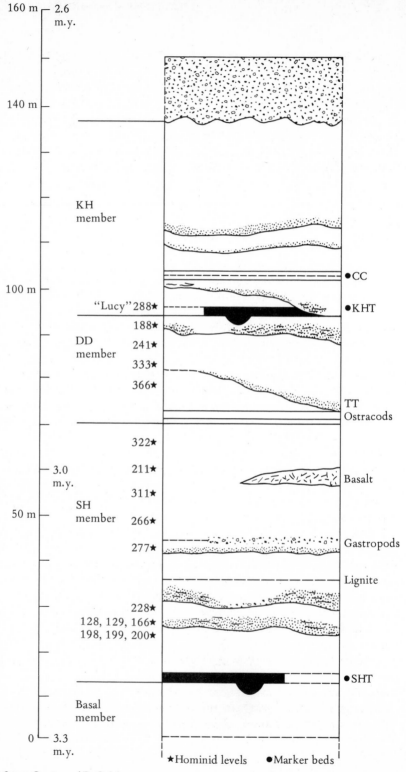

160 m — 2.6 m.y.	
140 m —	
	KH member
100 m —	●CC
	"Lucy" 288★ ●KHT
	188★
	DD member 241★
	333★
	366★ TT Ostracods
	322★
3.0 m.y.	211★ Basalt
50 m —	311★
	SH member 266★
	277★ Gastropods
	Lignite
	228★
	128, 129, 166★
	198, 199, 200★
	●SHT
	Basal member
0 — 3.3 m.y.	

★Hominid levels ●Marker beds

Source: Courtesy of D. G. Johanson.

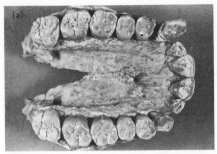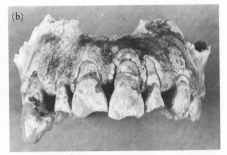

FIGURE 7-8 Hominids from Hadar, Ethiopia, date to between 2.6 and 3.3 m.y. old. This maxilla, AL 200, was originally attributed to *Homo*; it dates to about 3.2 m.y. ago. However, the maxillae of hominids show few distinctions between the different genera, and this individual has now been attributed *A. afarensis*. **(a)** Occlusal view. **(b)** Anterior view: The incisors on AL 200 show uneven wear which indicates that they may have be used to hold objects; the front teeth also show extensive chipping of the enamel, consistent with their use as tools. (Photographs courtesy of D. C. Johanson.)

The Hadar hominids reveal a wide spectrum of morphologic variability; but despite this variability all have been attributed to the primitive species *A. afarensis* (Johanson, White, and Coppens, 1978; Johanson and White, 1979). Two palates, Al 199 and Al 200 (Figure 7-8a,b), reportedly show a number of resemblances to other fossil material that has been allocated to *Homo erectus* (Johanson and Taieb, 1976). These two palates are from the lowest hominid levels at Hadar, about 4 m below the basalt dated to 3 m.y. ago. Other specimens, such as the temporal bone Al 166-9, show the heavy pneumatization typical of the robust australopithecines (Taieb et al., 1976). Whether these different morphologies are due to sexual dimorphism, as Johanson and White (1979) have suggested, or more than one species is present at Hadar is therefore uncertain.

The most recent individual from the entire Hadar series is AL 288 ("Lucy"; see Figures 6-4b and 6-6a), recovered just beneath the deposits that date to 2.6 m.y. B.P. This nearly complete skeleton demonstrates the gracile australopithecine features characteristic of this group. The morphologic similarities are particularly close to individuals from Sterkfontein, except that AL 288 may be smaller. Precise estimates of stature have not yet been published; but it is very probable that this individual was little more than 1 m tall.

Stone tools are not known from the lower levels at Hadar.

Lake Turkana The discoveries at Lake Turkana since 1969, when work first began there, have played a key role in our understanding of Plio-Pleistocene hominids. When Richard and Louis Leakey made their first helicopter landing on the eastern shore of the lake in 1967, our knowledge of human evolution was, in retrospect, very limited. The South

African material was of course known, but it was not absolutely dated. The presence of *Homo* there, or of even more than one form of australopithecine, was the subject of lively debate. The discoveries of fossil hominids at Olduvai Gorge, while of great importance, were fragmentary (with some notable exceptions) and few in number; only 34 hominids had been reported from the Gorge by 1971. The apparent coexistence of *"Zinjanthropus"* and *"Homo habilis"* occasioned much debate and little consensus. Mary Leakey's fine volume (1971a) on the archeological material from Beds I and II had not yet appeared. Moreover, in 1967, only a few scrappy hominid fragments were known from Laetolil and the Omo; Hadar had not so far yielded any fossil hominids. Until that time, fossil hominids appeared slowly and sedately and even the recovery of a small fragment of jaw or skull was the occasion for excitement and discussion.

Since 1969, however, more than 200 fossil hominids have been recovered from the Lake Turkana area, and the discovery has resulted in an almost exponential increase in our knowledge of Plio-Pleistocene human evolution. But more important, perhaps, some agreement is now appearing among the diversely trained scientists who study fossil hominids. Scientists from many different disciplines have had access to the Lake Turkana area and to the material recovered from it. As a result of the free exchange of ideas among them, a basic outline of the history (geologic, faunal, and cultural) of the area is widely understood and generally agreed upon. The coexistence of *Homo* and the australopithecines, suggested previously at Swartkrans and Olduvai and later at Omo and Hadar, is fully and almost unquestionably confirmed at Lake Turkana (see R. E. F. Leakey and Walker, 1976). The confirmation of this coexistence means that the widely accepted phyletic gradualism model of human evolution, which rested on the gradual evolution of a more primitive australopithecine into a more advanced *Homo*, is incorrect. Clearly, the more realistic model is more complex—and more interesting—than this "straight-line" theory.

As we will see, important problems still exist in regard to the Lake Turkana area in particular and to the wider questions of human evolution in general, but at least a larger body of data now exists on which to base our models and theories.

One of the major uncertainties is the date of the crucial KBS tuff. This volcanic tuff is widely distributed in the hominid-bearing deposits of the Lake Turkana area, and a date of 2.6 m.y. B.P. (Fitch and Miller, 1970) was initially regarded as firm. This tuff gained even more importance when the cranium of KNM ER 1470 and a *Homo*-like femur and pelvis were recovered from beneath it.

Since 1970, however, other tests have given different dates, thus reopening the problem of the KBS date. (These various dates are summarized in Table 7-10.) The dates for the KBS tuff now range from a low of 1.6 m.y. B.P. to a high of 2.6 m.y. B.P.

TABLE 7-10 Absolute dates for the KBS tuff

METHOD	DERIVED DATE (m.y. b.p.)	REFERENCE
Conventional potassium-argon	2.61 ∓ .26 1.60 ∓ .05 to 1.82 ∓ .04	Fitch and Miller, 1976 Curtis, Drake, Cerling, and Hempel, 1975
^{40}Argon-^{39} argon	2.61 ∓ .26 2.42 ∓ .01	Fitch and Miller, 1970 Fitch, Hooker, and Miller, 1976
Fission track	1.8 2.44 ∓ .08 1.98	Hurford, 1974 Hurford and Gleadow, 1976 Wagner, 1977

One way out of this confusion is to seek help from the paleontological record. Here, a more consistent pattern emerges which supports the younger dates. For example, a skull of *Equus*, the modern genus of horse, has been recovered from below the KBS at Lake Turkana. Yet the genus does not appear in Europe until 2.5 m.y. b.p. and not in the nearby Omo area until between 1.8 m.y. to 1.9 m.y. b.p. (Eisenmann, 1976). The fossil hippo *Hippopotamus gorgops* also occurs below the KBS but does not appear in the Omo until the same 1.8 m.y. to 1.9 m.y. period. Fossil pigs, such as *Mesochoerus limnetes*, also support the younger date. Evolutionary changes in the teeth of this species are well documented, yet changes in the individuals occurring below the KBS tuff are not matched in the Omo sequence until deposits of about 2 m.y. of age (Cooke, 1976). A number of other fossil forms also add support to a date of the KBS of about 1.8 m.y. b.p., which is thus its most probable age.

Geologically, there are several areas of hominid-bearing Plio-Pleistocene sediments in the Lake Turkana Basin (Table 7-11). Together, these sediments span a time from more than 3 m.y. to about 1 m.y. ago.

Ecologically, Plio-Pleistocene conditions in the Turkana Basin were much the same as those described for Omo and Hadar. A large lake has existed in the Basin since Miocene time, but since then there has been a progressive trend toward greater aridity. Thus a series of lake-margin, river or stream, and flood-plain environments were available to the early hominids in this area. Behrensmeyer (1975), in her study of the paleo-ecology of this area, has pointed out that *Homo* is more often found in association with lake-margin sediments, while the australopithecines[10] are more often in stream-channel situations away from the lake and are found in association with more open-country forms.

Archeological work has revealed two different tool assemblages in the Turkana Basin (Isaac, 1976a; Isaac, Harris, and Crader, 1976). The earliest

[10]Most of the australopithecines at Turkana are of the robust type.

TABLE 7-11 Biostratigraphy at Lake Turkana*

ILERET (AREAS 1-12)	KARARI ESCARPMENT (AREAS 129,130,131)	KBS RIDGE (AREAS 105,118)	KOOBI FORA RIDGE (AREA 104) (AREAS 102, 102)	TOOL INDUSTRY	SUGGESTED AGE (M.Y.)
Chari tuff					1.2
	Karari tuff				1.3
404,725,728, 731,739,740, 741,805,992, 993,1463, 1465,1466,1467				Karari Industry	
Okote tuff					1.4
729,733,803,806, 807,808,809,818, 1468	BBS tuff		Koobi Fora		1.5
Lower tuff 406,407,727,732, 801,802,815,819, 820,1170,1171, 1464,1591,1592		405,738,1476, 1477,1478,1479	164,810,811, 813,814,816, 997,998,3733	Tuff 403,730,734 736,737	KBS Industry	
KBS tuff 1590,1593,3228, 3728,1801	KBS tuff 1462,1469, 1470,1471,1472, 1473,1474, 1475,1481,1482, 1483,1500,1806	KBS tuff 3732			1.6-1.8
	Tulu Bor tuff				3.1

*Numbers refer to Kenya National Museum specimens (KNM ER); underlined specimens have been attributed to *Homo*.

Sources: Adapted from Brock and Isaac, 1974; additional data, Day, 1977.

of these assemblages is attributable to the Oldowan category, although Isaac has used the term "KBS industry" to identify it. The KBS industry is composed of the same six or so basic tools that constitute the typical Oldowan assemblages. The earliest tool assemblages in the Turkana area occur at the CPH site, 8 to 10 m below the KBS tuff. This very scanty grouping consists of choppers, discoids, and a few flakes.

The best known of the Oldowan Type tool sites in the Turkana Basin is the KBS site. This site is located within the tuff itself, where it has filled a small stream channel; it is probable that the hominids were occupying a dry stream channel. Such a seasonal channel may have been bordered by trees and bushes which offered protection for the hominids. Among the floral remains identified at the KBS site were the leaves of fig trees, leading Isaac to draw a biblical (although unconfirmed) parallel (see Isaac et al., 1976, p. 536).

Among the butchered animals found at the KBS site were porcupines, pigs, gazelles, and waterbuck. There is no way to determine whether these animals had been deliberately killed by the hominids, but their relatively small size would be appropriate for a human predator. The fact that they are all gathered in one place, along with a number of stone tools, would indicate that this may have been a home-base camp. Therefore, the animals were probably killed (or scavenged) elsewhere, then brought back to the camp area to be shared and consumed (Isaac et al., 1976).

Most of the artifacts at the KBS site were made from lava cobbles; there are a few core tools and a much larger quantity of flakes and debitage. Isaac points out that "tools, in the technical sense of secondarily trimmed, designed objects," constitute only about 5 percent of the total assemblage (Isaac et al., 1976, p. 538). Most of the artifacts are simply fortuitously shaped flakes or debitage. Among the stone tools are serveral pig and hippo tusks which may also have served some function.

The KBS tool industry has also been found in association with a single butchered hippo; here, the bones and tools are closely contained within so small an area that a direct link between them can scarcely be denied. Most of the tools here are small flakes, adding further documentation to the idea that the butchering of even a large animal can be carried out with small and unsophisticated tools.

The second artifactual industry identified in the Turkana Basin has been termed the "Karari assemblage"; this industry has no close parallel with other known assemblages between about 1.4 m.y. and 1.6 m.y. ago. It differs from the KBS and Oldowan assemblages in several ways. First, the tools are much larger. They are often formed of cobbles of basalt from which large flakes have been removed. Harris and Isaac (1976) have emphasized that such activities would require considerable strength, much different from that required to form the small KBS flakes. Second, the density of the tool accumulations is greater. This may indicate that tool manufacture and use had assumed greater importance and frequency than they had had earlier. Third, more tool types are present. The basic Oldowan tool kit is present in the Karari assemblages, along with the addition of simple bifaces and large pick-like tools. Finally, there is greater standardization of tool type, and recognizable tool types occur more frequently.

As at other east African sites, *Homo* and *Australopithecus* are contemporaneous at Lake Turkana. It is odd, however, that the evidence for the gracile form of australopithecine is very limited here. As pointed out above, this form is well represented in levels as early as 3.3 m.y. ago at Omo, and it was certainly present before 2.5 m.y. ago at Hadar. Since no major geologic or ecologic barrier exists between these areas, it is hard to understand the rarity of the gracile form at Turkana. The robust form, however, is very well represented. One of the best preserved of this group is the cranium KNM ER 406, recovered above the KBS tuff. A considerable amount of mandibular material is also referable to the robust form. The cranium KNM ER 732 may well represent a female of the robust group, and it indicates that a large amount of sexual dimorphism was present. The same broad expansion low on the skull and pneumatization are present in KNM ER 732, as are the flared cheekbones. The temporal lines, however, do not meet to form a crest.

Postcranial material referable to *Australopithecus* is also known from Turkana. A number of femoral fragments are known which demonstrate the small head and long, flattened neck characteristic of this group.

As indicated previously, the early presence of *Homo* at Lake Turkana is now well documented; this evidence includes cranial, dental, and postcranial material. Several femora, recovered from below the KBS tuff, indicate the presence of this genus there before at least 1.8 m.y. ago.

A complete femur (KNM ER 1481A) shows the large head and round neck that are characters of *Homo* femora. A pelvis (KNM ER 3228) also constitutes strong evidence of the genus *Homo* prior to the deposition of the KBS tuff. This pelvis is large and strongly built. It has a strong buttress of bone between the acetabulum and iliac crest (the iliac pillar) similar to that seen in the *Homo erectus* pelvis (OH 28; see Figure 8-8) from Bed IV, Olduvai Gorge (R. E. F. Leakey and Walker, 1976; Day, 1971a). Moreover, the acetabulum of KNM ER 3228 is large, indicating a large femoral head. These features, too, are hominine and are quite unlike the complex seen in *Australopithecus*.

Dental evidence of *Homo* may be seen in the mandible KNM ER 730 (see Figure 6-12) recovered from just below a tuff dated to 1.5 m.y. ago. This mandible has a number of similarities with the *Homo erectus* jaws from Peking, dating to the Middle Pleistocene.

Perhaps the clearest evidence of early *Homo* at Lake Turkana is seen in the beautifully preserved skull KNM ER 3733. This is the most complete early hominine skull known (see Figure 6-11 *a, b, c*). It was found below a tuff dated to 1.5 m.y. B.P. and above the KBS tuff; it may therefore be about 1.6 m.y. old. In both its details and its morphological pattern, this skull is very like others attributed to *Homo erectus*.

Other African Localities

At least two other African localities have yielded very limited evidence of Early Pleistocene hominids.

Natron In 1964 a well-preserved mandible was recovered at Peninj Stream, near Lake Natron in Tanzania. Its age, roughly equivalent with the middle of Bed II at Olduvai Gorge, may be about 1.4 m.y. B.P. (Isaac and Curtis, 1974). The mandible is clearly that of a robust australopithecine and is, in fact, a near fit with the cranium of OH 5 (L. S. B. Leakey and M. D. Leakey, 1964).

Chad The very fragmentary skull from Chad, in north central Africa, is more enigmatic. The specimen consists of a severely crushed frontal bone and facial portions. There is a well-developed brow ridge with minimal postorbital constriction, and the cranial capacity may be rather large.

Both the dating and the classification of this specimen have been unsatisfactory so far. The pattern of features is slightly more suggestive of *Homo* than of *Australopithecus*, although its original placement was in the latter category (Coppens, 1961a, b; 1962). Later, however, it was placed with "*Homo habilis*" (L. S. B. Leakey, Tobias, and Napier, 1964); other workers have placed it somewhere between the two genera (Tobias and Von Koenigswald, 1964; Coppens, 1965).

On the basis of paleontologic evidence, the lake deposits that have yielded the Chad hominid may date to the late Lower or early Middle Pleistocene.

The picture in Africa in the Pliocene and Early Pleistocene thus indicates the contemporaneous presence of an australopithecine lineage and a hominine lineage. By the end of the Early Pleistocene, some members of the genus *Homo* had left Africa and had rapidly spread over the eastern hemisphere. The hominids were apparently widespread in Europe and Asia at an early date.

EUROPE

No skeletal evidence of Plio-Pleistocene hominids is known from Europe. However, several localities have yielded cultural evidence of the hominids' presence about 1 m.y. ago. The best documented of these is Vallonet Cave (de Lumley et al., 1963) on the French Mediterranean coast, which was probably occupied at about 0.9 m.y. to 0.95 m.y. ago (de Lumley, 1975). Here, pebble tools and waste flakes were mixed with the remains of animals and shed antlers. The bones of a whale were also mixed in with this débris. It seems a good assumption that the local hominids found the whale dead on the nearby beach and brought parts of it back to the cave. A site at Grâce, near Amiens in the Somme Valley, may be contemporary with Vallonet (de Lumley, 1975). A number of other European sites containing crude stone tools have also been attributed, in a rather inexact way, to this time.

ASIA

China

Evidence of Plio-Pleistocene hominids has been found at various sites in China. At some localities the hominids were in association with *Gigantopithecus*. Other sites have yielded only tools dated to this time period. Therefore, although the evidence of Plio-Pleistocene hominids in China is very limited, it does serve to document human presence there at this time.

All the hominid evidence of this period in China consists of isolated teeth, on the basis of which it is very difficult to make definite taxonomic attributions below the level of the family Hominidae. We cannot be sure, therefore, whether these teeth represent *Homo* or *Australopithecus*. Gao-Jian (1975), in describing five teeth recovered in Hupei and Kwangsi Provinces, has pointed out that they are rectangular in shape and have low crowns and complex occlusal surfaces. He has concluded that although they share a number of features with *Homo erectus* from Choukoutien, they are closer morphologically to *Australopithecus africanus*. There is, however, no clear evidence of *Australopithecus* outside Africa.

Java

The story of the discovery of early hominids in Java (summarized in Table 7-12) is as remarkable as any in the history of studies of early hominids. The discovery of Neandertal in 1856 and the publication of Darwin's *Origin of Species* in 1859 provided a firm foundation for the scientific investigation of the evolution of humans. These two events, occurring so close in time, provided both the fossil evidence of an earlier human type and a theoretical framework in which the existence of such a type could be both explained and understood.

Among the pioneers in evolutionary studies was Ernst Haeckel. Much of Haeckel's studies were based on embryology; while conducting them, he had noted a close resemblance between the embryo of a gibbon and that of a human. He therefore concluded that humans may have evolved in

TABLE 7-12 Pleistocene hominids from Java

| | | | | HOMINIDS | | |
DATE	FORMATION	BEDS	CODE NUMBER	OTHER NAMES	PRESERVED PARTS	DATE OF DISCOVERY
"Upper Pleistocene"*	Ngongdong River Terrace		Ngongdong 1	Solo 1; "Homo (Javanthropus) soloensis"†	Calotte, adult female	1931–1933†
			Ngongdong 2	Solo 2	Frontal juvenile	
			Ngongdong 3	Solo 3	Calvarium, adult male	
			Ngongdong 4	Solo 3a‡	Fragment of parietal‡	
			Ngongdong 5	Solo 4	Skull fragments, subadult	
			Ngongdong 6	Solo 5	Calotte, adult male	
			Ngongdong 7	Solo 6	Calvarium, female	
			Ngongdong 8	Solo 7	Right parietal, subadult female	
			Ngongdong 9	Solo 8	Parietals, subadult male	
			Ngongdong 10	Solo 9	Calotte, adult female	
			Ngongdong 11	Solo 10	Calotte, adult female	
			Ngongdong 12	Solo 11	Calvarium, adult male	
			Ngongdong 13	"Tibia A"	Tibial shaft	
			Ngongdong 14	"Tibia B"	Tibial shaft	
0.5 m.y. B.P. §	Kabuh	Trinil	Trinil 1	"Anthropopithecus erectus"; "Anthropopithecus erectus"	RM_3	1891
			Trinil 2	"Pithecanthropus erectus"; "Pithecanthropus I"	Calotte	1891

*, †, ‡, § Notes appear on page 300.

(Continued)

TABLE 7-12 (continued)

DATE	FORMATION	BEDS	CODE NUMBER	OTHER NAMES	HOMINIDS	
					PRESERVED PARTS	DATE OF DISCOVERY
0.5 m.y. B.P. §	Kabuh	Trinil	Trinil 3	"P. erectus, Femur 1" "Anthropopithecus erectus"	Complete femur	1892
			Trinil 4	"Anthropopithecus erectus"; "Pithecanthropus erectus"; *Pongo*;¶ "Meganthropus"	LM$_2$	1892
			Trinil 5		LP$_3$	1898
			Trinil 6	"P. erectus, Femur 2"	Proximal right femur	1900
			Trinil 7	"P. erectus, Femur 3"	Shaft, left femur	1900
			Trinil 8	"P. erectus, Femur 4"	Shaft, right femur	1900
			Trinil 9	"P. erectus, Femur 5"	Shaft, left femur	1900
0.7 m.y. B.P.**		Sangiran	Sangiran 2	"P. erectus"; "Pithecanthropus 2"	Calotte	1937
0.83 m.y. B.P.			Sangiran 3	"Pithecanthropus 3"	Skull fragments, juvenile	1938
0.7 m.y. B.P.	Kabuh	Sangiran	Sangiran 7b		Isolated teeth	1937–1941
0.8 m.y. B.P.			Sangiran 8	"Meganthropus B"	Right mandible fragment	1952

§, ¶, ** Notes appear on page 300.

TABLE 7-12 (continued)

DATE	FORMATION	BEDS	HOMINIDS			
			CODE NUMBER	OTHER NAMES	PRESERVED PARTS	DATE OF DISCOVERY
0.8 m.y. B.P.	Kabuh	Sangiran	Sangiran 10	"Pithecanthropus 6"	Calotte, zygomatic	1963
			Sangiran 11		Isolated teeth	1963
			Sangiran 12	"Pithecanthropus 7"	Calotte	1965
			Sangiran 13		Skull fragments	1965
			Sangiran 14		Skull-base fragments	1966
			Sangiran 15		Left maxilla fragments	1968, 1969
			Sangiran 16	"Meganthropus?"	Isolated teeth	1969
			Sangiran 17		Cranium, teeth	1969
			Sangiran 18	"Pithecanthropus 8"	Skull fragments	1970
			Sangiran 19		Occipital fragments	1970
			Sangiran 20		Skull fragments	1970
			Sangiran 21		Mandible fragment	1973
1.9 m.y. ± 0.4 m.y. B.P.††	Putjangan‡‡	Djetis	Sambungmachan 1	"Mandible E"	Calotte	1973
			Modjokerto 1	"Homo modjokertensis"	Calvarium, infant	1936
			Sangiran 1a		Right maxilla	1936
			Sangiran 1b	"Mandible B"	Mandibular fragment	1936
			Sangiran 4	"Pithecanthropus 4"; "Pithecanthropus robustus"	Calvarium, maxilla	1938, 1939

(Continued)

††, ‡‡ Notes appear on page 300.

TABLE 7-12 (continued)

DATE	FORMATION	BEDS	CODE NUMBER	HOMINIDS		
				OTHER NAMES	PRESERVED PARTS	DATE OF DISCOVERY
1.9 m.y. ± 0.4 m.y. B.P.††	Putjangan‡‡	Djetis	Sangiran 5	"Pithecanthropus dubius"	Right maxilla	1939
			Sangiran 6	"Meganthropus 1"; "Meganthropus palaeojavanicus"	Right mandible	1941, 1950
			Sangiran 7a		Isolated teeth	1937, 1941
			Sangiran 9	"Mandible C"	Mandibular fragment	1960
			Sangiran 22	"Maxilla F"	Maxillary fragment	1974

*The Solo River deposits are dated only by their faunal remains; no absolute dates have yet been obtained.

†All the Solo hominids were recovered between 1931 and 1933, and all have been attributed to this taxon.

‡This small parietal fragment was found adhering to the skull of Ngongdong 3 and was originally attributed to that individual. However, since Ngongdong 3 already had parietal bones, this fragment must represent another individual.

§This date is based on potassium-argon (Von Koenigswald, 1964).

¶The attribution of this molar to *Pongo* was made by Hooijer (1948).

**These dates are based on potassium-argon (Von Koenigswald, 1964, 1968).

††This date is based on potassium-argon dating of pumice 8 m below the site of Modjokerto 1 (Jacob and Curtis, 1971; Jacob, 1972). The hominids date to a somewhat later time, perhaps about 1.3 m.y. B.P. (see text).

‡‡This is also spelled "Pucangan" (Jacob, 1973).

Sources: Data derived from Jacob, 1973; Oakley, Campbell, and Molleson, 1975; and Von Koenigswald, personal communication.

those areas where gibbons still lived, such as southeast Asia. Haeckel (1889) proposed the name "Pithecanthropus alalus" ("ape-man without speech") for this early human ancestor even though no fossil evidence of such a type had been found. Eugene Dubois, a young Dutch anatomist, accepted Haeckel's hypothesis and, with remarkable single-mindedness, decided he would find the "ape-man."[11] His medical training allowed him to obtain a post as medical officer in the Dutch possessions in southeast Asia. He was first sent to Sumatra in 1889 and his initial excavations there yielded only orangutan teeth. While in Sumatra, however, his avowed interest in early humans resulted in his being sent a skull which had recently been recovered at Wadjak in Java. Somehow managing to become posted to Java, he excavated the rock-shelter site at Wadjak, recovering a second skull and some postcranial material; this material was of Upper Pleistocene age and will be discussed in Chapter 9. Recognizing that the Wadjak material was relatively recent, Dubois searched for other sites to excavate in Java. He focused on the area around the village of Trinil, on the Solo River, in central Java. This area had long been a collecting ground for paleontologists interested in Late Tertiary material. Almost immediately, he recovered his first fossil hominid: a jaw fragment found at Kedung-Brubus in November 1890. In September 1891, he recovered a single fossilized tooth from the Solo riverbank at Trinil. With this stimulus, he then proceeded to remove the entire riverbank in the area where the tooth had been found. In October 1891, a skullcap **(calotte)** was found about 3 m from where the tooth had been recovered. Dubois was unsure whether these finds should be attributed to humans or to a form of chimpanzee. But the question was settled in August 1892 when a femur, clearly of human form, was recovered in the same area. Dubois (1894) then proposed the name "Pithecanthropus erectus" ("ape-man who walked erect"). These finds, from the Kabuh Formation, are of Middle Pleistocene age and will be discussed in Chapter 8.

Although Dubois's work was centered on the Trinil and Sangiran deposits of Middle and Upper Pleistocene age, he nevertheless provided a prime stimulus for other investigations of early hominids in Java. Early in the 1930s, Von Koenigswald began paleontological work on the island. In 1936, a child's skull, found near the village of Modjokerto in central Java, was brought to his attention. This skull is from a geologic level underlying the Kabuh Formation called the "Djetis beds," which are of Early Pleistocene age. Volcanic material taken from below the site where the child's skull was discovered has been dated with potassium-argon to 1.9 m.y. ± 0.4 m.y. ago (Jacob and Curtis, 1971; Jacob, 1972). This date,

---

[11]Herbert Wendt's book *In Search of Adam* (1956) provides an excellent description of the development of evolutionary theory and of the individuals who helped (or hindered) the process.

however, represents only a maximum age for the Djetis deposits; the actual time when hominids entered Java was probably somewhat later.

Java, as an island, presents special problems to immigrants; and, in the absence of any evidence of the use of water craft by hominids in the Early Pleistocene, we must assume entry over dry land. The waters which surround Java and other nearby islands, such as Sumatra, Borneo, Flores, and Timor, are relatively shallow. Therefore, even a small drop in sea level would expose a dry shelf of land between these island areas and the mainland of southeast Asia. Sea level has in fact fallen a number of times, during periods when glaciers were being formed. In the Late Cenozoic, the first evidence of widespread glaciation—and therefore of a drop in sea level—occurred about 3 m.y. ago (Berggren and Van Couvering, 1974). This seems too early for hominids to have entered Java. However, another drop in sea level occurred between 1.5 m.y. and 1.2 m.y. ago, and the first entry of hominids into Java probably occurred during this time range. A look at a map will confirm that hominids may have crossed Sumatra to reach Java; although no early human remains are known from there, it would be an interesting place to look. Borneo, too, may well have shared in this Early Pleistocene occupation in southeast Asia. As we will see later, stone tools, possibly referable to this period, have been found on the islands of Flores and Timor, just to the east of Java.

At present, the best evidence of Early Pleistocene hominids in Asia is to be found in the Djetis beds on the island of Java. At least six hominids have been identified from this time level. The Modjokerto child's skull is nearly complete, but none of the facial portion is present below the brow ridges. The age of the child at death was probably between 2 and 4 years, an estimate based on the fact that the fontanelle (the "soft spot") had just closed. It is remarkable, in fact, that so fragile a structure as a child's skull would have been preserved at all, much less in relatively good condition. The front portion of this skull is interesting in that the beginnings of both postorbital constriction and brow-ridge development can be seen. Von Koenigswald (1936) proposed the name "Homo modjokertensis" for the child but later decided that it should be included within "Pithecanthropus" (Von Koenigswald and Weidenreich, 1939).

Subsequently, a number of important hominid fossils were recovered from several other Javan sites containing Djetis-age faunas. In 1939 the recovery of portions of a large and remarkably robust skull was reported (Von Koenigswald and Weidenreich, 1939). The material, representing this individual first referred to as "Pithecanthropus 4" consists of the rear portion of the skull and the maxilla. The maxilla is of interest in that the canines are large and a gap, or diastema, is present between the lateral incisor and the canine. In living primates such a gap exists to accommodate a large and protrusive lower canine.

Even more remarkable for their large and robust development are the mandibular fragments called "Meganthropus." From 1939 through 1969, four fragmentary mandibles attributed to this genus were recovered. Since this material consists of only the sides of the jaws, the front teeth and the rest of the skull are not known. The size and robusticity of the first two specimens to be recovered so impressed Weidenreich that he incorporated them into his theory of a gigantic phase in human evolution. Other workers, notably J. Robinson, have tried to use them to demonstrate the existence of robust australopithecines outside Africa.

No hominid living sites have been identified in Early or Middle Pleistocene deposits in Java. Similarly, no cultural assemblages have been found in direct association with hominids from these time levels. However, a number of stone tools have been found in situations that suggest that they probably date to either the Early or the Middle Pleistocene (Mulvaney, 1970). These early Javan tools are termed the "Patjitanian industry." Hand axes made of flakes are a basic component of this industry; some of them are large—as much as 30 cm long and weighing up to 3 kg (Movius, 1944). These are not typical Acheulian hand axes but resemble stone tool industries found elsewhere in Asia. Some workers have suggested that the Patjitanian industry closely resembles the Tampanian industry from Malaysia and even the African Oldowan (Sieveking, 1958). The possible occurrence of similar tools on Timor and Flores islands is of particular interest (Glover and Glover, 1970). If the Patjitanian industry is indeed the industry of early *Homo* in southeast Asia, and if the tools on Flores and Timor are of the same type, hominids at this time must have been very widespread.

This spread of human populations, in the Early Pleistocene, into cooler and more temperate regions has important implications. It means that humans had by this time developed cultural abilities that sustained them outside the warmth and climatic stability of the equatorial regions. Since one of the major climatic features of temperate regions is a more marked difference between the seasons, this geographic expansion must have meant that humans were able to cope with a variable food supply and seasonal extremes in the weather. Morphological flexibility and dietary omnivory must have equipped humans well for this expansion.

SUMMARY

Investigations of Plio-Pleistocene hominid sites reveal the occurrence of several events and practices during that period.

1. *Occupation of the grasslands (c. 9 m.y. B.P.)* Although the hominids had first appeared in forest or forest-fringe environments, by the later Miocene they had moved into true grassland habitats.

2. *Emergence of two distinct genera (2 m.y. to 3 m.y.* B.P.*)*   The genera *Australopithecus* and *Homo* had clearly diverged by 2 m.y. ago, if not earlier; little is known, however, about their immediate ancestors. These genera had slightly different adaptive patterns in the grassland. *Australopithecus* may have maintained a diet and behavioral pattern much like that of their common ancestor, while *Homo* practiced a broadened subsistence base, involving the use of more meat.

3. *First artifacts (2 to 3 m.y.* B.P.*)*   The first stone tool assemblages appeared in east Africa by 2.5 m.y. B.P. Earlier assemblages based on bone, teeth, and horn materials have been postulated for Makapan in South Africa. Although this particular assemblage is controversial, it does form a logical precursor type of tool assemblage.

4. *Occupation of a home base (2 m.y. to 3 m.y.* B.P.*)*   The earliest hominid sites contain the remains of only one or a very few butchered animals. But by about 2 m.y. ago, the accumulation of a larger quantity of animals, stone tools, and toolmaking débris indicates that living activities were increasingly becoming focused, at least for a short period, on a single site.

5. *Increased use of meat; probable hunting (2 m.y. to 3 m.y.* B.P.*)*   The remains of various types of animals at a single site indicate the inclusion of meat in the hominid diet. The wide variety of animal remains found at some sites strongly suggests that at least some of these animals were actively sought rather than scavenged.

6. *Geographic expansion outside Africa (c. 1.5 m.y.* B.P.*)*   By at least 1.5 m.y. ago, some hominids had left Africa and soon after this time appeared in Java. Evidence suggests that only *Homo erectus* was involved in this expansion.

7. *Extinction of the genus Australopithecus (c. 1 m.y.* B.P.*)*   No evidence of the australopithecines is known after about 1 m.y. ago. There is evidence that this form remained localized in east and South Africa and became extinct without issue.

SUGGESTIONS FOR FURTHER READING

Bishop, W. W., and J. D. Clark (eds.), 1967. *Background to Evolution in Africa.* Chicago: University of Chicago Press.

Bishop, W. W., and J. Miller (eds.), 1972. *Calibration of Hominoid Evolution.* Edinburgh: Scottish Academic Press. (A series of papers dealing with various methods of dating.)

Broom, R. 1959, *Finding the Missing Link.* London: Watts. (A very readable and enjoyable description of the early australopithecine discoveries in South Africa.)

Butzer, K. 1971, *Environment and Archeology* (2d ed.). Chicago: Aldine-Atherton. (Good background information placing humans in their ecological context.)

Cole, S. 1975, *Leakey's Luck*. New York: Harcourt, Brace Jovanovich. (Strictly speaking, a biography of Louis Leakey, but in a broader sense, a description of the development of studies on early humans in east Africa.)

Coppens, Y., F. C. Howell, G. L. Isaac, and R. E. F. Leakey (eds.), 1976, *Earliest Man and Environments in the Lake Rudolf Basin*. Chicago: University of Chicago Press. (A series of detailed papers on various studies in this important area.)

Leakey, L. S. B. 1967, *Olduvai Gorge, 1951–1961*. Cambridge, England: Cambridge University Press. (Report on the early work at the Gorge.)

Leakey, M. D. 1971, *Olduvai Gorge*, Vol. 3. Cambridge, England: Cambridge University Press. (Report on the cultural materials from Beds I and II.)

Oakley, K. P., B. Campbell, and T. Molleson. 1971, *Catalog of Fossil Hominids: Europe*; 1975, *Catalog of Fossil Hominids: Americas, Asia and Australasia*; 1977, *Catalog of Fossil Hominids:* Africa (2d ed.). London: Trustees of the British Museum (Natural History). (This series of catalogs lists virtually every hominid found to date; it includes tabulated data on the history, stratigraphy, dating, cultural association, taxonomy, faunal associations, and current location of each specimen.)

8

HOMINIDS OF THE MIDDLE PLEISTOCENE:
(0.7 to 0.2 m.y. B.P.)

INTRODUCTION

The Middle Pleistocene,[1] as a phase in human evolution, presents some rather paradoxical features. There is, on the one hand, more homogeneity in human morphology and culture than was present in the Plio-Pleistocene. In fact, however, this homogeneity is more relative than real; variations due to individual variability, sexual differences, geographic adaptation, and evolutionary progression all occur. But the bounds of cultural and morphological variability are very clearly less than they had been during the Pliocene and Early Pleistocene.

Within the Middle Pleistocene, evidence of human populations in Europe and Asia becomes widely visible. There are a number of important sites of Middle Pleistocene age (Table 8-1), yielding a broad variety of information concerning the morphology and behavior of humans during this time. Some sites have revealed only cultural evidence: Torralba and

[1]Most paleontologists agree on placing the beginning of the Middle Pleistocene at the time of the last major reversal in the earth's magnetic field. The Brunhes-Matuyama reversal occurred at 0.7 m.y. B.P.; and since it was a worldwide event, it provides a widely acceptable datum point. (See Butzer and Isaac, 1975; Bishop and Miller, 1972.)

TABLE 8-1 Hominids of the Middle Pleistocene, 0.7 m.y. to 0.2 m.y. B.P.

m.y. B.P.	GLACIAL EPOCH	EUROPE	AFRICA	ASIA
0.2	Third Glacial *Riss* .3–.2	Arago Lazeret La Chaise Petralona(?)	Bodo ↑(?) Rabat(?) Littorina Cave	
0.3	Second Interglacial *Holsteinian* .4–3	Swanscombe Steinheim Bilzingsleben Montmaurin	Salé	Choukoutien
0.4	Second Glacial *Mindel* .65–4	Vértesszöllös Ubeidiya	Ternifine Lake Ndutu ↕ Olduvai Hominid 12 Olduvai Hominid 28	Lantian Trinil
0.6	First Interglacial *Cromerian* .7–65	Mauer (Heidelberg)		
0.7 1.1	First Glacial *Gunz* 1.1–.7			Sangiran

(?) = date questionable

Ambrona, in Spain, and Terra Amata, in France, have abundant and informative cultural remains but no human remains. On the other hand, sites at Steinheim and Heidelberg in Germany have yielded human bones but no artifacts.

With expansion into more northern latitudes, humans came into contact with a remarkable series of events in earth history: the Pleistocene ice ages. The ice advances of the Late Tertiary actually began in the Pliocene, but until the extensive occupation of Europe and Asia in the Middle Pleistocene, they were not an important factor in human history.

PLEISTOCENE ECOLOGY: THE ICE AGES

The Plio-Pleistocene Ice Ages are characterized by the repeated formation of large continental glaciers (glacials) alternating with periods of warmer climate (interglacials). Although most authors work with a simplified glacial chronology involving four major glacial advances (the Gunz, Mindel, Riss, and Würm), with possibly two minor glacial episodes preceding the Gunz, the situation is actually much more complicated than this simple system indicates. Kukla (1975), for example, has shown evidence of 17 major glacial-interglacial shifts in the last 1.6 m.y. Despite this apparent complexity, it may be useful, if not entirely accurate, to maintain the traditional fourfold division, while recognizing that this is a simplification of the actual situation.

The Plio-Pleistocene ice ages were experienced most strongly in the northern hemisphere. There the combination of high mountain ranges and continental climatic patterns allowed the formation, first, of mountain glaciers and then, through the subsequent fusion of these smaller ice masses, of vast continental ice sheets (Figure 8-1).

During the Pleistocene, glaciers appeared in mountain ranges in many parts of the world, but the greatest extent of the continental ice sheets occurred in two areas: northern Europe and North America. The glacial terminology used here relates to the Alpine sequence where the evidence for the Plio-Pleistocene ice ages was first studied. Different terminologies have been proposed for the northern European, Himalayan, Scandinavian, and North American sequences. It is thought that these sequences were broadly, but not exactly, contemporaneous; for example, a particular ice advance may have begun earlier in the northern, colder areas and slightly later in the southern and warmer areas. However, the glaciations were not local phenomena but reflected worldwide climatic conditions.

Whatever precise combination of climatic factors was ultimately responsible for the ice ages,[2] glaciers will begin to develop when more snow falls in the winter than melts in the summer. When this occurs, the ice packs in different areas will begin to consolidate and, as the weight of the ice mass increases, will gradually flow into surrounding areas. Such a major advance is called a "glacial period." Within such a period the ice does not continuously grow and move but will undergo phases of expansion and melting. A period of expansion within a glacial is called a "stadial"; a period of melting or regression within a glacial is called an "interstadial."

As ice accumulation continues within a glacial, water will steadily be drawn from the seas to feed the glaciers. The result is that as the glaciers

---

[2]A number of theories have been proposed to explain the occurrence of the ice ages: see Ewing and Donn, 1956; Donn and Ewing, 1966; Hays and Schackleton, 1976.

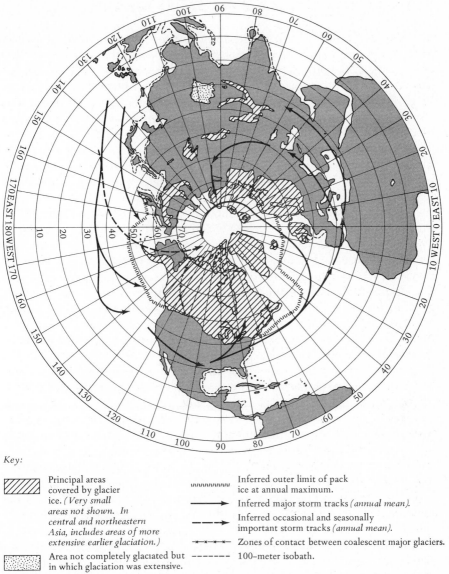

Key:

▨	Principal areas covered by glacier ice. *(Very small areas not shown. In central and northeastern Asia, includes areas of more extensive earlier glaciation.)*	

∿∿∿∿∿ Inferred outer limit of pack ice at annual maximum.

⟶ Inferred major storm tracks *(annual mean)*.

⟶ Inferred occasional and seasonally important storm tracks *(annual mean)*.

–×–×–×– Zones of contact between coalescent major glaciers.

▦ Area not completely glaciated but in which glaciation was extensive.

– – – – – – 100-meter isobath.

FIGURE 8-1 Glaciers in the Middle Pleistocene: extent of glaciers, pack ice, and storm tracks during the last glacial maiximum, northern hemisphere. (By permission of R. F. Flint.)

expand on land, the level of the seas decreases. Most geologists would agree that a maximum of 100 m to 150 m of water was withdrawn from the seas at glacial maxima, only to be replaced as the glaciers melted (Flint, 1947). If the continental glaciers remaining today on Greenland and

Antarctica, for example, were to melt entirely, the sea level would rise as much as 50 m.

The removal and then readdition of water to the seas have had the effect of opening up land connections at one time and then drowning them later. Such land connections have had an important effect on the entrance of humans into otherwise isolated areas. Their entrance into Java in the Early Pleistocene and into the New World in the Late Pleistocene was almost undoubtedly made possible by a lowering of sea levels during glacial episodes.

During the glacial episodes, the mean annual temperature in northern Europe may have been $-2°C$ or less (Butzer, 1971). During the maximum extent of the Pleistocene glaciers—the Mindel, or Second Glacial—ice covered 32,257,155 sq km in the northern hemisphere. During the Würm, ice covered 26,874,387 sq km. In contrast, today ice covers only about 15.5 million sq km of the entire surface of the earth (Flint, 1947).

In the nonglaciated areas of Europe and western Asia, very cold conditions prevailed with perhaps only 30 to 40 frost-free days per year. Such very cold conditions would favor the development of both pine forests and tundras. In some areas, for example, there were sparse forests of pine, spruce, and birch, and the open areas were dominated by plants of the genus *Artemisia* (Butzer, 1971). This is a large and important group of plants containing forms such as wormwood, tarragon, and other herbs, and, in the New World, sagebrush. The tundra plants, in the colder areas, formed a very valuable source of food for the large herds of grazing animals that were common during the glacial period in Europe and Asia. These tundra plants, such as mosses, lichens, and sedges, were a main food source for mammoths, reindeer, bison, and horses. These animals in turn provided an important food source for humans during that time.

Thus the Pleistocene forests and tundras, despite the very cold conditions, were well stocked with both plant and animal foods for human use. This was unquestionably an influential factor in the ability of humans to survive the glacial conditions. The cultural traditions of this time are marked by the progressively efficient ability of humans to exploit and utilize these tundra herds.

In the more southerly areas of Europe, cold, termperate forests with both deciduous and fir trees existed. Such forests were found from the northern shore of the Mediterranean to the southern shore of the Caspian Sea (Butzer, 1971).

Between the major glacial episodes, the ice masses melted entirely, and probably even the continental glaciers that exist today on Greenland and Antarctica also melted. Such periods of complete glacial disappearance are called "interglacials." It is probable that we are now in the early phase of an interglacial period that began about 11,000 years ago.

In Europe the interglacials can be characterized in a very general way as having been warmer and more moist than today. Such climatic conditions are indicated by the presence of plants and animals requiring warmth and moisture far to the north of their present distribution in the Second and Third Interglacials (Frenzel, 1968; Butzer, 1971).

Overall, both summer and winter conditions were warmer, with temperatures about 2°C to 4°C higher than today. Sea level may have been as much as 55 m higher than at present.

HOMO ERECTUS (1.5± c.0.25 m.y. B.P.)

The hominids of the Middle Pleistocene are usually placed within a single species, *Homo erectus*, which is generally thought to contain a number of geographic subspecies or races. Of the two or more hominid lineages present in the Pliocene and Early Pleistocene, *Homo erectus* was the survivor. Perhaps this species survived because its members possessed a breadth of subsistence activities, mobility, and offensive and defensive abilities that significantly surpassed those of the australopithecines. Perhaps *Homo erectus* possessed skills in communication which allowed the individual to assimilate, use, and pass on learned information more effectively. Perhaps members of the species possessed the ability to perceive and manipulate their environment in ever more complex and useful ways. Nevertheless, at some time prior to 1 m.y. ago, members of the genus *Homo* left Africa, eventually to colonize the world; the australopithecines did not go along.

As we have seen in Chapters 6 and 7, perhaps the most remarkable single feature within the Plio-Pleistocene hominids was the variation and diversity present in those populations. However, after about 1 m.y. ago, that variation diminished substantially and no definite evidence of the australopithecine line is known after that time. The remaining hominid lineage, usually referred to as *Homo erectus*, is no less notable for its geographic range than for its morphologic unity. Differences do occur, but they appear to be no greater than between living populations of *Homo sapiens*.

Recognition of this unity is relatively recent, however. Early workers, impeded by the slow exchange of information and of casts of the fossils, tended to view "their" hominids as special and distinctive specimens. As a result, many if not most new finds were placed in entirely new genera or species, so that by the late 1950s there was considerable proliferation of Middle Pleistocene hominid taxa. Taxonomic revision of these hominids was first undertaken by Campbell (1962, 1965), who suggested that the taxon *Homo erectus* should be reorganized to include "Sinanthropus pekinensis" ("Peking Man"), "Pithecanthropus erectus" ("Java Man"), and a number of other less well known specimens. Campbell, and later,

Howells (1966), concluded that the morphological variation present in the Middle Pleistocene hominids was probably at the subspecies or racial level.

CHARACTERISTICS

Important characteristics of *Homo erectus* are as follows:

Thick bones in skull and postcranium
Long, low skull (platycephaly)
Cranial capacity, 775 to 1400 cc; mean, approximately 1100 cc
Well-developed brow ridges (supraorbital tori)
Well-developed horizontal crest on occiput (occipital tori)
Strong angulation of occiput in lateral view
Maximum breadth of skull low on temporal bone
Protrusion of lower part of face (prognathism)
Upper and lower borders of mandible parallel
No chin
Geographic distribution: tropical and temperate areas of the Old World

MORPHOLOGY

Skull

The skull of *Homo erectus* is low-vaulted and long (platycephalic) (see Figure 8-2). The forehead is always lower and less vertically oriented than in *Homo sapiens*. It usually slopes gently back from the brow ridge. Some later *Homo erectus* individuals, such as those from Choukoutien and from Lake Ndutu, Tanzania (R. H. Clarke, 1976), have a more vertical, though still low forehead. The low forehead of *Homo erectus* undoubtedly reflects the small size of the frontal lobe of the brain (Weidenreich, 1943a).

All *Homo erectus* individuals have very large brow ridges (supraorbital tori). They are composed of a bar of bone which is continuous and thick over the root of the nose and then gently arches over each eye. In the Choukoutien skulls and KNM ER 3733 (see Figure 6-11) from Lake Turkana, there is a groove (the supratoral sulcus) along the upper margin of the brow ridges, but in other forms the torus merges smoothly and without interruption into the low forehead.

Although large brow ridges are a consistent character throughout the species, the internal structure of this feature is highly variable. In the Javan forms and in individuals from Bilzingsleben, Germany (Vlcek, 1978), Petralona, Greece, and Rhodesia, for example, the brow ridges overlie large, hollow frontal sinuses. In the Choukoutien skulls, on the other

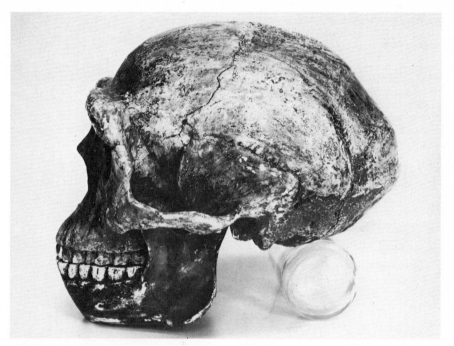

FIGURE 8-2 Skull of *Homo erectus*, lateral view. This reconstruction of the skull of "Peking Man" shows a pattern of characteristics found in *Homo erectus* throughout the very wide geographic and temporal range of this species: long skull, sharply angled occiput, sloping forehead, large brow ridges, and facial prognathism. Note also the absence of a chin. The Peking site dates from about 350,000 years ago.

hand, frontal sinuses are virtually nonexistent except for a very restricted, narrow area at the root of the nose. In these Chinese skulls, the interior of the brow ridges is not hollow but is filled with spongy, cancellous bone tissue (Weidenreich, 1943a). This variability leads us to the conclusion that brow ridge development is not functionally or directly related to large frontal sinuses; in fact, we understand very little about the functional base of large brow ridges.

In the temporal bone, the ear region shows a morphology distinct from that of *Homo sapiens*. In *Homo sapiens* the tympanic plate is more-or-less vertically oriented (see Figure 2-2*b*), but in *Homo erectus* the tympanic plate is obliquely oriented (Weidenreich, 1943a). *Australopithecus*, as pointed out in Chapter 6, has a nearly vertical tympanic plate, as in *Homo sapiens* (Tobias, 1967). In *Homo erectus* skulls from Choukoutien and Lake Ndutu (R. H. Clarke, 1976), the tympanic plate also differs from *Homo sapiens* in being greatly thickened; in fact, in the Choukoutien skulls it is 2 to 3 times the thickness of sapiens (Weidenreich, 1943a). As will be discussed below, such bone thickness appears to have been a general characteristic of this species.

TABLE 8-2   Occipital size and shape relationships

HOMINIDS	OCCIPITAL BREADTH (BIASTERIONIC BREADTH)	OCCIPITAL HEIGHT (LAMBDA-OPISTHION)	OCCIPITAL INDEX*
Homo sapiens (males)	107.9 ∓ 4.8	96.5 ∓ 5.9	89.4
Homo sapiens (females)	104.3 ∓ 4.7	94.2 ∓ 4.6	90.3
Archaic *Homo sapiens*			
Rhodesian	138	88	62.8
Omo 2	126	105	83.3
Skhul 5	116	92	79.3
Neandertals			
Tabun 1	119	90	75.6
La Chapelle	122	91	74.5
Shanidar 1	121	100	82.6
Homo erectus			
Swanscombe	123	94	76.4
OH 9	116	?	
Sangiran 4	130	79.5	61.2
Choukoutien (mean)	115	85	73.9
Solo (mean)	126.2	85.2	67.5
Australopithecus			
STS 5	76	58.5	77
OH 5	89.2	57.8	64.8
MLD 1	85	68	80

*Occipital index $= \dfrac{\text{occipital breadth} \times 100}{\text{occipital height}}$

Sources: *Homo sapiens*, Swanscombe, and La Chapelle, Weiner and Campbell, 1964; *Australopithecus*, Tobias, 1967; Choukoutien, Weidenreich, 1943a; Solo and Sangiran, Weidenreich, 1951; Shanidar, Stewart, 1977. Others, by the author on casts or originals.

The occipital bone is both shorter and broader than in *Homo sapiens* (Table 8-2). It is interesting that while the australopithecine occiput is absolutely much smaller than in hominines, the relationship between breadth and height of the bone is very similar in both the early hominines and the australopithecines. Note, however, the much greater absolute breadth of the occiput in the early hominines in comparison with the sapiens. Most of the early hominines have occipital breadths greater than 2 standard deviation units from the mean of the male sapiens. This is a very significant finding and indicates that the cranial base has been an area of active evolutionary change. Part of the greater breadth in the *Homo erectus* occiput is undoubtedly due to the great thickness of the bones, but this does not account for all the difference. The change in the length and breadth relationships of the hominine occiput may well reflect intrinsic, but undocumented, changes in the brain itself.

The shortness of the occipital bone is accentuated by the tight angulation of the occiput when viewed from the side. This small occipital angle is particularly marked in skulls from Asia (Java, and Choukoutien and Lantian in China), Africa (OH 9 and Ndutu) and Europe (Bilzingsle-ben). Some, such as individuals from Vértesszöllös, Hungary, and Swanscombe, England, however, show an occiput which has become higher and the angle therefore has become larger.

In *Homo erectus* the occipital bone is crossed horizontally by a large bar of bone called the occipital torus. The great development of this torus makes it a major character of the *Homo erectus* skull. Below the torus is an extensive area for attachment of the neck (or nuchal) muscles. These large neck muscles were a biomechanical necessity in view of the large, prognathous *Homo erectus* face, which would have added considerable weight to the front part of the cranium. In some individuals there is a distinct groove along the top of the occipital torus; the "supratoral sulcus" is present in skulls from Choukoutien (Weidenreich, 1943a) and Bilzings-leben (Vlcek, 1978).

In *Homo erectus* skulls from Choukoutien (Weidenreich, 1943a) and Vértesszöllös (Thoma, 1966; Wolpoff, 1971c), the occiput shows a horizon-tal division of the bone above the torus. The resultant extra bone in the upper part of the occiput is called an "inca bone" and is found occasionally in modern humans. Four of the five occipital bones from Choukoutien that were studied by Weidenreich had such inca bones. We cannot be sure if this incidence was typical of the frequency of this feature in the entire Chinese *Homo erectus* population, but the high precentage is worthy of note.

Cranial size for the species ranges from 775 cc to 1400 cc and thus overlaps with the sapients at the upper end of the range. In the Javan forms from both the Djetis and Kabuh beds, the average was probably about 900 cc. In the slightly later Chinese forms, the average was probably nearer 1000 cc (Weidenreich, 1943a; Table 8-3). Some individuals, such as the one from Vértesszöllös, reached approximately the *Homo sapiens* mean of 1400 cc (Thoma, 1966).

The parietal bones can be characterized as being "smaller, flatter, thicker and more rectangular" than in modern humans (Weidenreich, 1943a, p. 33). In sapients the parietals are more-or-less square and are strongly curved both front to back and up and down. The large size and curvature of these bones reflect the fact that in sapients the upper part of the vault has enlarged and the point of maximum skull breadth occurs high on the parietals. In contrast, the *Homo erectus* skull has the point of maximum breadth low in the mastoid region (Figure 8-3).

The mastoid, a pyramidal extension of the temporal bone just behind the ear, is well developed, as in *Homo sapiens*. However, in sapients the mastoid points straight downward, whereas in *Homo erectus* it is tucked under the skull and the tip of the pyramid points somewhat inward. The mastoid process provides a point of origin for the sternocleidomastoid muscle; this muscle, which inserts onto the sternum and the middle

TABLE 8-3 Cranial capacity in the early hominines

LOCALITY	FOSSIL(S)	CAPACITY, cc
Africa	KNM ER 3733	800–900 (estimated)
	OH 9	1067
	OH 12	727
Europe	Steinheim	1070
	Swanscombe	1325 (reconstructed)
	Petralona	1220
	Vértesszöllös	1400 (reconstructed)
Asia		
Java	Trinil 2	850
	Sangiran 2	775
	Sangiran 3	900
	Sangiran 4	750
	Sangiran 10	975
	Mean for Java	848
China	"Sinanthropus" 2	1030
	"Sinanthropus" 3	915
	"Sinanthropus" 10	1225
	"Sinanthropus" 11	1015
	"Sinanthropus" 12	1030
	Mean for Peking	1043
	Lantian	780

Sources: KNM ER 3733, R. E. F. Leakey and Walker, 1976; OH 9 and OH 12, Holloway, 1973; Europe, see Day, 1977 for references; Asia, see Tobias, 1967, for references.

portion of the clavicle, pulls the head forward and rotates it. This conformation of the mastoid may well reflect the broader skull base in *Homo erectus* discussed above.

Also on the side of the skull, a well-developed crest, called the supramastoidal crest, runs from the rear of the cheekbone onto the lateral portion of the occiput. This crest is present in sapients but is much slighter in its development and does not continue onto the occiput.

From the front (Figure 8-4), it can be seen that the face of *Homo erectus* was large. In some of the earlier forms, such as "Pithecanthropus" 4 and 8, the face is massive, and it is also very large in the somewhat later forms from China. By the end of the Middle Pleistocene, the face had become reduced and skulls from Steinheim, Germany, and Arago, France, show a less massive facial structure. Especially in the Steinheim skull, probably that of a female, the face is of a much lighter build and approaches that of sapients in overall size. A very interesting feature appears in the faces of individuals from Steinheim, Arago (Figure 8-5), Rhodesia, and Bodo, Ethiopia (Conroy et al., 1978). In these skulls, the maxilla, in the center of the face, has a swollen, inflated appearance. This feature becomes

FIGURE 8-3 Reconstructed skull of "Peking Man," posterior view. Note that the point of maximum skull breadth is low on the skull but not—as in *Australopithecus*—at the lowest point.

considerably accentuated in the skull of Neandertals, in the later Pleistocene (see Chapter 9). This inflation of the maxilla appears to reflect large maxillary sinuses. The Rhodesian and Bodo skulls have especially large maxillary sinuses. The Choukoutien skulls, however, have neither inflated maxillary sinuses nor inflation of the maxilla. Therefore, this maxillary expansion may be a feature of later Middle Pleistocene hominines.

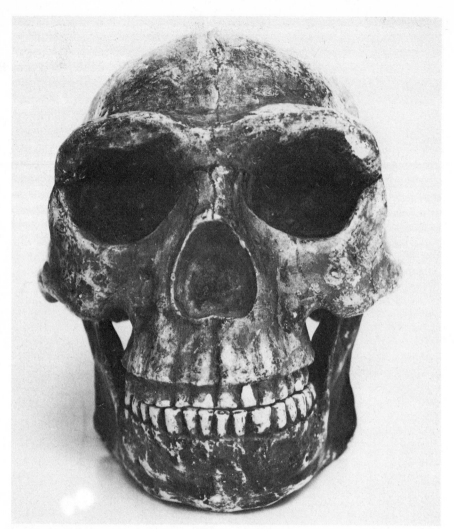

FIGURE 8-4 Reconstructed skull of "Peking Man," facial view. In this view, the low forehead is again evident. (Photograph by Gary Feinstein.)

Also, in the facial view, many *Homo erectus* skulls show a sagittal keel. This is not homologous with the sagittal crest, which in the robust australopithecines and in larger pongids represents an area of origin of the temporalis muscle. The temporalis in *Homo erectus* originates on the sides of the skull at about the same level as in sapiens.

The nasofrontal suture is usually horizontal, as in *Homo sapiens* and in contrast with the australopithecines.

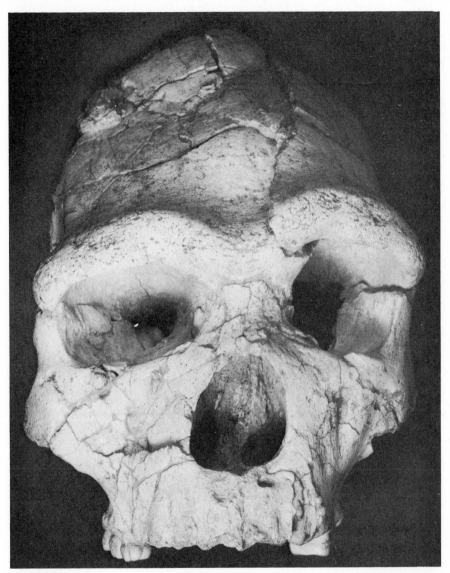

FIGURE 8-5 Skull from Arago, France, dated to about 300,000 years ago. This skull shows a combination of features characteristic of both *Homo erectus* and the Classic Neandertals: the central facial portion (the maxilla) has a slightly swollen or inflated appearance (this becomes exaggerated in the later Neandertals), and the brow ridges are rounded (this is particularly characteristic of the Classic Neandertals). (Photograph courtesy of H. de Lumley.)

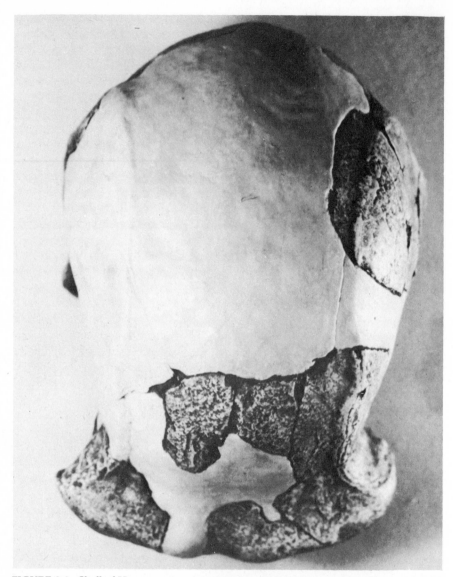

FIGURE 8-6 Skull of Homo erectus, superior view (OH 9). Compare this illustration with Figure 6-3; in contrast with the australopithecines, *Homo erectus* had a longer, less globular skull shape and showed considerable expansion across the frontal region, resulting in less postorbital constriction (Photograph of a cast, used with permission of Kenya National Museum.)

When viewed from above (Figure 8-6), the *Homo erectus* skulls show tight constriction of the frontal bone just behind the eyes. As in *Australopithecus*, but to a lesser degree, this postorbital constriction reflects a face which is large in relation to the size of the cranium. It is only when facial size becomes smaller and cranial size larger that postorbital constriction diminishes.

The base of the skull in all early hominids is poorly known. Weidenreich (1943a) and others have observed that the skull base may have been deliberately pulled out in order to reach and extract the brain. In any case, few specimens reveal the precise location and size of the foramen magnum. From the available evidence, however, it appears that the foramen magnum was placed far forward under the skull, as in sapients (Le Gros Clark, 1964), thus indicating that head position and body posture were similar in both groups. This supposition needs to be confirmed when more individuals with the base intact are discovered.

In those *Homo erectus* skulls in which the base is preserved, a crest of bone is present along the suture between the occipital bone and the mastoid portion of the temporal bone. This crest is situated along the medial side of the digastric sulcus, a deep groove just behind the mastoid. This crest, while it may occur in sapients, is never strongly developed in that group and was, in fact, never named as an anatomical feature until Weidenreich (1943a) described it as the "crista occipto-mastoidea" in the Choukoutien skulls. It has since been identified in the Swanscombe skull (Stewart, 1964) and in several Neandertals (see Chapter 9). It appears to have been a consistent feature of the early hominines.

One of the most remarkable and consistent morphological features of the *Homo erectus* skull is the thickness of the cranial bones (see Table 6-1). Weidenreich (1943a) first noted this increased thickness in the Choukoutien material, and his finding has since been confirmed as an important characteristic of the species. Moreover, all the known postcranial bones of the species also show such increased thickness.

The bones of the skull are formed of three layers: inner and outer tables consisting of dense cortical bone, and a middle layer, the diploe, formed of spongy, cancellous bone. In *Homo erectus* the skull thickness is produced by enlargement of the inner and outer tables and there is little change in the diploe layer. This is quite different from the increased thickness seen in some of the australopithecines. In the skulls of that group, in areas of strong muscle attachment, the outer table alone increases; the underlying layers of the bone remain very thin (see Figure 6-1). Also, in the more robust members of the australopithecines, the skull bones may become thickened because of expansion of the diploe layer, a process called pneumatization (discussed in Chapter 6). Although there is some pneumatization in the *Homo erectus* skull (particularly in the temporal bone), it is very minimal in comparison with the australopithecines.

We do not understand the function of these thick *Homo erectus* bones.

The thickness is clearly not related to muscular robusticity since only the outer portion of the bone is involved in hyperdevelopment of the musculature. It is, in fact, difficult to find any biomechanical correlate of this feature since such non–weight-bearing and nonstressed bones like the tympanic plate are involved. `Neither does it appear to be due to a pathological condition. Some types of anemia, for example, produce thicker bones, but in such cases it is the spongy portion of the bones, such as the diploe in the skull, that increases. It is in such spongy bone that red blood cells are manufactured, and expansion represents an effort by the body to produce more blood-forming tissue. Many other conditions, including various types of dietary deficiencies and aging, result in thinned, not thickened, bones. A genetic factor is most likely involved, but the adaptive significance (if any) of such a factor remains unknown.

Mandible

The mandible, too, contains a number of distinctive features. One of the most characteristic features of the *Homo erectus* jaw is that there is no chin. The later development of a chin in *Homo sapiens* is a reflection of a number of different evolutionary changes. One such evolutionary trend has been a reduction, from early to later hominines, in the overall size of the teeth. The result is that in *Homo sapiens* the bony, tooth-bearing margin of the mandible (the alveolus) has decreased in size while the lower portion of the jaw has remained much the same size. This reduced size of the alveolus is reflected in the diminished prognathism of later hominines. Thus, *Homo sapiens* is much more orthognathous than was *Homo erectus*.

A second trend relates to the rotary movement used by hominids in chewing their food. The rotation of the lower jaw, relative to the upper jaw, produces considerable biomechanical stressing along the lower margin of the jaw where some of the major chewing muscles attach. In order to withstand this stress, additional bone has been added along the lower margin of the hominid jaw, particularly at its front portion. *Homo erectus* produced this buttressing mostly on the inside of the jaw. This inner buttress, called the "mandibular torus," is particularly well marked in the Choukoutien individuals but is seen, in some degree of development, in virtually all early hominine jaws. In *Homo sapiens* the bony buttress, no longer on the inside of the jaw, has moved to the outer, lower margin of the jaw, thus contributing to the visible chin. It is interesting that at least one early hominine, KNM ER 730 from Lake Turkana, shows early indications of such chin development (Figure 6-12). In this individual there is a very slight triangular swelling of the bone in the lower front region of the mandible (Day and R.E.F. Leakey, 1973).

It is also interesting that another early hominid, from Kanam, Kenya, had its possible sapient status revoked when it was realized that its "chin" was actually a cancerous growth on the jaw (Tobias, 1960).

Another characteristic feature of most Middle Pleistocene mandibles is the presence of multiple mental foramina, also seen in some australopithecines. These foramina are seen in jaws from Java; from Choukoutien and Lantian in China; from Heidelberg, Germany; and from Montmaurin, France, and Ternifine, Algeria. Such multiple foramina also characterize the jaws of most pongids.

In most *Homo erectus* the sides of the jaw diverge slightly toward the rear. In many individuals (e.g., Sangiran 4, Choukoutien, and Heidelberg) the jaw reaches its greatest width at the level of M_3. In the later sapients, the jaw sides turn in at the level of M_2, where the greatest width is reached. Thus, the parabolic dental arcades, long regarded as a character of hominids in general, can be shown to be a specific feature of sapients.

A final feature of the *Homo erectus* mandible is that the tooth-bearing margin of the jaw is parallel with the lower margin of the jaw. Therefore, the height of the jaw under the incisors and under the molars is approximately the same. In *Homo sapiens*, by contrast, the front portion of the jaw is higher, so that the area under the molars is relatively lower.

Dentition

In most features, the dentition of *Homo erectus* closely approaches that of modern humans, although the teeth generally tend to be somewhat larger in the earlier group. The canines are similar in size and shape to those of *Homo sapiens*. In a few individuals, however, they tend to be slightly more conical and protrude slightly beyond the level of the other teeth. The incisors, especially those from Choukoutien, are apt to be concave (shovel-shaped) on their inner surface; such a feature is common in many living Asiatic and American Indian populations. The upper premolars in *Homo erectus* tend to have three roots (Weidenreich, 1937; Von Koenigswald, 1950), while a double, fused root is usual in modern humans. A newly discovered *Homo erectus* from Morocco also shows this feature (Ennouchi, 1975). Triple-rooted premolars are also reported in other early hominids as well. A skull from the Sterkfontein Extension site attributed to *Homo*, STW 53, also has such triple-rooted premolars. This specimen is particularly interesting in that its molars also show a multiplicity of roots (Hughes and Tobias, 1977). Moreover, most of the premolars from robust australopithecines at Swartkrans show triple-rooted premolars (Clarke and Howell, 1972; J. Robinson, 1953a).

In the molars, there is considerable variation in relative size. The general rule in modern sapients is for the first molar (M1) to be the largest and the last molar (M3) to be the smallest; such a pattern is also clearly seen in the Steinheim upper jaw. In other Middle Pleistocene hominids, however, the size of the molars is nearly equal or increases from front to back. In the Montmaurin mandible, for example, M3 is the largest molar tooth (Coon, 1962). The enamel of the unworn molars in *Homo erectus* is often finely wrinkled (crenulated), and a thickened rim of enamel (a cingulum) often occurs at the base of the crown. These are both primitive characteristics which are found in many australopithecines, particularly the robust group.

Postcranium

Of the few postcranial bones recovered for *Homo erectus*, only the femur is well known, with femoral material having been recovered from Java, Choukoutien, and east Africa. In terms of their external morphology, these bones differ little from *Homo sapiens*. The overall configuration, size, and shape are much the same in both groups. However, in terms of their internal morphology, visible on x-rays, important differences do exist. This fact has been the cause of some controversy, especially with regard to the five femora from the Trinil beds in Java. These bones, especially the complete and well-preserved "Pithecanthropus 1" femur recovered by Dubois (Figure 8-7), have a fully modern appearance to the unaided eye. Because of the clearly *H. erectus* nature of the cranial remains from these levels, it was originally concluded that both skull and leg bones could not have been derived from a single population. However, when the Javan bones were internally examined with the aid of x-rays, it could be seen that they did not closely resemble modern populations. In the *Homo erectus* femora from Choukoutien, Trinil, Bed IV at Olduvai, and Lake Turkana, the outer walls of the shaft (the cortex) are as much as twice as thick as the

FIGURE 8-7 Femur found by Eugene Dubois in 1891 at Trinil, Java, probably referrable to *Homo erectus*. This femur shows a remarkable pathological growth (probably myositis ossificans) which may have been a reaction of the outer tissues of the bone to an injury. Neither the injury nor this growth was incapacitating: the individual walked until death. (Photograph courtesy of M. H. Day.)

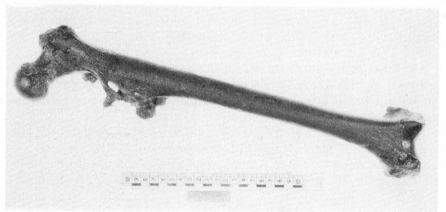

average for a comparative *Homo sapiens* population. The internal cavity (the medulla) is correspondingly reduced, so that the external or outer dimensions of the bones are roughly equivalent in both groups (Kennedy, 1973). The tibia also shows this pattern of thick shaft walls (Chia, 1975).

Another feature that distinguishes the femur of *Homo erectus* from that of *Homo sapiens* is the point at which the minimum diameter of the bone occurs. In *Homo sapiens*, this point is found about halfway along the shaft, but in *Homo erectus*, it occurs in the lower third of the bone. This may reflect some postural difference in the two groups. In modern humans, the femur is slanted inward so that the knees come close together or touch when the individual is standing. It seems likely that in *Homo erectus* the knees did not come close together and that the thigh did not slant inward at the knees as much as in modern humans (Kennedy, 1973).

The pelvis of *Homo erectus* is known from a single specimen, OH 28, recovered from Bed IV at Olduvai Gorge. In its major biomechanical features, this pelvis shows a close overall similarity with sapiens. However, a few features do distinguish it. The most important difference is in the presence of a strongly developed and vertically oriented pillar of bone which runs from the socket for the head of the femur (the acetabulum) to the top of the ilium (Figure 8-8). This "iliac pillar" appears to add strength and stabilization to the *Homo erectus* ilium (Day, 1971a). Moreover, the acetabulum is very large in comparison with sapiens, thus indicating that the femoral head in *Homo erectus* was very large. These two features taken together—a well-buttressed ilium and a large femoral

FIGURE 8-8 Pelvis of *Homo erectus* (OH 28). Note the large acetabulum, indicating a large femoral head, and the strongly marked iliac pillar running up to the crest of the ilium. Both of these features appear to have been characteristic of the *Homo erectus* pelvis. (Photograph by Gary Feinstein.)

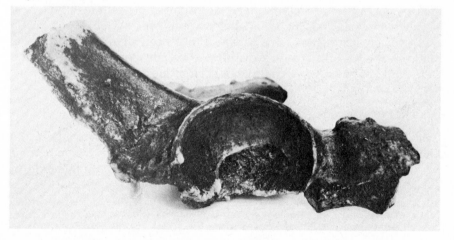

head—could indicate substantial body weight for *Homo erectus*, but this conjecture cannot be confirmed on the basis of present evidence. Finally, Day (1971a) also reports that the ischium of this pelvis shows a strong medial rotation, a feature not seen in sapiens.[3]

SKELETAL EVIDENCE FROM THE MIDDLE PLEISTOCENE

Human populations in the Middle Pleistocene were very widely distributed. Although we first saw evidence for such geographic extension into Europe and Asia in the Early Pleistocene, that earlier evidence was mostly archeological in nature. Now, however, we begin to see more skeletal remains of the hominids themselves.

First, or Cromerian, Interglacial (0.7 m.y. to 0.65 m.y. B.P.)

Within this first interglacial episode, we see skeletal evidence of humans in both Europe and Asia.

At present, the oldest hominid material from Europe is the Mauer or Heidelberg jaw. This complete and well-preserved mandible was recovered in 1907 from a sand pit in the town of Mauer, about 6 km east of the city of Heidelberg, Germany. The Mauer pit, long a source of Middle Pleistocene fauna, probably dates to a period about 0.7 m.y. ago (Cooke, 1972). The mandible was recovered from a layer about 20 m below the ground surface.

This jaw is very large and robust, and it is similar in some ways to the strongly built hominids from the slightly earlier Djetis beds in Java, which were discussed previously. Despite its robust build, however, the teeth are not remarkably large. There is no chin, but, as in other *Homo erectus* jaws, multiple foramina are present on the lower border beneath the premolars. An interesting sidelight on the Mauer jaw is Wendt's (1956) report that a skull possibly belonging to this individual had been recovered in the same sand pits after World War II. According to Wendt, however, the workers were afraid of having to account for a skull in their pits and destroyed it.

Second, or Mindel, Glacial (0.65 m.y. to 0.40 m.y. B.P.)

Asia A large number of human fossils have been recovered from the Middle Pleistocene Kabuh levels in Java. In China, both the important cave at Choukoutien and the sites in Lantian County date to this time.

---

[3]As pointed out in Chapter 6, a pelvis from Lake Turkana, KNM ER 3228, also shows this pattern of morphology. It is, however, perhaps a million years earlier in time than OH 28 and has not been formally attributed to *Homo erectus*.

JAVA   The dates for the Kabuh Formation, which contains the Trinil beds on the island of Java (see Table 7-12), indicate an age of about 0.83 m.y. to 0.5 m.y. B.P. (Jacob, 1973). Although some of the human material, especially from the Sangiran area, may date to the earlier time, the Trinil hominids seem to have come from a colder period and therefore probably date to Mindel times (Selenka and Blanckenhorn, 1911).

To date, 27 hominids have been recovered from Middle Pleistocene deposits on the island of Java (Jacob, 1973). The material has been recovered from three areas: near the village of Trinil, at Kedung Brubus, and near Sangiran, all located in central Java. Not all this material is well known to scientists. The material originally excavated by Dubois in the 1890s, mainly from Trinil and Kedung Brubus, has been stored at Leiden, Holland, for many years. This material includes the first "Pithecanthropus" skullcap (calotte), some teeth, and five femora. This material, stored in Europe and easily accessible to scholars, has long been available for study. However, most material recovered since 1931 is stored in Indonesia and has therefore been less frequently examined.

The five femora in the Leiden collection are of some interest. The first femur to be discovered by Dubois (called "Pithecanthropus 1") (Figure 8-7) is complete and well preserved, although it demonstrates a remarkable pathological growth. This femur was immediately recognized to be human, but the remaining four, which are not complete, were not so identified until years later when a museum assistant found them in storage boxes in Leiden. As pointed out previously, on external examination these femora have a very modern appearance quite in contrast with the clear *Homo erectus* nature of the skullcap. Chemical comparisons between the skullcap and the femora, using fluorine, uranium, and nitrogen, have shown that they could be of similar antiquity (Day and Molleson, 1973). X-ray examination of the internal structure of these femora has shown them to be thick-walled and to have other features similar to the Choukoutien and OH 28 femora; it therefore appears that they belong nearer to that group than to sapients.

In 1969, a nearly complete skull and face were recovered in the Sangiran area. Typical of other *Homo erectus* individuals, this skull (Sangiran 17) is low, with well-developed brow ridges and nuchal crest. The maximum skull breadth is placed low in the mastoid region and the cheekbones are very robust and broad. Although the teeth are very worn, the canine appears to be slightly larger than in the modern human (Jacob, 1973).

CHINA   Two other Asian sites, both in China, date also to this time. The site at Chenchiawo Village, Lantian County, Shensi Province, appears, on the basis of faunal correlations, to be slightly older than Choukoutien.

A skull, with parts of the face and mandible, was recovered in Lantian

County in 1965. The skull is remarkable for its small size, only about 780 cc (Woo, 1965). The brow ridges are very well developed and grade smoothly into the forehead. This structure is in contrast to the Choukoutien skulls, where there is a groove or depression between the upper margin of the brow ridges and the beginning of the forehead. There are multiple foramina on the mandible; the dentition is of interest in that the third molars appear to have been congenitally absent. This occurs occasionally in modern humans but is not known in other Middle Pleistocene fossils. Although no "chin" is present, a slight bulge marks the lower front region of the jaw (Woo, 1964).

Woo (1965) has pointed out that in its degree of robusticity, the Lantian individual more closely resembles the earlier Javan Djetis age populations than the later Chinese group. This robusticity is particularly apparent in the thickness of the skull walls, which in some dimensions are thicker than those of any other known *Homo erectus* individuals.

Perhaps the best-known and most informative of all Middle Pleistocene hominid sites in the cave at Choukoutien (Figure 8-9). The site contains the fragmentary remains of about 50 *Homo erectus* individuals as

FIGURE 8-9 The cave deposits at Choukoutien. The deposits are in a limestone cavern which provided a living site for *Homo erectus* over a long period of time in the Second Interglacial. Many of the human bones found here were in and around hearths and were mixed with animal bones; this may indicate that the hominids, like the animals, had been eaten. Table 8-4 correlates hominid loci with stratigraphic layers and excavation levels. (By permission of the British Museum—Natural History.)

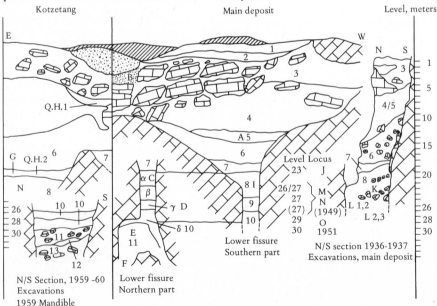

TABLE 8-4 Correlation of hominid loci with stratigraphic layers and excavation levels in Figure 8-9.

SITUATION	HOMINID LOCUS OR DATE OF FIND	LAYER	LEVEL
Main deposit and southern part of lower Fissure	A	5	
	B	3 or 4	
	I	8	22
	J	(8–9)	23
	K	8–9	24
	L	9	25
	M	9	26–27
	N	9–10	27
	1949	(9–10)	(27)
	O	(10)	29
	1951–53	10–11	30
Lower Fissure, northern part, and lower cave	C	∝	
	D	γ	
	E	11	
	F	11	
Kotzetang	G	Quartz Horizon 2	
	1959	10	27
Upper Travertine	H		

Note: Parentheses indicate probable but uncertain provenance or correlation.

Source: By permission of the British Museum (Natural History). (Data from Weidenreich, 1937, 1943a; and Black et al., 1933.)

well as hearths, stone tools, and a large vertebrate fauna. The cultural materials from Choukoutien will be discussed in the following section. (See also Figure 8-9 and Table 8-4.)

The large amount of data available on the hominids from Choukoutien is due almost entirely to Weidenreich's fine monographs (1936; 1937; 1941; 1943a). The morphology, on the whole, is as discussed in the anatomical definition of the species. Cranial capacity of the five skulls for which it can be determined ranges from 915 cc to 1225 cc and is slightly higher than for the Javan forms. All the skulls are low, broad, and thick-walled. Some of them retain a suture (the metopic suture) in the middle of the frontal bone; this feature occurs in some modern individuals but is rare.

EUROPE Only a single European site is known to contain Mindel-age hominids. Human material, consisting of an occipital bone and a few broken teeth, was recovered from Vértesszöllös, Hungary, in 1965. The occipital bone is of considerable interest since it shows evidence that it was derived from a skull of virtually modern size. Although this bone is broad and thick, as in typical *Homo erectus*, it is larger and has a more open, rounded profile than is usually found in that group (Thoma, 1966; Vertes, 1965,a, b). Cranial capacity of the skull may have been about 1400 cc, the average for modern humans.

Thus, it may be possible to identify, as early as the Second Glacial, the beginnings of the cranial increase that was to be a major characteristic of *Homo sapiens*. It may be significant, too, that hominids with cranial capacities at or near the sapient mean can be found in such widely separated geographic areas as Asia and Europe.

AFRICA Hominid remains dating to the period between 0.65 m.y. and 0.4 m.y. ago have been found both in north Africa and in Bed IV, Olduvai Gorge.

The site at Ternifine, Morocco, has yielded the earliest skeletal evidence of humans in the northern part of Africa, although cultural evidence suggests human presence there since the Early Pleistocene. The Ternifine site, dating to the late Mindel (Jaeger, 1975), contained three mandibles, part of a parietal, and a few teeth. The mandibles show a number of similarities with those from Choukoutien, despite the geographic separation. The similarities include parallel upper and lower borders to the jaw, multiple mental foramina, and the inner buttress or ridge of bone (torus mandibularis). The parietal bone is thick and curves in such a way as to indicate that the skull was moderate and the maximum breadth was placed near its lower border; the cranial capacity may have been about 1300 cc (Kochetkova, 1970).

OH 28, from Bed IV, Olduvai Gorge (Table 8-5), represents important evidence of the postcranial morphology of humans at this time. The human remains, consisting of a partial pelvis and femur, were described by Day (1971a). In that description, he noted that the OH 28 femur shared several similarities with femora recovered from Choukoutien and described by Weidenreich in 1941. In particular, the Chinese and African femora show front-to-back flattening of the upper part of the shaft (platymeria), a thick cortex, a thin medullary canal or cavity, and a low point of minimum shaft breadth. While the platymeria is not a feature of all Middle Pleistocene femora (e.g., Trinil), the other features do seem to represent a recurrent pattern during this time period.

The partial pelvis of OH 28 (see Figure 8-8) shows a number of similarities with the earlier KNM ER 3228 from Lake Turkana; among them are the strong buttressing of the ilium and the large acetabulum described previously.

OH 28 was in association with an Acheulian tool complex and the deposits in Bed IV may date to about 0.5 m.y. B.P. (M. D. Leakey, 1971b).

Further evidence of *Homo erectus* in Bed IV is seen in OH 12. Although the skull of this individual is very broken and incomplete, the thickened bones characteristic of this group are unmistakable.

TABLE 8-5   Hominids from Beds III and IV, Olduvai Gorge

POSITION	HOMINID NUMBER (OH)	DATE OF DISCOVERY	PARTS PRESERVED	TAXONOMIC STATUS	ASSOCIATED INDUSTRY
Bed IV, VEK,MNK	22	1968	Right half of mandible, P_3–M_2	cf. *Homo erectus*	None
Bed IVb, FLK	23	1963	Fragment of left mandible, P_4–M_2	cf. *Homo erectus*	Acheulian
Bed IVa, MNK	2	1935	Fragments of cranial vault	cf. *Homo erectus*	Inferred Acheulian
Bed IVa, VEK	12	1962	Fragments of cranial vault, palate and maxilla	*Homo erectus*	Inferred Acheulian
Bed IVa, Geological locality 54	25	1968	Fragments of left parietal	?	Inferred Acheulian
Bed IVa, WK	28*	1970	Femur, left pelvis	*Homo erectus*	Acheulian
Beds III, IVa JK West	29	1969	Fragment of molar, 2 incisors, phalanx	cf. *Homo erectus*	Acheulian
Beds III, IVa JK West	34	1962	Femur, fragmentary tibia	?	Acheulian

*See Figure 8-8.

Sources: Data from M. D. Leakey, 1971a; Day, 1977.

Although the dating is as yet uncertain, the skull and Acheulian artifacts from Lake Ndutu, Tanzania, may be broadly equivalent in time with OH 28. Acheulian tools, butchered animals, and a hominid skull were uncovered by the receding waters of Lake Ndutu, not far from Olduvai Gorge, during the dry season of 1972 (Mturi, 1976).

The cranium is quite complete and shows a number of similarities to the Choukoutien skulls. These features include large brow ridges, thick skull bones, and a small mastoid. But the individual also shows several features of a more modern configuration: more vertical skull walls with expansion of the upper part of the vault and a reduced supramastoid crest (Clarke, 1976). Only preliminary work has been completed on this skull, and the fact that the skull base, along with the foramen magnum, is preserved makes its ultimate description very desirable.

Second, or Holsteinian, Interglacial (0.4 m.y. to 0.3 m.y. B.P.)

In the Second, or Holsteinian, Interglacial, several important sites are known in Europe, and the occupation levels at Choukoutien continue on into this period; a single hominid is known from North Africa.

Africa   A nearly complete skull has recently been reported from deposits at Salé, Morocco. This skull has a capacity between 930 cc and 960 cc, thick skull walls, and pronounced postorbital constriction. A strong nuchal torus is present, but it is less pronounced and less angulated than in other Middle Pleistocene hominids. The greatest width is low, but the parietals are expanded outward so that the skull walls are more or less vertical (Jaeger, 1975).

Europe   Several European hominids are known from the so-called "Great Interglacial" between the Mindel and Riss glacial periods. One of the most interesting of them is the Steinheim cranium recovered in 1933 from a gravel pit at Steinheim an der Murr, near Stuttgart (Weinert, 1936). This is a nearly complete cranium, although the base of the skull is missing. On one side of the face, the brow ridge and orbit are badly damaged, perhaps from an injury at the time of death. As with the earlier Ternifine and Vértesszöllös individuals, Steinheim too shows some evidence of evolutionary advance in some features. The cranium is small (about 1175 cc), the skull is low, and the brow ridges are large. However, along with these typical *H. erectus* features are others of a more modern aspect. The face is relatively small and straight and does not protrude in the jaw region; it appears to be tucked under the brow ridges. Moreover, the point of maximum skull breadth is higher than in earlier *Homo erectus* individuals, indicating that while total cranial size is still small, skull shape is approaching that of sapiens. The teeth are small and the M^3 is particularly reduced, both more modern features. At the rear of the skull, the profile is rounded without the sharp angle. There is here, as in other individuals of the Middle Pleistocene, evidence of more advanced features.

No archeological material was found with the skull, and, despite the fact that it was recovered long ago, it has never been fully prepared or even adequately reported.

The site at Swanscombe, just south of London, has yielded cranial bones recovered under fortuitous circumstances. In June 1935, an occipital bone was recovered in a gravel pit near the banks of the Thames, and in March 1936, a left parietal was recovered nearby. Both bones fit together well, indicating that they came from the same individual. Some 20 years later, in July 1955, the right parietal was found, again making a perfect fit to form the rear and side portions of a skull.

These bones are thick and the maximum skull breadth is low; the cranial capacity is no more than 1325 cc. Complete anatomical studies have been performed on these three bones by Weiner and Campbell. They noted (1964) that one of the sinuses found in the lower portion of the skull (the sphenoidal sinus) continues onto the occipital bone. Such extension would be a very rare feature in modern humans. They reasoned that if the sphenoidal sinus was so well developed, the other sinuses of the skull, including those in the frontal bone, may also have been enlarged. Such enlargement, if indeed present, may result in large brow ridges and a face with proportions similar to Steinheim. Other features also resemble more typical *Homo erectus* individuals; these features included an occipitomastoid crest.

Recently, a thorium-uranium date of greater than 0.3 m.y. has been derived for this site (Butzer and Isaac, 1975); this date is consistent with the Second Interglacial aspect of the faunal remains.

Thus, these hominids in the Second Interglacial show a recurring complex of more advanced features mixed with typical *Homo erectus* characters. The most consistent advanced features seem to be increased cranial capacity and reduction in tooth size.

A cavesite at Petralona, in northern Greece, has yielded evidence of human occupation over a long period from Mindel through Third Interglacial times. Stone tools and hearths, as well as fragmentary human bones, have been found throughout the 4.5 m of débris which covers the rock floor of the cave (Poulianos, 1971). In 1960, human remains, originally reported to be those of a completely preserved individual lying on its right side, were discovered in the cave. The date of this individual may be between 0.25 m.y. (electron spin resonance studies) and 0.3 m.y. B.P. (uranium disequilibrium studies) (Papamarinopoulos, 1977). However, all but the skull of this individual was lost before controlled excavations began.

The skull in many ways is very similar to that of other typical *Homo erectus* individuals: the face is massive with well-developed brow ridges and the forehead is low. The point of maximum skull breadth is low and the occiput has a well-defined torus. Although the cranial capacity has not been directly determined, it is probably somewhat above the range for Choukoutien. This slightly larger size is reflected in a slightly more rounded profile at the back of the skull. Although no jaw was found, it must have been massive: even the large Mauer jaw is not large enough for the Petralona maxilla. A closer fit would be found in some of the Javan mandibles, such as "Pithecanthropus 4."

Multivariate analyses on this skull have indicated a close morphologic affinity with typical *Homo erectus*, particularly with individuals from Choukoutien (Stringer, 1974; Corruccini, 1975). Both studies, which used different forms of multivariate analyses, also showed a very close resemblance to the Rhodesian skull. This pattern of resemblance is interesting because the Rhodesian skull is from a later time period, probably dating to about 100,000 years ago.

Human remains were first found at the German site of Bilzingsleben in 1972. Since then, four hominid skull fragments and a single molar tooth have been recovered (Vlcek, 1978). Analysis of the skull fragments indicates a morphology close to OH 9 and to Sangiran 17 (Vlcek, 1978). The brow ridges are well developed, the skull bones are very thick, and the occiput is marked by a strong horizontal torus. The Bilzingsleben skull is too fragmentary to determine whether the signs of morphological change, present in other Mindel-Riss hominids, occur here as well. The bones were in association with a Clactonian flake industry (see below) and numerous butchered animal bones characteristic of the European Second Interglacial (Vlcek, 1978).

The skull from Bodo D'Ar, Ethiopia, must be regarded as undated although its general Middle Pleistocene age seems secure. Conroy et al. (1978) believe the skull should be between 0.7 m.y. and 0.125 m.y. old. The skull was found during 1976 and 1978 in the Awash River Valley, near the Plio-Pleistocene localities reported by Johanson. Stone tools and butchered hippos were found in association with the skull.

The skull shows many of the typical *Homo erectus* features: a sagittal keel on the vault, low point of maximum breadth, and extraordinarily thick skull bones. In fact, at one point on the skull the bone is one of the thickest ever reported for a hominid (see Table 6-1). However, the Bodo cranium also shows evidence of more advanced features, such as less postorbital constriction. Its overall morphological pattern may be closest to the Rhodesian skull (Conroy et al., 1978). (See Chapter 9.)

Third, or Riss, Glacial (0.3 m.y. to 0.12 m.y. B.P.)

Human remains are poorly known from this time period; both Europe and North Africa have yielded only limited materials.

Europe   The most informative human material from this period, correlating with the European Third Glacial, was found in the cave of Arago at Tautavel in France (see Figure 8-6). Three mandibles, a skull, a number of isolated teeth, and some skull fragments were found in the cave between 1969 and 1971 by Henri and Marie de Lumley. All this material clearly shows a complex of *H. erectus* and more advanced features. The mandibles, for example, are very broad, low, and robustly built, and they show resemblances to the Mauer jaw. The skull is of particular interest. It consists of the face and front part of the cranium; the rear portion has been broken away; it appears to have belonged to a male about 20 years of age. As in other *Homo erectus* individuals, the brow ridges are very pronounced and the postorbital constriction is strong. The prognathism of the lower portion of the face is considerable and the forehead is low and sloping.

Along with these typical *H. erectus* features, however, are some characteristics of later populations, particularly of the Neandertals. The center portion of the face, for example, has the swollen, puffed appearance seen in the Neandertal populations. (H. de Lumley and M. A. de Lumley, 1971; H. de Lumley, 1975.)

Africa   The north African material of Riss age is very fragmentary. The so-called "Rabat Man" from Morocco consists of numerous very small skull and jaw fragments; all apparently belonged to a young man about 16 or 17 years of age. The mandible is very broad and robust and has multiple foramina, like the Ternifine jaws. On the basis of the available information, therefore, the Rabat fragments seem to affirm the presence of *Homo erectus* in north Africa at this time. The very fragmentary material from nearby Littorina Cave also seems to share a number of characters with both Ternifine and Rabat.

BEHAVIOR

There is abundant evidence of human behavior patterns during the Middle Pleistocene. During this time, humans first began to occupy caves; and some caves, such as those at Choukoutien in China and Arago in France, contain excellent evidence of human occupation at this period. Other, equally informative data come from sites of open-air habitation, such as those at Torralba and Ambrona in Spain and Terra Amata in France.

DIETARY PRACTICES

An important behavioral characteristic of Middle Pleistocene populations was their very broad subsistence base. As we have seen, the roots of such omnivory extend back into the Pliocene; from then through the Middle Pleistocene, humans utilized and exploited many different food sources. Fruits, vegetables, seeds, and nuts, each in its season, must have provided valuable dietary elements. At Terra Amata in France, for example, fossilized human feces, called "coprolites,"[4] contain the pollen of *Genista*, the "broom plant," and the cave deposits at Choukoutien contain numerous remains of the hackberry.

Aquatic resources were not ignored. Shellfish such as clams, oysters, and mussels were used; the coprolites at Terra Amata also contain small amounts of mussel shell. Curiously, although shellfish exist in great numbers in some areas and are easy to gather, Middle Pleistocene humans never used them to any great extent. During the period from about 8,000 to 10,000 years ago, many human groups began to use shellfish as a staple in their diet, and their reliability as a food source allowed these populations to spend much of the year in one area. Such sites are marked by huge mounds of shells called "middens." Middle Pleistocene humans, however, used shellfish only sporadically and occasionally.

Meat, both scavenged and hunted, was also a part of the human diet. The usual Middle Pleistocene subsistence pattern, little changed from that of earlier times, was the killing of one or several animals. Sometimes the

---

[4]The study of coprolites provides some interesting insights into human dietary patterns; see Bryant and Williams-Dean, 1975.

animals were very large, such as elephants, rhinos, oxen, or horses; at other times, smaller game, including deer and beaver, were killed.

Many models of Middle Pleistocene human evolution have, in fact, stressed the importance of big-game hunting patterns to the social, cultural, and even physical development of humans (see Chapter 5). However, the significance of big-game hunting may have been stressed beyond its actual value to humans during this time. That they hunted elephants, bison, horses, and other large mammals cannot be doubted; but, as we have seen, such exploitation patterns had emerged long before the Middle Pleistocene. Moreover, it seems likely that regular, basic subsistence depended less on the big and dangerous species and more on plant foods and on smaller animal species with less dangerous defensive mechanisms.

One significant trend in human hunting patterns does emerge in the Middle Pleistocene, when humans first began the systematic exploitation of herds of animals. We have seen that in Olduvai Gorge small groups of herd animals were killed on a few occasions. This trend toward the exploitation of herds, rather than individual animals, increased during the Middle Pleistocene and reached its culmination during the Upper Pleistocene. Such a hunting pattern is a major prerequisite for the support of the larger and less migrant human populations that are characteristic of Upper Pleistocene and later times.

TOOLS

The cultural traditions of the Middle Pleistocene have often been divided into two major categories. Movius (1944), for example, has distinguished between a bifacial hand-ax tradition called the **"acheulian,"** centered in Africa, Europe, western Asia, and parts of India, and a **chopper–chopping tool** industry centered in eastern Asia. Movius interpreted these two traditions as representing long periods of separate cultural evolution which had occurred during relative geographic isolation. Others have attempted to explain the dichotomy on the basis that tool form follows function; differences in tool morphology and tool-kit composition would therefore reflect different subsistence activities.

The true nature of the dichotomy remains to be explained. It is probable, however, that no single explanation will suffice in revealing why tool assemblages, some in direct geographic and temporal contiguity, show major differences.

Acheulian

The term "Acheulian" was originally proposed for flaked stone tools found in a quarry near the village of Saint-Acheul on the Somme River in

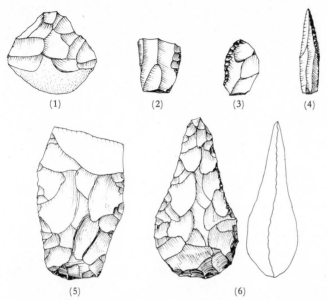

FIGURE 8-10 Acheulian assemblages. The Acheulian is known from many Middle Pleistocene sites in Africa, Europe, and western Asia; it is not found in eastern Asia. The most characteristic tool of Acheulian assemblages is the bifacially flaked hand ax. (1) Chopping tool; (2) burin; (3) scraper; (4) backed blade; (5) cleaver; (6) bifacial hand ax. (Scale: 0.5; drawings by Ross Sackett.)

northwest France (Rigollott, 1855) (Figure 8-10). As currently used, the term replaces a variety of names previously applied to lithic assemblages derived from a number of areas.

Europe:
Chellean
Abbevillian

Africa:
Victorian
Fauresmith
Stellenbosch

As we saw previously, Oldowan tools were made from random cobbles or rocks (cores) from which a few chips were removed to produce a cutting or shearing edge. The resultant tools show a wide variety of form and shape, reflecting the fact that the cobbles or pebbles were little modified from their original form. In the Acheulian manufacturing technique, on the other hand, a large flake was detached from the core and the flake itself was then chipped and trimmed in order to form a tool. Acheulian tools were more extensively modified than Oldowan tools and show greater standardization. This is especially true in later Acheulian assemblages where there is a high degree of consistency within the tool kits in terms of size, overall shape, and the number of flake scars.

The unifying, and indeed the definitive, aspect of the Acheulian complex is the presence of bifacially flaked hand axes. These hand axes, which are chipped or flaked from both faces (hence the term "biface"), have a cutting edge along most of the margin of both sides. They are usually oval in shape, with one end more-or-less pointed and the other rounded or left unflaked to serve as a butt. Tools like these occur in small numbers in Developed Oldowan B but, by definition, a stone tool assemblage becomes "Acheulian" when 40 to 60 percent of the tools show bifacial flaking (Kleindienst, 1962). Therefore, an Acheulian tradition is defined, not simply on the presence of bifacially flaked tools, but on the fact that such tools constitute a large portion of the total assemblage.

These hand axes seem to have served diverse purposes. In the Acheulian assemblage from Isimila in Tanzania, Howell (1961) observed that many of the hand axes show very little edge wear, indicating that they had not been used for rough jobs, such as dismembering animal carcasses. He concluded that the sharp edges and lack of battering imply that these tools had been used for preparing animal skins or for digging plant foods. In the Acheulian levels at Torralba in Spain, however, hand axes are found in direct association with butchered elephants and other large mammals; evidently in this case they had been used for very heavy duty work. It therefore seems possible to conclude that the Acheulian hand axes and the "scrapers" and "cleavers" also present in these assemblages were used in various ways and were not made specifically to perform a single type of task. However, a number of anthropologists have tried to draw a correlation between tool form and its function. Some years ago, Oakley (1964) of the British Museum suggested that Acheulian assemblages were found more often in grassland environments and that chopper-chopping tool complexes were recovered more often in forest areas. Such environmental differences could reflect the different ways in which they were used. Louis Binford (1972) has stated that small tools, such as scrapers, are more likely to have been used in the butchery of even very large animals. As we have seen previously, the association between butchery and very small tools can be observed even today. Conversely, at sites where bifacial tools are numerous, there tend to be very few bone remains (Isaac, 1976b).

In Africa, there does seem to be a correlation between the environmental setting and the presence of the Acheulian industry. Most of the Acheulian sites have been found in grasslands or open-country areas either in, or very near, stream channels. In the former case, it seems clear that the Acheulians were camping in dry stream channels; Mary Leakey has pointed out that some African groups still camp in such places because they can obtain subsurface water there by digging. At Olorgasailie in Kenya, the campsite was about 4 km away from the lake margin but within a sandy stream channel. In Europe, however, a number of Acheulian sites are found in more wooded areas but still in close association with water sources. At Swanscombe in England, campsites were located in a deciduous oak forest near the Thames. The kill and butchering sites at Torralba and Ambrona, in Spain, were located in a pine forest with swampy meadows in low-lying areas. At Terra Amata in Nice, France, the campsite was very near the Mediterranean shore.

All these sites show very short occupation times. Although many sites were frequently reoccupied, perhaps year after year, each stay apparently lasted only long enough for the consumption of the meat from a single hunt or the harvest of a single fruit or vegetable crop. The group then moved on, leaving behind a thin layer of occupational débris. The usual size of these groups seems to have been small. Analogy with living hunters and gatherers would indicate that the usual nomadic group consisted of a few nuclear families; 4 or 5 adult males and a total group size of about 20 to 25 seems a reasonable estimate. However, it is possible that, on occasion, several such bands may have come together, perhaps for certain activities or rituals (Howell, 1973). The large amount of meat killed and carried away at Torralba could indicate a group of 100 or more individuals (Freeman, 1975).

Throughout its very wide range, there is little important variation in the Acheulian stone tool kit; the oval, bifacial hand axes are a constant denomination throughout much of the Middle Pleistocene. However, some minor variations do occur, and of these, size is perhaps the most apparent. Some of the hand axes are, for example, very large. Some from the Lewa site in Kenya and Bed IV, Olduvai Gorge, are as much as 35 cm long; some from Olorgesailie weigh up to 3 kg. The ones from Olduvai, of white tabular quartzite, are beautifully made and carefully trimmed (Cole, 1963).

The stone tool assemblage forms just one component of the Acheulian industry. Excavations at a number of sites in east Africa, Europe, and southwest Asia have added further cultural components to our understanding of the behavior of Middle Pleistocene humans. Wood, for example, also provided a source of raw material in the Middle Pleistocene. At Kalambo Falls in Tanzania, Lehringen in Germany, Clacton in England, and Torralba in Spain, wooden spears have been identified; the spears in Germany and Spain were found near the remains of elephants and a well-preserved spear made from yew wood was found at the English site. At Terra Amata in France, H. de Lumley (1969) has identified the remains of what may have been a wooden bowl. Bone, too, was a source of raw material. At Terra Amata, an elephant leg bone had been hammered to a point; another had a fire-hardened point, and yet another was an awl-like tool. Also at the Spanish site, a number of elephant tusks had been trimmed to a point.

Of the large number of Acheulian occupation sites available, we might look at a few for more evidence of human behavioral patterns in the Middle Pleistocene.

Africa At Olduvai Gorge, the Acheulian complex first appeared about the middle of Bed II, some 1.2 m.y. ago (M. D. Leakey, 1975). By Bed IV times, which most of the recovered Acheulian sites represent, the lake at Olduvai had become much smaller and was probably saline. The known Acheulian sites are situated away from the lake margin, on or in stream channels; most of the streams were probably active only during the rainy season. However, permanent water must have been locally available; Mary Leakey notes that most of the Bed IV sites contain numerous remains of catfish, which require fresh water. Indeed, the site at TK, in Fish Gulley, contains the remains of numerous fish within the context of an occupation site.

It is interesting that the Developed Oldowan assemblages continue through Beds II, III, and IV and are therefore contemporaneous with the Acheulian. During the middle of Bed II times, the Oldowan assemblages first show the presence of rudimentary bifacial tools. Mary Leakey (1975) has suggested that the "concept of bifacial tools was almost certainly borrowed" from the Acheulians at this time. However, she points out that the makers of the Oldowan tools never achieved the technological proficiency of the Acheulians. The prime distinction between them seems to have been the inability of the Oldowan knappers to detach large flakes from their raw material. This distinction in tool-kit composition and technology continues into Europe and western Asia, where bifacial hand-ax traditions coexist with chopper–chopping tool assemblages in certain areas.

The site at Olorgesailie, Kenya, represents a series of repeated encampments by Acheulian humans. Several campsites have been uncovered by excavations and are, in fact, now on view to the public much as their occupants left them 400,000 years ago. One of the most interesting features of the Olorgesailie occupation sites contains evidence of a large baboon kill (Isaac, 1977). The remains of about 80 individuals of a large Pleistocene genus, *Simopithecus*, have been uncovered in one area. These remains include both juveniles and adults and may indicate that an entire troop was ambushed, perhaps as its members were sleeping. The remains of hippos, elephants, frogs, and fish have also been found at Olorgesailie. It is possible that rather sophisticated methods were used to capture the fish. J. D. Clark (1960) reports that a line of stones was placed near the margin of the Middle Pleistocene lake. Among groups now living in east Africa, such an arrangement often forms a fish weir that traps fish near the shore as the water level recedes in the dry season.

It is of interest that, although the tool assemblages at Olorgesailie are clearly Acheulian, a number of small variations are present in the tool kits from various levels and sites within the area. At the "cat walk" site, for example, the tools are very large—the hand axes are up to 30 cm long and 3 kg in weight. But at a site nearby, the tools are much smaller and a high proportion of them are formed on small flakes. Such differences could be attributed to bands or tribes with slightly different toolmaking traditions. Alternatively, the differences could reflect different activities.

Israel The site at Ubeidiya in Israel contains noteworthy examples of both Acheulian and Developed Oldowan; but here, instead of being contemporaneous, the two tool complexes seem to alternate. The lowest levels (14 archeological assemblages have been identified) contain a Developed Oldowan complex with many spheroids; this complex is very similar to that from middle and upper Bed II, at Olduvai Gorge (Bar-Yosef, 1975). Later, other assemblages appear that contain numerous bifacially flaked hand axes of Acheulian type. These groups are followed by still other tool kits with no bifaces but again containing spheroids.

The camp sites at Ubeidiya were occupied between 0.64 m.y. and 0.68 m.y. ago (Horowitz, Siedner, and Bar-Yosef, 1973). They seem to have been situated near a lake and swampy regions were in the area. Grasslands existed, probably in the lowlands, and the nearby hills were forested with oak and pistachio. Several hominid skull fragments and two teeth were recovered from a level containing Developed Oldowan tools (Tobias, 1966a). These bones are very broken and not much information is available from them. However, they are very thick, and such thickness is a characteristic of early members of the genus *Homo* and not of the australopithecines.

Europe FRANCE The site at Terra Amata in Nice was excavated by de Lumley in 1966 (H. de Lumley, 1969, 1975). The name "Terra Amata" refers to a blind alley in the port area where the site was uncovered during building operations. The site was apparently reoccupied, perhaps 11 times, for brief periods near the end of the Mindel Glaciation; the time of occupation was between 0.45 m.y. and 0.38 m.y. ago (H. de Lumley, 1975). Pollen analysis shows that pine and fir trees were common in the area then. The occupants of the site exploited a wide variety of the foods available in the neighborhood. At least eight species of large mammal including stags, elephants, boar, ibex, rhinos, and oxen, are present within the site. Most of them, however, were juveniles rather than adults. Small game, such as turtles, rabbits, birds, and rodents, is also present. The site of Terra Amata, then as now, was very close to the shores of the Mediterranean, and the resources of the sea were not ignored. A quantity of oyster, mussel, and limpet shells are present. More interesting, however, is the accumulation of fishbones and fish vertebrae, indicating that aquatic resources were not merely gathered but were probably more actively sought (H. de Lumley 1969; 1975).

With the evidence of structures from Beds I and II at Olduvai Gorge, it should come as no surprise that Middle Pleistocene humans, too, were building temporary living quarters. Perhaps the best evidence for this sort of activity in the Middle Pleistocene comes from Terra Amata. There, H. de Lumley found arrangements of stones and imprints of stakes which he interpreted as having formed the support for a number of huts built during the different occupation phases. These huts were oval, ranging from 7 m to 15 m in length and from 4 m to 6 m in width. Located in the center of the oval formed by the stakes was a second, linear arrangement of impressions, possibly indicating the support for a roof. It seems plausible that branches or brush were laid over an open framework of stakes. Within this arrangement were localized, dense concentrations of stone débris, probably indicating the stone-knapping areas. In fact, some of the flakes can be fitted back onto the core, indicating that they had been knapped in that same area. These concentrations encircle a barren area where the knapper sat. Also within the hut walls were the remains of fire hearths. These hearths, 30 cm to 50 cm in diameter, were shallowly scooped out of the sand. This evidence, and that from the roughly contemporaneous site at Vértesszöllös, Hungary, appear to constitute the earliest clear indications of the control of fire by humans. The behavioral implications of such control are very significant and will be explored in some detail below.

No human remains are known from Terra Amata, but two indirect pieces of evidence reveal some interesting information. A human footprint has been found at the site; this footprint is 24 cm long, and H. de Lumley (1975), using a formula which relates foot length to body height, has estimated that the individual was 1.56 m (just under 5 ft) tall. Such stature would be small for most *Homo sapiens,* but it is consistent with the stature estimations for the Choukoutien *Homo erectus* populations. Coprolites, or fossilized feces, found at Terra Amata indicate the ingestion of many kinds of vegetable foods. Most of the recognized plant species have a flowering period in late spring or early summer, and thus probably reveal the season when the site was occupied (Bryant and Williams-Dean, 1975).

Living structures have been identified in at least two other French sites of Middle Pleistocene age. At Lazeret, a structure 11 m by 3.5 m was erected just inside a cave entrance. The structure had two rooms, one of which was apparently for sleeping. ''In the back, two small fires had been lit directly on the ground. Round these, Acheulian hunters had put bedding made of seaweed covered with skins, as witnessed by the shells which had been attached to the seaweed and the ungual phalanges [finger bones] from carnivores" (H. de Lumley, 1975, p. 799). De Lumley further comments, "When [the hunters] left Le Lazeret after the winter sojourn, they put a wolf's skull just behind the cave entrance after having removed the brain through a hole 5 cm in diameter, into the right parietal. It is possible that by this gesture they sought to acquire some of the wolf's power" (p. 799). Oval huts, up to 5 m by 2.5 m in size, have also been identified at La Baume Bonne; these huts, which were occupied during a cold, wet phase of the Riss, had floors paved with cobbles, apparently to keep out the moisture. A rounded structure has also been identified at l'Atelier Commont (H. de Lumley, 1975).

SPAIN Two very important Middle Pleistocene sites are recognized in Spain, about 150 km northeast of Madrid in the province of Soria. The sites of Torralba and Ambrona were first investigated by a Spanish nobleman, the Marqués de Cerralbo, in the 1880s, and Clark Howell began major investigations there in the 1960s. These localities, which are roughly contemporaneous with Terra Amata, represent a series of extensive kill sites which, like the French site, were reused briefly over a period of time. The sites are located at an altitude of about 1100 m above sea level in a small stream valley, which was probably swampy in its lower levels during the time of occupation. It is in a geographic situation where the stream valley may well have served as a migration route for the large mammals that were killed there.

Animal remains found there are mostly those of large mammals: elephant, horse, red deer, ox, and rhino. Some of these animals were very large indeed. One of the male elephants was 5 m to 5.5 m tall and would have weighed about 9000 kg (10 tons). The meat provided by these kills was bounteous. Although only a few animals were killed at any one time, their size resulted in as much as 13,590 kg (about 30,000 lb) of meat for a single killing episode (Freeman, 1975).

Much evidence is available at Torralba concerning the hunting techniques, butchering practices, tool function, and even group size. For example, a great deal of charcoal is thinly but widely spread over the Torralba sites; Howell (1966, 1973) has postulated that fires may have been lit in the grassy upland areas in order to drive the animals into the low-lying swamps where they would become mired down. Then the hunters may have used large stones, which had been carried into the area, to batter the animals to death. There are, in fact, accumulations of stones which may be "deliberate stockpiles of ammunition" (Freeman, 1975); similar accumulations of stones were found at the Acheulian site of Isimila in Tanzania (Howell, 1961). Wooden spears, also found at the Torralba sites, may have been used too to kill the animals.

Freeman (1975) reports on a study designed to indicate the existence (if any) of significant correlations between type of tool and type of activity. Using a statistical procedure called "factor analysis," Freeman investigated several "data categories," such as animal parts, types of stone tools, and vegetable remains. One of the groupings or "constellations" produced by factor analysis includes choppers and chopping tools, scrapers, tusks, teeth, and nonlimb portions of the skeleton. This collection may indicate that the choppers and chopping tools were used in the initial butchering of the animals' remains. The bifacial tools more often occurred with the skulls of large animals, such as elephants and bovids. The hand axes may have been used to batter open the heavy skulls in order to expose the brains. The top portion of one elephant skull, for example, had been chopped away and hand axes were nearby. Many of the limb bones show evidence of battering and charring, indicating that the meat had been removed without moving the bones. But many body parts are missing; in fact, many of the "meatiest" portions of the long bones have been disarticulated and carried away. In one area of the site, several elephant long bones had been placed in a linear arrangement; Howell (1973) has suggested that these bones formed a "causeway" from the swampy kill area, thus enabling the hunters to carry some of the meat to firmer ground. This meat may have been removed to secondary butchering areas where it was further prepared for consumption.

This evidence from Torralba is a good measure of the degree of sophistication of Middle Pleistocene hunters. The recognition and use of an animal migration route, the use of fire to drive the animals, the use of the swampy areas to facilitate the kill, and the butchery practices all indicate forethought, planning, and the exchange of information on a wide variety of items. Communication, in the form of a mutually understood language, seems a vital necessity in such a pattern.

Chopper–Chopping Tool Complex

The second widespread cultural complex that existed in the Middle Pleistocene contains few or no hand axes (Figure 8-11). This culture is most common in eastern Asia, although it has also been identified in Europe and Great Britain. These tool complexes without hand axes have been identified by the following names (together with their locations):

Clactonian	(Great Britain)
Tayacian	(Continental Europe)
Buda	(Hungary)
Soan	(India)
Anyathian	(Burma)
Patjitanian	(Java)

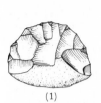   

(1) (2) (3) (4) (5)

FIGURE 8-11 Chopper–chopping tool assemblages. Tool assemblages such as these are found in Africa, Europe, and both western and eastern Asia. Tool forms similar to those illustrated here are known from Arago, France; Clacton-on-Sea, England; and Choukoutien, China. Assemblages of this type have no bifacially flaked hand axes. (1) Chopping tool; (2) pointed chopper; (3) scraper; (4) Levallois flake; (5) small point. (Scale: 0.5; drawings by Ross Sackett.)

Europe Many sites with a chopper–chopping tool complex are known from Middle Pleistocene-age deposits in continental Europe. The site at Vértesszöllös, near Budapest in Hungary, is of particular interest, since a human occipital bone and a few teeth were found there. These tools are exceptionally small; they range in size from 11 mm to 62 mm in length, with an average length of 2.5 cm. At Vértesszöllös, this industry, called the "Buda," is composed of over 3000 tools and flakes, yet not a single hand ax has been identified (Vertes, 1965a, b; Kretzoi and Vertes, 1965). The Vértesszöllös locality was apparently a living site, since a hearth has been found there. The level containing the hearth was deposited during an interstadial of the Mindel and dates to approximately 0.4 m.y. ago. As noted earlier, this evidence, along with similar findings from Terra Amata, is the earliest indication of the controlled use of fire.

The cavesite at Arago, near Tautavel in the French Pyrenees, also contains a chopper–chopping tool industry, termed the "Tayacian." H. de Lumley, who excavated the site, reports that these assemblages show a number of similarities with the Buda complex (1975). The cavesite was occupied a number of times and human remains have been found in levels dating to the early Riss Glacial, about 0.3 m.y. years ago.[5] The human skull at Arago had been left on a pile of animal bones within the cave. Since the back portion of the skull had been removed and a small flake inserted inside, the individual may have been eaten just as the horse, oxen, deer, and rhino had been (H. de Lumley, 1975).

Asia Although no occupation sites of Middle Pleistocene age are known from the island of Java, one site has yielded stone tools in association with

[5]An amino acid racemization date for Arago places its occupation between 0.22 m.y. and 0.32 m.y. ago; this is consistent with the faunal and geologic date of early Riss (Bada and Helfman, 1976).

the remains of *Homo erectus*. The Trinil beds at Sangiran have revealed a flake industry; the cranial remains of "Pithecanthropus 3" were recovered from the same site (Von Koenigswald and Ghosh, 1973a, b). The flake industry, containing numerous blades and scrapers, utilized various silicious materials, such as chalcedony, agate, and silicified wood. This material was probably obtained from a volcanic area about 50 km away (Von Koenigswald and Ghosh, 1973a).

A primary site containing a chopper–chopping tool industrial complex—and indeed the crucial Middle Pleistocene occupation site in Asia—is the cave at Choukoutien,[6] near Peking.

The cave at Choukoutien, like the caves in South Africa, was originally a lime mine, and the first fossils were found there by miners. Andersson, a geologist investigating the site in 1921, was the first to recognize the importance of the cave to studies of early humans. Noting that the small chunks of white quartz found in the cave-fill material were intrusive, he said, "Here is primitive man, now all we have to do is to find him!" (Black et al., 1933). Paleontological work began soon after Andersson's visit, and in 1923 a worn human tooth was found by Zdansky. This tooth, and a second one found subsequently, excited such interest that excavations were begun in 1927 by the Geological Survey of China and the Department of Anatomy at the Peking Union Medical College. Faculty at the Medical College, including Davidson Black and Franz Weidenreich, were later to become important figures in the analysis of "Peking Man." It was Davidson Black who, in 1927, proposed the nomen *"Sinanthropus pekinensis"* for this material. This proposal was based on a single tooth (the third one found) before any other human material had been recovered.

Work continued at Choukoutien until 1937, when war intervened; during the previous years, a large amount of faunal and human remains and artifactual material had been recovered. Work began again in 1949 and has continued, with relatively short interruptions, until the present.

During military actions in China between 1937 and 1945, all the fossil material disappeared. What happened to it is perhaps the single greatest mystery in paleoanthropology today. The Chinese believe that the Americans took the fossils (Chia, 1975); some Americans believe that either the Russians or the Japanese may have them. In fact, no one appears to know the truth. The loss of this material and that of the eight Upper Pleistocene hominids from the nearby "Upper Cave" are a serious loss to paleoanthropology. These losses are softened, however, by the fact that Weidenreich had made excellent casts of the "Peking Man" material and of three skulls from the Upper Cave before their disappearance.

More than 50 m of occupational débris exists in the Choukoutien cave,

---

[6]This site is known by a variety of names. "Locality 1" distinguishes it from the nearby sites "Localities 13 and 15." Another name, "Lower Cave," distinguishes its Middle Pleistocene levels from the "Upper Cave" deposits dating to the Upper Pleistocene.

and it has revealed a great deal of information regarding Middle Pleistocene humans in Asia (see Figure 8-9 and Table 8-4). The cave appears to have been reoccupied many times over a long span of time, perhaps as much as 200,000 years (Chia, 1975). On the basis of faunal correlations, the period of occupation may span the Late Mindel and early portions of the Second Interglacial.

The Choukoutien populations made tools from various raw materials; many types of rock, bones, and antlers were used, but no hand axes are known from these deposits.

A number of hearths that have been identified throughout the cave deposits contain accumulations of both artifactual and bone material. Bones of many food animals have been found within the ash layers. Human bones also occur within these levels; three skulls of "Peking Man" were found in the bottom part of one of the hearth areas. Many of the human skulls, and those of large mammals (particularly deer), have had their bottom and facial portions hacked away. The remaining skullcap may have served as a vessel of some sort (Weidenreich, 1943a).

The populations had a highly varied diet. Large animals, such as deer, pigs, horses, and bears, occur throughout the deposits. Small mammals are also well represented; rodents, hedgehogs, frogs, bats, and hares. Broken remains of numerous eggshells, many charred, have also been recovered (Chia, 1975). The only identifiable plant foods are the endocarps of hackberries, which may have provided an important seasonal food (Chaney, 1935). Human meat may also have been consumed; human remains are scattered throughout the deposit in much the same way as the faunal remains. Moreover, many of the human long bones show the same sort of spiral fractures as the faunal material, as if they too had been twisted and broken for the marrow; virtually all the human skulls appear to have been broken open deliberately (Weidenreich, 1943a).

At the present time, portions of about 50 individuals are known from the deposits. Many of these individuals (39.5 percent) appear to have been under 14 years old at the time of death, and only 2.6 percent seem to have survived to the age of 50 or more. Clearly, most of the Peking population died at an early age (Chia, 1975).

FIRE

To this point, most of the behavior patterns and activities of humans in the Middle Pleistocene can be traced to clear beginnings in the Early Pleistocene. Broadly based subsistence activities, including hunting and the building of temporary living structures, are just two of these patterns. However, Middle Pleistocene humans made a unique and singularly constructive cultural advancement, which might correctly be called an "invention." Beginning about 400,000 B.P., we see the first evidence of the controlled, deliberate use of fire. It may be argued that the control and preservation of fire is the single most important cultural invention in the Middle Pleistocene. It allowed humans to extend their geographic range even farther, to exploit the northern reaches of Europe and Asia during the interglacials, and to remain in the central and southern portions of those areas during glacial advances.

The social ramifications of the hearth are stunning. It provides a focus for activities; it defines both time and place for the exchange of ideas and information. Its light extends the working part of the day, so that toolmaking and hide preparation may be practiced and perhaps improved over a longer time span. And, in addition to facilitating these activities, it provides a focus for leisure during which activities not directly related to life sustenance may be carried on; it is easy to see the beginnings of art and storytelling during such leisure. In nonliterate societies, storytelling plays an extremely influential role. The repetition of events or legends provides the ideals and conventions of behavior; it defines the models of appropriate social and cultural responses. And the heroes and events of the legends bind people together and provide a source of mutual recognition. The hearth may well have been one of the important socializing factors in human evolution.

SUMMARY

Morphology: Hominid morphology in the Middle Pleistocene is, in contrast with that of the Plio-Pleistocene hominids, relatively homogeneous. All hominids of the time are placed within the single taxon *Homo erectus*.

1. Cranial capacity 775 to 1400 cc, with a mean of about 1100 cc
2. Skull vault low (platycephalic)
3. Strong muscle crests on the occiput
4. Well-developed brow ridges
5. Maximum skull breadth low in mastoid region
6. Mandible without chin
7. Thickened bones in skull, femur, and tibia; structure of other limb bones unknown

Distribution: Geographic: tropical and temperate regions of Old World. Time: 1.5 +m.y. to about 250,000 years ago

Behavior:

1. Very broad subsistence base
2. Big-game hunting

3. Erection of temporary living structures or occupation of caves
4. Two major tool industries
   a Acheulian: hand-ax industries very widespread in Africa, Europe, and western Asia; not known in eastern Asia
   b Chopper–chopping tool: without hand axes; also very widespread and extending into eastern Asia
5. Use and conservation of fire

Although human populations of the Middle Pleistocene are homogeneous relative to the enormous heterogeneity of the Plio-Pleistocene, these hominids are not without some evidence of diversity. Individuals from Java, China, east Africa (Bed II and Lake Turkana), and Europe (Mauer and Bilzingsleben) may be regarded as "typical" *Homo erectus,* showing a stable and consistent morphological pattern. Moreover, individuals in this "typical" group closely resemble individuals known in east Africa from far earlier time periods. For example, a cranium (KNM ER 3733) and a pelvis (KNM ER 3228) from Lake Turkana are very similar to skulls from Choukoutien and Bed IV, Olduvai Gorge (OH 28), although they are separated in time by more than a million years. This similarity in cranial size and shape and locomotor features indicates a very stable human gene pool at this period. Thus there is little, if any, evidence of gradual morphological change in the genus *Homo* from the Late Pliocene into the early Middle Pleistocene.

However, by approximately 0.5 m.y. ago (corresponding to the Second European Glacial), the first evidence of morphological change occurs. Some individuals, such as those at Vértesszöllös and Swanscombe, had somewhat larger cranial capacities. Others, like those at Steinheim, had smaller, less robust facial structures and skulls of more modern shape. There is, in fact, continuing controversy over whether individuals from Steinheim, Swanscombe, Vértesszöllös, and elsewhere represent *Homo erectus* or *Homo sapiens.* Their taxonomic position is not the significant question, however. The significance of these individuals, and the populations they represent no matter what they are labeled, is that we can see in them the first stirring toward the emergence of *Homo sapiens.*

SUGGESTIONS FOR FURTHER READING

Bordes, F. 1968. *The Old Stone Age,* New York: McGraw-Hill. (Contains a good, although brief, discussion of tools and tool assemblages from the Middle Pleistocene through the Upper Pleistocene.)

Butzer, K., and G. Isaac (eds.). 1975. *After the Australopithecines.* The Hague: Mouton. (A series of detailed and important papers of various aspects of the Middle Pleistocene. An important source book for this time period.)

Coon, C. 1962. *The Origin of Races*, New York: Knopf. (Although this book presents Coon's own view of racial origins, which has not found wide support, it contains excellent reviews of the fossil materials and is a good bibliographic source.)

Howell, F. C. 1960. "European and Northwest African Middle Pleistocene Hominids," *Current Anthropology*, **1**, 195–232. (An excellent review of the hominids of this time.)

Howells, W. W. 1966. *"Homo erectus,"* *Scientific American*, **215**(5), 46–53. (A good review of the group, including an overview of the history of studies of the Middle Pleistocene and later.)

Ovey, C. D., (ed.). 1964. "The Swanscombe Skull. A Survey of Research on a Pleistocene Site," in *Occasional Papers of the Royal Anthropological Institute of Great Britain and Ireland*, (London), no. 20, 1–215. (Contains a variety of papers covering topics from taxonomy to stratigraphy of this important site.)

Weidenreich, F. 1936. "The Mandibles of *Sinanthropus pekinensis*," *Paleontologica Sinica*, New Series D. no. **7**(4), 1–162.

Weidenreich, F. 1937. "The Dentition of *Sinanthropus pekinensis*," *Paleontologica Sinica*, New Series D, no. 1 (Whole Series, no. 101), 1–180.

Weidenreich, F. 1941. "The Extremity Bones of *Sinanthropus pekinensis*," *Paleontologica Sinica*, New Series D, no. 5 (Whole Series, no. 116), 1–150.

Weidenreich, F. 1943. "The Skull of *Sinanthropus pekinensis*," *Paleontologica Sinica*, New Series D, no. 10 (Whole Series, no.127), 1–485. (This series of descriptive and comparative works are classics in the field of palaeoanthropology. They constitute the most thorough analysis of any fossil hominid group ever made.)

HOMINIDS OF THE EARLY UPPER PLEISTOCENE
(250,000 to 25,000 B.P.)

INTRODUCTION

The Upper Pleistocene, covering the Eemian or Third Interglacial and the
Würm or Fourth Glacial periods, was a complex time in human development. During this period, the taxon *Homo sapiens* gradually emerged from
its Middle Pleistocene progenitors. This transitional process was slow and
uneven, and it was reflected in a number of different morphological and
behavioral manifestations. Thus, the Upper Pleistocene[1] was also a
complex period in terms of human cultural development. The Middle
Paleolithic Mousterian traditions gradually replaced the earlier Acheulian traditions, and these in turn were replaced during the middle of the
Fourth Glacial by the extremely diversified technologies of the Upper
Paleolithic.

---

[1]The terms "Pleistocene" and "Paleolithic" are sometimes confused. "Pleistocene" refers only
to the geological epoch; "Paleolithic" refers to stone tool assemblages.

TABLE 9-1   Comparative glacial chronologies in the Würm

YEARS B.P.	BORDES, 1968	BUTZER, 1971	MOVIUS, 1960	BERGGREN AND VAN COUVERING, 1974
			Main Würm, Main Phase	
15,000 —	————————			
	Würm III/IV	————————		→ Maximum: Main Würm
20,000 —	————————	Würm II		
			————————	
			Paudorf oscillation	
	Würm III		————————	
	————————	————————	Main Würm Early Phase	
			————————	
30,000 —	Würm II/III	Würm I/II	Würm I/II	
35,000 —			"Gottweig Interstadial"	
	————————			
40,000 —		————————		
	Würm II			
50,000 —				
		Würm I	Würm I	
55,000 —				
60,000 —				
70,000 —				→ Maximum: Early Würm
75,000 —	?	————————	————————	

ECOLOGICAL BACKGROUND

With the beginning of the Würm, glacial conditions returned to western Europe; the first cold period, or stadial, reached its maximum at about 70,000 years ago (Berggren and Van Couvering, 1974). However, there is little overall agreement among scholars concerning the chronology of geologic and climatic events during the last glacial, as Table 9-1 shows. Bordes (1968), for example, working with the French sequence, recognizes at least three interstadials, during which the glacial conditions became somewhat milder. Butzer (1971), however, working with the German evidence, identifies just one major interstadial and several smaller "oscillations" of improved climate. Despite such differences, all authorities identify interstadial conditions between roughly 30,000 to 40,000 years ago. This interstadial, called the "Würm I/II" in France and the "Würm II/III" in Germany, was the time of the first entrance of populations of anatomically modern type into western Europe. Figure 9-1 shows the distributions of glaciers in the early Würm.

FIGURE 9-1 European environments during the main Würm glacial. (By permission of Karl Butzer.)

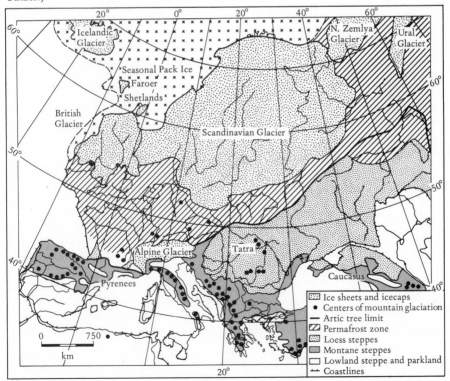

CULTURAL TRADITIONS

MIDDLE PALEOLITHIC: MOUSTERIAN

Tools

The origins of the Middle Paleolithic industries, collectively termed the "Mousterian," have roots that extend deep into the Middle Pleistocene. The earliest known Mousterian assemblages, at Ehringsdorf in East Germany, are dated to about 220,000 B.P. (Broecker et al., 1973). In Africa, early sites in Ethiopia containing Mousterian tools have been dated to 181,000 B.P. (Wendorf et al., 1975). The transition between Acheulian and Mousterian traditions was a very gradual process, however, and it was not until early in the Fourth Glacial period that the Mousterian became the dominant tool industry.

There are, in fact, few technological differences between the Acheulian and Mousterian assemblages. Hand axes, a major component of Acheulian assemblages, also occur at Mousterian sites; similarly, finely made flake tools, characteristic of the Mousterian, are found at Acheulian sites. It may be that the major distinctions between the Acheulian and Mousterian assemblages reflect the nature of the site and the diagnostic criteria of the archeologist more than any real technological or functional differences. For example, virtually all Acheulian materials have been found at open-air sites; conversely, much of the Mousterian materials have come from cavesites or rock-shelter sites. It is therefore possible that the different depositional environments of such sites may in some way determine the kinds of tools that are found within them.

However, in a very broad sense, the transition from Lower Paleolithic Acheulian assemblages to Middle Paleolithic Mousterian assemblages does appear to involve a few changes. These changes are more a matter of emphasis than of any real technological innovation. One such change was an improvement in the method of making tools, so that greater control over the final product was possible. Toward this end, the Levallois method, involving preparation of the core before the flakes were struck off, was developed. The origins of such core preparation are, however, seen within the Middle Pleistocene. A second factor, reflected in the transition from the Lower to the Middle Paleolithic, represents increasingly specialized activities by the human populations. Not only was there an increase in the number of tool types in the Middle Paleolithic, but these tools apparently served ever more precise functions. There was, moreover, a tendency toward the exploitation of fewer animal species, which were, however, used intensively. Thus, the very broad subsistence base of the Lower Paleolithic was gradually replaced by narrower, but more specialized, hunting patterns.

The Mousterian tool industry (Figure 9-2) was not a single tradition but probably represented several tool complexes, which have been defined

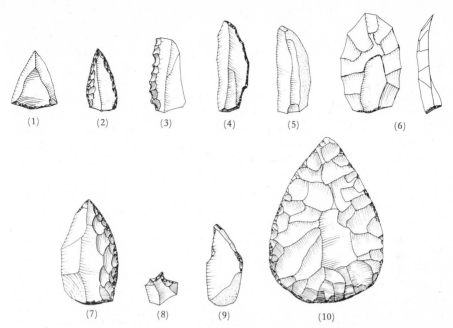

FIGURE 9-2 Tools of the Middle Paleolithic: the Mousterian. The Mousterian does not represent a single cultural tradition; rather, several types of Mousterian tool kits can be recognized. Among these are the Typical Mousterian, the Mousterian of Acheulian Tradition, the Quina-Ferrassie (or Charentian), and the Denticulate Mousterian. The tools shown here occur, in varying frequencies, in these traditions. Mousterian tools are most frequently, but not invariably, associated with hominids of the Neandertal type. At Qafzeh, in Israel, Mousterian tools are associated with hominids of a nearly modern morphology. (1) Levallois point; (2) Mousterian knife; (3) denticulate piece; (4) backed knife; (5) naturally backed knife; (6) Levallois flake; (7) side scraper; (8) borer; (9) burin; (10) cordiform biface. (Scale 0.5; drawings by Ross Sackett.)

and discussed by Bordes (1968). The Mousterian of Acheulian tradition, for example, appears to have been derived directly from Acheulian complexes. In some cases, typical bifacial hand axes transcend the Acheulian-Mousterian boundary and continue almost unchanged within the context of new tool assemblages. This is particularly clear in some of the east African assemblages, such as the Sangoan found near Lake Victoria. Other Mousterian assemblages have very few or no hand axes and appear to have been derived from chopping–chopper tool Clactonian backgrounds. The assemblages of the Quina-Ferrassie type, found mainly in the Charente area of France, are very similar in many respects to those of the Middle Pleistocene Clactonian site at High Lodge, England. Scrapers are very common in Quina-Ferrassie tool kits, forming up to 80 percent of some assemblages. Most of the sites associated with the classical Neandertals of the early Fourth Glacial, such as the Le Moustier site, contain this tool industry. Other Mousterian assemblages are termed "Typical"; fewer scrapers are found in these groups, and bifaces are very rare. Points, however, were well developed. The last of the important Mousterian assemblages is termed the "Denticulate"; they contain no hand axes and few scrapers or points, but denticulated or notched tools are common.

Therefore, with the exception of the Mousterian of Acheulian tradition, most Mousterian assemblages contain mostly small flake tools. There is a great variety of tool types in Mousterian assemblages; Bordes has recognized the existence of at least 60 different Mousterian tool categories (1968). Many of these tools are scrapers of one sort or another which seem to dominate many Mousterian assemblages.

Beyond the diversity of tool types, the Mousterian assemblages are also characterized by the previously mentioned method of tool manufacture called the "Levallois technique." The Levallois method involved careful preparation of the core so that the flake tool, when it was finally detached, had a predetermined form. Such careful preparation of the core meant that a high degree of control over size and shape of the resultant tool was possible. The Levallois technique represents a considerable advance in the level of sophistication over the previous methods of tool manufacture. As described in previous chapters, Oldowan tools were made by the detachment of a few small flakes from a core of convenient size and shape. Little alteration of the original stone took place. In the Acheulian method, more control was exercised in that the flake which formed the tool was often deliberately detached. But no preparation of the core took place; the flake was detached and then shaped and formed into the desired size and shape. In the Levallois method, however, the core was shaped before the flake was detached. Therefore, the size and shape of the final tool existed, not visibly in the raw material itself, but in the mind of the stone knapper. This would imply a level of intellectual perception, comprehension, and control that had not been demonstrated before.

The diversity in the Mousterian tool kits has been explained in several ways. Some archeologists, for example, have placed these kits within an evolutionary sequence. Thus, in this explanation, the Mousterian of Acheulian tradition would have been followed in a sequential fashion by the other Mousterian assemblages (see Mellars, 1970). However, Bordes (1972) has been able to document that at Combe Grenal, for example, no simple chronologic sequence occurred; the various assemblages are interspersed and alternate within the cave deposits. On the other hand, Bordes himself (1968) has argued that human groups with differing cultural backgrounds were responsible for the various assemblages. Still others (Binford and Binford, 1966, 1969; Freeman, 1966) have adopted a functional explanation, arguing that the different assemblages reflect differing exploitative and extractive processes.

In the end, we do not understand why these different assemblages existed. In many cases, however, a purely functional explanation is hard to accept; very similar tool kits seem to have existed under different sets of environmental conditions and, conversely, different tool kits seem to have existed under apparently very similar conditions.

Subsistence Patterns

The cultural diversity of the Middle Paleolithic assemblages is much greater than we saw in any of the Lower Paleolithic sites. At that time, humans were apparently exploiting a great variety of food sources, and many of the tool kits have an "all-purpose" aspect to them. The diversity of the Mousterian tool kits may represent specialization in subsistence patterns. Perhaps humans were focusing their major hunting and gathering activities on a smaller and more limited range of resources. In fact, we see evidence that in some areas, human subsistence was becoming so finely tuned that some groups were able to remain in the same area for prolonged periods. In southern France, for example, there is limited evidence that some Mousterian sites may have been occupied during the entire year (Bouchud, 1954). This trend continued into the Upper Paleolithic, where it became even more pronounced.

While some Mousterian populations may have had a relatively nonnomadic life, others appear to have followed or intercepted the large herds of tundra grazers on their yearly rounds. These herds, consisting mainly of bison, mammoths, reindeer, and horses, moved into the more southerly woodland areas in the winter and then, in the summer, moved north onto the vast tundras. A site at Salzgitter-Lebenstedt, in northern Germany, represents one such hunting camp. This site was occupied briefly but repeatedly about 48,000 years ago by a group of some 40 to 50 individuals (Tode et al., 1953; see also Butzer, 1971). At Salzgitter-Lebenstedt, 72 percent of the total faunal remains were reindeer, 14 percent were woolly mammoth, and about 5 percent each were bison and horses. Thus, the primary subsistence base was reindeer, although other large mammals were taken when available. Of great interest, however, is the presence of several types of birds and fish (which make up the remainder of the animal bones) in the kitchen débris at Salzgitter-Lebenstedt. Highly developed skills are necessary to catch birds like swans and duck or such fish as pike and perch. The tool kit, which is Mousterian of Acheulian tradition, reflects this diversified food-getting skill. There are worked reindeer antlers that may have served as clubs and bone points with barbs that may have been used as either spear points or harpoons.

Burials

Associated with Mousterian assemblages in the Early Würm, we see the first evidence of a remarkable human behavior pattern. At this time, humans began to bury their dead, doing so with a degree of care and consideration that indicates that they had made another of the quantum jumps that separate humans from their primate relatives.

The earliest known burials are of individuals of the classic Neandertal group in France. There is some evidence that the practice of ritual treatment of the dead may have begun as early as Würm I. In the cave of Regourdou, in the Dordogne area of France, an adult was buried with the bones of bear and deer under a small pile of ash and stones (Bonifay and Vandermeersch, 1962; Bonifay, 1964). The burial of an adult occurred during the first interstadial (Würm I-II) of the Würm at the cave of Arcy-sur-Cure in the Yonne area of France (Leroi-Gourhan, 1950).

More abundant evidence of human burial practices, however, occurs in the second stadial of the Würm, Würm II. Human burials at La Chapelle-aux-Saints, La Ferrassie, and Le Moustier have all been dated to this time. The burial at Le Moustier is typical of this period. Here a young man, about 15 years old, was laid on his side with his head resting on his forearm; the legs were drawn up slightly. Under his head were a few finely made stone tools, and a few joints of meat were nearby (Vallois, 1939). A very similar pattern was found far to the east in Uzbekistan, near Afghanistan; the cavesite is called Teshik-Tash. Here a young boy, also of the Neandertal group, was found in a shallow grave which had been marked with the horns of ibex; Mousterian tools were also found in this grave (Movius, 1953). At La Ferrassie, in France, a group burial, possibly representing a family, was found. In one area of the La Ferrassie rock shelter, nine small mounds were arranged in three rows of three; in one of these rows were the bones of a very small, perhaps stillborn, infant. The other mounds were empty, but perhaps at one time they had contained grave offerings. Near the nine small mounds were the graves of two adults, a male and a female who had been buried head to head. At the feet of the male were the graves of two more children; one about 3 years old and one about 10 years old (Piveteau, 1957; Heim, 1968).

One of the most remarkable series of human burials has been found in the Mousterian levels at Shanidar cave in northern Iraq (Solecki, 1957, 1960, 1961, 1971; Stewart, 1959, 1961, 1963, 1977) (Figure 9-3). The remains of eight individuals have been found in these levels, at least four of which represent deliberate burials. Shanidar 4, 6, 7, and 8 were found virtually superimposed in the central living area of the cave; Shanidar 6 and 7 were females and Shanidar 8 was an infant. Shanidar 4 was a male, about 45 years of age, who had been buried on his left side in a shallow, scooped-out area of the cave floor. When this man was placed in his grave, wildflowers, like the ones still growing on the nearby Iraqi mountains, were evidently placed with him. Pollen analysis of the soil surrounding the burial showed that at least eight species of flowers were present; these included hyacinths, daisies, hollyhocks, and bachelor's buttons, all of which bloom in the late spring or early summer (Solecki and Leroi-

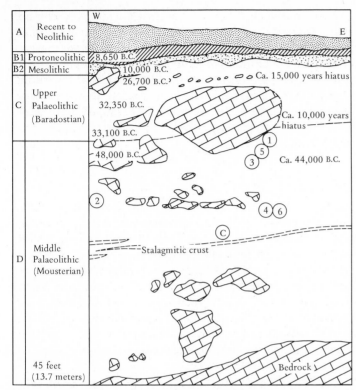

		W		
A	Recent to Neolithic			E
B1	Protoneolithic	8,650 B.C.		
B2	Mesolithic	10,000 B.C.		Ca. 15,000 years hiatus
		26,700 B.C.?		
C	Upper Palaeolithic (Baradostian)	32,350 B.C.		Ca. 10,000 years hiatus
		33,100 B.C.		
		48,000 B.C.	① ⑤ ③	Ca. 44,000 B.C.
			② ④⑥	
D	Middle Palaeolithic (Mousterian)	© Stalagmitic crust		
	45 feet (13.7 meters)			Bedrock

FIGURE 9-3 Section of cave deposits at Shanidar. The numbers in circles represent the adult burials; the circled "C" indicates the position of the infant skeleton Shanidar 7. (By permission of the British Museum.)

Gourhan, 1961; Leroi-Gourhan, 1968). It is an attractive thought to interpret these flowers as a burial offering, a custom that parallels some of our own burial practices. However, it is perhaps significant that at least six of the flower species in the Shanidar 4 burial have medicinal purposes that are recognized by people living in the area today (Solecki, 1971). Whatever interpretation we give these flowers, it is probable that we are witnessing a level of consciousness and thought process not unlike our own.

Shanidar 1, while not a deliberate burial, represents a very interesting individual. The right arm of this male, including the upper part of the humerus, scapula, and clavicle, have a withered appearance, indicating that the arm was apparently paralyzed, perhaps from birth. Stewart (1959) reported that the humerus had been cut off just above the elbow, during life; the healing at the severed end of the bone indicates that the individual survived the "surgery." If this was in fact surgery to remove a useless arm, it is the earliest evidence of surgical intervention of any sort. As probable compensation for his useless right arm, this individual must have used his front teeth a great deal; they are very worn. This man was not intentionally buried but was killed in a rockfall that apparently also killed Shanidar 5. They were not completely covered by the large rocks that fell from the ceiling, and the remainder of their bodies was covered with smaller stones. The remains of a small hearth containing burned animal bones was found near the bodies, and Solecki interprets these bones as indicators of a funeral meal (1960, 1971). Shanidar 3 was killed and buried by another rockfall; at the time of his death, he was recovering from a spear wound in his ribs (Stewart, 1977).

Ritual

Evidence of rituals other than those of burial is also present in the Early Würm in association with Mousterian tool assemblages. At Monte Circeo in Italy, for example, a human skull was found on the floor of a cave deep within a hillside. The skull, which is missing the mandible, had been severely damaged; the right temporal had been broken away and the foramen magnum was apparently broken outward. The skull was found within a circle of stones with its base up; no bones of the postcranium were found (Blanc, 1961). Evidently, this skull had been used in some sort of ritualized activity. At several sites, such as Regourdou in France and Drachenloch in Austria, numerous remains of cave bear (*Ursus spelaeus*) are further indication of ritualized activity.

Another aspect of such ritual behavior is a sense of symbolism, and there is accumulating evidence that Mousterians possessed a system of abstract thought. Bordes (1972) has found in the Mousterian levels at Pech de l'Aze numerous rectangles or triangles of manganese dioxide which he termed "pencils." Manganese dioxide leaves a black smear when rubbed, and many of the "pencils" show smoothing or rounding at one end. A small, flat slab of limestone may have served as a "palette." Numerous pieces of bone marked with zigzags or other patterns are also known from Mousterian sites (Marshack, 1972a, b, 1975), indicating the use of some sort of notational or indicative system.

Items of personal adornment are also known from Mousterian sites. At La Quina in France (H. Martin, 1910) and at Bacho Kiro in Bulgaria (see Marshack, 1975), large carnivore canine teeth were found with one end bored through to form a pendant. It is interesting, however, that no such items of adornment are known from Mousterian graves; the first such material does not appear as grave goods until the Upper Paleolithic.

UPPER PALEOLITHIC

By 40,000 years ago or perhaps even earlier, important changes in both human morphology and human culture had appeared. The cumulative effect of these changes was the emergence of anatomically modern humans and even more complex and diversified patterns of human behavior.

The cultural transition from Middle to Upper Paleolithic seems to have occurred, within the broad context of the Middle Würm, in a number of areas. The transition in western Europe is particularly well documented, but other areas also experienced, apparently independently, similar cultural changes.

While the transition from Middle to Upper Paleolithic is usually defined on the basis of the composition and technology of tool kits, it is really human behavior, in the broadest sense, and human morphology that were undergoing change. This transition can be examined from various viewpoints.

Tools

First, in terms of cultural changes, there was an important regionality in Upper Paleolithic industries. This trend toward localized development of certain cultural patterns is first seen in the Mousterian, where it contrasts with the broad cultural unity that is characteristic of the Lower Paleolithic. Within the Upper Paleolithic, then, we see a strong tendency for localized, regional cultural patterning. This is probably a reflection of hunting and gathering patterns which emphasized intense and efficient exploitation of local resources rather than a strictly migratory existence. Early indications of such patterns are seen in some of the Mousterian sites.

A further cultural characteristic of the Upper Paleolithic was an improved method of tool manufacture centering on the production of blades.[2] Blades are the dominant element in many Upper Paleolithic tool assemblages; they were struck from a prepared core in a way that resulted in the quick and efficient production of relatively large quantities of tools.

While the exact sequence of cultural tradition from the Middle Paleolithic through the Upper Paleolithic in western Europe is not typical of what happened elsewhere, it is indicative of the broad trends of cultural development at this time. The work of François Bordes (1968, 1972) has been especially important in documenting this time period in France. Bordes has indicated, for example, that in France the first of the Upper Paleolithic traditions, the Perigordian (Figure 9-4), evolved directly from the Mousterian of Acheulian tradition. The date of this transition in France may have been about 35,000 years ago;[3] the last Mousterian level at La Qunia is dated to 35,250 B.P. (Henri-Martin, 1964).

The Aurignacian (Figure 9-4) first appeared in France about 32,000

[2]A blade is a stone tool with parallel sides.

[3]Level VIII, Arcy-sur-Cure, with a Lower Perigordian carbon-14 date of 33,860±250 B.P. (Vogel and Waterbolk, 1963).

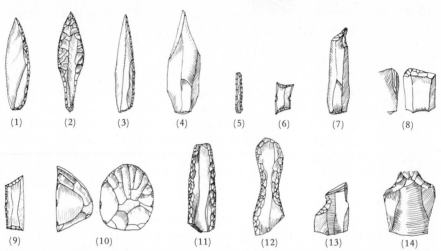

| (1) | (2) | (3) | (4) | (5) | (6) | (7) | (8) |

| (9) | (10) | (11) | (12) | (13) | (14) |

FIGURE 9-4 Tools of the Early Upper Paleolithic: the Perigordian and Aurignacian. Most of the tool forms which occur in the Early Upper Paleolithic also occurred in earlier assemblages; it was the relative importance of certain tools which changed. For example, blade tools with long, parallel sides are known from Mousterian assemblages; but they become numerically much more important in the Upper Paleolithic. Scrapers and burins also occur in relatively greater numbers in Upper Paleolithic assemblages. *Perigordian tools:* (1) Chatelperron knife; (2) Font-Robert point; (3) Gravette point; (4) dihedral burin; (5) Noailles burin; (6) backed bladelet; (7) borer; (8) Raysse burin; (9) truncated piece. *Aurignacian tools:* (10) carniate scraper; (11) retouched blade; (12) strangled blade; (13) busked burin; (14) nosed scraper. (Scale: 0.5; drawings by Ross Sackett.)

years ago; the Aurignacians did not replace the Perigordians but, in some cases, may have coexisted with them at least until Würm III, around 16,000 or 17,000 years ago. The Aurignacians seem to have been an intrusive group into western Europe and may have developed in the Near East; their appearance in western Europe is closely correlated in time with the first appearance there of anatomically modern *Homo sapiens*. Thus, sites such as Les Eyzies, where "Cro-Magnon Man" was discovered in 1868, contain Aurignacian material.

The Solutrean tradition was a very localized and very short-lived European industry, dating to between 19,000 and 17,000 years ago (Philip Smith, 1964). The Solutrean assemblages contain exquisite examples of the art of flint knapping. The characteristic laurel-leaf and willow-leaf points are often beautifully retouched; some were made too delicately to have served any subsistence function and may have been symbolic objects.

The final Upper Paleolithic tradition in western Europe was the Magdalenian, first appearing around 17,000 years ago. The Magdalenians seem to have been relatively poor stone knappers but worked extensively in bone. Very beautifully and carefully worked bone harpoons and barbs date to this time. Such artifacts testify to the Magdalenian exploitation of aquatic resources, particularly salmon and other fish of the salmon type.

Subsistence Patterns

Beyond tool technology and tool traditions, there are other characteristics of the Upper Paleolithic as compared with the Middle Paleolithic. One important feature of the Upper Paleolithic is an apparent increase in population size. Evidence of large settlement size first appears in Perigordian sites of the Bergerac region in France (Bordes, 1968). In many areas, Upper Paleolithic sites directly overlie earlier ones without interruption. However, while the Mousterian deposits may be confined to a cave or rock shelter and the area immediately around it, the Upper Paleolithic sites cover those same areas and then extend much beyond.

There are also important changes in the hunting patterns of the Upper Paleolithic. Mousterian and Acheulian groups usually killed only small numbers of animals; even at Torralba and Salzgitter-Lebenstedt, sites of many successive large mammal kills, never more than a few animals were killed at one time. The total number of large mammals at Salzgitter-Lebenstedt, for example, was about 110. In contrast, a site near Solutré, in France, has yielded the remains of over 10,000 horses which had been driven, at various times, over a cliff (Howell, 1973). At Predmost, in Czechoslovakia, the remains of about 600 woolly mammoths have been found (Butzer, 1971). It is apparent that although the source of food remained the same, the pattern of exploitation had changed.

There is also evidence that some groups were becoming very specialized in their subsistence patterns. In northwestern Europe some groups appear to have become almost entirely dependent on reindeer; these animals supplied the human populations with meat, with skins for clothing, and with bone and antler for tools (Butzer, 1971). A similar pattern, centering on the mammoth, seems to have developed in eastern Europe. At Predmost, for example, the scapulae and limb bones of the mammoths served as building materials for human dwellings.

Art

Art became an even more important vehicle for human expression in the Upper Paleolithic. It too had its roots in earlier times, but in the Upper Paleolithic it achieved a period of flowering and remarkable development. During this time, virtually every form of artistic expression appeared: wall or cave painting, object painting, and sculpture and carving, both in the round and in relief, appeared for the first time.

Cave painting is perhaps the most remarkable and visible of human artistic accomplishments at this time. It first appeared in Aurignacian sites about 28,000 years ago, and at present about 70 painted cave sites are known (Bordes, 1968). Some cave paintings are placed very deep in caves in almost inaccessible spots; some can be seen only from very awkward positions or angles. Some are superimposed, with many images crowded into a small area. The obvious conclusion is that the cave paintings were not intended for esthetic appreciation or for frequent viewing. Since many of the subjects were food animals or men dressed as food animals, perhaps they were made in an effort to control the food supply. They may, then, represent a form of sympathetic magic (see Ucko and Rosenfeld, 1967).

The sculpture and carving of the Upper Paleolithic are no less extraordinary; but here the purpose may have been different. Many of the carved figures are of human females; there is usually great exaggeration of the female sexual characteristics: large, pendulous breasts and large buttocks. Often the face and limbs are indicated in an almost offhand manner. Some such figurines were carved from bone or ivory; others, such as those from Dolni Vestonice, Czechoslovakia, were made of baked clay.

A large number of incised or engraved pieces of bone or ivory are known from Upper Paleolithic sites in western Europe. Some pieces show easily recognizable images, such as food animals, fish, or even flowers. Others bear only lines, dots, or angles in either a recurrent or a random pattern. Marshack (1972a, b), after studying some of these pieces with the aid of a microscope, concluded that Upper Paleolithic humans had a system of notation. In this system they could record the passage of events, such as days, seasons, or the lunar cycle. Some of the pieces show signs of having been incised over a period of time with different instruments. Others show smoothing and rounding from having been carried or handled many times.

HUMAN EVOLUTION IN THE EARLY UPPER PLEISTOCENE

The emergence of *Homo sapiens* from *Homo erectus* populations of the Middle Pleistocene (Table 9-2) did not begin with a sharp morphological or behavioral alteration. In fact, there appear to be no quantum differences between *Homo erectus* and early *Homo sapiens* populations; all differences seem to be quantitative shifts rather than qualitative jumps.

Yet, by the beginning of the Third Interglacial, the morphological stasis characteristic of the earlier Middle Pleistocene *Homo erectus* populations was disappearing. Within the Third Interglacial a number of different patterns of *erectus-sapiens* features are found. This patterning appears to have depended on the nature and frequency of genetic exchanges with other groups and local selective pressures. In some groups, the conservative, more primitive *erectus* features predominate; these groups are usually referred to as Neandertals.[4] In others, the *erectus* features are much

---

[4]"Neandertal" was originally spelled "Neanderthal," but since the German orthography was revised in 1913, the "h" following the "t" has been omitted.

TABLE 9-2 Hominids of the early Upper Pleistocene

YEARS B.P.	AFRICA	EUROPE AND WESTERN ASIA	ASIA
			Kow Swamp
20,000			Upper Cave, Choukoutien ?Solo Lake Mungo
30,000		Predmost Abri Pataud Chancelade Cro-Magnon	
40,000	Fish Hoek Eyasi Florisbad Huau Fteah	Qafzeh XVII Skhul Amud Tabun, B Tabun, C	
	Saldanha Irhoud	Le Moustier, La Quina Neandertal Spy La Chapelle-aux-Saints Shanidar, Gibraltar-Forbes Quarry	Niah Teshik-Tash
50,000 70,000 80,000		Tabun, E	
100,000	Rhodesian	Fontechevade Taubach Krapina Ganovece	?Mapa
150,000	Omo		
200,000	Casablanca Temara	Saccopastore Ehringsdorf	

? = date uncertain.

diminished or changed. The earliest members of this group are termed "archaic" *Homo sapiens*, followed some 30,000 to 40,000 years ago, by the appearance of "anatomically modern" *Homo sapiens*.

The transition from *erectus* to *sapiens* did not proceed in the same way or at the same speed in all areas of the human domain. In southwest Asia and parts of eastern Europe, for example, it may have progressed relatively rapidly. But in more peripheral areas of human occupation, such as parts of Africa and the islands of southeast Asia, the transition may have been much slower. It is, in fact, possible that in such areas, Middle and early Upper Pleistocene local populations may have become extinct without contributing to the modern sapient gene pool.

For some populations, a variety of factors may have acted together to slow down the rate of change. Although genetic exchange was probably possible among all contemporaneous populations, it is likely that some populations exchanged genes more frequently than did others. This could have been caused by the mutual recognition of a relationship, a similar language, or geographic proximity. Conversely, some groups may not have exchanged genes because of superficial physical differences (possibly skin color), inability to understand the other's language, or geographic distance. Moreover, the total human population was probably quite small; members of many groups may have spent their entire lives without ever seeing an individual from another group. The first encounter with an unfamiliar individual was probably a rare and significant event in the history of many human groups.

One result of these latter factors was that some populations may have existed more-or-less in isolation for long periods of time. Thus, changes, both genetic and cultural, that were occurring in other groups were not passed on to these isolated populations. Such a pattern may well have occurred in southeast Asia, where the Solo population on Java and the later Kow Swamp population in Australia retained some *Homo erectus* features (Thorne and Macumber, 1972) long after anatomically modern humans had appeared in other areas. Individuals from Broken Hill ("Rhodesian Man") in Zambia and Saldanha in South Africa may also reflect the effects of such isolation.

The problems of the classification of fossil groups and the paradoxes of the Linnaean system in paleotaxonomy were explored in Chapter 1. Nowhere are these problems and paradoxes more apparent and more difficult to resolve than in the classification of the human populations of the early Upper Pleistocene.

As we will see, the Neandertals differed from both archaic and modern *Homo sapiens* in features of the pelvis, the scapula, the hand (particularly the thumb), bone thickness, facial structure, and other characters. On this basis it can be argued that the archaic and modern *Homo sapiens* together show independently acquired or synapomorphic features in these structures. This would therefore indicate genetic separation and speciation. This line of evidence and logic would lead to the placement of the Neandertals in a separate species, *Homo neandertalensis* (Le Gros Clark, 1964).

However, there is some evidence that the Neandertals did exchange genes with clearly sapient populations. The site at Predmost, Czechoslovakia, dated to 26,000 years ago (Oakley, Campbell, and Molleson, 1971), for example, appears to contain hominids with a combination of Neandertal and archaic *Homo sapiens* features. Other sites appear to contain further evidence of genetic exchange.

The evidence for genetic exchange would therefore appear to fulfill the criteria for containing the Neandertals and *Homo sapiens* (both archaic and fully modern) in a single biospecies, separate at the subspecies or racial level. Thus, some workers have proposed two racially distinct taxa to contain these populations: *Homo sapiens neandertalensis* and *Homo sapiens sapiens* (Campbell, 1962). Although this approach will be followed here, and is indeed widely accepted in paleoanthropology today, the problem is not resolved with any degree of confidence.

HOMO SAPIENS NEANDERTALENSIS

History

The Neandertals (Table 9-3) occupy an important place in the study of human evolution. They are of historical importance, since an individual of this type was the first fossil hominid to be discovered. Therefore, they have figured prominently in the development of many theories on human evolution. Their geographic distribution was Europe, Africa, and western Asia; their temporal distribution, the Third Interglacial and Fourth Glacial.

The first individual of the Neandertal group to be discovered was the child from Engis, Belgium, found in association with Mousterian tools in 1829. In 1843, a Neandertal skull was uncovered at Forbes Quarry on Gibraltar. Both these finds were ignored, however, since no clear understanding of human evolution existed in the first half of the nineteenth century. In fact, the very existence of evolutionary change of any sort was very poorly conceived at that time. By 1856, however, when the bones of "Neandertal Man" were recovered from a cave in the Neander Valley near Düsseldorf, the stage was set for the interpretation of this individual as an early type of human. The bones of "Neandertal Man" were initially brought to a local schoolteacher, Fuhlrott, who recognized their importance. He took them to Schaafhausen, who had already presented his own theory of evolution in his book *The Stability and Transformation of Species* (see Wendt, 1956). Schaafhausen also recognized the importance of the fossilized bones and proposed the name "Homo primigenius"; he decided to display them at a congress of scientists meeting at Kassel in 1857. Fuhlrott and Schaafhausen presented their findings and concluded that "Homo primigenius" represented an early form of human. Harsh criticism and controversy began immediately. Some suggested that the bones were those of a Cossack who had been on the Rhine in 1814, while others

TABLE 9-3 Distribution of the Neandertals

	EUROPE				WESTERN ASIA			AFRICA
	FRANCE	GERMANY	ITALY	OTHERS	SOVIET UNION	ISRAEL	OTHERS	
15				*SPAIN* Bañolas (17,600) Piñar (D?)				
20						Amud (D?) B		*ETHIOPIA* Dire' Dawa (D?)
			Monte Circeo					
25						Galilee (D?)		

Left time axis labels:

WÜRM GLACIAL

WÜRM MAIN PHASE "WÜRM III"

WÜRM MAIN EARLY PHASE "WÜRM II"

PAUDORF OSCILLATION "II/III" INTERSTADIAL

	WÜRM I/II INTERSTADIAL "CLASSIC NEANDERTALS"	EARLY WÜRM / WÜRM I	RISS/WÜRM INTERGLACIAL / EEMIAN "EARLY NEANDERTALS"

Time scale (×1000 years): 30 — 40 — 50 — 60 — 70

La Quina
Le Moustier (B)
La Chapelle aux Saints
La Ferrasie (B)
Chateauneuf
Hortus (C?)
Pech de L'Aze
Roc de Marsal (B)

Salzgitter–Lebenstedt

Regourdou (B)
Monsempron
Neandertal

Fontechevade (C?)   Taubach

Ehringsdorf

GIBRALTER
Forbes Quarry
Devil's Tower

SWITZERLAND
St. Brais 40,000

BELGIUM
Spy
La Naulette

HUNGARY
Subalyuk

JERSY–CHANNEL
ISLANDS
St. Brelade 47,000

CZECHOSLOVAKIA
Sipka
Kulna
Ochoz
Sala (D?)

CZECHOSLOVAKIA
Ganovece

YUGOSLAVIA
Krapina

Saccopastorc
Quinzano

Dzhruchula (D?)
Teshik–Tash (B)
Starosel'e
Kiik Koba (B)

Tabun (B)
Layer C: 40,900
Shanidar Layer D
= 46,900

LEBANON
Ksar ' Akil (B)
>43,750
IRAQ

MOROCCO
'Aliya 30,000

LIBYA
Haua Fteah
47,000
MOROCCO
Irhoud (D?)
Tangier (D?)

Key: B = burial; C = cannibalized; CR = cremation; D? = date questionable.
Source: For references, see Oakley et al., 1971 and 1975.

Pathology

suggested that, instead, the bones were of an old Dutchman, a Celtic, or a hermit. Rudolf Virchow, a professor of anatomy of great prestige, also took a position against an evolutionary interpretation and proposed a pathological interpretation of the Neandertal bones. He suggested that the individual had suffered from rickets which, in later life, had been complicated by arthritis; he stated that the man had probably also been a moron.[5]

The pathological explanation of the distinctive Neandertal morphology gained widespread interest. Recently, both rickets (Ivanhoe, 1970) and syphilis (Wright, 1971) have been revived as explanations. In 1859, however, "Darwin's theory struck like a flash of lightning into the conflict" (Wendt, 1956, p. 222); and, although such explanations continued, the evolutionists have held the field since that time.

Some more recent anthropologists have attempted to place the various "Neandertal" populations within a cohesive and explanatory framework of human evolution; of the assorted explanations, the model proposed by Clark Howell has gained the widest acceptance. Howell's approach (1957) divides the very widespread and diverse populations of the Third Interglacial and early Fourth Glacial into three groups, each with a separate geographic, temporal, and evolutionary position. He first defined an "Early Neandertal" group which, in the Third Interglacial, demonstrated an overall morphology less exaggerated than that of the later Würm Neandertals. The "classic" Neandertals, which demonstrate the most pronounced and exaggerated morphological features, were, according to Howell, very restricted in both time and space. They were found in southwestern Europe early in the last glacial episode and had completely disappeared by the middle of the Würm. Howell concluded that such geographic and temporal restrictions would have been related to the development of the extreme classic morphology. Such factors as restriction of gene flow owing to isolation by the glaciers in the southern European mountains, the possibility of genetic drift working on small, isolated populations, and the increased selective pressures from the very cold, damp environment could have all operated in the production of a localized and distinctive morphology. A number of anthropologists have, in fact, emphasized the possibility that the classic morphological pattern may represent adaptations to the cold glacial climate (see Coon, 1962, 1964; Wolpoff, 1968a; Patté, 1955; Vallois, 1958). The third group, the "generalized" or "progressive" Neandertals, coexisted in time with the classic group but was found outside the areas of harsh glacial climate, predominantly in southwest Asia and North Africa.

Howell's original model may need some alteration, although his basic approach to the organization of hominids within this time span works well. For example, the term "Neandertal" should probably not be applied

[5]Wendt (1956) contains an excellent discussion of this controversy.

to all these populations. While it should be retained for the early group and for the historically important and morphologically distinctive classic group, the generalized group should probably be referred to as "archaic" *Homo sapiens*.

An important aspect of Howell's model, however, is that it is predicated on a split or division in the hominid stock at some time in the Middle Pleistocene. It appears that such a division did occur. The European classic Neandertals and the more generalized Asian and Near Eastern archaic *Homo sapiens* were contemporaneous in the Middle Würm (about 40,000 years ago) and perhaps even earlier. The hominids from Skhul and Qafzeh in Israel, for example, demonstrate a complex of characters which may best be described as "archaic modern" and are clearly not of the classic mode; yet they were contemporaneous with the European Neandertals.

However, Howell's evolutionary explanation of the split, resting on highly specialized cold adaptations in the classic group, is not entirely supported in the fossil record. For example, individuals from Gánovece, Czechoslovakia, Saccopastore, Italy and Fontechevade, France (see below), demonstrate much of the classic Neandertal pattern in the Third Interglacial during mild climatic conditions. While these individuals do exhibit slight variations from the later fully classic pattern, a significant portion of the morphological complex is present.

Why, then, do the classic Neandertals suddenly appear in relatively large numbers in the early Fourth Glacial? It is possible that what is being documented in the human fossil record at this time is not the presence of a new human group but, instead, a new pattern of human behavior. That new pattern is the deliberate burial of the dead which has resulted in the preservation of more individuals.

This idea would suggest that much of the distinctive classic Neandertal morphological pattern had been present before the early Würm, when the burials first appeared in considerable numbers. The suggestion here is that there is a direct correlation between the appearance of this group and the development of a pattern of deliberate burial. These events do coincide in the early Würm. It is possible, however, that genetic drift, reduced migration, and natural selection may have contributed to the population structure of the early Würm groups in western Europe. Such factors may have been especially contributory to the high degree of relative homogeneity in these populations. However, the origins of the morphologic pattern can probably be traced to progressive evolutionary changes within *Homo erectus* populations of the Middle Pleistocene; hints of this pattern were present in individuals from Arago, France, and Steinheim, Germany. The apparent florescence of this morphological pattern in the early Würm may therefore reflect the fact that these populations were being preserved in larger numbers than before.

Relationship of the Neandertals to Modern Humans

Since the classic Neandertals were the first human fossils to be discovered, it is perhaps inevitable that a proliferation of theories should surround their relationship with modern populations. These theories, which can be grouped into two categories, reflect rather different ways of viewing the total process of human evolution.

One approach involves the existence of a group of contemporaneous hominid lineages; there are a number of permutations of the polyphyletic or cladogenetic model of human evolution. Boule (1908, 1911–1913) and Keith (1925, 1931) were especially active in the initial development of the polyphyletic model. In his writings on classic Neandertals, for example, Boule stressed their "ape-like" and "brutal" appearance and concluded that they could not have given rise to modern humans. Moreover, at the time when both Boule and Keith were writing, the more modern-appearing contemporaries of the classic Neandertals, such as those from Skhul and Qafzeh, were not known. Therefore, they had to look elsewhere for the progenitors of modern humans. There were, in fact, many candidates for such a position in the early decades of this century. The "Piltdown Man," not shown to be fraudulent until 1953 (Weiner et al., 1953, 1955), was a prime candidate with its fully modern skull and ape jaw. "Galley Hill," a modern skeleton found in Early Pleistocene deposits in London, was also a strong contender. The Galley Hill skeleton was later shown to have been an intrusive burial into the early levels. Swanscombe and Fontechevade were also considered to be part of the pre-sapiens line.

The loss of "Piltdown" and "Galley Hill" was a serious blow to the pre-*sapiens* theory, as was the demonstration that Swanscombe closely resembled earlier Middle Pleistocene individuals (Breitinger, 1952; Wolpoff, 1971c; Stewart, 1960b, 1964). Louis Leakey, however, was not dismayed by the losses of the European pre-*sapiens* line but, instead, sought his own candidates in east Africa. In 1935 he suggested that remains from Kanam and Kanjera in Kenya might in fact be early members of that line. The exact age and taxonomic position of these fossils have continued to be surrounded with controversy, and in 1964 Leakey proposed *"Homo habilis"* as a still earlier member of the line leading to the modern human (L. S. B. Leakey, Tobias, and Napier, 1964). Moreover, he has removed both *Homo erectus* and the classic Neandertals from that line and placed them on a separate, and finally extinct, side branch (L. S. B. Leakey, 1973).

Weidenreich (1943b) and, later, Coon (1962) developed their polyphyletic theories somewhat differently. Both saw multiple, contemporaneous lineages of hominids all slowly and independently evolving toward *Homo sapiens*. Coon, in the *Origin of Races* (1962), which he dedicated to Weidenreich, has developed an especially comprehensive view of human evolution. He sees the existing races of *Homo sapiens* as having great time depth extending at least back into the Middle Pleistocene. He does not deny that human populations have migrated and that gene exchange has taken place, but he emphasizes the power of local selective pressures in consistently producing the same adaptive pattern. He has suggested, for example, that African *Homo erectus* Negroid populations of the Middle Pleistocene have evolved into living *Homo sapiens* Negroid populations. Similarly, there were Asian *Homo erectus* populations having strong morphologic affinities with living mongoloid populations in the same area. In other words, in Coon's view, the subspecific, or racial, category transcends the specific boundary, with the same subspecies, or race, existing in both *H. erectus* and *H. sapiens* populations. Both taxonomists and evolutionary biologists deny that this is possible. Moreover, simply in terms of probability, the chance that five separate races of *Homo erectus* could have evolved into *Homo sapiens* five separate times is exceedingly small.

The alternative to the polyphyletic approach is the unilinear, or anagenetic, approach. This theory involves the slow and gradual evolution of a single lineage through a series of grades or phases from primitive to advanced. The classic anagenetic view of human evolution would be *Australopithecus→Homo erectus→*Neandertal*→Homo sapiens*. Such a process would depend upon the phyletic gradualism model that was discussed in Chapter 1.

An important aspect of the anagenetic model is the concept of evolutionary grades. This means that within a certain span of time, all human populations would have arrived at a particular level or grade of evolution. Thus the classic Neandertals and the Javan Solo populations would be viewed as members of the same evolutionary grade. The necessity of justifying this position resulted in turning the erectus-like Solo population into "tropical Neandertalers" (Von Koenigswald, 1958).

The grade concept of the evolutionary process was initially developed by Hrdlicka, who, in 1927, first defined a "Neandertal phase" in human evolution. Hrdlicka was very influential in developing one of the important ramifications of this model. He felt that within a certain period of time, such as the Early Würm, all human populations would have achieved a certain level of evolutionary advancement. The idea that time and morphology were related in a very precise way led to the development of "morphological dating." Thus a fossil, found in an undated context, could be assigned to a time period solely on the basis of its appearance. Morphological dating has indeed long been a popular practice with anthropologists and archeologists alike. This idea has recently been revived in the taxonomic scheme of Campbell, who has defined hominid taxa on the basis of their distribution in time (1973). Thus, *Australopithecus* "became" *Homo* at 1.3 m.y. ago. The existence of *Homo* at a much earlier date and the sympatry of both genera until about 1 m.y. ago are expendable items of information used in an effort to make the fossil record tidy.

An anagenetic model of human evolution has been applied to humans in the Upper Pleistocene. Brace (1962, 1964) and Brose and Wolpoff (1971) have formulated the concept that the classic Neandertals of western Europe developed directly into anatomically modern humans. These authors have suggested that neither cultural nor morphological discontinuities existed between these groups, and therefore anatomically modern populations could have evolved from the classic group.

However, morphological discontinuities did exist. As is discussed below, the classic Neandertals show a morphology that is distinctive in both its separate features and its overall pattern.

Characteristics of *Homo sapiens neandertalensis*

Important characteristics are as follows:

Platycephalic skull

Large cranial capacity, 1300 cc to 1750 cc

Well-developed brow ridges with fusion of medial and lateral elements

Marked occipital torus with backward extension of the occiput into a bun

Maximum skull breadth at about midpoint, resulting in a barrel-shaped skull when viewed from the rear

Small mastoid, directed inward

Forward displacement of the face (facial prognathism)

Inflation of maxilla and no canine fossa

No chin

Anterior dentition usually larger than in modern humans

Taurodontism

Occipito-mastoid crest

Skull and postcranial bones thinner than in *Homo erectus* but thicker than in modern humans

Thumb joint more rounded and less saddle-shaped than in modern humans

Pelvis with thin, plate-like superior pubic ramus; large, triangular obturator foramen

Scapula with dorsal groove at axillary border

Long bones curved with large articular surfaces

Geographic distribution: Europe, Africa, western Asia

Temporal distribution: Third Interglacial, Fourth Glacial

Skull The Neandertal populations are characterized by having a long, platycephalic skull with a cranial capacity that is often above the mean for modern sapiens (Heim, 1970); cranial capacity ranges from about 1300 cc to about 1750 cc.

The facial portion is large and protrusive (Figure 9-5). Reference to

FIGURE 9-5 Shanidar 1, facial view. The large orbits, strongly marked brow ridges, and inflated maxilla characteristic of the Neandertals are apparent in this view. Several pathological conditions are also visible. The right side of the forehead has been damaged superficially (from blows?), and the damage to the left orbit may have resulted in blindness. The uneven wear on the front teeth may reflect greater use of the teeth as tools after loss of the use of the right arm. (Photograph courtesy of T. D. Stewart.)

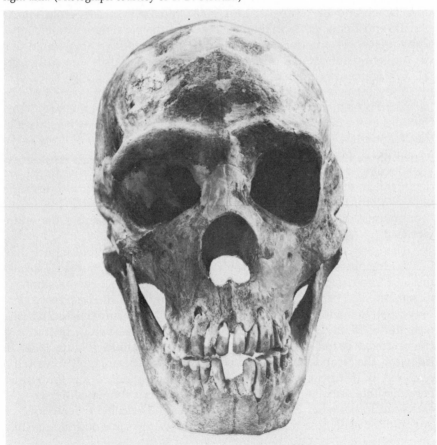

Table 6-3 will show that the facial height–cranial length indices of the Neandertals are higher than those for anatomically modern sapient types like Skhul 5 and Predmost. Moreover, the entire face appears to be displaced forward. Part of the forward displacement is due to the greatly enlarged facial (maxillary) sinuses, resulting in a distinctive, swollen appearance. As discussed in Chapter 8, this characteristic feature first appeared in earlier Middle Pleistocene individuals from France, Germany, and Greece (Arago, Steinheim, and Petralona). Because of this inflation of the central face, there is no depression near the root of the maxillary canine. This depression, called the "canine fossa," is a characteristic of modern sapiens. Associated with this enlargement and protrusion of the face is a very large nasal cavity. The nasal bridge is very high (Howells, 1970), and the nasal cavity is so large that, in some individuals, the nasal floor extends below the lower nasal margin and reaches to the level of the root tips of the upper teeth. This great expansion of the nasal cavity is seen in such individuals as Shanidar 1 and 2, from Iraq (Stewart, 1977); Amud, from Israel; and La Chapelle, La Quina, and La Ferrassie, from France (Suzuki and Takai, 1970). In modern sapiens, the nasal floor extends little, if any, below the anterior nasal margin. Some authorities have stated that the forward displacement of the face in the Neandertals is due entirely to this enlargement of the nasal cavity (Coon, 1962).

The protrusion of the central part of the face is emphasized by the backward placement of the facial bones toward the sides of the face. Thus, the sides of the orbits and the cheekbones both slant strongly backward in the Neandertals (Howells, 1970).

In the frontal region there is usually a sloping or retreating forehead; well-developed brow ridges are present (Figure 9-6). The brow ridges are distinctive in that they demonstrate fusion of the medial portion (over the nose) with the lateral portions into a single bony torus (Howell, 1957). This "continuous" brow ridge is usually of equal thickness across the entire forehead.

The occipital bone remains broad, as in *Homo erectus*, but higher than in most members of that group (see Table 8-2). The small, inwardly turned mastoid process reflects this great occipital breadth. The position of maximum skull breadth is usually placed higher than in *Homo erectus* but lower than in modern sapiens. Thus, the point of maximum breadth in the Neandertal skull is placed about midway on the vault, giving it a characteristic barrel shape when viewed from behind (Figure 9-7). In sideview, the Neandertal occipital bone protrudes considerably toward the rear and is distinctive in that it appears to pop out along the suture between the occipital and parietal bones. This pronounced backward extension forms what French anthropologists have called a "chignon" or bun. On the skull base the occipital bone shows the same occipito-mastoid

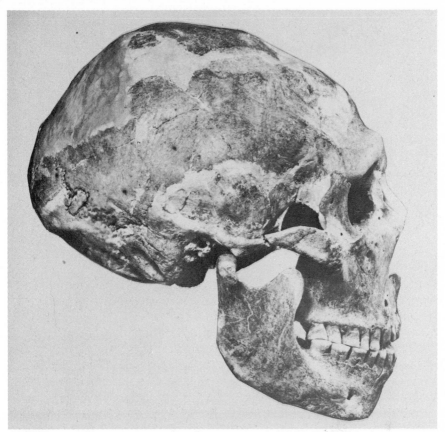

FIGURE 9-6 Shanidar 1, lateral view. This view shows the occipital bun which accentuates the great length of the Neandertal skull. Note also the large jaws and teeth and the absence of a chin. (Photograph courtesy of T. D. Stewart.)

crest identified on *Homo erectus* skulls (Stewart, 1961, 1964, 1977; Weiner and Campbell, 1964). This crest marks the boundary between the mastoid portion of the temporal bone and the occipital bone.

The mandible clearly reflects the forward displacement of the Neandertal face. In this group, the third molar usually sits well forward of the leading edge of the vertical ramus of the mandible while in modern sapients this tooth is usually hidden in the side view (Figure 9-6). The mandible is large and robustly built and there is usually no chin, although some individuals show incipient development of a chin. Thus, Shanidar 1 is reported as having a slightly developed chin (Stewart, 1977). The back margin of the jaw, where the horizontal ramus turns into the vertical

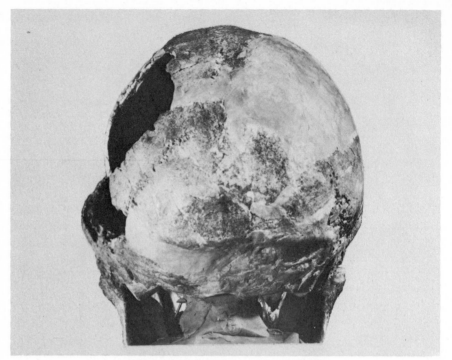

FIGURE 9-7 Shanidar 1, posterior view. The rounded, barrel shape of the Neandertal skull is apparent here. This shape contrasts strongly with earlier hominids such as *Australopithecus* and *H. erectus,* in which the greatest breadth occurs very low on the skull; and with modern *H. sapiens,* in which the upper part of the skull has expanded outward. (Photograph courtesy of T. D. Stewart.)

ramus (the gonial angle), is typically very rounded in Neandertals (Boule and Vallois, 1957; Stewart, 1977). In modern sapiens, this area is more angular (see Figure 9-11 for comparison).

The Neandertal mandible often shows multiple mental foramina, as does the jaw of *Homo erectus.* These are seen in individuals from La Chapelle, La Naulette, and La Quina in France (Coon, 1962) and Shanidar in Iraq (Stewart, 1977).

It is interesting that the Neandertal jaw joint (the temporo-mandibular joint) often shows signs of osteoarthritis. Such arthritic changes in the jaw joint have been identified in individuals from Krapina, Yugoslavia (Gorjanovic-Kramberger, 1906), La Chapelle, La Ferrassie and La Quina, France (Straus and Cave, 1957), Tabun on Mount Carmel, Israel (McCown and Keith, 1939), and Shanidar, Iraq (Stewart, 1977).[6]

[6]Alexandersen (1967) contains an excellent general discussion of this material.

Osteoarthritis is often regarded as a disorder related to excessive stress on the joints involved (see Jurmain, 1977). There is, in fact, some evidence from dental wear, particularly on the front teeth, that the Neandertals were using their teeth for a variety of jobs (Alexandersen, 1967; Brace, 1967; Coon, 1962). These jobs may have involved the softening of skins (Brace, 1967; Coon, 1962).[7] Arthritic temporo-mandibular joints also appear in some non-Neandertal individuals from the Upper Paleolithic such as Skhul 5 from Mount Carmel, Israel (McCown and Keith, 1939), and Cro-Magnon from France (Vallois, 1949).

In the dentition, the incisors are often large, in many cases as large as in *Homo erectus*. Moreover, the inner or lingual surface of the incisors often has well-developed tubercles of enamel at the gum line (McCown and Keith, 1939; Coon, 1962; Stewart, 1977). Conversely, the cheek teeth are usually no larger than in modern sapiens, and the third molar is often very small (Le Gros Clark, 1964).

Neandertal molars and premolars often have enlarged pulp cavities and fused roots; this condition is called **taurodontism.** It is also known from a number of *Homo erectus* individuals including those from Heidelberg and Choukoutien. Taurodontism may be related to a delay in the development of the roots. The result is that the roots do not form completely and the pulp cavity, as a consequence, enlarges downward (Gleiser and Hunt, 1955). This would appear to be a neotenous condition.

Postcranium A number of distinctive features and patterns have been identified in the vertebral column, scapula, pelvis, and limb bones of the Neandertals.

VERTEBRAL COLUMN Although neck or cervical vertebrae are known from a number of Neandertal individuals, such as those from La Chapelle, La Quina, Spy, and Krapina, little comprehensive or comparative work has been done on this material. Boule and Vallois (1957) did study some of the European Neandertal vertebrae, but their conclusion that they closely resembled those of a chimp rather than of a human was never widely accepted. Since then, Stewart (1962b) has studied the cervical vertebrae from Shanidar and has identified several ways in which they differ from those of modern humans. These differences, however, are slight and indicate that the Neandertal vertebral column, in the neck region at least, did not differ qualitatively from that of modern sapiens.

For example, in modern sapiens the articular facets (where one vertebra rests on the next) are placed obliquely to the plane of the vertebral column, thus enhancing the curvature of the spine in the neck area. In

---

[7]Not everyone agrees that the Neandertals were using their teeth as tools. For alternative points of view, see Wallace (1975) and Patricia Smith (1976).

Shanidar 2 these facets are placed in a less oblique orientation, apparently decreasing the cervical curve slightly. Boule and Vallois (1957) thought the curve would have been eliminated completely; but this apparently was not the case (see Straus and Cave, 1957).

Another feature concerns the orientation of the posterior spinous process. In modern sapiens this process of bone (which protrudes from the rear portion of the vertebrae) points strongly downward. In Shanidar 2, the posterior spinous process is less obliquely oriented and points strongly backward. This is particularly true in the last cervical vertebra (C 7) in which the posterior spinous process deviates only 9.5° from the horizontal axis of the vertebral body (Stewart, 1962b).

SCAPULA   A distinctive morphological pattern has been identified in the scapula of the Neandertals. Stewart (1962a), while noting that the scapula has high variability in modern humans, found that individuals from La Ferrassie (1 and 2), Krapina, Neandertal, Shanidar (1), and Tabun (1) all shared a similar pattern. More recently, this same pattern has also been identified in the skeleton from Amud, Israel (Suzuki and Takai, 1970). Stewart has noted that in Neandertal individuals, there was a well-developed groove or sulcus on the outside (the dorsal aspect) of the scapula on the border nearest the arm. In modern sapiens, the groove is usually present on the under side (the ventral aspect) closest to the ribs.

Trinkaus (1977) has suggested that this dorsal groove may reflect very strong rotator muscles of the upper arm. The teres minor muscle attaches onto the dorsal surface of the scapula along the outer or axillary margin. The function of this muscle, along with two others, is to rotate the humerus outward and to help maintain the head of the humerus in the joint during this activity. The presence of the dorsal sulcus, Trinkaus argues, provides additional attachment area and therefore greater power for the teres minor muscle.

Overall, this evidence of strong lateral rotation of the humerus would reinforce other evidence of strong inner or medial rotation in the upper arm. This would mean that while the Neandertals had great power in their upper arms, this power was delicately counterpoised so that the strength of teres minor and the other lateral rotators was balanced by that of the inward rotators. Therefore, manual dexterity and precision of action were possible along with the muscular power.

PELVIS   The pelvis (or os coxa) of the classic Neandertals (Figure 9-8) also has several distinctive morphological features. The os coxa is composed of three separate bones—the ilium, ischium, and pubis—which become fused by adulthood. The most distinctive of the classic Neandertal pelvic features occurs in the pubis. The top bar or superior ramus of the pubis is narrowed

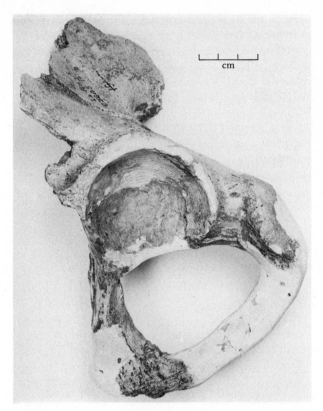

FIGURE 9-8 Pelvis of Neandertal (La Ferrassie I). The large obturator foramen and thin superior pubic ramus are characteristic of this group. (Photograph courtesy of E. Trinkhaus and the Musée de l' Homme.)

in its vertical dimension and is elongated relative to that of modern humans. The thinness of the superior ramus results in an enlarged obturator foramen. This pattern of characters occurs in hominids over a wide geographic range in the early Upper Pleistocene. It has been found in os coxae from La Ferrassie 1 and Krapina in Europe and Tabun 1, Shanidar, and Amud in the Near East (Trainkaus, 1976).

Limb Bones The limb bones of the Neandertals also present evidence of a distinctive morphological pattern. The bones of the arm and leg are characterized by being very robust, rather short, and often very curved in comparison with those of modern humans. Moreover, the joint and articular surfaces are frequently very large. These large joint areas are, in fact, a remarkable feature of these bones.

HAND   Musgrave (1970, 1971, 1973), in studying the Neandertal hand, has pointed out several ways in which it differed from that of modern sapients. For example, the Neandertal hand was characterized by having very short proximal phalanges and long distal phalanges, the reverse of the usual relationship in modern groups. Thus, the overall length of the Neandertal hand was not different from that of modern sapients, but the component bones did vary in their relative sizes.

The thumb (Figure 9-9) is of particular interest. Musgrave found that the proximal surface of the first metacarpal was more rounded and less saddle-shaped or concave than in modern humans. Such a structure may have meant that the Neandertals lacked the ability to bring the pulp surface of the index finger to oppose the pulp surface of the thumb in a full precision grip (see Chapter 2). The usual grip in the Neandertal hand may

25
mm

FIGURE 9-9   Thumb of Neandertal (La Ferrassie I). Several features distinguish the Neandertal thumb from that of modern humans: the large articular surfaces; the broad, flat distal phalanges; and a more rounded surface on the proximal surface of the first metacarpal. Thus, the articular facet between the trapezium and the first metacarpal was evidently less well developed than in modern humans: Neandertals may have lacked full opposability of the thumb. (Photographs taken by A. Featherstone; provided courtesy of J. Musgrave.)

therefore have been a "key grip" where the pulp of the thumb was brought against the side of the index finger. A further characteristic of the Neandertal hand bones is that they, like other bones in the postcranium, had large articular surfaces; thus, the Neandertal finger joints must have been rather large. Musgrave concluded by noting that the distal phalanges of the fingers were very broad and flat and probably supported a large pulp surface on the ends of the fingers. Such a large pulp surface would have been an important advantage in a cold climate in providing additional heat resources for the fingers. It is interesting that Musgrave detected this particular pattern of morphology in widely scattered individuals of early Würm date. He found it not only in western European individuals, such as those at La Ferrassie and La Chapelle in France and at Spy in Belgium, but also in those at Kiik-Koba in the Crimea and at Krapina in Yugoslavia.

FEMUR   Although comprehensive studies on Neandertal long bones are rare, several Neandertal femora have been included in one broad analysis of early hominid femora (Kennedy, 1973). The results demonstrated that while most features could individually be included within the modern sapient range, several features were outside the range of variation for a modern comparative group. For example, all Neandertal long bones are characterized by large articular surfaces, as the Neandertal femoral head demonstrates. In a sample of modern sapients, the males had a mean vertical femoral head diameter of 49 mm; the femoral head of the original Neandertal[8] was 56.2 mm; that from Spy, Belgium, was 52.5 mm.

A further distinctive feature of the Neandertal femur was a strong curvature or bowing from front to back. In the same modern sapient group, the males had a mean curve subtense height of 6 mm, while in the original Neandertal femur, the subtense height was 12.4 mm, outside the range of variation of the comparative group. Other long bones, particularly the radius and ulna, show similar strong curvatures.

As pointed out in Chapter 8, a characteristic of early hominines is the presence of thick cortical bone; the Neandertals, while having less thick bones than *Homo erectus*, were well above the mean values of the modern comparative group. For example, the thickness of the outer cortex at the very top of the femoral shaft in the male sapients had a mean of 7.2 mm. In the original Neandertal femur, this value was 12 mm, again outside the range of variation of modern sapients.

TALUS   Although Trinkaus (1975) has concluded that the foot of the Neandertals showed no functional difference from modern sapients, it

[8]The term "original" is used here to distinguish a part of the first Neandertal skeleton discovered (in 1856 in Germany) from the Neandertals as a group.

does have several distinctive features. First, the foot phalanges show the same shortening of the proximal phalanges and lengthening of the distal phalanges seen in the hand. Second, the neck of the talus appears to be more obliquely oriented than in modern *Homo sapiens* (see Table 6-6). Thus, the horizontal neck angle of Shanidar 2 is 29° (Stewart, 1977) and of La Chapelle, 23° (Day, 1977). Although these figures are not outside the range of variation for modern humans, they are well above the mean values.

Locomotion and Posture   After the French anthropologist Boule had studied the La Chapelle-aux-Saints skeleton (1923), he concluded that Neandertals stood and moved rather differently from modern humans. He stated that the Neandertals stood with knees bent, that the S-shaped curve in the spine was less than in modern humans, and that the foot rested on the ground on its outer surface. The English anatomist Elliot-Smith (1924) perpetuated a picture of "uncouth and repellent Neandertal Man." He emphasized that the "half-flexed legs of a peculiarly ungraceful form, [and the] unbroken curve of the neck and back in place of the alteration of curves which is one of the graces of the truly erect *Homo sapiens* . . . combined to complete the picture of unattractiveness." As late as 1956, some authors (see Straus and Cave, 1957), while eliminating the more subjective aspects of this description, reconstructed all Neandertals as being stoop-shouldered, bent-kneed, semierect, shuffling bipeds.

This description was finally shown to be false when Straus and Cave (1957) examined the actual remains of the "old man" from La Chapelle-aux-Saints. They found that this individual, who had provided the prototype for Neandertal posture and locomotion, had been severely afflicted with osteoarthritis. This progressive and deforming bone disease had, in fact, severely affected the man's posture and movement. However, analysis of other individuals who did not have pathological bone disorders showed that they more closely resembled the modern human in their fully erect posture, curvatures of the spinal column, and the way they transmitted weight into the foot. Thus, while the "old man" at La Chapelle-aux-Saints may, indeed, have had severe postural problems, as do some modern people with osteoarthritis, other Neandertals moved and stood much as modern *Homo sapiens* does.

HOMO SAPIENS SAPIENS

Populations included here under the taxon of *Homo sapiens sapiens* are contained in two groups: an "archaic" group and an "anatomically modern" group. Their geographic distribution was both hemispheres. Temporal distribution for archaic *Homo sapiens* is late Third Interglacial into early Fourth Glacial; for modern *Homo sapiens* 30,000 B.P. to the present.

The origins of the archaic group may extend back as early as 130,000 years B.P.; archaic sapiens from the Kibish Formation in Ethiopia have been dated to this time. A long time period separates these earliest archaic sapiens from the next appearance of this group in the fossil record. At some 40,000 years ago, archaic sapiens appeared widely in the Old World; at about the same time, they may also have made their entry into the New World. Sapient populations dating to about 40,000 years ago are found in such widely spaced areas as South Africa, north Africa, southwest Asia, southeastern Asia, and perhaps the west coast of the United States.[9] This very broad geographic distribution is strong evidence that the archaic sapiens had emerged at a considerably earlier period.

The archaic sapiens are very heterogeneous and differ from fully modern members of the group in a number of ways. Archaic individuals, for example, often show large brow ridges, large teeth, occipital buns, facial prognathism, or other features found in more primitive groups, such as the Neandertals. These primitive features are frequently combined with more modern features, such as a more vertical forehead, formation of a chin, presence of a canine fossa, or limbs without the Neandertal curvatures and robusticity. Individuals from the Kibish levels in Ethiopia, Florisbad in South Africa, Eyasi in Tanzania, and Skhul in Israel are among those placed in this archaic group.

Between about 30,000 to 40,000 years ago, populations that can be called modern *Homo sapiens* appeared. Qafzeh, in Israel, Fish Hoek in South Africa, Niah in Borneo, and Cro-Magnon in France can be placed in this group (see Table 9-4).

Characteristics of Archaic and Modern *Homo sapiens sapiens*

Important characteristics are as follows.

More vertical forehead than in earlier groups

Cranial capacity, 900 cc to 2300 cc; mean, 1400 cc

Brow ridges absent to moderate; never a continuous bar or torus

Occipital rounded without bun or strong torus

Maximum skull breadth high on parietals

Mastoid small to moderate in size but oriented down rather than inward

Face orthognathous to moderately prognathous; lower face never displaced forward

Canine fossa present

[9]There is a great deal of controversy surrounding the time of the first human entry into the New World. Some authorities accept a much later date (10,000 to 20,000 years B.P.) for this event.

TABLE 9-4 Distribution of anatomically modern *Homo sapiens*

	EUROPE						AFRICA	ASIA		NEW WORLD	
TIME	FRANCE	GREAT BRITAIN	CZECHOSLOVAKIA	ITALY	SOVIET UNION	OTHERS		AUSTRALIA	OTHERS	CALIFORNIA	OTHERS
10	Bruiniquel (11,750)	Gough's Cave 10,000 Kent's Cavern 10,000 (Nos. 1 & 2) Sun Hole 12,000		Arene Candide (B) 10,330 Moritzo 13,000 Grimaldi Baousso da Torre Barma del Caviglione (B)	Kostenki (B) 11,000	*YUGOSLAVIA* Sandalja 12,230 *NETHERLANDS* Beegden 13,000	*EGYPT* Kom Ombo (2) 13,070	Kow Swamp (B) (10,000) Talgai (12,000) Keilor (12,900)	*JAVA* Wadjak (D?) Solo (D?)	Arlington Springs (10,000)	*MEXICO* Tepexepan 11,000 *WASHINGTON* Marmes 11,000 B *MINNESOTA* (D?) *PERU* Guitarreo Cave 12,560 *TEXAS* Midland <14,700
15	Chancelade Roc de Sers (B)				Kostenki 14,300		*TANZANIA* Olduvai Hominidi (B) 16,000 *SUDAN* Singh 17,000			Laguna Beach 17,150	*TENNESSEE* Natchez (D?)
20	Abri Pataud, Bed 2 21,940	Paviland (B) 18,000 Badger Hole 18,000 Kent's Cavern (No. 4)		Barma Grande (B) Grotte des Enfants (B, CR)	Akhshtyr 19,500 Afontova Gora 20,900 Sungir (B) 21,800	*POLAND* Maszycka (C) *GERMANY* Oberkassel (B, D?)	*MOROCCO* Taforalt (1) 21,000 *ZAMBIA* Mumbwa 22,000		*CHINA* Upper Cave 18,340 Ordos (D?) *PHILLIPPINES* Tabon (23,200)		
25	Cro Magnon (B) Pavlov (B) Combe Capelle (B)		Predmost (B) 26,000 Pavlo (B) 26,000 Brno Mladec					Lake Mungo 25,000 (B, CR)		Los Angeles 23,600	

WÜRM GLACIAL — WÜRM MAIN PHASE "WÜRM III"

PAUDORF OSCILLATION II/III INTERSTADIAL — MAIN EARLY PHASE "WÜRM II"

ALBERTA,
CANADA
Taber
> 30,000

La Jolla
44,000

Del Mar
48,000

BORNEO
Niah 40,000

SOUTH
AFRICA
Fish Hoek
35,000
Eyasi
35,000
Florisbad
39,000

Border Cave
45,000

ISRAEL
Skhul
Qafzeh

YUGOSLAVIA
Velika Pecina
33,000

ETHIOPIA
Omo 130,000

Dolni
Vestonice
29,000
(B, C)

Les Cottés
31,000

30 — 40 — 50 — 60 — 70

WÜRM I/II   WÜRM I   RISS/WÜRM INTERGLACIAL EEMIAN

Key: B = burial; C = cannibalized; CR = cremation; D? = date questionable.

Source: For references, see Oakley et al., 1971 and 1975.

Chin present

Long bones without strong curvatures or large articular surfaces

Bone thickness less than in *Homo erectus* and Neandertals

Geographic distribution: both hemispheres

Temporal distribution: archaic *H. sapiens*, late Third Interglacial into early Fourth Glacial; modern *H. sapiens*, 40,000 B.P. to present

HOMINIDS OF THE THIRD INTERGLACIAL

EUROPE

East Germany

The earliest human remains from the Third Interglacial were found in two quarries at Ehringsdorf, a suburb of Weimar in East Germany. A date of greater than 220,000 B.P. has recently been obtained on uranium-thorium ratios from travertine at Fisher's Quarry (Kukla, in Butzer and Isaac, 1975, p. 897). Since the dated material overlies the hominid level, this represents a minimum age; the presence of a warm type of fauna reinforces the probability of an interglacial age.

In 1908 two small skull fragments were found at Fisher's Quarry at Ehringsdorf, and in 1925 a fragmentary human skull, lacking the face, was found there. The cranium (Ehringsdorf 9) demonstrates many features characteristic of the later, Würm-age classic Neandertals but has a high, nearly vertical forehead (Weidenreich, 1927, 1928).

The high forehead, along with Weidenreich's restoration (which probably made the skull too large), has resulted in many different interpretations of the Ehringsdorf skull. Until this important skull is restudied and possibly reconstructed, no final conclusions can be made.

Further discoveries were made at nearby Kampfe's Quarry between 1909 and 1916; they consist of the very fragmentary remains of seven individuals. An adult mandible, Ehringsdorf 6, originally called the "Weimar Jaw," shows pronounced alveolar prognathism and lack of a chin, and in these features resembles later classic Neandertals. The entire dentition, however, is rather small and the third molar is especially reduced. A similar pattern is reproduced in the child's mandible, Ehringsdorf 7. As pointed out previously, Mousterian tools are known from both Ehringsdorf sites. They may, in fact, be the earliest evidence of the Mousterian.

A third travertine quarry, at nearby Taubach, yielded two teeth, recovered in 1908. They were found in association with a warm fauna and probably also date to the Eemian; Boule and Vallois (1957) reported that the

Taubach site may, in fact, have been a living site. Mousterian tools, broken and burned animal bones, and traces of hearths were found here, but apparently no systematic excavation has ever been made. The two teeth, one from an adult and the other from a child, seem very similar to the Ehringsdorf teeth (Virchow, 1917; Boule and Vallois, 1957). A recent thorium-uranium date indicates that these teeth may be about 125,000 years old; this date is fully consistent with an Eemian age (Broecker et al., 1973).

Saccopastore, Italy

Also associated with Mousterian tools and dating to the last interglacial are two skulls found at Saccopastore, near Rome, between 1929 and 1935. In both, the full pattern of classic Neandertal features is present except that the occipital bone is more rounded and less protuberant than in the later classic group. The cranial capacity, about 1300 cc for each individual, is somewhat less than is usually found in the Würm Neandertals. As in the Ehringsdorf individuals, the third molar is much reduced.

Fontechevade, France

Remains of at least three individuals have been recovered from deposits of the last interglacial age at Fontechevade, near Charente, in France; they were associated with a Tayacian tool assemblage (Henri-Martin, 1947). The very broken condition of the skull bones and their association with food animals could mean that they too were the remains of human meals (Vallois, 1958).

Although these skull bones are in very fragmentary condition, several interesting features are present. Estimates on the most complete of the skulls (Fontechevade 5) indicate a cranial capacity of about 1450 cc (Boule and Vallois, 1957); the bones, however, are thick and the skull seems to have been broad across the base. Both this partial skull and a small fragment consisting of just the central part of the forehead (Fontechevade 4) show no clear evidence of brow ridge formation. For this reason the Fontechevade individuals have been used to indicate the presence of anatomically modern humans at an early date. However, Trinkaus (1973) has recently pointed out that Fontechevade 4 (Fontechevade I, in his paper) is probably a juvenile, and as such, shares a similar degree of brow ridge development with classic Neandertal juveniles from Gibraltar, La Quina, and Engis. He has also pointed out that the frontal region in Fontechevade 5 (Fontechevade II, in his paper) is too incomplete for any definitive reconstruction.

Corruccini (1975) has recently studied the parietal bones of the more complete individual and has noted the presence of a number of features shared with both the earlier individual from Steinheim and Würm-age classic Neandertals. This study and others (Sergi, 1953); Weiner and Campbell, 1964) would seem to affirm a close morphologic affinity between the Fontechevade individuals and the classic Neandertals.

Gánovece, Czechoslovakia

In 1926, human remains were found near Gánovece, Czechoslovakia. They include a natural endocranial cast made from travertine; such a cast would have formed when highly mineralized spring water seeped into a skull and gradually replaced the organic tissues of the brain. The cast, of a brain about 1320 cc in size, shows several similarities with earlier Swanscombe and contemporary Saccopastore individuals in terms of overall size and shape. Moreover, the occipital region seems to have been more "bun-like" and protuberant, as in the later classic Neandertals (Vlcek, 1955).

Krapina, Yugoslavia

The rock-shelter site at Krapina, near Zagreb in Yugoslavia, was first excavated by Gorjanovic-Kramberger in 1899. On the basis of faunal comparisons, the site probably dates to late in the Riss-Würm Interglacial. Nine occupation levels were discovered. Gorjanovic-Kramberger identified the cultural remains from the occupation levels as Mousterian (1899, 1905, 1906). Others, however, have identified Acheulian and Aurignacian components within the site (Skerlj, 1958).

Human remains at Krapina have all been recovered from a single occupation level, the third level from the bottom. These remains are extremely fragmented and consist of 649 identified pieces (Coon, 1964). Much of the fragmentation is due to the fact that early excavations were carried out by means of dynamite. However, some of the bones are charred and may represent the remains of cremations or cannibalism. At least 14 individuals, and possibly as many as 28, are present at Krapina (Oakley Campbell, and Molleson, 1971).

Because of the extreme fragmentation of the bones, the morphological features of the population are difficult to ascertain. Several features are visible, however. The size of the two adult skulls that are complete enough for estimation ranges from 1200 cc to 1450 cc. An interesting feature is that the skulls appear to be very broad and relatively short (Coon, 1964); skulls of other fossil humans are usually longer and narrower. The brow ridges appear to be well developed.

A fragmented pelvis shows the thin, plate-like superior pubic ramus characteristic of the classic Neandertals (Trinkaus, 1976).

AFRICA

Kibish, Ethiopia

An interesting situation, perhaps indicative of a large amount of interpopulation heterogeneity, can be seen in the two individuals[10] found in the Kibish Formation near the Omo River in Ethiopia (Figure 9-10). They were found by Richard Leakey in 1967 and have been dated to 130,000 years B.P. with uranium-thorium (Butzer, Brown, and Thurber, 1969). Kibish 1 shows a robust but modern appearance, with rounded occipital, minimal development of the brow ridges, and a chin present on the mandible. The skull of Kibish 2, however, shows a rather different picture. This skull, although found on the surface, is reportedly contemporaneous with Kibish 1. It has a marked occipital angle, low position of maximum skull breadth, and a sloping forehead. Both individuals may have had a cranial capacity near the sapient mean of 1400 cc (Day, 1971b).

If the date of 130,000 years is confirmed for the Kibish skulls, then they would seem to represent the earliest of the archaic *Homo sapiens*.

Broken Hill, Zambia

"Rhodesian Man" Further south in Africa, the remains of several individuals have been recovered from a lead and zinc mine at Broken Hill in Zambia. Beginning in 1921, a nearly complete skull, a maxilla, a pelvis, three femora, a tibia, and a humerus were found in the mine. These were originally called "Rhodesian Man."

The skull shows a rather remarkable appearance that resulted in its being placed in a new species, "Homo rhodesiensis," by Woodward in 1921. Portions of the postcranial remains were later referred to an entirely new hominid taxon, "Cyphanthropus rhodesiensis," or "stooping man," by Pycraft in 1928. However, this taxon was a reflection more of a poor understanding of the bony remains (Le Gros Clark, 1928) than of any truly distinctive features. Recently, a date of 110,000 years old has been obtained on this material from amino acid racemization in isoleucine (Bada, Schroeder, Protsch, and Berger, 1974).

The capacity of the skull is rather small, about 1280 cc, and the skull bones are not remarkably thick. The brow ridges are among the largest in any hominid and are similar to those of OH 9. The length of the face is one of the largest ever recorded; only the face of the Neandertal from La Ferrassie is longer (Coon, 1962). The teeth of the upper jaw (no mandible is known) are very large and, in fact, approach those of the Chinese and Javanese *Homo erectus* in size. Such a pattern would indicate a morphologi-

---

[10]A third individual is represented by a very small piece of frontal bone.

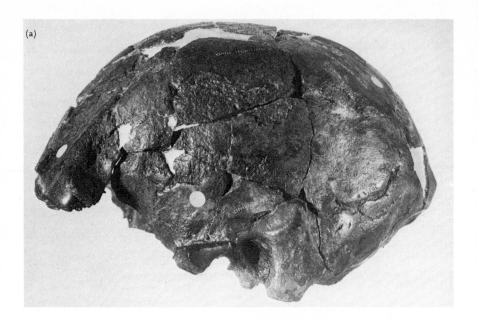

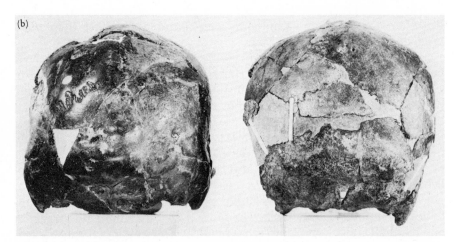

FIGURE 9-10   **(a)** Skull of Kibish II, lateral view. This skull, from Ethiopia, may represent the earliest evidence of *Homo sapiens sapiens*. This archaic form of the species shows a sloping forehead, a very large occipital torus, and a flattened nuchal or occipital plane. **(b)** Skulls of Kibish I and II, posterior views. Although these skulls appear to have been contemporaneous, they show a considerable range of variation. Kibish II, on the left, has the maximum skull breadth very low in the mastoid region, as in earlier hominines, while in Kibish I the maximum breadth is placed high, as in modern humans. (Photographs courtesy of M.H. Day.)

cal affiliation with earlier *Homo erectus* populations. This affiliation has recently been statistically confirmed in multivariate studies indicating that the Rhodesian skull and femora are similar to earlier Middle Pleistocene hominids (Kennedy, 1973; Stringer, 1974).

HOMINIDS OF THE EARLY WÜRM

EUROPE

The main proliferation of the classic Neandertals lies within western Europe in the early Würm. The major sites are given in Tables 9-5 and 9-6, and the morphology of these individuals has been discussed earlier. As originally defined by Howell (1957), the classic Neandertals were confined strictly to western Europe in the early Fourth Glacial. Indeed, the dynamics of his hypothesis rested on such restriction, and many subsequent authors, either implicitly or explicitly, have followed this concept. However, during the Early Würm, individuals outside of western Europe can be seen to demonstrate either the full range of the classic pattern or significant parts of it.

During the first interstadial of the Würm, about 35,000 years ago, an anatomically modern population entered western Europe. It brought with it the Aurignacian cultural tradition, a tool technology new to western Europe. The evidence of the human remains supports the evidence of this technology in indicating the presence of a new population.

These intrusive populations are generally termed the "Cro-Magnons" after the rock-shelter site in the Vézére River valley where the first individual of this type was recovered in 1868. Since that time, other sites containing Aurignacian archeological material have been discovered in Germany, Spain, Italy, and other parts of southern France. This material is documentation that the Aurignacian, unlike the Perigordian, was not a local phenomenon but possibly a large-scale population movement. Reference to Table 9-6 will show the distribution of this material and the nature of the known remains.

Of the human material associated with the European Aurignacian, individuals from Cro-Magnon and the various Grimaldi caves are best known. The morphological pattern encountered in the Near East is also apparent here. Brow ridge development is slight; the skulls are large, with almost no facial prognathism; the limb bones are straight, without the pronounced curvatures present in the classical group.

One Aurignacian site is of particular interest, since a strong indication of Neandertal features persists in some individuals until a relatively late period. The open-air occupation site at Predmost, Czechoslovakia, is dated to 26,000 B.P. The remains of at least 29 individuals have been recovered.

TABLE 9-5 Mousterian sites containing human remains

LOCATION	DATE	MATERIAL PRESENT	BURIAL
Belgium			
Engis	Würm	Cranium, postcranium; child	Possible
Fond de Forêt	Würm	Femur	Possible
La Naulette	Würm	Cranium, postcranium; adult	Possible
Great Britain			
St. Brelade, Jersey (Channel Islands)	47,000 B.P. (Early Würm)	Cranium, postcranium; adult	Possible
France			
Arcy-sur-Cure	Würm I; Würm I–II	Teeth, cranium; adult; n = 2	Deliberate
Bau de l'Aubesier	Würm II	Teeth	Possible
La Chapelle-aux-Saints	Würm II	Cranium, postcranium	Deliberate
Chateau sur Charente	End of Würm or Würm II	Cranium, postcranium; child	Possible
Combe Grenal	Würm II	Cranium, postcranium; n = 2	Possible
La Ferrassie	Würm II	Cranium, postcranium; n = 2	Deliberate
Hortus	Würm II	Cranium, postcranium; n = 38 (food débris; cannibalism?)	Possible
Marillac	Würm II	Cranium	Possible
Le Moustier	Würm II	Cranium, postcranium; n = 2	Deliberate
Pech de l'Aze	Würm I or II	Cranium; child	Possible
La Quina	Würm II	Cranium, postcraniuu; n = 22	Possible
Regourdou	Würm I	Cranium, postcranium	Deliberate
Roc de Marsel	Würm I–II or Würm II	Cranium, postcranium; child	Deliberate
Germany			
Weimar-Ehringsdorf	Riss-Würm	Cranium, postcranium; n = 9	Possible
Gibraltar			
Devil's Tower	Würm	Cranium; child	Possible
Forbes Quarry	Würm	Cranium, postcranium; adult	Possible
Hungary			
Subalyuk	Early Würm	Cranium, postcranium; adult and child; n = 2	Possible

Italy			
Bisceglie	Würm I or II	Femur	Possible
Circeo	Würm I or II	Cranium and 4 mandibles; n = 4(?)	Skull only
Quinzano	Riss-Würm	Occiput	Possible
Saccopastore	Riss-Würm	Cranium; n = 2	Possible
Spain			
Cariguela (Piñar)	Würm	Cranium; n = 6	Possible
Cova Negra	Würm I	Cranium	Possible
Soviet Union			
Akhshtyr'	Early Würm	Tooth	Possible
Kiik-Koba	Early Würm	Postcranium; adult and child	Deliberate
Sterosel'e	Early Würm (?)	Cranium, postcranium; child and adult	Possible
Teshik-Tash	Early Würm	Cranium, postcranium; child	Deliberate
Krapina	Riss-Würm	Cranium, postcranium; n = 14+	Possible
Libya			
Haua Fteah	47,000 B.P.	2 mandibles	Possible
Morocco			
Irhoud	30,000 B.P.	Cranium, postcranium; n = 3	Possible

Source: See Oakley, Campbell, and Molleson, 1971, 1977, for references.

TABLE 9-6 Aurignacian sites containing human remains

LOCATION	DATE	MATERIAL PRESENT	BURIAL
Czechoslovakia			
Brno	Würm II (?)	Cranium, postcranium	Ocher burial, covered with mammoth scapula
France			
La Combe	Würm III	Tooth	Possible
Les Cottes Vienne	Würm III	Cranium, postcranium	Possible
Cro-Magnon	Würm III	Cranium, postcranium; n = 5	Deliberate
Les Roches	Würm III	Cranium; child	Possible
Les Rois	Würm III	Mandible, teeth; child	Possible
Germany			
Fuhlinger	?	Cranium	Possible
Honert	?	Mandible, teeth; child	Possible
Sirgenstein	?	Cranium, teeth	Possible
Italy			
Grimaldi			
Baousso da Torre	?	Cranium, postcranium; n = 3	Ceremonial burials, red ocher and perforated shells, traces of animal pelt
Barma del Caviglione	?	Cranium, postcranium; child	Ceremonial burial, red ocher and perforated shells, traces of animal pelt
Barma Grande	?	Cranium, postcranium; n = 6	Ceremonial burial with bone and shell ornaments; number 4 burnt; postcranium of number 1 destroyed in quarrel
Grotte des Enfants	?	Cranium, postcranium; child and adult	Ceremonial burial

Eighteen of them were in a communal grave which had been covered with a limestone slab and the scapulae of mammoths; the burials were tightly flexed. Some of the buried individuals showed cuts or incisions on the long bones, indicating that the meat may have been removed from the bones (Matiegka, 1934).

The Predmost population, like the earlier Skhul population (described below), was very heterogeneous. Some individuals have large brow ridges and occipital buns, while others show a more sapient morphology. Yet this site is dated well after the first anatomically modern humans entered western Europe.

WESTERN ASIA

Kiik-Koba, Russian Crimea

The child from Kiik-Koba in the Russian Crimea demonstrates classic Neandertal features in the scapula and in the curvature and robusticity of the long bones. Vlcek (1973) concluded that this child closely resembled its western European contemporaries in the early Würm.

Teshik Tash, Uzbekistan

Another child, this one from Uzbekistan near the Afghanistan border, also seems to resemble the European classic Neandertals in many important features. This boy, about 9 years of age at death, had a large skull with a capacity of 1490 cc, heavy, continuous brow ridges, bun-shaped occiput, large nasal cavity, and large teeth. All these features are close morphologically to the western group. On the other hand, the face is not markedly prognathous, the maxilla is only slightly inflated, and the long bones are relatively gracile without the strong bowing and curvatures seen in the classic group (see Coon, 1962; Weidenreich, 1945b; Movius, 1953). In both the Crimean and the Uzbekistan site, the cultural associations are Mousterian.

The Early Würm hominids from the Near East and north Africa also show the pattern of the western European classics but with certain small differences. For example, the three fragmentary skulls from Jebel Irhoud, Morocco, have long, low skulls, small mastoids, no canine fossa, and large brow ridges. They differ from the European group, however, in having a more rounded occiput without the characteristic bun of the classics (Ennouchi, 1962a, b, 1968, 1969).

Israel

Tabun, Mount Carmel In Tabun Cave, on Mount Carmel in Israel, fragmentary remains of two hominids also show some features of the classic Neandertals; they were recovered from Layer C, which has a radiocarbon date of 40,900±1000 B.P. (Vogel and Waterbolk, 1963). Tabun 1, a female about 156 cm (5 ft 1 in) tall, shows large, continuous brow ridges, platycephalic skull with retreating forehead, large, thick incisors, and very curved long bones like the European group. However, the occiput is rounded without the characteristic bun and the face is not markedly prognathous. The mandible (Tabun 2) is large and robust, and its breadth suggests a very broad skull base; the incisors are broad and thick, but a chin is present (McCown and Keith, 1939). These were found in association with Mousterian tools of Levallois tradition.

Skhul, Mount Carmel   The rock shelter at Skhul neighbors Tabun Cave on Mount Carmel. Skhul, which is virtually a cemetery, contains the buried remains of 10 individuals. Material from this site has been dated with amino acid racemization to between 31,000 and 33,000 B.P., thus making its occupation later in time than that at Tabun (Bada and Helfman, 1976).

The individuals from Skhul show a great deal of heterogeneity. Skhul 4, for example, has large brow ridges, a platycephalic skull with a large cranial capacity (1554 cc), but no canine fossa, no occipital bun, and no facial prognathism. Skhul 5 (Figure 9-11) has a very similar morphology but with a more vertical forehead and greater skull height. The postcranial remains of most of the individuals have a very modern appearance with none of the classic Neandertal features. Skhul 7 and Skhul 9, however, have curved long bones very similar to those of Tabun 1 and the western European classics.

Some anthropologists have interpreted the Skhul population as transitional between the classics and anatomically modern humans. However, this supposition seems unlikely, since fully modern individuals are known at an earlier date, further east and in southern Africa.

Qafzeh   A similar pattern of heterogeneity is seen at Qafzeh Cave, also in Israel. Bed XVII, containing most of the hominids, has been dated to 33,000 B.P. with amino acid racemization, and thus was contemporary with Skhul. The hominids from Qafzeh, recovered between 1934 and 1967, have never been adequately described; however, some data are available. Qafzeh 6 has a high vertical forehead, large mastoid, and chin similar to the individuals of more sapient appearance at Skhul. Others, however, have larger brow ridges and large teeth, indicating a wide range of variation (Howells, 1974).

The cultural associations at Qafzeh Cave are highly significant. Vandermeersh (1972) reports that Bed XVII, the level of the hominids, contains Mousterian tools of Levallois tradition. Here, in direct association, are Mousterian tools with *Homo sapiens* of the archaic type. Their presence

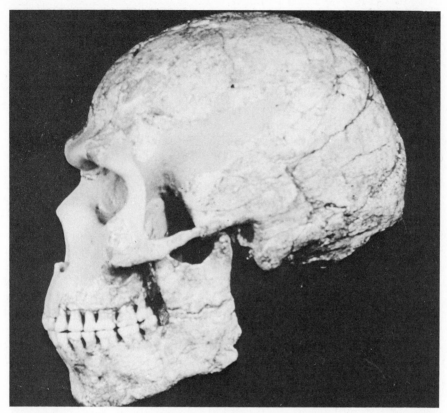

FIGURE 9-11 Skull of archaic *Homo sapiens* (Skhul 5). This skull is a good example of the archaic form of the species which was widespread in Europe, Africa, and the Near East between 25,000 and 35,000 years ago. Although there is some brow-ridge formation and facial prognathism, the forehead is high and vertical and the occiput is rounded; there is a chin. (Photograph of a cast.)

indicates that hominids other than Neandertals made tools of the Mousterian type, a point long disputed by some archeologists.

Amud Remains of at least four individuals were recovered from Amud Cave, near Lake Tiberias, between 1961 and 1964; and one of these (Amud 1) is virtually a complete individual. Absolute dating on Amud Cave has proven difficult, but all indications point to an age between 35,000 and 40,000 B.P.; this would correspond to the interstadial between Early Würm and Main Würm glacial advances. Amud 1 and Mousterian artifacts were recovered from the same cave levels.

The skull of Amud 1 has a cranial capacity of 1740 cc, possibly the largest of any fossil hominid (Suzuki and Takai, 1970). Overall, it shares many similarities with the classic Neandertals: it is platycephalic, the brow ridges are large, the maxilla is inflated, and there is considerable facial prognathism. In the rear view, the skull has the same barrel-shaped outline characteristic of the western group. The incisors are thick and the third molar in the mandible is set well forward of the jaw ramus.

The postcranium, however, shows a combination of classic characters and more modern sapient features. The pelvis has the thin superior pubic ramus characteristic of the classic group. The limbs are straight without the robust curvatures of other Neandertals. The stature of 174 cm (about 5 ft 8 in) was somewhat taller than the European groups.

Shanidar, Iraq

The important cavesite at Shanidar, Iraq, has already been discussed in terms of its burials. Of the eight individuals recovered there, Shanidar 1 and Shanidar 4 are the best known. Both show many of the features encountered in the western classic Neandertals. The cranial capacity is large, about 1700 cc in Shanidar 1. The skulls are platycephalic with receding foreheads. There is considerable maxillary inflation and no canine fossa is present. The features of the dentition, especially in the thick incisors, are also similar to the classic group. On the other hand, the brow ridges, although large and thick, are not continuous, as in the western European group.

AFRICA

Africa south of the Sahara shows a very heterogeneous mixture of populations during the Upper Pleistocene.

Florisbad

The Florisbad skull from South Africa is dated to around 38,500±2000 B.P. (Bada, Protsch, and Schroeder, 1973). This skull is of the archaic sapient type with a low, vaulted skull and moderate brow ridge formation and prognathism (Howells, 1973). The skull from Eyasi, Tanzania, may also be of this type (Protsch, 1975). Three individuals have been recovered from this site, dating to about 34,000 B.P. (Oakley et al., 1977).

Fish Hoek

The skull from Fish Hoek, South Africa, however, is apparently of fully modern sapient morphology. This is a large skull without brow ridges and a very small amount of facial prognathism. It is dated to 35,000 B.P. (Bada,

Schroeder, and Carter, 1974). Protsch, who has studied much of this material, has claimed that fully modern sapiens appeared in South Africa before they emerged elsewhere (1975). However, he has not provided the morphological or anatomical studies that would be necessary to validate his claim.

EASTERN ASIA

During the early Upper Pleistocene, the islands of southeastern Asia also contain evidence of heterogeneous populations.

Solo, Java

The Solo population from Java consists of 11 calvaria and 2 tibiae, which were discovered between 1931 and 1933 (Figure 9-12). These human remains have never been adequately dated. The Ngandong beds (see Table 7-12) in which they were found contain an Upper Pleistocene fauna with many species which still live in Java, although a few of the Ngandong species are remnants from earlier Middle Pleistocene levels. One species in

FIGURE 9-12   Skull of Solo 9. Although the Solo skulls from Java apparently date from the Upper Pleistocene, they have a number of features similar to *Homo erectus*. These similarities include both overall pattern (compare this illustration with Figure 8-2) and small, anatomical details. (Photograph of a cast.)

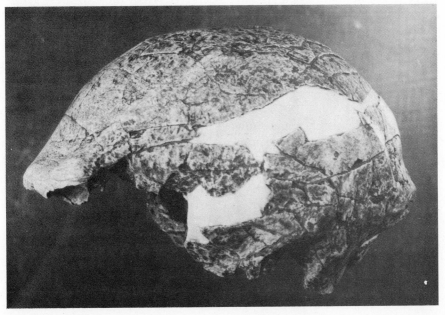

the Ngandong fauna, however, may be of some use in determining the climatic conditions at the time of deposition. A crane, *Grus grus*, today has its home far to the north in China; its presence in the Ngandong deposits may indicate the prevalence of colder conditions in its usual home range. That may therefore suggest that the Ngandong fauna, and the included hominids, were living in a cold period of the Early Würm (see Weidenreich, 1951).

When Weidenreich died in 1948, he had nearly completed the anatomical description of the Solo population, but he had not written his conclusions. His monograph, published in 1951, ends as he left it, in mid-sentence. The skulls as described by Weidenreich are of extraordinary interest. Only the skullcap portion remains on each individual; the facial portion is missing on each, and only one individual retains a skull base. The cranial capacity is low, ranging between 1035 and 1255 cc; the skulls are platycephalic, with retreating foreheads and large brow ridges. The occiput is sharply angled and the maximum skull breadth is low. The skull bones are very thick, approximately equal to the thickness of the Peking skulls (Weidenreich, 1951). Throughout his monograph, Weidenreich repeatedly points to morphological similarities between the Solo and Peking individuals; indeed, in their overall size, shape, and morphology, they are very close.

The circumstances surrounding the presence of the Solo population on the terrace of the Solo River are unclear. Apparently the site represents a living area; although no hearths and only a few stone tools were found, over 25,000 faunal fragments have been recovered. Most of these faunal remains represent deer and cattle, and also rhinos, hippos, and elephants. The skulls were found among the faunal remains, all lying base up. They were not found, however, within any localized area of the site but were scattered through it. Weidenreich concluded that the skulls may have been used as stone bowls, and there is considerable cultural parallel for such a practice from both modern and Upper Paleolithic populations.

The stone tools reportedly "disappeared" before they could be studied; Weidenreich noted, however, that some of the tools were stone balls 67 mm to 92 mm in diameter. Others were small scrapers or small triangular flakes. Stingray barbs were also found—far from the sea and a further indication of human activity.

Four of the skulls reveal signs of injuries that had healed prior to death; two individuals show nearly identical square-shaped depressions which penetrate the outer bone table of the skull.

Borneo

At present, one of the earliest modern *Homo sapiens* individuals comes from Niah Cave on the island of Borneo in levels dated to 41,500±1000 B.P.

(Harrisson, 1958, 1959; Brothwell, 1960). This individual, an adult female, was very delicate in build and resembled some modern southeast Asians, particularly those on New Guinea (Birdsell, 1979). There are no brow ridges, the forehead is vertical, and the occiput is smooth and rounded.

Australia

To the south, Australia has revealed evidence of entry at least 40,000 years ago. This entry poses certain problems, since Australia—unlike Java and other southeast Asian islands—was never connected to the mainland. Australia and New Guinea occupy a separate tectonic plate and are separated from the rest of Asia by deep water. Therefore, early humans needed some sort of watercraft to enter Australia.

Archeological evidence of human occupation at Lake Mungo, New South Wales, dates to 32,750 B.P. (Bowler, Thorne, and Polack, 1972). Table 9-7 shows that a number of sites in Australia date to between 20,000 and 32,000 years ago.

A cremated and very fragmented human skeleton has been found at Lake Mungo in levels dated to 25,500±1,000 B.P. This individual, like the Niah individual, has a fully modern appearance and shares a number of similarities with living native Australian populations. The Lake Mungo individual, a female, is significant in that it represents the earliest known cremation-burial. The individual was burned and the remaining bones

TABLE 9-7   Early sites in Australia, 20,000 to 32,000 years B.P.

SITE	DATE, YEARS B.P.	TYPE OF REMAINS	REFERENCE
Burrill Lake, NSW	20,760 ± 80	Rock shelter, charcoal	Barbetti and Allen, 1972
Nawamoyn, NT	21,450 ± 380	Rock shelter, charcoal	Mulvaney, 1969
Koonalda Cave, SA	21,900 ± 540	Cave, charcoal	Barbetti and Allen, 1972
Devil's Lair, WA	24,600 ± 800	Cave, charcoal	Dortch and Merrilees, 1973
Malangangerr, NT	24,800 ± 1600	Rock shelter, charcoal	Mulvaney, 1969
Lake Mungo 5, NSW	24,020 ± 1480	Shell midden	Barbetti and Allen, 1972
Lake Mungo 1, NSW	25,500 ± 1000	Human cremation	Barbetti and Allen, 1972
Lake Yantara, NSW	26,200 ± 1100	Hearth	Barbetti and Allen, 1972
Lake Menindee, NSW	26,300 ± 1500	Hearth	Barbetti and Allen, 1972
Kosipe, TPNG	26,450 ± 880 / 26,870 ± 590	Open site, charcoal	White et al., 1970
Lake Mungo 3, NSW	30,780 ± 520	Oven, charcoal	Barbetti and Allen, 1972
Keilor, V	31,600 ± 1100	River terrace, charcoal	Barbetti and Allen, 1972
Lake Mungo 2, NSW	32,750 ± 1250	Unionid shell	Barbetti and Allen, 1972

Abbreviations: NSW = New South Wales; NT = Northern Territory; SA = South Australia; TPNG = Territory of Papua and New Guinea; V = Victoria; WA = Western Australia.

Source: Data adapted from R. Jones, 1973.

were broken and buried in a small, rounded depression (Bowler et al., 1972).

At Kow Swamp in the state of Victoria, a different morphological pattern is demonstrated. Over 40 burials have been recovered from the site, dating to 10,070±250 B.P. (Thorne and Macumber, 1972).

These skulls show a remarkable morphological pattern: they are long and low with retreating foreheads, large brow ridges, strong occipital angulation, prognathous faces, and thickened skull bones (Figure 9-13). The best interpretation is that the Kow Swamp population represents a group whose gene pool had remained relatively unchanged since Middle Pleistocene times.

The two populations of Kow Swamp and Solo form an interesting puzzle. Both groups show a pattern of morphology very similar to that of

FIGURE 9-13   Skull of Kow Swamp 5, dated to about 10,000 years ago. Note the sloping forehead, large brow ridges, and facial prognathism. These are characteristics of more archaic *Homo sapiens* which had disappeared from other areas of the world by this date. (Photograph courtesy of A. Thorne.)

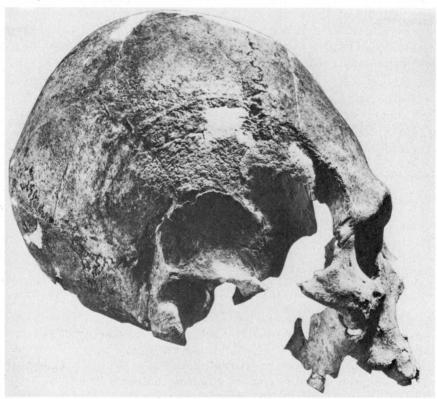

Homo erectus long after this pattern had apparently disappeared in other parts of the world. One possible interpretation is that this pattern represents the effects of long-term isolation from other human populations that were moving toward a more sapient morphology. It is indeed logical that such isolation may have occurred in these areas. Java would have been periodically cut off by high sea levels from the rest of southeast Asia. Middle Pleistocene populations there could have continued, relatively unchanged, until the sea-level regressions of the Early Würm reestablished contact. Similarly, immigrations into Australia may have been very rare in the Upper Pleistocene. The necessity of watercraft probably meant that only a very few groups crossed the 50 or so miles of open water between Australia and its nearest neighbor on the other side of the tectonic plate. In an area as vast as Australia, contact between groups may have been a rare event and gene pools may have continued more-or-less in isolation. This situation in itself is an adequate demonstration of the dangers in correlating time and morphology. If we did not have the absolute radiocarbon dates for Lake Mungo and Kow Swamp, morphological dating would demand that these groups be reversed in time.

THE NEW WORLD

The evidence, then, indicates that *Homo sapiens* populations clearly existed in widely spaced areas of the Old World by about 40,000 years ago. Early evidence of the existence of *Homo sapiens* is also found in the New World. Although there are numerous hominid and archeological sites that may date to between 20,000 and 40,000 years ago, various problems are connected with the acceptance of these early dates.

First, few New World sites dating to early periods have been excavated under controlled conditions. Consequently, the antiquity of many remains was not recognized until years after their discovery, when both archeological and geological contexts had been lost. Second, many finds are too fragmentary or too old for radiocarbon dating. Therefore, many of the early dates for the New World have been obtained with the relatively new technique of amino acid racemization. Although the newness of this technique has not limited the acceptance of amino acid dates for the Old World, such dates for the New World are inexplicably controversial.

The most complete skull of an early hominid from the New World has been recovered from Del Mar, near San Diego in California (Figure 9-14). It has been dated by amino acid racemization to 48,000 years ago (Bada et al., 1974). The morphology of this skull is like that of early Upper Pleistocene *Homo sapiens* from Africa and western Asia. It has facial prognathism, moderate brow ridges, and a low, sloping forehead. It is closer to the archaic *sapiens* than to more modern groups.

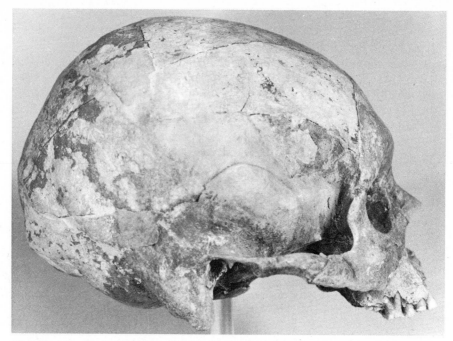

FIGURE 9-14 Skull of Del Mar. This skull, found on the coast of southern California, has been dated to 48,000 years B.P. by amino acid racemization. Although this early date has not yet been confirmed by other dating methods, the long, low shape of the skull and the prognathic profile are unlike most later California Indians. (Photograph courtesy of J. Austin and the San Diego Museum of Man.)

SUMMARY

After the long morphological stasis of the Middle Pleistocene, human evolution entered another vigorous phase which culminated in the Upper Pleistocene. Beginning with the Third Interglacial, the morphological pattern of *Homo erectus* began disappearing and patterns closer to those of modern humans started to appear.

By the middle of the Third Interglacial, two hominine morphological patterns had been established. One, a more conservative line, is termed "Neandertal." By early in the Fourth Glacial, the classic Neandertals had achieved a very distinctive, even exaggerated, morphological pattern. Although most common in western Europe, they are also found in north Africa and southwest Asia. The Neandertals preserve many features, such as thickened bones, occipito-mastoid crest, small, inwardly projecting mastoid, and great occipital breadth, that are found in earlier *Homo erectus* populations. These characteristics indicate that the Neandertals were a very conservative group, retaining many primitive traits. The full extent of their similarity (or dissimilarity) with *Homo erectus* is not known because our knowledge of the earlier species is incomplete.

The second major group to appear within the early Upper Pleistocene was more progressive and closer to the morphological pattern of modern humans. The archaic *Homo sapiens* of the Third Interglacial gave way to anatomically modern sapient populations beginning by 40,000 years ago, when they existed in widely scattered areas of the Old World and perhaps had even entered the New World.

The classification of the Neandertals and the sapient groups of more modern appearance has long proved troublesome and the issue is not yet resolved. The morphological distinctiveness and apparent primitiveness of both the early and classic Neandertals argue strongly for placement in a separate species. Yet, there is evidence that they may have interbred with the anatomically modern groups. Both their brain size and structure and the evidence of their cultural remains suggest that the Neandertals had intellectual abilities equal to those of groups much more modern in overall appearance.

For these reasons, the Neandertals are most often regarded as a subspecies of *Homo sapiens, H.s.neandertalensis.*

SUGGESTIONS FOR FURTHER READING

Garrod, D., and D. Bate. 1937. *The Stone Age of Mount Carmel. Vol. 1; Excavations at the Wady el Mughara.* Oxford, England: Clarendon.

Howell, F. C. 1952. "Pleistocene Glacial Ecology and the Evolution of 'Classic' Neandertal Man," *Southwestern Journal of Anthropology,* **8,** 377–410. (A fine, useful paper which examines the ecological conditions experienced by human populations in the Fourth Glacial.)

Howell, F. C. 1957. "Evolutionary Significance of Variation and Varieties of 'Neanderthal Man'," *Quarterly Review of Biology,* **32,** 330–347. (This paper outlines Howell's hypothesis of cold adaptation-isolation in the production of the Neandertal morphology. The entire volume commemorates the hundredth anniversary of the discovery of "Neanderthal Man" and contains a number of useful papers.)

Howells, W. W. 1974. "Neanderthals: Names, Hypotheses and Scientific Method," *American Anthropologist,* **76,** 24–38. (This short, interesting paper contains some useful ideas on the morphology, classification, and evolution of the Neandertals.)

Marshack, A. 1972. *The Roots of Civilization,* New York: McGraw-Hill. (This beautifully produced book deals with the earliest evidence of human artistic activities.)

McCown, T., and A. Keith. 1939. *The Stone Age of Mount Carmel, Vol. 2; The Fossil Human Remains from the Levalloiso-Mousterian.* Oxford, England: Clarendon. (This volume, together with that by Garrod and Bate (1937), constitutes a fine interdisciplinary approach to the study of the important hominid sites on Mount Carmel.)

Suzuki, H., and F. Takai. 1970. *The Amud Man and His Cave Site,* Tokyo: Keigaku Publishing Co. (An excellent interdisciplinary examination of the Amud site; contains very complete comparative data on Upper Pleistocene hominids.)

Ucko, P., and A. Rosenfeld. 1967. *Palaeolithic Cave Art,* London: World University Library. (An examination of western European cave art.)

Weidenreich, F. 1951. "The Morphology of Solo Man," *Anthropological Papers, American Museum of Natural History* 43(3), 205–290. (Like Weidenreich's examination of the Choukoutien hominids, this paper constitutes a very important contribution to the comparative and descriptive anatomy of fossil hominids.)

10

SUMMARY

The primates are among the oldest orders of mammals, and their evolution (Figure 10-1) has presented a variety of fascinating, and at times paradoxical, events and processes.

In some instances, the evolution of a primate line has proceeded slowly and visibly, and the fossil record clearly documents the small steps leading from one taxon to another. For example, the line of Eocene prosimians leading from *Pelycodus* through *Notharctus* to *Smilodectes* was one such case of phyletic gradualism. The emergence of the living gorillas from the Miocene form *Proconsul major* and the evolution of the living hylobatids from the Oligocene genus *Aeolopithecus* are other instances of the type of slow evolutionary progressions that Darwin envisioned. In other cases, however, the evolution of a group of primates may have proceeded relatively rapidly. Because of the speed of such evolution, there are fewer intermediate forms to be preserved in the fossil record. The family Hominidae may provide a case in point. The hominids were originally forest dwellers or forest-fringe dwellers, but near the end of the Miocene they moved into grassland habitats. With this move they underwent a period of rapid evolutionary change and diversification. Such punctuated equilibria, resulting in the rapid appearance of a number of new forms in the fossil record, often occur when a group occupies a new habitat.

409

410

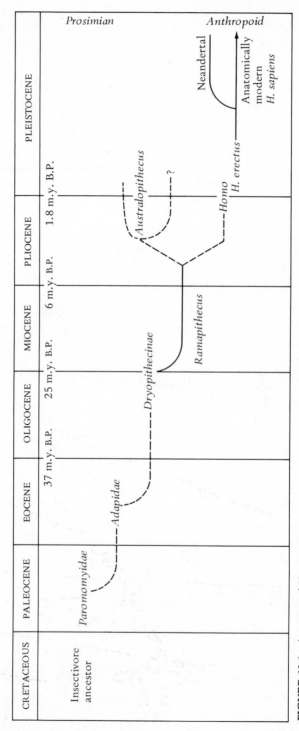

FIGURE 10.1 Ancestry of *Homo sapiens*.

When viewed in the long time perspective of the Cenozoic and in comparison with many other mammalian orders, the evolution of the primates has been very conservative. Despite the fact that they have radiated widely and entered a variety of habitats, most primates are morphologically quite generalized. They retain the clavicle, unfused lower limb bones, and five-rayed hands and feet of the earliest land mammals. This conservatism is one of the most interesting and significant facets of primate evolution: Radiation and adaptation have occurred without true morphological specialization. This pattern is quite unlike the evolutionary patterns of other animal groups where geographic radiation and adaptation are almost always accompanied by morphological specializations.

Yet, a few primates, while retaining this underlying generalized morphology, show fascinating patterns of more specialized morphology. Among the prosimians, the long-fingered, insect-grubbing aye-aye (genus *Daubentonia*) is an example. The brachiating "biped" of the Late Miocene, *Oreopithecus*, and the dramatically named *Gigantopithecus* are others. The hominids too show an unusual pattern of specializations. The most important of these specializations involve the neurological and locomotor systems. The first permits a high degree of intermodel linkages that result in complex language, memory, planning, initiative, and learning abilities. The second involves an almost unique locomotor system that has resulted in morphological changes throughout the body.

The conservatism typical of most primates is somewhat paradoxical in view of the antiquity of the order. The first primates, contemporaries of the dinosaurs, began to diverge from their insectivore ancestors late in the Cretaceous.

The Late Cretaceous was a time of far-reaching changes in both the plant and animal kingdoms. Many animal groups, including the dinosaurs, disappeared from the fossil record at this time. In the plant world, the formerly dominant ferns and cycads, occupants of warm, moist places, gave way to angiosperms, more tolerant of cooler and drier conditions. The radiation of the angiosperms was, in fact, one of the outstanding events of the Late Cretaceous; this radiation resulted in the development of the forest ecosystems which have become a major feature of the Cenozoic landscape. A number of animals moved into the expanding forests during the Late Cretaceous, and among them were the primates.

The earliest primates, members of the family Paromomyidae, show a pattern of dental changes away from that of their insectivore ancestors. Insectivores depend on sharp teeth at the front of the mouth to immobilize and pierce their prey quickly. The paromomyid primates show a reduction of the anterior teeth and an expansion of the chewing surfaces of the cheek teeth. This change would indicate that piercing and shearing actions were far less important in early primate feeding patterns than were chewing and grinding. Thus, the emergence of the first primates seems to reflect a dietary shift away from insectivory toward herbivory.

The origin of the primates demonstrates an example of the feedback and "initial kick" models discussed in Chapter 1. In a feedback model, evolution is viewed as both a cause and an effect mechanism. Thus, to ensure survival, a change on one level of organization (the genetic, for example) may necessitate, and even demand, complementary changes on other levels (such as the social or behavioral). The "initial kick" is any change that distorts or disrupts a population's equilibrium within its environment. Thus, the "initial kick" is an event (genetic mutation, behavioral change, or environmental shift) that sets the stage for a new pattern of evolutionary interactions.

The expanding angiosperm forests of the Late Cretaceous provided an evolutionary opportunity (an "initial kick") for animals that could make their living in the trees; the primates were among those that accepted the challenge.

It can, in fact, be argued that the major features of primate anatomy are related to their early success in the trees. For example, rapid, agile movement through the multiple strata of the trees is enhanced by stereoscopic vision, which provides depth perception. Swift and accurate movement in the trees is additionally facilitated, not only by acute vision, but also by grasping, flexible hands and feet. Survival is further enhanced by mental processes that permit a high degree of curiosity and exploration of the habitat. When such mental processes are part of the full intellectual pattern of learning, the result is a broad range of adaptive capabilities and responses.

During the Eocene, the primates extended their range into most of the major land areas: Europe, Asia, North America, and Africa all have evidence of primates at this time. Several new types of primates appeared, including the first lemur-like and tarsier-like forms, and, late in the Eocene, the first anthropoids or higher primates. It seems most likely that the anthropoids were derived from one of the lemur-like groups, possibly within the Adapidae. Although we are not sure exactly where this evolutionary change occurred, we do know that in many areas during the Late Eocene, temperatures declined and formerly reliable and persistent water sources showed seasonal drying. Such increased seasonality may have placed a premium, not on morphological specialization, but on flexible, adaptable behavior patterns which permitted a wide range of responses in diet, locomotion, selection of nesting places, etc. This possibility supports the concept that the major thrust of primate evolution has rested on increasing morphological and behavioral adaptability and laterality of response.

By Oligocene times, the suborder Anthropoidea had experienced considerable divergence. Although virtually all knowledge of Oligocene primates is based on a single site, at Fayum in Egypt, nevertheless their diversity, particularly among the hominoids or great apes, is remarkable. One Egyptian Oligocene genus, *Aeolopithecus*, may have provided the ancestral stock for the gibbons; another genus, *Aegyptopithecus*, may have supplied the ancestral stock for the very widespread dryopithecines of the Miocene. A third genus, *Apidium*, may be ancestral to the "swamp ape" *Oreopithecus* of the European Miocene.

The dryopithecines are, in fact, one of the most interesting and far-flung groups of Miocene mammals. One genus of this group, *Proconsul*, first appeared in east Africa in the Early Miocene. Since Africa was still separated from the rest of the world at this time, we can safely assume an African origin for the group. By about 16 m.y. ago, however, the African continental plate joined with the Eurasian plate, and the dryopithecines left to colonize many parts of the Old World.

By Middle Miocene times, these hominoids were very widespread, but although they entered a variety of habitats in both tropical and temperate areas of the Old World, they did not become morphologically specialized. Therefore, although some splitting and diversification did occur, the conservatism of their morphological evolution is remarkable.

In order to understand the genesis of their diversification, we must look again to the environment. The drying and cooling trends of the earlier Tertiary continued unabated into the Miocene. By the Middle Miocene the forests, once continuous over much of the earth's surface, had broken up, and grassland areas began to expand. Like the angiosperm forests of the Late Cretaceous, the grasslands of the Middle Miocene provided new opportunities for evolution. Moreover, the diminution of the forests placed a greater premium on that space, increasing competition for its progressively limited resources. This competition may itself have provided the stimulus (or "initial kick") for further evolution in the great apes. Some apes, for example, may have begun exploiting the higher portions of the trees; others, the lower branches. Still other primates, losers in the competition for the trees, may have moved onto the forest floor. Such actions would serve to lessen the increasing competition for ecological space which must have existed at that time.

Out of this situation of decreasing forests and increasing grasslands, at least two new forms of primate emerged to make adaptations to the savannas. One was *Gigantopithecus* from the Middle and later Miocene of northern India. This genus had broad, flat cheek teeth, indicating the exploitation of a harsh vegetarian diet. Even the canines, long and pointed in most primates, were flattened and incorporated into the chewing apparatus in this genus. So successful was its adaptation that it survived at least until the Middle Pleistocene, with no apparent evidence of change.

The earliest hominids, the genus *Ramapithecus*, also emerged from the competitive pressures of the Middle Miocene forests. The remains of these hominids are found in deposits indicating that they lived near the margin between the forest and the grassland. Not only would the competitive pressures have been intense in this limited space, but also, in such a diversified mosaic environment, the selective pressures for flexible, innovative behavior patterns would have been high. Like *Gigantopithecus*, *Ramapithecus* also showed dental adaptations to a coarse, hard, or fibrous diet.

By late in the Middle Miocene, *Ramapithecus* could be found in Africa, Europe, India, and Asia. Yet, again, little morphological diversity is apparent. However, by the Late Miocene or Early Pliocene, the ramapithecines had moved into full grassland habitats and a period of rapid evolutionary diversification followed. By 2 m.y. to 3 m.y. ago, a variety of hominids is evident in the fossil record. One group, the genus *Australopithecus*, contains a variety of diverse forms. Some, particularly in east Africa, were very large and were characterized by large, flat molars, reduced anterior dentition, and sagittal crests for the large chewing muscles. Some of the South African australopithecines showed this same pattern but were less robust. Still others, from both east and South Africa, were very small and gracile without the extreme dental characters. All were bipedal. The australopithecines probably maintained much the same dietary pattern as the ramapithecines; that is, mainly fruits, grasses, and seeds, with perhaps small amounts of scavenged or hunted meats.

The other group to appear at this time, the genus *Homo*, contains the direct ancestors of the modern human. This group showed a progressive decrease in size of the whole dental apparatus, increased brain size, and growing dependence on tools. While vegetable foods still formed part of the diet in *Homo*, meat, especially hunted meat, took on an importance not encountered elsewhere among the primates. As pointed out earlier, the regular consumption of hunted meat provided another example of the feedback process. In fact, it can be argued that the increasing importance of meat in the diet of one line of early hominids may have provided the "initial kick" for the emergence of the group we now call *Homo*.

The particular feedback mechanism involved here has already been discussed in detail. It involves cooperation, food sharing, use of a home base, and cultural accessories, including container objects and tools for butchery. Behavioral evolution makes a particularly important contribution to this feedback system in that large and dangerous animals may have been killed, not through close physical contact with spears or knives, but through drives or traps. The selective pressures for increased intellectual and learning capabilities are obvious here. Consumers of seeds and grasses do not wage an intellectual or a dangerous battle with their food; hunters do.

The origin of hominid bipedality and its relationship to this feedback system are unclear. Since both forms of Plio-Pleistocene hominid, *Australopithecus* and *Homo*, demonstrate this rare and almost unique locomotor pattern, we can assume that it was part of the morphological pattern inherited from their common ancestor. In order for bipedality to have been selected for (as indeed it obviously was), it must have increased survival in some way. But why become bipedal at all? It makes balance more precarious, exposes the ventral organs to attack, and reduces maximum speed. Some anthropologists have suggested that bipedality improves carrying ability. The Koshima macaques assume a bipedal position to carry several food items; to transport only a single item, they carry it in their mouths or hold it in one hand and move tripedally. Carrying tools does not seem to have been important for the earliest hominids, however. The earliest stone tools do not appear until about 2.5 m.y. ago, more than a million years after the first evidence of hominid bipedality. Moreover, the earliest known tools were not offensive or defensive weapons that indeed could have increased survival but were, instead, small chips of stone used in butchering. Missiles, spears, blunt objects, and knives date to later periods and are usually carried singly anyway. Carrying infants is another possibility, but, mechanically, babies fit into the single-object category. The origin of one of the human's most unique features—bipedality—thus remains an enigma.

The fossil record indicates that the two lines of hominid had coexisted for at least 1 m.y. (from 2 m.y. to 1 m.y. ago) and perhaps for much longer. But, by 1 m.y. ago, the genus *Australopithecus* disappeared from the fossil record; only *Homo*, now in the form of *Homo erectus*, survived. By at least 1.5 m.y. ago, members of the genus *Homo* had left Africa, and by at least 1.3 m.y. ago, they had arrived in the Far East.

In the Middle Pleistocene, a period of evolutionary stasis again occurred, and the crazy-quilt variability of the Plio-Pleistocene is no longer evident. Changes and variability occurred in *Homo erectus*, but all populations seem to have been remarkably alike until around the last interglacial. At about this time or perhaps a little earlier, evolution made another move forward and the human line bifurcated again. One line conservatively retained much of the *Homo erectus* morphology while developing a few progressive features, such as a larger brain and a more complex cultural pattern. This lineage consisted of the Neandertals. Their center of distribution appears to have been western Europe, but they are also known from north Africa and western Asia as well.

The other line went through a phase of more active evolution and developed a morphology, cranially and postcranially, much like modern humans. The earliest hominids of nearly modern type are known from Ethiopia and date to about 130,000 years ago. By 40,000 to 50,000 years ago, anatomically modern humans were very widespread and had possibly entered the New World. By at least 30,000 years ago, modern humans had reached western Europe; although the Neandertals hung on in some areas until about 20,000 years ago, they were no longer the dominant population in western Europe.

The physical and morphological differences between *Homo erectus* and

Homo sapiens are present and identifiable, but they appear to be minimally important to survival. No individual features, or even group of features, can be singled out as having provided improved adaptive fitness for *Homo sapiens*. Efficient locomotor capability, efficient eye-hand coordination, and advanced brain structure are all long-standing characters of the Hominidae; they are not special features of the sapiens. Yet, *Homo erectus* with its distinctive morphology gave way to *Homo sapiens*. If it was not morphological improvement that permitted sapient dominance, then it must have been the acquisition of superior behavioral characteristics. Behavior does not enter the fossil record except indirectly and incompletely, and we can only guess at the behavioral adaptations and modifications which allowed *Homo sapiens* to cope and survive in larger numbers than *Homo erectus*. Perhaps it was better technology (although this is not apparent in the record of the early sapiens), perhaps it was more stable group structure, or better cooperation and acknowledgment of interdependencies which permitted *Homo sapiens* to replace *Homo erectus*.

In the final analysis, the practice of paleoanthropology, as in other sciences, relies on the available evidence. Unlike other scientists, however, paleoanthropologists, paleontologists, and archeologists have access to only part of the total original information. The limitations of the fossil record mean that we cannot play our scientific game with a full deck. We judge cultures only by their imperishable remains; and we judge breathing, moving, functioning, and behaving organisms only by their bones and teeth. Thus, the models we build of organisms and environments and behaviors of the past are based in part on induction, in part on deduction and, to be honest, in part on intuition. While one hopes that the third process is firmly based on the first two logical ones, one knows that is not always so. Nevertheless, the reconstruction of the human past presented here seems to fit well with the available empirical evidence. Only further discoveries and analyses will determine its correctness.

APPENDIX:
DATING TECHNIQUES

The ability to date specimens is vital in evolutionary studies. Knowledge of temporal relationships of material under study is a prerequisite to understanding the phylogenetic relationships of fossils and eventually reconstructing a group's history and emergence. This appendix deals with the most common dating techniques. It divides them into two categories: (1) absolute dating techniques, which result in dates in years; and (2) relative dating techniques, which place specimens in relation to one another.

ABSOLUTE DATING TECHNIQUES

With absolute dating techniques, an absolute age, in years, is obtained. These methods are sometimes called "chronometric techniques."

RADIOCARBON (CARBON^{14}), CONVENTIONAL METHOD

A small fraction of the normal carbon, C^{12}, in living organisms is "heavy" carbon, carbon^{14} (or C^{14}). This radioactive isotope decays at a regular rate. One-half the C^{14} in a sample decays in 5730 years; this period is termed its "half-life." Reducing the organic sample to a gas (usually CO_2) and counting the beta emissions with a gas proportional counter will indicate the amount of C^{14} remaining. The remaining or undecayed amount of C^{14} will give an indication of the years elapsed since the death of the organism. A "dead" sample (one with no remaining C^{14}) is older than the 50,000 to 70,000 years covered by this method.

417

Material Used   Organic materials, such as bone collagen, charcoal, wood, and peat, can be dated with this technique. Carbonates, such as shells, caliche, calcitic travertines, and calcite tufas can also be dated; but because of their increased susceptibility to contamination or for other geochemical reasons, they may yield unrelia' .e dates.

Period   Ages from 0 to 50,000 years can be radiocarbon-dated. Isotopic enrichment may extend this period to 70,000 years (Haring et al., 1958).

Advantages   This technique permits direct dating of organic materials.

Disadvantages   Contamination of samples with "newer" carbon may occur in a variety of ways: wrapping specimens in paper, using preservatives with an organic base, percolation of groundwaters, exchange reactions, roots, etc. The amount of organic material required for dating depends on the size of the counters used; several grams of charcoal, wood, or bone may be needed. In practice, often an entire long bone, such as a femur or tibia, is destroyed in producing the CO_2 gas.

Terminology   Two conventions are used in writing radiocarbon dates. First, carbon[14] dates are followed by "B.P." (before present). The "present" is conventionally determined as 1950. Second, all radiocarbon dates are followed by the name of the laboratory where the date was determined and by the number of the run: thus, GrN - 2203 is the number of the Groningen laboratory run which determined the radiocarbon age of the Piltdown skull (620 $\mp$ 100 B.P.). Other laboratory codes are: LJ = La Jolla; C = Chicago; Y = Yale; abbreviations for other labs are found in issues of *Radiocarbon* (see References below).

References

American Journal of Science. *Radiocarbon.* Published annually and listing all radiocarbon dates determined for each year, beginning in 1959.

Haring, A., A. E. DeVries, and H. DeVries. 1958. "Radiocarbon Dating Up to 70,000 Years with Isotopic Enrichment," *Science,* **128,** 472–473.

Libby, W. 1955. *Radiocarbon Dating* (2d ed.). Chicago: University of Chicago Press.

Olsson, I. U. (ed.). 1970. *Radiocarbon Variations and Absolute Chronology,* 12th Nobel Symposium. New York: Wiley.

RADIOCARBON, DIRECT METHOD

This is a new method of radiocarbon dating which attempts to measure directly the ratio of carbon[14] to carbon[12]. A cyclotron or other linear accelerator is used as a mass spectrometer to determine the gas ratios.

Material Used   The same as that used for the conventional method.

Period   40,000 to 100,000 years.

Advantages   Much smaller amounts of materials are required than in the conventional method: 1 to 100 mg versus several grams in the conventional method. The direct method is potentially more accurate and covers a greater time span.

Disadvantages   The material may undergo possible contamination with N^{14}, which is very similar to the C^{14} atom (Nelson et al., 1977, report that they have solved this problem).

References

Bennett, C. L., R. P. Beukens, M. R. Clover, H. E. Gove, R. B. Liebert, A. E. Litherland, K. H. Purser, and W. E. Sondheim. 1977. "Radiocarbon Dating Using Electrostatic Accelerators: Negative Ions Provide the Key," *Science*, **198,** 508–510.
Muller, R. A. 1977. "Radioisotopic Dating with a Cyclotron," *Science*, **196,** 489–494.
Nelson, D. E., R. G. Korteling, and W. R. Stott. 1977. "Carbon-14: Direct Detection at Natural Concentrations," *Science*, **198,** 507–508.

POTASSIUM-ARGON (K/A)

The isotope potassium^{40} (K^{40}) decays to its daughter isotope A^{40}; this method determines the ratio of these two isotopes in a mass spectrometer.

Material Used   Suitable materials include potassium-bearing rocks, such as igneous or once-molten forms like lava and tuffs; sedimentary rocks, such as glauconite or clays.

Period   The half-life of K^{40} is very long (1.3 billion years). In practice, samples less than 0.5 m.y. cannot be dated unless they are very rich in potassium (such as sanidine and leucite). In theory, potassium-rich samples as young as 5000 years can be dated with this method. The maximum period is the age of the earth.

Advantages   This method is useful over a long time span.

Disadvantages   A prime assumption of this method is that no argon^{40} (or only negligible amounts) existed in the sample originally and that all A^{40} is the result of natural decay. A number of geological processes and events can, however, upset or distort the amount of argon. Later thermal events which reheat the rocks may result in argon loss; such "overprinting" can give an anomalously young date. Inclusion of extraneous argon from surrounding rocks can add argon, thus increasing the apparent age of the deposit.

References

Brown, F. H. 1972. "Radiometric Dating of Sedimentary Formations in the Lower Omo Valley, Ethiopia," in W. W. Bishop and J. A. Miller (eds.), *Calibration of Hominoid Evolution*. Edinburgh: Scottish Academic Press. Pp. 273–287.

Dalrymple, G. E., and M. A. Lanphere (eds.). *Potassium-Argon Dating*. San Francisco: Freeman.

Fitch, F. J. 1972. "Selection of Suitable Material for Dating and the Assessment of Geological Error in Potassium-Argon Determinations," in W. W. Bishop and J. A. Miller (eds.), *Calibration of Hominoid Evolution*. Edinburgh: Scottish Academic Press. Pp. 77–92.

ARGON^{40}–ARGON^{39} (A^{40}/A^{39})

Argon^{39} is produced by potassium^{39} during neutron irradiation in the laboratory. The amount of this artificially produced isotope is then compared with the amount of argon-40 produced during natural isotopic decay. In A^{40}/A^{39} age-spectrum analysis, the irradiated sample is heated in increments and the isotopic content of the gas is analyzed at each increment with a mass spectrometer. This method is useful in evaluating samples which may have been contaminated during their geologic history. The step heating allows the "newer" argon to be released first, leaving the older original argon, which will be released by higher temperatures.

Material Used   Same as in K/A dating.

Period   Same as in K/A dating.

Advantages   This method requires a very small amount of material, and it can be used on minerals with low potassium content. It can detect both argon loss and the presence of exotic elements in the sample.

Disadvantages   The method is still new and unexplained, anomalous dates have occasionally been obtained.

References

Curtis, G. H., T. Drake, T. Cerling, and Hempel. 1975. "Age of KBS Tuff in Koobi Fora Formation, East Rudolf, Kenya," *Nature*, **258**, 359–398.

Fitch, F. J., and J. A. Miller. 1976. "Conventional Potassium-Argon and Argon-40/Argon-39 Dating of Volcanic Rocks from East Rudolf," in Y. Coppens, F. Howell, G. Isaac, and R. Leakey (eds.), *Earliest Man and Environments in the Lake Rudolf Basin*. Chicago: University of Chicago Press. Pp. 123–147.

Miller, J. A. 1972. "Dating Pliocene and Pleistocene Strata Using the Potassium-Argon and Argon-40/Argon-39 Methods," in W. W. Bishop and J. A. Miller (eds.), *Calibration of Hominoid Evolution*. Edinburgh: Scottish Academic Press. Pp. 63–76.

FISSION TRACK

The uranium isotope U^{238} decays through the process of spontaneous fission at the rate of 10^{16} per year. This method counts the proportion of uranium atoms which have fissioned; this proportion is related to the total uranium content, per unit, of the sample. Chemical etching of the tracks enlarges them so that they may be counted with the use of an optical microscope.

Material Used   Rocks containing U^{238}: apatite, mica, zircon, pumice, sphene, obsidian (natural glass), tektites.

Period   20 to 5 X 10^9 years.

Advantages   Laboratory techniques are simple and low in cost.

Disadvantages   The tracks may fade in certain rocks, leading to incorrect age estimates. It is assumed that uranium concentration is homogeneous throughout the rock sample; this may not always be true, thus giving an anomalous date.

References
Fleischer, R. L., and H. R. Hart, Jr. 1972. "Fission Track Dating: Techniques and Problems," in W. W. Bishop and J. A. Miller (eds.), *Calibration of Hominoid Evolution*. Edinburgh: Scottish Academic Press. Pp. 135–170.

AMINO ACID RACEMIZATION

The proteins of living organisms contain amino acids with L isomers; after death the L isomers are gradually replaced by nonprotein D isomers. This replacement process is termed "racemization." Racemization dating uses the ratio of D to L isomers to determine the years elapsed since the death of the organism. The racemization rate is temperature-dependent; therefore the rate must be calibrated for a particular site or area. This calibration is usually done through obtaining a C^{14} date and a D/L ratio on the same sample. The C^{14} date permits a rate of racemization to be calculated which is specific for a particular amino acid from a particular site. Once the rate is determined, samples outside the range of C^{14} can be dated from the same site.

Material Used   Any proteinaceous organic material may be dated with this method.

Period   Each amino acid racemizes at a different rate; therefore, each has a different period. Aspartic acid: 5,000 to 100,000 years. Isoleucine: Up to 500,000 years.

Advantages This method uses very small amounts of organic material, usually no more than a few grams. The range of applicability is potentially broad.

Disadvantages Calibration of the racemization rate is required for each site or area. It is assumed that the temperature (and therefore the reacemization rate) has been constant at a particular site; this may not always be true.

References

Bada, J. L., and P. M. Helfman. 1975. "Amino Acid Racemization Dating of Fossil Bones," *World Archeology*, **7**, 160–173.

Bada, J. L., and R. Protsch. 1973. "Racemization Reaction of Aspartic Acid and Its Use in Dating Fossil Bones," *Proceedings of the National Academy of Science, U.S.A.*, **70**, 1331–1334.

Bada, J. L., R. A. Schroeder, R. Protsch, and R. Berger. 1974. "Concordance of Collagen-Based Radiocarbon and Aspartic-Acid Racemization Ages," *Proceedings of the National Academy of Science, U.S.A.*, **71**, 914–917.

RELATIVE DATING TECHNIQUES

In relative dating techniques, objects, fossils, or sites are dated not in years but instead in relation to other objects, fossils, or sites. Thus, the resolution of relative dating methods does not extend beyond the determination that something is younger than, older than, or contemporaneous with something else.

PALEOMAGNETIC DATING

The dipolar magnetic field of the earth has undergone a number of reversals. When molten, iron compounds in rocks (usually hematite or magnetite) will align themselves parallel with the earth's magnetic field. Thus, in times of "normal" polarity these elements will align themselves with the magnetic north pole; during a "reversed" period they will become aligned with the south magnetic pole. This alignment can be determined either in the laboratory or with portable field equipment. The reversals are of irregular length. A long polarity-episode interval (1 m.y.) is termed a "polarity epoch" and is named after a particular scientist: e.g., the "Brunhes epoch." A shorter interval is termed a "polarity event" and is named after the site where it was first identified: e.g., the "Olduvai event." The determination of a polarity profile for a site will permit that site to be cross-correlated with other sites. Radiometric dating, with K/A, for example, of levels within the stratigraphic profile enhances the usefulness of such cross-correlations.

Materials Used This technique is suitable for rocks containing magnetic components which have been molten and archeological materials such as fired bricks.

Period This method can cover 0-4.5 m.y. Although evidence of field polarity remains in the rocks, the probable errors in K/A dates beyond 4.5 m.y. will exceed the length of most polarity events or epochs. Therefore, the resolution of K/A dating is insufficient for use beyond this time period.

Advantages With its time range, Paleomagnetic dating is a powerful tool for temporally cross-correlating sites. Since polarity intervals are world-wide events, geographic distance is no barrier to such correlations.

Disadvantages Without radiometric control, the polarity profiles may be ambiguous. Thus a particular pattern of reversed and normal polarities may recur within a geologic column, making correlation difficult.

References
Cox, A. 1969. "Geomagnetic Reversals," *Science,* **163,** 237–246.
Cox, A. 1972. "Geomagnetic Reversals—Their Frequency, Their Origin and Some Problems of Correlation," in W. W. Bishop and J. A. Miller (eds.), *Calibration of Hominoid Evolution.* Edinburgh: Scottish Academic Press. Pp. 93–106.
Dalrymple, G. B. 1972. "Potassium-argon Dating of Geomagnetic Reversals and North American Glaciations," in W. W. Bishop and J. A. Miller (eds.), *Calibration of Hominoid Evolution.* Edinburgh: Scottish Academic Press. Pp. 107–134.

FLUORINE DATING

Soluble fluorides are present in most groundwaters. When organic materials are buried, the fluorine ions in the groundwater are gradually absorbed, replacing the hydroxyl ions in the hydroxy-apatite which is a principal component in bone tissue. This process produces fluorapatite. Bones buried for the same length of time (the bones of a single individual, or associated fauna, or both) will have a similar amount of fluorine. This amount is usually determined by chemical methods.

Material Used Bones and teeth may be dated in this way.

Period Dating is by relative time placement.

Advantages This method provides a test of contemporaneity between bone and dental material recovered from a single site. Since the fluorapatite is very stable, it is not removed in subsequent reworking of the deposit. If reworking is suspected, the fluorapatite levels may give an indication of the original depositional site of the materials.

Disadvantages The method cannot be used to evaluate relative ages of different sites, since the soluble fluorides in groundwater vary widely from place to place.

References

Oakley, K. P. 1963. "Fluorine, Uranium and Nitrogen Dating of Bone," in E. Pyddoke (ed.), *The Scientist in Archaeology*. London: Phoenix House. Pp. 111–119.

Oakley, K. P. 1969. "Analytical Methods of Dating Bones," in D. Brothwell and E. Higgs (eds.), *Science in Archaeology*. London: Thames and Hudson. Pp. 35–45.

NITROGEN DATING

Approximately 20 percent of the collagen in bone is composed of nitrogen. After death the nitrogen is gradually lost. Local conditions will affect the rate at which the nitrogen is lost but bones buried for a similar length of time at the same site will show a similar amount of nitrogen.

Material Used Bones and teeth.

Period Relative time placement.

Advantages This method provides a test of contemporaneity for materials recovered from a single site.

Disadvantages The method cannot be used to determine relative ages of material recovered from different sites, since many local factors affect nitrogen loss.

References See the entries for fluorine dating.

URANIUM DATING

Uranium is present in small amounts in most groundwaters. As the groundwater percolates through buried organic materials, the uranium replaces the calcium ions in the hydroxy-apatite of the bones and teeth. Organic materials buried for a similar length of time in a single site will show a similar amount of uranium.

Materials Used   Bones and teeth.

Period   Relative time placement.

Advantages   No organic material is destroyed in the analysis, since the beta emissions of the material are measured with a geiger counter.

Disadvantages   This method cannot be used to determine relative ages of material recovered from different sites, since many local factors affect the rate of uranium uptake.

References   See the entries for fluorine dating.

GLOSSARY

abductor   A muscle which moves a bone away from the midline of the body.

adaptive radiation   Rapid morphological diversification of a group, usually upon entering a new habitat.

adductor   A muscle which moves a bone toward the midline of the body.

allopatric populations   Two or more populations of a species that do not live in the same geographic area.

alveolar prognathism   Projection of the tooth-bearing portions of the jaws.

analogous structures   Features that are similar in function and superficial form in different organisms but that differ in their origin. Example: the wings of insects, birds, and bats.

anterior   Situated in front of the midline; toward the front or ventral surface.

anthropoidea   A suborder of the primates containing monkeys, apes, and humans.

arboreal theory   A theory of primate origins stating that the major distinctive primate features evolved in response to the pressures of living in trees.

auditory bulla   An expanded, bubble-like part of the primate temporal bone containing the structures of the middle ear.

B.P   Before the present time (literally "before present"); a notation conventionally given with radiometric dates, in which "the present" is considered to be 1950.

bilophodont   A condition of the molar teeth of the Old World monkeys. The two mesial cusps (protocone and paracone) are joined by a ridge or loph; the two distal cusps (metacone and hyponone) are similarly joined by a ridge.

binomial   Literally, "two names." The classificatory system devised by Linnaeus in which an organism is designated by a genus and species name; e.g., *Homo sapiens*, *Australopithecus africanus*. By convention, Linnaean binomials are italicized or underlined.

426

bipedal Locomotor function or habit involving only the hind limbs.

bovid A member of the family Bovidae (within the Artiodactyla) containing such forms as cows, sheep, and bison.

buccal The cheek side (of a tooth, for example).

brachiation Locomotor function or habit involving the upper limbs in a swinging, arm-over-arm progression.

bunodont Tooth cusp, particularly on the molars, that is low and rounded.

calotte The skullcap without the face or basal portions.

calvarium The skull and face.

carpal One of the eight bones of the wrist.

ceboidea A primate superfamily containing the New World monkeys.

cenozoic Geologic era comprising the Paleocene through the Recant; it began about 70 m.y. ago. Also called the "Age of Mammals."

cercopithecoidea A superfamily of the primates containing the Old World monkeys.

cingulum A rim or ridge of enamel on the teeth below the occlusal surface. It may be on the inner side (lingual cingulum) or outer side (buccal cingulum), or it may completely surround the tooth. (Plural, "cingula.")

convergent evolution Similar evolutionary histories in animals that are not closely related. Example: dolphins (mammals) and sharks (chondrichthyes).

coronal suture A major suture or division in the prosimian brain. It runs lengthwise (fore and aft) along both front sides of the brain. It does not occur in the anthropoid brain, which has a crosswise or central suture. The term also applies to a suture in the bones of the skull. It runs from side to side between the frontal and parietal bones.

cortex An anatomical term meaning the outer layer of a structure. In the long bones, the cortex is the dense outer tube of bone; the brain cortex is the gray matter covering the cerebral hemispheres.

crenulation Occlusal surfaces of teeth (usually the molars) which are wrinkled, as in orangs and in some australopithecines.

deciduous dentition The milk teeth, conventionally identified by a small "d"; for example, dm_1 designates the deciduous first lower molar.

dendrite A long, thread-like body which transmits a nerve impulse toward the nerve cell.

dental formula A convention used to describe the numbers of different kinds of teeth in each half of the jaw. For example, 2123 means 2 incisors, 1 canine, 2 premolars, and 3 molars.

diastema A gap in the tooth row; in the primate upper jaw, it is between the I^2 and the C^-; in the lower jaw, it is between the C. and P_3.

distal In a limb, the part that is away or farthest from the trunk; in a tooth, the part that is away from the front of the mouth.

ectotympanic A small plate of bone which, in tarsiers and the higher primates, forms the external auditory tube.

foramen magnum A large hole in the base of the skull through which the spinal cord passes. In quadrupeds, it is placed at the rear of the skull; in bipeds, near the center of the skull.

founder effect Result occurring when populations split or fragment, so that a new local group contains a random distribution of the gene frequencies of the parent group and may therefore differ significantly from it.

generalized   The condition of an organism or a body part not showing specialized adaptations for a particular function or habitat.

genetic drift   Random or chance changes in a gene pool, of minimal importance in large populations, but possibly having a marked effect on small, isolated gene pools.

graminovorous   Having a dietary practice of eating grains, seeds, or other small, hard objects. (Also termed "granivorous.")

hallux   The big toe.

heteromorphic   Having different or variable form, as in heteromorphic premolars (one premolar sectorial, one premolar bicusped).

hominidae   Primate family containing humans and their close ancestors (*Ramapithecus, Australopithecus, Homo erectus*). The corresponding adjective or noun is "hominid."

hominine   Member of the genus *Homo* (*H. erectus, H. sapiens*).

hominoidea   Primate superfamily containing the great apes, humans, and fossils. The corresponding adjective or noun is "hominoid."

homologous structures   Features that have a similar evolutionary development and history. They may or may not have a similar function. Example: the wing of a bird and the arm of a human.

homomorphy   Similarity in form, as in the homomorphic (identical) premolars of *Homo sapiens*.

illium   The largest bone in the pelvis; it is rounded and tightly curved in hominids, long and blade-like in other primates.

inferior   That portion of a bone or body part farthest from the head.

in situ   Literally, "in place." In paleoanthropology, it refers to a bone, artifact, or other material which was found where it had originally been deposited.

interglacial   A warm period between two glacial periods; for example, the Riss/Würm (or Third) Interglacial.

interstadial   A warmer period within a glacial period; for example, the Würm I/II Interstadial.

ischium   A small bone of the pelvis placed beneath and behind the hip joint. In some primates, such as baboons, it supports the ischial callosities.

lateral   Situated away from the midline of the body.

lingual   The tongue side—of a tooth, for example.

m.y   Million years.

mandible   The lower jaw.

maxilla   The upper jaw.

medial   Placed toward the midline of the body.

mesial   In a tooth, the part toward the front of the mouth.

mesozoic   Geologic era lasting from c. 200 m.y. ago to 70 m.y. ago; often called the "Age of Reptiles."

metacarpal   One of the five long bones in the hand between the wrist bones (the carpals) and the finger bones (the phalanges).

metatarsal   One of the five long bones in the foot between the ankle region and the toes.

molariform   Having the shape or form of a molar; a grinding tooth with several cusps. The premolars of the robust australopithecines and *Gigantopithecus* were molariform.

monophyletic Having a single line of descent.

neoteny The rentetion of fetal or juvenile features in the adult form. A possible explanation for some hominid characteristics.

neuron A nerve cell.

nuchal Literally, the "neck." Often used to indicate the place, on the rear of the skull, where the neck muscles attach. The nuchal crest is a horizontal bar of bone raised on the skull of some *Homo erectus* individuals where very large neck muscles attached.

opposability The ability of the thumb to rotate so that its pulp surface can meet the pulp surface of one or more of the fingers.

orthognathous Literally, "straight-jawed." A straight or flat face without protrusion of the jaws.

paleoencephalon Phylogenetically, the oldest part of the brain.

palynology The study of fossil pollen and plant spores; used to reconstruct past environments.

parallel evolution Similar evolutionary histories in animals that are closely related. Example: New World and Old World monkeys.

petrosal bulla An expanded area in the petrous portion of the temporal bone which, in primates, contains the structures of the middle ear. A definitive characteristic of the primates; also called the "auditory bulla."

phalange One of the small bones of the fingers or toes.

pharynx The tube connecting the nose and mouth with the gastric tube; it contains the speech organs.

phenotype The visible expression of the genes; the appearance of an organism.

phyletic gradualism A type of evolutionary progression where one species gradually evolves or emerges from another; the type of evolution originally described by Darwin. No splitting of lineages is involved.

phylogenetic The evolutionary relationships between organisms.

platycephalic Literally, "flat-headed," the term refers to a skull shape in which the forehead and vault are low.

pollex The thumb.

polyphyletic Descending from more than one ancestral line, as an animal group whose ancestry is found in two or more groups.

Pongidae Primate family containing the great apes (chimps, gorillas, and orangs), living and fossil.

postorbital Bony encircling enclosure of the eye. In primates the encirclement has been accomplished by the downward expansion of the frontal and upward expansion of the zygomatic (also called the "malar") bones.

postorbital plate Enclosure of the eye behind the postorbital bar. In primates, this plate has been formed by expansion of the zygomatic, alisphenoid, and frontal bones.

posterior Situated behind the midline; toward the back or dorsal surface.

prehensile Having the ability to grasp objects. All primates have a prehensile hand; some, such as most New World monkeys, have a prehensile tail.

prognathous Protruding, as of the jaws.

Prosimii A suborder of the primates containing the lemurs, lorises, and tarsiers.

pubis A small bone of the pelvis, in front of and medial to the hip joint. The right and left pubes meet at the midline and form the **pubic symphysis.**

punctuated equilibrium   A mode of evolutionary progression marked by uneven rates of change. This tempo contrasts with that of **phyletic gradualism,** which has a slow and even pace.

quadrupedal   Walking on all four limbs.

Quaternary   The most recent period of the Cenozoic, containing the Pleistocene and the Holocene or Recent epochs.

ramus   Literally, "branch." For example, the mandible is characterized by a horizontal ramus which contains the teeth and a vertical or ascending ramus which articulates with the skull.

sagittal crest   A crest of bone in the midline of the skull which forms along the area of origin of the temporalis muscle. It is found in some large pongids (particulalry in males) and in some robust australopithecines.

sectorial   A single cusped, pointed tooth, such as the sectorial P_3 of most nonhuman primates. A semisectorial tooth is one with a large outer and a small inner cusp; such a tooth is found in the P_3 of some early hominids.

specialized   An organism or body part showing definite and clear-cut adaptations to a particular function or habitat.

speciation   The evolutionary development of new species.

stadial   A cold period within a glacial period. (See **Interstadial.**)

stereoscopic vision   Overlapping of the visual fields so that depth perception is produced. A characteristic of the primates.

superior   That portion of a bone or body part nearest the head.

sympatric populations   Two or more populations of a species living in a geographically contiguous or overlapping area.

symplesiomorphic characters   Shared characters which have been inherited from a common ancestral form; also called "characters of common inheritance."

synapomorphic characters   Characters developed after separation from an ancestral form: also called "characters of independent acquisition."

talon   Literally, "heel." An area of enamel developed behind the trigon in primate molars; it carries the entocone, hypocone, and hypoconule. (For lower teeth, add the suffix "id": thus, talonid, entoconid, hypoconid, hypoconulid.)

tarsal   One of the seven small bones in the ankle region.

taxon   A unit or category of classification. (Plural, "taxa.")

temporal bone   A bone of the skull containing, in primates, the middle ear structures and jaw joint.

tertiary   A period of the Cenozoic containing the Paleocene, Eocene, Oligocene, Miocene, and Pliocene.

torus   A bar or heavy ridge of bone; for example, the supraorbital torus or the nuchal torus. (Plural, "tori.")

trigon   The mesial two- or three-cusped area of primate molars inherited from the primitive mammalian ancestors; it carries the protocone, paracone, and metacone. (For lower teeth, add the suffix "id": thus, protoconid, paraconid, metaconid. The paraconid is usually absent in the higher primates.)

trochlea   A spindle-shaped area of bone which provides a smooth articular area for another bone. For example, the trochlea on the distal humerus articulates with the proximal ulna.

BIBLIOGRAPHY

Aaronson, J., T. Schmitt, R. Walter, M. Taieb, J. Tiercelin, D. Johanson, C. Naeser, and A. Nairn. 1977. "New Geochronologic and Palaeomagnetic Data for the Hominid-Bearing Hadar Formation of Ethiopia," *Nature,* **267,** 323–327.

Aguirre, E. 1970. "Identificacíon de 'Paranthropus' en Makapansgat," *Crónica del XI Congreso Nacional de Arqueología, Mérida* (Mexico), 1969. Pp. 98–124.

Alexandersen, V. 1967. "The Pathology of the Jaws and the Temporomandibular Joint," in D. R. Brothwell and A. T. Sandison, (eds.), *Diseases in Antiquity.* Springfield, Ill.: Charles C. Thomas. Pp. 551–595.

Andrews, P. 1970. "Two New Fossil Primates from the Lower Miocene of Kenya," *Nature,* **228,** 537–540.

Andrews, P. 1971. "*Ramapithecus wickeri* Mandible from Fort Ternan, Kenya," *Nature,* **231,** 192.

Andrews, P. 1974. "New Species of *Dryopithecus* from Kenya," *Nature,* **249,** 188–190.

Andrews, P. 1976. "Taxonomy and Relationship of Fossil Apes." Paper delivered at the Sixth International Primate Congress, Cambridge, England.

Andrews, P. 1978. "A Revision of the Miocene Hominoidea of East Africa," *Bulletin, British Museum (Natural History),* Geology Series, **30**(2).

Andrews, P., and H. Tobien. 1977. "New Miocene Locality in Turkey and Evidence on the Origin of *Ramapithecus* and *Sivapithecus,*" *Nature,* **268,** 699–701.

431

Andrews, P., and J. Van Couvering. 1975. "Palaeoenvironments in the East African Miocene," in F. Szalay (ed.), *Approaches to Primate Paleobiology, Contributions to Primatology*. Basel, Switzerland: Karger, vol. 5, pp. 62–103.

Andrews, P., and A. Walker. 1976. "The Primate and Other Fauna from Fort Ternan, Kenya," in G. Isaac and E. McCown (eds.), *Human Origins*. Menlo Park, Calif.: W. A. Benjamin. Pp. 279–306.

Ankel, F. 1965. "Der Canalis Sacralis als Indicator fur die lange der Caudalregion der Primaten," *Folia Primatologia*, **3**, 263–276.

Anonymous. 1972. "Confusion over Fossil Man," *Nature*, **232**, 294–295.

Anonymous. 1979. "Difficulties in the Definition of new Hominid Species," *Nature*, **278**, 400–401.

Ardrey, R. 1961. *African Genesis*. New York: Atheneum.

Avis, V. 1962. "Brachiation: The Crucial Issue for Man's Ancestry," *Southwestern Journal of Anthropology*, **18**, 119–148.

Azzaroli, A. 1970. "Villefranchian Correlations Based on Large Mammals," *Giornale de Geologia*. (Pisa), **35**(1), 111–131.

Bada, J., and P. Helfman. 1976. "Application of Amino Acid Racemization Dating in Palaeoanthropology and Archeology." Paper delivered at Colloque I, Union Internationale des Sciences Préhistoriques et Protohistoriques, Nice, France, Sept. 13–18.

Bada, J., R. Protsch, and R. Schroeder, 1973. "The Racemization Reaction of Isoleucine used as a Palaeotemperature Indicator," *Nature*, **241**, 394–395.

Bada, J., R. Schroeder, and G. Carter. 1974. "New Evidence for the Antiquity of Man in North America Deduced from Aspartic Acid Racemization," *Science*, **184**, 791–793.

Bada, J., R. Schroeder, R. Protsch, and R. Berger. 1974. "Concordance of Collagen-based Radiocarbon and Aspartic-Acid Racemization Ages," *Proceedings of the National Academy of Science (U.S.A.)*, **71**, 914–917.

Bakker, R. T. 1975. "Dinosaur Renaissance," *Scientific American*, **232**, 58–78.

Barbetti, M., and H. Allen. 1972. "Prehistoric Man at Lake Mungo, Australia, by 34,000 years B.P.," *Nature*, **240**, 46.

Bartholomew, G., and J. Birdsell. 1953. "Ecology and the Protohominids," *American Anthropologist*, **55**, 481–498.

Bar-Yosef, O. 1975. "Archaeological Occurrences in the Middle Pleistocene of Israel," in K. Butzer and G. Isaac (eds.), *After the Australopithecines*. The Hague: Mouton. Pp. 571–604.

Basmajian, J. 1967. *Muscles Alive: Their Functions Revealed by Electromyography* (2d ed.). Baltimore: Williams & Wilkins.

Bauchot, R., and H. Stephan. 1966. "Donnes nouvelles sur l'encephalisation des insectivores et des prosimiens," *Mammalia*, **30**, 160–196.

Bauchot, R., and H. Stephan. 1969. "Encephalisation et niveau evolutif chez les simiens," *Mammalia*, **33**, 225–275.

Behrensmeyer, A. K. 1975. "The Taphonomy and Paleoecology of Plio-Pleistocene Vertebrate Assemblages East of Lake Rudolf, Kenya," *Bulletin of the Museum of Comparative Zoology*. Cambridge, Mass.: Harvard University Press, **147**(10), 473–578.

Berger, W. 1952. "Neue Ergebnisse der Tertiarbotanik im Weiner Beckan," *Neues Jahrbuch für* Geologie and Palaeontologie. Stuttgart W. Germany: Monatshefte.

Berggren, W., and J. Van Couvering. 1974. "The Late Neogene: Biostratigraphy, Geochronology and Paleoclimatology," *Paleogeography, Paleoclimatology, Paleoecology*, **16**(1/2), 1–216.

Bernor, R. 1973. "Hominoid Evolution: A Biogeographical Approach," *Anthropology, UCLA*, **5**(1), 1–87.

Binford, L. 1972. "Contemporary Model Building: Paradigms and the Current State of Palaeolithic Research," in D. L. Clarke (ed.), *Models in Archaeology*. London: Methuen, P. 109.

Binford, S. 1968. "A Structural Comparison of Disposal of the Dead in the Mousterian and the Upper Paleolithic," *Southwestern Journal of Anthropology*, **24**, 139–154.

Binford, S. R., and L. R. Binford. 1966. "A Preliminary Analysis of Functional Variability in the Mousterian of Levallois Facies," in J. D. Clark and F. C. Howell (eds.), *American Anthropologist, Special Publication* no. 68, 238–295.

Binford, S. R., and L. R. Binford. 1969. "Stone Tools and Human Behavior," *Scientific American,* **220**, 70–84.

Birdsell, J. 1979. "A Reassessment of the Age, Sex and Population Affinities of the Niah Cranium." Paper given at the annual meeting, American Association of Physical Anthropologists, San Francisco.

Bishop, W. W. 1976. "Pliocene Problems Relating to Human Evolution," in G. Isaac and E. McCown (eds.), *Human Origins*. Menlo Park, Calif.: W. A. Benjamin.Pp. 139–154.

Bishop, W., and G. Chapman. 1970. "Early Pliocene Sediments and Fossils from the Northern Kenya Rift Valley," *Nature*, **226**, 914–918.

Bishop, W., and J. D. Clark (eds.). 1967. *Background to Evolution in Africa*. Chicago: University of Chicago Press.

Bishop, W., F. Fitch, and J. Miller. 1969. "New Potassium-Argon Age Determinations Relevant to the Miocene Fossil Mammal Sequence in East Africa," *American Journal of Science*, **267**, 669–699.

Bishop. W. W., and J. A. Miller (eds.). 1972. *Calibration of Hominoid Evolution*. Edinburgh: Scottish Academic Press.

Bishop, W., and M. Pickford. 1975. "Geology, Fauna and Palaeoenvironments of the Ngorora Formation, Kenya, Rift Valley," *Nature*, **254**, 185–192.

Black, D., T. Chardin, C. Young, and W. Pei. 1933. "Fossil Man in China," *Geological Survey of China, Memoir Series A* (11).

Blanc, A. 1961. "Some Evidence for Ideologies of Early Man," in S. Washburn (ed.), *Social Life of Early Man*. Chicago: Aldine-Atherton. Pp. 119–136.

Bock, W. 1965. "The Role of Adaptive Mechanisms in the Origins of Higher Levels of Organization," *Systematic Zoology*, **14**, 272–297.

Bock, W. 1970. "Microevolutionary Sequences as a Fundamental Concept in Macroevolutionary Models," *Evolution*, **24**, 704–722.

Bock, W. 1972. "Species Interactions and Macroevolution," in T. Dobzhansky, M. Hecht, and W. Steere (eds.), *Evolutionary Biology*, **5**, 1–24.

Bock, W. 1973. "Examining Macroevolutionary Events by Sequential Species Analysis," in *Proceedings of the Seventeenth International Zoological Congress*.

Bohlin, B. 1946. "The Fossil Mammals from the Tertiary of Tabun-buluk." *Report of the Sino-Swedish Expedition to the N.W. Provinces of China*. Vol. 6(4).

Bolk, L. 1926. *Das Problem der Menschwerdung*. Jena, E. Germany: Gustav Fischer.

Bonifay, E. 1964. "La Grotte du Regourdou (Montignac, Dordogne), Stratigraphie et Industrie Lithique Moustérienne," *Anthropologie* (Paris), **68**, 49–64.

Bonifay, E., and B. Vandermeersch. 1962. "Dépôts rituels d'ossements d'ours dans de gisement moustérien du Regourdou (Montignac, Dordogne)," *Comptes Rendus de l'Académie de Sciences* (Paris), Series D, **255**, 1635–1636.

Bonis, L. de, G. Bouvrain, D. Geraads, and J. Melentis. 1974. "Première découverte d'un Primate hominoide dans de Miocène supérieur de Macédoine (Grèce)," *Comptes Rendus de l'Académie de Sciences* (Paris), Series D, **281**, 379–382.

Bonis, L. de, G. Bouvrain, and J. Melentis. 1975. "Nouveaux restes de Primates hominoides dans le Vallésien de Macédoine (Greece)," *Comptes rendus de lAcadémie de Sciences* (Paris), Series D, **281**, 379-382.

Bonis, L. de, and J. Melentis. 1977. "Un nouveau genre de Primate hominoide dans le Vallésien (Miocène supérieur) de Macédoine," *Comptes Rendus de l'Académie de Sciences* (Paris), Series D, **284**, 1393–1396.

Bonnefille, R. 1975. "Palynological Evidence for an Important Change in the Vegetation of the Omo Basin Between 2.5 and 2.0 m.y.," in Y. Coppens, C. Howell, G. Isaac, and R. Leakey (eds.), *Earliest Man and Environments in the Lake Rudolf Basin.* Chicago: University of Chicago Press. Pp. 421–431.

Bordes, F., 1968. *The Old Stone Age.* New York: McGraw-Hill.

Bordes, F., 1972. *A Tale of Two Caves.* New York: Harper & Row.

Borisiak, A. A. 1962. "A Survey of Fossil Sites of Tertiary Land Mammals in the U.S.S.R.," *International Geological Review,* **4**(7), 863–864.

Bouchud, J. 1954. "La Renne et le problème des migrations," *Anthropologie* (Paris), **58**, 79–85.

Boule, M. 1908. "L'Homme fossile de la Chapelle-aux-Saints (Corrèze)," *Anthropologie* (Paris), **19**, 519–525.

Boule, M. 1911. "L'Homme fossile de la Chapelle-aux-Saints," *Annales de Paleontologie,* **6**(3,4), 109–172.

Boule, M. 1912. "L'Homme fossile de la Chapelle-aux-Saints," *Annales de Paleontologie,* **7**(2,3,4), 85–192.

Boule, M. 1913. "L'Homme fossile de la Chapelle-aux-Saints," *Annales de Paleontologie,* **8**(1), 1–270.

Boule, M. 1923. *Fossil Men.* Edinburgh: Oliver & Boyd.

Boule, M., and H. Vallois. 1957. *Fossil Men.* New York: The Dryden Press.

Bowler, J., A. Thorne, and H. Polack. 1972. "Pleistocene Man in Australia: Age and Significance of the Mungo Skeleton," *Nature,* **240**, 48–50.

Bown, T. 1976. "Affinities of *Teilhardina* (Primates, Omomyidae) with Description of a New Species from North America," *Folia Primatologia,* **25**, 62–72.

Bown, T., and P. Gingerich. 1973. "The Paleocene Primate *Plesiolestes* and the Origin of the Microsyopidae," *Folia Primatologia,* **19**, 1-8.

Brace, C.L. 1962. "Refocusing on the Neanderthal Problem," *American Anthropologist,* **64**, 729–741.

Brace, C. L. 1964. "The Fate of the 'Classic' Neanderthals: A Consideration of Hominid Catastrophism," *Current Anthropology,* **6**, 3–43.

Brace, C. L. 1967. "Environment, Tooth Form and Size in the Pleistocene," *Journal of Dental Research,* **46**, 806–819.

Brady, J. V. 1955. *Emotional Behavior Handbook of Physiology* (J. Field, ed.), Sec. 1, vol. 3, 1529–1552.

Brain, C. K. 1958. "The Transvaal Ape Man Bearing Deposits," *Memoirs of the Transvaal Museum* (Pretoria), **11**, 78–80.

Brain, C. K. 1967. "Hottentot Food Remains and Their Bearing on the Interpretation of Fossil Bone Assemblages," *Scientific Papers of the Namib Research Station* (Pretoria), **32**, 1–11.

Brain, C. K. 1970. "New Finds at the Swartkrans Australopithecine Site," *Nature*, **225**, 1112–1119.

Brain, C. K. 1976a. "A Re-Interpretation of the Swartkrans Site and Its Remains," *South African Journal of Science*, **72**, 141–146.

Brain, C. K. 1976b. "Some Principles in the Interpretation of Bone Accumulations Associated with Man," in G. Isaac and E. McCown (eds.), *Human Origins*. Menlo Park, Calif: W. A. Benjamin. Pp. 97–116.

Branco, W. 1897. "Die Menschenahnlichen Zahne aus dem Bohnerz der Schwabishen," *Alb. Jh. Vaterl. Naturk. Wurtt.*, **54**, 1.

Breitinger, E. 1952. "Zur Morphologie und systematischer Stellung des Schadelfragmentes von Swanscombe," *Homo*, **3**, 131–133.

Brock, A., and G. Isaac. 1974. "Paleomagnetic Stratigraphy and Chronology of Hominid-Bearing Sediments East of Lake Rudolf, Kenya," *Nature*, **247**, 344–348.

Brock, A., P. McFadden, and T. Partridge. 1977. "Preliminary Palaeomagnetic Results from Makapansgat and Swartkrans," *Nature*, **266**, 249–250.

Broecker, W., J. Goddard, D. Mania, and G. Kukla. 1973. (MS. in preparation.) Referenced in K. Butzer and G. Isaac (eds.), *After the Australopithecines*. The Hague: Mouton. P. 897.

Broom, R. 1936. "New Anthropoid Skull from South Africa," *Nature*, **138**, 486–488.

Broom, R. 1939. "A Restoration of the Kromdraai Skull," *Annals of the Transvaal Museum* (Pretoria), **19**, 327.

Broom, R. 1959. *Finding the Missing Link*. London: Watts.

Broom, R., and J. Robinson. 1949. "A New Type of Fossil Man," *Nature*, **164**, 322–323.

Broom, R., and J. Robinson. 1950. "Man Contemporaneous with Swartkrans Ape Man," *American Journal of Physical Anthropology*, New Series 8, 151–156.

Broom, R., and J. Robinson. 1952. "Swartkrans Ape Man, *Paranthropus crassidens*," *Memoirs of the Transvaal Museum* (Pretoria), **6**, 1–124.

Broom, R., J. Robinson, and G. Schepers. 1950. "Sterkfontein Ape-Man, Plesianthropus," *Memoirs of the Transvaal Museum*, (Pretoria) **4**, 1–117.

Broom, R., and G. Schepers. 1946. "The South African Fossil Ape-Men: The Australopithecinae," *Memoirs of the Transvaal Museum* (Pretoria), **2**, 1–272.

Brose, D., and M. Wolpoff. 1971. "Early Upper Paleolithic Man and Late Middle Paleolithic Tools," *American Anthropologist*, **73**, 1156–1194.

Brothwell, D. R. 1960. "Upper Pleistocene Human Skull from Niah Cave, Sarawak," *Sarawak Museum Journal*, **9**, 323–349.

Brown, F., and K. LaJoie. 1971. "Correlation of K-AR Dates for Omo Valley Formations," *Nature*, **229**, 483–485.

Brown, F., and W. P. Nash. 1976. "Radiometric Dating and Tuff Morphology of Omo Group Deposits," in Y. Coppens, F. Howell, G. Isaac, and R. Leakey (eds.), *Earliest Man and Environments in the Lake Rudolf Basin*. Chicago: University of Chicago Press. Pp. 50–63.

Brown, W. L., Jr. 1958. "Some Zoological Concepts Applied to Problems in Evolution of the Hominid Lineage," *American Scientist*, **46**, 151–158.

Brown, W. L., Jr., and E. O. Wilson. 1956. "Character Displacement," *Systematic Zoology*, **5**, 49–65.

Bryant, V. M., and G. Williams-Dean. 1975. "The Coprolites of Man," *Scientific American*, **232**(1), 100–109.

Buettner-Janusch, J. 1966. *The Origins of Man*. New York: Wiley.

Buettner-Janusch, J. 1973. *Physical Anthropology: A Perspective*. New York: Wiley.

Butzer, K. 1971. *Environment and Archeology: An Ecological Approach to Prehistory* (2d ed.). Chicago: Aldine-Atherton.

Butzer, K. 1974. "Paleoecology of South African Australopithecines: Taung Revisited," *Current Anthropology*, **15**, 367–426.

Butzer, K. 1976. "Lithostratigraphy of the Swartkrans Formation," *South African Journal of Science*, **72**, 136–141.

Butzer, K. 1978. "Geo-ecological Perspectives on Early Hominid Evolution," in C. Jolly (ed.), *Early Hominids of Africa*. London: Duckworth.

Butzer, K., F. Brown, and D. Thurber. 1969. "Horizontal Sediments of the Lower Omo Valley: The Kibish Formation," *Quaternaria*, **11**, 15–39.

Butzer, K., and G. Isaac (eds.). 1975. *After the Australopithecines*. The Hague: Mouton.

Bygott, J. D. 1972. "Cannibalism among Wild Chimpanzees," *Nature*, **238**, 410–411.

Cachel, S. 1975. "The Beginnings of the Catarrhini," in R. Tuttle (ed.), *Primate Functional Morphology and Evolution*. The Hague: Mouton.

Cain, A. J. 1954. *Animal Species and Their Evolution*. London: Hutchinson.

Campbell, B. 1962. "The Systematics of Man," *Nature*, **194**, 225–232.

Campbell, B. 1965. "The Nomenclature of the Hominidae," *Publications of the Royal Anthropological Institute of Great Britain and Ireland*, no. 22.

Campbell, B. 1966. *Human Evolution*. Chicago: Aldine.

Campbell, B. 1972. "Conceptual Progress in Physical Anthropology: Fossil Man," *Annual Review of Anthropology*, **1**, 27–54.

Campbell, B. 1973. *Human Evolution: An Introduction to Man's Adaptations*. Chicago: Aldine.

Campbell, B. (ed.). 1976. *Humankind Emerging*. Boston: Little, Brown.

Campbell, B., and R. Bernor. 1976. "The Origin of the Hominidae: Africa or Asia?" *Journal of Human Evolution*, **5**, 441–454.

Carney, J., A. Hill, J. Miller, and A. Walker. 1971. "Late Australopithecine from Baringo District, Kenya," *Nature*, **230**, 509–514.

Carpenter, C. R. 1940. "A Field Study in Siam of the Behavior and Social Relations of the Gibbon *(Hylobates lar)*," *Comparative Psychology Monographs*, **16**, 1–212.

Cartmill, M. 1972. "Arboreal Adaptations and the Origin of the Order Primates," in R. Tuttle (ed.), *The Functional and Evolutionary Biology of Primates*. Chicago: Aldine. Pp. 97–122.

Cartmill, M. 1974. "Rethinking Primate Origins," *Science*, **184**, 436–442.

Chance, M. R. H. 1964. "Social Behavior and Primate Evolution," in M. F. A. Montagu (ed.), *Culture and the Evolution of Man*. New York: Oxford University Press. Pp. 84–129.

Chaney, R. W. 1933. "A Tertiary Flora from Uganda," *Journal of Geology*, **41**, 702–709.

Chaney, R. W. 1935. "The Occurrence of Endocarps of *Celtis barbouri* at Chou Kou Tien," *Bulletin of the Geological Society of China*, **14**(2).

Chang, Y-Y, L-H Wang, and X-R Dong. 1975. "Discovery of a *Gigantopithecus* Tooth from Bama District in Kwangsi," *Vertebrata Palasiatica*, **13**(3), 153.

Chavaillon, J. 1967. "La Préhistoire éthiopienne à Melka Kontouré," *Archeologia*, **19**, 56–63.

Chavaillon, J. 1976. "Evidences for Technical Practices of Early Pleistocene Hominids, Shungura Formation, Lower Valley of the Omo, Ethiopia," in Y. Coppens, C. Howell, G. Isaac, and R. Leakey (eds.), *Earliest Man and Environments in the Lake Rudolf Basin*. Chicago: University of Chicago Press. Pp. 563–575.

Chesters, K. I. M. 1957. "The Miocene Flora of Rusinga Island, Lake Victoria, Kenya," *Palaeontographica*, **101**(B), 30–71.

Chia, Lan-Po. 1975. *The Cave Home of Peking Man*. Peking: Foreign Languages Press.

Chow, M. C. 1958. "Mammalian Faunas and Correlations of Tertiary and Early Pleistocene of South China," *Journal of the Paleontological Society of India*, **3**, 123–130.

Chow, M. C. 1961. "A New Tarsioid Primate from the Lushi Eocene, Honan," *Vertebrata Palasiatica*, **5**(1), 1–5.

Clark, J. D. 1960. "Human Ecology during Pleistocene and Later Times in Africa South of the Sahara," *Current Anthropology*, **1**, 307–324.

Clark, J. D. 1969. *Kalambo Falls Prehistoric Site*. Cambridge, England: Cambridge University Press.

Clarke, R. H. 1976. "New Cranium of *Homo erectus* from Lake Ndutu, Tanzania," *Nature*, **262**, 485–487.

Clarke, R. J., and C. Howell, 1972. "Affinities of the Swartkrans 847 Hominid Cranium," *American Journal of Physical Anthropology*, **37**, 319–336.

Clarke, R. J., C. Howell, and C. K. Brain. 1970. "More Evidence for an Advanced Hominid from Swartkrans," *Nature*, **225**, 1217–1222.

Clemens, W. 1974. "*Purgatorius*, an Early Paromomyid Primate, (Mammalia)," *Science*, **184**, 903–905.

Colbert, E. H. 1935. "Siwalik Mammals in the American Museum of Natural History," *Transactions, American Philosophical Society*, **26**, 1–401.

Colbert, E. H. 1938. "Fossil Mammals from Burma in the American Museum of Natural History," *Bulletin of the American Museum of Natural History*, **74**, 255–436.

Colbert, E. H. 1973. *Wandering Lands and Animals*. New York: Dutton.

Cole, S. 1963. *Prehistory of East Africa*. New York: Macmillan.

Cole, S. 1975. *Leakey's Luck*. New York: Harcourt, Brace Jovanovich.

Conroy, G. 1976. "Primate Postcranial Remains from the Oligocene of Egypt," *Contributions to Primatology*. Basel, Switzerland: Karger, vol. 8.

Conroy, G., and J. Fleagle. 1972. "Locomotor Behavior in Living and Fossil Pongids," *Nature*, **237**, 103–104.

Conroy, G., C. Jolly, D. Cramer, and J. Kalb. 1978. "Newly Discovered Fossil Hominid Skull from the Afar Depression, Ethiopia," *Nature*, **276**, 67–70.

Cooke, H. B. S. 1958. "Observations Relating to Quaternary Environments in East and Southern Africa," *Transactions of the Geological Society of South Africa*, **61** (Annexeure), 1–73.

Cooke, H. B. S. 1967. "The Pleistocene Sequence in South Africa and Problems of Correlation," in W. W. Bishop and J. D. Clark (eds.), *Background to Evolution in Africa*. Chicago: University of Chicago Press. Pp. 175–184.

Cooke, H. B. S. 1968. "The Fossil Mammal Fauna of Africa," *Quarterly Review of Biology*, **43**, 234–264.

Cooke, H. B. S. 1972. "The Fossil Mammal Fauna of Africa," in A. Keast, F. Erk, and B. Glass (eds.), *Evolution, Mammals and Southern Continents*. Albany: State University of New York Press. Pp. 89–128.

Cooke, H. B. S. 1976. "Suidae from Plio-Pleistocene Strata of the Rudolf Basin," in Y. Coppens, F. Howell, G. Isaac, and R. Leakey (eds.), *Earliest Man and Environments in the Lake Rudolf Basin*. Chicago: University of Chicago Press. Pp. 251–264.

Coon, C. 1962. *The Origin of Races*. New York: Knopf.

Coon, C. 1964. "Comment on the Fate of the 'Classic' Neanderthals: A Consideration of Hominid Catastrophism," *Current Anthropology*, **5**, 21–22.

Coppens, Y. 1961a. "Découverte d'un Australopithécine dans le Villafranchien du Tchad," *Comptes Rendus de l'Académie de Sciences*, Series D, Paris, **252**, 3851–3852.

Coppens, Y. 1961b. "Un Australopithèque au Sahara (Nord Tchad)," *Bulletin, Société Préhistorique Français*, **58**, 756–757.

Coppens, Y. 1962. "Prises de date pour les gisements paléontologiques quaternaires et archéologiques découverts au cours mission de deux mois dans le nord du Tchad," *Bulletin, Société Préhistorique Français*, **59**, 260–267.

Coppens, Y. 1965. "L'Hominien du Tchad," *Comptes Rendus de l'Académie de Sciences*, Paris, Series D, **260**, 2869–2871.

Coppens, Y., F. C. Howell, G. L. Isaac, and R. E. F. Leakey (eds.). 1976. *Earliest Man and Environments in the Lake Rudolf Basin*. Chicago: University of Chicago Press.

Corruccini, R. 1975. "The Interaction between Neurocranial and Facial Shape in Hominid Evolution," *Homo*, **26**, 136–139.

Coryndon, S., and R. Savage. 1973. "The Origin and Affinities of African Mammal Faunas," in N. F. Hughes (ed.), *Organisms and Continents through Time*. London: Palaeontology Association, Systematics Association, Pub. no. 9, pp. 121–135.

Crusafont, M., and J. Hürzeler. 1961. "Les Pongidés Fossiles d'Espagne," *Comptes Rendus de l'Académie de Sciences* (Paris), Series D, **254**, 582–584.

Crusafont, M., and J. Hurzeler. 1969. "Catálogo comentado de los Póngides fossiles de Espagne," *Acta Geológica Hispánica*, (Barcelona), **4**, 44–48.

Crusafont-Pairo, M., and J. M. Golpe-Posse. 1973. "New Pongids from the Miocene of Valles Penedes Basin (Catalonia, Spain)," *Journal of Human Evolution*, **2**, 17–23.

Curtis, G., T. Drake, T. Cerling, and Hempel. 1975. "Age of KBS Tuff in Koobi Fora Formation, East Rudolf, Kenya," *Nature*, **258**, 395–398.

Dart, R. 1925. "*Australopithecus africanus*: The Man Ape of South Africa," *Nature*, **115**, 195–199.

Dart, R. 1934. "Dentition of *Australopithecus africanus*," *Folia Anatomica Japonica*, **12**, 207–221.

Dart, R. 1948a. A (?) Promethean Australopithecus from Makapansgat Valley," *Nature*, **162**, 375.

Dart, R. 1948b. "The Makapansgat Proto-human *Australopithecus prometheus*," *American Journal of Physical Anthropology*, **6**, 259–284.

Dart, R. 1960. "The Status of *Gigantopithecus*," *Anthropologischer Anzeiger* (Stuttgart), **24**, 139–145.

Darwin, C. 1859. *On the Origin of Species by Means of Natural Selection, or the Preservation of Favored Races in the Struggle for Life*. London: J. Murray.

Darwin, C. 1871. *The Descent of Man and Selection in Relation to Sex*. London: J. Murray.

Davis, D. D. 1964. "The Giant Panda: A Morphological Study of Evolutionary Mechanism," *Fieldiana Zoology Memoirs*. Pp. 1–339.

Davis, P. R., and J. R. Napier. 1963. "A Reconstruction of the Skull of *Proconsul africanus*," *Folia Primatologia*, **1**, 20–28.

Day, M. H. 1969a. "Femoral Fragment of a Robust Australopithecine from Olduvai Gorge, Tanzania," *Nature*, **221**, 230–233.

Day, M. H. 1969b. "Omo Human Skeletal Remains," *Nature*, **222**, 1135–1138.

Day, M. H. 1971a. "Postcranial Remains of *Homo erectus* from Bed IV, Olduvai Gorge, Tanzania," *Nature*, **232**, 383–387.

Day, M. H. 1971b. "The Omo Human Skeletal Remains," in F. Bordes (ed.), *The Origin of Homo sapiens*. Paris: UNESCO. Pp. 31–35.

Day, M. H. 1976. "Hominid Postcranial Material from Bed I, Olduvai Gorge," in G. Isaac and E. McCown (eds.), *Human Origins*. Menlo Park, Calif.: W. A. Benjamin. Pp. 363–376.

Day, M. H. 1977. *Guide to Fossil Man* (3d ed.). Chicago: University of Chicago Press.

Day, M. H. 1978. "Functional Interpretation of the Morphology of Postcranial Remains of Early African Hominids," in C. Jolly (ed.), *Early Hominids of Africa*. London: Duckworth.

Day, M. H., and R. E. F. Leakey. 1973. "New Evidence of the Genus *Homo* from East Rudolf, Kenya: I," *American Journal of Physical Anthropology*, **39**, 341–354.

Day, M. H., and T. Molleson. 1973. "The Trinil Femora," in M. H. Day (ed.), *Human Evolution*. Symposium for the Study of Human Biology, no. 11. London: Taylor and Francis. Pp. 127–154.

Day, M. H., and J. R. Napier. 1961. "The Two Heads of Flexor Pollicis Brevis," *Journal of Anatomy* (London), **95**, 123–130.

Day, M. H., and J. R. Napier. 1963. "Functional Significance of the Deep Head of Flexor Pollicis Brevis in Primates," *Folia Primatologia*, **1**, 122–134.

Day, M. H., and J. R. Napier. 1964. "Hominid Fossils from Bed I, Olduvai Gorge, Tanganyika. Fossil Foot Bones," *Nature*, **201**, 967–970.

Day, M. H., and J. R. Napier. 1966. "A Hominid Toe Bone from Bed I, Olduvai Gorge, Tanzania," *Nature*, **211**, 929–930.

Day, M. H., R. E. F. Leakey, A. C. Walker, and B. A. Wood. 1975. "New Hominids from East Rudolf, Kenya: I," *American Journal of Physical Anthropology*, **42**, 461–476.

Day, M. H., and B. A. Wood. 1968. "Functional Affinities of the Olduvai Hominid 8 Talus," *Man*, **3**, 440–455.

de Bonis, L. *see* Bonis, L. de.

Delson, E. 1978. "Models in Early Hominid Phylogeny," in C. Jolly (ed.), *Early Hominids of Africa*. London: Duckworth, pp. 517–542.

Delson, E., and P. Andrews. 1975. "Evolution and Interrelationships of the Catarrhine Primates," in W. P. Luckett and F. S. Szalay (eds.), *Phylogeny of the Primates: A Multidisciplinary Approach*. New York: Plenum, pp. 405–446.

Delson, E., N. Eldredge, and I. Tattersall. 1977. "Reconstruction of Hominid Phylogeny: A Testable Framework Based on Cladistic Analysis," *Journal of Human Evolution*, **6**, 263–278.

de Lumley, H. *see* Lumley, H. de.

Desmond, A. 1975. *Hot-Blooded Dinosaurs: A Revolution in Palaeontology*. New York: The Dial Press.

Dewey, J., W. Pittman, B. Ryan, and J. Bonnin. 1973. "Plate Tectonics and the Evolution of the Alpine System," *Bulletin of the Geological Society of America*, **84**, 3137–3180.

Donn, W. L., and M. Ewing. 1966. "A Theory of the Ice Ages, III," *Science*, **152**, 1706.

Dorf, E. 1940. "Relationship between Floras of Type Lance and Fort Union Formations," *Bulletin of the Geological Society of America*, **51**, 213–235.

Dorf, E. 1942. "Upper Cretaceous Floras of the Rocky Mountain Region, II, Flora of the Lance Formation," *Carnegie Institute of Washington*, Pub. 508, 1–167.

Dorf, E. 1955. "Plants and the Geologic Time Scale," *Geological Society of America*, *Special Paper*, no. 62.

Dortch, C. E., and D. Merrilees. 1973. "Human Occupation of Devil's Lair, Western Australia, during the Pleistocene," *Archaeology and Physical Anthropology of Oceania*, **8**(2), 89–115.

Dubois, E. 1894. "*Pithecanthropus erectus*, eine menschenaehnliche Ubergangsform aus Java," Batavia: Landesdruckerei.

Dubois, E. 1895, "Résumé d'une communication sur le *Pithecanthropus erectus* du Pliocene de Java," *Bulletin de la Société de Géologie*, **9**, 151–160.

Dubois, E. 1897. "Ueber drei ausgestorbene Menschenaffen," *N. Jahrbuch Min. Geol. Palaont*, Vol. **1**.

Dunbar, C. 1956. *Historical Geology*. New York: Wiley.

Eckhart, R. 1972. "Population Genetics and Human Origins," *Scientific American*, **226**(1), 94–103.

Edwards, W. 1936. "The Flora of the London Clay," *Proceedings of the Geological Association*, **47**, 22–31.

Eisenmann, V. 1976. "A Preliminary Note on the Equidae from the Koobi Fora Formation, Kenya," in Y. Coppens, F. Howell, G. Isaac, and R. Leakey (eds.), *Earliest Man and Environments in the Lake Rudolf Basin*. Chicago: University of Chicago Press. Pp. 234–237.

Eldredge, N., and S. Gould. 1972. "Punctuated Equilibria: An Alternative to Phyletic Gradualism" in J. Schopf (ed.), *Models in Paleobiology*. San Francisco: Freeman, Cooper. Pp. 82–115.

Eldredge, N., and I. Tattersall. 1975. "Evolutionary Models, Phylogenetic Reconstruction, and Another Look at Hominid Phylogeny," in F. Szalay (ed.), *Approaches to Primate Paleobiology, Contributions to Primatology*. Basel, Switzerland: Karger, vol. 5, pp. 218–242.

Elftman, N., and J. Manter. 1935. "Chimpanzee and Human Feet in Bipedal Walking," *American Journal of Physical Anthropology,* **20,** 69–79.

Elliott-Smith, G. 1912. "The Evolution of Man," *Smithsonian Institute Annual Report,* p. 553.

Elliott-Smith, G. 1924. *The Evolution of Man.* London: Oxford University Press, pp. 69–70.

Ennouchi, E. 1962a. "Un Crâne d'homme ancien au Jebel Irhoud (Maroc)," *Comptes Rendus de l'Académie de Sciences* (Paris), Series D, **254,** 4330–4332.

Ennouchi, E. 1962b. "Un Néanderthalien; L'Homme du Jebel Irhoud (Maroc)," *Anthropologie* (Paris), **66,** 279–299.

Ennouchi, E. 1968. "Le Deuxieme Crâne de l'Homme d'Irhoud," *Annales de Paléontologie (Vertébrés),* **54,** 117–128.

Ennouchi, E. 1969. "Présence d'un enfant Néanderthalien au Jebel Irhoud (Maroc)," *Annales de Paléontologie (Vertébrés),* **54,** 251–265.

Ennouchi, E. 1975. "New Discovery of an Archanthropine in Morocco," *Journal of Human Evolution,* **4,** 441–443.

Evernden, J., and G. Curtis. 1965. "Potassium Argon Dating of Late Cenozoic Rocks in East Africa and Italy," *Current Anthropology,* **6,** 343–385.

Evernden, J., D. Savage, G. Curtis, and C. James. 1964. "K-Ar Dates and Cenozoic Mammalian Chronology of North America," *American Journal of Science,* **262,** 145–198.

Ewing, M., and W. Donn. 1956. "A Theory of Ice Ages," *Science,* **123,** 1061.

Filhol, H. 1873. "Sur un nouveau genre de lémurien fossile: Recemment découverte dans les gisements de phosphate de chaux du Quercy," *Comptes Rendus de l'Académie de Sciences (Paris),* **77,** 1111–1112.

Fitch, F., P. J. Hooker, and J. A. Miller. 1976. "$^{40}AR/^{39}AR$ Dating of the KBS Tuff in Koobi Fora Formation, East Rudolf, Kenya," *Nature,* **263,** 740–744.

Fitch, F., and J. Miller. 1970. "Radioisotopic Age Determinations of Lake Rudolf Artifact Site," *Nature,* **226,** 226–228.

Fitch, F., and J. Miller. 1976. "Conventional Potassium/Argon and Argon-40/Argon-39 Dating of Volcanic Rocks from East Rudolf," in Y. Coppens, F. Howell, G. Isaac, and R. Leakey (eds.), *Earliest Man and Environments in the Lake Rudolf Basin.* Chicago: University of Chicago Press. Pp. 123–147.

Fleagle, J., E. Simons, and G. Conroy. 1975. "Ape Limb Bone from the Oligocene of Egypt," *Science,* **189,** 135–137.

Flint, R. F. 1947. *Glacial Geology and the Pleistocene Epoch.* New York: Wiley.

Forsyth-Major, C. I. 1900. "A Summary of Our Present Knowledge of Extinct Primates from Madagascar," *Geological Magazine,* **7,** 492–499.

Frayer, D. 1973. "*Gigantopithecus* and Its Relationships to *Australopithecus,*" *American Journal of Physical Anthropology,* **39,** 413–426.

Freeman, L. 1966. "The Nature of Mousterian Facies in Cantabrian Spain," *American Anthropologist,* **68,** 230–237.

Freeman, L. 1975. "Acheulian Sites and Stratigraphy in Iberia and the Maghreb," in K. Butzer and G. Isaac (eds.), *After the Australopithecines.* The Hague: Mouton. Pp. 661–744.

Frenzel, B. 1968. "The Pleistocene Vegetation of Northern Eurasia," *Science,* **161,** 637–649.

Freyberg, B. von. 1950. "Das Neogen-Gebiet nordwestlich Athen," *Analecta Geologica Helvetica*, **3**, 65–86.

Frisch, J. 1968. "Individual Behavior and Intertroop Variability in Japanese Macaques," in P. Jay (ed.), *Primates*. New York: Holt. Pp. 243–252.

Gantt, D., D. Pilbeam, and G. Steward. 1977. "Hominoid Enamel Prism Patterns," *Science*, **198**, 1155–1157.

Gao-Jian. 1975. "*Australopithecus* Teeth Associated with *Gigantopithecus*," *Vertebrata Palasiatica*, **13**(2).

Gause, G. 1934. *The Struggle for Existence*. Baltimore: Williams & Wilkins.

Gazin, C. L. 1958. "A Review of the Middle and Upper Eocene Primates of North America," *Smithsonian Miscellaneous Collections*, **136**, 1–112.

Genet-Varcin, E. 1969. *A la Récherche du Primate Ancêtre de l'Homme*. Paris: Boubée.

Gentry, A. 1970. "The Bovidae (Mammalia) of the Fort Ternan Fossil Fauna," in L. Leakey and R. Savage (eds.), *The Fossil Vertebrates of Africa*, Vol. 2. London: Academic. Pp. 243–324.

George, T. N. 1956. "Biospecies, Chronospecies and Morphospecies," in P. Sylvester-Bradley (ed.), *The Species Concept in Palaeontology*, Systematics Association, Pub. no. 2. London: E. W. Classey. Pp. 123–137.

Gervais, P. 1872. "Sur un Singe Fossile d'espèce non encore décrite, qui a été découverte au Monti-Bamboli (Italie)," *Comptes Rendus de l'Académie de Sciences* (Paris), 1217–1223.

Geschwind, N. 1964. "Development of the Brain and Evolution of Language," *Monograph Series in Language and Linguistics*, **17**, 155–169.

Geschwind, N. 1972. "The Organization of Language and the Brain," in S. Washburn and P. Dolhinow (eds.), *Perspectives on Human Evolution*, Vol. 2. New York: Holt. Pp. 382–394.

Gingerich, P. 1972. "Molar Occlusion and Jaw Mechanics of the Eocene Primate *Adapis*," *American Journal of Physical Anthropology*, **36**, 359–368.

Gingerich, P. 1973. "The Anatomy of the Temporal Bone in the Oligocene Anthropoid *Apidium* and the Origin of Anthropoidea," *Folia Primatologia*, **19**, 329–337.

Ginsberg, L. 1961. "Découverte de *Pliopithecus antiquus* B1. dans le falum sauv-ignéen de Noyant-sur-le-Lude (Maine et Loire)," *Comptes Rendus de l'Académie de Sciences* (Paris), Series D, **252**, 585–587.

Gleiser, I., and E. Hunt. 1955. "The Permanent Mandibular First Molar, Its Calcification, Eruption and Decay," *American Journal of Physical Anthropology*, **13**, 253–284.

Glover, I. C., and E. A. Glover. 1970. "Pleistocene Flaked Stone Tools from Timor and Flores," *Mankind*, **7**, 188–190.

Golz, D. 1976. "Eocene Artiodactyla of Southern California," *Natural History Museum of Los Angeles County, Scientific Bulletin*, **26**, 1–85.

Goodall, J. 1964. "Tool-Using and Aimed Throwing in a Community of Free-living Chimpanzees," *Nature*, **201**, 1264–1266.

Goodman, M. 1962a. "Evolution and Immunological Species Specificity of Human Serum Proteins," *Human Biology*, **34**, 104–150.

Goodman, M. 1962b. "Immunochemistry of the Primates and Primate Evolution," *Annals of the New York Academy of Sciences*, **102**, 219–234.

Goodman, M. 1963. "Man's Place in the Phylogeny of the Primates as Reflected in

Serum Proteins," in S. Washburn (ed.), *Classification and Human Evolution*. Chicago: Aldine. Pp. 204–234.

Goodman, M. 1967. "Effects of Evolution on Primates Macromolecules," *Primates*, **8**, 1–22.

Gorjanovic-Kramberger. K. D. 1899. "Der Palaolithische Mensch und Seine Zietgenessen aus dem Diluvium von Krapina in Croatien," *Mitteilungen der Anthropologischen Gesellschaft* (Vienna), **29**, 65-68.

Gorjanovic-Kramberger. K. D. 1905. "Die Variationen am Skelette der Altdiluvialen Menschen," *Glasnik Hrvatskaoga Narodoslovnoga Drustva* (Zagreb), **16**, 72–75, 377–381.

Gorjanovic-Kramberger, K. D. 1906. *Der Diluviale Mensch von Krapina in Croatien*. Wiesbaden, W. Germany: C. W. Kreidels Verlag.

Gould, S. J. 1975. "The Child as Man's Real Father," *Natural History*, **74**(5), 18–22.

Gould, S. J. 1977. *Ontogeny and Phylogeny*. Cambridge, Mass.: Harvard University Press.

Gray, J. E. 1825. "Outline of an Attempt at the Disposition of the Mammalia into Tribes and Families with a List of the Genera Apparently Appertaining to Each Tribe," *Annals of Philosophy*, New Series, **10**, 337–344.

Green, R. 1961. "Palaeoclimatic Significance of Evaporites," in A. E. M. Nairn (ed.), *Descriptive Palaeoclimatology*. New York: Interscience.

Greenfield, L. O. 1972. "Sexual Dimorphism in *Dryopithecus africanus*," *Primates*, **13**, 395–410.

Greenfield, L. O. 1973. "Note on the Placement of the Most Complete 'Kenyapithecus africanus' Mandible," *Folia Primatologia*, **20**, 274–279.

Gregory, W. K. 1916. "Studies on the Evolution of Primates," *Bulletin of the American Museum of Natural History*, **35**, 239–355.

Gregory, W. K. 1920. "On the Structure and Relations of *Notharctus*, an American Eocene Primate," *Memoirs of the American Museum of Natural History*, New Series, **3**, 49–243.

Gregory, W. K., and M. Hellman. 1923. "Notes on the Type of Hesperopithecus haroldcookii," *American Museum Novitates*, no. 53. P. 1.

Gregory, W. K., and M. Hellman. 1939a. "The South African Fossil Man Apes and the Origin of the Human Dentition," *Journal of the American Dental Association*, **26**, 558–564.

Gregory, W. K., and M. Hellman, 1939b. "The Dentition of the Extinct South African Man Ape, *Australopithecus (Plesianthropus) transvaalensis* Broom," *Annals of the Transvaal Museum* (Pretoria), **19**, 339–373.

Gregory, W. K., M. Hellman, and G. Lewis. 1938. "Fossil Anthropoids of the Yale-Cambridge Indian Expedition of 1935," *Carnegie Institute of Washington*, Pub. 495, 1–27.

Gregory, W. K., J. E. Hill, and J. H. McGregor. 1957. "Primates," in *Encyclopedia Britannica*, vol. 18, pp. 485–490. Chicago: Encyclopedia Britannica.

Groves, C. 1970. "*Gigantopithecus* and the Mountain Gorilla," *Nature*, **226**, 973.

Gutgesell, V. J. 1970. "'Telanthropus' and the Single Species Hypothesis: A Reexamination," *American Anthropologist*, **72**, 565–609.

Haeckle, E. 1868. *Naturlicke Schopfungsgeschichte*. Berlin: Georg Reimer.

Haeckle, E. 1889. *History of Creation*. London: Kegan Paul, Trench, Trubner & Co.

Hall, J. W., and J. J. Norton. 1967. "Palynological Evidence of Floristic Change across the Cretaceous-Tertiary Boundary in Eastern Montana," *Paleogeography, Paleoclimatology, Paleoecology,* **3,** 121–131.

Hamilton, W., III., R. E. Buskirk, and W. H. Buskirk. 1975. "Defensive Stoning by Baboons," *Nature,* **256,** 488–489.

Hardin, G. 1960. "The Competitive Exclusion Principle," *Science,* **131,** 1291–1297.

Harding, R. J., and S. Strum. 1976. "The Predatory Baboons of Kekopey," *Natural History,* **85**(3), 46–53.

Harris, J., and G. Isaac. 1976. "The Karari Industry: Early Pleistocene Archaeological Evidence from the Terrain East of Lake Turkana, Kenya," *Nature,* **262,** 102–107.

Harrisson, T. 1958. "Carbon-14 Dated Palaeoliths from Borneo," *Nature,* **181,** 792.

Harrisson, T. 1959. "New Archaeological and Ethnological Results from Niah Caves, Sarawak," *Man,* **59,** 1–8.

Hay, R. L. 1976. *Geology of Olduvai Gorge.* Berkeley: University of California Press.

Hays, J. D. and R. M. Shackleton. 1976. "Variations in the Earth's Orbit; Pacemaker of the Ice Ages," *Science,* **194,** 1121.

Heim, J. L. 1968. "Les restes néanderthaliens de La Ferrassie I. Nouvelles données sur la stratigraphie et inventaire des squelettes," *Comptes Rendus de l'Académie de Sciences* (Paris), Series D, **266,** 576–578.

Heim, J. L. 1970. "L'encephale Neandertalien de l'Homme de La Ferrassie," *Anthropologie* (Paris), **74,** 527–572.

Helgren, D. M., and K. Butzer. 1974. "Alluvial Terraces of the Lower Vaal Basin: Reply," *Journal of Geology,* **82,** 665–667.

Hennig, W. 1950. *Grundzuge einer Theorie der Phylogenetischen Systematik.* Berlin: Deutscher Zentralverlag.

Hennig, W. 1966. *Phylogenetic Systematics.* Urbana: University of Illinois Press.

Henri-Martin, G. 1947. "L'Homme Fossile Tayacien de la Grotte de Fontechevade," *Comptes Rendus de l'Academie de Sciences* (Paris), Series D, **225,** 766–767.

Henri-Martin, G. 1964. "La Dernière Occupation Moustérienne de La Quina (Charente), Datation par le Radio-carbone," *Comptes Rendus de l'Academie de Sciences* (Paris), Series D, **258,** 3533.

Heywood, V. H., and J. McNeill (eds.). 1964. *Phenetic and Phylogenetic Classification,* Systematics Association, Pub. no. 6. London: E. W. Classey.

Hill, W. C. Osman. 1953–1962. *Primates: Comparative Anatomy and Taxonomy.* Edinburgh: Edinburgh University Press. 5 vols.

Hill, W. C. Osman. 1968. "The Genera of Old World Monkeys and Apes," in A. B. Chiarelli (ed.), *Taxonomy and Phylogeny of Old World Primates with Reference to the Origin of Man.* Turin, Italy: Rosenburg and Sellier.

Hill, W. C. Osman. 1972. *Evolutionary Biology of the Primates.* London: Academic.

Hockett, C., and R. Ascher. 1964. "The Human Revolution," *Current Anthropology,* **5,** 135–168.

Hofer, H. 1969. "The Evolution of the Brain of Primates: Its Influence on the form of the Skull," *Annals of the New York Academy of Science,* **167,** 341–356.

Hofer, H., and J. Wilson. 1967. "An Endocranial Cast of an Oligocene Primate," *Folia Primatologia,* **5,** 148–152.

Holloway, R. 1966. "Cranial Capacity, Neural Reorganization and Hominid Evolution: A Search for More Suitable Parameters," *American Anthropologist,* **68,** 103–121.

Holloway, R. 1967. "Evolution of the Human Brain: Some Notes toward a Synthesis between Neural Structure and the Evolution of Complex Behavior," *General Systems*, **12**, 3–19.

Holloway, R. 1970. "Australopithecine Endocast (Taung Specimen, 1924): A New Volume Determination," *Science*, **168**, 966–968.

Holloway, R. 1972. "New Australopithecine Endocast, SK 1585, from Swartkrans, South Africa," *American Journal of Physical Anthropology*, **37**, 173–186.

Holloway, R. 1973. "Endocranial Volumes of Early African Hominids and the Role of the Brain in Human Mosaic Evolution," *Journal of Human Evolution*, **2**, 449–459.

Holloway, R. 1974. "The Casts of Fossil Hominid Brains," *Scientific American*, **231**(1), 106–115.

Hooijer, D. A. 1948. "Prehistoric Teeth of Man and of the Orang-utan from Central Sumatra, with notes on the Fossil Orang-utan from Java and Southern China," *Zoologische Mededelinger Rijks Museum Van Natuurlijke Historie te Leiden*, **29**, 272–280.

Hooijer, D. A. 1968. "A Rhinoceros from the Late Miocene of Fort Ternan, Kenya," *Zoologische Mededelinger Rijks Museum Van Natuurlijke Historie te Leiden*, **43**, 77–92.

Hooijer, D. A., and V. J. Maglio. 1974. "Hipparions from the Late Miocene and Pliocene of Northwestern Kenya," *Zoologische Verhandelinger Rijks Museum van Natuurlijke Historie Leiden*, (134).

Hopson, J., and F. Crompton. 1969. "Origins of Mammals," *Evolutionary Biology*, **3**, 15–71.

Hopwood, A. T. 1933. "Miocene Primates from Kenya," *Journal of the Linnaean Society (Zoology)*, **38**, 437–464.

Horowitz, A. 1975. "Preliminary Palaeoenvironmental Implications of Pollen Analyses of Middle Breccia from Sterkfontein," *Nature*, **258**, 417–418.

Horowitz, A., G. Siedner, and O. Bar-Yosef. 1973. "Radiometric Dating of the Ubeidiya Formation, Jordan Valley, Israel," *Nature*, **242**, 186–187.

Howell, F. C. 1952. "Pleistocene Glacial Ecology and the Evolution of 'Classic' Neanderthal Man," *Southwestern Journal of Anthropology*, **8**, 377–410.

Howell, F. C. 1957. "Evolutionary Significance of Variation and Varieties of 'Neanderthal Man'," *Quarterly Review of Biology*, **37**, 330–347.

Howell, F. C. 1960. "European and Northwest African Middle Pleistocene Hominids," *Current Anthropology*, **1**, 195–232.

Howell, F. C. 1961. "Ismila: A Paleolithic Site in Africa," *Scientific American*, **205**(4), 119–129.

Howell, F. C. 1966. "Observations on the Earlier Phases of the European Lower Paleolithic," *American Anthropologist*, **68**, 88–201.

Howell, F. C. 1969. "Remains of Hominidae from Pliocene/Pleistocene Formations in the Lower Omo Basin, Ethiopia," *Nature*, **223**, 1234–1239.

Howell, F. C. 1973. *Early Man*, Chicago: Time-Life.

Howell, F. C. 1976. "Overview of the Pliocene and Earlier Pleistocene of the Lower Omo Basin, Southern Ethiopia," in G. Isaac and E. McCown (eds.), *Human Origins*. Menlo Park, Calif: W. A. Benjamin. Pp. 227–268.

Howell, F. C., and Y. Coppens. 1976. "An Overview of Hominidae from the Omo Succession," in Y. Coppens, F. Howell, G. Isaac, and R. Leakey (eds.), *Earliest*

Man and Environments in the Lake Rudolf Basin. Chicago: University of Chicago Press. Pp. 522–532.

Howell, F. C., Y. Coppens, and J. de Heinzelin. 1974. "Inventory of Remains of Hominidae from Pliocene/Pleistocene Formations of the Lower Omo Basin, Ethiopia," *American Journal of Physical Anthropology,* **40,** 1–16.

Howell, F. C., and B. Wood. 1974. "An Early Hominid Ulna from the Omo Basin, Ethiopia," *Nature,* **249,** 174–176.

Howells, W. W. 1966. *"Homo erectus," Scientific American,* **215**(5), 46–53.

Howells, W. W. 1970. "Mt. Carmel Man: Morphological Relationships," *Proceedings of the 8th International Congress of Anthropological and Ethnological Sciences,* Tokyo and Kyoto, 1968. **1,** 269–272.

Howells, W. W. 1973. *Evolution of the Genus Homo.* Reading, Mass: Addison-Wesley.

Howells, W. W. 1974. "Neanderthals: Names, Hypotheses and Scientific Method," *American Anthropologist,* **76,** 24–38.

Hrdlicka, A. 1927. "The Neanderthal Phase of Man," *Journal of the Royal Anthropological Institute,* **57,** 249–274.

Hrdlicka, A. 1935. "The Yale Fossils of Anthropoid Apes," *American Journal of Science,* **229,** 34–39.

Hsu, K. 1972. "When the Mediterranean Dried Up," *Scientific American,* **227**(6), 26–36.

Hsu, K., W. Ryan, and M. Cita. 1973. "Late Miocene Desiccation of the Mediterranean," *Nature,* **242,** 240–244.

Hughes, A. R. 1954. "Hyenas vs. Australopithecines as Agents of Bone Accumulation," *American Journal of Physical Anthropology,* **12,** 476–486.

Hughes, A. R. and P. V. Tobias. 1977. "A Fossil Skull Probably of the Genus *Homo* from Sterkfontein, Transvaal," *Nature,* **265,** 310–312.

Hurford, A. J. 1974. "Fission Track Dating of a Vitric Tuff from East Rudolf, North Kenya," *Nature,* **249,** 236–237.

Hurford, A. J., and A. J. Gleadow. 1976. "Fission Track Dating of Pumice from the KBS Tuff, East Rudolf, Kenya," *Nature,* **263,** 738–740.

Hürzler, J. 1949. "Neubeschreibung von *Oreopithecus bambolii Gervais,*" *Schweizerische Palaeontologische Abhandlungen,* **66,** 1-20.

Hürzeler, J. 1958. *"Oreopithecus bambolii Gervais:* A Preliminary Report," *Verhandlungen der Naturforschenden Gesellschaft in Basel,* **69,** 1–49.

Huxley, J. 1942. *Evolution, the Modern Synthesis.* London: Allen & Unwin.

Isaac, G. 1967. "The Stratigraphy of the Peninj Group—Early Middle Pleistocene Formations West of Lake Natron, Tanzania," in W. W. Bishop and J. D. Clark (eds.), *Background to Evolution in Africa.* Chicago: University of Chicago Press. Pp. 229–257.

Isaac, G. 1971. "The Diet of Early Man: Aspects of Archaeological Evidence from Lower and Middle Pleistocene Sites in Africa," *World Archeology,* **2,** 278–298.

Isaac, G. 1972. "Comparative Studies of Pleistocene Site Locations in East Africa," in P. Ucko, R. Tringham, and G. Dimblebey (eds.), *Man, Settlement and Urbanism.* Morristown, N.J.: Schenkman. Pp. 165–176.

Isaac, G. 1976a. "Plio-Pleistocene Artifact Assemblages from East Rudolf, Kenya," in Y. Coppens, F. Howell, G. Isaac, and R. Leakey (eds.), *Earliest Man and Environments in the Lake Rudolf Basin.* Chicago: University of Chicago Press. Pp. 552–564.

Isaac, G. 1976b. "The Activities of Early African Hominids: A Review of the

Archaeological Evidence from the Time Span Two and a Half to One Million Years Ago," in G. Isaac and E. McCown (eds.), *Human Origins*. Menlo Park, Calif.: W. A. Benjamin. Pp. 483–514.

Isaac, G. 1977. *Olorgesailie: Archeological Studies of a Middle Pleistocene Lake Basin in Kenya*. Chicago: University of Chicago Press.

Isaac, G., and G. H. Curtis. 1974. "Age of Early Acheulian Industries from the Peninj Group, Tanzania," *Nature*, **249**, 624–627.

Isaac, G., J. Harris, and D. Crader. 1976. "Archeological Evidence from the Koobi Fora Formation," in Y. Coppens, F.Howell, G. Isaac, and R. Leakey (eds.), *Earliest Man and Environments in the Lake Rudolf Basin*. Chicago: University of Chicago Press. Pp. 533–551.

Isaac, G., R. Leakey, and K. Behrensmeyer. 1971. "Archaeological Traces of Early Hominid Activities East of Lake Rudolf, Kenya," *Science*, **173**, 1129–1134.

Isaac, G., and E. McCown (eds.). 1976. *Human Origins*. Menlo Park, Calif.: W. A. Benjamin.

Ivanhoe, F. 1970. "Was Virchow Right about Neanderthal?" *Nature*, **227**, 577–579.

Jacob, T. 1972. "The Absolute Date of the Djetis Beds at Modjokerto," *Antiquity*, **41**, 148.

Jacob, T. 1973. "Paleoanthropological Discoveries in Indonesia with Special Reference to the Finds of the Last Two Decades," *Journal of Human Evolution*, **2**, 473–485.

Jacob, T., and G. Curtis. 1971. "Preliminary Potassium Argon Dating of Early Man in Java," *Contributions to the University of California Research Facility*, no. 12, p. 50.

Jaeger, J. J. 1975. "The Mammalian Faunas and Hominid Fossils of the Middle Pleistocene of the Maghreb," in K. Butzer and G. Isaac (eds.), *After the Australopithecines*. The Hague: Mouton. Pp. 399–418.

Jepsen, G. 1963. "Eocene Vertebrates, Coprolites and Plants," *Bulletin, Geological Society of America*, **74**, 673–684.

Jerison, H. J. 1973. *Evolution of the Brain and Intelligence*. New York: Academic.

Johanson, D. C., and M. Taieb. 1976. "Plio-Pleistocene Hominid Discoveries in Hadar, Ethiopia," *Nature*, **260**, 293–297.

Johanson, D. C., and T. D. White. 1979. "A Systematic Assessment of Early African Hominids." *Science*, **203**, 321–330.

Johanson, D. C., T. D. White, and Y. Coppens. 1978. "A New Species of the Genus *Australopithecus* (Primates: Hominidae) from the Pliocene of Eastern Africa," *Kirtlandia*, **28**, 1–14.

Jolly, A. 1972. *The Evolution of Primate Behavior*. New York: Macmillan.

Jolly, C. 1970. "The Seed Eaters: A New Model of Hominid Differentiation Based on a Baboon Analogy," *Man*, **5**, 5–26.

Jolly, C. 1973. "Changing Views on Hominid Origins," *Yearbook of Physical Anthropology*, **16**, 1–17.

Jones, R. 1973. "Emerging Picture of Pleistocene Australians," *Nature*, **246**, 278–281.

Jouffroy, F. K., and J. Lessertisseur. 1960. "Les Spécialisations anatomiques de la main chez les singes à progression suspendue," *Mammalia*, **24**, 93–151.

Jurmain, R. 1977. "Stress and the Etiology of Osteoarthritis," *American Journal of Physical Anthropology*, **46**, 353–366.

Kawai, M. 1965. "Newly Acquired Precultural Behavior of the Natural Troop of Japanese Monkeys on Koshima Islet," *Primates*, **6**, 1–30.

Keast, A. 1968. "Evolution of Mammals on Southern Continents," *Quarterly Review of Biology*, **43**, 225–233.

Keast, A., F. Erk, and B. Glass (eds.). 1972. *Evolution, Mammals and Southern Continents*. Albany: State University of New York Press.

Keith, A. 1925. *The Antiquity of Man* (2d ed.). London: Williams & Norgate.

Keith, A. 1931. *New Discoveries Relating to the Antiquity of Man*. London: Williams & Norgate.

Kennedy, G. E. 1973. *The Anatomy of Lower and Middle Pleistocene Femora*. Dissertation, University of London.

Kielan-Jaworowska, Z. 1975. "Late Cretaceous Mammals and Dinosaurs from the Gobi Desert," *American Scientist*, **63**, 150–159.

Kleindienst, M. R. 1961. "Variability with the Late Acheulian Assemblages in East Africa," *South African Archaeological Bulletin*, **16**, 35–52.

Kleindienst, M. R. 1962. "Components of the East African Acheulian Assemblage: An Analytic Approach," in C. Mortelmans and J. Nenquin (eds.), *Actes du IVe Congrès Panafricain de Préhistoire et de l'Etude du Quaternaire*, Tervueren (Belgium), **3**, 81–111.

Kochetkova, V. I. 1970. "Reconstruction de l'endocrane de l'*Atlanthropus mauritanicus* et de l'*Homo habilis*," *Proceedings of the 8th International Congress of Anthropological and Ethnological Sciences*, **1**, 102–104.

Kohl-Larsen, L. 1943. *Auf den Spuren des Vormenschen*, vol. 2. Stuttgart, W. Germany:

Kollmann, J. 1905. "Neue Gedanken über das alter Problem von der Abstammung des Menschen," *Korrespondenzblatt der deutschen Gesellschaft für Anthropologie Ethnologie und Urgeschichte*, (Braunschweig), **36**, 9.

Kortlandt, A. 1967. "Experimentation with Chimpanzees in the Wild," in D. Starch (ed.), *Progress in Primatology*, Stuttgart, W. Germany: D. Fischer.

Kortlandt, A., and M. Kooij. 1963. "Protohominid Behavior in Primates," in J. R. Napier (ed.), *The Primates*, Symposium of the Zoological Society of London, **10**, 61–88.

Kräusel, R. 1961. "Palaeobotanical Evidence of Climate," in A. E. M. Nairn (ed.), *Descriptive Palaeoclimatology*, New York: Interscience.

Kretzoi, M. 1975. "New Ramapithecines and *Pliopithecus* from the Lower Pliocene of Rudabanya in Northeastern Hungary," *Nature*, **257**, 578–581.

Kretzoi, M., and L. Vertes. 1965. "Upper Biharian (Intermindel) Pebble Industry Occupation Site in Western Hungary," *Current Anthropology*, **6**, 74–87.

Kukla, G. 1975. "Loess Stratigraphy of Central Europe," in K. Butzer and G. Isaac (eds.), *After the Australopithecines*. The Hague: Mouton. Pp. 99–188.

Kuhn, T. S. 1962. *The Structure of Scientific Revolutions*. Berkeley: University of California Press.

Kummer, H. 1968. "Social Organization of Hamadryas Baboons, A Field Study," *Bibliotheca Primatologica*, no. 6, Basel, Switzerland: Karger.

Kummer, H. 1971. *Primate Societies*. Chicago: Aldine.

Kummer, H., and F. Kurt. 1963. "Social Units of a Free Living Population of Hamadryas Baboons," *Folia Primatologia*, **1**, 1–16.

Kurten, B. 1966. "Holarctic Land Connexions in the Early Tertiary," *Commentationes Biologicae Societas Scientiarum Fennica*. (Helsingfors), **29**, 1–5.

Kurten, B. 1969. "Continental Drift and Evolution," *Scientific American*, **220**(3), 54–65.

Kurten, B. 1971. *The Age of Mammals*. New York: Columbia University Press.

Kurten, B. 1972. *Not from the Apes*. New York: Pantheon.

Kyrnine, P. D. 1937. "Petrography and Genesis of the Siwalik Series," *American Journal of Science*, **34**, 422–446.

Lack, D. 1947. *Darwin's Finches*. London: Cambridge University Press.

Lartet, E. 1837. "Note sur la découverte récente d'un mâchoire de singe fossile," *Comptes Rendus de l'Académie de Sciences* (Paris), **4**, 85–93.

Lartet, E. 1856. "Note sur la découverte récente d'un mâchoire de singes superieurs," *Comptes Rendus de l'Académie de Sciences* (Paris), **43**.

Leakey, L. S. B. 1935. *Stone Age Races of Kenya*. London: Oxford University Press.

Leakey, L. S. B. 1962. "A New Lower Pliocene Fossil Primate from Kenya," *Annals and Magazine of Natural History*, Series 13, **4**, 689–696.

Leakey, L. S. B. 1967a. *Olduvai Gorge 1951–1961*. Cambridge, England: Cambridge University Press.

Leakey, L. S. B. 1967b. "An Early Miocene Member of the Hominidae," *Nature*, **213**, 155–163.

Leakey, L. S. B. 1968. "Lower Dentition of *Kenyapithecus africanus*," *Nature*, **217**, 827–830.

Leakey, L. S. B. (ed.). 1969. *Fossil Vertebrates of Africa*, Vol 1. London: Academic.

Leakey, L. S. B. 1973. "Was *Homo erectus* Responsible for the Hand-axe Culture?" *Journal of Human Evolution*, **2**, 493–497.

Leakey, L. S. B., and M. D. Leakey. 1964. "Recent Discoveries of Fossil Hominids in Tanganyika: At Olduvai and Near Lake Natron," *Nature*, **202**, 5–7.

Leakey, L. S. B., P. V. Tobias, and J. R. Napier. 1964. "A New Species of the Genus *Homo* from Olduvai Gorge," *Nature*, **202**, 7–9.

Leakey, M. D. 1970. In C. K. Brain, J. Robinson, F. C. Howell, and M. D. Leakey, "New Finds at the Swartkrans Australopithecine Site," *Nature*, **225**, 1112–1119.

Leakey, M. D. 1971a. *Olduvai Gorge:* Vol. 3. Cambridge, England: Cambridge University Press.

Leakey, M. D. 1971b. "Discovery of Postcranial Remains of *Homo erectus* and Associated Artifacts in Bed IV at Olduvai Gorge, Tanzania," *Nature*, **232**, 380–383.

Leakey, M. D. 1975. "Cultural Patterns in the Olduvai Sequence," in K. Butzer and G. Isaac (eds.), *After the Australopithecines*. The Hague: Mouton. Pp. 477–494.

Leakey, M. D., R. J. Clarke, and L. S. B. Leakey. 1971. "New Hominid Skull from Bed I, Olduvai Gorge, Tanzania," *Nature*, **232**, 308–312.

Leakey, M. D., and R. L. Hay, 1979. "Pliocene Footprints in the Laetolil Beds at Laetoli, Northern Tanzania," *Nature*, **278**, 317–323.

Leakey, M. D., R. L. Hay, G. H. Curtis, R. E. Drake, M. K. Jackes, and T. D. White. 1976. "Fossil Hominids from the Laetolil Beds," *Nature*, **262**, 460–466.

Leakey, R. E. F. 1971. "Further Evidence of Lower Pleistocene Hominids from East Rudolf, North Kenya," *Nature*, **231**, 241–245.

Leakey, R. E. F. 1973a. "Further Evidence of Lower Pleistocene Hominids from East Rudolf, North Kenya," *Nature*, **242**, 170–173.

Leakey, R. E. F. 1973b. "Evidence for an Advanced Plio-Pleistocene Hominid from East Rudolf, Kenya," *Nature*, **242**, 447–450.

Leakey, R. E. F. 1974. "Further Evidence of Lower Pleistocene Hominids from East Rudolf, North Kenya, 1973," *Nature,* **248,** 653–656.

Leakey, R. E. F. 1976. "New Hominid Fossils from the Koobi Fora Formation in Northern Kenya," *Nature,* **261,** 574–576.

Leakey, R. E. F., K. Butzer, and M. Day. 1969. "Early *Homo sapiens* Remains from the Omo River Region of South-West Ethiopia," *Nature,* **222,** 1137–1143.

Leakey, R. E. F., and A. Walker. 1976. "*Australopithecus, Homo erectus* and the Single Species Hypothesis," *Nature,* **261,** 572–574.

Leakey, R. E. F., and B. Wood. 1973. "New Evidence for the Genus *Homo* from East Rudolf, Kenya," *American Journal of Physical Anthropology,* **39,** 355–368.

Le Gros Clark, W. E. 1928. "Rhodesia Man," *Man,* **28,** 206–207.

Le Gros Clark, W. E. 1945. "Note on the Paleontology of the Lemuroid Brain," *Journal of Anatomy* (London), **79,** 123–126.

Le Gros Clark, W. E. 1947. "Observations on the Anatomy of the Fossil Australopithecinae," *Journal of Anatomy* (London), **81,** 300–333.

Le Gros Clark, W. E. 1962. *Antecedents of Man* (2d ed.). Edinburgh: Edinburgh University Press.

Le Gros Clark, W. E. 1964. *The Fossil Evidence for Human Evolution* (2d ed.). Chicago: University of Chicago Press.

Le Gros Clark, W. E. 1965. *History of the Primates* (9th ed.). London: British Museum (Natural History).

Le Gros Clark, W. E. 1967. *Man Apes or Ape Men?* New York: Holt.

Le Gros Clark, W. E., and L. S. B. Leakey. 1951. "The Miocene Hominoidea of East Africa," *Fossil Mammals of Africa,* Vol. 1. London: British Museum (Natural History).

Leroi-Gourhan, André. 1950. "La Grotte du Loup, Arcy-sur-Cure (Yonne)," *Bulletin de la Société Préhistorique Française* (Paris), **47,** 268.

Leroi-Gourhan, Arlette. 1968. "Le Néanderthalien IV de Shanidar," *Bulletin de la Société Préhistorique Française, Comptes Rendus de Séances Mensuelles* (Paris), **65,** 79–83.

Lewis, G. E. 1934. "Preliminary Notice of the New Man-Like Apes From India," *American Journal of Science,* **27,** 161–181.

Lewis, G. E. 1937a. *Siwalik Fossil Anthropoids.* Doctoral thesis, Yale University.

Lewis, G. E. 1937b. "Taxonomic Syllabus of Siwalik Fossil Anthropoids," *American Journal of Science,* **34,** 139–147.

Lewis, O. J. 1965. "The Evolution of the mm. Interossei in the Primate Hand," *Anatomical Record,* **153,** 275–283.

Lewis, O. J. 1972. "Osteological Features Characterizing the Wrists of Monkeys and Apes, with a Reconsideration of This Region in *Dryopithecus (Pronconsul) africanus,*" *American Journal of Physical Anthropology,* **36,** 45–57.

Levins, R. 1968. *Evolution in Changing Environments: Some Theoretical Explorations.* Princeton, N.J.: Princeton University Press.

Lieberman, P. 1968. "Primate Vocalizations and Human Linguistic Ability," *Journal of the Acoustical Society of America,* **44,** 1574–1584. (Reprinted in Lieberman, 1972.)

Lieberman, P. 1972. "Primate Vocalizations and Human Linguistic Ability," in S.

Washburn and P. Dolhinow (eds.), *Perspectives on Human Evolution*, Vol. 2. New York: Holt. Pp. 444–468.

Lillegraven, J. 1976. "Didelphids (Marsupialia) and Uintasorex (? primates) from Later Eocene Sediments of San Diego County, California," *Transactions, San Diego Society of Natural History*, 18(5), 85–112.

Linnaeus, C. 1735. *Systema naturae per regna tria naturae*. Stockholm: Holmiae.

Linnaeus, C. 1750. *Systema naturae per regna tria naturae* (10th ed.). Stockholm: Holmiae.

Lisowski, F., G. H. Albrecht, and C. E. Oxnard. 1976. "African Fossil Tali: Further Multivariate Morphometric Studies," *American Journal of Physical Anthropology*, 45, 5–18.

Lovejoy, O. 1973. "The Gait of Australopithecus," *Yearbook of Physical Anthropology*, 17, 147–161.

Lovejoy, O. 1975. "Biomechanical Perspectives of the Lower Limb of Early Hominids," in R. Tuttle (ed.), *Primate Functional Morphology and Evolution*. The Hague: Mouton.

Lovejoy, O. 1978. "A Biomechanical Review of the Locomotor Diversity of Early Hominids," in C. Jolly (ed.), *Early Hominids of Africa*, London: Duckworth, pp. 403–430.

Lovejoy, O., K. Heiple, and A. Burnstein. 1973. "The Gait of *Australopithecus*," *American Journal of Physical Anthropology*, 38, 757–779.

Lumley, H. de 1969. "A Paleolithic Camp at Nice," *Scientific American*, 220(5), 42–50.

Lumley, H. de 1975. "Cultural Evolution in France and Its Paleoecological Setting During the Middle Pleistocene," in K. Butzer and G. Isaac (eds.), *After the Australopithecines*. The Hague: Mouton. Pp. 745–808.

Lumley, H. de, S. Gagniere, L. Barral, and R. Pascal. 1963. "La Grotte du Vallonet, Roquebrune-Cap Martin (A.M.)," *Bulletin, Musée d'Anthropologie et Préhistoire de Monaco*, 10, 5–20.

Lumley, H. de, and M-A. de Lumley. 1971. "Découvertes des restes humaines antenéandertaliens dâtés du début du Riss à la Caune de l'Arago (Tautavel, Pyrenées-Orientales)," *Comptes Rendus de l'Académie de Sciences* (Paris), Series D, 272, 1739–1742.

Lydekker, R. 1879. "Further Notices of Siwalik Mammalia," *Records, Geological Survey of India*, 12, 33–52.

Maglio, V. J. 1971. "The Nomenclature of Intermediate Forms: an Opinion," *Systematic Zoology*, 20, 370–373.

Maglio, V. J. 1972. "Vertebrate Faunas and Chronology of Hominid-Bearing Sediments East of Lake Rudolf, Kenya," *Nature*, 239, 379–385.

Maglio, V. J. 1973. "Origin and Evolution of Elephantidae," *Transactions, American Philosophical Society*, 63, 1–149.

Mann, A., and E. Trinkaus. 1974. "Neanderthal and Neanderthal-like Fossils from the Upper Pleistocene," *Yearbook of Physical Anthropology*, 17, 169–193.

Marshack, A. 1972a. *The Roots of Civilization*. New York: McGraw-Hill.

Marshack, A. 1972b. "Upper Paleolithic Notation and Symbol," *Science*, 178, 817–828.

Marshack, A. 1972c. "Cognitive Aspects of Upper Paleolithic Engraving," *Current Anthropology*, **13**, 445–477.

Marshack, A. 1975. "Some Implications of the Paleolithic Symbolic Evidence for the Origin of Language." Paper given at the Conference on Origins and Evolution of Language and Speech, New York Academy of Science, Sept. 22–25, 1975.

Martin, H. 1910. "Les Couches du Gisement de La Quina et Leur Age," *Comptes Rendus du Congrès de Préhistorique de Française* (Tours), 125–128.

Martin, R. D. 1968. "Towards a New Definition of Primates," *Man*, **3**, 376–401.

Martin, R. D. 1975. "Ascent of the Primates," *Natural History*, **84**(3), 53–60.

Martyn, T., and P. V. Tobias. 1967. "Pleistocene Deposits and New Fossil Localities in Kenya," *Nature*, **215**, 476–480.

Maruyama, M. 1963. "The Second Cybernetics: Deviation Amplifying Mutual Causal Processes," *American Scientist*, **51**, 164–179.

Mason, R. J. 1962. *Prehistory of the Transvaal*. Johannesburg, S. Africa: Witwatersrand University Press.

Mason, R. J. 1965. "Makapansgat Limeworks Fractured Stone Objects and Natural Fracture in Africa," *South African Archaeological Bulletin*, **20**, 3–16.

Matiegka, J. 1934. *Homo předmostensis. Fosilní člověk z Předmosti na Moravě*, Vol. 1. Prague: I. Lebky.

Matthew, W. E. 1904. "The Arboreal Ancestry of the Mammalia," *American Naturalist*, **38**, 811–818.

Mayr, E. 1950. "Taxonomic Categories of Fossil Hominids," *Cold Spring Harbor Symposium on Quantitative Biology*, **15**, 109–118.

Mayr, E. 1963. *Animal Species and Evolution*. Cambridge, Mass.: Belknap Press, Harvard University Press.

Mayr, E. 1970. *Population, Species and Evolution*. Cambridge, Mass.: Belknap Press, Harvard University Press.

Mayr, E. 1976. *Evolution and the Diversity of Life*. Cambridge, Mass.: Belknap Press, Harvard University Press.

McBurney, C., J. Trevor, and L. Wells. 1953. "The Hauah Fteah Fossil Jaw," *Journal of the Royal Anthropological Society*, **83**, 71–85.

McClure, F. A. 1943. "Bamboo as Panda Food," *Journal of Mammalia*, **24**, 267–268.

McCown, T., and A. Keith. 1939. *The Stone Age of Mount Carmel. Vol. 2: The Fossil Human Remains from the Levalloiso Mousterian*. Oxford, England: Clarendon Press.

McGrew, W. C., and C. Tutin. 1973. "Chimpanzee Tool Use in Dental Grooming," *Nature*, **241**, 477–478.

McHenry, H. 1972. *Postcranial Skeleton of Early Pleistocene Hominids*. Ph.D. thesis, Harvard University.

McHenry, H. 1973. "Early Hominid Humerus from East Rudolf, Kenya," *Science*, **180**, 739–741.

McHenry, H. 1975. "Biomechanical Interpretation of the Early Hominid Hip," *Journal of Human Evolution*, **4**, 343–355.

McHenry, H., and R. Corruccini. 1975. "Distal Humerus in Hominoid Evolution," *Folia Primatologia*, **23**, 227–244.

McKenna, M. 1960. "4 Mile Fauna," *University of California, Geological Science Publication*, **37**, 1–130.

McKenna, M. 1961. "A Note on the Origin of Rodents," *American Museum Novitates*, **2037**, 1–5.

McKenna, M. 1963. "The Early Tertiary Primates and Their Ancestory," *Proceedings of the 16th International Congress on Zoology*, **4**, 69–74.

McKenna, M. C. 1966. "Palaeontology and the Origin of the Primates," *Folia Primatologia*, **4**, 1–25.

Mellars, P. 1970. "Some Comments on the Nature of 'Functional Variability'," *World Archaeology*, **2**, 74–89.

Merrick, H., J. de Heinzelin, P. Haesaerts, and F. C. Howell. 1973. "Archaeological Occurrences of Early Pleistocene Age from the Shungura Formation, Lower Omo Valley, Ethiopia," *Nature*, **242**, 572–575.

Merrick, H., and J. Merrick. 1976. "Archeological Occurrences of Earlier Pleistocene Age, from the Shungura Formation," in Y. Coppens, F. Howell, G. Isaac, and R. Leakey (eds.), *Earliest Man and Environments in the Lake Rudolf Basin*. Chicago: University of Chicago Press. Pp. 574–584.

Mivart, St. G. 1873. "On Lepilemur and Cheirogaleus and on the Zoological Rank of the Lemuridae," *Proceedings of the Zoological Society of London, 1873*. Pp. 484–510.

Montagu, M. F. A. 1962. "Time, Morphology and Neoteny in the Evolution of Man," in M. F. A. Montagu (ed.), *Culture and the Evolution of Man*. New York: Oxford University Press. Pp. 324–342.

Moore, G. W., and M. Goodman. 1968. "Phylogeny and Taxonomy of the Catarrhine Primates," in A. B. Chiarelli (ed.), *Taxonomy and Phylogeny of Old World Primates*. Turin, Italy: Rosenburg and Sellier.

Morbeck, M. 1975 *"Dryopithecus africanus* Forelimb," *Journal of Human Evolution*, **4**, 20–38.

Morgan, E. 1972. *Descent of Woman*. New York: Stein and Day.

Movius, H. L., Jr. 1944. "Early Man and Pleistocene Stratigraphy in South and Eastern Asia," *Papers of the Peabody Museum of Archaeology and Ethnology* (Harvard University), **19**, 1–125.

Movius, H. L., Jr. 1948. "The Lower Paleolithic Cultures of Southern and Eastern Asia," *Transactions of the American Philosophical Society*, **38**, 330–420.

Movius, H. L., Jr. 1953. "The Mousterian Cave of Teshik-Tash, South-eastern Uzbekistan, Central Asia," *Bulletin of the American School of Prehistoric Research*, **17**, 11–71.

Movius, H. L., Jr. 1960. "Radiocarbon Dates and Upper Paleolithic Archeology in Central and Western Europe," *Current Anthropology*, **1**, 355–391.

Movius, H. L., Jr. 1975. "Excavations of the Abri Pataud, Les Eyzies (Dordogne)," *Peabody Museum of Archaeology and Ethnology* (Harvard University), Bulletin 30, vol. 1.

Mturi, A. A. 1976. "New Hominid From Lake Ndutu, Tanzania," *Nature*, **262**, 484–485.

Muller, J. 1968. "Palynology of the Pedawan and Plateau Sandstone Formations in Sarawak, Malaysia," *Micropaleontology*, **14**, 1–37.

Mulvaney, D. J. 1969. *The Prehistory of Australia*. London: Thames and Hudson.

Mulvaney, D. J. 1970. "The Patjitanian Industry: Some Observations," *Mankind*, **7**, 184–187.

Musgrave, J. 1970. *An Anatomical Study of the Hands of Pleistocene and Recent Man.* Thesis, Cambridge University.

Musgrave, J. 1971. "How Dextrous Was Neanderthal Man?" *Nature,* **233,** 538–541.

Musgrave, J. 1973. "The Phalanges of Neanderthal and Upper Palaeolithic Hands," in M. H. Day (ed.), *Human Evolution,* Symposium for the Study of Human Biology, no. 11. London: Taylor and Francis. Pp. 59–86.

Nairn, A. E. M. (ed.). 1961. *Descriptive Paleoclimatology.* New York: Interscience.

Nairn, A. E. M. (ed.). 1964. *Problems in Paleoclimatology.* London: Interscience.

Napier, J. 1962. "Fossil Hand Bones from Olduvai," *Nature,* **196,** 409–411.

Napier, J. 1967. "The Antiquity of Human Walking," *Scientific American,* **216**(7), 56–66.

Napier, J. 1970. "Paleoecology and Catarrhine Evolution," in J. Napier and P. Napier (eds.), *Monkies: Evolution, Systematics and Behavior.* New York: Academic. Pp. 53–96.

Napier, J., and P. Davis. 1959. "The Forelimb and Associated Remains of *Proconsul africanus,*" *Fossil Mammals of Africa,* **16,** 1–69. London: British Museum (Natural History).

Napier, J., and P. Napier. 1967. *Handbook of Living Primates.* London: Academic.

Negus, V. E. 1949. *Comparative Anatomy and Physiology of the Larynx.* London: William Hanemann.

Oakley, K. P. 1956. "The Earliest Fire Makers," *Antiquity,* **30,** 102–107.

Oakley, K. P. 1964. *Frameworks for Dating Fossil Man.* Chicago: Aldine.

Oakley, K. P. 1974. "Revised Dating of the Kanjera Hominids," *Journal of Human Evolution,* **3,** 257–258.

Oakley, K. P., B. Campbell, and T. Molleson. 1971. *Catalog of Fossil Hominids, Part 2, Europe.* London: Trustees of the British Museum (Natural History).

Oakley, K. P., B. Campbell, and T. Molleson. 1975. *Catalog of Fossil Hominids, Part 3: Americas, Asia, Australasia.* London: Trustees of the British Museum (Natural History).

Oakley, K. P., B. Campbell, and T. Molleson. 1977. *Catalog of Fossil Hominids, Part 1: Africa* (2d ed.). London: Trustees of the British Museum (Natural History).

Odum, E. P. 1959. *Fundamentals of Ecology.* Philadelphia: Saunders.

Olson, E. 1944. "Origin of Mammals Based upon Cranial Morphology of the Therapsid Sub-Orders," *Geological Society of America, Special Paper,* no. 55, 1–136.

Osborn, H. F. 1902. "American Eocene Primates and the Supposed Rodent Family Mixodectidae," *Bulletin of the American Museum of Natural History,* **16,** 169–214.

Ovey, C. D. (ed.). 1964. *The Swanscombe Skull: A Survey of Research on a Pleistocene Site; Occasional Papers of the Royal Anthropological Institute* (London), no. 20, pp. 1–215.

Oxnard, C. 1972. "Some African Fossil Foot Bones: A Note on the Interpolation of Fossils into a Matrix of Extant Species," *American Journal of Physical Anthropology,* **37,** 3–12.

Oxnard C. 1973. *Form and Pattern in Human Evolution.* Chicago: University of Chicago Press.

Oxnard, C. 1974. "Functional Inferences from Morphometrics: Problems Posed by

Uniqueness and Diversity among The Primates," *Systematic Zoology,* **22,** 409–424.

Papamarinopoulos, S. 1977. "The First Known European," *Bulletin of the University of Edinburgh,* **13**(10).

Partridge, T. 1973. "Geomorphological Dating of Cave Openings at Makapangat, Sterkfontein, Swartkrans and Taung," *Nature,* **246,** 75–79.

Patté, E. 1955. *Les Néanderthaliens.* Paris: Masson et Cie.

Patterson, B., A. K. Behrensmeyer, and W. D. Sill. 1970. "Geology and Fauna of a New Pliocene Locality in Northwestern Kenya," *Nature,* **226,** 918–921.

Patterson, B., and W. W. Howells. 1967. "Hominid Humeral Fragment from Early Pleistocene of Northwestern Kenya," *Science,* **156,** 64–66.

Pearson, K. 1926. "On the Coefficient of Racial Likeness," *Biometrika,* **18,** 105–117.

Pearson, K., and J. Bell. 1919. *A Study of the Long Bones of the English Skeleton,* Drapers Company Research Memoirs, Biometric Series IX. London: Cambridge University Press.

Pei, W. C. 1957. "Giant Ape's Jaw Discovered in China," *American Anthropologist,* **59,** 834–838.

Penfield, W., and R. Roberts. 1959. *Speech and Brain Mechanisms.* Princeton, N.J.: Princeton University Press.

Penrose, L. S. 1954. "Distance, Size and Shape," *Annals of Eugenics* (London), **18,** 337–343.

Pettet, A. 1975. "Defensive Stoning by Baboons," *Nature,* **258,** 549.

Pickford, M. 1975. "Late Miocene Sediments and Fossils from the Northern Kenya Rift Valley," *Nature,* **256,** 279–284.

Pilbeam, D. 1967. "Man's Earliest Ancestors," *Science Journal,* **3,** 47–53.

Pilbeam, D. 1969. "Tertiary Pongidae of East Africa: Evolutionary Relationships and Taxonomy," *Peabody Museum Bulletin* (Yale), no. 31, 1–85.

Pilbeam, D. 1970. "*Gigantopithecus* and the Origins of the Hominidae," *Nature,* **225,** 516–519.

Pilbeam, D., G. Meyer, C. Badgley, M. Rose, M. Pickford, A. Behrensmeyer, and S. Shah. 1977. "New Hominoid Primates from the Siwaliks of Pakistan and Their Bearing on Hominoid Evolution," *Nature,* **270,** 689–694.

Pilbeam, D., and E. Simons. 1971. "A Gorilla-sized Ape from the Miocene of India," *Science,* **173,** 23–27.

Pilgrim, G. E. 1910. "Notices of New Mammalian Genera and Species from the Tertiary of India," *Record of the Geological Survey of India,* **40,** 63–71.

Pilgrim, G. E. 1915. "New Siwalik Primates and Their Bearing on the Question of the Evolution of Man and the Anthropoidea" *Record of the Geological Survey of India,* **45,** 1–74.

Pilgrim, G. E. 1927. "A *Sivapithecus* Palate and Other Primate Fossils from India," *Paleontologia India,* New Series, **14,** 1–26.

Piveteau, J. 1957. *Traité de Paléontologie.* Paris: Masson et Cie.

Pohlig, H. 1895. "*Paidopithex rhenansus* N.g.; N. sp., le singe anthropomorphe du pliocène rhénan," *Bulletin de la Société Belge de Géologie,* **9,** 149–151.

Poulianos, A. 1971. "Petralona: A Middle Pleistocene Cave in Greece," *Archeology,* **24,** 6–11.

Prasad, K. N. 1964. "Upper Miocene Anthropoids from the Siwalik Beds of Haritalyangar, Himachal Pradesh, India," *Palaeontology*, **7**, 124–134.

Preuschoft, H. 1973. "Body Posture and Locomotion in Some East African Miocene Dryopithecinae," in M. H. Day (ed.), *Human Evolution*, Symposium for the Study of Human Evolution, no. 11. London: Taylor and Francis. Pp. 13–46.

Protsch, R. 1975. "The Absolute Dating of Upper Pleistocene Sub-Saharan Fossil Hominids and Their Place in Human Evolution," *Journal of Human Evolution*, **4**, 297–322.

Pycraft, W., G. Elliott-Smith, M. Yearsley, J. Carter, R. Smith, A. Hopwood, D. Bate, and W. Swindon. 1928. *Rhodesia Man and Associated Remains*. London: Clowes.

Radinsky, L. 1967. "The Oldest Primate Endocast," *American Journal of Physical Anthropology*, **27**, 385–388.

Radinsky, L. 1970. "The Fossil Evidence of Prosimian Brain Evolution," in C. Norback and W. Montagna (eds.), *The Primate Brain: Advances in Primatology*, Vol. 1. New York: Appleton-Century-Crofts. Pp. 209–224.

Radinsky, L. 1974. "The Fossil Evidence of Anthropoid Brain Evolution," *American Journal of Physical Anthropology*, **41**, 15–28.

Radinsky, L. 1975. "Primate Brain Evolution," *American Scientist*, **63**, 656–663.

Reid, E. M., and M. E. Chandler. 1933. *The London Clay Flora*. London: Trustees of the British Museum (Natural History). Pp. 1–561.

Remane, A. 1950. "Bemerkungen über *Gigantopithecus blacki*," in H. Weinert (ed.), *Über die neuen Vorund und Frühmenschenfundi aus Afrika, Java, China and Frankreich. Zeitschrift fur Morphologie und Anthropologie* (Stuttgart, W. Germany), **42**, 113–148.

Remane, A. 1960. "Die Stellung von *Gigantopithecus*," *Anthropologischer Anzeiger*, **24**, 146–159.

Remane, A. 1961. "Problème der Systematik der Primaten," *Zeitschrift für Wissenschaftliche Zoologie*, **165**, 1–34.

Riesenfeld, A. 1956. "Multiple Infraorbital and Mental Foramina in the Races of Man," *American Journal of Physical Anthropology*, **14**, 85–100.

Rigollott, D. 1855. *Memoire sur des instruments en silex trouvés a Saint-Acheul, prés de Amiens*. Amiens, France.

Robins, R. H. 1964. *General Linguistics*. Bloomington: Indiana University Press.

Robinson, B. 1967. "Vocalizations Evoked from the Forebrain in *Macaca mulatta*," *Physiological Behavior*, **2**, 345–354.

Robinson, B. 1972. "Contrasts between Human and Other Primate Vocalizations," in S. Washburn and P. Dolhinow (eds.), *Perspectives on Human Evolution*, Vol. 2. New York: Holt. Pp. 438–443.

Robinson, J. 1953a. "Telanthropus and Its Phylogenetic Significance," *American Journal of Physical Anthropology*, **11**, 445–501.

Robinson, J. 1953b. "Meganthropus, Australopithecines and Hominids," *American Journal of Physical Anthropology*, **11**, 1–38.

Robinson, J. 1954. "The Genera and Species of the Australopithecinae," *American Journal of Physical Anthropology*, **12**, 181–200.

Robinson, J. 1955. "Further Remarks on the Relationship between 'Meganthropus' and *Australopithecus africanus,"* *American Journal of Physical Anthropology,* **13,** 429–446.

Robinson, J. 1959. "A Bone Implement from Sterkfontein," *Nature,* **184,** 583–585.

Robinson, J. 1961. "The Australopithecines and Their Bearing on the Origin of Man and of Stone Tool Making," *South African Journal of Science,* **57,** 3–13.

Robinson, J. 1963. "Adaptive Radiation in the Australopithecines and the Origin of Man," in F. Howell and F. Bouliere (eds.), *African Ecology and Human Evolution.* Chicago: Aldine. Pp. 385–416.

Robinson, J. 1965. "Homo 'habilis' and the Australopithecines," *Nature,* **205,** 121–124.

Robinson, J. 1972. *Early Hominid Posture and Locomotion.* Chicago: University of Chicago Press.

Robinson, J., and R. Mason. 1959. "Occurrence of Stone Artifacts with *Australopithecus* at Sterkfontein," *Nature,* **180,** 521–524.

Robinson, J., and R. Mason. 1962. "Australopithecines and Artifacts at Sterkfontein," *South African Archaeological Bulletin,* **17,** 87–125.

Robinson, J., and D. Steudel. 1973. "Multivariate Discriminate Analysis of Dental Data Bearing on Early Hominid Affinities," *Journal of Human Evolution,* **2,** 509–527.

Robinson, P. 1968. "Paleontology and Geology of the Badwater Creek Area, Central Wyoming with a Discussion of Material from Utah," *Annals, Carnegie Museum,* **39,** 307–326.

Romer, A. S. 1945. *Vertebrate Paleontology* (2d ed.). Chicago: University of Chicago Press.

Rose, K. D. 1975. "The Carpolestidae: Early Tertiary Primates from North America," *Bulletin, Museum of Comparative Zoology,* **147,** 1–74. Cambridge, Mass.: Harvard University Press.

Russell, D. 1959. "Le Crâne de *Plesiadapis,"* *Bulletin of the Geological Society of France,* **1,** 312–314.

Russell, D. 1967. "Sur Menatotherium et l'âge Paléocène du gisement de menat (Puy-de-Dôm)," *Probl. Actuels Pal.* (Paris), **163,** 483–489.

Sampson, G. 1974. *The Stone Age Archaeology of Southern Africa.* New York:

Sarich, V. 1968. "The Origin of the Hominids: An Immunological Approach," in S. L. Washburn and P. Jay (eds.), *Perspectives on Human Evolution, Vol. 1.* New York: Holt. Pp. 94–121.

Sarich, V. 1970. "Primate Systematics with Special Reference to Old World Monkeys," in J. Napier and P. Napier (eds), *Old World Monkeys.* New York: Academic. Pp. 17–24.

Sarich, V., and A. Wilson. 1967. "Immunological Time Scale for Hominid Evolution," *Science.* **158,** 1200–1203.

Sarich, V., and A. Wilson. 1973. "Generation Time and Genomic Evolution," *Science,* **179,** 1144–1147.

Sartono, S. 1973. "Observations on a Newly Discovered Jaw of *Pithecanthropus modjokertensis* from the Lower Pleistocene of Sangiran, Central Java," *Proceedings: Koninklijke nederlandse akademie van Wetenschappen* (Amsterdam), Series B, **77,** 25–31.

Schaffer, W. 1968. "Character Displacement and the Evolution of the Hominidae," *American Naturalist*, **102**, 559–571.

Schlosser, M. 1887. "Die Affen, Lemuren, Chiropteren, Insectivoren, Marsupialier, Creodonten und Carnivoren," *Beitrage zur Paläontologie Oesterreich-Ungarns und Orients*, **6**, 1–227.

Schlosser, M. 1911. "Beitrage zur Kenntnis der Oligozanen Landsaugetiere aus dem Fayum, Agypten," *Beitrage zur Paläontologie Oesterreich-Ungarns und Orients*, **24**, 51–167.

Schön, M., and L. Ziemer. 1973. "Wrist Mechanism and Locomotor Behavior of *Dryopithecus (Proconsul) africanus*," *Folia Primatologia*, **20**, 1–11.

Schopf, T. S. M. (ed.). 1972. *Models in Paleobiology*. San Francisco: Freeman, Cooper and Co.

Schuchert, C. 1955. *Atlas of Paleogeographic Maps of North America*. New York: Wiley.

Schultz, A. H. 1930. "The Skeleton of the Trunk and Limbs of Higher Primates," *Human Biology*, **2**, 303–438.

Schultz, A. 1933. "Observations on the Growth, Classification and Evolutionary Specializations of Gibbons and Siamangs," *Human Biology*, **5**, 212–385.

Schultz, A. 1937. "Proportions, Variability and Asymmetries of the Long Bones of the Limbs and the Clavicles in Man and Apes," *Human Biology*, **9**, 281–328.

Schwalbe, B. 1915. "Uber den Fossilen Affen *Oreopithecus bambolii*," *Zeitschrift für Morphologie und Anthropologie* (Stuttgart, W. Germany), **19**, 149–254.

Schwarzback, M. 1963. *Climates of the Past, an Introduction to Paleoclimatology*. Princeton, N.J.: Van Nostrand.

Selenka, L., and M. Blanckenhorn. 1911. "Die Pithecanthropus—Schlichten auf Java," *Geologische und Palaeontologische Ergebnisse der Trinil Expedition (1907–1908)*. Leipzig, E. Germany.

Sergi, S. 1908. "Di una classificatione razionale dei gruppi unami," *Atti del Società Italiana per il Progresso delle Scienze*, (Rome).

Sergi, S. 1953. "I Profanerantropi di Swanscombe e di Fontechevade," *Rivista di Antropologia* (Rome), **40**, 65–72.

Seymour, R. S. 1976. "Dinosaurs, Endothermy and Blood Pressure," *Nature*, **262**, 207–208.

Shariff, G. A. 1953. "Cell Counts in the Primate Cerebral Cortex," *Journal of Comparative Neurology*, **98**, 381–400.

Sieveking, A. 1958. "The Paleolithic Industry of Kota Tampan, Perak, Northwestern Malaya," *Asian Perspectives*, **11**, 91–102.

Simons, E. 1960. "*Apidium* and *Oreopithecus*," *Nature*, **186**, 824–826.

Simons, E. 1961a. "Notes on Eocene Tarsioids and a Revision of Some Necrolemurinae," *Bulletin, British Museum (Natural History), Geology*, Series, 5(3), 45–75.

Simons, E. 1961b. "On the Phyletic Position of *Ramapithecus*," *Postilla*, (57) 1–5.

Simons, E. 1963. "A Critical Reappraisal of Tertiary Primates," in J. Buettner-Janusch (ed.), *Evolutionary and Genetic Biology of Primates (I)*. New York: Academic. Pp. 65–129.

Simons, E. 1964. "On the Mandible of *Ramapithecus*," *Proceedings, National Academy of Science*, **51**, 528–535.

Simons, E. 1965. "New Fossil Apes from Egypt and the Initial Differentiation of Hominoidea," *Nature*, **205**, 135–139.

Simons, E. 1967. "The Earliest Apes," *Scientific American,* **217**(6) 28–35.

Simons, E. 1967. "Fossil Primates and the Evolution of Some Primate Locomotor Systems," *American Journal of Physical Anthropology,* **26**, 241–254.

Simons, E. 1969. "The Late Miocene Hominid from Fort Ternan, Kenya," *Nature,* **221**, 448–451.

Simons, E. 1972a. *Primate Evolution.* New York: Macmillan.

Simons, E. 1972b. "Notes on Early Tertiary Prosimii." Paper delivered at the Research Seminar on Prosimian Biology, London, April 1972.

Simons, E. 1974. "Diversity among the Early Hominids: A Vertebrate Paleontologist's Viewpoint." Paper delivered at the Wenner-Gren Conference, Jan. 26–Feb. 2, 1974. (Now published in C. Jolly (ed.). 1978. *Early Hominids of Africa.* London: Duckworth, pp. 543–566.)

Simons, E. 1977. "*Ramapithecus,*" *Scientific American,* **236**(5), 28–35.

Simons, E., and S. Chopra. 1969. "*Gigantopithecus* (Pongidae, Hominoidea): A New Species from North India," *Postilla,* (138) 1–18.

Simons, E., and P. C. Ettel. 1970. "*Gigantopithecus,*" *Scientific American,* **222**(1), 76–85.

Simons, E., and D. Pilbeam. 1965. "Preliminary Revision of the Dryopithecinae (Pongidae, Anthropoidea)," *Folia Primatologia,* **3**(2–3), 81–152.

Simons, E., and D. Pilbeam. 1971. "Humerus of *Dryopithecus* from Saint Gaudens, France," *Nature,* **229**, 406–407.

Simons, E., and D. Pilbeam. 1972. "Hominoid Paleoprimatology," in R. Tuttle (ed.), *Functional and Evolutionary Biology of Primates.* Chicago: Aldine. Pp. 36–62.

Simons, E., D. Pilbeam, and S. Boyer. 1971. "Appearance of Hipparion in the Tertiary of the Siwalik Hills of North India, Kashmir and West Pakistan," *Nature,* **229**, 408–409.

Simons, E., and D. E. Russell. 1960. "The Cranial Anatomy of *Necrolemur,*" *Breviora,* **127**, 1–14. Cambridge, Mass.: Museum of Comparative Zoology, Harvard University.

Simpson, G. G. 1945. "The Principles of Classification and a Classification of Mammals," *Bulletin of the American Museum of Natural History,* **85**, 1–350.

Simpson, G. G. 1947. "Holarctic Mammalian Faunas and Continental Relationships during The Cenozoic," *Bulletin of the Geological Society of America,* **58**, 613–688.

Simpson, G. G. 1951a. "The Species Concept," *Evolution,* **5**, 285–298.

Simpson, G. G. 1951b. *Horses.* New York: Oxford University Press.

Simpson, G. G. 1953. "Evolution and Geography," Condon Lecture. Corvallis: University of Oregon Press.

Simpson, G. G. 1955. "The Phenacolemuridae, a New Family of Early Primates," *Bulletin of the American Museum of Natural History,* **105**, 411–441.

Simpson, G. G. 1961. *Principles of Animal Taxonomy.* New York: Columbia University Press.

Skerlj, B. 1958. "Were Neanderthalers the Only Inhabitants of Krapina?" *Bulletin Scientifique Conseil des Académies de la RPF de Yugoslavia* (Zagreb), **4** 44.

Sloan, R. 1969. "Cretaceous and Paleocene Terrestrial Communities of Western North America," *Proceedings of the North American Paleontological Convention,* Vol. E, 427–453.

Smith, J. M. 1966. "Sympatric Speciation," *American Naturalist,* **100**, 637–650.

Smith, Patricia. 1976. "Dental Pathology in Fossil Hominids. What Did the Neandertals do with Their Teeth?" *Current Anthropology*, **17**(1), 149–151.

Smith, Philip. 1964. "The Solutrean Culture," *Scientific American*, **211**(2), 86–94.

Smith, W. 1799. "Order of the Strata, and Their Imbedded Organic Remains, in the Neighborhood of Bath; Examined and Proved Prior to 1799." London.

Smith, W. 1816. *Strata Identified by Organized Fossils, Containing Prints on Colored Paper of the Most Characteristic Specimens in Each Stratum*. London: W. Arding.

Sneath, P. H., and R. Sokal. 1962. "Numerical Taxonomy," *Nature*, **193**, 855–860.

Solecki, R. 1957. "Shanidar Cave," *Scientific American*, **197**(5), 59–64.

Solecki, R. 1960. "Three Adult Neanderthal Skeletons from Shanidar Cave, Northern Iraq," *Smithsonian Report for 1959*. Pp. 603–635.

Solecki, R. R. 1961. "New Anthropological Discoveries at Shanidar, Northern Iraq," *Transactions of the New York Academy of Science*, Series 2, **23**, 690–699.

Solecki, R. 1971. *Shanidar, the First Flower People*. New York: Knopf.

Solecki, R., and A. Leroi-Gourhan. 1961. "Palaeoclimatology and Archaeology in the Near East," *Annals of the New York Academy of Science*, **95**, 729–739.

Sperber, G. H. 1974. *Morphology of the Cheek Teeth of the Early South African Hominids*. Thesis, University of Witwatersrand, Johannesburg, S. Africa.

Stanley, S. 1973. "Effects of Competition on Rates of Evolution with Special Reference to Bivalve Mollusks and Mammals," *Systematic Zoology*, **22**, 486–506.

Steininger, R. 1967. "Ein Weiterer Zahn von *Dryopithecus* (Mammalia, Pongidae) aus dem Miozan des Weiner Beckens," *Folia Primatologia*, **7**, 243–275.

Steininger, F., F. Rogl, and E. Martini, 1976. "Current Oligocene/Miocene Biostratigraphic Concept of the Central Paratethys (Middle Europe)," *IGCP Project 73/1/25: Stratigraphic Correlation Tethys—Paratethys Neogene, Newsletter on Stratigraphy*, **4**(3), 174–202.

Stekelis, M. 1966. *Archaeological Excavations at Ubeidiya, 1960–1963*. Jerusalem: Israel Academy of Sciences and Humanities.

Stephan, H. 1969. "Quantitative Investigations on Visual Structures in Primate Brains," *Proceedings of the Second International Congress of Primatology*, **3**, 34–42.

Stewart, T. D. 1959. "The Restored Shanidar I Skull," *Smithsonian Report for 1958*. Pp. 473–480.

Stewart, T. D. 1960a. "The Form of the Pubic Bone in Neanderthal Man," *Science*, **131**, 1437–1438.

Stewart, T. D. 1960b. "Indirect Evidence of the Primitiveness of the Swanscombe Skull," *American Journal of Physical Anthropology*, **18**, 363.

Stewart, T. D. 1961. "The Skull of Shanidar II," *Sumer*, **17**, 97–106.

Stewart, T. D. 1962a. "Neanderthal Scapulae with Special Reference to the Shanidar Neanderthals from Iraq," *Anthropos*, **57**, 779–800.

Stewart, 1962b. "Neanderthal Cervical Vertebrae with Special Attention to the Shanidar Neanderthals from Iraq," *Bibliotheca Primatologia*, **1**, 130–154.

Stewart, T. D. 1963. "Shanidar Skeletons IV and VI," *Sumer*, **19**, 8–26.

Stewart, T. D. 1964. "A Neglected Primitive Feature of the Swanscombe Skull," in C. Ovey (ed.), *The Swanscombe Skull: A Survey of Research on a Pleistocene Site: Occasional Papers of the Royal Anthropological Institute* (London), no. 20, 151–159.

Stewart, T. D. 1977. "The Neanderthal Skeletal Remains from Shanidar Cave, Iraq:

A Summary of Findings to Date," *Proceedings of the American Phiosophical Society*, **121**(2), 121–165.

Stock, C. 1933. "An Eocene Primate from California," *Proceedings of the National Academy of Science*, **19**, 954–959.

Stock, E. 1934. "A Second Eocene Primate from California," *Proceedings of the National Academy of Science*, **20**, 150–154.

Stock, C. 1938. "A Tarsiid Primate and a Mixodected from the Poway Eocene, California," *Proceedings of the National Academy of Science*, **24**, 288–293.

Straus, W., Jr. 1963. "The Classification of *Oreopithecus*," in S. L. Washburn (ed.), *Classification and Human Evolution*. Chicago: Aldine. Pp. 146–177.

Straus, W., Jr., and A. Cave. 1957. "Pathology and Posture of Neanderthal Man," *Quarterly Review of Biology*, **32**, 340–363.

Straus, W., Jr., and M. A. Schön. 1960. "Cranial Capacity of *Oreopithecus bambolii*," *Science*, **132**, 670–672.

Stringer, C. 1974. "A Multivariate Study of the Petralona Skull," *Journal of Human Evolution*, **3**, 397–404.

Sudré, J. 1975. "The First Early Paleogene African Prosimian, *Azibius* trerki, n. gen., n. sp., from the Northwest Sahara," *Comptes Rendus de l'Académie de Sciences* (Paris), Series D., **280**, 1539–1542.

Suzuki, H., and F. Takai. 1970. *The Amud Man and His Cave Site*. Tokyo: Keigaku Publishing Co.

Swindler, D., and C. Wood. 1973. *An Atlas of Primate Gross Anatomy*. Seattle: University of Washington Press.

Sylvester-Bradley, P. C. (ed.). 1956. *The Species Concept in Palaeontology*. London: Systematics Association, Pub. no. 20.

Szalay, F. 1968a. "The Beginnings of Primates," *Evolution*, **22**, 19–36.

Szalay, F. 1968b. "Origins of the Apatemiyidae (Mammalia, Insectivora)," *American Museum Novitates*, no. 2352, 1–11.

Szalay, F. 1970. "Late Eocene *Amphipithecus* and the Origins of the Catarrhine Primates," *Nature*, **227**, 355–357.

Szalay, F. 1971. "On the Cranium of the Late Paleocene Primate *Plesiadapis tricuspidens*," *Nature*, **230**, 324–325.

Szalay, F. 1972a. "Cranial Morphology of the Early Tertiary *Phenacolemur and Its Bearing on Primate Phylogeny*," *American Journal of Physical Anthropology*, **36**, 59–76.

Szalay, F. 1972b. "Primate Phylogeny and the Prosimian-Anthropoid Dichotomy." Paper delivered at the Research Seminar on Prosimian Biology, London, April 1972.

Szalay, 1973. "New Paleocene Primates and a Diagnosis of the New Suborder Paromomyiformes," *Folia Primatologia*, **19**, 73–87.

Szalay, F. 1975a. "Where to Draw the Nonprimate-Primate Taxonomic Boundary," *Folia Primatologia*, **23**, 158–163.

Szalay, F. 1975b. "Phylogeny of Primate Higher Taxa: The Basicranial Evidence," in W. P. Luckett and F. S. Szalay (eds.), *Phylogeny of the Primates*, New York: Plenum, pp. 91–125.

Taieb, M., D. C. Johanson, Y. Coppens, and J. L. Aronson. 1979. "Geological and

Palaeontological Background of Hadar Hominid Site, Afar, Ethiopia," *Nature*, **260**, 289–297.

Tattersall, I. 1969a. "Ecology of North Indian *Ramapithecus*," *Nature*, **221**, 451–452.

Tattersall, I. 1969b. "More on the Ecology of North Indian *Ramapithecus*," *Nature*, **224**, 821–822.

Tekkaya, I. 1974. "A New Species of Tortonian Anthropoid (Primates, Mammalia) from Anatolia," *Bulletin Mineral Research and Exploration Institute of Turkey* (Ankara), **83**, 148–165.

Teleki, G. 1974. "The Omnivorous Chimpanzee," *Scientific American*, **228**(1), 32–42.

Thenius, E. 1958. "Tertiarstratigraphie und Tertiäre Hominoiden-funde," *Anthropologischer Anzeiger* (Stuttgart, W. Germany), **22**, 66–77.

Thoma, A. 1966. "L'occipital de l'Homme mindélien de Vérteszöllös," *Anthropologie* (Paris), **70**, 495–533.

Thorne, A., and P. Macumber. 1972. "Discoveries of Late Pleistocene Man at Kow Swamp, Australia," *Nature*, **238**, 316–319.

Tobias, P. V. 1960. "The Kanam Jaw," *Nature*, **185**, 946–947.

Tobias, P. V. 1965a. "*Australopithecus, Homo habilis* and Tool-Using and Tool-Making," *South African Archaeological Bulletin*, **20**, 167–192.

Tobias, P. V. 1965b. "New Discoveries in Tanganyika," *Current Anthropology*, **6**(4), 391–399.

Tobias, P. V. 1966a. "Fossil Hominid Remains from Ubeidiya, Israel," *Nature*, **211**, 130–133.

Tobias, P. V. 1966b. "A Reexamination of the Kedung Brubus Mandible," *Zoologische Meduligen* (Leiden), **41**, 307–320.

Tobias, P. V. 1967. *Olduvai Gorge, vol. 2: The Cranium and Maxillary Dentition of Australopithecus (Zinjanthropus) boisei*. Cambridge, England: Cambridge University Press.

Tobias, P. V. 1971. *The Brain in Hominid Evolution*. New York: Columbia University Press.

Tobias, P. V. 1972. " 'Dished Faces,' Brain Size and Early Hominids," *Nature*, **239**, 468–469.

Tobias, P. V. 1973. "Implications of the New Age Estimates of the Early South African Hominids," *Nature*, **246**, 79–83.

Tobias, P. V. 1976a. "African Hominids: Dating and Phylogeny," in G. Isaac and E. McCown (eds.), *Human Origins*. Menlo Park, Calif.: W. A. Benjamin. Pp. 377–422.

Tobias, P. V. 1976b. "Important Fossil Skull Found at Sterkfontein," *South African Journal of Science*, **72**, 227.

Tobias, P. V., and G. Von Koenigswald. 1964. "A Comparison between the Olduvai Hominines and Those of Java and Some Implications for Hominid Phylogeny," *Nature*, **204**, 515–518.

Tode, A., F. Preul, K. Richter, and A. Kleinschmidt. 1953. "Die Untersuchung der Paläolithischen Freilandstation von Salzgitter-Lebenstedt," *Eiszeitalter und Gegenw*, **3**, 144–220.

Trevor, J. C. 1947. "The Physical Characters of the Sandawe," *Journal of the Royal Anthropological Institute*, **77**, 61–78.

Trinkaus, E. 1973. "A Reconsideration of the Fontechevade Fossils, *American Journal of Physical Anthropology*, **39**, 25–35.

Trinkaus, E. 1975. *A Functional Analysis of the Neanderthal Foot.* Thesis, University of Pennsylvania.

Trinkaus, E. 1976. "The Morphology of European and Southwest Asian Neanderthal Pubic Bones," *American Journal of Physical Anthropology,* **44,** 95–103.

Trinkaus, E. 1977. "A Functional Interpretation of the Axillary Border of the Neanderthal Scapula," *Journal of Human Evolution,* **6,** 231–234.

Tuttle, R. 1969. "Knuckle Walking and the Problem of Human Origins," *Science,* **166,** 953–961.

Ucko, P., and A. Rosenfeld. 1967. *Palaeolithic Cave Art.* London: World University Library.

Vallois, H. 1939. "La découverte du Squelette du Moustier," *Anthropologie* (Paris), **49,** 776–778.

Vallois, H. 1949. "Paleopathologie et Paleontologie humaine," *Homenaje a Don Luis de Hayos Sainz,* **1,** 333.

Vallois, H. 1958. "La Grotte de Fontechevade, 2d Partie: Anthropologie," *Archives, Institute de Paleontologie Humaine,* **29,** 8.

Vallois, H., and B. Vandermeersch. 1975. "The Mousterian Skull of Qafzeh (Homo VI): An Anthropological Study," *Journal of Human Evolution,* **4,** 445–455.

Van Couvering, J. A. 1972. "Radiometric Calibration of the European Neogene," in W. W. Bishop and J. A. Miller (eds.), *Calibration of Hominoid Evolution.* Edinburgh: Scottish Academic Press. Pp. 247–272.

Van Couvering, J. A., and J. A. Miller. 1971a. "Late Miocene Marine and Non-Marine Time Scale in Europe," *Nature,* **230,** 559–563.

Van Couvering, J. A., and J. A. Miller. 1971b. "Miocene Stratigraphy and Age Determinations, Rusinga Island, Kenya," *Nature,* **221,** 628–632.

Van Couvering, J. A., and J. Van Couvering. 1976. "Early Miocene Mammal Fossils from East Africa," in G. Isaac and E. McCown (eds.), *Human Origins.* Menlo Park, Calif.: W. A. Benjamin. Pp. 155–208.

Van Lawick-Goodall, J. 1968. "The Behavior of Free Living Chimpanzees in the Gombe Stream Reserve," *Animal Behavior Monographs,* **1,** 161–311.

Van Lawick-Goodall, J., H. Van Lawick, and C. Packer. 1973. "Tool Use in Free Living Baboons in the Gombe National Park, Tanzania," *Nature,* **241,** 212–213.

Van Valen, L. 1965. "A Middle Paleocene Primate," *Nature,* **207,** 435–436.

Van Valen, L. 1969. "A Classification of the Primates," *American Journal of Physical Anthropology,* **30,** 295–296.

Van Valen, L., and R. Sloan. 1965. "The Earliest Primates," *Science,* **150,** 743–745.

Vandermeersch, B. 1972. "Récentes découvertes de squelettes humains à Qafzeh (Israel): Essai d'interprétation," in F. Bordes (ed.), *The Origins of Homo sapiens.* Paris: UNESCO. Pp. 49–53.

Verdcourt, B. 1963. "The Miocene Non-Marine Mollusca of Rusinga Island, Lake Victoria and Other Localities in Kenya," *Palaeontographia,* **121**(A), 1–37.

Vertes, L. 1965a. "Discovery of *Homo erectus* in Hungary," *Antiquity,* **39,** 303.

Vertes, L. 1965b. "Typology of the Buda Industry, Pebble Tool Industry from the Hungarian Lower Paleolithic," *Quaternaria,* **7,** 185–195.

Virchow, H. 1917. "Der Taubacher Zohn des Prähistorischen Museums der Universität Jena," *Prähistorische Zeitschrift* (Berlin), **9,** 1–18.

Vlcek, E. 1955. "The Fossil Man of Gánovce, Czechoslovakia," *Journal of the Royal Anthropological Institute,* **85,** 163–171.

Vlcek, E. 1973. "Postcranial Skeleton of a Neandertal Child from Kiik-Koba, U.S.S.R.," *Journal of Human Evolution*, **2**, 537–544.

Vlcek, E. 1978. "A New Discovery of *Homo erectus* in Central Europe," *Journal of Human Evolution*, **7**, 239–252.

Vogel, J., and H. T. Waterbolk. 1963. "Groningen Radiocarbon Dates," *Radiocarbon*, **5**, 166.

Von Bonin, G. 1963. *The Evolution of the Human Brain*. Chicago: University of Chicago Press.

Von Koenigswald, G. H. R. 1936. "Erste Mitteilung über einen fossilen Hominiden aus dem alt pleistocan Ostjavas," *Proceedings, The Academy of Science*, Amsterdam, **39**, 1000–10009.

Von Koenigswald, G. H. R. 1950. "Fossil Hominids from the Lower Pleistocene of Java," *Proceedings, 18th International Geological Congress*, Part 9, 959.

Von Koenigswald, G. H. R. 1952. "*Gigantopithecus blacki* von Koenigswald, a Giant Fossil Hominoid from the Pleistocene of South China," *Anthropological Papers of the American Museum of Natural History*, **43**(4), 291–325.

Von Koenigswald, G. H. R. 1956. *Meeting Prehistoric Man*. London: Thames and Hudson.

Von Koenigswald, G. H. R. 1957. "Remarks on *Gigantopithecus* and Other Hominoid Remains from Southern China," *Proceedings: Koninklijke nederlandse akademie van Wetenschappen* (Amsterdam), Series B, **60**, 153–159.

Von Koenigswald, G. H. R. (ed.). 1958. *Hundert Jahre Neanderthaler*. Koln, W. Germany: Bohlau Verlag.

Von Koenigswald, G. H. R. 1962. "Potassium-Argon Dates for the Upper Tertiary," *Proceedings: Koninklijke nederlandse akademie van Wetenschappen* (Amsterdam), Series B, **65**, 31.

Von Koenigswald, G. H. R. 1964. "Potassium Argon Dates for Early Man: Trinil," *Report, 6th INQUA Congress, 1961* (Warsaw), **4**, 325–327.

Von Koenigswald, G. H. R. 1965. "Critical Observation upon the So-called Higher Primates from the Upper Eocene of Burma," *Proceedings: Koninklijke nederlandse akademie van Wetenschappen* (Amsterdam), Series B, **68**, 165.

Von Koenigswald, G. H. R. 1968. "Das absolute Alter des *Pithecanthropus erectus* Dubois," in G. Kurth (ed.), *Evolution und Hominisation* (2d ed.). Stuttgart, W. Germany: G. Fischer Verlag. Pp. 195–203.

Von Koenigswald, G. H. R. 1969. "Miocene Cercopithecoidea and Oreopithecoidea from the Miocene of East Africa," in L. S. B. Leakey (ed.), *Fossil Vertebrates of Africa*. Vol. 1. London: Academic. Pp. 39–52.

Von Koenigswald, G. H. R. 1972. "Ein unterkiefer einesfossilen Hominoiden aus dem Unterpliozan Griechlands," *Proceedings: Koninklijke nederlandse akademie van Wetenschappen* (Amsterdam), Series B, **75**, 385–394.

Von Koenigswald, G. H. R. 1973. "*Australopithecus, Meganthropus* and *Ramapithecus*," *Journal of Human Evolution*, **2**, 487–491.

Von Koenigswald, G. H. R., and A. K. Ghosh. 1973a. "Stone Implements from the Trinil Beds of Sangiran, Central Java, I," *Proceedings: Koninklijke nederlandse akademie van Wetenschappen* (Amsterdam), Series B, **76**, 1–19.

Von Koenigswald, G. H. R., and A. K. Ghosh. 1973b. "Stone Implements from Central Java, II," *Proceedings, Koninklijke nederlandse akademie van Wetenschappen* (Amsterdam), Series B, **76**, 20–34.

Von Koenigswald, G. H. R., and F. Weidenreich. 1939. "The Relation between *Pithecanthropus* and *Sinanthropus*," *Nature*, **144**, 926.

Vrba, E. 1974. "Chronological and Ecological Implications of the Fossil Bovidae at the Sterkfontein Australopithecine Site," *Nature*, **250**, 19–23.

Vrba, E. 1975. "Some Evidence of Chronology and Paleoecology of Sterkfontein, Swartkrans and Kromdraai from the Fossil Bovidae," *Nature*, **254**, 301–304.

Wagner, G. A. 1977. "Fission-Track Dating of Pumice from the KBS Tuff, East Rudolf, Kenya," *Nature*, **267**, 649.

Walker, A. 1967. "Patterns of Extinction among the Subfossil Madagascan Lemuroids," in P. S. Martin (ed.), *Pleistocene Extinctions*. New Haven, Conn.: Yale University Press.

Walker, A. 1969. "Fossil Mammal Locality on Mount Elgon, Eastern Uganda," *Nature*, **223**, 591–596.

Walker, A. 1973. "New *Australopithecus* Femora from East Rudolf, Kenya," *Journal of Human Evolution*, **2**, 545–555.

Walker, A. 1976. "Remains Attributed to *Australopithecus* in the East Rudolf Succession," in Y. Coppens, F. Howell, G. Isaac, and R. Leakey (eds.), *Earliest Man and Environments in the Lake Rudolf Basin*. Chicago: University of Chicago Press. Pp. 484–489.

Walker, A., and P. Andrews. 1973. "Reconstruction of the Dental Arcades of *Ramapithecus wickeri*," *Nature*, **244**, 313–314.

Wallace, J. 1975. "Did La Ferrassie I Use His Teeth as a Tool?" *Current Anthropology*, **16**(3), 393–396.

Wallace, J. 1978. "Evolutionary Trends in the Early Hominid Dentition," in C. Jolly (ed.), *Early Hominids of Africa*, London: Duckworth, pp. 285–310.

Warick, R. 1950. "The Relation and Direction of the Mental Foramina to the Growth of the Human Mandible," *Journal of Anatomy* (London), **84**, 116–120.

Washburn, S. 1950. "Origin and Evolution of Man. Analysis of Primate Evolution," *Cold Spring Harbor Symposium on Quantitative Biology*, **15**, 67–77.

Washburn, S. 1957. "*Australopithecus*: The Hunters or the Hunted?" *American Anthropologist*, **59**, 612–614.

Washburn, S. 1959. "Speculations on the Interrelations of the History of Tools and Biological Evolution," *Human Biology*, **31**, 21–31.

Washburn, S. 1960. "Tools and Human Evolution," *Scientific American*, **203**(3), 62–75.

Washburn, S., and I. DeVore. 1961. "Social Life of Baboons and Early Man," in S. Washburn (ed.), *Social Life of Early Man*, Viking Fund Publications in Anthropology, Vol. 31. Chicago: Aldine. Pp. 91–105.

Weidenreich, F. 1927. "Der Schadel von Weimar-Ehringsdorf," *Verhandlungen der Gesellschaft fur physische Anthropologie* (Stuttgart, W. Germany), **2**, 34–41.

Weidenreich, F. 1928. *Der Schadelfund von Weimar-Ehringsdorf*. Jena, E. Germany:

Weidenreich, F. 1936. "The Mandibles of *Sinanthropus pekinensis*," *Paleontologica Sinica*, New Series D, 7 no. 4, 1–162.

Weidenreich, F. 1937. "The Dentition of *Sinanthropus pekinensis*," *Paleontologica Sinica*, New Series D, no. 1 (Whole Series, no. 101), 1–180.

Weidenreich, F. 1941. "The Extremity Bones of *Sinanthropus pekinensis*," *Paleontologica Sinica*, New Series D, no. 5 (Whole Series, no. 116), 1–150.

Weidenreich, F. 1943a. "The Skull of *Sinanthropus pekinensis*: A Comparative Study

of a Primitive Hominid Skull," *Paleontologica Sinica*, New Series D, no. 10 (Whole Series, no. 127), 1–485.

Weidenreich, F. 1943b. "The 'Neanderthal Man' and the Ancestors of *Homo sapiens*," *American Anthropologist*, **45**, 39–48.

Weidenreich, F. 1945a. "Giant Early Man from Java and South China," *Anthropological Papers, American Museum of Natural History*, **40**, 1–134.

Weidenreich, F. 1945b. "The Palaeolithic Child from the Teshik-Tash Cave in Southern Uzbekistan (Central Asia)," *American Journal of Physical Anthropology*, **3**, 21–32.

Weidenreich, F. 1946. *Apes, Giants and Men*. Chicago: University of Chicago Press.

Weidenreich, F. 1951. "The Morphology of Solo Man," *Anthropological Papers, American Museum of Natural History*, **43**(3), 205–290.

Weiner, J., and B. Campbell. 1964. "The Taxonomic Status of the Swanscombe Skull," in C. D. Ovey (ed.), *The Swanscombe Skull: A Survey of Research on a Pleistocene Site; Occasional Papers of the Royal Anthropological Institute* (London), no. 20, 175–209.

Weiner, J., K. P. Oakley, and W. E. Le Gros Clark. 1953. "The Solution of the Piltdown Problem," *Bulletin, British Museum* (Natural History), Geology, **2**(3), 139–146.

Weiner, J., K. P. Oakley, and W. E. Le Gros Clark. 1955. "Further Contributions to the Solution of the Piltdown Problem," *Bulletin, British Museum* (Natural History), Geology, **2**(6), 225–287.

Weinert, H. 1936. "Der Urmenschenschadel von Steinheim," *Zeitschrift fur Morphologie und Anthropologie* (Stuttgart, W. Germany): **35**, 463–518.

Weinert, H. 1950. "Über die Neuen Vor-und Frühmenschenfunde aus Afrika, Java, China und Frankreich," *Zeitschrift fur Morphologie und Anthropologie* (Stuttgart, W. Germany), **42**, 113–148.

Wells, L. H. 1969. "Faunal Subdivision of the Quaternary of Southern Africa," *South African Archaeological Bulletin*, **24**, 93–95.

Wendorf, F., R. L. Laury, R. Schild, C. V. Haynes, and P. Damon. 1975. "Dates for the Middle Stone Age of East Africa," *Science*, **187**, 740–742.

Wendt, H. 1956. *In Search of Adam*. Boston: Houghton Mifflin.

White, T. D. 1975. "Geomorphology to Paleoecology: *Gigantopithecus* Reappraised," *Journal of Human Evolution*, **4**, 219–233.

White, T. D. 1977. "New Fossil Hominids from Laetolil, Tanzania," *American Journal of Physical Anthropology*, **46**, 197–230.

Whitworth, T. 1958. "Miocene Ruminants of East Africa," *Fossil Mammals of Africa*, No. 15. London: British Museum (Natural History). Pp. 1–50.

Wilson, A. C., and V. Sarich. 1969. "A Molecular Time Scale for Human Evolution," *Proceedings, National Academy of Science*, **63**, 1088–1093.

Wilson, J. 1966. "A New Primate from the Earliest Oligocene, West Texas: Preliminary Report," *Folia Primatologia*, **4**, 227–248.

Wilson, J. Tuzo (ed.). 1972. *Continents Adrift*. San Francisco: Freeman.

Wolberg, D. 1970. "The Hypothesized Osteodontokeratic Culture of the Australopithecinae: A Look at the Evidence and the Opinions," *Current Anthropology*, **11**(1), 23–37.

Wolpoff, M. 1968a. "Climatic Influence on the Skeletal Nasal Aperture," *American Journal of Physical Anthropology*, **29**, 405–424.

Wolpoff, M. 1968b. " 'Telanthropus' and the Single Species Hypothesis," *American Anthropologist,* **70,** 477–493.

Wolpoff, M. 1970a. "Metric Trends in Hominid Dental Evolution," *Studies in Anthropology, Case Western Reserve University* (Cleveland), **2,** 1–244.

Wolpoff, M. 1970b. "The Evidence for Multiple Hominid Taxa at Swartkrans," *American Anthropologist,* **72,** 576–607.

Wolpoff, M. 1971a. "Competitive Exclusion among Lower Pleistocene Hominids: The Single Species Hypothesis," *Man,* **6,** 601–614.

Wolpoff, M. 1971b. "Is the New Composite Cranium from Swartkrans a Small Robust Australopithecine?" *Nature,* **230,** 398–401.

Wolpoff, M. 1971c. "Is Vérteszöllös II an Occipital of European *Homo erectus?*" *Nature,* **232,** 567–568.

Wolpoff, M. 1973. "Posterior Tooth Size, Body Size and Diet in South African Gracile Australopithecines," *American Journal of Physical Anthropology,* **39,** 375–393.

Woo, J. K. 1957. "*Dryopithecus* Teeth from Keiyuan, Yunnan Province," *Vertebrata Palasiatica,* **1,** 25–32.

Woo, J. K. 1962. "The Mandibles and Dentition of *Gigantopithecus,*" *Paleontologica Sinica,* New Series D (11), 65–94.

Woo, J. K. 1964. "A Newly Discovered Mandible of the *Sinanthropus*-type *Sinanthropus lantianensis,*" *Scientia Sinica,* **13,** 801–811.

Woo, J. K. 1965. "A Preliminary Report on a Skull of *Sinanthropus lantianensis,* of Lantian, Shensi," *Scientia Sinica,* **14**(7), 1032–1035.

Woo, J. K. 1966. "The Skull of Lantian Man," *Current Anthropology,* **7**(1), 83–86.

Woo, J. K., and M. Chow. 1957. "New Material of the Earliest Primate Known in China," *Vertebrata Palasiatica,*1(4), 267–272.

Wood, A. 1962. "The Early Tertiary Rodents of the Family Paramyidae," *Transactions, American Philosophical Society,* New Series, **52,** 1–261.

Wood, B. 1973. "A *Homo* Talus from East Rudolf, Kenya," *Journal of Anatomy* (London), **117,** 203–204.

Wood, B. 1974. "Olduvai Bed I Postcranial Remains," *Journal of Human Evolution,* **3,** 373–378.

Wood, B. 1976. "Remains Attributed to *Homo* in the East Rudolf Succession," in Y. Coppens, F. Howell, G. Isaac, and R. E. F. Leakey (eds.), *Earliest Man and Environments in the Lake Rudolf Basin.* Chicago: University of Chicago Press. Pp. 490–506.

Wood-Jones, F. 1916. *Arboreal Man.* London: E. Arnold.

Woodward, A. S. 1921. "A New Cave Man from Rhodesia, South Africa," *Nature,* **108,** 371–372.

Wright, D. J. M. 1971. "Syphilis and Neanderthal Man," *Nature,* **229,** 409.

Zapfe, H. 1958. "The Skeleton of *Pliopithecus (Epipliopithecus vindobonensis)* Zapfe and Hurzeler," *American Journal of Physical Anthropology,* **16,** 441–458.

Zapfe, H. 1960. "Die Primatenfunde aus der miozänen Spaltenfullung von Neudorf an der March (Děvinská Nová Ves) Tschechoslowakei. Mit Anhang: Der Primatenfund aus dem Miozan von Klein Hadersdorf in Niederoesterreich," *Schwiezerische Palaeontologische Abhandlungen,* **78,** 4–293.

Zwell, M. 1972. "On the Supposed '*Kenyapithecus africanus*' Mandible," *Nature,* **240,** 236–240.

INDEX

INDEX

Abbevillian assemblage, 337
Acheulian tools, 188, 252, 282, 336–341,
    349, 354–356, 390
Adapidae, 86, 412
Adapis, 50, 52, 86, 88
Adaptive radiation:
    of hominids, 238
    of hominoids, 117, 134, 144–145
    of mammals, 27
    of primates, 69
Aegyptopithecus, 97, 116, 413
    brain of, 109
    dentition of, 107–108
    ear region of, 52, 105, 109, 130
    postcranium of, 108–109
    skull of, 50–109
    tail of, 49, 109
Aeolopithecus, 107, 116, 128, 409, 413
Ambrona, Spain, 307, 335, 339, 343
Amphipithecus, 96, 97, 101

Amud, Israel, 376, 380, 381, 399–400
Anagenetic evolution, 373
Anatomically modern man (see *Homo
    sapiens sapiens*, anatomically mod-
    ern)
Angiosperms, 26, 27, 69, 411, 412
    defined, 26
Anthropoid origins, 102–104, 112
    lemuroid ancestor, 103, 110
    tarsoid ancestor, 109
Anyathian industry, 344
Apidium, 52, 116, 164, 413
    A. moustafi, 101, 105
    A. phiomense, 101, 105
Arago, France, 316, 319, 334, 335, 345,
    376
Arboreal theory, 28, 29
    criticism of, 31–36
Arcy-sur-Cure, France, 358, 361
Ardrey, R., 206

Art, Paleolithic, 363–364
Auditory bulla (see Petrosal bulla)
Aurignacian industry, 361–363, 390, 393, 396
Australopithecus:
  morphology: brain, 221–222
    cranium, 216, 218, 220, 222–224
    dentition, 227
    locomotion, 231, 233–234
    lower Limb, 231, 233–237
    mandible, 227–229
    pelvis, 231, 233
    premaxilla, 224
    upper limb, 229–231
    vertebrae, 233–234
  presence in Asia of, 296, 303
  species of: *A. afarensis,* 215, 216, 226, 238, 282–283, 289
    A. africanus, 8, 163, 207, 208, 215, 216, 238, 259, 282–283
    A. boisei, 8, 208, 215, 216, 218, 220, 221, 224, 226, 286
    A. robustus, 8, 207, 208, 215, 216, 218, 220, 221, 226, 260, 286
"Australopithecus prometheus," 267
  (*See also* Makapan, South Africa)
Azibius, 98

Bacho Kiro, Bulgaria, 360
Bifacial tools, 338
  (*See also* Acheulian tools)
Bilzingsleben, Germany, 315, 333–334, 349
  (See also *Homo erectus,* distribution of, in, Europe)
Bodo, Ethiopia, 316, 317, 334
Bone tools, 255, 262, 268, 269, 272, 347, 357, 362
Boule, M.:
  La Chapelle-aux-Saints, study of, 384
  polyphyletic model, development of, 372
Brace, C. L., 374
Brain, C. K., 265, 270
Branisella, 99
Breccia, 256
Broca's area, 221–222

Broken Hill (*see* Rhodesian "Man," Zambia)
Broom, R., 259, 261, 267
Buda industry, 344–345
Burials, human, 357–360, 403

Campbell, B., 4, 210, 373
Candir, Turkey, 122, 124, 158
Canine fossa, 376, 374
Cannibalism, 345, 347, 389, 390, 397
Carpolestidae, 77–79, 81, 85
Chad, 209, 295
Chellean assemblage, 337
Chemeron, Kenya, 213
Chesowanja, Kenya, 216
Chignon (*see* Occipital bun)
Chopper-chopping tools, 336, 344–347
Choukoutien, China:
  cave, 328–329, 346–347
  hominids, 311, 313–318, 321–324, 328–329, 335, 349, 390
  (See also *Homo erectus,* distribution of, in China)
Chronospecies, 210
Chumashius, 96
Clacton, England, 339
Clactonian, industries, 334, 344, 355
Cladistics, 19, 20
Clark, W. E. Le Gros, 19, 29, 36, 88
  arboreal theory, 29
  australopithecines, 170, 207, 260
  dryopithecine locomotion, 144
  total morphological pattern, 37
Coon, C., polyphyletic model, development of, 372
Coprolite, 335–342
Cro-Magnons, 362, 379, 385, 393
"Cyphanthropus rhodesiensis" (*see* Rhodesian "Man," Zambia)

Dart, R., 151, 215, 257, 259, 267
  Osteodontokeratic tools, 267–269
Darwin, C., 1, 6
Dating techniques:
  absolute, 417–422
    amino acid racemization, 421–422

Dating techniques:
  absolute: argon^{40}—argon^{39}, 420
    fission track, 421
    potassium-argon (K/A), 274, 419
    radiocarbon (C^{14}): conventional method, 417–418
      direct method, 418–419
  relative, 422–425
    fluorine, 327, 423–424
    nitrogen, 327, 424
    paleomagnetic, 422–423
    uranium, 327, 424–425
Day, M., 209, 330
Debitage, 252
Del Mar, San Diego, 405
Dendropithecus, 116, 128
Dental formula, 56
Djetis beds, Java, 301–302, 326
Dolni Vestonice, Czechoslovakia, 364
Drachenloch, Austria, 360
Dryopithecinae, 104, 107, 116, 117
  classification of, 131–137
  cranium of, 141
  dentition of, 135, 139
  femora of, 143
  forelimb of, 141–143
  locomotion of, 141–143
  mandible of, 139–141
Dryopithecus, 49, 101, 116, 133
  D. fontani, 131, 133, 134, 137
  "D. macedoniensis," 125
  D. laietanus, 133, 134, 137
Dubois, E., 143n., 301, 324, 327
Dwelling structures:
  La Baume Bonne, 343
  l'Atelier Commont, 343
  Lazeret, 342–343
  Olduvai Gorge, 276, 278–279
  Terra Amata, 342
Dyseolemur, 95

Ehringsdorf, German, 354, 388
Elliott-Smith, G., 28, 384
Engis, Belgium, 367, 389
Eyasi, Tanzania, 385

Fauresmith assemblage, 337
Fayum, Egypt, 100–101
Feedback, 2, 4, 12, 60, 185, 191, 239, 244, 414
Fire, evidence of, 268, 342, 345, 347–348
Fish, Hoek, South Africa, 385, 400–401
Fisher's Quarry, 388
Flake tools, 252
Florisbad, South Africa, 385, 400
Fontechevade, France, 371, 372, 389–390
Footprints, human: Laetolil, 214
    Terra Amata, 342
Forbes Quarry, Gibraltar, 367
Fort Ternan, Kenya, 13, 121–122, 153, 198

Galley Hill, England, 372
Gamble's Cave, Kenya, 274
Ganovece, Czechoslovakia, 371, 390
Garusi, Tanzania, 282
Generalized, 13, 14, 36
Gibraltar, 367, 389
Gigantopithecus, 116, 117, 126, 145–152, 170, 411
  associated with hominids, 150, 295
  discovery of, 149–150
  ecology, 150
  species of: G. bilaspurensis, 147, 148
    G. blacki, 147–152
Gregory, W., 259–260
Grimaldi Caves, Monaco, 393

Hadar, Ethiopia, 192, 216, 229, 238, 287, 289
  (See also Australopithecus, species of: A. afarensis)
Haeckel, E., 296, 301
Heidelberg, Germany, 323, 326, 307, 349
"Hesperopithecus," 121n.
Hipparion, 17, 124–126, 148
Hoanghonius, 96
Hominid origins:
  ancestral form, 158–159
  Bartholomew, G., and J., Birdsell, 191–192

Hominid origins:
   geographic location of, 122, 158, 170,
      171
   habitat and, 206–207
   hockett C., and R. Ascher, 194
   Jolly, C., 195–197
   Morgan, E., 197
   neoteny in, 199
Hominadae:
   characteristics of: behavior, 184
      brain, 180
      dentition, 172
      jaw biomechanics, 172–174
      locomotion, 174–180
      speech, 181–184
   classification of: Middle Pleistocene,
      306, 311–312
      Miocene, 115, 124, 152–158
      Plio-Pleistocene, 207–212, 215–
      216
      Upper Pleistocene, 366–367, 370–
      371, 384–385
   origin of, 122, 158, 170–171
Homo:
   morphology: cranium, 240, 242
      dentition, 242–243
      early members, 238–239
      femora, 243
      mandible, 243
      taxonomy, 207
   origin of, 244
"Homo africanus," 211
   (See also Australopithecus, species of:
      A. africanus)
Homo erectus:
   behavior of: diet, 335–336
      dwelling structures, 342–343
      fire, use of, 268, 342, 345, 347–348
      tools: acheulian, 336–344
         bone, 340
         chopper-chopping, 336, 341–344
         spears, 339, 343
   distribution of: in Africa, 281, 330–
      332, 334
      in China, 315, 327, 331, 335
      in Europe, 326, 329, 332, 334–335
      in Java, 220, 326–327

Homo erectus:
   morphology: bone thickness, 321–322
      cranium, 294, 312–318, 321–322,
         331, 332
      dentition, 323–324
      femur, 324–325, 327, 330
      mandible, 322–323
      pelvis, 294, 325–326, 330
      ulna, 281
Homo habilis, 372
   at Chad, 295
   criticism of, 209–210
   morphology of, 208–209
   at Olduvai, 277, 281
   at Sterkfontein, 263
"Homo modjokertensis," 302
   (See also Homo erectus, distribution
      of: in Java)
"Homo primigenius," 367
   (See also Homo sapiens neandertalensis)
"Homo rhodesiensis" (see Rhodesian
   "Man," Zambia)
Homo sapiens neandertalensis:
   history of, 367, 370
   morphology: cranium, 375–377
      dentition, 379
      femora, 383
      hand, 382
      locomotion, 384
      pelvis, 380–381
      scapula, 380
      talus, 383–384
      vertebrae, 379–380
   pathology, 359, 360, 375, 378–379,
      384
   relationship of, to modern humans,
      372–374
Homo sapiens sapiens:
   anatomically modern: first appear-
      ance of, 384
      morphology, 55, 385
   archaic: distribution of, 365, 384, 385,
      388
      first appearance of, 384–385
      morphology, 386
Howell, F. C., 370
Hrdlicka, A., 163, 164, 373

Ice Ages, 308–311
"Initial kick," 5, 412
  in hominids, 194, 195, 214
Insectivores, 27, 411
Intergalacial:
  defined, 308
  Great, 332
Isaac, G., 253, 293, 338
Isimila, Tanzania, 338, 343

Jebel Irhoud, Morocco, 397
Jolly, C., 152, 195

Kabuh Formation, Java, 301, 326, 327
Kalambo Falls, Tanzania, 339
Kampfe's Quarry, 388
Kanam, Kenya, 209, 274, 322, 372
Kanapoi, 192, 214, 248
Kanjera, Kenya, 274, 372
Karari assemblage, 252, 293–294
KBS (Kay Behrensmeyer's Site):
  industry, 293
  site, 293
  tuff, 290–291
Keith, A., 372
"Kenyapithecus wickeri," 153
  (See also *Ramapithecus*)
Kibish, Ethiopia, 385, 391
  (See also *Homo sapiens sapiens*, ar-
    chaic)
Kiik-Koba, U.S.S.R., 397
Kohl-Larsen, L., 282
Kow Swamp, Australia, 366, 404
Krapina, Yugoslavia, 378–381, 383,
  390
Kromdraai, South Africa, 267
Kummer, H., 193

La Baume Bonne, France, 343
La Chapelle-aux-Saints, France, 358,
  376, 378, 379, 383, 384
Laetolil, Tanzania, 216, 282–283
  (*See also* Footprints; Garusi, Tan-
    zania)

LaFerrassie, France, 358, 376, 378, 380,
  381, 383, 391
Lake Mungo, Australia, 403
Lake Natron, Tanzania, 216, 295
Lake Rudolf (*see* Lake Turkana, Kenya)
Lake Turkana, Kenya, 11*n.*, 229–230,
  238, 286, 289–295, 324, 349
  archaeological sites: dating, 290–291
    hominids, 291–295
    Karari industry, 252–253, 291,
      293–294
    Oldowan (KBS) industry, 293
La Naulette, France, 378
Lantian, China, 315, 323, 327–328
  (See also *Homo erectus*, distribution
    of, in China)
La Quina, France, 360, 361, 376, 378, 379,
  389
l'Atelier Commont, France, 343
Lazeret, France, 342
Leakey, L. S. B., 131, 153, 170, 273–274,
  372
Leakey, M. D., 132, 170, 255, 256, 274,
  276, 339
Leakey, R. E. F., 274, 289
Lehringen, Germany, 339
Le Moustier, France, 358
Les Eyzies, France, 362
Lewa, Kenya, 339
Limnopithecus, 106, 107, 116
  L. legetet, 120, 121
Littorina Cave, Morocco, 335
Lothagam, Kenya, 213
"Lucy" (AL 288), 226, 227, 229, 231, 232,
  263, 282, 289
  (See also *Australopithecus*, species of:
    A. afarensis)
Lukeino, Kenya, 118, 122, 214
Lunate sulcus, 221, 259
Lushius, 96

McHenry, H., 233
Magdalenian tradition, 362–363
Mandibular torus, 322
Makapan, South Africa, 216, 267–272
  Osteodontokeratic tools, 268–272

Mauer (*see* Heidelberg, Germany)
Mayr, E., 210
Megaladapis, 50
"Meganthropus," 151
   "*M. africanus*" 282
      (See also *Australopithecus*, species
         of: *A. afarensis*)
   "*M. paleojavanicus*", 211, 298–300, 303
      (See also *Homo erectus*, distribution
         of, in Java)
Mental foramina, 227, 229, 322, 378
Microsyopidae, 98
Modjokerto, Java, 301, 302
   (See also *Homo erectus*, distribution
      of: in Java)
Monte Circeo, Italy, 360
Montmaurin, France, 323
Morphological dating, 210, 373
Mousterian, the
   African, 354, 355
   European, 351, 354–357
Mousterian rituals, 360
Mousterian traditions: Acheulian tradi-
      tion, 355, 357
   Denticulate, 356
   Quina-Ferrassie, 355
   typical, 356

Nannopithex, 90, 93
Ndutu, Tanzania, 315, 331
Neandertal "Man", 1, 11, 364, 367, 370–
      374, 380, 383, 407
   (See also *Homo sapiens neandertalensis*)
Necrolemur, 90–91, 93
Neoteny, 61, 379
Ngandong Beds, Java, 400
Ngorora, Kenya, 118, 122, 214
Niah, Borneo, 385, 402–403
Notharctus, 50, 86, 89, 91, 97, 409

Occipital bun, 374, 376
Oldowan tools, 188, 252–256, 265, 276,
      277, 282, 337, 356
   developed, 254–255, 338, 340, 341
   typical, 253
"Oldoway Man" (OH 1), 273

Olduvai Gorge, 208, 216, 272–282, 330
   Bed I & lower Bed II, 274, 276, 342
   Bed IV, 324, 339, 340
   middle & upper Bed II, 280–282, 340,
      349
Olduvai hominids:
   OH 1, 273
   OH 3, 281
   OH 4, 209
   OH 5, 217, 219, 223, 224, 245, 274, 276,
      290, 295
   OH 6, 209
   OH 7, 208, 217, 247, 277
   OH 8, 209, 235, 237
   OH 9, 247, 281, 315, 320, 333, 391
   OH 12, 330
   OH 13, 209, 210, 281
   OH 14, 209
   OH 20, 277
   OH 24, 209, 210, 276, 277
   OH 28, 244, 294, 325, 327, 330, 349
   OH 36, 281
Oligopithecus, 101, 128
Olorgasailie, Kenya, 339, 340–341
Omo River Basin, Ethiopia, 209, 216,
      238, 283, 286–287
   Kibish Formation, hominids, 385, 391
   Shungura Formation, 286–287
      archaeological sites, 252
      hominids, 230, 282
   Usno Formation hominids, 283, 286
Oreopithecus, 48, 49, 105, 106, 116, 117,
      121*n*., 411
Osteodontokeratic tools, 267–272
Ouranopithecus, 125, 126

Paleolithic:
   Lower, 354
   Middle, 351, 354–360
   Upper, 351, 360–364
Paleopathology:
   Homo sp. indet. (KNM ER 730) 242
   Kanam jaw, 209, 322
   Neandertals, 370, 375, 378–379, 384
   Shanidar, 359, 360
   Solo, 402
"Paranthropus robustus," 211, 265, 267

Parapithecus:
  P. fraasi, 101, 105
  P. grangeri, 101, 106
Paromomyidae, 50, 70–72, 75–76, 85, 98, 99, 411
Pasalar, Turkey, 122–124, 145, 158
Patjitanian industry, 303, 344
Pech de l'Aze, France, 360
Pelycodus, 17, 89, 97, 103, 409
Peninj (*see* Lake Natron, Tanzania)
Perigordian industry, 361–363
Petralona, Greece, 333, 220, 376
Petrosal bulla, 31, 36, 52, 53
Phenacolemur, 75–76, 80
Phyletic gradualism, 7, 210, 290, 373, 409
Picrodontidae, 76–77, 81, 85
Piltdown "Man," 259, 372
"Pithecanthropus alalus," 301
  (See also Homo erectus, distribution of, in Java)
"Pithecanthropus erectus," 301, 311
  (See also *Homo erectus*, distribution of, in Java
Plagiaulacoid dentition, 78, 81
Plesiadapidae, 35, 77, 79–81
Plesiadapis, 49, 73–74, 79–81, 102
"Plesianthropus transvaalensis," 261
  (See also *Australopithecus,* species of: *A. africanus*
Pliopithecus, 49, 107, 110, 116, 121, 144
  P. antiquus, 124, 128–131
  P. hernajaki, 128–131
  P. vindobonensis, 128–131, 143
Pneumatization, 208, 216, 220
Pondaugia, 96, 97, 101
Potwar Plateau, Pakistan, 123, 126
Predmost, Czechoslovakia, 363, 367, 376, 393
Pre-*sapiens,* 272
Preconsul, 116, 121
  morphology: forelimb, 142–143
    locomotion, 142–143
    premaxilla, 224
    skull, 141
  species: *P. africanus,* 132–134, 141–143, 224
    P. major, 134, 140, 144, 409
    P. nyanzae, 132–134, 158

Propliopithecus, 106–107, 128
Punctuated equilibrium, 10, 11, 21
  in hominids, 409
  in hominoids, 145
Purgatorius, 82
  ceratops, 70–72, 75
  unio, 71, 75
Pyrgos, Greece, 124, 158

Qafzeh, Israel, 317, 372, 385, 398–399

Rabat, Morocco, 334–335
Ramapithecus, 11, 13, 121, 122, 126, 127, 139, 145, 197, 207, 224, 413
  ancestor of, 158–159
  diet, 163
  ecology: in Africa, 121, 122
    in Asia, 126–128
    in Europe, 124–125
  morphology, 159
    dentition, 160–163
      microstructure, 162
      wear, 162–163
    face, 160
    mandible, 159–160, 173
      biomechanics of, 172–174
  species of: *R. freybergi* 158
    R. punjabicus 152, 158
    R. wickeri 158
Rangwapithecus, 115, 159
  R. gordoni, 134
  R. vancouveringi, 134
Regourdou, France, 358, 360
Rhodesian "Man," Zambia, 220, 316, 317, 333, 334, 366
Robinson, J., 209–211, 223
Rudabanya, Hungary, 124

Saccopastore, Italy, 371, 389, 390
Saldanha, South Africa, 366
Salé, Morocco, 332
Salzgitter-Lebenstedt, Germany, 357, 363
Sangoan assemblage, 355
Sarich, V., 81, 164, 190*n.*

Shanidar, Iraq, 358–359, 378–381, 400
Shoshonius, 95
Shungura formation (*see* Omo River Basin, Ethiopia)
"Sinanthropus pekinensis," 311, 346
    (*See also* Choukoutien, China; *Homo erectus*, distribution of, in China
Sivapithecus, 126, 145
    S. darwini, 122, 145, 158
    S. indicus, 146, 147
    S. meteai, 146
    S. sivalensis, 146
Skhul, Israel, 371, 372, 376, 379, 385, 398
Smilodectes, 89
Smith-Woodwood, A., 259, 391
Soan industry, 344
Solo, Java, 366, 401–402, 404–405
Solutrean tradition, 362
Specialized, 13, 14, 36
Speciation, 6–9
Species:
    biospecies, 15, 18
    chronospecies, 18
    morphospecies, 18
Spy, Belgium, 379, 383
Steinheim, Germany, 307, 316, 323, 332, 349, 376, 390
Sterkfontein, South Africa, 216, 221, 261–263
    extension site, 209, 262–263, 323
    type site, 219, 224, 229, 233, 263, 277
Swanscombe, England, 232–233, 315, 321, 339, 349, 372, 390
Swartkrans, South Africa, 216, 263–267, 323
    Homo, 265–266
        "Telanthropus," 263, 265, 266
        tools, 265

Tabun, Israel, 378, 380, 381, 397
Tampanian industry, 303
Taubach, Germany, 388
Taung, South Africa, 215, 257, 259–261
Taurodontism, 374, 379
Tayacian industry, 344, 389
"Telanthropus," 263, 265, 266

Ternifine, Morocco, 323, 330, 332, 335
Terra Amata, France, 307, 335, 339, 340, 341
Teshik-Tash, U.S.S.R., 358, 397
Tetonius, 94
Tobias, P., 207–208, 260, 269
Tools, archaeological assemblages: Abbevillian, 337
    Acheulian, 188, 252, 282, 336–341, 344, 349, 354–356, 3o0
    Anyathian, 344
    Aurignacian, 361–363, 390, 393, 396
    Buda, 344–345
    Chellean, 337
    chopper-chopping, 336, 344–347, 349
    Clactonian, 334, 344, 355
    earliest, 287, 293, 304
    Fauresmith, 337
    Karari, 252, 253, 291, 293–294
    KBS, 293
    Levallois method in manufacture of, 354–356
    Magdalenian, 362–363
    Mousterian, 351, 354–357, 388–390, 394–395, 397–399
    nonlithic: bone, 255, 262, 268, 269, 272, 347, 357, 362
        horn, 268
        teeth, 255–256, 265
        wood, 268–272, 339, 340, 343, 347
    Oldowan, 188, 252–256, 265, 276, 277,, 282, 337, 338, 340, 341, 356
    Osteodontokeratic, 267–269
    Patjitanian, 303, 344
    Perigordian, 361–363
    Sangoan, 355
    Soan, 344
    Solutrean, 362
    Stellenbosh, 337
    Tampanian, 303
    Tayacian, 344, 389
    Victorian, 337
Torralba, Spain, 306, 335, 338, 339, 343–344, 363
Trinil beds, Java, 327, 346

Ubeidiya, Israel, 209, 341
Usno formation (*see* Omo River Basin, Ethiopia)

Vallonet Cave, France, 295
Vertesszollos, Hungary, 315, 329–330, 332, 342, 345, 349
Victorian assemblage, 337
Virchow, R., 370
Vrba, E., 261–263, 265

Wadjak, Java, 301
Washakius, 95
Weidenreich, F., 151, 303, 329, 372, 388, 402
Weimar jaw (*see* Ehringsdorf, Germany)
Wolpoff, M., 210
Wood-Jones, F., 28

"Zinjanthropus," (OH 5), 217, 219, 223, 224, 245, 276, 277, 290, 295